Publisher's Letter

Graham Jones, President

It is official, after over a year in lockdown, people are overwhelmingly seeking to explore and fill their time with memorable experiences, from boating to camping to space travel. In our industry, boating has surpassed milestones never before seen. Recreational boating is seeing record sales numbers, inventory shortages and unprecedented demand. All of this means there is a large influx of new customers entering our waterways and industry.

With a lot of boaters just learning their new vessel or taking to the water on an unknown adventure, it means we will all likely have an encounter with someone just learning the ropes. I encourage everyone who loves boating to think about your first steps on a boat, or the first few months (or even years) when entering this lifestyle. There is a learning curve, mistakes are made and you likely needed help from someone with more experience than you. As boaters, we know it is our job to help one another and I want to reinforce that in today's environment.

At Waterway Guide we are doing our part by focusing on the customer experience through safe and informed boating. We want to keep these new boaters in their boats for a long time, taking them from a hobby to a lifestyle. We _____ along 75 years' worth of local knowledge of destinations, channel information and ports across our waterways is as valuable as it gets, especially for a new boater. Information can instill confidence in any boater to take that trip they never felt was possible, enhance the voyage and hopefully keep a lot of these new boaters around for a while.

The data also shows that many of these new boaters are younger and less experienced. While a positive sign for the future of our industry, Waterway Guide's challenge in today's environment is digital delivery of our content across many devices and platforms. So we continue to innovate. In March of 2021 we launched the new Waterway Guide mobile app for iOS. This is an effort to optimize our planning tools for mobile devices and provide an easy way for boaters to consume our content and interact with it in the same place. The result is a culmination of our popular cruising guides mixed with our expansive map-based planning tool, Waterway Explorer (waterwayguide.com). Please give it a download and let us know your thoughts.

As more boaters splash their boats into our beautiful waterways, our team is standing by and committed to help making the experience of planning and traveling by boat easier, safer and more enjoyable.

Thank you for playing your part in this and we look forward to seeing you on the water!

Graham Jones, President

WATERWAY GUIDE OFFICES

Corporate/Production Office
16273 General Puller Hwy.
P.O. Box 1125
Deltaville, VA 23043
804-776-8999
804-776-6111 (fax)
www.waterwayguide.com

BOOK SALES

waterwayguide.com/shipstore
800-233-3359

F O U N D E D   I N   1 9 4 7

Publisher	**JEFF JONES** jjones@waterwayguide.com
President	**GRAHAM JONES** graham@waterwayguide.com
Editor-in-Chief	**ED TILLETT** etillett@waterwayguide.com
Managing Editor	**JANI PARKER** jparker@waterwayguide.com
Graphic Design/ Production Manager	**SCOTT MCCONNELL** scott@waterwayguide.com
Operations Manager	**HEATHER SADEG** heather@waterwayguide.com
Marketing & Advertising Traffic Manager	**ETHAN JETT** ethan@waterwayguide.com
Book Sales Manager	**LINDA JERNIGAN** linda@waterwayguide.com
Sales & Marketing Manager	**KELLY CROCKETT** kelly@waterwayguide.com
Senior Advisor/ Skipper Bob Editor	**TED STEHLE** tstehle@waterwayguide.com
News Editor	**LISA SUHAY** lisa@waterwayguide.com
Web Master	**MIKE SCHWEFLER**
Office Assistant	**LEON HOLZMAN**

NATIONAL SALES

GRAHAM JONES   graham@waterwayguide.com

REGIONAL MARKETING REPRESENTATIVES

KELLY CROCKETT   kelly@waterwayguide.com

PETE HUNGERFORD   pete@waterwayguide.com

RAY CLARK   ray@waterwayguide.com

REGIONAL CRUISING EDITORS

MARK BAKER
SCOTT RICHARD BERG
MICHAEL CAMERATA
MATT & LUCY CLAIBORNE
CAPT. GEORGE & PAT HOSPODAR
MICHAEL O'REILLY & ANN PHILLIPS
MARY & THERON RODRIGUEZ
BOB SHERER (CONTRIBUTING EDITOR)

CUBA CRUISING EDITORS

ADDISON CHAN
NIGEL CALDER (CONTRIBUTING EDITOR)

@Waterway Guide   **@waterway_guide**

Printed in Canada

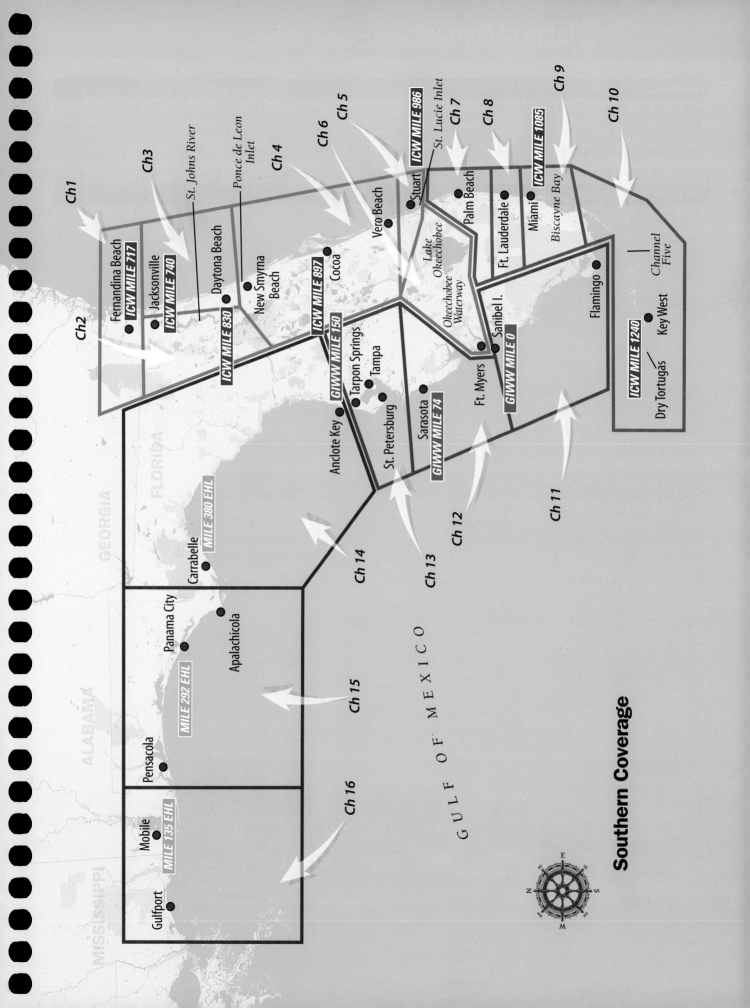

Southern Coverage

Table of Contents 2022 Southern Edition

INLETS: ST. JOHNS RIVER ENTRANCE TO CAPE FLORIDA INLET

FLORIDA'S UPPER EAST COAST   SECTION 1

Cruising south on the ICW, mariners enter Florida at Mile 714. As you cross Cumberland Sound and the St. Marys River, the broad expanses of the marsh-bordered Georgia ICW give way to the narrower, more protected and more populated Florida route. Below St. Lucie Inlet, the coastline becomes truly tropical, with a profusion of palm trees and exotic flowers. The Florida ICW is well marked and easy to follow.

Table of Contents 2022 Southern Edition

FLORIDA'S LOWER EAST COAST — SECTION 2

More than 300 miles of mostly navigable inland waterways carve through the Fort Lauderdale area, making it the "Venice of America." It is well known as a yachting center and boating amenities and services are readily available. Fort Lauderdale to Miami is known as "Florida's Gold Coast," and it glimmers with glamour and charm. Extending in a sweeping southwesterly curve from Miami and the mainland, the Florida Keys offer the cruising boater an environment unlike other waterway areas. In many ways, the Keys resemble the islands of the Bahamas. However, a main highway and a total of 18.94 miles of bridges tie them together.

FLORIDA'S WEST COAST — SECTION 3

Zoologically and geographically, Florida's lower west coast differs substantially from the east. The cruising, too, is entirely different. The sophistication, glamour and luxury so prevalent on the east coast comes in more measured doses here. The pace is slower, the atmosphere more relaxed and the amenities somewhat more limited and spaced farther apart, but the cruising is superb.

UPPER GULF COAST — SECTION 4

Florida's Panhandle, stretching from Carrabelle or Apalachicola on the eastern end to Pensacola and Perdido Bay on the west, is sometimes called the Forgotten Coast. It can be reached in one of three ways: From the east, either directly across the Gulf of Mexico or by skirting the Big Bend area just offshore; or from the west, where the inland rivers of the midwest merge into Mobile Bay.

INDEXES

The Islands of the

BAHAMAS

fly away

Discover 16 unique island destinations sprinkled across 100,000 square miles of uninhabited cays and the world's clearest water. The Islands of The Bahamas – Fly Away.

Plan your getaway at Bahamas.com

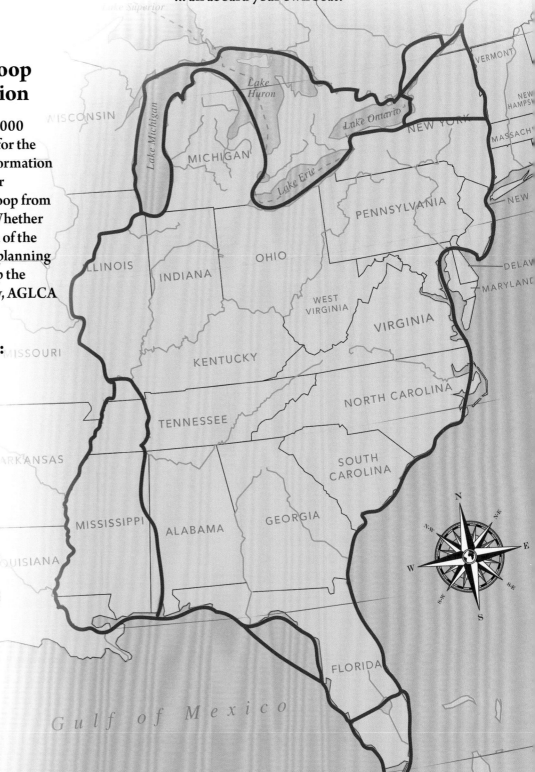

Waterway Guide's on-the-water Cruising Editors bring us firsthand information about the navigation, news and trends along the waterways we cover. In addition to contributing to the annual guide, they provide daily updates on the Waterway Explorer at www.waterwayguide.com. We are pleased to introduce you to our crew.

Mark Baker and his partner, Ann, have been avid "part-time liveaboards" since purchasing their 37-foot, shoal-draft, racer/cruiser 12 years ago. Since that time they have put over 10,000 nautical miles under the keel and have personally made all repairs and upgrades to their sailboat. Favorite sailing grounds include Penobscot Bay, ME; Narragansett Bay, RI; The Florida Keys; The Bahamas; and beautiful Florida Bay and The Everglades. They enjoy meeting new folks in the towns and cities along the way and also seeking out secluded spots to enjoy the natural world and to experience some good ol' gunkholing. Ann is a talented birdwatcher and Mark enjoys underwater photography and the study of geology. As former teachers, both are practitioners of lifelong learning.

Scott Richard Berg is a lifelong boater and full-time cruiser with five decades of experience on a range of vessels from el Toro prams to a 135-foot Baltic Trader. He operated CHARDONNAY BOATWORKS, a full service marine repair company, for many years from a series of cruising sailboats (all named *CHARDONNAY*). A full-time delivery captain, Scott holds a 100-ton Masters License, is a past president of the Seven Seas Cruising Association, an ABYC Certified Master Technician and holds an Amateur Extra Class radio license. Scott is once again cruising the east coast of the U.S. after spending several years at the Capital Yacht Club in Washington, DC.

Michael Camarata started sailing in the early 1970s when he bought a car-top sailboat with his future wife, Carol Zipke. Within a few years they had a sailing dinghy and had TWO sails to deal with! Boats got larger and more complicated in the following decades. They now live aboard a 44-foot catamaran, *Infinite Improbability*, which is likely their last upgrade. Originally they cruised Long Island Sound out to Nantucket and north of the Cape Cod Canal but now, having sold all their "dirt-based" property, cruise from southern New England to the Florida Keys with the seasons, mostly via the ICW. They moor near the Mystic, CT, area in the summer and Marathon, FL, in the winter.

Capts. Matt & Lucy Claiborne are full-time cruising sailors and storytellers. After college, Matt and Lucy lived on a 32-foot sailboat in the Florida Keys. Even while working in the "real-world" as professors at a university, they continued cruising and camping with a trailerable 21-foot cuddy cabin. In 2014, they cast off on a full-time sailing adventure on a 38-foot Lagoon catamaran. Both Matt and Lucy have USCG Master and FAA pilot licenses. They are full-time digital nomads who work from their boat. Their favorite offices are quiet anchorages; their favorite coworkers are dolphins and pelicans. Matt and Lucy are passionate about education and helping new boaters fulfill their cruising dreams. In 2019, they purchased their "forever dream boat"–a Cabo Rico 38 named *Dulcinea*. After a year outfitting for off-the-grid living and long-distance cruising, you'll now find them cruising Chesapeake Bay, the ICW, Bahamas and beyond with their adventure dog, Chelsea.

Capt. George & Patricia Hospodar have been boaters for over 45 years and have cruised more than 50,000 miles together aboard two sailboats and their 48-foot Symbol motor yacht, *Reflection*. George has been a 100-ton licensed U.S. Coast Guard Captain for 30 years. He and Pat are proud Platinum Loopers, lifetime members of the America's Great Loop Cruisers' Association and New Jersey Harbor Hosts. Together they have authored two popular boating books: "Reflection on America's Great Loop" and "The Great Loop Experience from Concept to Completion" as well as serving as Cruising Editors for Waterway Guide publications. They have also been featured speakers at many boat shows, TrawlerFests and other nautical events.

Michael O'Reilly & Ann Phillips came to sailing by first messing about with canoes and kayaks while living on the Canadian shore of Lake Superior. Sailing replaced the smaller boats and over the last 15-plus years they have enjoyed many extended summer cruises. After completing a cruise through four of the five Great Lakes, they spent a few years exploring Lake Ontario and the Thousand Islands. One season was spent traveling the St. Lawrence River all the way to Newfoundland, which is the current "home" for their boat. Mike is a long-time freelance journalist, writing mostly about the sciences. With the transition to this new watery life, Mike now spends most of his work time writing about traveling, destinations and cruising. Ann is an accomplished photographer. Together they are chronicling their life afloat.

Mary & Tharon Rodriguez are Cruising Editors for the fresh waters of Lake Michigan and Lake Huron. They have been sailing for under a decade but have sailed Michigan to the Bahamas and everything in between. Their sailing vessel is *Tipsy Gypsy*, a 36-foot Nonsuch docked in their home port of Muskegon, MI. They are both digital nomads, working and cruising on a regular basis. They are based back in Michigan after multiple years of living aboard on the east coast. If you see them around, be sure to say hi! They are fun-loving, adventure-seeking, mid-westerners with a whole lot to offer our team. Learn more about these young cruisers at www.maryandtharon.com

Bob & Ann Sherer started sailing in 1985 with charters in Maine, Florida and the Caribbean followed by their first sailboat in 1986 which then lead to a 38-foot Ericson, followed by their present boat, a 42-foot Beneteau 423 in 2004. They started their yearly cruises on the ICW from New York to Key West in 2010 and Bob became known as Bob423, the person to follow for advice navigating through the many shoals of the ICW. He published his first *ICW Cruising Guide* in 2015 and has published an updated edition every year. The guide not only includes charts to avoid groundings but also tips learned from years of boating and a review of basic and advanced topics covering the ICW and is available on Amazon.com in paperback and eBook formats.

In 2018, Bob joined Waterway Guide as an on-the-water Editor, specializing in the Atlantic ICW and maintaining the Waterway Guide alerts for the ICW. That same year, Bob started the ICW Cruising Guide Facebook page, which has grown to 13,500 members. His most recent efforts include the publishing of Bob423 Tracks in GPX format for free downloading, which follow the deep-water path around the shoals of the ICW to enable a less stressful cruise in staying out of the mud. He is routinely consulted by NOAA, the USACE, and the Coast Guard on matters affecting the boating public. Bob and Ann reside 9 months of the year aboard their latest boat, a 42-foot Beneteau 423 sailboat, with their fearless dog, Hoolie, a Brittany.

Addison Chan is an experienced software entrepreneur, a world traveler and a committed sailing cruiser. He is the founder of Land and Sea Software Corp. which has engineered a revolutionary platform to produce mobile friendly, piracy-resistant, interactive content for traditional publishers. Waterwayguide Media is using the platform to provide its users with an enhanced digital experience that always delivers the most currently available information to mobile devices.

Addison and his wife, Pat, have traveled extensively through Cuba, Mexico and the Bahamas on their 42-foot Catalina sailboat, acquiring deep local knowledge over the years. The depth of his local knowledge and understanding of local culture is evident in his work as the coauthor of *Waterway Guide Cuba,* which is the gold standard of cruising guides for Cuba. His latest project has the working title of "A Handbook for Comfortable Cruising in The Bahamas" which will be representative of a new breed of interactive cruising guides. He is active within the cruising community and maintains the popular Cuba, Land and Sea and Bahamas Land and Sea groups on Facebook.

Other Contributors
Waterway Guide gathers information and photos from a variety of sources, including boaters, marinas, communities and tourism divisions. We would like to thank everyone who contributed to this edition.

About Our NOAA Chart Extracts

The U.S. Department of Commerce National Oceanic and Atmospheric Administration (NOAA) has advanced its plan of phasing out the updating and printing of nautical charts effective February 2021. Under the new practice NOAA will revise and refresh vector data that will be available to Electronic Navigational Charts (ENC) platforms only. The standardized data can be used by chart plotters and other map applications for creating visual displays of depths, aids to navigation (ATONS), points of interest and extensive details related to navigation, tides, shorelines, hazards and more. Updating of paper charts by NOAA will conclude in 2025, as will chart number references. For those who want printed outputs of nautical charts at various scales for specific geographic areas, the charts may still be obtained using several methods and suppliers. Visit www.noaa.gov for details.

Waterway Guide's objective is to offer the most up-to-date information available through use of NOAA's data superimposed on appropriate base maps. Because the printed charts from NOAA that have served us over the years are no longer supported, and have been supplanted by a new method of management and distribution of information, the chart extracts in this publication have been designed to address our distinctive editorial objectives.

Waterway Guide participated in workshops and seminars to develop a working relationship with NOAA and arrived at solutions for displaying acceptable levels of navigation and situational awareness in our various media platforms. Using NOAA-supplied vector data superimposed on geographically accurate base maps that were generated and supplied by Aqua Map, our publications now contain uncomplicated extracts of the geographical areas described in the accompanying text and tables throughout our guidebooks. The chartlets, as we identify them, contain shorelines, ATONS, water depths, landmarks, street and city names when available, and locations of marinas, all at sufficient levels of detail and scale for ease of interpretation. The chartlets are provided for reference only and not to be used for navigation.

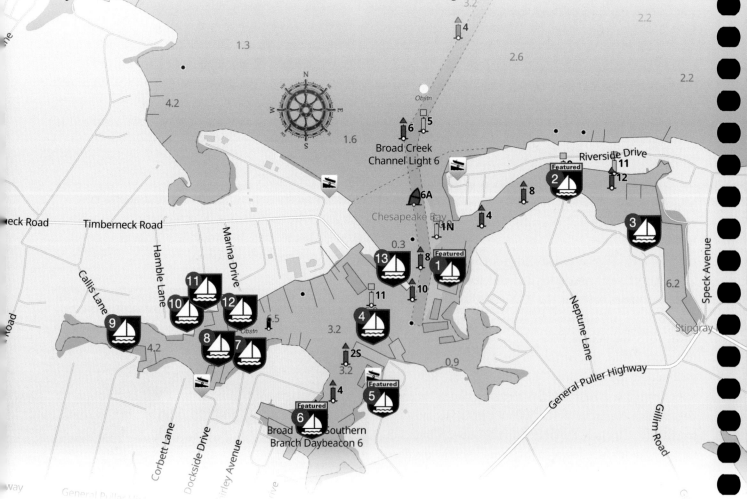

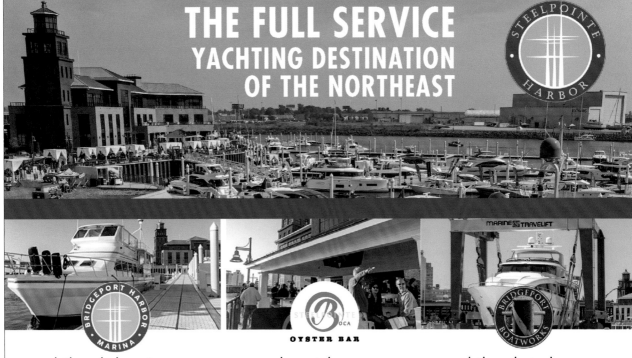

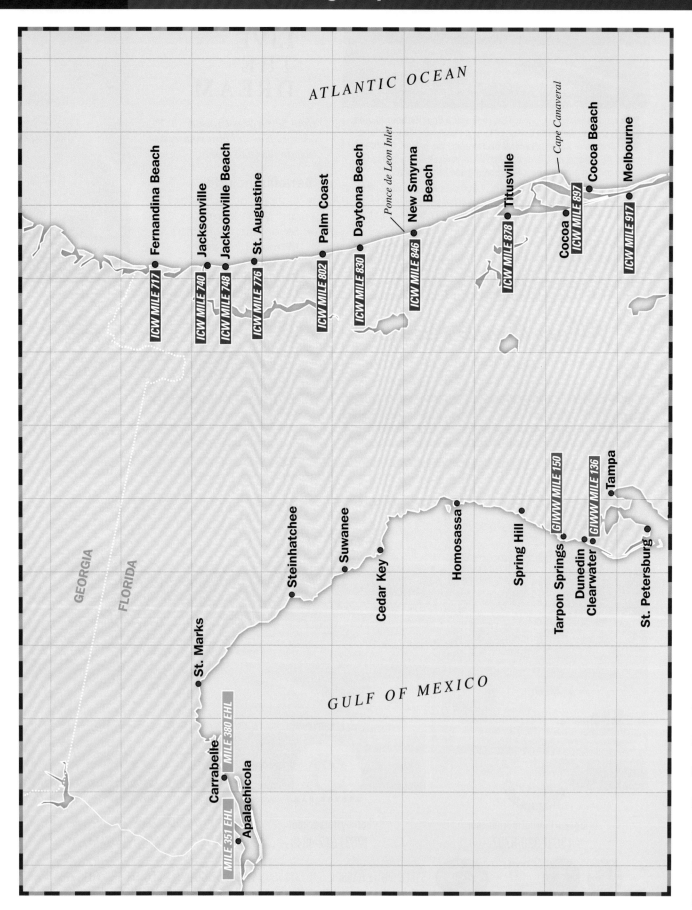

ATLANTIC OCEAN

Cape Canaveral

Ponce de Leon Inlet

Fernandina Beach
Jacksonville
Jacksonville Beach
St. Augustine
Palm Coast
Daytona Beach
New Smyrna Beach
Titusville
Cocoa
Cocoa Beach
Melbourne

ICW MILE 717
ICW MILE 740
ICW MILE 748
ICW MILE 776
ICW MILE 802
ICW MILE 830
ICW MILE 846
ICW MILE 878
ICW MILE 897
ICW MILE 917

GEORGIA
FLORIDA

Steinhatchee
Suwanee
Cedar Key
Homosassa
Spring Hill
Tampa
Tarpon Springs
Dunedin
Clearwater
St. Petersburg

GIWW MILE 150
GIWW MILE 136

St. Marks

Carrabelle
MILE 380 EHL
Apalachicola
MILE 351 EHL

GULF OF MEXICO

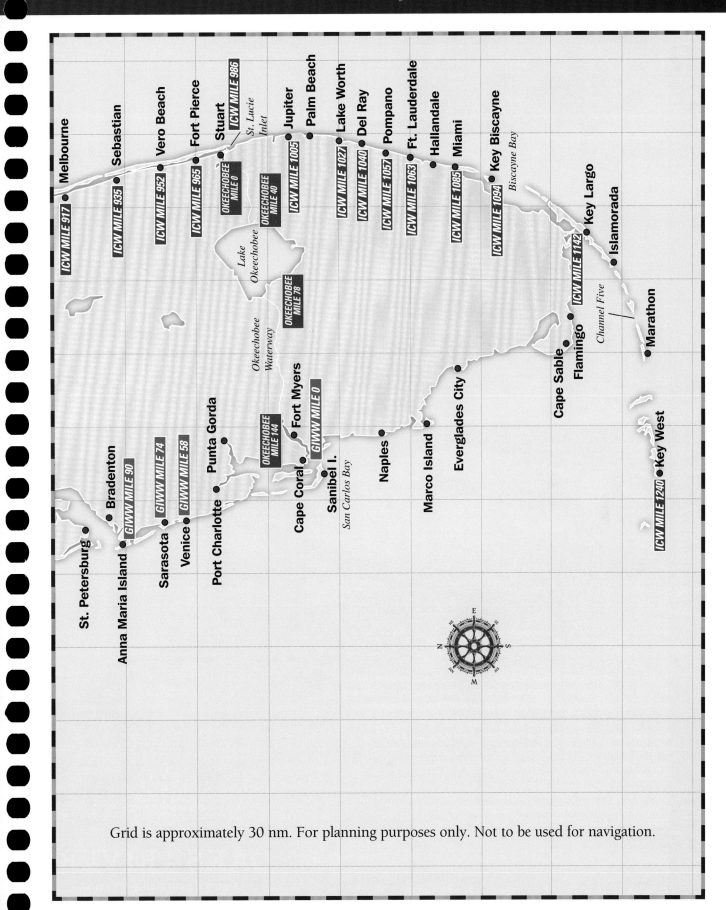

Melbourne

Sebastian

Vero Beach

Fort Pierce

Stuart

St. Lucie Inlet

Jupiter

Palm Beach

Lake Worth

Del Ray

Pompano

Ft. Lauderdale

Hallandale

Miami

Key Biscayne

Biscayne Bay

Key Largo

Islamorada

Marathon

ICW MILE 917

ICW MILE 935

ICW MILE 952

ICW MILE 965

ICW MILE 986

ICW MILE 1005

ICW MILE 1027

ICW MILE 1040

ICW MILE 1057

ICW MILE 1063

ICW MILE 1085

ICW MILE 1094

ICW MILE 1142

OKEECHOBEE MILE 0

OKEECHOBEE MILE 40

OKEECHOBEE MILE 78

Lake Okeechobee

Okeechobee Waterway

Channel Five

Cape Sable

Flamingo

Everglades City

Marco Island

Naples

Sanibel I.

San Carlos Bay

Cape Coral

Fort Myers

GIWW MILE 0

OKEECHOBEE MILE 144

Punta Gorda

Port Charlotte

Venice

Sarasota

GIWW MILE 58

GIWW MILE 74

GIWW MILE 90

Bradenton

Anna Maria Island

St. Petersburg

Key West

ICW MILE 1240

E
NE
N
SE
S
SW
W
NW

Grid is approximately 30 nm. For planning purposes only. Not to be used for navigation.

SKIPPER'S HANDBOOK

Port Security

The U.S. Coast Guard and Customs and Border Patrol–both components of the Department of Homeland Security–handle port security in the United States. Local law enforcement agencies and the FBI also have a role in port security at the local and regional level. Each year more than 11 million maritime containers arrive at our seaports. At land borders, another 11 million arrive by truck and 2.7 million by rail. Homeland Security is responsible for knowing what is inside those containers, whether it poses a risk to the American people and ensuring that all proper revenues are collected.

As an example, one in five food items is now imported. American consumers demand fresh limes and blueberries all year round and, as a result, during the winter months in the U.S. nearly 80 percent of the fresh fruits and vegetables on our tables come from other countries. With the ever-increasing amount of trade, the agricultural risks to the United States grow. The threat to crops and livestock is real.

In response to this threat and others, the U.S. Coast Guard has established "protection zones" around all U.S. Navy vessels, tank vessels and large-capacity cruise vessels, even when underway. U.S. Navy bases, U.S. Coast Guard bases and some shoreside facilities such as nuclear power plants are also in protection zones. Non-military vessels (this means YOU) are not allowed within 100 yards of these protection zones. To do so can rack up serious civil penalties and even imprisonment.

These protection zones vary from port to port and from facility to facility but ignorance of the protection zones is not a viable excuse. Having said that, law-abiding boaters sometimes find themselves unable to comply with the letter of the law without hitting a jetty, for example. In such cases, common sense and good communication should prevail.

America's Waterway Watch Program

Government officials view the recreational boating community as an ally. We can do our part (and perhaps stave off more stringent regulations and surveillance measures) by becoming familiar with the Coast Guard's America's Waterway Watch program. Think of it as a neighborhood watch program for the waterways.

It is not the intent of America's Waterway Watch to spread paranoia or to encourage spying on one another and it is not a surveillance program; it is instead a simple deterrent to potential terrorist activity. The purpose of the program is to allow boaters and others who spend time along the water to help the authorities counter crime and terrorism. To report suspicious behavior, call the National Response Center at 877-249-2824 (877-24WATCH). For immediate danger to life or property, call 911 or contact the U.S. Coast Guard on Marine VHF Channel 16.

Staying safe and responsible requires a little forethought and vigilance on your part. Following the steps outlined below will help ensure a trouble-free journey and keep you and your crew out of the headlines.

Be Prepared

■ Before you leave, check the current charts for the area in which you will be traveling and identify any security areas. Security zones are highlighted and outlined in magenta with special notes regarding the specific regulations pertaining to that area.

■ Check the latest *Local Notice to Mariners* (available online at www.navcen.uscg and posted at some marinas) and identify any potential security areas that may not be shown on the chart.

■ Prior to your departure, listen to VHF Channel 16 for any Sécurité alerts from the Coast Guard (departing cruise ships, U.S. Navy vessels, fuel tankers, etc.) for the area you will be cruising.

■ Talk to other boaters in your anchorage or marina about the areas where you will be traveling. They may have tips and suggestions on potential security zones or special areas they may have encountered along the way.

Stay Alert While Underway

■ Mind the outlined magenta security areas noted on your charts.

■ Look for vessels with blue or red warning lights in port areas and, if approached, listen carefully and strictly obey all instructions given to you.

■ Keep your VHF radio switched to VHF Channel 16 and keep your ears tuned for bulletins, updates and possible requests for communication.

■ Avoid commercial port operation areas, especially those that involve military, cruise line or petroleum facilities. Observe and avoid other restricted areas near power plants, national monuments, etc.

■ If you need to pass within 100 yards of a U.S. Navy vessel for safe passage, you must contact the U.S. Navy vessel or the Coast Guard escort vessel on VHF Channel 16 to let them know your intentions.

■ We advise that if government security or the U.S. Coast Guard hails you, do exactly what they say, regardless of whether or not you feel their instructions have merit.

Additional Resources

Atlantic Intracoastal Waterway Association:
www.atlanticintracoastal.org.

America's Waterway Watch:
www.americaswaterwaywatch.org

Department of Homeland Security:
www.dhs.gov

U.S. Customs and Border Protection:
www.cbp.gov

Customs Reporting Procedures

Operators of small pleasure vessels, arriving in the U.S. from a foreign port are required to report their arrival to Customs and Border Patrol (CBP) immediately. The master of the vessel reports their arrival at the nearest Customs facility or other designated location. These reports are tracked in the Pleasure Boat Reporting System. An application to lawfully enter the U.S. must be made in person to a CBP officer at a U.S. port-of-entry when the port is open for inspection.

CBP has designated specific reporting locations within the Field Offices that are staffed during boating season for pleasure boats to report their arrival and be inspected by CBP. The master of the boat must report to CBP telephonically and be directed to the nearest Port of Entry to satisfy the face-to-face requirement, or report to the nearest designated reporting location, along with the boat's passengers for inspection.

You may be required to rent a car or take a cab to the nearest airport or federal office several miles away for the inspection. These offices are often closed on weekends. If your arrival is after working hours, you are required to stay on board and clear in the next morning. You must, however, clear in within 24 hours of your arrival. Everyone on board, regardless of nationality, has to report in person. U.S. nationals must take their passports or passport cards. All non-U.S. Nationals should take their passports with valid visas and a Green Card, if held. Take your boat papers, either U.S. documentation or state registration with state decal number. You should also present a list of firearms and ammunition on board.

Clearing In with the ROAM App

Travelers arriving by boat into many popular U.S. ports can check into the country on their phones or tablets. The Reporting Offsite Arrival–Mobile (ROAM) app is the official replacement for the Local Boater Option (LBO) and Small Vessel Reporting System (SVRS) programs that have been used over the years. These programs required an initial interview to get in but usually resulted in a quick phone call instead of a face-to-face meeting to re-enter the U.S.

If you have a www.Login.gov account, you can log into the app immediately. If you need a password, the app directs you to the website. Then it walks you through the steps, including entering the specifics for each person on board and for your vessel. Once you've entered all of the details and submitted it for a review, an officer may initiate a video call to discuss the trip or to ask any necessary questions. All of this happens directly inside the app. Of course, there are still instances where in-person reporting is required. If you require an I-94, need to pay customs fees or duties, or need to obtain a cruising permit, you will still need to check in in-person. Boaters are still required to have a current fee decal onboard.

Now that the app has been implemented on a larger scale, travelers entering by boat in the Great Lakes; most of the East Coast (Delaware to Florida); Texas and San Diego, CA; and the U.S. territories in the Caribbean can use the app. New locations are continually being added, and because the program is new, it's probably a good idea to call your port of arrival to ensure they are using the ROAM app.

To download the ROAM app, just search the Apple App Store or the Google Play Store on your device. For more information, visit the CBP website or contact the CBP office at your port of arrival.

Additional Resources

U.S. Customs and Border Control:
www.cbp.gov/travel/pleasure-boats-private-flyers

Designated Port of Entry (Key West):
301 Simonton St., Ste. 20, 305-296-5411

Florida's Sojourner Permit

Florida has a unique form of short-term registration of a vessel called a Sojourner Permit. This is a temporary registration that is most applicable to those non-residents who leave their boats in a marina for the entire winter season.

The permit is required for any vessel owned by a non-Florida resident that is registered in another state or federally documented and that stays in Florida waters for more than 90 days or is used in Florida waters more than 183 days in a 12-month period. U.S. Coast Guard documented vessels from another state may also apply for a Sojourner Permit and will be granted an additional 1 year of use in Florida waters.

The intent is to ensure that boats used in Florida are registered in Florida, thus making them taxable under Florida's law regarding items purchased out of state but stored or used in Florida. However, under the Sojourner permit, your stay is deemed temporary and no tax is collected if you meet all of the following conditions:

1. You are a legal resident of another state
2. You have owned the boat 6 months or longer
3. You have shown no intent to use the boat in Florida at or before the time of purchase
4. The boat has been in use 6 months or longer within the taxing jurisdiction of another state.

Florida law requires that a vessel be registered in a U.S. jurisdiction at the time the boat enters Florida waters so as to be eligible for the initial 90-day grace period. Individual county tax offices issue the Sojourner Permit. State law is subject to local interpretation, depending on the tax district. Therefore, if you are going to keep a boat in Florida longer than the allotted 90 days, you will want to educate yourself in advance. Note that this is related to the USE tax and not the SALES tax on a vessel purchased in the State of Florida. Also, the Sojourner Permit applies only to Florida and does not supersede, cancel or impair the home-state registration of the vessel. A $50.00 non-resident commercial vessel fee is charged if the vessel is being used for commercial purposes.

VHF Communications

Skippers traveling the U.S. inland waterways use their VHF radios almost every day to contact other vessels and bridgetenders, make reservations at marinas, arrange to pass other vessels safely and conduct other business. Waterway Guide has put together the following information to help remove any confusion as to what frequency should be dialed in to call bridges, marinas, commercial ships or your friend anchored down the creek.

Remember to use low power (1 watt) for your radio transmission whenever possible. If you are within a couple of miles of the responding station (bridge, marina or other craft), there is no need to broadcast at 25 watts and disturb the transmissions of others 25 miles away.

Channel Usage Tips

■ VHF Channel 16 (156.8 MHz) is by far the most important frequency on the VHF-FM band. VHF Channel 16 is the international distress, safety and calling frequency.

■ If you have a VHF radio on your boat, Federal Communications Commission (FCC) regulations require that you maintain a watch on either VHF Channel 09 or 16 whenever you are underway and the radio is not being used to communicate on another channel. Since the Coast Guard does not have the capability of announcing an urgent marine information broadcast or weather warning on VHF Channel 09, it recommends that boaters remain tuned to and use VHF Channel 16.

■ Recreational craft typically communicate on VHF Channels 68, 69, 71, 72 or 78A. Whenever possible, avoid calling on VHF Channel 16 altogether by prearranging initial contact directly on one of these channels. No transmissions should last longer than 3 minutes.

■ The Coast Guard's main working VHF Channel is 22A and both emergency and non-emergency calls generally are switched there to keep VHF Channel 16 clear. Calling the Coast Guard for a radio check on VHF Channel 16 is prohibited.

■ Radio-equipped bridges on the Atlantic ICW use VHF Channel 09 with a few exceptions.

■ The Bridge-to-Bridge Radio Telephone Act requires many commercial vessels, including dredges and tugboats, to monitor VHF Channel 13. VHF Channel 13 is also the frequency used by bridges in several states.

Distress Calls

MAYDAY: The distress signal "MAYDAY" is used to indicate that a vessel is threatened by grave and imminent danger and requests immediate assistance.

PAN PAN: The urgency signal "PAN PAN" is used when the safety of the ship or person is in jeopardy.

SÉCURITÉ: The safety signal "SÉCURITÉ" is used for messages about the safety of navigation or important weather warnings.

VHF Channel 16 is the distress call frequency. The codeword "MAYDAY" is the international alert signal of a life-threatening situation at sea. After a MAYDAY message is broadcast, VHF Channel 16 must be kept free of all traffic, other than those directly involved in the rescue situation, until the rescue has been completed.

If you hear a MAYDAY message and no one else is responding, it is your duty to step in to answer the call, relay it to the nearest rescue organization and get to the scene to help. Remember, a MAYDAY distress call can only be used when life is threatened. For example, if you have run on the rocks but no one is going to lose their life, that is NOT a MAYDAY situation.

> Note: The Coast Guard has asked the FCC to eliminate provisions for using VHF Channel 09 as an alternative calling frequency to VHF Channel 16 when it eliminates watch-keeping on VHF Channel 16 by compulsory-equipped vessels. Stay tuned for updates.

How to Make a Distress Call

MAYDAY! MAYDAY! MAYDAY!

This is: Give your vessel name and call sign.

Our position is: Read it off the GPS or give it as something like "2 miles southwest of Royal Island." (Your rescuers must be able to find you!)

We are: Describe what's happening (e.g., on fire/hit a reef/sinking).

We have: Report how many people are on board.

At this time we are: Say what you're doing about the crisis (e.g., standing by/abandoning ship).

For identification we are: Describe your boat type, length, color, etc. (so your rescuers can more readily identify you).

We have: List safety equipment you have (e.g., flares/ smoke/ocean dye markers/EPIRB).

We will keep watch on Channel 16 as long as we can.

VHF Channels	
09	Used for radio checks and hailing other stations (boats, shoreside operations). Also used to communicate with drawbridges in Florida.
13	Used to contact and communicate with commercial vessels, military ships and drawbridges. Bridges in several states monitor VHF Channel 13.
16	***Emergency use only.*** May be used to hail other vessels, but once contact is made, conversation should be immediately switched to a working (68, 69, 71, 72, 78A) VHF channel.
22	Used for U.S. Coast Guard safety, navigation and Sécurité communications.
68 69 71 72 78A	Used primarily for recreational ship-to-ship and ship-to-shore communications.

Rules of the Road

Anyone planning to cruise U.S. waterways should be familiar with the rules of the road. *Chapman Piloting: Seamanship and Small Boat Handling* and *The Annapolis Book of Seamanship* are both excellent on-the-water references with plentiful information on navigation rules. For those with a penchant for the exact regulatory language, the U.S. Coast Guard publication *Navigation Rules: International–Inland* covers both international and U.S. inland rules. (Boats over 39.4 feet are required to carry a copy of the U.S. Inland Rules at all times.)

Following is a list of common situations you may likely encounter on the waterways. Make yourself familiar with them, and if there is ever a question as to which of you has the right-of-way, let the other vessel go first.

Sailors need to remember that a boat under sail with its engine running is considered a motorboat.

Passing or Being Passed:

■ If you intend to pass a slower vessel, try to hail them on your VHF radio to let them know you are coming.

■ In close quarters, BOTH vessels should slow down, which normally allows the faster vessel to pass quickly without throwing a large wake onto the slower boat.

■ Slower boats being passed have the right-of-way and passing vessels must keep clear of these slower vessels.

■ As you pass a slower boat, take a look back to see how they were affected by your wake. Remember: YOU are responsible for your wake. It is the law to slow down and it is common courtesy.

At Opening Bridges:

■ During an opening, boats traveling with the current go first and generally have the right-of-way.

■ Boats constrained by their draft, size or maneuverability (e.g., dredges, tugs and barges) take priority.

■ Standard rules of the road apply while circling or waiting for a bridge opening.

Tugs, Freighters, Dredges & Naval Vessels:

■ These vessels are usually constrained by draft or their inability to easily maneuver. For this reason, you will almost always need to give them the right-of-way and keep out of their path.

■ You must keep at least 100 yards away from any Navy vessel. If you cannot safely navigate without coming closer than this, you must notify the ship of your intentions over VHF Channel 16.

■ Keep a close watch for freighters, tugs with tows and other large vessels while offshore or in crowded ports. They often come up very quickly, despite their large size.

■ It is always a good practice to radio larger vessels (VHF Channel 13 or 16) to notify them of your location and your intentions. The skippers of these boats are generally appreciative of efforts to communicate with them. This is especially true with dredge boats on all the waterways.

Additional Resources

U.S. Coast Guard Boating Safety Division:
www.uscgboating.org

U.S. Coast Guard Navigation Center:
www.navcen.uscg.gov

In a Crossing Situation:

- When two vessels under power are crossing and a risk of collision exists, the vessel that has the other on her starboard side must keep clear and avoid crossing ahead of the other vessel.

- When a vessel under sail and a vessel under power are crossing, the boat under power is usually burdened and must keep clear. The same exceptions apply as per head-on meetings.

- On the Great Lakes and western rivers (e.g., the Mississippi River system), a power-driven vessel crossing a river shall keep clear of a power-driven vessel ascending or descending the river.

Power Vessels Meeting Any Other Vessel:

- When two vessels under power (either sailboats or powerboats) meet "head-to-head," both are obliged to alter course to starboard.

- Generally, when a vessel under power meets a vessel under sail (i.e., not using any mechanical power), the powered vessel must alter course accordingly.

- Exceptions are vessels not under command, vessels restricted in ability to maneuver, vessels engaged in commercial fishing or those under International Rules such as a vessel constrained by draft.

Two sailboats meeting under sail:

- When each has the wind on a different side, the boat with the wind on the port side must keep clear of the boat with the wind on the starboard side.

- When both have the wind on the same side, the vessel closest to the wind (windward) will keep clear of the leeward boat.

- A vessel with wind to port that sees a vessel to windward but cannot determine whether the windward vessel has wind to port or starboard will assume that windward vessel is on starboard tack and keep clear.

Keep Watch for Crab Pots!

While crab pots with marker buoys are not intentionally placed inside navigational channels, they sometimes break loose and find their way there. The terms "pot" refers to the enclosed traps (usually a framework of wire) used to catch crabs in shallow waters. The attached retrieval markers can range from colorful buoys to empty milk jugs (or anything else that floats). Most buoys are painted in a color that contrasts the water surface but some are black or even dark blue, which are especially difficult to see in the best of conditions. You do NOT want to get a line wrapped around your prop so it is advisable to have a spotter on the foredeck when traversing fields of pots.

Coast Guard Requirements

The U.S. Coast Guard stands watch at all times to aid vessels of all sizes and the persons on board. In some areas, you can quickly reach the Coast Guard by dialing *CG on a cellular phone. If you have a question of a non-emergency nature, the Coast Guard prefers that you telephone the nearest station. As always, if there is an emergency, initiate a "MAYDAY" call on VHF Channel 16.

In addition to aiding boaters in distress, the Coast Guard also enforces maritime law and conducts safety inspections. While a Coast Guard boarding can be unnerving, if you are responsible and prepared, it will only take 15 to 30 minutes and will be a non-event. First, have your boat in order. This includes having your vessel documentation, registration and insurance documents on hand, as well as your passport. Organize this in a binder and keep it in the nav station so you don't have to fumble around looking for documents and paperwork. You will need to acknowledge the location of any weapons on board and show a permit (when required by state law). The officers will likely focus on areas with the largest safety concerns including the following.

Note that state and local requirements are also considered. If there is a minor violation, they may give you a written warning explaining what needs to be fixed to be in compliance. If you are found with a small violation and correct it quickly, then this will merely be a chance to interact with those whose goal is to keep you as safe as possible on the water.

Life Jackets: One Type I, II, II or V per person plus one Type IV throwable device is required. PFDs must be U.S. Coast Guard-approved, wearable by the intended user and readily accessible. The Type IV throwable device must be located so that it is immediately available.

Visual Distress Signals: All vessels 16 feet and over must be equipped with minimum of 3 day-use and 3 night-use or 3 day/night combination pyrotechnic devices. Non-pyrotechnic substitutes are orange flag (for day use) and electric S-O-S signal light (for night use). Flares must be up to date (e.g., not expired).

Sound Producing Devices: A whistle, horn, siren, etc. capable of a 4-second blast audible for 0.5 mile must be on board for use during periods of reduced visibility. Boats 65 feet and over must have a bell and one whistle or horn required to signal intentions.

Navigation Lights: All powered vessels under 12 meters (39.4 feet) must have working navigational lights and an independent all-around anchor light. Sailboats under power are considered powerboats and must follow "power" rules.

Fire Extinguisher: U.S. Coast Guard-approved, marine-type fire extinguishers are required on any boat with enclosed fuel or engine spaces, enclosed living spaces or permanent (not movable by one person) fuel tanks. They must be in good working condition and readily accessible. (Number of units required depends on vessel length.)

Ventilation: Boats built after August 1, 1980, with enclosed gasoline engines must have a powered ventilation system with one or more exhaust blowers.

Backfire Flame Arrester: All gasoline-powered inboard/outboard or inboard motor boats must be equipped with an approved backfire flame arrester.

Pollution Placard: It is illegal to discharge oil or oily waste into any navigable waters of the U.S. Boats over 26 feet must display a durable oily waste pollution placard of at least 5 by 8 inches in a prominent location.

MARPOL Trash Placard: It is illegal to dump plastic trash anywhere in the ocean or navigable waters of the U.S. Boats over 26 feet must display a durable trash placard at least 4 by 9 inches in a prominent location.

Navigation Rules: Boats 39.4 feet and over must have a copy of current Navigation Rules on board. You can download a copy at www.uscgboating.org.

Marine Sanitation Devices: The discharge of treated sewage is allowed within 3 nm of shore except in designated "No Discharge Zone" areas. The Coast Guard will check that overboard discharge outlets can be sealed (and remain sealed if within 3 nm of shore).

Reference Materials

U.S. Coast Guard Local Notice to Mariners

The U.S. Coast Guard provides timely marine safety information for the correction of all U.S. Government navigation charts and publications from a wide variety of sources, both foreign and domestic via the *Local Notice to Mariners*. These are divided by district, updated weekly and available as a PDF at www.navcen.uscg.gov. (Select LNMs tab at top of page.)

Cruising Guides

- *ICW Cruising Guide (by Bob423)*, Robert A. Sherer

- *Skipper Bob Cruising Guides*, Ted Stehle (editor)

Navigation

- *A Boater's Guide to Federal Requirements for Recreational Boaters.* Covers equipment requirements, navigation rules and aids to navigation, a sample float plan and safety and survival tips. Can be downloaded as a PDF at www.uscgboating.org/images/420.PDF.

- *NAVIGATION RULES, INTERNATIONAL—INLAND*, U.S. Dept. of Homeland Security. The U.S. Coast Guard requires all vessels over 39 feet carry this book of the national and international rules of the road. Can be downloaded as a PDF at www.navcen.uscg.gov.

- *U.S. Coast Pilot (1-5)*, NOAA. Includes piloting information for coasts, bays, creeks and harbors. Also includes tide tables and highlights restricted areas. Updated weekly and can be downloaded as a PDF at www.nauticalcharts. noaa.gov/publications/coast-pilot/index.html.

- *U.S. Chart No 1. (Chart Symbols)*. Describes the symbols, abbreviations and terms used on NOAA nautical charts. Available online at www. nauticalcharts.noaa.gov/publications/us-chart-1.html.

- *U.S. Aids to Navigation System* is a downloadable guide from the U.S. Coast Guard with basic information on the recognition of U.S. Aids to Navigation System (ATONS). Find it at www.uscgboating.org/images/486.PDF.

Maintenance

- *Boatowner's Mechanical & Electrical Manual* (4th Edition), Nigel Calder

- *Boatowner's Illustrated Electrical Handbook*, Charlie Wing

- *Boat Mechanical Systems Handbook*, David Gerr

Seamanship

- *Anchoring: A Ground Tackler's Apprentice*, Rudy and Jill Sechez

- *Boater's Pocket Reference*, Thomas McEwen

- *Chapman Piloting & Seamanship* (68th Edition), Charles B. Husick

- *Eldridge Tide and Pilot Book* (Annual), Robert E. and Linda White

- *Heavy Weather Sailing* (7th Edition), Peter Bruce

- *Nigel Calder's Cruising Handbook*, Nigel Calder

- *Offshore Cruising Encyclopedia*, Steve & Linda Dashew

- *The Annapolis Book of Seamanship* (4th Edition), John Rousmaniere

- *The Art of Seamanship*, Ralph Naranjo

- *World Cruising Essentials*, Jimmy Cornell

First Aid & Medical

- *Advanced First Aid Afloat* (5th Edition), Dr. Peter F. Eastman

- *DAN Pocket Guide to First Aid for Scuba Diving*, Dan Orr & Bill Clendenden

- *First Aid at Sea*, Douglas Justin and Colin Berry

- *Marine Medicine: A Comprehensive Guide* (2nd Edition), Eric Weiss and Michael Jacobs

- *On-Board Medical Emergency Handbook: First Aid at Sea*, Spike Briggs and Campbell Mackenzie

About the Weather

Every day on the water can't have balmy breezes, abundant sunshine and consistently warm weather; however, staying out of bad weather is relatively easy if you plan ahead. The National Weather Service (NWS) provides mariners with continuous broadcasts of weather warnings, forecasts, radar reports and buoy reports over VHF-FM and Single Side Band (SSB) radio. There are almost no areas on the Atlantic ICW where a good quality, fixed-mount VHF cannot pick up one or more coastal VHF broadcasts. Also, there is no substitute for simply looking at the sky, and either stay put or seek shelter if you don't like what you see.

Reading the Skies

Water and metal are excellent conductors of electricity, making boating in a thunderstorm a risky prospect. While the odds of a given boat being hit are small, the consequences are severe and deadly. Do not try and play the odds! The best advice if you are out on the water and skies are threatening is get back to land and seek safe shelter, but that's not always practical for cruisers who live aboard or are not near land.

Thunderstorms occur when air masses of different temperatures meet over inland or coastal waters. An example of this would be when air with a high humidity that is warm near the ground rises and meets cooler air, which condenses and creates water droplets. This releases energy, which charges the atmosphere and creates lightning. This is why thunderstorms are a daily occurrence between March and October near southern waterways.

A tell-tale sign of a thunderstorm is cumulonimbus clouds: those tall clouds with an anvil-shaped (flat) top. Thunderstorms can also precede even a minor cold front. Keep in mind that thunderstorms generally move in an easterly direction so if you see a storm to the south or southwest of you, start preparing.

Don't Wait Until It's Too Late!

Almost all lightning will occur within 10 miles of its parent thunderstorm, but it can strike much farther than that. Also, the current from a single flash will easily travel for long distances. Because of this, if you see lightning or hear thunder, you CAN get struck!

Weather Apps (Free)
Boat Weather
Buoycast: NOAA Marine Forecast
National Hurricane Center Tracker
NOAA Marine Weather Radar
NOAA Weather
PredictWind
Wind Alert
Windfinder
Windy
Weather Online
Accuweather (www.accuweather.com)
BoatUS Hurricane Tracking & Resource Center (www.boatus.com/hurricanes/tracking)
Buoy Weather (www.buoyweather.com)
Coastal Marine Forecast (www.weather.gov/marine)
National Hurricane Center (www.nhc.noaa.gov)
National Weather Service (www.weather.gov)
Passage Weather (www.passageweather.com)
Predict Wind (www.predictwind.com)
Sailflow (www.sailflow.com)
The Weather Channel (www.weather.com)
Windfinder (www.windfinder.com)

The ability to see lightning will depend on the time of day, weather conditions and obstructions, but on a clear night it is possible to see a strike more than 10 miles away. Thunder can also be heard for about 10 miles, provided there is no background noise such as traffic, wind or rain.

If you see lightning, you can determine the distance by timing how long it takes before you hear thunder. The old rule that every 5 seconds of time equals 1 mile of distance works well. So if it takes 20 seconds to hear thunder after you see lighting, then the storm is 4 miles away. Time to drop anchor and "hunker down"!

Lightning Safety Tips

Lightning tends to strike the tallest object and boats on the open water fit this profile. The lightning will try to take the most direct path to the water, which is usually down the mast on a sailboat or the VHF antenna on a powerboat. However, both sailboats and powerboats with cabins–especially those with lightning protection systems properly installed–are relatively safe, provided you keep a few things in mind:

■ Before the storm strikes, lower, remove or tie down all antennas, fishing rods and flag poles.

■ Stay down below and in the center of the cabin. Avoid keel-stepped masts and chain plates (on sailboats) and large metal appliances such as microwaves or TVs. Remove any metal jewelry.

■ Disconnect the power and antenna leads to all electronics including radios. Do not use the VHF radio unless absolutely necessary.

■ If you are stuck on deck, stay away from metal railings, the wheel, the mast and stays (on sailboats) or other metal fittings. Do not stand between the mast and stays as lightning can "side-flash" from one to the other.

■ Stay out of the water and don't fish or dangle your feet overboard. Salt water conducts electricity, which means that it can easily travel through the water toward you.

■ Don't think rubber-soled deck shoes will save you; while rubber is an electric insulator, it's only effective to a certain point. The average lightning bolt carries about 30,000 amps of charge, has 100 million volts of electric potential and is about 50,000°F.

If You Are Struck:

1. Check people first. Many individuals struck by lightning or exposed to excessive electrical current can be saved with prompt and proper cardiopulmonary resuscitation (CPR). Contrary to popular belief, there is no danger in touching persons after they have been struck by lightning.

2. Check the bilge as strikes can rupture through-hull fittings and punch holes in hulls. Props and rudders are natural exit points on boats.

3. Check electronics and the compasses. Typically everything in the path of the lightning is destroyed on the way down to the water including instruments, computers and stereos.

4. Consider a short haul to check the bottom thoroughly. Lightning strikes sometimes leave traces of damage that may only be seen when the boat is out of the water.

Don't Rush Back Out

Because electrical charges can linger in clouds after a thunderstorm has passed, experts agree that you should wait at least 30 minutes after a storm before resuming activities. And remember: If you can hear thunder, you can still be struck by lightning!

Natural Seasickness Remedies

■ *Take slow, deep breaths.* This helps soothe upset stomach and dizziness.

■ *Focus on the horizon.* Keep your body still and head facing forward and watch a stationary object. Taking the helm always helps.

■ *Ginger can help.* Eat ginger snaps, drink ginger tea or ginger ale or digest in capsule form ahead of time.

■ *Peppermint works too.* Sucking on a peppermint candy, drinking peppermint tea or breathing in peppermint oil dabbed on a cloth can help with stomach issues.

■ *Try acupuncture wristbands.* Apply pressure to specific points on your wrist to reduce nausea.

Float Plan

BoatU.S.

1. Phone Numbers

Coast Guard:_____

Marine Police:_____

Local TowBoatU.S. Company:_____

2. Description of the Boat

Boat Name:_____Hailing Port:_____

Type:_____Model Year:_____

Make:_____Length:_____Beam:_____Draft:_____

Color, Hull:_____Cabin:_____Deck:_____Trim:_____Dodger:_____

Other Colors:_____# of Masts:_____

Distinguishing Features:_____

Registration No:_____Sail No:_____

Engine(s) Type:_____Horsepower:_____Cruising Speed:_____

Fuel Capacity, Gallons:_____Cruising Range:_____

Electronics/Safety Equipment Aboard

VHF Radio:_____Cell Phone:_____CB:_____SSB:_____

Frequency Monitored:_____Loran:_____SatNav:_____

Depth Sounder:_____Radar:_____GPS:_____

Raft:_____Dinghy:_____EPIRB:_____A/B/C/406M
(Indicate Type)

3. Trip Details

Owner/Skipper (Filing Report):_____

Phone:_____Age:_____

Address:_____

Additional Persons Aboard, Total:_____

Name:_____Age:_____

Address:_____Phone:_____

Boating Experience:_____

Name:_____Age:_____

Address:_____Phone:_____

Boating Experience:_____

Name:_____Age:_____

Address:_____Phone:_____

Boating Experience:_____

Name:_____Age:_____

Address:_____Phone:_____

Boating Experience:_____

Name:_____Age:_____

Address:_____Phone:_____

Boating Experience:_____

Departure Date/Time:_____Return No Later Than:_____

Depart From:_____

Marina (Home Port):_____Phone:_____

Auto Parked At:_____

Model/color:_____Lic. #_____

Destination Port: _____

_____ETA:_____No Later Than:_____

Phone:_____

Anticipated Stopover Ports:_____

_____ETA:_____No Later Than:_____

Phone:_____

_____ETA:_____No Later Than:_____

Phone:_____

_____ETA:_____No Later Than:_____

Phone:_____

_____ETA:_____No Later Than:_____

Phone:_____

_____ETA:_____No Later Than:_____

Phone:_____

Plan Filed With:_____

Name:_____Phone:_____

Get in the habit of filing a Float Plan. It can assure quicker rescue in the event of a breakdown, stranding or weather delay. Fill out the permanent data in Sections 1 and 2. Then, make enough copies to last for the season. If you file a Float Plan with someone not at your home, such as a harbormaster or boating friend, be sure to notify them as soon as you return. Don't burden friends or authorities with unnecessary worry and responsibility if you are safe.

Check your *BoatU.S. Towing Guide*. Some listed companies will accept a verbal Float Plan via telephone or VHF.

Ditch Bag Checklist

Rescue Items

☐ Functioning, registered EPIRB

☐ Handheld VHF radio (waterproof or in sealed pouch with extra batteries)

☐ Sea anchor, drogue and line

☐ Manual inflation pump

☐ Selection of flares (parachute and handheld) and smoke signals

☐ Strobe light (may be present in inflatable PFD)

☐ Flashlight & batteries (headlamp is ideal)

☐ Whistle (may be present in inflatable PFD)

☐ Signal mirror

☐ Handheld GPS or compass (for position)

☐ Small pair of binoculars (to confirm a boat or plane spotting before using flares)

Survival Items

☐ Sponges and bailer (with handle)

☐ Patch kit for inflatable dinghy or life raft (or emergency clamps)

☐ Water (individually sealed or in collapsible containers)–at least 2 gallons per person

☐ Emergency food rations and can opener (if needed)

☐ Power Bars

☐ Prescription medications

☐ Seasickness medications/remedies

☐ First aid kit

☐ Multipurpose tool or sailor's knife

☐ Waterproof matches

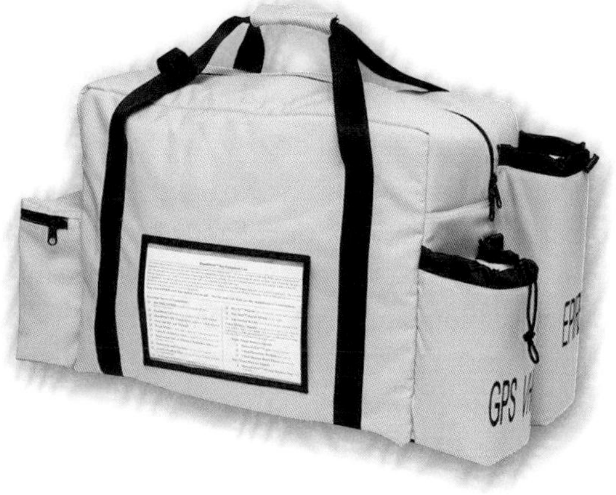

Other Items

☐ Solar blanket

☐ Heavy-duty coated gloves

☐ Duct tape

☐ Sewing kit

☐ Simple fishing gear (line, jigs, hooks, etc.)

☐ Polypropylene line

☐ Waterproof sunscreen and zinc oxide

☐ Bug repellent

☐ Ziploc bags (gallon size)

☐ Paper and pen in Ziploc bag

☐ Spare prescription glasses and sunglasses (polarized to reduce glare)

☐ Laminated copies of passports or license

☐ Cash ($50 in small bills)

☐ Copy of the yacht's papers (including insurance)

Tropical Weather & Hurricanes

While all coastal areas of the country are vulnerable to the effects of a hurricane (especially from June through November), the Gulf Coast, Southern and Mid-Atlantic states typically have been the hardest hit. But northern locales aren't immune; several destructive hurricanes have dealt a blow to areas in New England over the last 100 years including Hurricane Sandy in 2012 and Matthew in 2016. While hurricanes can create vast swaths of devastation, ample preparation can help increase your boat's chances of surviving the storm.

According to the National Weather Service, a mature hurricane may be 10 miles high with a great spiral several hundred miles in diameter. Winds are often well above the 74 mph required to classify as hurricane strength, especially during gusts. Hurricane damage is produced by four elements: tidal surge, wind, wave action and rain.

Distance from Eye	Force Level	Wind Speed
150 miles	Force 8	34–40 knots
100 miles	Force 11	56–63 knots
75 miles	Force 12	over 64 knots

- Tidal surge is an increase in ocean depth prior to the storm. This effect, amplified in coastal areas, may cause tidal heights in excess of 15 to 20 feet above normal. Additionally, hurricanes can produce a significant negative tidal effect as water rushes out of the waterways after a storm.

- Wind gusts can exceed reported sustained winds by 25 to 50 percent. For example, a storm with winds of 150 mph might have gusts of more than 200 mph, according to the National Weather Service.

- Wave action is usually the most damaging element of a hurricane for boaters. The wind speed, water depth and the amount of open water determine the amount of wave action created. Storm surges can transform narrow bodies of water into larger, deeper waters capable of generating extreme wave action.

- Rainfall varies but hurricanes can generate anywhere from 5 to 20 inches or more of rain.

Hurricane Categorization

CATEGORY	PRESSURE	WIND SPEED	SURGE
1	Above 980 mb (Above 28.91 in.)	64–82 knots (74–95 mph)	4–5 ft. (1–1.5 m)
Visibility much reduced. Maneuvering under engines just possible. Open anchorages untenable. Danger of poorly secured boats torn loose in protected anchorages.			
2	965–979 mb (28.50–28.91 in.)	83-95 knots (96–110 mph)	6-8 ft. (1.5–2.5 m)
Visibility close to zero. Boats in protected anchorages at risk, particularly from boats torn loose. Severe damage to unprotected boats and boats poorly secured and prepared.			
3	945–964 mb (27.91–28.50 in.)	96-113 knots (111–130 mph)	9-12 ft. (2.5–3.5 m)
Deck fittings at risk and may tear loose, anchor links can fail and unprotected lines will chafe through. Extensive severe damage.			
4	920–944 mb (27.17-27.91 in.)	114-135 knots (131–155 mph)	13-18 ft. (3.5–5.4 m)
Very severe damage and loss of life.			
5	Below 920 mb (Below 27.17 in.)	Above 135 knots (131–155 mph)	Above 18 ft. (Above 5.4 m)
Catastrophic conditions with catastrophic damage.			

If your boat is in a slip, you have three options: Leave it where it is (if it is in a safe place); move it to a refuge area; or haul it and put it on a trailer or cradle. Some marinas require mandatory evacuations during hurricane alerts. Check your lease agreement and talk to your dockmaster before a hurricane if you are uncertain. Keep in mind that many municipalities close public mooring fields in advance of the storm. In some localities, boaters may be held liable for any damage that their boat inflicts to marina piers or property; check locally for details. Because of this, rivers, canals, coves and other areas away from large stretches of open water are best selected as refuges.

Consult your insurance agent if you have questions about coverage. Many insurance agencies have restricted or canceled policies for boats that travel or are berthed in certain hurricane-prone areas. Review your policy and check your coverage as many insurance companies will not cover boats in hurricane-prone areas during the June through November hurricane season. Riders for this type of coverage are notoriously expensive.

Preparing Your Boat

■ Have a hurricane plan made up ahead of time to maximize what you can get done in the amount of time you will have to prepare (no more than 12 hours in some cases). Plan how to tie up the boat or where to anchor before a hurricane is barreling down on you. Make these decisions in advance!

■ Buy hurricane gear well in advance. When word of a hurricane spreads, local ship stores run out of storm supplies (anchors and line, especially) very quickly.

■ Strip everything that isn't bolted down off the deck of the boat (e.g., canvas, sails, antennas, bimini tops, dodgers, dinghies, dinghy motors, cushions, unneeded control lines on sailboats) as this will help reduce windage and damage to your boat. Remove electronics and valuables and move them ashore.

■ Any potentially leaky ports or hatches should be taped up. Dorades (cowls) should be removed and sealed with deck caps.

■ Make sure all systems on board are in tip-top shape in case you have to move quickly. Fuel and water tanks should be filled, bilge pumps should be in top operating condition and batteries should be fully charged.

■ You will need many lengths of line to secure the boat; make certain it is good stretchy nylon (not Dacron). It is not unusual to string 600 to 800 feet of dock line on a 40-foot-long boat in preparation for a hurricane. If you can, double up your lines (two for each cleat) as lines can break during a strong storm. Have fenders and fender boards out and make sure all of your lines are protected from chafing.

■ If you are anchored out, use multiple large anchors; there is no such thing as an anchor that is too large. If you can, tie to trees with a good root system such as mangroves or live oaks. Mangroves are particularly good because their canopy can have a cushioning effect. Be sure mooring lines include ample scope to compensate for tides 10 to 20 feet above normal.

■ Lastly, do not stay aboard to weather out the storm. Many people have been seriously injured (or worse) trying to save their boats during a hurricane. Take photos of the condition in which you left your boat and take your insurance papers with you.

Returning Safely After the Storm

■ Before hitting the road, make sure the roads back to your boat are open and safe for travel. Beware of dangling wires, weakened docks, bulkheads, bridges and other structures.

■ Check your boat thoroughly before attempting to move it. If returning to your home slip, watch the waters for debris and obstructions. Navigate carefully as markers may be misplaced or missing.

■ If your boat should sink, arrange for engine repairs before floating it but only if it is not impeding traffic. Otherwise, you will need to remove it immediately. Contact your insurance company right away to make a claim.

Additional Resources

National Hurricane Center: www.nhc.noaa.gov

BoatUS Hurricane Tracking & Resource Center: www.boatus.com/hurricanes

Dealing With Onboard Waste

Up until the late 1980s, many boaters simply discharged their untreated sewage overboard into the water. After a revision to the Clean Water Act was passed in 1987, the discharge of untreated sewage into U.S. waters within the 3-mile limit was prohibited. Shortly thereafter, pump-out stations became a regular feature at marinas and fuel docks throughout the U.S. waterways.

Simply stated, if you have a marine head installed on your vessel and are operating in coastal waters within the U.S. 3-mile limit (basically all of the waters covered in the guide you are now holding), you need to have a holding tank and you will obviously need to arrange to have that tank pumped out from time to time.

Government regulation aside, properly disposing of your waste is good environmental stewardship. While your overboard contribution to the waterways may seem small in the grand scheme of things, similar attitudes among fellow boaters can quickly produce unsavory conditions in anchorages and small creeks. The widespread availability of holding tank gear and shoreside pump-out facilities leaves few excuses for not doing the right thing.

No-Discharge Zones

- No-Discharge means exactly what the name suggests: No waste, even waste treated by an onboard Type I marine sanitation device (MSD), may be discharged overboard. All waste must be collected in a holding tank and pumped out at an appropriate facility.

- Keep in mind that there are some areas that forbid overboard discharge of any waste including gray water from showers or sinks. Familiarize yourself with local regulations before entering new areas to ensure you don't get hit with a fine.

The Law

- If you have a marine head onboard and are operating on coastal waters within the U.S. 3-mile limit (basically all of the waters covered in this guide), you need to have an approved holding tank or Type I MSD. In a No-Discharge area even a Type I MSD system must have a holding tank.

- All valves connected to your holding tank or marine head that lead to the outside (both Y-valves AND seacocks) must be wire-tied, padlocked or absent of the valve handle and in the closed position. Simply having them closed without the (non-releasable) wire ties will not save you from a fine if you are boarded.

- You may discharge waste overboard from a Type I MSD in all areas except those designated as No-Discharge Zones. A Type I MSD treats waste by reducing bacteria and visible solids to an acceptable level before discharge overboard.

- While small and inconvenient for most cruisers, "Port-A-Potties" meet all the requirements for a Type III MSD as the holding tank is incorporated into the toilet itself.

Pump-Out and Holding Tank Basics

- Some marinas are equipped with pump-out facilities, normally located at the marina's fuel dock. Note that some marinas charge a fee for the service.

- Several municipalities and local governments have purchased and staffed pump-out boats that are equipped to visit boats on request, especially those at anchor. Radio the local harbormaster to see if this service is available in the area you are visiting. There is normally a small fee involved.

- You will want to keep an eye out on your holding tank level while you are cruising, especially if you are getting ready to enter an area where you many not have access to proper pump-out services for a few days. Plan a fuel stop or marina stay to top off the fuel and water tanks and empty the other tank before you set out into the wild.

Marine Sanitation Devices

■ Type I MSD: Treats sewage before discharging it into the water using maceration. The treated discharge must not show any visible floating solids and must meet specified standards for bacteria content. Raritan's Electro Scan and Groco's Thermopure systems are examples of Type I MSDs. Not permitted in No-Discharge Zones.

■ Type II MSD: Type II MSDs provide a higher level of waste treatment than Type I units and are larger as a result. They employ biological treatment and disinfection. These units are usually found on larger vessels due to their higher power requirements. These may not be discharged in No-Discharge Zones.

■ Type III MSD: Regular holding tanks store sewage until the holding tank can either be pumped out to an onshore facility or at sea beyond the U.S. boundary waters (i.e., 3 miles offshore).

Penalties and Fines

■ Misuse or failure to equip a vessel with a Marine Sanitation Device may result in a non-criminal infraction with a $56 penalty.

■ Illegal dumping/discharge of a Marine Sanitation Device may result in a non-criminal infraction with a $250 penalty.

Additional Resources

BoatU.S. Guide to Overboard Discharge:
www.boatus.com/foundation/guide/
environment_7.html

EPA Listing of No-Discharge Zones:
www.epa.gov/vessels-marinas-and-ports/
no-discharge-zones-ndzs-state

Distances: Fernandina Beach to Key West, FL

Inside Route Distances - Fernandina Beach, Florida to Key West, Florida
(nautical and statute miles)

	Key West	Flamingo	Marathon	Matecumbe Harbor	Tavernier	Miami	Port Everglades	Fort Lauderdale	Port of Palm Beach	Jupiter	Fort Myers	Moore Haven	Clewiston	Port Mayaca	Stuart	Salerno	Fort Pierce	Vero Beach	Melbourne	Eau Gallie	Cocoa	Titusville	New Smyrna Beach	Daytona Beach	Marineland	St. Augustine	Jacksonville	Fernandina Beach	Norfolk, VA
Norfolk, VA	1061	1050	1045	1017	999	947	927	925	885	873	975	926	915	892	865	860	839	827	798	795	780	764	735	722	692	676	659	623	•
Fernandina Beach	458	427	422	394	378	324	304	303	262	251	353	303	292	269	242	237	216	204	175	172	157	141	113	99	69	53	36	•	717
Jacksonville	454	423	418	390	374	320	300	299	258	247	349	299	288	265	238	233	212	200	171	168	153	137	108	95	65	49	•	41	758
St. Augustine	405	374	369	341	324	271	251	249	209	197	299	250	239	216	189	184	163	151	122	119	104	88	59	46	16	•	56	60	778
Marineland	389	358	353	325	309	255	235	234	193	182	284	235	223	200	173	169	148	136	106	103	89	72	44	30	•	18	75	79	796
Daytona Beach	359	328	323	295	279	225	205	204	163	152	254	204	193	170	143	138	117	105	76	73	58	42	14	•	35	53	109	114	831
New Smyrna Beach	345	315	309	282	265	211	191	190	150	18	240	191	180	157	130	125	104	92	63	59	45	28	•	16	51	68	124	130	846
Titusville	317	286	281	253	237	183	163	162	121	110	212	163	151	128	101	97	76	64	34	31	17	•	32	48	83	101	158	162	879
Cocoa	301	270	264	237	220	166	146	145	105	93	195	146	135	112	85	80	59	47	18	14	•	20	52	67	102	120	176	181	898
Eau Gallie	286	255	250	223	206	152	132	131	90	79	181	132	120	97	70	66	45	33	3	•	16	36	68	84	119	137	193	198	915
Melbourne	283	252	247	219	203	149	129	128	87	76	178	128	117	94	67	62	41	29	•	14	21	39	72	87	122	140	197	201	918
Vero Beach	254	223	217	190	173	119	99	98	58	46	148	99	88	65	38	33	12	•	34	38	54	74	106	121	157	174	230	235	952
Fort Pierce	242	211	205	178	161	107	87	86	46	34	136	87	76	53	26	21	•	14	47	52	68	87	120	135	170	188	244	249	966
Salerno	224	193	188	161	144	90	70	69	28	17	119	70	58	35	8	•	24	38	71	76	92	112	144	159	194	212	268	273	990
Stuart	229	198	193	165	149	95	75	74	33	22	111	61	50	27	•	9	30	44	77	81	98	116	150	165	199	217	274	278	995
Port Mayaca	256	225	220	192	176	122	102	101	60	49	83	34	23	•	31	40	61	75	108	112	129	147	181	196	230	248	305	310	1026
Clewiston	279	248	243	215	199	145	125	124	83	72	61	11	•	26	58	67	87	101	135	138	155	174	207	222	257	275	331	336	1053
Moore Haven	290	259	254	227	210	156	136	135	94	83	49	•	13	40	70	81	100	114	148	152	168	188	220	235	270	288	344	349	1066
Fort Myers	339	309	303	276	259	205	185	184	144	132	•	56	70	96	128	137	157	170	205	208	224	244	276	292	327	344	402	406	1122
Jupiter	207	177	171	144	127	73	53	52	12	•	152	96	83	56	25	20	39	53	87	91	107	127	159	175	209	227	284	289	1005
Port of Palm Beach	196	165	160	132	116	62	42	41	•	14	166	108	96	69	38	32	53	67	100	104	121	139	173	188	222	241	297	302	1018
Fort Lauderdale	155	125	119	92	75	21	1	•	47	60	212	155	143	116	85	79	99	113	147	151	167	186	219	235	269	287	344	348	1064
Port Everglades	154	123	118	91	74	20	•	1	48	61	213	156	144	117	86	80	100	114	148	152	168	188	220	236	270	289	345	350	1067
Miami	134	104	98	71	54	•	23	24	71	84	236	180	167	141	109	104	123	137	171	175	191	211	243	259	293	312	368	373	1090
Tavernier	83	52	47	19	•	62	85	86	133	146	298	242	229	203	171	166	185	199	234	237	253	273	305	321	356	373	430	435	1150
Matecumbe Harbor	65	35	29	•	22	82	105	106	152	166	318	261	247	221	190	185	205	219	252	257	273	291	323	339	374	392	449	453	1170
Marathon	42	34	•	33	54	113	136	137	184	197	349	292	280	253	222	216	236	250	284	288	304	323	356	372	407	425	481	486	1203
Flamingo	73	•	39	40	60	120	142	144	190	204	356	296	285	259	228	222	243	257	290	293	311	329	362	377	412	430	486	491	1208
Key West	•	84	48	75	96	154	177	178	226	239	390	334	321	295	264	258	278	292	326	329	346	365	397	413	448	466	522	527	1244

Distances: St. Johns River, FL

Distances on St. Johns River, Florida (nautical and statute miles)															
	Lake Harney	Sanford	Astor-Volusia	Georgetown	Leesburg	Moss Bluff Lock	Silver Springs	Welaka	Crescent City	Palatka	Doctors Lake Inlet	Jacksonville	Broward River (mouth)	Intracoastal Waterway	Mayport	St. Johns River (mouth)
St. Johns River (mouth)	161	143	109	95	162	145	136	86	89	68	32	20	12	4	2	•
Mayport	159	141	107	93	160	143	134	84	87	66	30	18	10	2	•	2
Intracoastal Waterway	157	139	105	91	158	141	132	82	85	64	28	16	8	•	2	5
Broward River (mouth)	149	131	97	83	150	133	124	74	77	56	20	8	•	9	12	14
Jacksonville	141	123	89	75	142	125	116	66	69	48	12	•	9	18	21	23
Doctors Lake Inlet	129	111	77	62	129	112	104	54	56	36	•	14	23	32	35	37
Palatka	93	75	41	26	94	76	68	18	20	•	41	55	64	74	76	78
Crescent City	101	83	49	35	102	85	76	26	•	23	64	79	89	98	100	102
Welaka	75	57	23	8	75	58	50	•	30	21	62	76	85	94	97	99
Silver Springs	123	105	71	56	31	14	•	58	87	78	120	134	143	152	154	157
Moss Bluff Lock	131	113	79	65	17	•	16	67	98	87	129	144	153	162	165	167
Leesburg	148	131	96	82	•	20	36	86	117	108	148	163	173	182	184	186
Georgetown	66	49	14	•	94	75	64	9	40	30	71	86	96	105	107	109
Astor-Volusia	52	34	•	16	110	91	82	26	56	47	89	102	112	121	123	125
Sanford	18	•	39	56	151	130	121	66	96	86	128	142	151	160	162	165
Lake Harney	•	21	60	76	170	151	142	86	116	107	148	162	171	181	183	185

Distances: Key West to Apalachicola, FL

Coastwise and Inside Route Distances – Key West, FL to Apalachicola, FL
(nautical miles)

	Apalachicola, FL	Carrabelle, FL	St. Marks, FL	Cedar Key, FL	Tarpon Springs, FL	Clearwater, FL	Tampa, FL	St. Petersburg, FL	Bradenton, FL	Sarasota, FL	Venice, FL	Port Boca Grande, FL	Fort Myers, FL	Naples, FL	Everglades, FL	Cape Sable, FL	Flamingo, FL	Matecumbe Harbor, FL	Marathon, FL	Key West, FL
Key West, FL	406	389	367	310	250	234	232	218	210	186	172	144	134	96	88	57	70	65	42	-
Marathon, FL	408	391	389	313	253	237	235	221	213	189	174	146	136	100	80	31	37	29	-	
Matecumbe Harbor, FL	411	394	392	316	255	240	237	224	215	191	177	149	139	103	81	32	35	-		
Flamingo, FL	396	379	377	301	240	225	222	209	200	176	162	134	124	88	66	17	-			
Cape Sable, FL	379	362	360	284	223	208	205	192	183	159	145	117	107	71	49	-				
Everglades, FL	350	334	332	255	195	179	177	163	155	131	116	88	79	38	-					
Naples, FL	316	299	297	221	160	145	143	129	120	96	82	54	44	-						
Fort Myers, FL	297	280	278	202	142	126	124	110	102	78	63	35	-							
Port Boca Grande, FL	262	245	244	167	107	91	89	75	67	43	28	-								
Venice, FL	234	218	216	139	79	63	61	47	39	15	-									
Sarasota, FL	221	204	202	125	65	49	42	33	25	-										
Bradenton, FL	209	193	191	114	54	38	36	22	-											
St. Petersburg, FL	202	186	184	107	47	31	18	-												
Tampa, FL	218	202	200	123	63	47	-													
Clearwater, FL	174	157	155	79	18	-														
Tarpon Springs, FL	164	147	145	68	-															
Cedar Key, FL	118	101	91	-																
St. Marks, FL	69	52	-																	
Carrabelle, FL	25	-																		
Apalachicola, FL	-																			

Routes used in table:
- Hawk Channel – between Marathon and Key West
- Northwest Channel (Key West) and outside to places between Cape Sable and San Carlos Bay, thence inside to Anclote Keys, thence outside to St. George Sound.

Distances from Everglades northward are inside via Big Marco River and Gordon Pass.

Florida Anchoring Restrictions

For over a decade, Florida legislators have grappled with the rules of anchoring. Following the completion of an 8-year pilot program conducted by the U.S. Fish & Wildlife Service that provided insight into the multitude of issues associated with vessels anchoring in the state's waterways, the Florida legislature approved House Bill 7043 that codified anchoring regulations in the state. The regulations, which offer clear guidance and specific requirements for boaters, localities, public safety agencies and law enforcement, went into effect July 1, 2017.

It is illegal for any vessel to be at anchor any time during the period between one-half hour after sunset and one-half hour before sunrise in the following areas:

- The section of Middle River lying between Northeast 21st Court and the ICW in Broward County.

- Sunset Lake in Miami-Dade County.

- The sections of Biscayne Bay in Miami-Dade County lying between: Rivo Alto Island and Di Lido Island; San Marino Island and San Marco Island; and San Marco Island and Biscayne Island

Exceptions
- If the vessel suffers a mechanical failure that poses an unreasonable risk of harm to the vessel or the persons onboard unless the vessel anchors. The vessel may anchor for three business days or until the vessel is repaired, whichever occurs first.

- If imminent or existing weather conditions in the vicinity of the vessel pose an unreasonable risk of harm to the vessel or the persons onboard unless the vessel anchors. The vessel may anchor until weather conditions no longer pose such risk. During a hurricane or tropical storm, weather conditions are deemed to no longer pose an unreasonable risk of harm when the hurricane or tropical storm warning affecting the area has expired.

- During special events, including public music performances, local government waterfront activities or fireworks displays. A vessel may anchor for the lesser of the duration of the special event or three days.

- Vessels engaged in recreational fishing if the persons onboard are actively tending hook and line fishing gear or nets.

The bill provides that citations will result in a mandatory court appearance and a $50 civil penalty. Those failing to show up for court may be found guilty of a misdemeanor of the second degree, with more severe penalties.

The Bottom Line
House Bill 7043 effectively prevents cities, towns, counties or other municipal entities from passing laws or ordinances preventing boaters from anchoring. HB 7043 now provides specific language related to where vessels may anchor in proximity to marinas, docks, boatyards, mooring fields, superyacht repair facilities and other vessels.

As of July 2021, the State of Florida has enacted a law that allows municipal governments and counties to manage anchorages. Be advised that regulations and laws will change for many designated and favorite anchorages in the state. Boaters should be aware of local ordinances before choosing an anchorage. Law enforcement will most likely be polite and understanding if you don't know the rules, but pulling up anchor and moving is not an activity you want to engage in after settling in following a day underway.

These new measures also provide guidance on the definitions of derelict vessels, use of unpermitted moorings and proof of pump-out when anchored for 10 days or longer in permitted mooring fields or No-Discharge Zones.

Dinghy Restriction in Miami Beach
It is also important to note that in the City of Miami Beach it is unlawful to tie a dinghy to a canal wall to visit the city. The city is also strictly enforcing the 20-minute limit for the dinghy dock at the end of 17th St. These restrictions carry stiff civil fines.

GPS Waypoints

The following list provides selected waypoints for the waters covered in this book. The latitude/longitude readings are taken from government light lists and must be checked against the appropriate chart and light list for accuracy. Some waypoints listed here are lighthouses and should not be approached too closely as they may be on land, in shallow water or on top of a reef. Many buoys must be approached with caution, as they are often located near shallows or obstructions. The positions of every aid to navigation should be updated using the Coast Guard's *Local Notice to Mariners* (www.navcen.uscg.gov/lnm).

The U.S. Coast Guard will continue to provide Differential GPS (DGPS) correction signals for those who need accuracy of 10 meters or less, even though most GPS receivers now come with an internal capability for receiving differential signals.

> *Prudent mariners will not rely solely on these waypoints to navigate. Every available navigational tool should be used at all times to determine your vessel's position.*

Florida East Coast

LOCATION	LATITUDE	LONGITUDE
St. Marys Entrance Lighted Buoy STM	N 30° 42.900'	W 081° 14.650'
St. Johns Lighted Buoy STJ	N 30° 23.583'	W 081° 19.133'
St. Augustine Lighted Whistle Buoy STA	N 29° 54.917'	W 081° 15.283'
Ponce de Leon Inlet Lighted Bell Buoy 2	N 29° 04.767'	W 080° 53.483'
Cape Canaveral App. Chnl. Lig. Buoy 8	N 28° 23.867'	W 080° 33.433'
Fort Pierce Inlet Lighted Buoy 2	N 27° 28.650'	W 080° 15.417'
St. Lucie Entrance Lighted Buoy 2	N 27° 10.017'	W 080° 08.383'
Lake Worth Inlet Lighted Buoy LW	N 26° 46.367'	W 080° 00.600'
Boca Raton Inlet North Jetty Light 2	N 26° 20.167'	W 080° 04.183'
Hillsboro Inlet Entrance Lighted Buoy HI	N 26° 15.133'	W 080° 04.467'
Port Everglades Lighted Buoy PE	N 26° 05.500'	W 080° 04.767'
Bakers Haulover Inlet Jetty Light	N 25° 53.933'	W 080° 07.183'
Miami Lighted Buoy M	N 25° 46.100'	W 080° 05.000'

Florida Keys

LOCATION	LATITUDE	LONGITUDE
Biscayne National Park N. Lig. Buoy N	N 25° 38.733'	W 080° 05.367'
Fowey Rocks Light	N 25° 35.433'	W 080° 05.800'
Triumph Reef Light 2TR	N 25° 28.267'	W 080° 06.917'
Pacific Reef Light	N 25° 22.267'	W 080° 08.517'
Carysfort Reef Light	N 25° 13.317'	W 080° 12.683'
Elbow Reef Light 6	N 25° 08.667'	W 080° 15.500'
Molasses Reef Light 10	N 25° 00.717'	W 080° 22.583'
Davis Reef Light 14	N 24° 55.550'	W 080° 30.167'
Alligator Reef Light	N 24° 51.100'	W 080° 37.133'
Tennessee Reef Light	N 24° 44.767'	W 080° 46.933'
Coffins Patch Light 20	N 24° 40.550'	W 080° 57.500'
Sombrero Key Light	N 24° 37.667'	W 081° 06.650'
Big Pine Shoal Light 22	N 24° 34.117'	W 081° 19.550'
Looe Key Light 24	N 24° 32.800'	W 081° 24.150'
American Shoal Light	N 24° 31.500'	W 081° 31.167'
Pelican Shoal Light 26	N 24° 30.367'	W 081° 35.983'
Stock Island Approach Channel Light 32	N 24° 28.483'	W 081° 44.533'
Key West Ent. Lighted Whistle Buoy KW	N 24° 27.683'	W 081° 48.033'
Key West NW Chan. Ent. Lig. Bell Buoy 1	N 24° 38.867'	W 081° 53.967'
Sand Key Light	N 24° 27.233'	W 081° 52.650'
Cosgrove Shoal Light	N 24° 27.467'	W 082° 11.100'
Twenty-Eight Foot Shoal Light	N 24° 25.800'	W 082° 25.533'
Halfmoon Shoal Light WR2	N 24° 33.500'	W 082° 28.433'
Rebecca Shoal Light	N 24° 34.733'	W 082° 35.117'

LOCATION	LATITUDE	LONGITUDE
Dry Tortugas Light	N 24° 38.000'	W 082° 55.233'
New Ground Rocks Light	N 24° 40.000'	W 082° 26.650'
Ellis Rock Light	N 24° 38.950'	W 082° 11.033'
Smith Shoal Light	N 24° 43.100'	W 082° 55.300'

Florida Bay and West Coast

LOCATION	LATITUDE	LONGITUDE
Bullfrog Banks Light BB	N 24° 50.733'	W 081° 20.567'
Arsenic Bank Light 1	N 24° 52.250'	W 080° 53.017
East Cape Light 2	N 25° 05.000'	W 081° 04.967'
Northwest Cape Light 4	N 25° 12.833'	W 081° 11.750'
Little Shark River Entrance Light 1	N 25° 19.350'	W 081° 09.233'
Broad Creek Light 6	N 25° 26.317'	W 081° 12.200'
Lostmans River Light 8	N 25° 32.567'	W 081° 14.983'
Pavilion Key Light 10	N 25° 40.917'	W 081° 21.400'
Cape Romano Shoals Light	N 25° 41.300'	W 081° 38.783'
Indian Key Pass Light 1	N 25° 47.983'	W 081° 28.067'
Coon Key Light	N 25° 52.900'	W 081° 37.933'
Capri Pass Light 2	N 25° 58.500'	W 081° 46.267'
Gordon Pass Shoal Light	N 26° 05.483'	W 081° 48.683'
San Carlos Bay Light SC	N 26° 25.133'	W 081° 57.550'
Sanibel Island Light	N 26° 27.183'	W 082° 00.850'
Charlotte Harbor Ent. Lig. Bell Buoy 2	N 26° 39.850'	W 082° 19.567'
Venice Inlet Light 1	N 27° 06.767'	W 082° 28.217'
Big Sarasota Pass Light 1	N 27° 15.567'	W 082° 33.767'
New Pass Entrance Light NP	N 27° 18.917'	W 082° 35.883'
Longboat Pass Approach Light LP	N 27° 25.850'	W 082° 41.850'
Southwest Channel Ent. Lig. Bell Buoy 1	N 27° 32.333'	W 082° 48.600'
Tampa Bay Lighted Buoy T	N 27° 35.317'	W 083° 00.717'
Pass-A-Grille Entrance Light PG	N 27° 40.583'	W 082° 46.017'
Johns Pass Light JP	N 27° 46.500'	W 082° 48.033'

LOCATION	LATITUDE	LONGITUDE
Clearwater Pass Channel Light 1	N 27° 58.267'	W 082° 50.850'
Anclote Anchorage South Ent. Light 1	N 28° 08.283'	W 082° 51.950'
Anclote River Entrance Light 1	N 28° 10.383'	W 082° 49.533'
Anclote Anchorage North Ent. Light 2	N 28° 15.050'	W 082° 52.900'
Homosassa Bay Entrance Light 2	N 28° 41.433'	W 082° 48.650'
Crystal River Lighted Buoy 2	N 28° 47.517'	W 082° 58.583'
Withlacoochee River Entrance Light 1	N 28° 58.133'	W 082° 49.717'
Cedar Keys Main Channel Light 1	N 29° 04.000'	W 083° 04.550'
Cedar Keys NW Channel App. Light 2	N 29° 08.483'	W 083° 07.850'
Suwannee River, Alligator Pass Light 2	N 29° 14.583'	W 083° 11.783'
Suwannee R., McGriff Pass Daybeacon 1	N 29° 18.583'	W 083° 12.017'
Steinhatchee River Light 1	N 29° 39.383'	W 083° 27.433'
St. Marks River Lighted Buoy SM	N 30° 04.300'	W 084° 10.800'
Carrabelle Channel Lighted Bell Buoy 2	N 29° 44.550'	W 084° 39.200'
St. George Island W Jetty Lig. Buoy 1	N 29° 36.167'	W 084° 57.217'
St. Joseph Bay Lig. & Ent. Rg. A Rear Lig.	N 29° 55.100'	W 085° 22.833'
St. Andrew Bay Ent. Lig. Whistle Buoy SA	N 30° 05.500'	W 085° 46.433'
Choctawhatchee Bay Ent. Lig. Whi. By CB	N 30° 22.250'	W 086° 30.900'
Pensacola Bay Ent. Lig. Gong Buoy 1	N 30° 16.267'	W 087° 17.550'

Alabama

LOCATION	LATITUDE	LONGITUDE
Perdido Pass Ent. Lig. Whistle Buoy PP	N 30° 15.517'	W 087° 33.400'
Mobile Entrance Lighted Horn Buoy M	N 30° 07.517'	W 088° 04.117'

Bridge Basics

Bridges have to be factored in when planning a trip. Depending on where you cruise, you may be dependent on bridge openings; a particular bridge's schedule can often decide where you tie up for the evening or when you wake up and get underway the next day. While many are high (over 65 feet) and some usually remain open (such as railroad bridges), others are restricted for different hours in specific months, closed during rush hours and/or open on the quarter-hour, half-hour or even at 20 minutes and 40 minutes past the hour.

To add to the confusion, the restrictions are constantly changing. Just because a bridge opened on a certain schedule last season does not mean it is still on that same schedule. Changes are posted in the Coast Guard's *Local Notice to Mariners* reports, which can be found online at www.navcen.uscg.gov/lnm. It is also a good idea to check locally to verify bridge schedules before your transit.

Calling a Bridge

Most bridges monitor VHF Channel 09, designated by the Federal Communications Commission as the "bridgetender channel." Bridges in NC and VA still answer on VHF Channel 13, as do the locks in the Okeechobee.

In any waters, it is a good idea to monitor both the bridge channel and VHF Channel 16–one on your ship's radio and one on a handheld radio, if your main set doesn't have a dual-watch capability–to monitor oncoming commercial traffic and communications with the bridgetender.

When using VHF, always call bridges by name and identify your vessel by name and type (such as sailing vessel or trawler) and whether you are traveling north or south. If you are unable to raise the bridge using VHF radio, use a horn signal.

If the gates do not come down and the bridge does not open after repeated use of the radio and the horn, call the Coast Guard and ask them to call the bridgetender on the land telephone line, or you may be able to call the bridge directly. Phone numbers for many bridges are given in the following Bridges & Locks section, although some of the numbers are not for the actual bridgetender, but for a central office that manages that bridge. Some bridges are not required to open in high winds. If you encounter a bridge that won't open, it is prudent to drop the hook in a safe spot until the situation is resolved.

Swing bridges have an opening section that pivots horizontally on a central hub, allowing boats to pass on one side or the other when it is open.

Lift bridges normally have two towers on each end of the opening section that are equipped with cables that lift the road or railway vertically into the air.

Most bridges carry a tide board to register vertical clearance at the center of the span. (Note that in Florida waters the tide board figure–and the one noted on the chart–is generally for a point that is 5 feet toward the channel from the bridge fender.) In the case of arched bridges, center channel clearance is frequently higher than the tide gauge registers. So check your chart and the tide boards and, unless it specifically notes that vertical clearance is given "at center," you may be able to count on a little extra height at mid-channel under the arch of the bridge. Some bridges may bear signs noting extra height at center in feet.

Because many bridges restrict their openings during morning and evening rush hours to minimize inconvenience to vehicular traffic, you may need to plan an early start or late stop to avoid getting stuck waiting for a bridge opening.

Pontoon bridges consists of an opening section that must be floated out of the way with a cable to allow boats to pass. Do not proceed until the cables have had time to sink to the bottom.

Bascule bridges are the most common type of opening bridge you will encounter. The opening section has one or two leaves that tilt vertically on a hinge like doors being opened skyward.

Bridge Procedures:

■ First, decide if it is necessary to have the drawbridge opened. You will need to know your boat's clearance height above the waterline before you start. Drawbridges have "clearance gauges" that show the closed vertical clearance with changing water level but a bascule bridge typically has 3 to 5 feet more clearance than what is indicated on the gauge at the center of its arch at mean low tide. Bridge clearances are also shown on NOAA charts.

■ Contact the bridgetender well in advance (even if you can't see the bridge around the bend) by VHF radio or phone. Alternatively, the proper horn signal for a bridge opening is one prolonged blast (four to six seconds) and one short blast (approximately one second). Bridge operators sound this signal when ready to open the bridge, and then usually the danger signal–five short blasts–when they are closing the bridge. The operator of each vessel is required by law to signal the bridgetender for an opening, even if another vessel has already signaled. Tugs with tows and U.S. government vessels may go through bridges at any time, usually signaling with five short blasts. A restricted bridge may open in an emergency with the same signal. Keep in mind bridgetenders will not know your intentions unless you tell them.

■ If two or more vessels are in sight of one another, the bridgetender may elect to delay opening the bridge until all boats can go through together.

■ Approach at slow speed and be prepared to wait as the bridge cannot open until the traffic gates are closed. Many ICW bridges, for example, are more than 40 years old and the aged machinery functions slowly.

■ Once the bridge is open, proceed at no-wake speed. Keep a safe distance between you and other craft as currents and turbulence around bridge supports can be tricky.

■ There is technically no legal right-of-way (except on the Mississippi and some other inland rivers) but boats running with the current should always be given the right-of-way out of courtesy. As always, if you are not sure, let the other boat go first.

■ When making the same opening as a commercial craft, it is a good idea to contact the vessel's captain (usually on VHF Channel 13), ascertain his intentions and state yours to avoid any misunderstanding in tight quarters.

■ After passing through the bridge, maintain a no-wake speed until you are well clear and then resume normal speed.

Locks & Locking Through

Many rivers in North America are a series of pools created by dams. When the dams also include locks, navigation is possible beyond the dam. Locks are watertight chambers with gates at each end. They raise and lower boats from one water level to the next. Many cruisers find locking through a pleasant experience and part of the adventure of boating.

Lock Types

- Conventional lift locks are single chambers that raise and lower boats.

- Flight locks are a series of conventional lift locks.

- Hydraulic lift locks have water-filled chambers supported by rams or pistons that move in opposite directions. The movement of one chamber forces the movement of the other via a connected valve. The chamber in the upper position adds sufficient water to cause it to drop, forcing the lower chamber to rise. The chambers have hinged gates fore and aft that contain the water and allow boats to enter or leave.

- Marine railways convey boats over obstacles, usually a landmass, by containing boats in a gantry crane that moves over the land and deposits the boat on the other side of the obstruction.

River locks are usually conventional lift locks. The dam deepens water around shoals and the lock allows vessels to bypass the dam. Conventional lift locks work by gravity alone. Water passively flows into or out of the lock. When the lock is filling, the valve at the upper end of the lock is opened and water flows in. The downstream lock gate is closed, preventing the escape of the water. This is the time of greatest turbulence in the locks and the time of greatest vigilance for boaters. When the upper water level is reached, the upper lock gate opens to allow boats to exit or enter.

When the lock empties, both lock doors are closed, a valve on the lower end of the lock is opened and water exits. This creates a surge of water outside the lock but inside the lock, the water recedes like water in a tub. When the water level in the lock is the same as the lower river level, the lower lock gate opens and vessels leave.

Locking Protocol

Call ahead on VHF Channel 13 (or sound three blasts) for permission to lock through. Indicate whether you are northbound (upbound) or southbound (downbound). Your presence and communication indicate to the locktender your desire to lock through.

Wait a safe distance from the lock or find an anchorage nearby and within sight of the lock.

Prepare for locking by placing large fenders fore and aft and having lines ready. Fender boards are useful because they protect your fenders and provide a skid plate against the dirt and algae on the lock wall.

When approaching the lock, stay back to allow outbound vessels to clear the lock. Do not enter until signaled to do so. Signals vary. Look for a telephone/pull rope at the lock wall; listen for a whistle blast–one long and one short blast or three blasts; look for a "traffic" light–green, yellow or red. Follow directions given by the locktender. The order of priority is:

1. U.S. Military

2. Mail boats

3. Commercial passenger boats

4. Commercial tows

5. Commercial fishermen

6. Pleasure Craft

When the locktender turns on the green light or calls for you to enter, enter in the order that boats arrived at the lock. The longest waiting boat goes first, unless directed by the locktender, who may call boats in according to size and the configuration of the lock. Do not jump the line, do not scoot in front of others and defer to faster boats so you do not have them behind you after you leave the lock.

When entering the lock, leave no wake, heed instruction and respect other boaters. If they are having trouble and appear unsettled, stand by until they are secure. Listen to the directives of the locktenders. Some lock systems require all line handlers to wear personal flotation devices (PFDs). Crew members on the bow should wear PFDs.

You will be directed by the locktender to a place along the lock wall. You will find an inset mooring pin (floating bollard), vertical cable or a rope.

- If there is a floating bollard, secure the boat to the pin via a center cleat by wrapping the line around the pin then back to the boat cleat.

- If there is a vertical cable, wrap the line around the cable and bring it back to the boat; the loop will ride up or down the cable.

- If there is a drop-down line, bring the line around a cleat and hold it. DO NOT TIE THE LINES!

If you are asked to provide a line, throw it to the locktender. After the locktender has secured it, take the bitter end and wrap–but do not tie– around a cleat. Attend the bow and the stern, and adjust the line(s) as the boat rises or falls in the lock chamber.

In crowded locks, move forward as far as you can to make room for others coming in behind you. Small boats may raft to bigger boats. Set adequate fenders for fending off another vessel.

Inside the lock chamber, turn off engines when secure. Exhaust fumes contained in the lock chamber are an irritant to people in small, open boats. Attend the lines at all times. Be prepared for turbulence when the lock fills. Never use hands or feet to fend a boat off a lock wall. Stay alert to other boats. Be prepared to quickly cut a line if needed.

When the lock reaches its determined depth/height, the locktender will loosen the line and drop it to you if you are using a line attached at the top of the lock. After receiving a whistle blast by the locktender, recover any lines used, and prepare to exit. Leave the lock in the same order as entering. Do not rush ahead of those in front of you.

Bridge & Lock Schedules

KEY:

Statute Miles from ICW Mile 0
Vertical Clearance

Drawbridge clearances are vertical, in feet, when closed and at Mean High Water in tidal areas. Bridge schedules are subject to schedule changes due to repairs, maintenance, events, etc. Check Waterway Explorer at waterwayguide.com for the latest schedules or call ahead.

FLORIDA BRIDGES MONITOR (THE) CHANNEL 09

Florida's East Coast ICW

720.7 / 5' — **Kingsley Creek Railroad Bridge:** Usually open

720.8 / 65' — **Thomas J. Shave, Jr. Twin Bridges:** Fixed. (Also known as **Kingsley Creek Hwy. Bridges**.)

739.2 / 65' — **SR 105 (Sisters Creek) Bridge:** Fixed

St. Johns River

13.1 / 169' — **Napoleon Bonaparte Broward Bridge:** Fixed. (Also known as **Dames Point Bridge**.)

21.8 / 86' — **John E. Mathews Bridge:** Fixed

22.8 / 135' — **Isaiah D. Hart Bridge:** Fixed. (Also known as **Hart-Commodore Point Bridge**.)

24.7 / 40' — **Main Street Bridge:** Opens on signal except from 7:00 a.m. to 8:30 a.m. and from 4:30 p.m. to 6:00 p.m., Mon. through Sat. (except federal holidays), when the draw need not open.

24.8 / 75' — **Acosta Bridge:** Fixed

24.9 / 5' — **Florida East Coast Railroad Bridge:** Usually open, displaying flashing green lights to indicate that vessels may pass. When a train approaches, large signs on both the upstream and downstream sides of the bridge flash "Bridge Coming Down," the lights go to flashing red, and siren signals sound. After an 8-minute delay, the draw lowers and locks if there are no vessels under the draw. The draw remains down for a period of 8 min. or while the approach track circuit is occupied. After the train has cleared, the draw opens and the lights return to flashing green.

25.4 / 75' — **Fuller Warren Bridge:** Fixed

35.1 / 65' — **Henry H. Buckman, Sr (I-295) Bridge:** Fixed. (Also known as **Three-Mile Bridge**.)

51.4 / 45' — **Shands Bridge:** Fixed. (Note: A new fixed 65-foot vertical clearance bridge has been in the planning stages for several years.)

79.8 / 65' — **Memorial Bridge:** Fixed

90.2 / 7' — **Buffalo Bluff Railroad Bridge:** Usually open

122.2 / 20' — **Astor Bridge:** Opens on signal. (Note: Open bascule overhangs channel at a height of 72 feet and overhead power cable is 70 feet.)

138.2 / 15' — **SR 44 (Whitehair) Bridge:** Opens on signal

156.2 / 7' — **Port of Sanford Railroad Bridge:** Usually open

156.3 / 45' — **US 17/US 92 Bridge:** Fixed

156.6 / 45' — **I-4 (St. Johns River Veterans Memorial) Bridges:** Fixed

Florida's East Coast ICW (cont.)

742.1 / 65' — **Wonderwood Dr. (SR 116) Bridge:** Fixed

744.7 / 65' — **Atlantic Boulevard (SR 814) Bridge:** Fixed

747.5 / 65' — **B.B. McCormick (U.S. 90) Bridge:** Fixed. (Also known as **Jacksonville Beach Bridge**.)

749.5 / 65' — **Butler Boulevard (SR 202) Bridge:** Fixed. (Also known as **Pablo Creek Bridge**.)

758.8 / 65' — **Palm Valley (SR 210) Bridge:** Fixed

775.8 / 65' — **Francis and Mary Usina (SR A1A/Vilano Beach) Bridge:** Fixed

777.9 / 18' — **Bridge of Lions (SR A1A):** Opens on signal, except from 7:00 a.m. to 6:00 p.m., when the draw need only open on the hour and half-hour; however, the draw need not open at 8:00 a.m., 12 noon and 5:00 p.m. Mon. through Fri. (except federal holidays). In addition, from 7:00 a.m. to 6:00 p.m. on Sat., Sun. and federal holidays, the draw need only open only on the hour and half-hour (904-824-7372). (Note: Additional 4 feet of vertical clearance observed at center of bridge.)

FLORIDA BRIDGES MONITOR 《VHF》 CHANNEL 09

780.3 / **65'** — **SR 312 Bridges:** Fixed

788.6 / **25'** — **Crescent Beach (SR 206) Bridge:** Opens on signal (904-461-4094)

803.0 / **65'** — **Hammock Dunes Bridge:** Fixed. (Also known as **Palm Coast Hwy. Bridge.**)

810.6 / **65'** — **SR 100 (Moody Blvd./Flagler Beach) Bridge:** Fixed

816.0 / **15'** — **Bulow (L.B. Knox) Bridge:** Opens on signal (386-441-0777)

824.9 / **65'** — **SR 40 Bridge** Fixed. (Also known as **Ormond Beach Bridge.**)

829.1 / **65'** — **Seabreeze Bridges:** Fixed

829.7 / **22'** — **Main Street Bridge:** Opens on signal (386-441-0777)

830.1 / **65'** — **International Speedway Blvd.:** Fixed

830.6 / **65'** — **Memorial Bridge:** Fixed (Note: Bridge under construction. Expect delays.)

835.5 / **65'** — **A1A Port Orange Relief Bridge:** Fixed. (Note: Vertical clearance may be as low as 63 feet on a high tide. Also known as **Dunlawton Ave. Bridge.**)

845.0 / **24'** — **George E. Musson/Coronado Beach (SR 44) Bridge:** Opens on signal, except from 7:00 a.m. until 7:00 p.m. daily, when the draw opens only on the hour and half hour. 386-424-2024. (Note: Hydraulic bridge; slow in opening.)

846.5 / **65'** — **Harris Saxon (South Causeway) Bridge:** Fixed. (Also known as **New Smyrna Bridge.**)

869.2 / **27'** — **Allenhurst (Haulover Canal) Bridge:** Opens on signal (321-867-4859). (Note: Manatee feeding area. Proceed slowly.)

876.6 / **7'** — **NASA (Jay-Jay) Railroad Bridge:** Usually open, displaying flashing green lights to indicate that vessels may pass. When a train approaches, the lights go to flashing red, and the draw lowers and locks if there are no vessels under the draw. The draw remains down for a period of 5 min. or while the approach track circuit is occupied. After the train has cleared, the draw opens and the lights return to flashing green.

878.9 / **65'** — **A. Max Brewer (SR 406) Bridge:** Fixed

885.0 / **27'** — **NASA Causeway (SR 405) Bridge:** Opens on signal, except from 6:30 a.m. to 8:00 a.m. and 3:30 p.m. to 5:00 p.m. Mon. through Fri. (except federal holidays), when the draws need not open (321-867-7200). (Also known as **Indian River Twin Bridges** or **Addison Point Twin Bridges.**)

894.0 / **65'** — **Bennett Causeway Bridges:** Fixed

897.4 / **65'** — **Hubert Humphrey (FL 520) Bridges:** Fixed. (Also known as Merritt Island [Cocoa] Twin Bridges.)

909.0 / **65'** — **Pineda Causeway Bridge:** Fixed

914.4 / **65'** — **Eau Gallie Causeway (SR 518) Bridge:** Fixed

918.2 / **65'** — **Melbourne Causeway (SR 516) Bridge:** Fixed

943.3 / **65'** — **Wabasso Bridge:** Fixed

951.9 / **66'** — **Merrill P. Barber (SR 60) Bridge:** Fixed. (Also known as **Vero Beach Bridge.**)

953.2 / **65'** — **Alma Lee Loy (SR 656/17th Street) Bridge:** Fixed

964.8 / **26'** — **SR A1A North Causeway (Banty Saunders) Bridge:** Opens on signal (772-468-3993).

965.8 / **65'** — **Peter B. Cobb Memorial (SR A1A) Bridge:** Fixed. (Also known as **Fort Pierce Bridge.**)

981.4 / **65'** — **Jensen Beach Causeway (Frank A. Wacha, SR 707A) Bridge:** Fixed

984.9 / **65'** — **Ernest Lyons (SR A1A) Bridge:** Fixed

Skipper's Handbook

Okeechobee Waterway (East to West)

3.4 / 65' — **Evans Crary (SR A1A) Bridge:** Fixed

7.3 / 65' — **Roosevelt (US 1) Bridge:** Fixed

7.4 / 7' — **Florida East Coast Railroad Bridge:** Usually in the fully open position, displaying flashing green lights to indicate that vessels may pass. When a train approaches, the navigation lights go to flashing red and a horn sounds four blasts, pauses, and then repeats four blasts. After an 8-min. delay, the draw lowers and locks, if there are no vessels under the draw. The draw remains down for a period of 8 min. or while the approach track circuit is occupied. After the train has cleared, the draw opens and the lights return to flashing green. Note: Only 50 feet of charted horizontal clearance.

7.4 / 14' — **Old Roosevelt (Dixie Highway) Bridge:** Opens on signal. The draw opens on signal, except from 7:00 a.m. to 6:00 p.m., Mon. through Fri. (except federal holidays), when the draw need open only on the hour and half hour. However, the draw need not open between 7:30 a.m. and 9:00 a.m. and 4:00 p.m. and 5:30 p.m. except at 8:15 a.m. and 4:45 p.m. On Saturdays, Sundays, and federal holidays from 8:00 a.m. to 6:00 p.m. the draw need open only on the hour, 20 minutes after the hour, and 40 minutes after the hour. When the adjacent railway bridge is in the closed position at the time of a scheduled opening the draw need not open, but it must then open immediately upon opening of the railroad bridge to pass all accumulated vessels. 772-692-0321

9.5 / 54' — **Palm City (SR 714) Bridge:** Fixed

10.9 / 55' — **Southwest Martin Highway Bridge:** Fixed

14.0 / 56' — **I-95 Twin Bridges:** Fixed

14.5 / 55' — **Florida Turnpike Bridges:** Fixed

15.1 — **St. Lucie Lock:** Opens on signal, 7:00 a.m. to 5:00 p.m. Last lockage at 4:30 p.m. Normally make fast on south wall. 772-287-2665

17.1 / 56' — **SR 76A Bridge:** Fixed

28.1 / 55' — **Indiantown (SR 710) Bridge:** Fixed

28.2 / 7' — **Seaboard System (Indiantoen) Railroad Bridge:** Opens on signal, except from 10:00 p.m. to 6:00 a.m., when the bridge opens on signal only if at least 3-hour notice is given. 772-597-3822

38.0 / 7' — **Florida East Coast Railroad Bridge:** Usually in the fully open position, displaying flashing green lights to indicate that vessels may pass. When a train approaches, it will stop and a crewmember will observe the waterway for approaching vessels, which will be allowed to pass. Upon manual signal, the bridge lights will go to flashing red, and the horn will sound four blasts, pause then repeat four blasts. The draw will lower and lock, if there are no vessels under the draw. After the train has cleared, the draw will open, and the lights will return to flashing green. (Note: Vertical clearance when open is 49 feet, setting the overhead clearance for the OCWW.) The bridge is not constantly tended.

38.8 / 55' — **US 98/441 Bridge:** Fixed

39.1 — **Port Mayaca Lock:** Opens on signal, 7:00 a.m. to 5:00 p.m. Last lockage at 4:30 p.m. Normally make fast on south wall. 561-924-2858

60.7 / 11' — **Belle Glade Dike (CR 717) Bridge:** Opens on signal from 7:00 a.m. to 6:00 p.m., Mon. through Thurs., and from 7:00 a.m. to 7:00 p.m., Fri. through Sun. At all other times, the draw need not be opened for the passage of vessels. Manual operation. (May not open in winds in excess of 20 mph.) 561-996-3844

75.5 — **Clewiston Lock:** Normally open. If the lock is closed due to high lake levels, an operator will be on site.

78.0 — **Moore Haven Lock:** Opens on signal, 7:00 a.m. to 5:00 p.m. Last lockage at 4:30 p.m. Normally make fast on south wall. 863-946-0414

78.3 / 5' — **Seaboard System (Moore Haven) Railroad Bridge:** Opens on signal, except from 10:00 a.m. to 6:00 a.m., when the draw need not open. (Note: Normally open. Manual operation.)

78.4 / 55' — **Moore Haven (US 27) Bridges:** Fixed

93.5 — **Ortona Lock:** Opens on signal, 7:00 a.m. to 5:00 p.m. Last lockage at 4:30 p.m. Normally make fast on south wall. 863-946-0414

FLORIDA BRIDGES MONITOR (((VHF))) CHANNEL 09

103.0 **28'** **La Belle (SR 29) Bridge:** Opens on signal, except from 7:00 a.m. to 9:00 a.m. and from 4:00 p.m. to 6:00 p.m., Mon. through Fri. (except federal holidays), when the bridge need not open. The bridge will open from 10:00 p.m. to 6:00 a.m. on signal only if at least 3-hour notice is given. 863-674-4663

108.2 **9'** **Fort Denaud Bridge:** Opens on signal, except from 10:00 p.m. to 6:00 a.m., when the bridge will open on signal only if at least 3-hour notice is given. 863-675-2055

116.0 **23'** **Alva Drawbridge:** Opens on signal, except from 10:00 p.m. to 6:00 a.m., when the bridge will open on signal only if at least 3-hour notice is given. 239-278-2704

121.4 **W.P. Franklin Lock:** Opens on signal from 7:00 a.m. to 5:00 p.m. Last lockage at 4:30 p.m. Normally make fast on south wall. 239-694-5451

126.3 **27'** **Wilson Pigott Drawbridge:** Opens on signal, except from 10:00 p.m. to 6:00 a.m., when the bridge will open on signal only if at least 3-hour notice is given.

128.9 **55'** **I-75 Bridge:** Fixed

129.9 **5'** **SCL Railroad Bridge:** Usually open. (Note: Span overhangs channel when open, resulting in a vertical clearance of 55 feet.)

134.6 **56'** **Edison Bridges:** Fixed

135 **55'** **US 41/Caloosahatchee River Bridge:** Fixed

138.6 **55'** **Midpoint Memorial Bridge:** Fixed

142 **55'** **Cape Coral Bridge:** Fixed

Florida's East Coast ICW (cont.)

995.9 **21'** **Hobe Sound (SR 708) Bridge:** Opens on signal (772-546-5234).

1004.1 **25'** **Jupiter Island (CR 707) Bridge:** Opens on signal (561-746-4261). (Hail as "707 Bridge.")

1004.8 **26'** **US 1 (Jupiter) Bridge:** Opens on signal (561-746-4907).

1006.2 **35'** **Indiantown (SR 706) Bridge:** Opens on the hour and half-hour.

1009.3 **35'** **Donald Ross Bridge:** Opens on the hour and half-hour (561-626-3030).

1012.6 **24'** **PGA Boulevard Bridge:** Opens on the hour and half-hour (561-626-3030).

1013.7 **25'** **Parker (US 1) Bridge:** Opens on the quarter and three-quarter hour (561-626-5445).

1017.2 **65'** **Blue Heron (SR A1A) Bridge:** Fixed

1020.8 **21'** **Flagler Memorial (SR A1A) Bridge:** Opens on the quarter hour and three-quarter hour. When the security zone is enforced, the draw will remain closed to navigation from 2:15 p.m. to 5:30 p.m. with the exception of a once an hour opening at 2:15 p.m., 3:15 p.m., 4:15 p.m. and 5:15 p.m. (weekdays only) if vessels request an opening (561-833-7339).

1022.6 **21'** **Royal Park (SR 704) Bridge:** Opens on the hour and half-hour. When the security zone is enforced, the draw will remain closed to navigation from 2:15 p.m. to 5:30 p.m. with the exception of a once an hour opening at 2:15 p.m., 3:15 p.m., 4:15 p.m. and 5:15 p.m. (weekdays only) if vessels request an opening (561-655-5617).

1024.7 **14'** **Southern Boulevard (SR 700/80) Bridge:** Opens on the quarter hour and three-quarter hour. When the security zone is enforced, the draw may be closed without advance notice to permit uninterrupted transit of dignitaries across the bridge (561-833-8852). (Note: Construction of a replacement 21-foot vertical clearance bascule bridge is proceeding with an expected completion date of late 2021. The temporary bridge, located north of the existing bridge, has a vertical clearance of 14 feet in the closed position and 64 feet in the open position with a 125-foot navigable channel. Expect delays.)

1028.8 **35'** **Lake Avenue (SR 802) Bridge:** Opens on signal (561-540-2516).

1031.0 **21'** **E. Ocean Avenue (Lantana) Bridge:** Opens on the hour and half-hour (561-582-2320).

1035.0 **21'** **E. Ocean Avenue (Boynton Beach) Bridge:** Opens on the hour and half-hour (561-733-0214).

1035.8 **25'** **E. Woolbright Rd. (SE 15th Street) Bridge:** Opens on signal (561-732-6461).

1038.7 **9'** **George Bush Boulevard Bridge:** Opens on signal (561-276-5948).

1039.6 **12'** **Atlantic Avenue (SR 806) Bridge:** Opens on the quarter hour and three-quarter hour (561-276-5435).

FLORIDA BRIDGES MONITOR (VHF) CHANNEL 09

1041.0
30'
Linton Boulevard Bridge: Opens on the hour and half-hour (561-278-1980). (Note: Actual vertical clearance may be as low as 27 feet. Call ahead to verify.)

1044.9
25'
Spanish River Boulevard Bridge: Opens on the hour and half-hour (561-395-5417).

1047.5
19'
Palmetto Park Bridge: Opens on the hour and half-hour (561-392-5903).

23'
Haven Ashe (SR A1A) Bridge (to ocean): Opens on signal. (Also known as **Boca Raton Inlet Bridge**.)

1048.2
9'
Camino Real Bridge: Opens on the hour, 20 min. past the hour and 40 min. past the hour (561-392-5903).

1050.0
21'
Hillsboro Boulevard (SR 810) Bridge: Opens on the hour and half-hour (954-428-1090).

13'
SR A1A (Hillsboro Inlet) Bridge (to ocean): Opens on signal, except from 7:00 a.m. to 6:00 p.m., the draw will open only on the hour, quarter hour, half-hour, and three-quarter hour.

1055.0
15'
NE 14th Street Bridge: Opens on the quarter hour and three-quarter hour (954-942-6909).

1056.0
15'
Atlantic Boulevard (SR 814) Bridge: Opens on the hour and half-hour (954-941-7119).

1059.0
15'
Commercial Boulevard (SR 870) Bridge: Opens on the hour and half-hour (954-772-3987).

1060.5
22'
Oakland Park Boulevard Bridge: Opens on the quarter hour and three-quarter hour (954-566-3711).

1062.6
25'
East Sunrise Boulevard (SR 838) Bridge: Opens on the hour and half hour (954-564-6986). On the first Sat. in May, the draw need not open from 9:45 p.m. to 10:45 p.m. The draw also need not open from 4:00 p.m. to 6:00 p.m. on both Sat. and Sun. of that weekend.

1064.0
24'
East Las Olas Boulevard Bridge: Opens on the quarter hour and three-quarter hour (954-463-0842). On the first Sat. in May, the draw need not open from 9:45 p.m. to 10:45 p.m. The draw also need not open from 4:00 p.m. to 6:00 p.m. on both Sat. and Sun. of that weekend.

New River (North & South Forks)

1.4
16'
SE 3rd Avenue Bridge: The draw opens on signal, except from 7:30 a.m. to 9:00 a.m. and 4:30 p.m. to 6:00 p.m., Mon. through Fri. (except federal holidays), when the draw need not open.

2.3
21'
Andrews Avenue Bridge: The draw opens on signal, except from 7:30 a.m. to 9:00 a.m. and 4:30 p.m. to 6:00 p.m., Mon. through Fri. (except federal holidays), when the draw need not open. The draw need not open for inbound vessels when the draw of the Florida East Coast Railroad Bridge is in the closed position for the passage of a train.

2.5
4'
Florida East Coast Railroad Bridge: Usually in the fully open position, displaying flashing green lights to indicate that vessels may pass. When a train approaches, the navigation lights go to flashing red and a horn sounds four blasts, pauses, and then repeats four blasts then the draw lowers and locks. After the train has cleared, the draw opens and the lights return to flashing green. The bridge shall not be closed more than 60 minutes combined for any 120-minute time period beginning at 12:01 a.m.

2.7
20'
William H. Marshall (7th Avenue) Bridge: The draw opens on signal, except from 7:30 a.m. to 9:00 a.m. and 4:30 p.m. to 6:00 p.m., Mon. through Fri. (except federal holidays), when the draw need not open.

0.9
21'
Davie Boulevard Bridge: (Located on South Fork.) The draw opens on signal, except from 7:30 a.m. to 9:00 a.m. and 4:30 p.m. to 6:00 p.m., Mon. through Fri. (except federal holidays), when the draw need not open.

2.0
55'
I-95 Twin Bridges: (Located on South Fork.) Fixed

2.1
2'
SCL Railroad Bridge: (Located on South Fork.) Opens on signal. Usually open if no train is approaching.

4.4
21'
SR 84 Bridge: (Located on South Fork.) Opens on signal if at least a 24 hour notice is given. Call 954-776-4300 (no VHF).

4.5
40'
I-595 Bridge: Fixed

FLORIDA BRIDGES MONITOR (VHF) CHANNEL 09

Florida's East Coast ICW (cont.)

1065.9 | **55'**
SE 17th Street (Brooks Memorial) Bridge: Opens on the hour and half-hour (954-524-7783).

1069.4 | **22'**
Dania Beach Boulevard (SR A1A) Bridge: Opens on the hour and half-hour (954-922-7833).

1070.5 | **22'**
Sheridan Street Bridge: Opens on the quarter hour and three-quarter hour (954-922-7833).

1072.2 | **25'**
Hollywood Beach Boulevard (SR 820) Bridge: Opens on hour and half-hour (954-922-3366).

1074.0 | **26'**
Hallandale Beach Boulevard (SR 858) Bridge: Opens on the quarter hour and three-quarter hour (954-456-6630).

1076.3 | **65'**
William Lehman Causeway (SR 856) Bridge: Fixed

1078.0 | **30'**
NE 163rd Street (SR 826) Bridge: Opens on signal, except from 7:00 a.m. to 6:00 p.m. on Mon. through Fri. (except federal holidays) and from 10:00 a.m. to 6:00 p.m. on Sat., Sun., and federal holidays, when the draw need open only on the quarter hour and three-quarter hour. (Also known as **Sunny Isles Bridge**.)

32'
Bakers Haulover Inlet Bridge (to ocean): Fixed

1081.4 | **16'**
Broad Causeway Bridge: Opens on signal, except from 8:00 a.m. to 6:00 p.m., when the draw need open only on the quarter hour and three-quarter hour (305-891-2221).

1084.6 | **25'**
West 79th Street Bridge: Opens on signal, except from 7:00 a.m. to 7:00 p.m., Mon. through Fri. (except federal holidays), when the draw need only open on the hour and half hour (305-758-1834).

1087.2 | **56'**
Julia Tuttle Causeway Bridge: Fixed (Note: Bridge is less than standard ICW vertical clearance of 64 feet and sets the controlling vertical clearance for the ICW.)

1088.6 | **12'**
Venetian Causeway Bridge (West): Opens on signal, except from 7:00 a.m. to 7:00 p.m., Mon. through Fri. (except federal holidays), when the bridge need only open on the hour and half-hour (305-358-6258).

1088.8 | **65'**
MacArthur Causeway Bridges: Fixed

1089.3 | **65'**
Dodge Island Bridge: Fixed

1089.4 | **22'**
Dodge Island Railroad Bridge: Usually open (unless train is approaching).

Miami River

23' | **0.1**
Brickell Avenue Bridge: Opens on signal, except from 7:00 a.m. to 7:00 p.m., Mon. through Fri. (except federal holidays), when the draw need only open on the hour and half-hour; however, from 7:35 a.m. to 8:59 a.m., 12:05 p.m. to 12:59 p.m. and 4:35 p.m. to 5:59 p.m., the draw need not open.

75' | **0.2**
Metro Train Bridge: Fixed

21' | **0.3**
South Miami Avenue Bridge: Opens on signal, except from 7:35 a.m. to 8:59 a.m., 12:05 p.m. to 12:59 p.m. and 4:35 p.m. to 5:59 p.m., Mon. through Fri. (except federal holidays), when the draw need not open.

75' | **0.4**
Retro Rail/M Path Bridge: Fixed

11' | **0.5**
SW Second Avenue Bridge: Opens on signal, except from 7:35 a.m. to 8:59 a.m., 12:05 p.m. to 12:59 p.m. and 4:35 p.m. to 5:59 p.m., Mon. through Fri. (except federal holidays), when the draw need not open.

75' | **0.6**
I-95 Twin Bridges: Fixed

18' | **0.9**
SW 1st Street Bridge: Opens on signal, except from 7:35 a.m. to 8:59 a.m., 12:05 p.m. to 12:59 p.m. and 4:35 p.m. to 5:59 p.m., Mon. through Fri. (except federal holidays), when the draw need not open.

35' | **1.0**
W Flagler Street Bridge: Opens on signal, except from 7:35 a.m. to 8:59 a.m., 12:05 p.m. to 12:59 p.m. and 4:35 p.m. to 5:59 p.m., Mon. through Fri. (except federal holidays), when the draw need not open.

12' | **0.5**
N 5th Street Bridge: Opens on signal, except from 7:35 a.m. to 8:59 a.m., 12:05 p.m. to 12:59 p.m. and 4:35 p.m. to 5:59 p.m., Mon. through Fri. (except federal holidays), when the draw need not open.

22' | **2.0**
NW 12th Avenue Bridge: Opens on signal, except from 7:35 a.m. to 8:59 a.m., 12:05 p.m. to 12:59 p.m. and 4:35 p.m. to 5:59 p.m., Mon. through Fri. (except federal holidays), when the draw need not open.

75' | **2.2**
Dolphin Expressway Bridge: Fixed

17' | **2.6**
NW 17th Avenue Bridge: Opens on signal.

25' | **3.2**
NW 22nd Avenue Bridge: Opens on signal.

21' | **3.5**
NW 27th Avenue Bridge: Fixed

FLORIDA BRIDGES MONITOR ((VHF)) CHANNEL 09

Florida Keys

1091.6 / 76' — **Rickenbacker Causeway Bridge:** Fixed

1126.9 / 65' — **Card Sound Road Bridge:** Fixed

1134.1 / 65' — **Jewfish Creek (US 1) Bridge:** Fixed

1152.0 / 15' — **Tavernier Creek Bridge:** Fixed

1156.0 / 27' — **Snake Creek Bridge:** Opens on signal, except from 8:00 a.m. to 6:00 p.m., when the draw need open only on the hour.

1157.0 / 10' — **Whale Harbor Channel Bridge:** Fixed

1162.0 / 7' — **Teatable Key Relief Bridge:** Fixed

1162.1 / 10' — **Teatable Key Channel Bridge:** Fixed

1163.0 / 27' — **Indian Key Channel Bridge:** Fixed

1164.5 / 10' — **Lignumvitae Channel Bridge:** Fixed

1168.5 / 10' — **Channel Two Bridge:** Fixed

1170.0 / 65' — **Channel Five Bridge:** Fixed

1176.0 / 23' — **Long Key Viaduct Bridge:** Fixed

1179.0 / 8' — **Toms Harbor Cut Bridge:** Fixed

1180.0 / 7' — **Toms Harbor Channel Bridge:** Fixed

1188.0 / 13' — **Vaca Cut Bridge:** Fixed

1194.0 / 19' — **Knight Key Channel Bridge:** Fixed

1197.0 / 65' — **Seven Mile Bridge:** Fixed. (Also known as **Moser Channel Bridge**.)

1205.0 / 20' — **Bahia Honda Bridges:** Fixed

1209.0 / 11' — **Spanish Harbor Channel Bridge:** Fixed

1215.0 / 15' — **Pine Channel Bridge:** Fixed. (Also known as **Little Torch Key Bridge**.)

1215.0 / 40' — **Niles Channel Bridge:** Fixed

1217.5 / 15' — **Kemp Channel Bridge:** Fixed

Florida's Gulf ICW (GIWW)

34.3 / 22' — **Boca Grande Swing Bridge:** Opens on signal, except from 7:00 a.m. to 6:00 p.m., Mon. through Fri., when the draw opens on the hour and half-hour. On Sat., Sun. and federal holidays the draw opens every 15 min. (Note: Vessels must request an opening.)

43.5 / 26' — **Tom Adams Bridge:** Opens on signal. (Also known as **Manasota Key Bridge**.)

49.9 / 26' — **Manasota Bridge:** Opens on signal. (Note: Actual clearance may be closer to 23 feet.)

54.9 / 25' — **Tamiami Trail (Circus) Bridges:** Opens on signal.

56.6 / 30' — **Venice Avenue Bridge:** Opens on signal, except from 7:00 a.m. to 4:30 p.m., Mon. through Fri. (except holidays), when the draw opens only at 10 min. after the hour, 30 min. after the hour and 50 min. after the hour. Between 4:35 p.m. and 5:35 p.m., the draw need not open.

56.9 / 30' — **KMI (Hatchett Creek) Bridge:** Opens on signal, except from 7:00 a.m. to 4:20 p.m., Mon. through Fri. (except federal holidays), when the draw opens only on the hour, 20 min. after the hour and 40 min. after the hour. Between 4:25 p.m. and 5:25 p.m., the draw need not open. On Sat., Sun. and federal holidays from 7:30 a.m. to 6:00 p.m. the draw will open only on the hour and every 15 min. thereafter.

59.3 / 14' — **Albee Road Bridge:** Opens on signal. (Also known as **Casey Key Bridge**.)

63.0 / 9' — **Blackburn Point Bridge:** Opens on signal.

68.6 / 18' — **Stickney Point (SR 72) Bridge:** Opens on signal, except from 6:00 a.m. to 7:00 p.m. daily, when the draw need open only on the hour and half hour .

71.6 / 25' — **Siesta Drive Bridge:** Opens on signal, except from 6:00 a.m. to 7:00 p.m. daily, when the draw need open only on the hour and half hour.

73.6 / 65' — **Ringling Causeway (SR 789) Bridge:** Fixed

23' — **New Pass (SR 789) Bridge (to Gulf):** The draw need only open on the hour, 20 min. past the hour, and 40 min. past the hour from 7:00 a.m. to 6:00 p.m. From 6:00 p.m. to 7:00 a.m., the bridge will open on signal only if at least 3-hour notice is given.

17' — **Longboat Pass (SR 789) Bridge (to Gulf):** Opens on signal.

FLORIDA BRIDGES MONITOR CHANNEL 09

87.4 / **22'** — **Cortez (SR 684) Bridge:** Opens on signal, except from 6:00 a.m. to 7:00 p.m. daily, when the draw need open only on the quarter hour and three-quarter hour.

89.2 / **24'** — **Anna Maria (SR 64/Manatee Avenue West) Bridge:** Opens on signal, except from 6:00 a.m. to 7:00 p.m. daily, when the draw need open only on the quarter hour and three-quarter hour.

65' — **Bob Graham Sunshine Skyway Bridge (to Tampa Bay):** Fixed

113.0 / **25'** — **Pinellas Bayway Structure 'E' Bridge:** Opens on signal, except from 7:00 a.m. to 9:00 p.m. daily, when the draw need open only on the hour and half hour.

114.0 / **65'** — **Pinellas Bayway Structure 'C' Bridge:** Fixed (Note: May be less than charted clearance.)

114.0 / **11'** — **Pinellas Bayway Structure 'B' Bridge:** Fixed

114.0 / **18'** — **Pinellas Bayway Structure 'A' Bridge:** Fixed

117.7 / **23'** — **Corey Causeway (SR 693) Bridge:** Opens on signal, except from 8:00 a.m. to 7:00 p.m., Mon. through Fri., and from 10:00 a.m. to 7:00 p.m., Sat., Sun. and federal holidays, when the draw need only open only on the hour, 20 min. after the hour and 40 min. after the hour.

118.9 / **21'** — **Treasure Island Causeway Bridge:** Opens on signal, except from 7:00 a.m. to 7:00 p.m., Mon. through Fri., when the draw will open on the hour, 20 min. after the hour and 40 min. after the hour and on the quarter hour and three-quarter hour on Sat., Sun. and federal holidays.

27' — **Johns Pass Drawbridge (to Gulf):** Opens on signal.

122.8 / **25'** — **Welch Causeway (SR 699) Bridge:** Opens on signal, except from 9:30 a.m. to 6:00 p.m. on Sat., Sun. and federal holidays, when the draw opens only on the hour, 20 min. after the hour and 40 min. after the hour.

126.0 / **20'** — **Park Boulevard (SR 248) Bridge:** Opens on signal.

129.3 / **25'** — **Indian Rocks Beach (CR 694) Bridge:** Opens on signal.

131.8 / **75'** — **Belleair Beach Causeway Bridge:** Fixed

74' — **Clearwater Pass (SR 183) Bridge (to Gulf):** Fixed

136.0 / **74'** — **Clearwater Memorial Causeway (SR 60) Bridge:** Fixed

141.9 / **24'** — **Dunedin Causeway Drawbridge:** Opens on signal. (Note: May be closer to 18 feet than charted clearance.)

GIWW, East of Harvey Lock (EHL)

361.4 / **65'** — **Bryant Patton (SR 300) Bridge:** Fixed. (Also known as **Apalachicola–St. George Island Bridge**.)

351.4 / **65'** — **John Gorrie Memorial (U.S. 98/319) Bridge:** Fixed

347.0 / **11'** — **Apalachicola Northern Railroad Bridge:** Maintained in the fully open-to-navigation position and untended.

329.3 / **65'** — **Elgin Bayless (SR 71) Bridge:** Fixed. (Also known as **White City Bridge**.)

75' — **U.S. 98/SR 30 Bridge (to Gulf):** Fixed. (Also known as **Port St. Joe Bridge**.)

315.4 / **65'** — **Overstreet (SR 386) Bridge:** Fixed

295.4 / **50'** — **Dupont (US 98) Bridge:** Fixed

284.6 / **65'** — **Hathaway (US 98) Bridge:** Fixed

271.8 / **65'** — **West Bay Creek (SR 79) Bridge:** Fixed

250.4 / **65'** — **Clyde B. Wells & Choctawhatchee Bay (US 331/SR 83) Bridge:** Fixed

234.2 / **64'** — **Mid-Bay (SR 293) Bridge:** Fixed

49' — **William T. Marler (US 98/SR 30) Bridge (to Gulf):** Fixed. (Also known as **Destin Bridge**.)

223.1 / **50'** — **Brooks Memorial Bridge:** Fixed

206.7 / **50'** — **Navarre Beach Causeway (CR 399) Bridge:** Fixed

189.1 / **65'** — **Bob Sikes (Pensacola Beach/SR 399) Bridge:** Fixed

171.8 / **73'** — **Gulf Beach Highway (SR 292) Bridge:** Fixed

ALABAMA BRIDGES MONITOR CHANNEL 13

54' — **Perdido Pass (SR 182) Channel Bridge (to Gulf):** Fixed

158.7 / **73'** — **Foley Beach Expressway Bridge:** Fixed

154.9 / **73'** — **Gulf Shores Parkway (SR 59) Bridges:** Fixed

127.8 / **83'** — **Dauphin Island Causeway Bridges** Fixed

Fort Pierce Inlet

Cruising the "inside waterway" (the ICW) is a bit like driving down I-95. There are areas where every amenity and convenience you need is but an exit away (especially in FL), and then there are stretches with only marsh and woods as far as the eye can see (mostly in SC and GA). And like I-95 there is constant construction, many speed-restricted areas and several bridges to pass under. (The lowest bridge clearance on the ICW is the Julia Tuttle Causeway at Mile 1087.1 in Miami, which is 56 feet.) The main difference between the highway and the waterway is the "road maintenance." With federal funding for dredging being scarce, shoaling has been more commonplace on the ICW and the "projected depths" on the NOAA charts can no longer be considered valid. This, alone, will drive (pun intended) some vessels to take the offshore (Atlantic Ocean) route.

Offshore Runs: Some boaters choose the offshore run to save time or to get a break from the bridge openings and speed restrictions. Many sailboats will take this option to turn off the engine and unfurl the sails. You may be forced to take the offshore route due to vessel draft or vertical clearance. Regardless of your reasons for exiting the ICW, there are numerous inlets along the coast that will allow you to duck in or back out should the weather turn. Keep in mind that not all inlets are navigable and some are treacherous under certain conditions. This section will assist you in recognizing those but it is still important to study the charts,

pay attention to the weather and seek current local knowledge before proceeding on an offshore run.

Overall Mileage: Heading north or south, many skippers mistakenly assume that they will shorten their trips by going out to sea and running down the coast. The distances shown here–both inside (ICW) and outside (from inlet to inlet)–demonstrate that this is not necessarily true. Keep in mind that even if outside distances from sea buoy to sea buoy are virtually the same as the ICW distances, the mileage in and out to the buoys adds to the total coastwise figure.

Cautions and Warnings: Before you begin an offshore passage, take an honest accounting of your vessel, your crew and yourself. Is each of you up to the task? Is the vessel properly outfitted? Do you have the necessary safety equipment, charts, long distance communications gear such as single sideband radio (SSB), an Emergency Position Indicating Radio Beacon (EPIRB) and life raft? Do you and your crew have adequate experience in boating and navigation to attempt an offshore coastal passage?

Check the weather using as many sources as possible. If you have access to weather routing services, they are a good option, particularly for longer offshore passages. You are seeking a weather window with enough space on each side to get you safely out and back in, with room for unexpected contingencies.

Of course, always file a float plan with a reliable person. A sample float plan is provided in the Skippers Handbook of this guide. You might also look into the free app BoatSafe Free, which allows you to create a float plan and email it to participants or emergency contacts.

Entering & Exiting: Plan your trip so that you enter in daylight, with the tide, particularly if your boat is slow or underpowered. Remember that wind against tide can create short, steep waves in an inlet that can quickly make even a ship channel impassable for slower boats. If conditions are bad when you reach the sea buoy for an inlet, you may find yourself being driven ashore by wind or waves and unable to find the inlet buoys. It may be better to remain well offshore in rough conditions, possibly continuing to a better inlet.

Be advised that the markers at some inlets are moved on a regular basis and the buoys should be honored. Should you find yourself at an inlet and needing direction, a call on VHF Channel 16 for local knowledge is likely to bring you a response. Sea Tow and TowBoatU.S. are two other knowledgeable sources. The Coast Guard may also be able to assist you, but only if it is indeed an emergency.

Resources: Prior to your voyage, there are a number of online sources that can familiarize you with the inlets, including the following:

- **Waterway Explorer** (www.waterwayguide.com): Provides chart and satellite views of the inlets plus cruising details from local boaters.

- **United States Coast Pilot** (www.nauticalcharts. noaa.gov): Nine-volume annual publication distributed by the Office of Coast Survey (NOAA) to supplement nautical charts.

- **Local Notice to Mariners** (www.navcen.uscg. gov, then select the LNMs tab): Weekly updates provided by the U.S. Coast Guard to provide corrections to navigational publications and nautical charts.

- **Tide Tables** (www.tidesandcurrents.noaa.gov): Provided by NOAA to provide tidal predictions (highs and lows) for specific areas.

Florida's East Coast Inlets

Recommended (big ship) inlets in this section are denoted with this symbol:

Gulf Coast Inlets

The big ship channels on the Gulf Coast (not shown here) are:

- Boca Grande Pass
- Tampa Bay Entrance
- St. Andrew Bay Entrance
- St. Joseph Bay Entrance
- Pensacola Bay Entrance
- Mobile Bay Entrance

There are several smaller channels (labeled as "Passes") that are available for smaller vessels. See Waterway Explorer for details (www. waterwayguide.com).

Big Ship Inlet Distances

St. Johns River Entrance to Port Canaveral Inlet:
150 nm (outside)/173 sm (ICW)

Port Canaveral Inlet to Fort Pierce Inlet:
65 nm (outside)/75 sm (ICW)

Fort Pierce Inlet to Lake Worth Inlet:
45 nm (outside)/52 sm (ICW)

Lake Worth Inlet to Port Everglades Inlet:
40 nm (outside)/46 sm (ICW)

Port Everglades Inlet to Government Cut:
20 nm (outside)/23 sm (ICW)

Note: In keeping with standard NOAA conventions, outside (ocean) distances are measured in nautical miles (nm), while ICW distances are measured in statute miles (sm):

1 nm = 1.15 sm

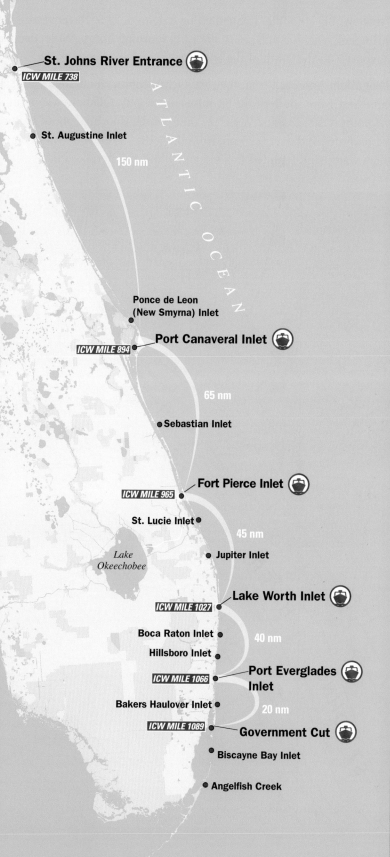

St. Johns River Entrance
ICW MILE 738

St. Augustine Inlet

ATLANTIC OCEAN

150 nm

Ponce de Leon
(New Smyrna) Inlet

Port Canaveral Inlet
ICW MILE 894

65 nm

Sebastian Inlet

Fort Pierce Inlet
ICW MILE 965

St. Lucie Inlet

45 nm

Lake
Okeechobee

Jupiter Inlet

Lake Worth Inlet
ICW MILE 1027

Boca Raton Inlet

40 nm

Hillsboro Inlet

ICW MILE 1066   Port Everglades
Inlet

Bakers Haulover Inlet

20 nm

ICW MILE 1089   Government Cut

Biscayne Bay Inlet

Angelfish Creek

Sea Buoy: RW sea buoy "SJ" is located at N 30° 23.600'/W 81° 19.140'.

Overview: Big ship inlet frequented by freighters, U.S. Naval vessels and commercial fishermen, especially shrimpers, who you will see in the early morning hours. Wide, deep and trouble-free entrance. Naval Station Mayport is to the south of the entrance.

Navigation: Approach from the east. Ocean approach landmark is St. Johns Light, which stands 83 feet above the shore and 1 nm south of the St. Johns north jetty. Offshore waypoint is located nearly 3 nm from the jetties. Use waypoint N 30° 23.860'/ W 81° 22.000', which is located about halfway between flashing red buoy "4" and flashing red buoy "6" and over 0.25 nm from the jetties. Follow buoys in. Landmarks include a tower at Jacksonville Beach and a water tank (painted in a red and white checkerboard design) at the naval station.

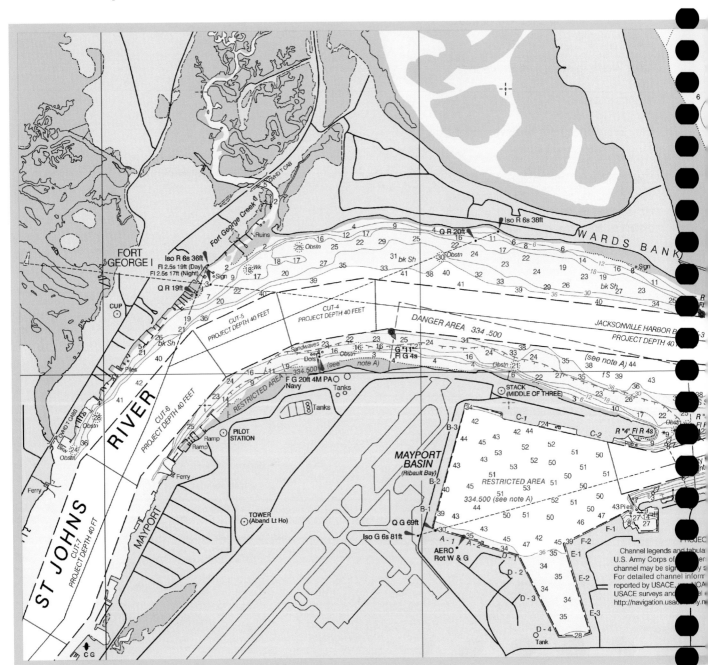

Cautions and hazards: None, other than the large vessel traffic, which can be heavy at times. Slower boats are well advised to pick their tide coming in here, or settle down for a very long transit; the tide can run up to 3 to 4 knots.

Depth: See interactive charts on Waterway Explorer at www.waterwayguide.com.

ICW connection: Mile 738 of the ICW is 5 nm from the jetties. If going south, be sure of your markers; there is an underwater jetty at the south entrance to the ICW channel. The current here can also quickly push you out of the channel. Caution is advised.

Nearest recommended inlet: It is approximately 30 nm to the St. Marys (Cumberland Sound) Entrance.

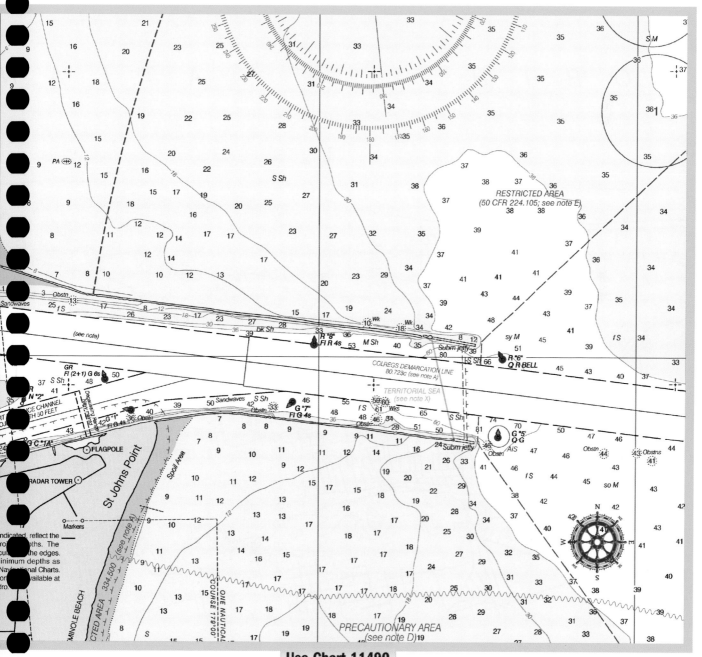

Use Chart 11490

St. Augustine Inlet

Sea Buoy: RW sea buoy "STA" is east and north of N 29° 55.000'/W 81°15.230'.

Overview: Located north of Anastasia State Park.

Navigation: From the sea buoy, proceed slightly south of east towards the inlet, paying close attention to the markers. You will see a tall cross ahead on shore providing an approximate range to the inlet, which will help you to orient yourself. Once past Cape Francis on the south, bear to the middle and south side of the channel as you proceed. There is a large shoal at marker "2A." Stay on the south side of the inlet. If headed north once inside the inlet, note that you keep red nun buoy "60" to port, as that is part of the ICW.

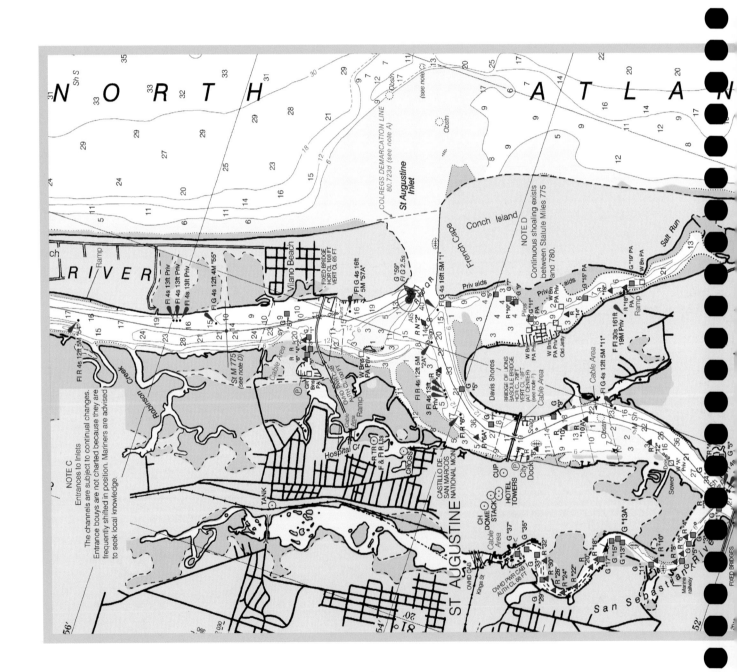

Cautions and hazards: There is some infrequent dredging activity in this inlet, but it should be regarded as a fair weather-only inlet with no protection until well inside the inlet. There are extensive shoals with breaking water to the north and south of the inlet extending well offshore. Proceed with caution at slow speed as the temporary markers–which are frequently moved by the USCG to mark deeper water–can be very difficult to see. The currents in this inlet are very powerful and dictate appropriate boat handling skills as well as advanced local knowledge.

Depth: See interactive charts on Waterway Explorer at www.waterwayguide.com.

ICW connection: Connects directly to the ICW at Mile 776. If going north, stay closest to the eastern side of the channel to avoid the marked shoal to port.

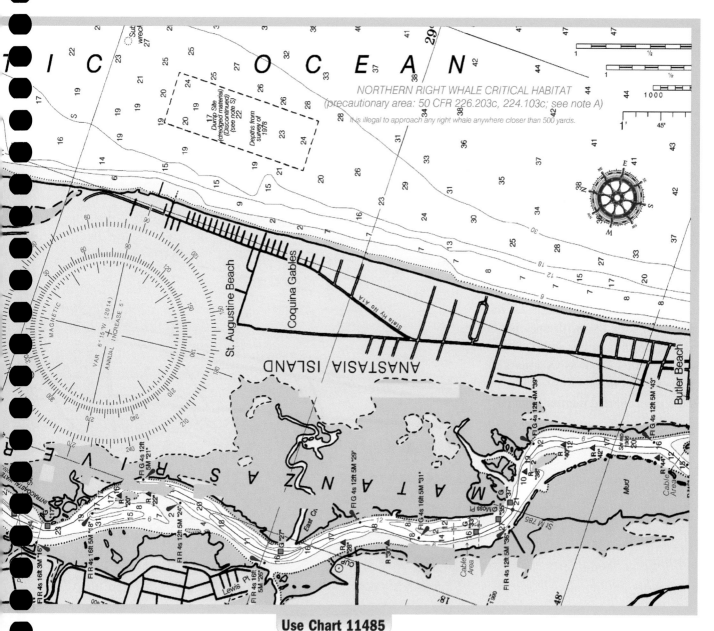

Use Chart 11485

Sea Buoy: Red buoy "2" is located at N 29° 04.700'/W 80° 53.700'.

Overview: Used extensively by locals and sport fishermen and convenient point to enter or leave the ICW between Daytona and Cape Canaveral. Sometimes referred to as New Smyrna Inlet. This is a fair weather inlet only.

Navigation: Coming from the offshore waypoint, the jetty on the north side of the inlet provides protection from north and northeast swells. Hold close to the jetty until inside the inlet, as there is a shoal building north and east from green buoy "7." The USCG station is located on the south channel of the inlet and will respond to calls for inlet conditions, and the local TowBoat US is up to date on local conditions. Both can be hailed on VHF Channel 16.

Webcam: For a live view of the inlet visit www.volusia.com/explore-a-city/ponce-inlet.

Cautions and hazards: Seemingly constant reclamation, dredging and seawall construction, yet shoaling has been reported in the approaches both north and south of the inlet coming from the ICW. Inlet markers are continually moved by the USCG to reflect deep water. Expect substantial traffic at all hours. This is a fair weather inlet only, particularly for weather out of the south and east, which creates large swells into the inlet. Local knowledge is strongly advised before using this inlet.

Depth: See interactive charts on Waterway Explorer at www.waterwayguide.com.

ICW connection: The inlet is 2.5 miles from ICW Mile 840 with one channel leading north, another south. The north channel is not as well marked as the south channel until well inside and shows charted depths of just 7 feet MLW.

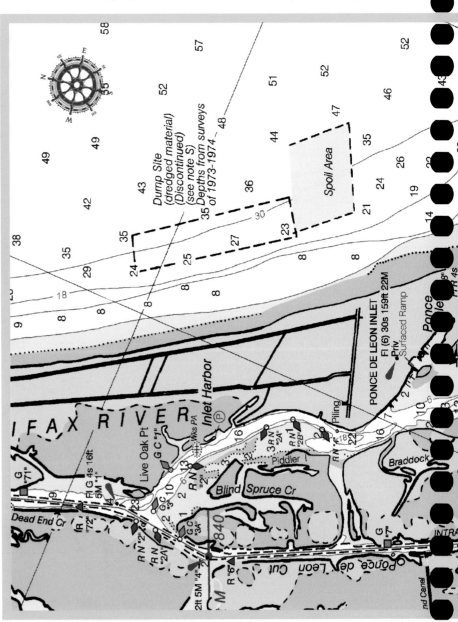

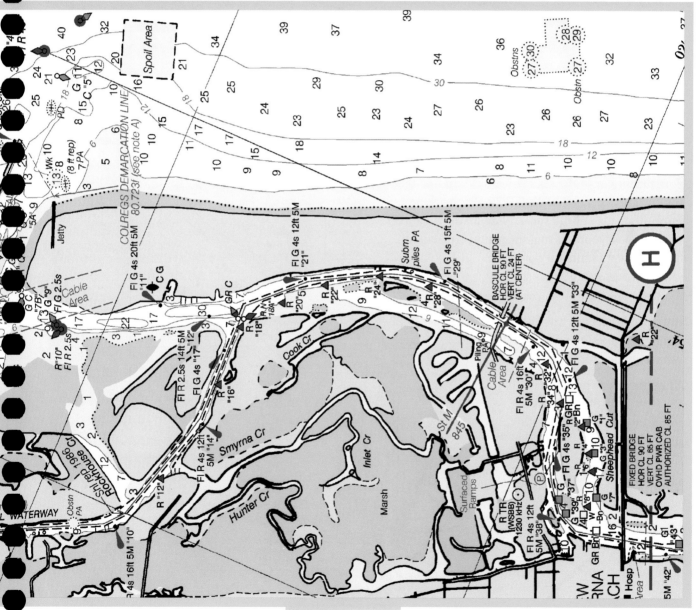

Use Chart 11485

Sea Buoy: Flashing red buoy "4" (2.5 sec) is located at N 28° 22.560'/W 80° 31.740'.

Overview: Well-marked, deep ship inlet protected from the north by the long and shallow Southeast Shoal off Cape Canaveral. The lock inside the inlet eliminates current, making this one of the easier to use inlets on the Florida coast.

Navigation: Southbound cruisers can make for N 28° 23.490'/W 80° 33.000' after rounding red buoy "4," while northbound craft could go in much closer, at N 28° 24.570'/W 80° 34.480'. The channel is well marked; simply run down the channel, turning due west at Middle Reach. Lock operating hours are 6:00 a.m. to 9:30 p.m., 365 days a year. (The observation area is open 6:00 a.m. to 9:00 p.m.) Lockage takes 20 to 30 minutes.

Webcam: For a live view of the inlet visit www. portcanaveralwebcam.com.

Cautions and hazards: Coming from the north, the Southeast Shoal off Cape Canaveral keeps boaters several miles offshore. Stay east of W 80° 27.000' before turning in to the sea buoy after rounding red buoy "4" at N 28° 23.470'/W 80° 29.100' marking the southern edge of the shoal. Note that this cuts off the offshore waypoint. From the south, cruisers can approach from within 0.5 nm of the shore in depths greater than 20 feet MLW.

Depth: See interactive charts on Waterway Explorer at www. waterwayguide.com.

ICW connection: Inlet is 7.5 nm from ICW Mile 894 (across the Banana River and through the Barge Canal).

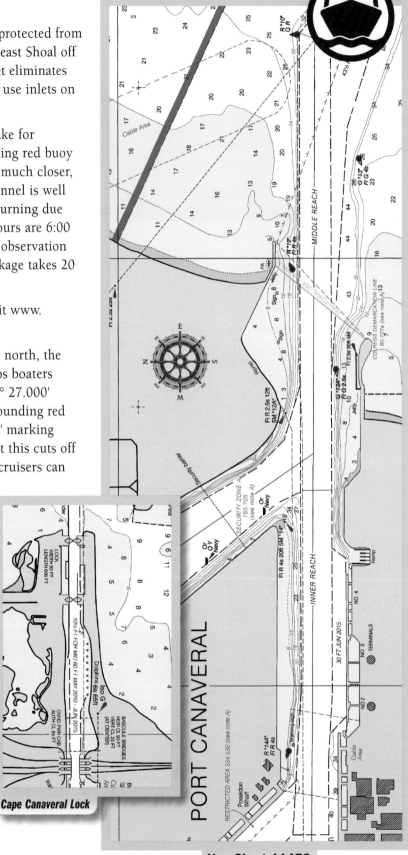

Cape Canaveral Lock

Use Chart 11478

Sebastian Inlet

Sea Buoy: No sea buoy. Steer to waypoint N 27° 51.675'/W 80° 26.500', which will place you directly east of the inlet.

Overview: This is the only charted inlet between Cape Canaveral and Fort Pierce and is a local knowledge, fair-weather inlet used largely by smaller recreational fishing boats. Crossed by a fixed bridge (A1A) with 37-foot vertical clearance.

Navigation: If you must enter, do so only from the east using the waypoint; there is an unmarked shoal blocking any approach from the south. From the waypoint, proceed due east keeping to the center of the jetties. There are no buoys and only a light at the end of the north jetty. A 3,000-foot-long by 100-foot-wide and 9-foot-deep channel provides access to the ocean, but as with all ocean inlets, a cautious approach is warranted, as shoaling is ever present and continuous.

Webcam: For a live view of the inlet visit www.sebastianinletcam.com.

Cautions and hazards: Swift cross currents and the resulting shifting channel make navigation difficult without up-to-date local information. The currents in this area can also affect travel on the ICW.

Depth: See interactive charts on Waterway Explorer at www.waterwayguide.com.

ICW connection: The inlet is 2 nm from ICW Mile 935 (across the Indian River) over an area of 5- to 6-foot depths following privately maintained aids.

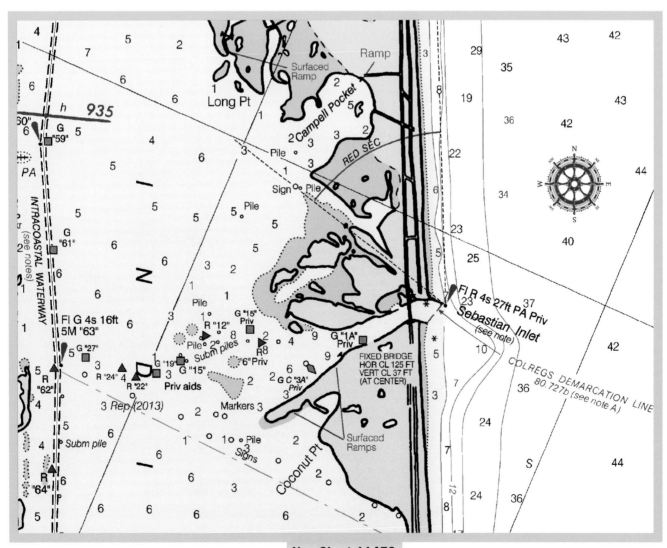

Use Chart 11472

Sea Buoy: Red sea buoy "2" is located at N 27° 28.640'/W 80° 15.410' (1.5 nm seaward of the channel).

Overview: This is a big ship inlet and one of the best and easiest inlets on Florida's east coast. Currents are strong; slower boats will want to have the tide favoring their passage. There is an inner channel and a turning basin.

Navigation: Above waypoint takes you 1.5 nm from the channel in deep water. Smaller craft can approach in over 20 feet MLW to green buoy "5" and red buoy "6" at N 27° 28.160'/W 80° 16.900', which is just 0.2 nm from the jetties.

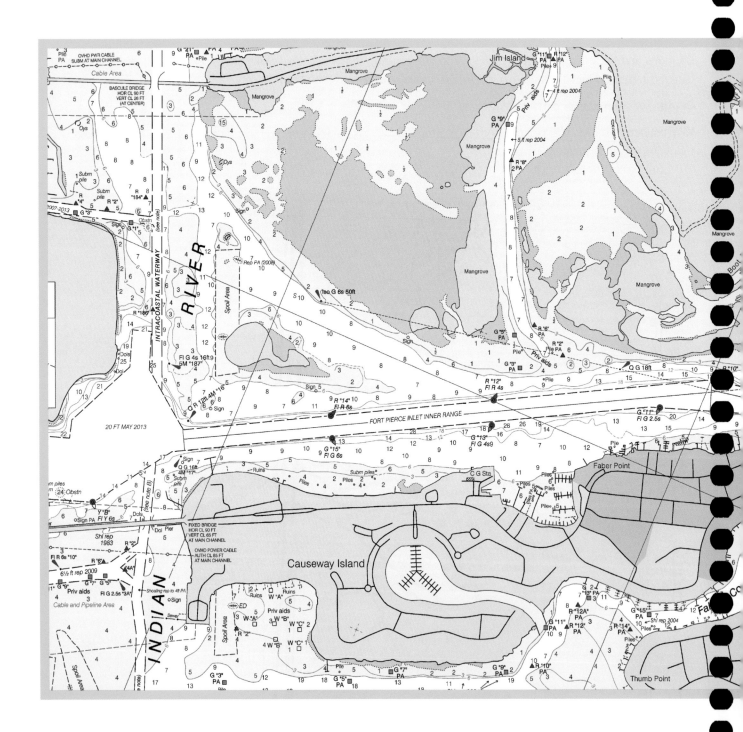

Webcam: For live view of the inlet visit www.visitstlucie.com/fort-pierce-inlet-webcam.

Cautions and hazards: Watch for the many small fishing boats throughout the channel. Eastbound swells can create rough conditions within the inlet proper, preventing smaller boats from leaving.

Depth: See interactive charts on Waterway Explorer at www.waterwayguide.com.

ICW connection: Connects directly to the ICW at Mile 965.

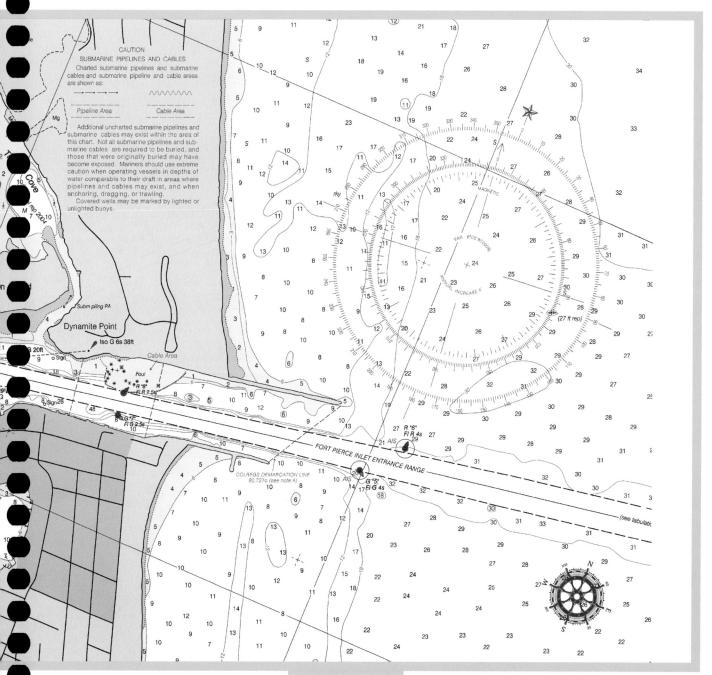

Use Chart 11475

Sea Buoy: Flashing red buoy "2" (4 sec) is located at N 27° 10.000'/W 80° 08.380'.

Overview: This marks the intersection of the Indian River, Saint Lucie, Okeechobee Waterway and ICW (hence "The Crossroads"). Used by sport fishermen, megayachts and offshore sailors.

Navigation: The entrance marker at N 27° 10.000'/ W 80° 08.380' can be used as an entrance waypoint. The jetties are visible directly west of this point.

Webcam: For a live view of the inlet visit www.stlucieinlet.com.

Cautions and hazards: Conveniently located and frequently dredged but requires caution due to problematic shoaling. Jetty to the north and small breakwater to the south offer protection once inside, although protection from the south is marginal in east to southeast winds. The USCG has placed temporary markers denoting best water. Local knowledge should be obtained before using this inlet. The current can be strong.

Depth: See interactive charts on Waterway Explorer at www.waterwayguide.com.

ICW connection: ICW is approximately 1 nm away at Mile 988. Due to constant shoaling, several temporary buoys have been placed between the inlet and the ICW.

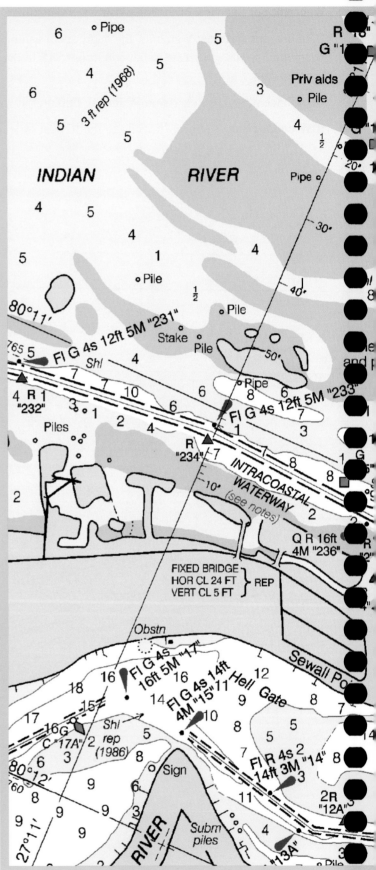

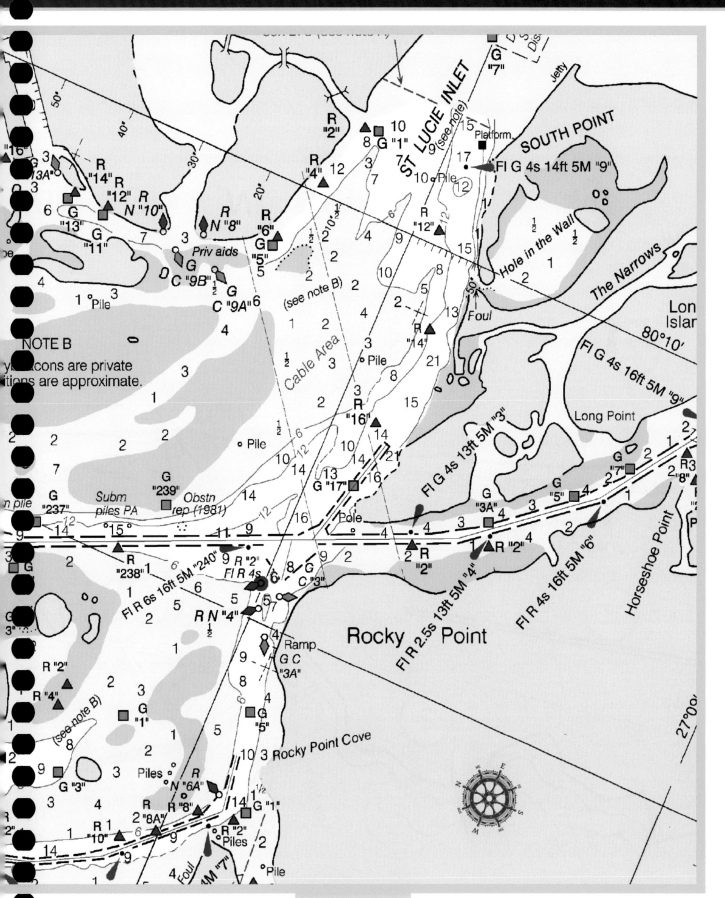

NOTE B

ys ... cons are private
... tions are approximate.

ST LUCIE INLET

SOUTH POINT

Hole in the Wall

The Narrows

Lon
Islar

Long Point

Horseshoe Point

Rocky Point

Rocky Point Cove

Fl G 4s 14ft 5M "9"

Fl G 4s 16ft 5M "9"

Fl G 4s 13ft 5M "3"

Fl R 2.5s 13ft 5M "4"

Fl R 4s 16ft 5M "6"

Fl R 6s 16ft 5M "240"

Cable Area

(see note B)

Sea Buoy: No sea buoy. Steer to waypoint N 26° 56.620'/ W 80° 03.790' (0.4 nm east of the inlet).

Overview: Fair weather inlet only. Prone to severe shoaling and cited by the USCG as "not navigable without local knowledge."

Navigation: If you must enter, proceed in a westerly direction from the waypoint to the markers on the jetties. Once inside the jetties, depths increase substantially.

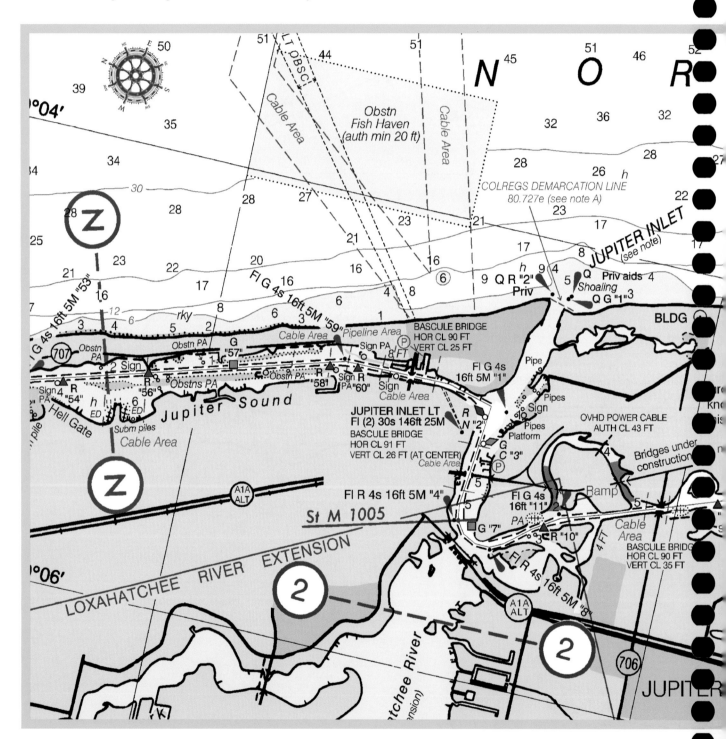

Webcam: For a live view of the inlet visit www.evsjupiter.com.

Cautions and hazards: Severe shoaling to both the north and south of the entrance. With any swell, mariners should divert to another inlet. The inlet is considered impassable in a northeast swell of any size.

Depth: See interactive charts on Waterway Explorer at www.waterwayguide.com.

ICW connection: Connects directly to the ICW at Mile 1005.

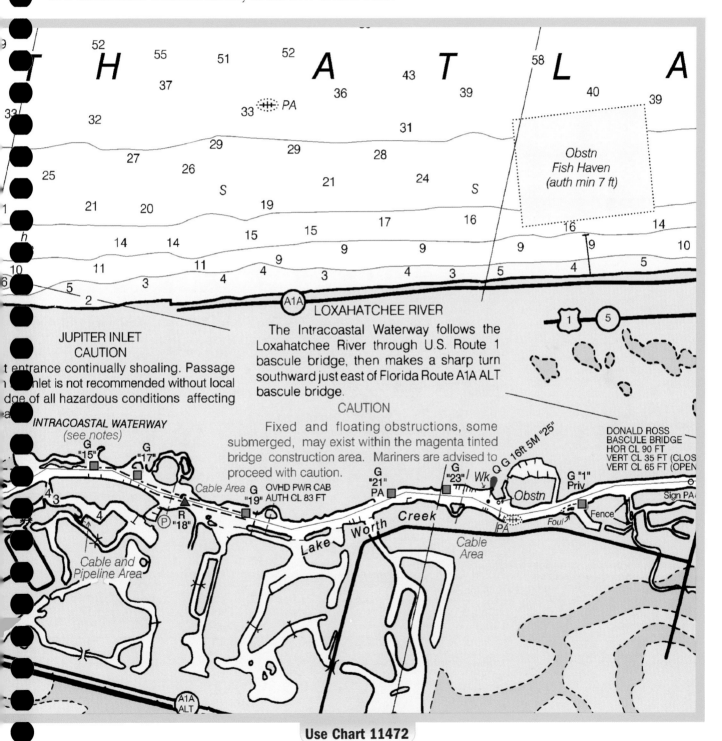

Use Chart 11472

Lake Worth (Palm Beach) Inlet

Sea Buoy: RW sea buoy "LW" is located at N 26° 46.360'/W 80° 00.610' (1.1 nm east of the jetties).

Overview: Deep, easily navigable big ship inlet that is sometimes referred to as the Palm Beach Inlet. Vessels returning from the Bahamas can clear Customs and Immigration here.

Navigation: Straight shot from the sea buoy with no hazards of any sort. There is a long jetty to the south and a much shorter one to the north.

Webcam: For a live view of the inlet visit www.pbcgov.com/webcams/lwi.

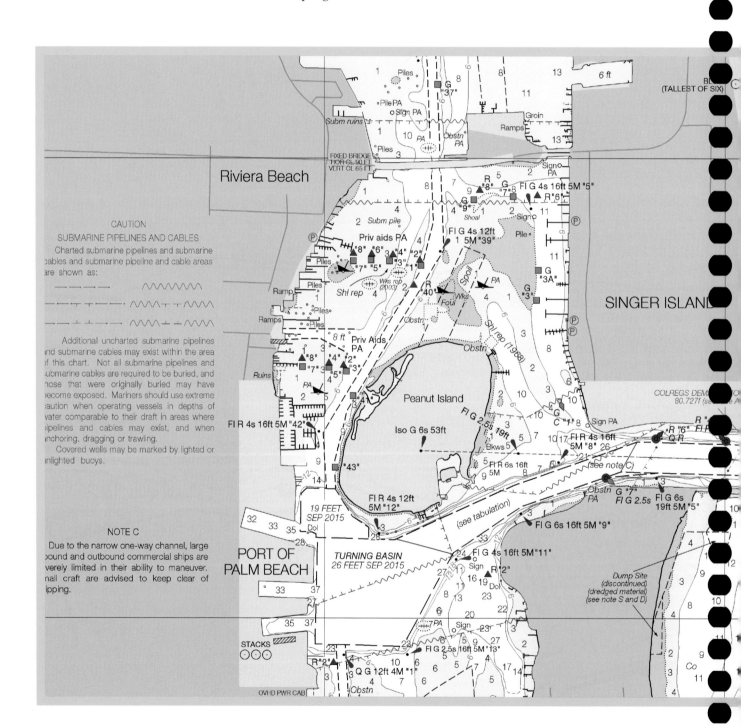

Cautions and hazards: Large commercial vessels frequently use this inlet. Further in, many small fishing boats can cause problems, particularly beside Peanut Island. Currents are strong but do not cause much difficulty in the inlet.

Depth: See interactive charts on Waterway Explorer at www.waterwayguide.com.

ICW connection: Connects directly to the ICW at Mile 1027.

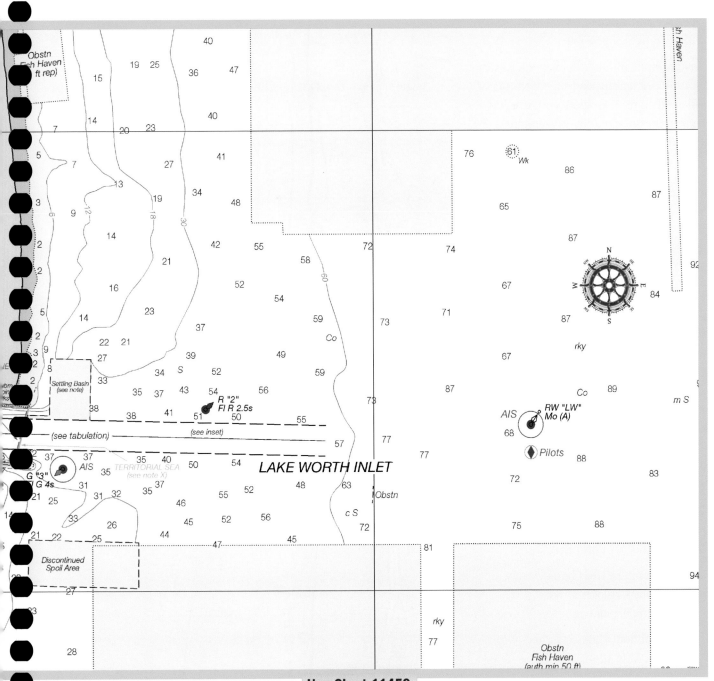

Use Chart 11459

Sea Buoy: No sea buoy. Steer to N 26° 20.150'/W 80° 04.270' and pick up the quick flashing green buoy "1" on the south jetty and quick flashing red buoy "2" on the north jetty.

Overview: Narrow, dredged cut located 5 nm northward of Hillsboro Inlet Light. Boca Raton Inlet (A1A) Bascule Bridge (23-foot vertical clearance) crosses the inlet and opens on signal. Continue to Hillsboro Inlet if possible.

Navigation: Tall, pink Boca Raton Resort & Club is a landmark visible from many miles offshore. The inlet's entrance has short jetties marked by private lights. Be sure to request a bridge opening upon arrival in the inlet to avoid circling in the strong current. It is strongly recommended to head south of green buoy "1" (south jetty) and approach the inlet from the south.

Webcam: For a live view of the inlet visit www.video-monitoring.com/beachcams/bocainlet.

Cautions and Hazards: There is heavy traffic in the area, especially on weekends. Local knowledge is required, as shoaling outside the inlet can limit access at low tide. Depths change frequently due to shoaling and shifting sandbars, and swift-moving currents cause swells where the outflow meets the ocean. The inlet channel and markers are not charted and transit is considered dangerous. Be aware that the current usually reverses in the ICW as it passes the Boca Raton Inlet.

Depth: See interactive charts on Waterway Explorer at www. waterwayguide.com.

ICW connection: Connects directly to the ICW at Mile 1048.

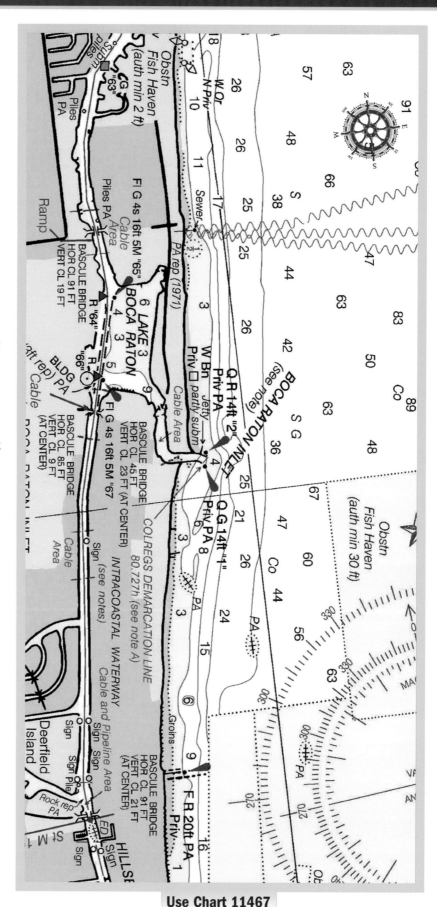

Use Chart 11467

Hillsboro Inlet

Sea Buoy: RW sea buoy "HI" is located at N 26° 15.070'/W 80° 04.630' (approximately 0.4 nm from the inlet). A course to the northwest (paying close attention to the green day marks and lighted buoys) will bring you past the jetty.

Overview: Frequently used and offers reliable 7-foot MLW depths; nevertheless this inlet requires attentiveness when entering.

Navigation: Easily identified by 136-foot high Hillsboro Lighthouse. Hillsboro Inlet Bascule Bridge (13-foot closed vertical clearance) inside the inlet opens on signal, except from 7:00 a.m. to 6:00 p.m., the drawspans need only open only on the hour, quarter-hour, half-hour and three-quarter hour. Due to the very strong currents in this inlet, vessels should contact the bridgetender before entering the inlet.

Webcam: For a live view of the inlet visit www.hillsborolighthouse.org/inlet-cam.

Cautions and Hazards: A southeast wind against a tide situation can kick up a short, vicious chop that can set an unwary boater onto the shoals to the south of the inlet. More than one vessel has been bounced onto the bottom here in the troughs. Currents to 6 knots have been reported. There is a 64-foot clearance power cable at the bridge.

Depth: See interactive charts on Waterway Explorer at www.waterwayguide.com.

ICW connection: Connects directly to the ICW at Mile 1053.

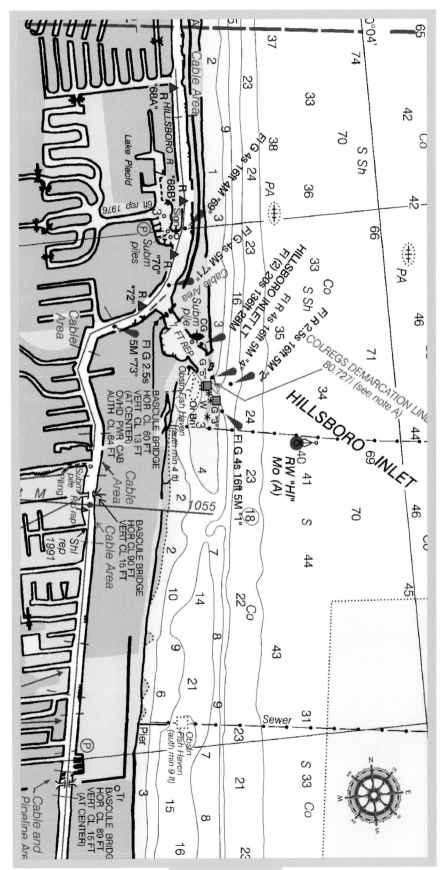

Use Chart 11467

Sea buoy: RW sea buoy "PE" is located at N 26° 05.500'/ W 80° 04.790'. From the sea buoy, head due west into the cut.

Overview: This big ship inlet, located 9 nm south of Hillsboro Inlet, is also known as Fort Lauderdale Inlet. Wide, deep, straight and completely free of hazards; accommodates naval vessels, container ships, freighters and cruise ships. Be aware that larger vessels will often be escorted and have an enforced security perimeter.

Navigation: At the turning basin, swing south into the ICW, or north to the ICW and the various marinas of Fort Lauderdale.

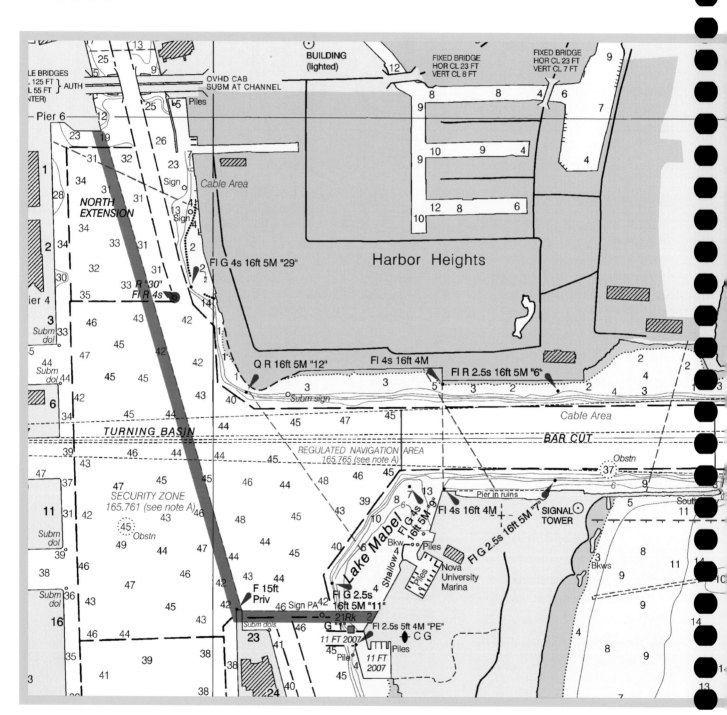

Webcam: For a live view of the inlet visit www.portevergladeswebcam.com. Fort Lauderdale ICW can be seen at www.ftlauderdalewebcam.com.

Cautions and hazards: Frequent large ship traffic in and out of this inlet necessitate a careful watch, particularly at night and in poor weather. The cut can get bouncy with sportfishing boats running in and out at high speeds.

Depth: See interactive charts on Waterway Explorer at www.waterwayguide.com.

ICW connection: Connects directly to the ICW at Mile 1066.

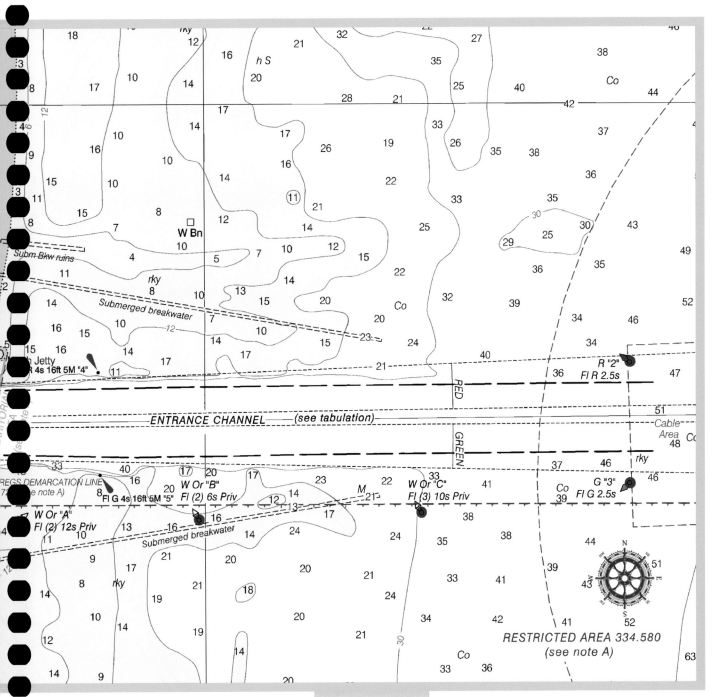

Use Chart 11470

Sea Buoy: No sea buoy. Steer to waypoint
N 25° 54.000'/W 80° 06.730'.

Overview: Popular and busy with local recreational fishermen and tour boats.

Navigation: There are no markers, other than a light on the south side of the inlet and once you have turned north, deep water is close to the shore on your port side. The inlet has a fixed bridge (A1A) with 32-foot vertical clearance.

Cautions and hazards: Strictly a fair-weather inlet for cruising vessels due to problems with continual ICW shoaling. Cruisers would be wise to forgo this inlet in favor of Miami's Government Cut (8 nm to the south) or Port Everglades Inlet (11.5 nm to the north). Mariners are advised to exercise extreme caution while transiting the area.

Depth: See interactive charts on Waterway Explorer at www.waterwayguide.com.

ICW connection: Proceed due east into the inlet, turning south once inside to head for the ICW Mile 1080. Severe shoaling exists in the vicinity of Biscayne Bay buoy "7B" on the ICW. The shoal protrudes into the channel on the east side, which reduces the channel width by approximately half of the charted width. Biscayne Bay Buoy "7B" has been relocated by USCG to mark the best water.

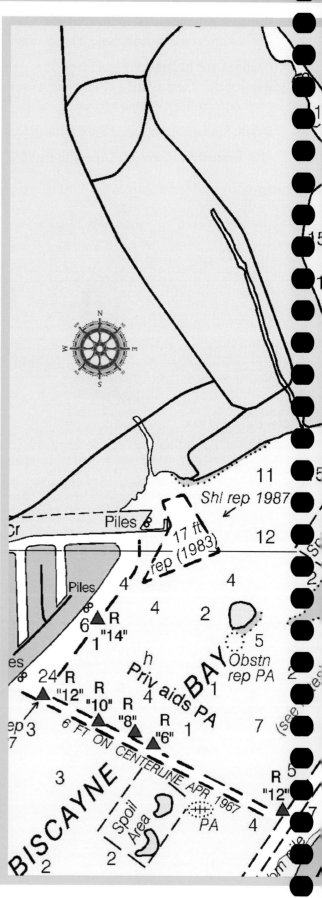

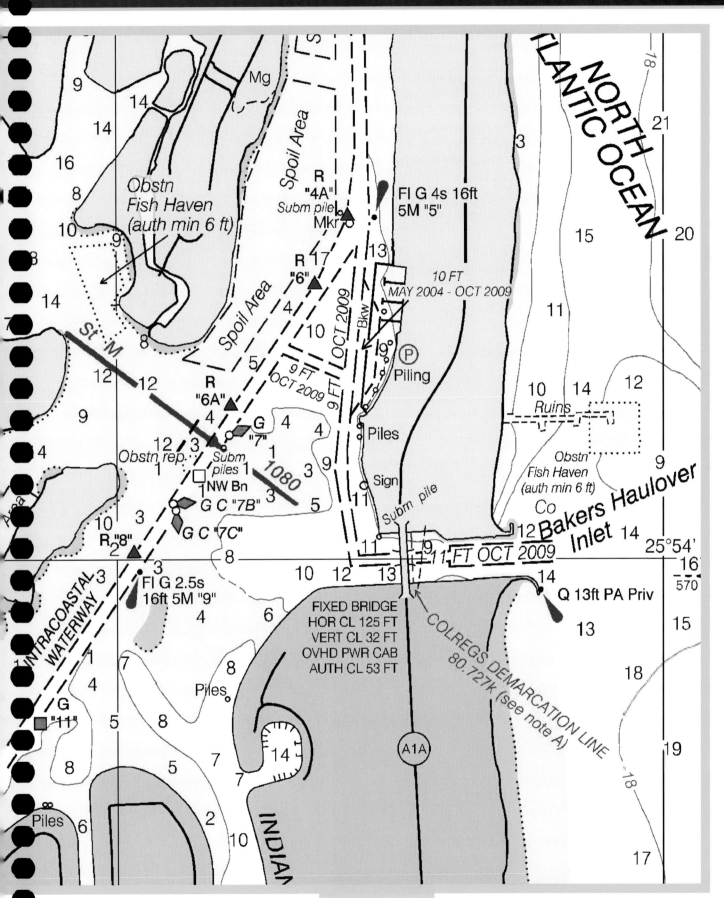

NORTH ATLANTIC OCEAN

Spoil Area

Mg

9

14

14

16

8

10

Obstn
Fish Haven
(auth min 6 ft)

8

9

14

7

St M

12

12

9

Obstn rep.

12   3

1

NW Bn

3

10

4

R "8"

2

3

INTRACOASTAL WATERWAY

1

Area

G
"11"

8

7

4

5

8

8

5

6

Piles

Spoil Area

R
"4A"
Subm pile
Mkr

R "6"

17

4

10

Spoil Area

5

R
"6A"

4

G
"7"

Subm
piles   1

1

1080

G C "7B"

G C "7C"

3

8

FI G 2.5s
16ft 5M "9"

4

6

7

7

Piles

14

A1A

INDIAN

2

10

9 FT OCT 2009

9 FT
OCT 2009

FI G 4s 16ft
5M "5"

13

10 FT
MAY 2004 - OCT 2009

Bkw

9

P
Piling

Piles

Sign

4

4

3

9

11

Subm pile

4

5

11

10   12   13

FIXED BRIDGE
HOR CL 125 FT
VERT CL 32 FT
OVHD PWR CAB
AUTH CL 53 FT

3

15

11

10   14   12

Ruins

Obstn
Fish Haven
(auth min 6 ft)

Co

9

Bakers Haulover
Inlet   14

12

11 FT OCT 2009

9

Q 13ft PA Priv

14

13

COLREGS DEMARCATION LINE
80.727k (see note A)

18

17

18

21

20

15

11

18

16
570

15

19

25°54'

Use Chart 11467

Government Cut (Miami) Inlet

Sea Buoy: RW sea buoy "M" is located at
N 25° 46.088'/W 80° 04.998'.

Overview: This big ship inlet is wide and deep and is free of hazards. Runs between Miami Beach (to the north) and Fisher Island (to the south).

Navigation: In settled conditions, use the waypoint
N 25° 45.400'/W 80° 06.880', which brings you in to just over 0.5 nm from the jetties; otherwise, the sea buoy at N 25° 46.130'/W 80° 04.960' is the preferable waypoint. Follow a course of 253° M inside the channel, then 299° M from green buoy "7" through the jetties. Closures are announced on VHF Channel 16. During closures, Fisherman's Channel south of Dodge Island is the alternate inlet. It is similarly free of hazards, although when entering from the ICW heading south, leave buoys "53A" and "55" well to port before turning in to the channel due to shoaling extending into the channel.

Webcam: For a live view of the inlet visit www.portmiamiwebcam.com.

Cautions and hazards: A car ferry runs between Dodge Island and Fisher Island with frequent crossings. Both channels are subject to strong currents.

Depth: See interactive charts on Waterway Explorer at www.waterwayguide.com.

ICW connection: Connects directly to the ICW at Mile 1089.

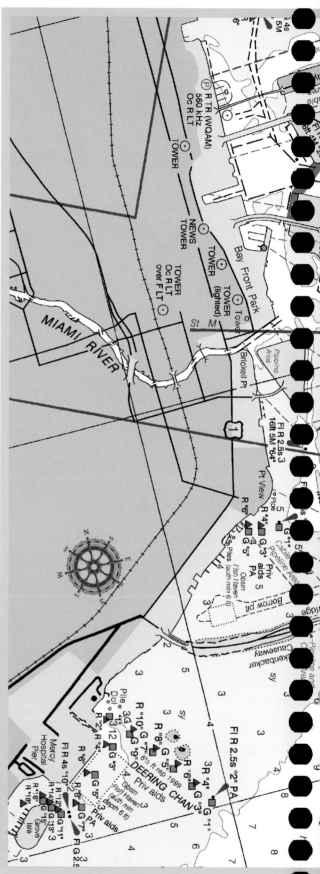

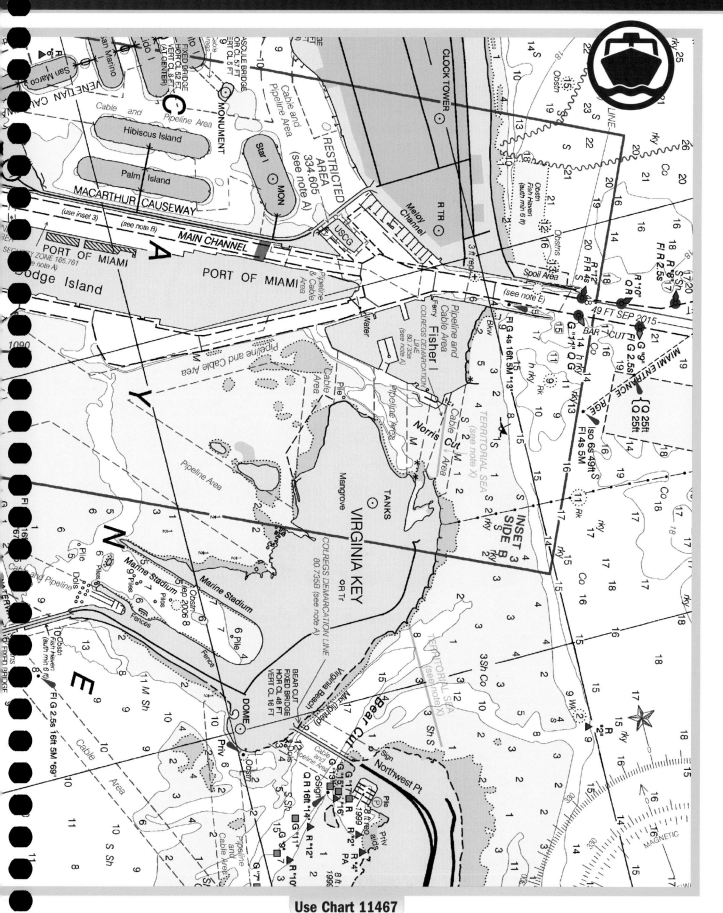

Use Chart 11467

Cape Florida (Biscayne Bay) Inlet

Sea buoy: Use flashing (4 sec) 37-foot Biscayne Channel Light "6M" located at N 25º 38.742'/W 80º 05.373'.

Overview: This inlet is primarily used by cruisers heading to the islands. Located 6 nm south of Miami.

Navigation: Pass Biscayne Channel Light to port, then continue to entrance buoy green "1" and follow the marked channel.

Cautions and hazards: Local knowledge should be obtained before entering this inlet for the first time. It is a well-marked channel, but attention is required in some shallow areas (7 to 9 feet).

Depth: See interactive charts on Waterway Explorer at www.waterwayguide.com.

ICW connection: Connects to ICW (0.5 nm) at Mile 1094.

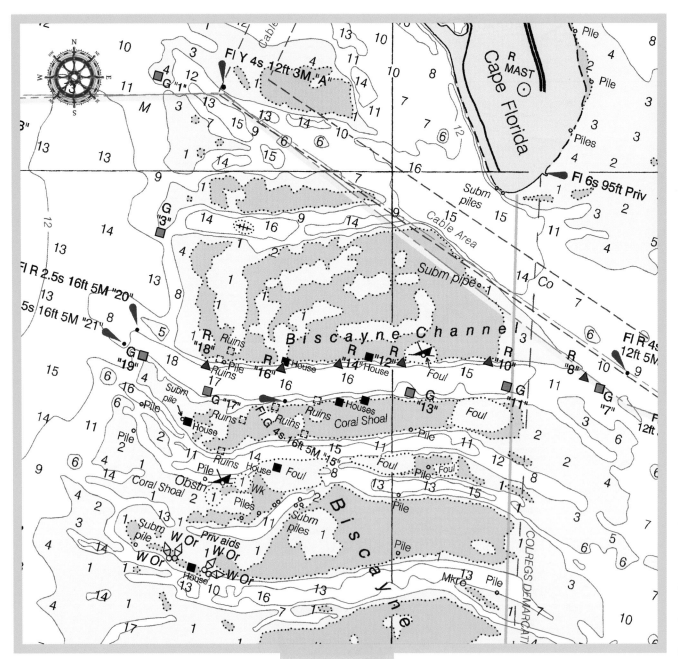

Use Chart 11465

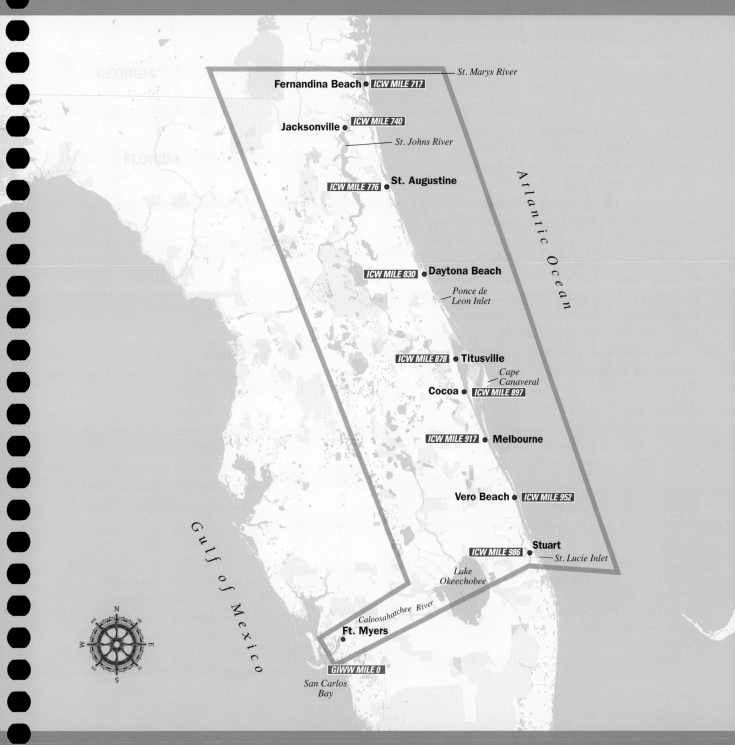

Mile 715-Mile 740

■ NAVIGATION NOTES

Cruising south on the Intracoastal Waterway (ICW) boaters enter the mouth of the Amelia River and the State of Florida at Mile 714. As you cross the St. Marys River and enter the State of Florida you will notice a change in the characteristics of the ICW.

Georgia's long, open sounds and wide rivers gradually transform into a series of creeks and rivers connected by narrow land cuts, and you will see much more development and boat traffic will increase. For the 370 or so miles to Miami navigational aids are plentiful and marinas and urban centers intensify as you travel south.

The Upper Florida ICW is well marked and easy to follow. Track of your position by checking off markers on the chart as you pass. Take extra care where inlet, river and ICW channels meet; a few moments' study of the chart ahead of time will prevent confusion in those areas where a buoy system changes direction or marker numbering resets. Be prepared as these areas are also prone to shoaling and markers may be repositioned.

With a few exceptions, the ICW here is protected from strong winds and is usually free of rough water. Tidal range is more than 7 feet at Fernandina and currents up to 4 knots may be encountered between Fernandina and Haulover Canal, especially at inlets and narrows. Tidal variances and currents decrease as you head south to Miami.

NO WAKE ZONE

No Wake Zones, Idle Speed Zones and various Speed Limit restrictions are in effect throughout the waterways included in this chapter. Exercise diligence in knowing the regulations by observing signs and other markers. Enforcement is always present. As always, be courteous to other vessels and avoid manatees and other marine life.

Manatee zones also have speed restrictions that are strictly enforced. Many are seasonal and the posted signs may be difficult to read so keep an eye out for them. Speed restrictions are subject to change. Always obey speeds as posted.

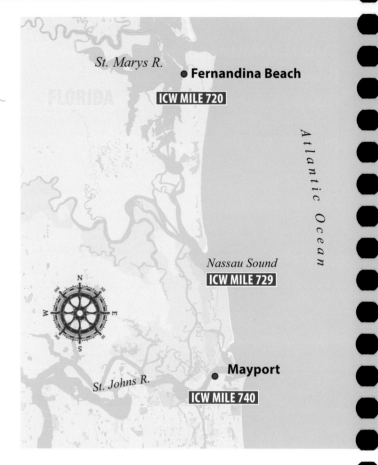

Crab Pot & Trap Markers

The terms "pot" and "trap" are somewhat interchangeable when referring to the enclosed traps (usually a framework of wire) used to catch crabs in shallow waters. The attached retrieval markers or "pots" can range from colorful buoys to empty milk jugs (or anything else that floats). They are so ubiquitous that some creeks and rivers along the ICW are clogged with pots making navigation tricky. Dark-colored markers are especially difficult to see in the best of conditions.

You do NOT want to get a line wrapped around your prop so it is advisable to have a spotter on the foredeck when traversing fields of pots. While it is against the law to place crabpots with marker buoys inside navigational channels, they sometimes break loose and find their way there. Crab pots can, however, assist with navigation. On many stretches of the ICW they delimit the channel and can often warn operators when they stray to the edge of the channel.

Fernandina Beach

Reminder: All mileage on the ICW is measured in statute rather than nautical miles (1 nm = 1.15 mile).

Docking & Anchoring

Much of Florida's eastern ICW channel is narrow with shallow edges and anchorages are sometimes widely spaced. As the population continues to increase, favorite anchorages become more crowded or re-designated. Good anchorages are still available if you plan ahead but not all allow shore access. Holding is generally good but keep in mind that the strong currents in the ICW may require extra scope and swing room. Also remember that most currents in the ICW run with the tides and ebb and flood currents might differ significantly. If possible pick a protected spot where tidal effects are minimal such as behind a causeway.

Use of an anchor light is important and required by law and, in some places, you will be ticketed for not having one on at night. Florida restrictions on anchoring are changing on a regular basis. Plan your stops in advance and be sure to check that anchoring is allowed at your chosen stop.

The same space shortage applies to marina dockage so you should reserve ahead or plan to arrive early at your chosen marina during the winter cruising season. Most dockmasters make every effort to find room for one more and the friendliness of the boating community more than makes up for the crowded conditions.

■ FERNANDINA BEACH AREA

ICW Mile 716 to Mile 720

Tracing the ICW route south you can trace timelines in history as well. Amelia Island has enjoyed a colorful history. In its earlier years pirates and smugglers used it as their stronghold and rum runners continued the tradition during Prohibition. Eight different flags have flown over Amelia Island, among them the standard of the Conquistadors and the French Huguenots, the British Union Jack and the Stars and Bars of the Confederacy.

The island's historic past can be explored at Fort Clinch State Park at the northern tip. The park has an impressive Civil War era fort and several walking trails but boats are not permitted to beach along the park's

Amelia River, FL

FERNANDINA BEACH AREA		Largest Vessel	VHF	Total Slips	Approach/ Dockside Depth	Floating Docks	Gas/ Diesel	Repairs/ Haulout	Min/Max Amps	Pump-Out Station
1. Tiger Point Marina (WiFi) MM 715.3	(904) 277-2720	55	16	50	7.0 / 8.0	F		RH	30 / 50	
2. Port Consolidated MM 716.5	(904) 753-4258	285	16	13	50.0 / 30.0		D			
3. Oasis Marinas at Fernandina Harbor (WiFi) MM 716.7	(904) 310-3300	250	16		18.0 / 8.0	F	GD		30 / 100	P
4. Amelia Island Marina (WiFi) MM 721.0	(904) 277-4615	110	16	147	5.0 / 6.0	F	GD	RH	30 / 50	P

(WiFi) Wireless Internet Access (onSpot) Dockside WiFi Facility
Visit www.waterwayguide.com for current rates, fuel prices, website addresses and other up-to-the-minute information.
(Information in the table is provided by the facilities.)

Scan here for more details:

shoreline. Contact the park if planning a visit.

Florida's northernmost city, Fernandina Beach, is on Amelia Island. The historic downtown district is located next to the waterfront and has several restaurants, taverns and gift shops. See "Goin' Ashore: Fernandina Beach, FL" in this chapter for more information.

NAVIGATION: Use NOAA Chart 11489. Markers are constantly being moved along the channel inside Amelia Island and we recommend you have the latest chart editions. Leaving Cumberland Sound southwards the ICW enters the Amelia River. Initially all hazards are close to shore, although flashing green buoy "5" is reported to be sinking.

Past the Fernandina Beach waterfront, there has been continual shoaling and reported groundings in the vicinity of red daybeacons "14" and "16" near mile 718. It is advised to favor the green side as you pass the industrial facility on Amelia Island. Stay well off these red makers. Depths of 4.5 feet MLW have been reported 250 feet off red daybeacon "16." Take a wide turn southward around flashing green "1" rounding the point immediately south of the shoal area.

After passing daybeacon "16" gradually turn due west towards newly added red daybeacon "18A" and continue towards the western shore. When abreast of red daybeacon "18A" turn 90 degrees to port and pass green daybeacons "1A" and "1B" to port. Turn 45 degrees to port at "1B" until reaching within 300 feet of the eastern shore. Run along the 12-foot contour line giving red daybeacon "2" a wide berth (at least 150 feet off) to avoid a charted shoal at Mile 719.3 extending from the west shore behind. After rounding the point of land head for flashing green "3." Stay in the channel for a minimum 9 feet MLW. Waterway Explorer (www.waterwayguide.com) provides a helpful chart of the Fernandina Beach shallows showing the new buoys and the recommended route.

The Amelia River breaks off to the west from the ICW at Mile 719.8 just southwest of the mouth of Jackson Creek. The ICW turns south here and enters Kingsley Creek. Two bridges span the ICW at Mile 720.7–Kingsley Creek Railroad Bridge and the high-rise **Thomas J. Shave, Jr. Twin Bridges** (also known as the Kingsley Creek Twin Bridges). Some charts may be off here. Maintain the visual center for 20 feet MLW approaching the bridges.

Note that the high-level bridges along this stretch are unofficially considered to be among the "lowest" of the 65-foot bridges on the ICW; expect no more than 64 feet at high tide. If in doubt check the clearance boards and go through at half tide. With the wide tidal range (7 feet) currents can be unexpectedly strong.

Although the **Kingsley Creek Railroad Bridge** (5-foot closed vertical clearance) is usually open, trains hauling logs to the area's paper mills can delay your journey. The bridge gives no warning when it is going to close and it does not have a VHF radio. If you are in this area and you hear train whistles be aware that the bridge could close as you approach it.

After passing beneath the bridges you could see either a wide expanse of water or mud flats on either side of the channel depending on the state of the tide. Keep in the center of the dredged channel (20-foot MLW depths) as it shoals quickly on both sides.

Dockage: At Mile 715.3 is the entrance to Egans Creek (east of the ICW), which leads to Tiger Point Marina, the first marina you will encounter as you enter Florida from the north. This is a full-service repair yard with limited transient slips.

Boats with large tankage can find great prices for diesel and gas at Port Consolidated (Mile 716.5). There

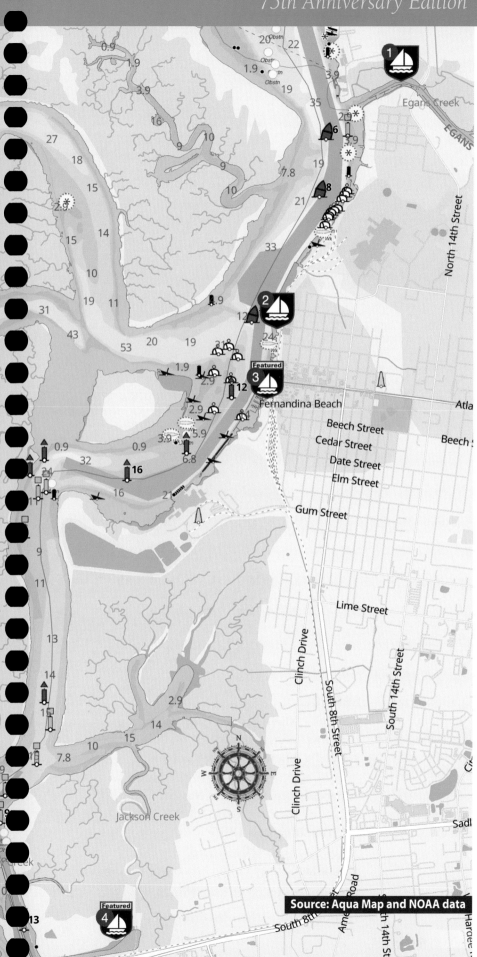

Source: **Aqua Map and NOAA data**

is a 100-gallon minimum. It is best to approach their fixed commercial dock at higher tides. Many commercial vessels fuel here so there may be a wait. Transient dockage is not available.

Oasis Marinas at Fernandina Harbor is at Mile 716.7. Slips (included 30 slips reserved for transients) are on concrete floating docks. Advance reservations are recommended for this popular facility.

Amelia Island Marina is on the east side just north of the bridges at Mile 720.6. This full-service marina offers haul-out capabilities and personalized boat service. They also have a courtesy car and an on-site boat club for rentals. The narrow channel leading to the marina should be traversed with a mid-tide or higher. There is good protection here in strong winds when other marinas may be too exposed but the transient slips fill quickly in bad weather so call ahead to check availability.

Anchorage: The mooring area in Fernandina Beach Moorings & Anchorage is marked with yellow buoys but anchoring is still permitted outside the marked area in 7 feet MLW. Anchored boats may use the dinghy dock and showers at Fernandina Harbor Marina for a modest fee. If you choose to anchor take care that your swing circle does not extend into the channel or the mooring area. Also make sure that you have adequate scope on your anchor for the varying depths and sometimes fast-moving current. (This may be difficult due to the moorings.) Although it is a relatively short dinghy ride to the marina dinghy dock, the anchorage and mooring areas are open to winds, wakes and considerable tidal current.

GOIN' ASHORE
FERNANDINA BEACH, FL

The downtown historic district of Fernandina Beach, a 50-block section surrounding Centre St., is an attractive and popular gingerbread seaport dating from the 1850s, when Florida's first cross-state railroad ran from Fernandina to Cedar Key. The area is listed on the National Historic Register and is a wonderful cruising stopover with many great restaurants, shops and supplies within an easy walk of the marina area and waterfront.

SERVICES

1. **Amelia Island Animal Hospital**
   1470 S. 8th St. (904-261-7153)
2. **Amelia Island Welcome Center**
   102 Centre St. (904-277-0717)
3. **Baptist Medical Center Nassau**
   1250 S. 18th St. (904-321-3500)
4. **Fernandina Post Office**
   401 Centre St. (800-275-8777)
5. **Nassau County Public Library of Fernandina**
   25 N. 4th St. (904-530-6500)

ATTRACTIONS

6. Amelia Island Lighthouse

Florida's oldest lighthouse was built in 1838 and is located on Egans Creek. Tours are available for a fee and pre-registration is required (904-310-3350).

7. Amelia Island Museum of History

Located in an old jail at 233 S. 3rd St. (904-261-7378) with docent-led tours of homes, pubs and even ghost hangouts (for a fee).

8. Maritime Museum of Amelia Island

Maritime history, pirate lore and marine artifacts are showcased at 115 S. 2nd St. (904-432-7086). Open Tuesday through Saturday; call for hours and admission fee.

9. Marlin & Barrel Rum Distillery

The distillery is co-located with the Maritime Museum at 115 S. 2nd St. (904-556-3837). Stop in for a sampling and stay to hear about the distilling process.

SHOPPING

10. Amelia Island Paint, Hardware & Marine Supply

Good selection of hardware and boating staples at 516 Ash St. (904-261-6604).

11. Fantastic Fudge

The fudge at 218 Centre St. (904-277-4801) is made the old fashion way using a copper kettle, marble slab tables and a recipe that dates back to 1887.

12. The Book Loft

A large selection of new and used books at 214 Centre St. (904-261-8991).

MARINA

13. Fernandina Harbor Marina

1 S. Front St. (904-261-2660)

Oyster Bay Harbour Marina off Lanceford Creek is private and does not accept transients; however, room to anchor here in 15 to 20 feet MLW or just to the north in Bells River in 12 to 15 feet MLW.

Another anchorage option is north of the factory/paper mill on the ICW channel between red daybeacons "14" and "16" south of Fernandina Beach. Watch for the two shallow spots. There is good holding and wind protection from the south but no wake protection and there is a strong current.

The Amelia River breaks off to the west of the ICW at Mile 719.8 at Piney Island with 6-to 7-foot MLW depths. Although it is preferred over Jackson Creek to the north, it is also quite narrow. Enter slowly with the depth sounder on. Be sure to lay out plenty of scope due to the swift currents but also be aware of your swing room.

■ TO ST. JOHNS RIVER ENTRANCE

Fernandina Beach to Sawpit Creek–ICW Mile 721 to Mile 730

The ICW follows a chain of rivers, creeks and cuts south from Amelia Island. With a tidal range of 6 feet or more this stretch is known for strong currents and changing shoals. This area has only light development but don't be distracted by the natural beauty and keep a watch on your course and depth sounder.

NAVIGATION: Use NOAA Chart 11489. South from the Kingsley Creek Railroad Bridge (usually open) and the high-rise Thomas J. Shave, Jr. Twin Bridges to flashing red "14," shoaling reduces depths along the west side of the channel to 5- to 8-foot MLW depths. Pass daybeacon "16" by 400 feet off and turn due west towards red daybeacon "18A."

Pass flashing red "24" by 170 feet off and, otherwise, try to split the ATONs. There is a 9.0 MLLW spot just north of the marker. It's less than 100 feet long, then it's deeper both north and south of the shallow spot.

Just past flashing red "28" (about Mile 724) you will pass Amelia City,

tucked into a bend on the east side of the river. You will see bulkheads, some private docks and a few houses.

The shallowest part of the south Amelia River is between red daybeacon "34" and red daybeacon "38."

> ⚠️
>
> Because this is such a changeable area remember to be on the alert for shoaling and the possibility that there may be additional aids in place when you make passage here. This stretch is dredged frequently but shoaling is a continual problem. Specific problem areas are described below.

- There is a 9.0 MLLW passage close to flashing green "37" but the channel is narrow and you can easily stray into 5-foot MLW depths. To avoid doing so, split red daybeacon "32" and the docks to the east. Pass 100 feet off flashing green "33" and aim for flashing green "37" until halfway then turn to split red daybeacon "36" and flashing green "37," where you should have 11 feet MLW. If you turn too soon you will find 5 feet MLW.

- Between red daybeacons "42" and "44" there are two spots showing 11- to 12-foot MLW on charts. Both spots have shoaled to 5 MLW or less. Pass by

both spots to the green side following the deeper water (18 feet MLW).

- From quick-flashing red "46" head southwest splitting red daybeacon "46A" and flashing green "47." Shoaling at the river junction prevents a direct line to the ICW cut. This is an area that experiences continual shoaling so watch your depth as you pass.

The lower portion of Amelia Island is home to a large and lovely resort community of Amelia Island Plantation. Dockage is not available on the premises.

The current across Nassau Sound's ocean inlet at the southern end of Amelia Island may be very strong so watch your set and drift. Slow boats may have to crab across. The deepest water is closer to the inlet. The **George Crady Bridge** (15-foot fixed vertical clearance) and the **SR A1A Bridge** (21-foot fixed vertical clearance) block access to Nassau Sound Inlet for most boats. North of the bridges quick-flashing red "46" stands on a 16-foot mast and marks the turn to the entrance to the ICW cut leading southward.

Anchorage: The ICW channel hugs the Amelia Island shore south of Amelia City. To the west another deep channel meets the entrance to Alligator Creek. It is safer to enter this channel from the south of the ICW

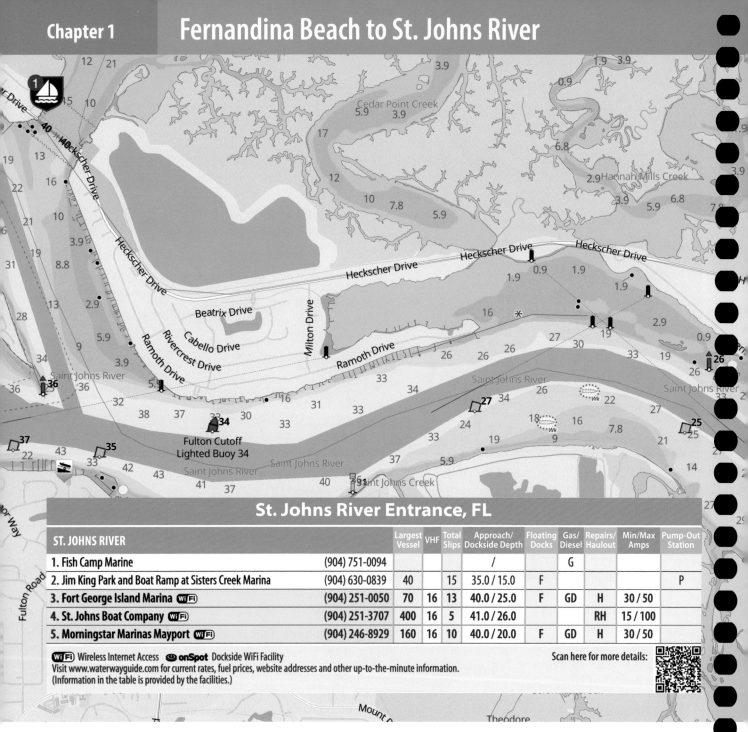

St. Johns River Entrance, FL

ST. JOHNS RIVER		Largest Vessel	VHF	Total Slips	Approach/ Dockside Depth	Floating Docks	Gas/ Diesel	Repairs/ Haulout	Min/Max Amps	Pump-Out Station
1. Fish Camp Marine	(904) 751-0094				/		G			
2. Jim King Park and Boat Ramp at Sisters Creek Marina	(904) 630-0839	40		15	35.0 / 15.0	F				P
3. Fort George Island Marina **WiFi**	(904) 251-0050	70	16	13	40.0 / 25.0	F	GD	H	30 / 50	
4. St. Johns Boat Company **WiFi**	(904) 251-3707	400	16	5	41.0 / 26.0			RH	15 / 100	
5. Morningstar Marinas Mayport **WiFi**	(904) 246-8929	160	16	10	40.0 / 20.0	F	GD	H	30 / 50	

WiFi Wireless Internet Access **onSpot** Dockside WiFi Facility
Visit www.waterwayguide.com for current rates, fuel prices, website addresses and other up-to-the-minute information.
(Information in the table is provided by the facilities.)

Scan here for more details:

by turning to the northwest from flashing green "37." Be careful here; the entrance is shallow, carrying only 6-foot MLW depths, increasing to 8-foot MLW depths off Alligator Creek. Be aware that tugboats have been observed taking a shortcut through this anchorage area at high tide.

Just to the south it is also possible to anchor at the mouth of Harrison Creek inside green daybeacon "39" in 9 feet MLW with excellent holding in mud. Stay close to shore to avoid shoaling.

Sawpit Creek & Gunnison Cut–ICW Mile 730 to Mile 734

NAVIGATION: Use Chart 11489. Between ICW Miles 730 and 735 the shorelines close in somewhat as the channel runs through narrow land cuts and two natural creeks. The dredged channel is now near center of the natural course of the creek. Follow the aids to navigation as positioned and note that temporary markers may be present. Sawpit Creek and Gunnison Cut lead to Sisters Creek and the St. Johns River crossing.

Source: Aqua Map and NOAA data

Anchorage: If you can navigate the shoal entrance, there is excellent holding in mud at Mile 731 opposite flashing red "48." Anchor behind the island between the bridges over Nassau Sound and the ICW where you will find at least 7 feet MLW. Expect a strong current.

Side Trip: Fort George River–ICW Mile 735

Fort George Island Cultural State Park makes an attractive side trip. The park features Indian mounds, the Kingsley Plantation, wildlife sanctuary and lush jungle growth.

NAVIGATION: Use NOAA Chart 11489. At Mile 735 the ICW meets the Fort George River. One mile east of the ICW channel, Fort George Island Cultural State Park can be accessed from the river. The ICW channel is quite narrow here and some shoaling has been reported so it's best to slow down and closely monitor depths.

Anchorage: Enter the Fort George River at flashing red "72." Once inside, the river the water will deepen and you can enjoy a beautiful anchorage at Fort George Island. Drop the hook in 6 to 15 feet MLW with excellent holding in mud. Hug the southern shore for deeper water

and be mindful of your swinging room and the state of the tide. The tidal range is about 6 feet here. The anchorage is exposed to the northwest. Anchor just past the plantation, which you can explore with your dinghy.

Sisters Creek–ICW Mile 735 to Mile 740

NAVIGATION: Use NOAA Chart 11489. South of the ICW junction with the Fort George River the ICW route runs a straightforward path through Sisters Creek to the St. Johns River. (The ICW picks up on the other side at Pablo Creek.) As you travel along some sections of Sisters Creek you may see the superstructures of large ships headed up or down the St. Johns River. The **Napoleon Bonaparte Broward Bridge** (locally known as Dames Point Bridge) at the western end of Blount Island can be used as a landmark when you are headed south.

The pilots and captains of large vessels in this area always announce their approach and intentions at the Sisters Creek and St. Johns River intersection via Sécurité warnings. Listen on VHF Channel 16. Smaller vessels in the area should stay clear of these large vessels.

Watch for shoaling on both sides near Mile 735 from flashing red "72" to flashing red "74" where the Fort George River enters into Sisters Creek. Pass flashing red "72" in the middle of the channel then favor the green side of the channel to avoid the shoaling north of green daybeacon "73." Note that green can "73A" has been added south of the mouth of the Fort George River to direct cruisers away from shoals forming to the east. The ICW channel is quite narrow here so it's best to slow down and monitor depths closely. Switch over to the red side of the channel by this marker and then return to the center of the channel by flashing red "74."

Favor the east bank just south of flashing red "82" on Sisters Creek as frequent shoaling results in 6- to 8-foot MLW depths along the west bank. The **SR 105 (Sisters Creek) Bridge** at Mile 739.2 has 65-foot fixed vertical clearance. Expect heavy currents when passing under the bridge and approaching the St. Johns River.

Crossing the St. Johns River where the river meets the ICW can present problems to lightly powered vessels due to the strong currents (2 to 3 knots on the ebb), obstructed visibility and continuous commercial traffic. Observe markers closely until you are safely into the ICW land cut (Pablo Creek) across the St. Johns River. This area has a clearly marked channel that should be very carefully followed. Note that the shipyard on the east side where Sisters Creek meets the St. Johns River creates a blind spot for small boats heading into the river.

Stay alert for large ships traversing the St. Johns River. Shipping traffic may be heavy. Keep in mind that large, oceangoing vessels have the right of way.

The land cut from this point southward through the Jacksonville Beach area is well marked. The entrance from the St Johns River into Pablo Creek has been dredged and the course of the ICW has been moved westward towards a large spoil island. Buoys have been repositioned to show the way through but they are small and often hard to see in hazy conditions and you must pass them by at least 50 feet off.

Follow the markers carefully to stay on the channel's centerline and be prepared to squeeze over for tugs with barges. Note that you cannot proceed directly from flashing green "5" to green daybeacon "7" and must bend around the turn.

Dockage: The City of Jacksonville operates the Jim King Park and Boat Ramp at Sisters Creek Marina. The facility has floating concrete face docks on either side of the SR 105 (Sisters Creek) Bridge at Mile 739 but the approach and dockside depths are shallow. Dockside water, restrooms and pump-out service are available. Dockage is complimentary for 72 hours. The current is strong but manageable. There is also a large boat ramp area that causes congestion, particularly on weekends. There is additional free overnight dockage with dockside water and restrooms that can handle larger cruising boats in the small creek just north and west of the launching area. Expect 6 feet MLW here.

Anchorage: It is possible to anchor near SR 105 (Sisters Creek) Bridge at Mile 739. Drop the hook north of Sisters Creek Bridge for 8 to 11 feet MLW with good holding in mud; however, it is exposed to north winds.

St. Johns River Entrance–ICW Mile 740

The jetties of the St. Johns River Entrance are 5 nm from Mile 738 of the ICW. This is one of the safest and easiest gateways from the Atlantic Ocean. This entrance is used by ocean freighters, military vessels and recreational craft. Cruisers use this inlet as an entry and departure point for passages along the coast.

Significant local traffic comes from the busy marinas at Mayport (2 miles upriver) and on the ICW (5 miles upriver). Operators should stay alert, especially when rounding curves and in poor visibility situations. It is 150 nm south from St. Johns River Entrance to the next big ship entrance at Port Canaveral Inlet.

NAVIGATION: Use NOAA Charts 11489, 11490 and 11491.The ocean approach landmark is St. Johns Light, which stands 83 feet above the shore 1 mile south of the St. Johns River north jetty. The light shines from a square white tower and is easy to spot from the ocean. The St. Johns River red and white sea buoy, flashing Morse (A) "STJ," is located 3 miles east of the jetties and guides boaters into the marked inlet channel.

Other landmarks include a tower at Jacksonville Beach and a water tank (painted in a red and white checkerboard design) at the Mayport Naval Air Station. Other water tanks line the beaches to the south.

Inside the jetties the St. Johns River runs unobstructed and naturally deep past the Mayport Basin, which is usually occupied by enormous naval craft. The basin is off-limits to recreational craft except in extreme emergencies.

Tidal range on the St. Johns River varies from 5 feet at its mouth to 1 foot just south of Jacksonville. While the natural current of the St. Johns River is extremely slow, tidal current typically ranges between 1 to 2 knots and are strongest on ebb.

The town of Mayport, located 3 miles inside the entrance jetties on the south side of the river, is an important commercial and sportfishing center that provides dockage for cruising boats. Mayport is a good place to lay over before you start your cruise up the St. Johns River as supplies are readily available here. A Coast Guard station is located at the south end of the Mayport

waterfront as well as a private luxury residential and marina project (Fort George Harbour).

> A ferry runs across the St. Johns River from Mayport Village to Fort George Island weekdays on the hour and half-hour between 6:00 a.m. and 7:00 p.m. On weekends it runs from 7:00 a.m. to 8:30 p.m. The ferry operates every day (including holidays).

Dockage: On the south side of the river, Morningstar Marinas Mayport provides transient dockage, a fully-stocked Ship's Store and concierge services. They also have a full-service mechanic on site.

On the north side of the river is Fort George Island Marina, which is mostly a storage facility but they do have a few transient slips. The marina is rooted in maritime history and surrounded by historic landmarks that can be easily be explored on foot or by bicycle.

St. Johns Boat Company is a full-service boatyard that can handle all manner of services and repairs. They also offer bulk diesel fueling (with 24-hour notice) and emergency towing and welcome participation from subcontractors and boat crews (DIY).

■ NEXT STOP

The splendid St. Johns River, which winds its way from Mayport to Sanford, is decribed in the following chapter. Cruisers continuing south on the ICW will find the route resuming in Chapter 3: "St. Johns River to New Smyrna Beach."

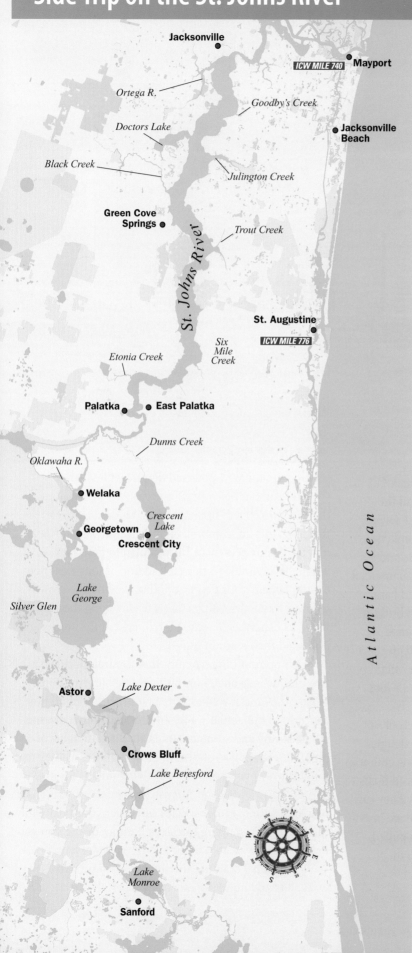

■ NAVIGATION NOTES

The St. Johns River is one of the few north-flowing rivers in the U.S. and travels 248 miles from the heart of central Florida to Mayport. The St. Johns River is a cruising ground with reliably mild winter weather and interesting towns, villages and secluded anchorages that should not be missed. The beauty is astounding and the cruising is wonderful. This is the route to the City of Jacksonville and is well worth the effort.

Residential areas with private piers line the shores south of Jacksonville to the Green Cove Springs area but the trees have been carefully preserved making it difficult to see some of the houses. The river is less developed and more scenic farther south. Part of the river is a wildlife sanctuary and many skippers make this beautiful trip an annual cruise. Shoreside development includes state parks, fish camps (both primitive and luxurious) and a few proper marinas, some large and some small.

In its narrow, winding sections, subtropical vegetation and heavy stands of trees grow right down to the water's edge. Its sloughs, creeks, oxbows and backwaters are often choked with water hyacinths but restraining fences and bulkheads help keep most of this floating vegetation out of the channel.

NO WAKE ZONE

No Wake Zones, Idle Speed Zones and various Speed Limit restrictions are in effect throughout the waterways included in this chapter. Exercise diligence in knowing the regulations by observing signs and other markers. Enforcement is always present. As always, be courteous to other vessels and avoid manatees and other marine life.

Cruising Conditions

From the intersection of the St. Johns River and the ICW at ICW Mile 739.5, you are likely to meet several types of commercial vessels, from freighters, tankers and container ships to tugs towing large barges and even cruise ships. Upriver from Jacksonville commercial traffic consists mostly of the occasional tug and barge.

Overhead clearance is set by a series of fixed bridges. Upstream from Jacksonville the Henry H. Buckman Sr. (I-295) Bridge at Mile 35.1 has a clearance of 65 feet, but the most significant is the Shands Bridge at Mile 51.4 (opposite Red Bay Point), which carries a 45-foot vertical clearance.

Snags are seldom a problem in main channels of the St. Johns River, but approach side streams and sloughs carefully. Keep a sharp eye out for the ubiquitous crab trap markers, which vary from commercially produced floats to plastic bottles, and may drift into the channels. They can be tough to spot. Some are painted black, some are heavily fouled with dark vegetation and some are even pulled under water by the current.

A good outboard-powered dinghy will enhance your pleasure in discovering the varied scenery along the St. Johns River's upper reaches. (Note, however, that alligators are common enough to warrant wariness in letting your pets roam.) If you plan to gunkhole, it would be advisable to carry a lead line or long boat pole to supplement your depth sounder. We find the crowd-sourced Navionics Sonar Charts useful along the St. Johns River, as fishermen have explored most of the creeks and uploaded their soundings.

It is important to recognize that Central Florida has two unique, seasonal, non-biting flying hazards–blind mosquitoes and lovebugs. The first is neither blind nor a mosquito but actually a freshwater midge that swarms in late spring and summer and is attracted to lights at night. Lovebugs also swarm in great numbers as they mate into bizarre "push me-pull you" flying unions for a short period in April/May and August/September but are active only in daytime. Either species can cover your boat with their fiberglass-staining carcasses. Inquire before you get here to learn if a hatch of these pests is underway.

Recreational craft use the river year-round. On weekends and holidays, especially when the weather is

Jacksonville, Florida

good, parts of the river carry heavy traffic. You will see everything from mid-sized cruisers and small runabouts to bass boats and personal watercraft, all in a great hurry to reach their destinations. Fishing is good but remember that you need a Florida fishing license if you are between 16 and 65 years old.

River Currents, Tides & Depths

Skippers of sailboats with auxiliary power or low-powered motor cruisers should check their tidal current tables before starting upriver to Jacksonville from the ICW or Atlantic Ocean entrance. River currents meeting strong ocean tides can create tricky conditions, especially near Jacksonville's cluster of downtown bridges.

Currents are more important than tidal range as the ebb in the river can run 2 to 3 knots making for a slow passage for underpowered boats. Up-to-date NOAA Tide Tables (available at www.tidesandcurrents.noaa.gov) give corrections to the Shands Bridge at Red Bay Point near Green Cove Springs. The average maximum flood given is 0.9 knots and the average maximum ebb is 0.6 knots.

The next noteworthy location is Tocoi, approximately 15 miles upriver. Current past Tocoi can be strongly influenced by the water level in the upper (southern) part of the river, which varies with seasonal rainfall. Summer is wet while winter is dry. Crosscurrents can be strong enough to make docking difficult for the unwary.

The spring range (full and new moon) at Mayport can exceed 5 feet and at Palatka, around 1.5 feet. Wind and rainfall affect depths dramatically in the upper reaches. Lake Monroe (Mile 164) may be 5 feet deeper after summer rains and storms than at the end of a dry winter in March. The river currents are strongest when the water is high and draining rapidly into the ocean. Usually a current sets with the tide as far as Lake George. South of the lake the weak current sets downstream (northward).

There's another variable: the St. Johns River Authority operates a system of dams and canals that control the water in connected lakes so cruisers may encounter unexpected water level changes in the entire network. One useful indicator is the depth of Lake Monroe at the navigable headwaters of the river.

St. Johns River Area, FL

TROUT RIVER		Largest Vessel	VHF	Total Slips	Approach/ Dockside Depth	Floating Docks	Gas/ Diesel	Repairs/ Haulout	Min/Max Amps	Pump-Out Station
1. Seafarer's Marina **WiFi**	(904) 765-8152	80	16	75	10.0 / 10.0				30 / 50	P

WiFi Wireless Internet Access ● **onSpot** Dockside WiFi Facility
Visit www.waterwayguide.com for current rates, fuel prices, website addresses and other up-to-the-minute information. (Information in the table is provided by the facilities.)

Scan here for more details:

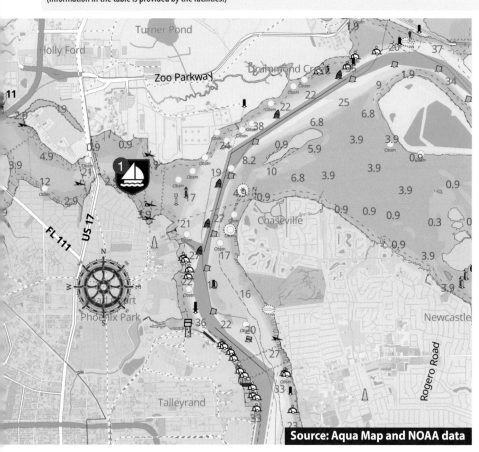

Source: Aqua Map and NOAA data

■ JACKSONVILLE AREA

Southbound on the ICW the waterway crosses the St. Johns River just west of Mile Point about 5 miles from the St. Johns River Entrance and a little over 1 mile west of Mayport. At that point the ICW leaves Sisters Creek and enters Pablo Creek at red nun "2" (Mile 740) for the run south. In this chapter, however, we are going to make a turn to starboard and then travel south "up" the St. Johns River (red markers to starboard), which flows from the heart of central Florida northward for 248 miles to the

Atlantic Ocean at Mayport.

The route to Jacksonville is a big ship channel that generally follows the wide, natural course of the river and is simple to run. The main precaution is to avoid commercial traffic. The channel is well marked and many markers are lighted for nighttime passage. There are no intricate ranges and the next light or marker is always within sight. For the most part deep water prevails alongside the marked channel, although there are some partially submerged wrecks and shoals near the edge so it is best to stay within

the marked channel. Our mileage guide starts with Mile 0 at the mouth of Sisters Creek.

To Jacksonville

NAVIGATION: Use NOAA Chart 11491. (NOAA Chart covers the mouth of the St. Johns River from the Atlantic Ocean to the Ortega River just past downtown Jacksonville.)

While currents gradually decrease upriver on the St. Johns River, the flow runs up to 3 knots at first and can be a major factor near the downtown Jacksonville bridges where the river narrows. If you require an opening contact the operator of the **Main Street Bridge–St. Johns River** on VHF Channel 09 well before approach (Mile 24.7). Plan your trip for a fair current by calculating slack before flood and maximum flood at Mile Point (at flashing red buoy "22") on the St. Johns River to get an interval of time to arrive at the ICW crossing.

The United States Coast Pilot (Volume 4) points out four critical traffic areas on the St. Johns:

1. Junction of the St. Johns River and the ICW
2. Dames Point Turn
3. Trout River Cut
4. Commodore Point

Commercial vessels must give a Sécurité call on VHF Channel 13 to avoid meeting one another at these points. Recreational boats do not need

GOIN' ASHORE

JACKSONVILLE, FL

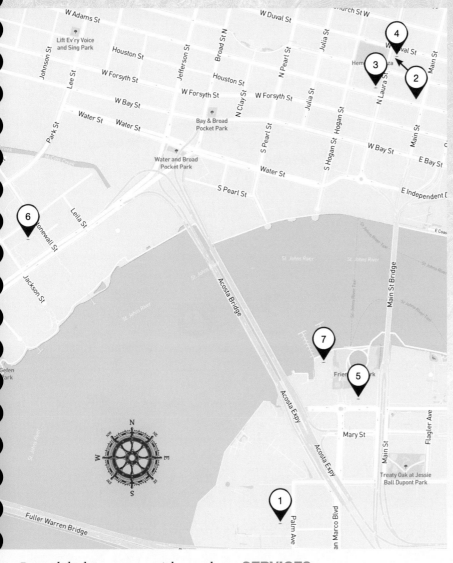

ATTRACTIONS

4. Museum of Contemporary Art
Changing exhibits and permanent works of art can be viewed at 333 N. Laura St. (904-366-6911).

5. Museum of Science & History (MOSH)
Features interactive exhibits of native wildlife and home to the Bryan-Gooding Planetarium (1025 Museum Cir., 904-396-6674).

SHOPPING

6. The Fresh Market
Upscale grocery store with local produce, prepared eats, wine and more at 150 Riverside Ave. (904-665-0180).

MARINA

7. River City Brewing Co. & Marina
835 Museum Cir.
(904-398-2299)

Beyond the busy commercial area, the Jacksonville waterfront is delightful. Tranquil riverside parks and open space line both banks of the river. A variety of dining options and shops are only a block away from the 2-mile-long Northbank Riverwalk. Across the river is the 1.25-mile wooden zigzag boardwalk known as Southbank Riverwalk. A highlight is the Friendship Fountain, a huge, circular fountain with jets of water that shoot as high as 120 feet into the air.

SERVICES

1. Baptist Medical Center Jacksonville
4050 Town Center Pkwy.
(904-202-6800)

2. Jacksonville Public Library
303 N. Laura St.
(904-630-2665)

3. Visit Jacksonville
208 N. Laura St. #102
(904-798-9111)

St. Johns River, FL

ARLINGTON		Largest Vessel	VHF	Total Slips	Approach/ Dockside Depth	Floating Docks	Gas/ Diesel	Repairs/ Haulout	Min/Max Amps	Pump-Out Station
1. Arlington Marina, Inc. WiFi	(904) 743-2628	60	16	30	16.0 / 5.0	F	GD	H	30 / 50	
JACKSONVILLE										
2. Metropolitan Park Marina	(904) 630-0839	80		78	30.0 / 15.0	F			30 / 50	P
3. River City Brewing Co. & Marina WiFi	(904) 398-7918	90	16	31	18.0 / 13.0	F	GD		30 / 50	

WiFi Wireless Internet Access onSpot Dockside WiFi Facility
Visit www.waterwayguide.com for current rates, fuel prices, website addresses and other up-to-the-minute information.
(Information in the table is provided by the facilities.)

Scan here for more details:

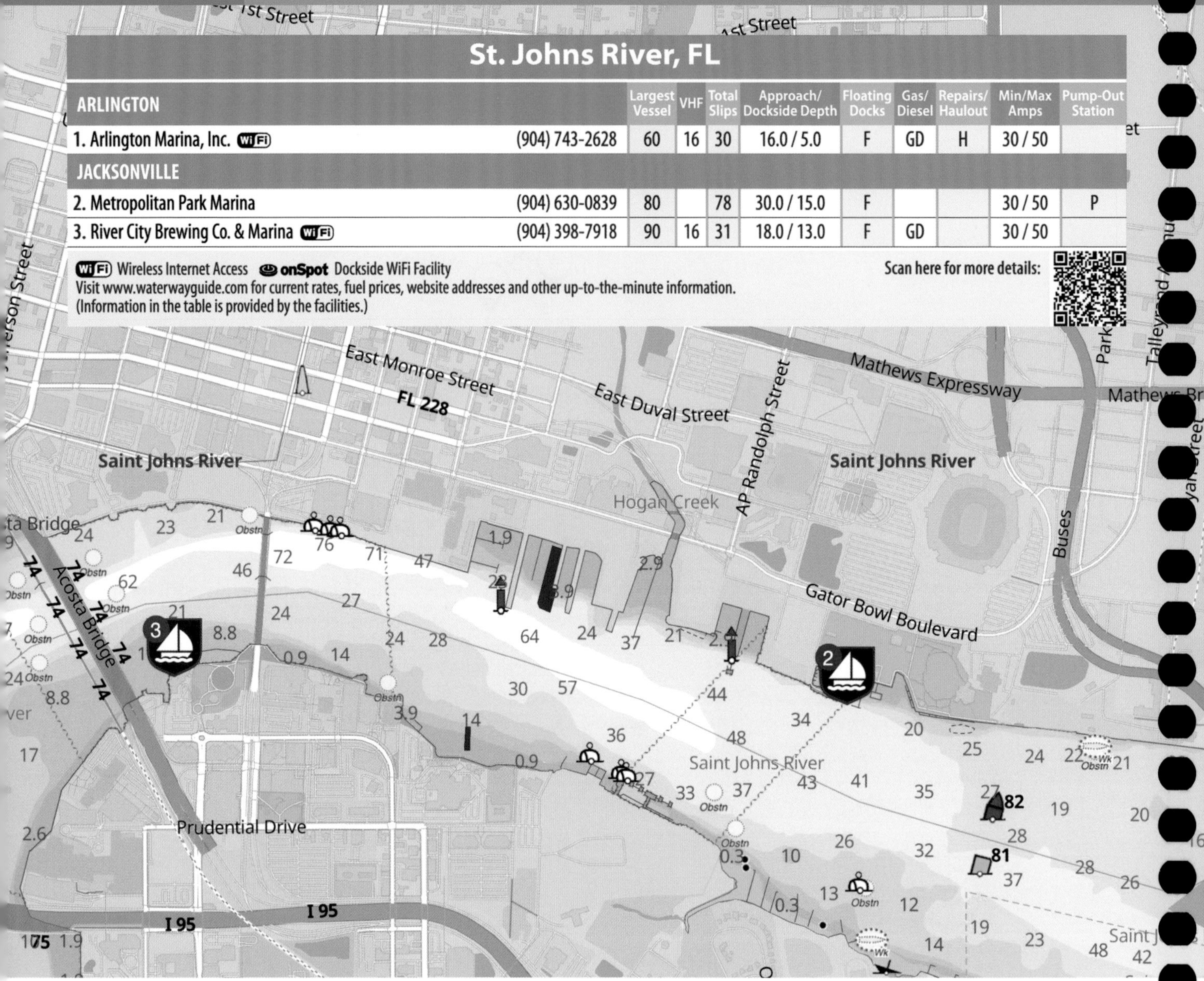

to do so (as you will have enough maneuvering room to stay out of the way) but you should monitor VHF Channel 13 so you will know whether you will be meeting a big ship or a tug with tow.

Dames Point–Fulton Cutoff

West of Sisters Creek and the ICW the channel enters wide and straight Dames Point–Fulton Cutoff, which is frequently dredged to eliminate a bend in the St. Johns River's natural course. The impressive high-level **Napoleon Bonaparte Broward Bridge** across the St. Johns River and Mill Cove is locally known as **Dames Point Bridge**.

Mainly a complex of wharves, warehouses and a container terminal, Blount Island (created by dredge spoil)

is on the north side of the Dames Point–Fulton Cutoff channel. Although the loop behind the island is deep, three low bridges (with 5-, 8- and 10-foot fixed vertical clearances) prevent a complete circuit. Blount Island Marine Terminal Entrance Channel (Back River) pierces Blount Island from the Dames Point–Fulton Cutoff Channel; it is entirely commercial. Recreational craft should not attempt to anchor or fish in the channel.

Anchorage: You may anchor off Little Marsh Island east of Blount Island and across the Blount Island East Channel if necessary but be sure to stay clear of the channel. Watch for pot markers and do not interfere with the private docks along Little Marsh Island. There is no place to go ashore here and it is very busy with commercial traffic.

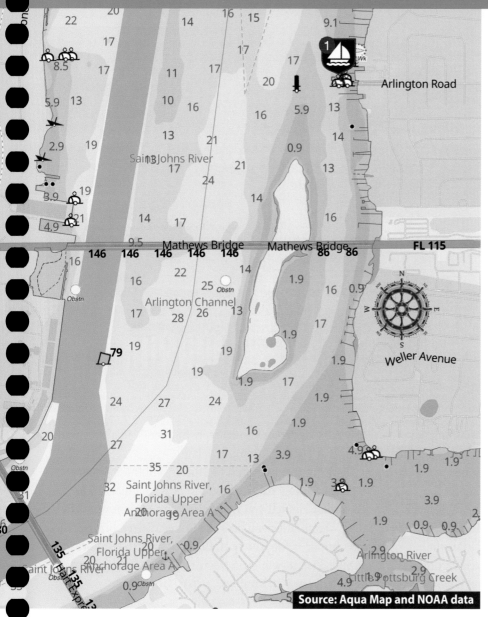

Source: Aqua Map and NOAA data

red daybeacon "2" and green daybeacon "3," which mark the Trout River Channel.

The fixed 29-foot fixed vertical clearance **Trout River (U.S. 17) Bridge** and **CSX Transportation Railroad Bridge** cross the river a short distance upstream. The 2-foot closed vertical clearance railroad swing bridge is not tended and is usually open. The lights change to flashing red and a horn continuously sounds while the draw closes when a train approaches.

Dockage: Twin daybeacons red "2" and green "3" mark the entrance to the family-friendly Seafarer's Marina on the Trout River, which has some transient space and dockside and approach depths of 10 feet MLW. Groceries and restaurants are nearby.

City of Jacksonville–Mile 25

Following the Civil War Jacksonville became a popular winter resort due to its mild climate, low labor costs and easy rail access. Jacksonville International Airport, 10 miles north of the city, has commercial air service to all major cities. See more in "Goin' Ashore: Jacksonville, FL" in this chapter.

NAVIGATION: Use NOAA Chart 11491. From the ICW crossing the river generally winds in an east-west direction until it broadens at Hendricks Point in South Jacksonville and turns south. Most of the development is on the western shore, south of the Ortega River, ranging from summer cabins and elegant homes to large commercial complexes. The heavily industrialized riverfront (with the largest deep water harbor on the southern Atlantic

A better anchorage is at Reed Island (across from Blount Island) in at least 10 feet at MLW with good holding in mud. It is, however, open to north and south wind and wakes from river traffic. Depths may be less than charted.

Trout River

NAVIGATION: Use NOAA Chart 11491. The unmarked Broward River requires local knowledge and is blocked off by a wharf extending 500 yards from shore as well as the

SR 105 Bridge (20-foot fixed vertical clearance) crossing the entrance. Many shallow-draft local boats use the Trout River just 2 miles to the south. (Note that the dinghy dock at the Jacksonville Zoo on the Trout River was destroyed by Hurricane Irma and there are plans to rebuild but no estimated timeframe.)

To access the Trout River turn off the main St. Johns River channel between flashing red buoys "64" and "66" into the Trout River and then pick up

St. Johns River

coast) begins just off the Trout River near flashing red "64." Tugs and barges cross the river channel at all hours of the day and night so be cautious in this area.

The St. Johns River runs wide and deep past the yards and wharves. About 12 miles past the high-level Napoleon Bonaparte Broward Bridge at Mile 13.1 (locally known as Dames Point Bridge). At Mile 21.8 is the red **John E. Mathews Bridge** (86-foot fixed vertical clearance) followed by the green high-level **Isaiah D. Hart Bridge** (locally known as the **Hart-Commodore Bridge**) at Mile 22.8.

The four remaining Jacksonville bridges are less than 1 mile apart. Starting from the east is the unmistakable blue **Main Street Bridge** (Mile 24.7), the high-level **Acosta Bridge** (Mile 24.8), the **Florida East Coast Railroad Bridge-St. Johns River** (Mile 24.9) and the high-level **Fuller Warren Bridge** (Mile 25.4).

The 40-foot closed vertical clearance Main Street Bridge opens on signal except from 7:00 a.m. to 8:30 a.m. and from 4:30 p.m. to 6:00 p.m., Monday through Saturday (except federal holidays), when the draw need not open for the passage of vessels. The 5-foot closed vertical clearance Florida East Coast Railroad Bridge is automated and is normally in the fully open position displaying flashing green lights to indicate that vessels

may pass. Trains cross relatively frequently at slow speed. Expect at least a 20-minute delay.

Barge traffic is common in the area of these bridges. Contact the tugboat skippers on VHF Channels 13 or 16 so they can tell you how to stay out of their way. The river widens after you pass the Fuller Warren Bridge. The next bridge is the **Henry H. Buckman Sr. (I-295) Bridge** at Mile 35.1, a twin-span, high-rise structure that carries eight lanes of I-295 traffic.

> Rather than calling the Coast Guard directly for navigation information, listen to the *Local Notice to Mariners* broadcast on VHF Channel 22A at 8:15 a.m. and 6:15 p.m. daily.

Dockage: Mind the current when docking in this area as it is strong. It is best to arrive at slack tide as the current can make docking interesting. The first facility you encounter when headed to Jacksonville is Arlington Marina, Inc. (before the John E. Mathews Bridge), which has transient space for vessels up to 80 feet at floating concrete docks.

The City of Jacksonville operates the 78-slip Metropolitan Park Marina on the north bank of the river adjacent to TIAA Bank Field, home of the Jacksonville Jaguars football team and the tent-like pavilion of Metropolitan Park. This facility is intended for public use and does not charge for dockage except during special events such as football games and concerts. The marina has no showers or laundry facilities but shore power is available via a kiosk on the dock (for a small fee) as well as a pump-out station. Water is also available at each dock. Transients may tie up here on a space-available basis for up to 72 hours.

Anchorage: You can anchor near the John E. Mathews Bridge between Exchange Island and the Arlington waterfront. Holding ground is best at Exchange Island North Side north of the bridge in 9- to 11-foot MLW depths. With the wind is out of the north you might elect to anchor in 8 to 20 feet MLW on the southern side of the bridge at Exchange Island South Side. (Expect some bridge traffic noise here in a north wind.) Traffic in the main channel might jostle you on either side of the bridge. Just north of the anchorage is a dock for tugs. Note that local folks may party late on the island during weekends. You may also see college rowing teams honing their skills against the swift current.

■ TO PALATKA

Through the 1920s-vintage classic Ortega River Bridge lies a busy series of marinas and yards aptly named "Jacksonville Marina Mile." Because of its low clearance in an area of high marine traffic, this is the most frequently opened drawbridge in Florida (about 15,000 openings per year).

The northwest bank of the Ortega River is almost a solid wall of yards, marinas and boatbuilders. The southwest shore is entirely residential with private docks and wooded plots. The only problem in finding a berth here may be choosing among the yards and marinas, many of which welcome transients.

All of the marinas are close to Roosevelt Square, which is only five blocks from the waterfront. It has a large variety of shore amenities (restaurants and shops, a pharmacy, a West Marine and a large grocery store). There is also convenient city bus service here that runs to downtown Jacksonville.

> ⚠️ Note that depending on your draft and clearance, fuel may not be available between Ortega River and Monroe Harbor (where diesel can be delivered as needed by truck with a two-day advance notice).

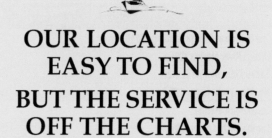

Ortega River, FL

ORTEGA RIVER		Largest Vessel	VHF	Total Slips	Approach/ Dockside Depth	Floating Docks	Gas/ Diesel	Repairs/ Haulout	Min/Max Amps	Pump-Out Station
1. The Marina at Ortega Landing **WiFi**	(904) 387-5538	130	16	192	6.0 / 6.0	F			30 / 100	P
2. Ortega River Marina **WiFi**	(904) 389-1199	60	16	99	7.0 / 6.0	F			30 / 50	P
3. Sadler Point Marine Center	(904) 384-1383	50	16	65	6.0 / 8.0			RH	30 / 50	P
4. Huckins Yacht Corp. WiFi	**(904) 389-1125**	**80**	**20**		**6.0 / 6.0**	**F**		**RH**	**30 / 50**	
5. Cedar Point Marina	(904) 384-5577	80		24	12.0 / 6.0	F			30 / 50	
6. Lamb's Yacht Center **WiFi**	(904) 384-5577	120	16	240	8.0 / 7.0		GD	RH	30 / 100	P

WiFi Wireless Internet Access   **onSpot** Dockside WiFi Facility
Visit www.waterwayguide.com for current rates, fuel prices, website addresses and other up-to-the-minute information.
(Information in the table is provided by the facilities.)

Scan here for more details:

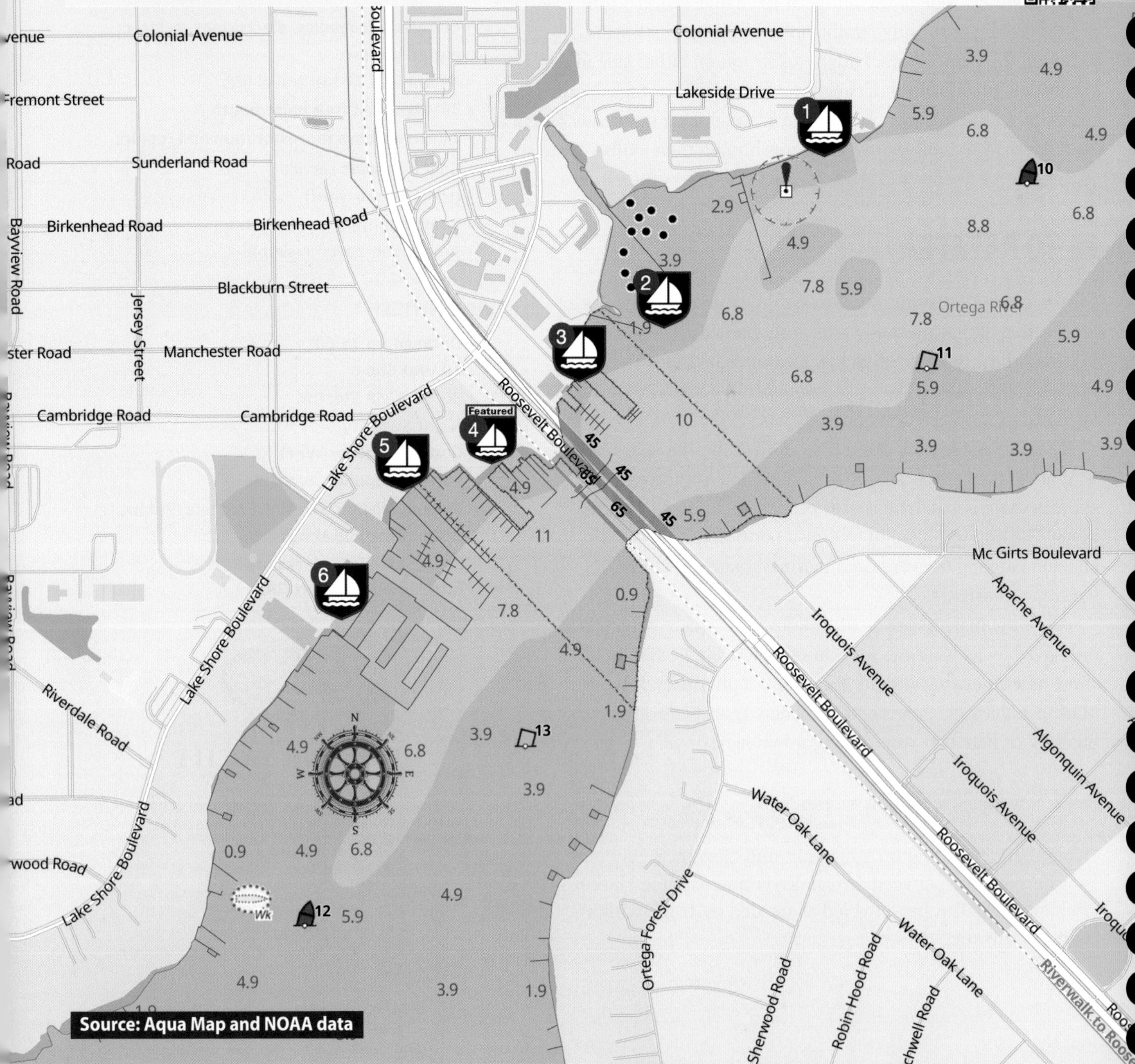

Source: Aqua Map and NOAA data

If you are planning on continuing south on the St. Johns River, this is the last place to conveniently provision and fuel the boat. There are stores along the St. Johns but you will need ground transportation to get to most of them, which could be a problem in some of the small, out-of-the-way places you'll encounter.

NAVIGATION: Use NOAA Chart 11491. While heading due south from the Fuller Warren Bridge, delay your westward turn to the Ortega River until you pass flashing red "2" in the St. Johns River and the orange-white daybeacon marking the shoal extending south off Winter Point. A series of private buoys mark a channel from the mouth of the Ortega River to the marinas beyond the bridge. Be sure your charts are up-to-date. If in doubt, follow a local boat in and mind the charted obstructions and pilings north of Sadler Point.

Large local yachts use the entrance regularly. Depths here are 5 to 8 feet MLW in the river (with shallower spots) so watch the depth sounder and proceed slowly, especially if you have a draft of 5 feet or more. The tidal range is about 1 foot.

For the deepest water give a wide berth to the shoal off Sadler Point and line up for the **Ortega River Bridge** after you are clear of the shallow water. The bridge has 9-foot closed vertical clearance and opens on signal. Depths are relatively consistent at 5 to 8 feet MLW beyond the fixed **Roosevelt Blvd. Bridge** (45-foot vertical clearance). The busy **CSX Transportation Railroad Bridge** (opens on signal) crosses the Ortega River just past the Roosevelt Blvd. Bridge (45-foot vertical clearance).

Dockage: In the basin beyond the Ortega River Bridge the well-kept The Marina at Ortega Landing is the first marina to on the northwest shore. This popular marina has full cruiser amenities including a pool and hot tub, loaner bikes and a free laundry.

Next upstream is the Ortega River Marina with transient slips on floating docks. It is close to a West Marine, other shopping, restaurants and public bus stops. Advance reservations are required.

Sadler Point Marine Center, the last facility before the Roosevelt Blvd. Bridge (45-foot vertical clearance), is a full-service boatyard and Yamaha Service Center.

Several marinas are beyond the 45-foot fixed vertical clearance Roosevelt Blvd. Bridge and the CSX Transportation Railroad Bridge (usually open). Immediately to starboard past the railroad bridge is Huckins Yacht Corp., known for its beautiful custom yachts. Frank Pembroke Huckins was instrumental in designing the famous PT boats of World War II. They offer major restorations and large repairs and are well known for excellent workmanship but do not have reserved transient slips. Call ahead.

Nearby Cedar Point Marina has dockage to 80 feet and some reserved transient space. To the south the large full-service Lamb's Yacht Center has transient slips to 120 feet and extensive repair capabilities. They are capable of hauling power cats.

Anchorage: A few boats can anchor on the south shore between the Ortega River Bridge and the Roosevelt Blvd. Bridge in 6- to 7-foot MLW depths with good holding in mud. At publication time anchoring in the Ortega River is unrestricted, despite some local attempts to prohibit it. Be a considerate cruising neighbor.

Jacksonville

St. Johns River

Huckins Yacht Corporation

Ortega River

Ortega River, FL

ORTEGA RIVER		Largest Vessel	VHF	Total Slips	Approach/ Dockside Depth	Floating Docks	Gas/ Diesel	Repairs/ Haulout	Min/Max Amps	Pump-Out Station
1. Florida Yacht Club-PRIVATE	(904) 387-1653	70	16	73	8.0 / 6.0	F			30 / 50	

(WiFi) Wireless Internet Access onSpot Dockside WiFi Facility
Visit www.waterwayguide.com for current rates, fuel prices, website addresses and other up-to-the-minute information.
(Information in the table is provided by the facilities.)

Scan here for more details:

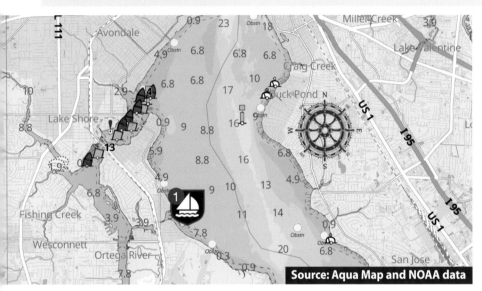

Source: Aqua Map and NOAA data

To Doctors Lake–Mile 32

The St. Johns River seems to transform itself into a lake immediately beyond the Ortega River with widths averaging a couple of miles or more for most of the 54 miles to Palatka. This section is great for sailing although strong winds out of the north or south can kick up quite a chop. Deep water stretches from shore to shore, providing plenty of room for sailboats to make long, pleasant tacks. Be aware that there are also some submerged hazards, particularly as you near Green Cove Springs. A well-marked channel indicates the safest route.

About 2 miles south of the Henry H. Buckman Sr. (I-295) Bridge on the west side of the St. Johns River is Doctors Lake. The lake is 4 miles long with 7- to 10-foot MLW depths extending almost to its banks; however, the **Park Ave.** **(U.S. 17) Bridge** with 37-foot fixed vertical clearance spans the entrance making this unaccessible to most sailboats. The lake is beautiful and well protected and its wooded shores are dotted with homes, many with their own docks.

NAVIGATION: Use NOAA Chart 11492. Even when the going is tranquil it is wise to run compass courses for each lengthy reach between the daybeacons and lights so you always have a good idea of your position. Note that green daybeacon "15" shown on older charts at Mile 35 has been removed. This country is great for fishing and crabbing but the bobbing floats of the commercial crabber's pots–some of which are dark and difficult to see–are numerous enough to warrant close attention.

Along the St. Johns River shoreline watch for the remnants of old docks (possibly submerged) and other hazardous debris. The Henry H. Buckman Sr. (I-295) Bridge at Mile 35.1 has 65-foot fixed vertical clearance.

If headed to Doctors Lake swing wide around Orange Point keeping well off red daybeacon "2," which has been repositioned farther away from shore. Stay clear of the shoaling on both sides of Doctors Inlet and steer toward the middle of the entrance. To enter Doctors Lake you must be able to pass under the 37-foot fixed vertical clearance Park Ave. (U.S. 17) Bridge.

Dockage: About 2 miles past the entrance to the Ortega River at Pirates Cove on the western shore is the private Florida Yacht Club. It is one of the country's oldest yacht clubs and is open only to its members and members of clubs that belong to the Florida Council of Yacht Clubs or by advanced approval from the Board of Directors.

Doctors Lake Marina is located just inside the Park Ave. (U.S. 17) Bridge on the south shore of Doctors Inlet with slips for vessels to 65 feet and competitively priced gas and diesel. Eight miles of paths for walking and bicycling provide access to restaurants, laundry, pharmacies and a grocery.

Anchorage: Beyond Goodbys Creek on the eastern side of the river you can anchor in Plummers Cove between Beauclerc Bluff and the Henry H. Buckman Sr. (I-295) Bridge.

St. Johns River, FL

DOCTORS LAKE		Largest Vessel	VHF	Total Slips	Approach/ Dockside Depth	Floating Docks	Gas/ Diesel	Repairs/ Haulout	Min/Max Amps	Pump-Out Station
1. Doctors Lake Marina **WiFi**	(904) 264-0505	65		100	7.0 / 6.0		GD	R	30 / 50	P

WiFi Wireless Internet Access **onSpot** Dockside WiFi Facility
Visit www.waterwayguide.com for current rates, fuel prices, website addresses and other up-to-the-minute information.
(Information in the table is provided by the facilities.)

Scan here for more details:

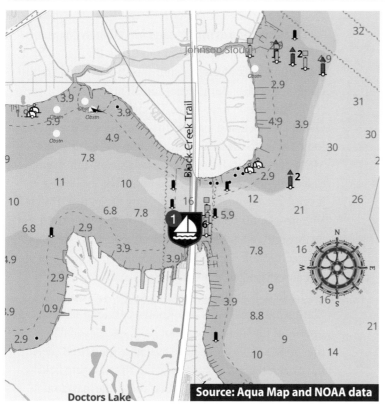

Doctors Lake

Source: Aqua Map and NOAA data

The entrance is straightforward. Just avoid the shoal off Beauclerc Bluff, which is marked by green daybeacon "9." Go in at the approximate middle of the bight while being careful to dodge the pot markers that sometimes pepper both the entrance and interior. Choose your weather carefully as this anchorage has no protection from the west. Anchor in depths of 6 to 8 feet MLW. The holding is good in mud. Expect to hear some noise from the naval air station across the river at Piney Point and from I-295.

If you can clear the 37-foot fixed vertical clearance Park Ave. (U.S. 17) Bridge and wish to anchor in Doctors Lake do so with care because the holding in some places is poor with very fine, soft silt. Be certain to power down on your hook and check it frequently. Choose your location according to wind protection. Mill Cove, Sugarhouse Cove and Macks Point are all good choices.

To Green Cove Springs–Mile 44

The town of Green Cove Springs is on a very shallow, pretty cove off the St. Johns River at Mile 44. Here the long piers of a World War II Navy facility jut out into the river. These piers clearly show up on the chart for the area.

Green Cove Springs took its name from the sulfur mineral spring found here. The waters here have long reputed to have medicinal qualities and attracted many famous visitors in the late 1800s and early 1900s. Today visitors will find the spring in the midst of a city park fringed with fine old homes. St. Mary's Episcopal Church, built in the late 19th century, is an elegant riverfront structure.

The town is home to St. Brendan's Isle (www.sbimailservice.com), a well-known mail forwarding service used by many cruisers.

NAVIGATION: Use NOAA Charts 11487 and 11492. Almost directly across the St. Johns River from Doctors Lake is Julington Creek with the fixed **Julington Creek Bridge** with 15-foot vertical clearance. Depths are shallow beyond the bridge so sound your way in. Inside the opening the creek shoals quickly to 4-foot MLW depths or less, especially on the north side.

Just north of Green Cove Springs at Mile 40 Black Creek empties into the west side of the St. Johns River just north of Green Cove Springs on the western bank of the St. Johns River at Wilkies Point. The creek is deep, placid, unspoiled and offers a microcosm of the world's subtropical rivers. If you make the trip in late spring or summer don't be surprised if you disturb a slumbering alligator along the banks.

The **U.S. 17 (SR 15) Bridge** at the entrance has a fixed vertical clearance of 30 feet and upstream are two additional bridges, each with a fixed vertical clearance of 20 feet. An overhead cable with an authorized vertical clearance of 47 feet also crosses the creek about 2 miles above the first bridge. If you can get under all of these

St. Johns River, FL

JULINGTON CREEK		Largest Vessel	VHF	Total Slips	Approach/ Dockside Depth	Floating Docks	Gas/ Diesel	Repairs/ Haulout	Min/Max Amps	Pump-Out Station
1. Mandarin Holiday Marina	(904) 268-1036	50	16	150	6.0 / 6.0		GD	RH	30	P
2. Julington Creek Marina St. Johns River	(904) 337-6924	40	16	326	6.0 / 5.0		G	H	30	P

WiFi Wireless Internet Access   **onSpot** Dockside WiFi Facility
Visit www.waterwayguide.com for current rates, fuel prices, website addresses and other up-to-the-minute information.
(Information in the table is provided by the facilities.)

Scan here for more details:

Source: Aqua Map and NOAA data

Dockage/Moorings: Mandarin Holiday Marina is located before the fixed Julington Creek Bridge, while Julington Creek Marina is after the 15-foot fixed vertical clearance bridge. Both accept transients.

To the south Green Cove Springs City Pier allows visitors to dock and explore the amenities of the city. The long pier with the octagonal pavilion has 8- to 9-foot MLW depths. Twelve slips are available on a first-come, first-served basis and an envelope will be available for leaving the payment in the drop box at the pier. Holland Marine is a full-service yacht maintenance and repair facility and offers long-term dry storage for vessels up to 65 feet, both power and sail. Reynolds Park Yacht Center can accommodate transient vessels and has a full-service yard. There is an airstrip nearby. Green Cove Springs Marina has slips but is best known as a long-term storage option. If the marina does not have space available at the dock, a mooring may be available (although there have been reports of sunk boats in the mooring field). Call ahead for details. Note that these marinas do not sell gas or diesel.

Anchorage: Julington Creek is shoaling so sound your way in and check the depth of your full swing circle if you choose to anchor here. For larger boats the more exposed Old Bull Bay at Julington Creek's mouth is a good anchorage with shelter from north through southeast winds. You will find 7- to 8-foot MLW depths on a line between the points of land and 4 to 6 feet MLW closer to the Julington Creek Bridge. This attractive area is especially good for dinghy exploration.

Boats that clear the 30-foot vertical clearance US 17 (SR15) Bridge can anchor in Black Creek in at least 15 feet MLW with excellent all-around protection. Most of the bottom here is sticky black mud offering good holding for a well-set hook. Taller air-draft boats can anchor outside the first bridge in all but east winds.

At Green Cove Springs you can anchor just north of the town in the mouth of Governors Creek in 8 feet MLW

(or have your mast unstepped at a nearby marina), you can cruise upriver to the headwaters and the town of Middleburg, which was founded in the early 19th century but with possible genealogical roots to the original St. Augustine settlement. A grocery store is a pleasant walk from the Middleburg waterfront but there are no transient docks.

When transiting the Green Cove Springs area stick to the marked channel to avoid both charted shoals and possible submerged obstructions.

At Mile 51.4 the Shands Bridge sets the overhead clearance for the upper St. Johns River with 45-foot fixed vertical clearance. (Construction of a new replacement 65-foot bridge is scheduled for completion in 2023.)

Palatka Memorial Bridge

with fair holding in mud. There is a boat ramp and a dinghy dock here. The anchorage is open to north through east winds and has quite a bit of highway noise but provisions are available within an easy walk. Should you choose to head upstream watch for the charted overhead power lines (30-foot vertical clearances) and fixed bridges (8- and 11-foot vertical clearances, respectively).

Across the river between Popo Point and the Shands Bridge at Orangedale (Mile 41.5) is another anchorage. Note the shoal water south of Hallowes Cove, as well as the 3-foot MLW spot northeast of flashing red "20." Enter well southeast of flashing red "20" avoiding the charted cable area. Holding is excellent in 7 to 10 feet MLW but protection is good only from the northeast.

Palatka–Mile 75.1

Palatka retains the ambiance of an old river town. A city park along the riverfront has picnic shelters, boat ramps and restrooms, as well as brick-paved residential streets that run beneath grand old oaks hung with Spanish moss. A 1-mile walk from the marinas south of the high-rise Memorial Bridge will bring you to Ravine Gardens State Park. The 59-acre state park was built in 1933 around

natural ravines. Nature trails wander among thousands of azaleas and other ornamental plants growing near streams and ravines. The park is open daily from 8:00 a.m. to sundown.

NAVIGATION: Use NOAA Charts 11487 and 11492. It is a 28-mile journey along the river's wooded and narrow banks from Green Cove Springs to Palatka. Fish weirs (stakes) and numerous pot markers populate the river hereabouts. When transiting the Green Cove Springs area stick to the marked channel to avoid both charted shoals and possible submerged obstructions. Beam winds, particularly from the west, can be very strong here so mind the chart plotter or remain lined up on the visual ranges if you have a deeper draft.

Most recreational boats will have enough depth anywhere in the center of the river here. Palatka's high and low tides happen about 7.25 and 8.5 hours, respectively, after Mayport's tides. The water depth in the channel ranges from 8 to 12 feet at MLW. The tidal range is about 1 foot.

Your journey of the St. Johns River ends at Mile 51.4 if you cannot pass under the 45-foot fixed vertical clearance **Shands Bridge**. (Completion on replacement 65-foot

St. Johns River, FL

GREEN COVE SPRINGS AREA		Largest Vessel	VHF	Total Slips	Approach/ Dockside Depth	Floating Docks	Gas/ Diesel	Repairs/ Haulout	Min/Max Amps	Pump-Out Station
1. Green Cove Springs City Pier	(904) 297-7060			12	8.0 / 8.0	F			30 / 50	
2. Holland Marine	(904) 284-3349	65		15	10.0 / 10.0	F		RH	30 / 50	
3. Reynolds Park Yacht Center WiFi	(904) 284-4667	400	16	70	12.0 / 6.0	F		RH	30 / 200+	P
4. Green Cove Springs Marina WiFi	(904) 284-1811	100	16	21	14.0 / 11.0	F		RH	30 / 50	P

WiFi Wireless Internet Access   onSpot Dockside WiFi Facility
Visit www.waterwayguide.com for current rates, fuel prices, website addresses and other up-to-the-minute information. (Information in the table is provided by the facilities.)

Scan here for more details:

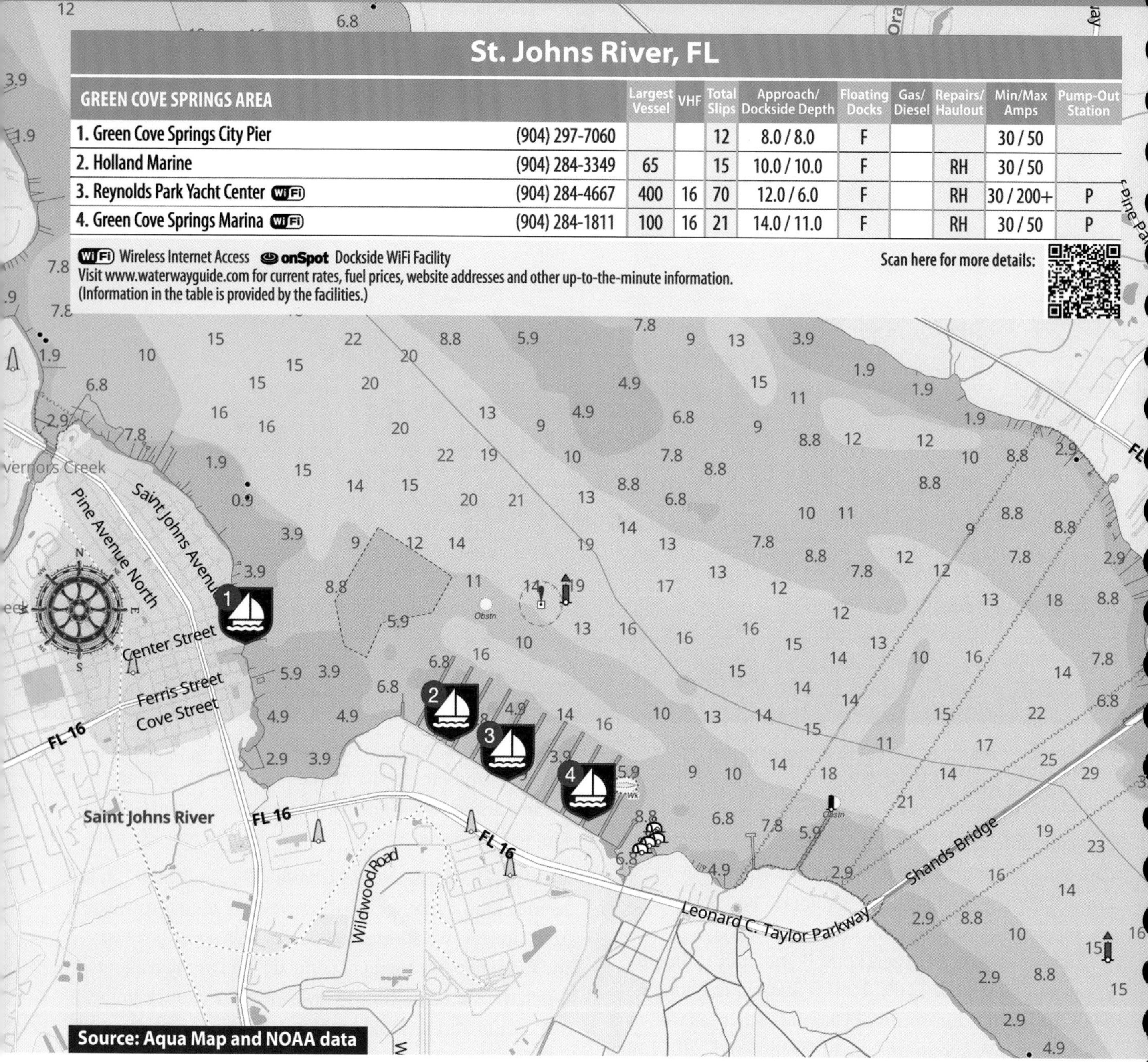

Source: Aqua Map and NOAA data

bridge is scheduled for completion in 2023.)

Heading south from Green Cove Springs the St. Johns River is wide and relatively deep all the way to Palatka. There are shoals near the shorelines (some marked) but keeping to the visual center of the river should suffice. Midline depths decrease from about 20 feet MLW at the Shands Bridge to 8 feet MLW just north of Palatka.

An exception is a series of charted but unmarked shoals starting south of green daybeacon "27" at Mile 60 and ending at Mile 62. These begin off Willis Point and end off Tocoi Creek and carry a minimum depth of 5 feet

MLW. The safer water is closer to the east side of the river for this stretch. Only one range remains in this section of the river. If you need the deepest water, align the 6-second flashing green on Racy Point with the quick-flashing green to its south as a back range past Ninemile Point. For most vessels there is enough water outside this channel.

A well-marked channel begins at flashing red "42" approaching Forrester Point at Mile 72. This channel takes a wide turn around Forrester Point and aligns with a final range for the commercial channel to Hog Eye Point near Palatka. The main hazard on this turn is just west of

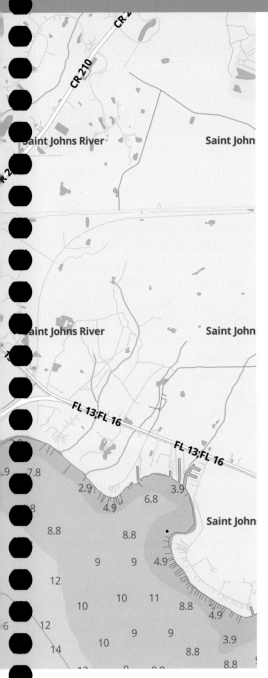

flashing red "42A" off Rice Creek.

Dockage: Trout Creek Marina across the river and south of Green Cove Springs may have space for you on their floating docks. Note that the marina is located beyond a fixed bridge with vertical clearance of 17 feet.

Closer to Palataka, Crystal Cove Resort Marina is part of a resort hotel with a few slips. Another hotel with a few slips is Quality Inn & Suites

Riverfront just north of Memorial Bridge. Call ahead for slip availability. The Palatka Town Dock south of the bridge is available for daytime stops only. It may be busy with small boats on weekends.

A short distance south is Palatka City Dock with fairly narrow slips and a T-head space, which is occasionally taken by a river cruise boat. Space is available on a first-come, first-served basis for up to 48 hours. It is free but with no amenities and is exposed to a strong easterly wind but otherwise is a good place for a temporary tie up. There is a boat ramp nearby. Shopping and restaurants are a few blocks away.

Boathouse Marina is south of the town dock with slips with full amenities. This marina has an Old Florida vibe and solid facilities. Head for the dock approximately midway between flashing green "1" and flashing red "2." Approach and dockside depths of 8 feet MLW are reported. The town is just 3 blocks away. Contact the marina in advance for reservations.

Corky Bell's Seafood and Steak at Gator Landing (386-325-1094) is at Devils Elbow in East Palatka (across from flashing red "6"). They have a dock and will let you do some nearby shopping if you eat a meal there. Nearby are a large hardware store, a drugstore and an independent grocery store.

Anchorage: To the southeast of the Shands Bridge, Trout Creek enters the St. Johns River on the north side of Palmo Cove around the east end of Jack Wright Island (Mile 48). Trout Creek is a popular anchorage but note that there is a fixed bridge about 0.5 miles up the creek. The official listed vertical clearance is 14

feet at high water but locals report a few feet more. Trout Creek is a deep and picturesque stream. For boats that cannot clear the bridge Palmo Cove is an alternative anchorage with protection from all but west winds.

About 4 miles upriver (south) from the Shands Bridge there is a scenic cove on the west side of the river south of Bayard Point and north of an unmarked shoal northeast of Clark Creek. Depths are 9 to 10 feet MLW in Bayard Point Cove, which is protected from the northwest and offers good holding in sandy mud. Sound your way in while dodging the pot markers that are often set here.

Farther south and on the east side of the St. Johns River is Solano Cove with 6- to 7-foot MLW depths and good holding. It is open to the northwest through south. To the south at Mile 62.5 is a remote, quiet anchorage at Deep Creek with all-around protection and good holding in mud. It has a tricky entrance, however, that is best navigated with Navionics Sonar Chart.

There is some anchoring room south of the Memorial Bridge on the west side of the river between the bridge and the Palatka City Dock. There is good depth here (12 to 15 feet MLW) with good holding in mud and silt. Sound your way in and use an anchor light at night making sure to stop well off the channel to clear tug and barge traffic. Stay to the north to avoid shoal areas.

Avoid Wilson Cove, which is situated south of Memorial Bridge on the west side of the river. An old sawmill here was removed years ago but abandoned wrecks, stumps and sunken logs make passage treacherous.

St. Johns River, FL

GREEN COVE SPRINGS AREA		Largest Vessel	VHF	Total Slips	Approach/ Dockside Depth	Floating Docks	Gas/ Diesel	Repairs/ Haulout	Min/Max Amps	Pump-Out Station
1. Trout Creek Marina	(904) 342-2471			13	7.0 /	F	GD		30	

WiFi Wireless Internet Access **onSpot** Dockside WiFi Facility
Visit www.waterwayguide.com for current rates, fuel prices, website addresses and other up-to-the-minute information.
(Information in the table is provided by the facilities.)

Scan here for more details:

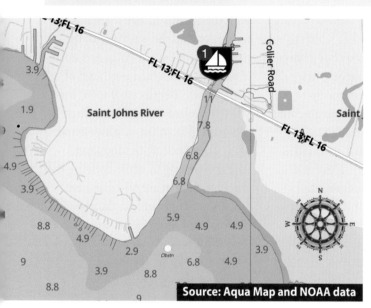

Source: Aqua Map and NOAA data

The south end of Porters Cove, approximately 3.3 miles upriver from Memorial Bridge at Mile 79.5, offers good protection from the west and fair protection from the northwest and southwest. The cove has wooded banks and is between the overhead power cables at River Crest and flashing red "12" on the west side of the river. Sound your way in to anchor in 8- to 10-foot MLW depths.

> Keep an eye out for the plentiful osprey nests here, which have Spanish moss woven in with the usual twigs and sticks. All the way to Lake Monroe osprey architecture (nest building) on the daybeacons grows more profuse so pay attention when reading the markers.

All types of wildlife call this home including playful otters, lazily swimming manatees and sleepy alligators sunning along the shore.

■ TO LAKE MONROE

To Welaka–Mile 95

From Palatka upriver to Welaka (about 20 miles away) the relatively narrow St. Johns River has navigational aids and adequate depths for barge traffic. Many of the boats you will encounter here are fishing skiffs and rented pontoon boats. Use caution around the rental boats as their skippers may not be highly skilled in the art of boat handling. Fish traps, stakes and submerged pilings are sometimes along the edge of the marked channel and require your attention at all times so follow the markers carefully, cruise slowly and take no shortcuts.

At the foot of Murphy Island is winding Dunns Creek, a wilderness stream with a bridge with fixed vertical clearance of 45 feet near its entrance and a controlling depth of 5 feet. It leads through 8 miles of untamed country to Crescent Lake (about 10 miles long with depths of 7 to 13 feet MLW). The creek itself has several very sharp turns but both Dunns Creek and the Murphy Creek side channel make for lovely gunkholing.

Now a sleepy hamlet with friendly residents Welaka was once a bustling steamboat depot for the transportation of wood, produce and tourists. Nowadays elegant antique steamboats rendezvous up the Ocklawaha River to its headwaters at Silver Springs, one of Florida's early tourist attractions. Welaka is a good stopover area about halfway up the river. You might want to visit the Welaka National Fish Hatchery and Aquarium where striped bass are hatched and grown for reintroduction to other rivers.

NAVIGATION: Use NOAA Charts 11487 and 11495. Once past the common mouths of Murphy and Dunns Creeks proceed marker to marker. Two hard sand shoals extend from Murphy Island almost into the south side of the channel. Favor the north side of the river just before and at flashing green "23" to avoid shoaling and submerged pilings.

Near green daybeacon "27" at Mile 90.2 the **Buffalo Bluff Railroad Bridge** (7-foot closed vertical clearance) is normally open but closes 20 to 30 minutes before trains arrive usually several times a day. The bridgetender responds on VHF Channel 09 and is usually on duty during the day. You will not see the bridge until you approach green daybeacon "27." You have to get closer still before you will spot the draw on the southeast

St. Johns River, FL

PALATKA		Largest Vessel	VHF	Total Slips	Approach/ Dockside Depth	Floating Docks	Gas/ Diesel	Repairs/ Haulout	Min/Max Amps	Pump-Out Station
1. Crystal Cove Resort Marina	(386) 328-4000			45	5.0 / 5.0		GD	R	30 / 50	
2. Quality Inn & Suites Riverfront WiFi	(386) 328-3481	100		21	25.0 / 8.0				30	
3. Palatka City Dock	(386) 329-0103	50		14	9.0 / 6.0	F			30	P
4. Boathouse Marina WiFi	(386) 328-2944	60	16	40	8.0 / 8.0				30 / 50	P

WiFi Wireless Internet Access onSpot Dockside WiFi Facility
Visit www.waterwayguide.com for current rates, fuel prices, website addresses and other up-to-the-minute information.
(Information in the table is provided by the facilities.)

Scan here for more details:

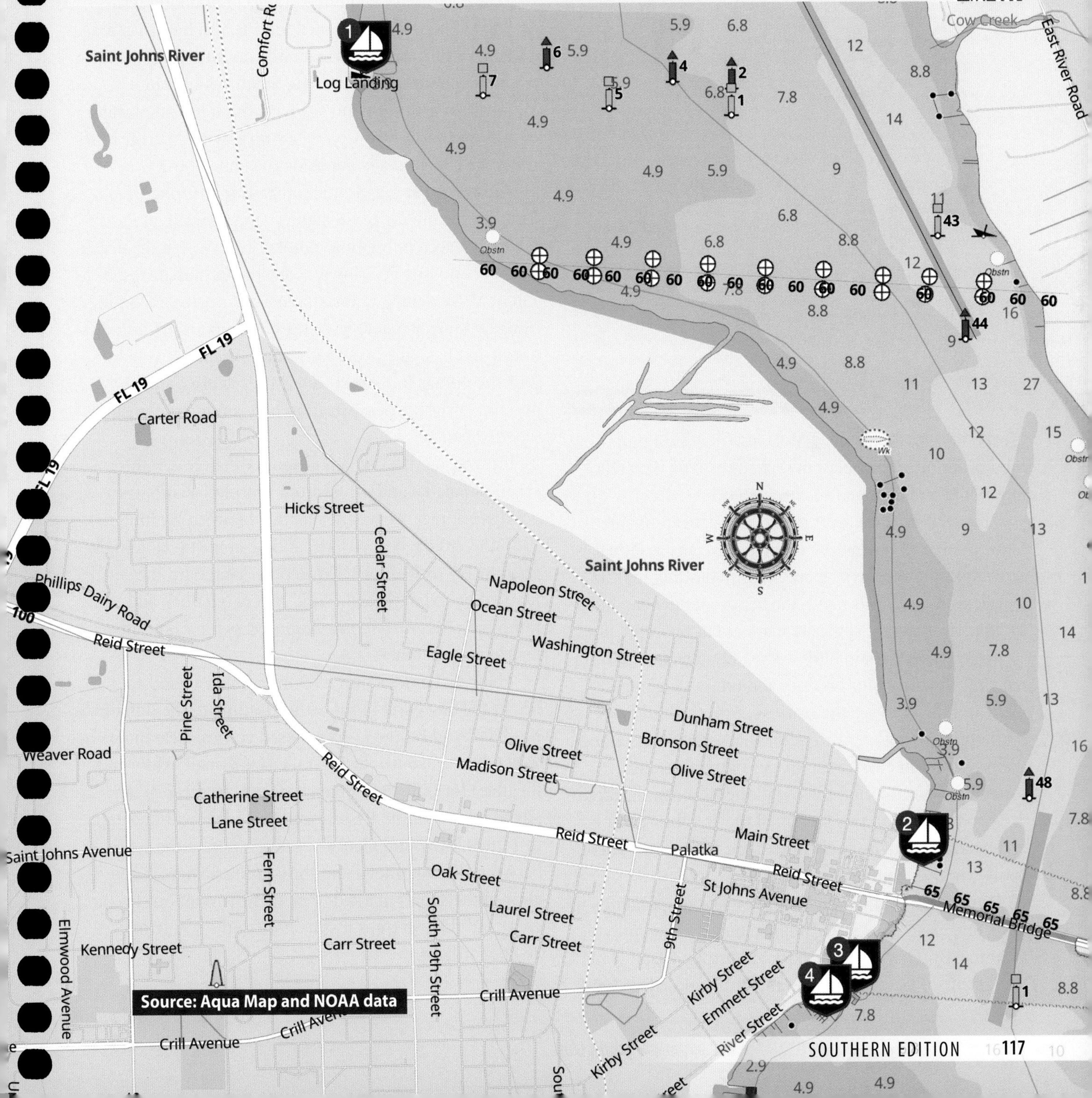

Source: Aqua Map and NOAA data

St. Johns River, FL

PALATKA		Largest Vessel	VHF	Total Slips	Approach/ Dockside Depth	Floating Docks	Gas/ Diesel	Repairs/ Haulout	Min/Max Amps	Pump-Out Station
1. Gibson Dry Docks **WiFi**	(386) 325-5502	49		20	6.0 / 6.0			RH	30	

WiFi Wireless Internet Access ⊜ **onSpot** Dockside WiFi Facility
Visit www.waterwayguide.com for current rates, fuel prices, website addresses and other up-to-the-minute information.
(Information in the table is provided by the facilities.)

Scan here for more details:

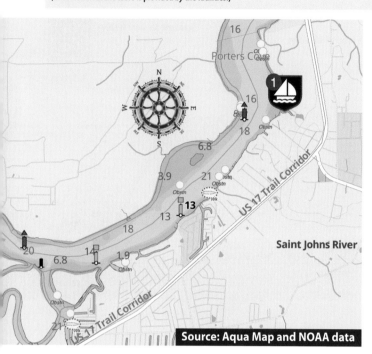

Saint Johns River

Source: Aqua Map and NOAA data

(port) side close to shore. The Coast Guard has proposed modifications to the operating schedule to be remotely monitored and operated so check ahead.

This section of the river has several dangerous shoals. Show particular care as you approach Welaka in either direction from red daybeacon "42A" to flashing red "52." Check your chart and watch the depth sounder carefully for mid-river shoals; some are marked but many are not.

Between the Buffalo Bluff Railroad Bridge and flashing red "52" the early morning sun and ground fog might make it difficult to see the markers. Also the bird nests built on the pilings obscure some marker numbers along the way and can change the shapes of triangles into squares. Close attention to your plotter is recommended.

Also note that in this section of the St. Johns River crabbers are about as likely to set their traps (also called "pots") in the channel as out of it.

Dockage: At Mile 12 Gibson Dry Docks specializes in dry storage and allows DIY improvements or can provide a contractor. There is a free dock at Murphy Island (Mile 84.7) with 20 feet MLW. It is somewhat exposed to the

southwest and southeast and wakes. Acosta Creek Marina near red daybeacon "42A" is built around a charming old Florida river house and offers transient and long-term dockage. The well-maintained marina also has dry storage and a DIY yard. Several restaurants dot the river within a couple of miles of the marina. Small vessels can try Welaka City Dock–Bryant's Whar, which has good water depths and short finger piers but no services. Larger boats might be able to dock alongside the end.

Anchorage: A snug anchorage is in Murphy Creek. Enter in the middle of the Dunns Creek mouth at Rat Island between pilings and pot markers. Watch the depth sounder and proceed slowly; you should find at least 5- to 7-foot MLW depths in the channel but depths are far less outside. Murphy Creek is to starboard about 0.5-mile ahead and has pilings on both sides. Anchor anywhere past the pilings in 7- to 20-foot MLW depths. Crab pots are the only signs of civilization here among the pristine wooded banks.

Browns Landing, which is approximately 7.5 miles south of Palatka and across from Murphy Island, has a good anchorage. Leave the channel between flashing red "16" and red daybeacon "18" and head north. Holding is good in 10- to 14-foot MLW depths. Watch for the shoal marked by red daybeacon "18." There is a dock and boat ramp located here offering shore access for your four-legged crewmembers.

About 1.5 miles south of Dunns Creek a good spot lies in the first bend of the S-turn leading to the Buffalo Bluff Railroad Bridge (7-foot closed vertical clearance). When headed south the 0.5-mile sign (small, white and illegible) for Buffalo Bluff anchorage is between green daybeacon "25" and flashing red "26." You will find 14 to 17 feet MLW and plenty of swing room in the space between the daybeacon and the southeast shore. Keep clear of the shoals marked "Emergent Vegetation" on the chart and the fish traps just inshore to the south and set an anchor light.

Astor Bridge

There is a comfortable anchorage near Seven Sisters Island; however, shore access for pets may be difficult to find. Behind Stokes Island you will be well protected in 8- to 9-foot MLW depths. Several places around Turkey Island have good holding and 8- to 17-foot MLW depths but watch for shoals near green daybeacon "43" and flashing green daybeacon "45" and around the islets at the entrance. Anchor inside past the islets.

Side Trip: The Cross-Florida Canal–Mile 89

A couple of miles beyond the Buffalo Bluff Railroad Bridge, the entrance to the Cross-Florida Greenway (www.floridastateparks.org/Cross-Florida) (officially named the Marjorie Harris Carr Cross Florida Greenway) is to starboard and marked by red-green "C" opposite Trout Island. A series of historic events transformed this corridor from one of the nation's largest uncompleted public works project to a 110-mile greenway.

The Cross-Florida Greenway offers hiking, biking, equestrian and paddling trails, boat ramps, fishing spots and campgrounds. If you fancy an exploration of Old Florida and have a fast dinghy it can make a fine side trip. The section to Rodman Reservoir and a 9-mile canal on the west coast at Yankeetown were the only two portions of the canal completed before public opposition–caused by environmental concerns and right-of-way problems–halted the project in 1971. Every few years (in winter) the water is drawn down to a much lower level. Contact the Office of Greenways and Trails at 352-236-7143 for the latest canal conditions and clearances.

Weleka to Lake George–Mile 95 to Mile 107

The second largest lake in the State of Florida (with the first being Lake Okeechobee) is Lake George, located 75 miles south of Jacksonville. This 11-mile-long lake is 5 miles wide and can be rough when winds are strong up or down its length.

Lake George is the site of a Navy bombing range. As the NOAA charts show the bombing range runs parallel to the channel along three sets of pilings and encompasses much of the eastern half of the lake. The rim is marked by tall pilings while shorter pilings mark the target area. Avoid it!

St. Johns River, FL

WELAKA AREA		Largest Vessel	VHF	Total Slips	Approach/ Dockside Depth	Floating Docks	Gas/ Diesel	Repairs/ Haulout	Min/Max Amps	Pump-Out Station
1. Acosta Creek Marina **WiFi**	(386) 467-2229	120	16	40	16.0 / 12.0		GD	RH	30 / 50	P
2. Welaka City Dock-Bryant's Wharf **WiFi**	(386) 467-9800			10	15.0 / 10.0	F				

WiFi Wireless Internet Access **onSpot** Dockside WiFi Facility
Visit www.waterwayguide.com for current rates, fuel prices, website addresses and other up-to-the-minute information.
(Information in the table is provided by the facilities.)

Scan here for more details:

Two beautiful springs in the Ocala National Forest on the west shore of Lake George draw many visitors by boat and by road: Salt Springs and Silver Glen Springs. In settled weather you can anchor a short distance offshore and dinghy into the shallow creeks that lead to the springs. These two springs feature crystal-clear water at a constant 72 degrees year-round. Bring a mask and snorkel and enjoy watching the underwater wildlife. Go on a weekday to avoid crowds.

NAVIGATION: Use NOAA Chart 11495. South of Welaka to Lake George a good part of the channel is dredged. Pay attention to markers, watch for lateral drift and keep the depth sounder on because it is easy to get out of the channel. In some spots depths are only 2 to 3 feet MLW on both sides. Follow the channel carefully from red daybeacon "54" to flashing red daybeacon "58" and again between red daybeacon "60" and flashing green daybeacon "65" as it is narrow with shoaling on both sides.

> Two antique ferries cross the channel in this area that deserve your attention. Hurricane Irma destroyed the Fort Gates Ferry landing about 4 miles south of Welaka at Mile 101. The ferry crossed just south of the overhead power cable between Buzzards Point and Mount Royal at flashing green "61A." It was the oldest operating ferry in Florida and its future is uncertain. A second ferry is 8 miles south of Welaka at Mile 105 (Georgetown) south of flashing red "70." It provides the only vehicular connection between the mainland and Drayton Island.

Markers for the channel across Lake George are easy to see and 9- to 11-foot MLW depths prevail elsewhere. A hyacinth fence at the south end of the lake looks like a long set of bridge fenders. The channel across the Volusia Bar is between the fenders while outside it are rocks and declining depths. There are no range markers on Lake George.

Salt Springs is at the head of a long, winding creek west of green daybeacon "3" just after you enter the lake from the north. Silver Glen Springs (a state park) is farther south, west of green daybeacon "9." Both have marked entrances but not much water depth unless the river is high after rainfall.

Dockage: On the north side of Lake George, Georgetown Marina, Lodge & RV Park has seven transient slips and reports 5.5-foot dockside depths.

Anchorage: A good secluded anchorage is in the curve east and behind Buzzards Point (Mile 99.5) in 13 feet MLW. Entering from the west turn off the channel halfway between flashing green "59" and red "60" avoiding the charted 6-foot MLW shoal. Leaving the anchorage follow the water's edge in 13 feet MLW until a course due south brings you to flashing green "61A" avoiding the 3-foot MLW shoal to starboard. The anchorage is protected in northerly and easterly winds but is also prone to wakes from local fishing boats.

Another pretty spot to drop the hook is 1.5 miles south of Little Lake George in Fruitland Cove on the eastern shore of the St. Johns River at Mile 101. You will find good shelter here from north through east winds and the many houses along the shore prevent feelings of isolation. Watch the depth sounder and you can anchor out of the channel by flashing green "63A" in 8 to 11 feet MLW. Avoid the cable area shown on the chart.

Lake George to Hontoon Landing– Mile 118 to Mile 138

The river deepens towards Astor about 4 miles south of Lake George. Fishing camps and waterside restaurants surround the Astor Bridge. Waterfront homeowners with docks and boat slips in the Astor area have rigged various devices–PVC pipes, float lines, fences, etc.–to keep water hyacinths from building up and choking access to the river. Without such devices the docks become surrounded by plant life and look as if they were constructed inland.

From here to Lake Monroe you may be joined by bald eagles, anhingas, ibises, herons and egrets. In the cool months alligators migrate south beyond Sanford to Lake Harney but if the winter is warm chances are you will find

Source: Aqua Map and NOAA data

many of them in the river. Manatee regulations upriver from Astor are strictly enforced.

NAVIGATION: Use NOAA Chart 11495. The **Astor Bridge** at Mile 122.2 monitors VHF Channels 09 and 16 and opens on signal. Note that the 20-foot closed vertical clearance bridge span hangs over the channel when open at a height of 72 feet and the overhead power cable here is at 70 feet. Two other cables (Internet and phone) are a few feet lower but none should be a problem for boats that can clear the other fixed bridges on the river.

Dredged cuts have eliminated many turns in the St. Johns River channel. Bars block entrance to many of the oxbows that show deep water inside. Overhanging foliage sometimes obscures daybeacons adding confusion to some of the cuts where the natural course of the river makes abrupt turns off the channel (with some turns actually wider than the channel itself). The markers are there, however, so go slow, pay attention and enjoy the beauty of this special place.

Lake Dexter is 4.5 miles south of Astor as the crow flies and less than 20 miles from Lake Monroe. On the river, however, it is more like 30 miles through a wilderness broken only by a few marinas. The route is well marked but if you lose your concentration you will quickly find yourself aground.

There are No-Wake Zones on both sides of the **Rt. 44 (Whitehair) Bridge** at Mile 138.2. The bridge has 15-foot closed vertical clearance and opens on signal.

Dockage: Astor Bridge Marina & Motel has transient slips and rooms for rent should you want to get off the boat for a night or two. The Blackwater Inn is just across the street with a restaurant located above the Inn. They may be able to provide an overnight slip.

Flanking the Rt. 44 (Whitehair) Bridge (Mile 138.2) is St. Johns Marina & KOA with 12 reserved transient slips and St. Johns Marina South with slips to 50 feet and offering some repairs.

Anchorage: On the south side of Lake George near flashing green daybeacon "19" you will find all-around protection in 5 to 10 feet MLW at Zinder Point. Just 2 miles south is a nice spot by Morrison Island with excellent holding in mud in 5 to 6 feet MLW.

Farther south there are two unnamed loops with anchoring options. The first is between red buoys "30" and "32" and has good holding in mud and 8 to 10 feet MLW. The second, known locally as Catfish Bend,

St. Johns River, FL

GEORGETOWN		Largest Vessel	VHF	Total Slips	Approach/ Dockside Depth	Floating Docks	Gas/ Diesel	Repairs/ Haulout	Min/Max Amps	Pump-Out Station
1. Georgetown Marina, Lodge & RV Park (WiFi) MM 72.0	(386) 467-2002	70	16	7	12.0 / 5.5		G		30 / 50	P

(WiFi) Wireless Internet Access · onSpot Dockside WiFi Facility
Visit www.waterwayguide.com for current rates, fuel prices, website addresses and other up-to-the-minute information.
(Information in the table is provided by the facilities.)

Scan here for more details:

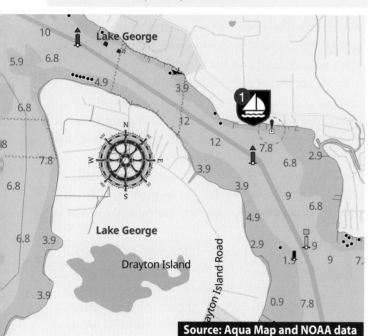

Source: Aqua Map and NOAA data

is located between red daybeacons "36" and "38" and just north of Crows Bluff. This has good holding and protection in at least 6 feet MLW. Sound your way in. If you do not have time for the entire trip to Sanford, Crows Bluff is a good place to turn around and start back downriver (i.e., north).

An anchorage at Drigger Island (Mile 136.9) at flashing green "41" is shallow (5 to 7 feet MLW) but has excellent holding in mud and all-around protection.

Hontoon Landing to Lake Monroe– Mile 138 to Mile 156

NAVIGATION: Use Chart 11498. The winding river from Hontoon Landing to Lake Monroe has narrow channels, land cuts, water hyacinths and snags, but there are good navigational aids. This waterway is extremely beautiful with an abundance of birds, turtles and manatees.

Blue Springs State Park is just south of flashing green "71." The springs are worth exploring. Hontoon Island Park and Blue Springs State Park are independent of each other but share a common manatee area that is carefully

monitored by the marine patrol. If you are moving too fast (and even auxiliary sailboats sometimes do) expect to get a ticket or at least a warning.

At flashing red "96" the narrow entrance to the Wekiva Reach is almost totally obscured by water hyacinths. Although a boat with a 5-foot draft can be taken several miles up the Wekiva River's entrance is tricky. Explore this river only with local knowledge.

Dockage: At Hontoon Landing (Mile 143.5), Holly Bluff Marina has limited transient dockage (two slips) and offers repairs. Nearby Hontoon Landing Resort & Marina reports 45 reserved transient slips.

Just south of Hontoon Landing, Hontoon Island State Park offers dockage along the St. Johns' western shore opposite green daybeacon "55." The park offers picnic tables, grills, spotless showers and a nature trail. The dock must be approached from the south; head for the face dock. The water is reported to be 6 feet MLW on the approach. (Larger boats will have to dock on the dock T ends.) There is water and shore power at the docks for a nominal fee and a small store on site. This spot is especially popular on summer weekends.

Fishermen, campers and picnickers frequently use the free pedestrian ferry, which crosses the river between the island and the mainland. The ferry operates daily from 8:00 a.m. to one hour before sunset. Hontoon Island State Park has a leash law to prevent your pet from falling prey to an alligator. You will also see a lot of manatees in the area. Be sure to respect the "Idle Speed Only" signs.

Anchorage: Real wilderness lies on the Hontoon Dead River at Hontoon Landing. Leave the St. Johns at red daybeacon "50" and proceed as far into the river as you like. Anchor in 10- to 15-foot MLW depths with mud, silt and good holding. The protection is very good from all directions with almost no current. Be sure to bring along a camera and fishing gear because you may not find a prettier place and the fishing is fantastic. This is a busy area on weekends when the state park is most popular.

Starks Landing Loop at Mile 146.8 near red daybeacon "70" is a little-used river loop behind the island off the

St. Johns River, FL

ASTOR		Largest Vessel	VHF	Total Slips	Approach/ Dockside Depth	Floating Docks	Gas/ Diesel	Repairs/ Haulout	Min/Max Amps	Pump-Out Station
1. Astor Bridge Marina & Motel (WiFi)	(386) 749-4407			60	8.0 /		G		30 / 50	P

(WiFi) Wireless Internet Access   (onSpot) Dockside WiFi Facility
Visit www.waterwayguide.com for current rates, fuel prices, website addresses and other up-to-the-minute information.
(Information in the table is provided by the facilities.)

Scan here for more details:

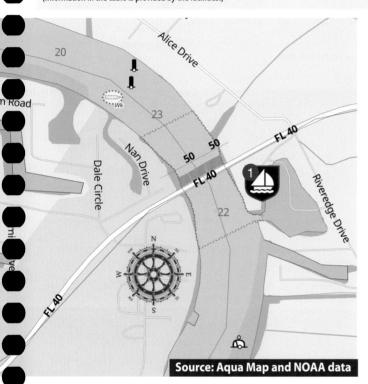

Source: Aqua Map and NOAA data

western bank. Enter at the north end by flashing green "69" and proceed slowly as this is a manatee refuge and depths are less than charted with shoaling to less than 5 feet MLW. The bottom is soft mud. Be sure to show an anchor light. You can dinghy to the beach just past the entrance to Blue Springs.

More oxbows are at Emanuel Bend and Butchers Bend. Emanuel Bend, a favorite anchorage for locals, is at Mile 153 across from the Wekiva River between green daybeacons "95" and "97." Both ends are navigable but the south end should be avoided as it is very narrow and may be full of hyacinths and overhanging trees plus other debris on the bottom. There may be campers on the island. Depths are less than the NOAA chart indicates. Enter Butchers Bend at Mile 156 at either end. Expect 7.5-foot MLW depths at the north entrance at flashing green daybeacon "109" and 6-foot MLW depths at the south at green daybeacon "111." This pretty spot is popular with locals and fishermen. Eagles, manatees and turtles like it too.

Lake Monroe (Sanford)

Sanford, located at the southeast side of Lake Monroe, was at one time an important river port and the largest celery-producing area in the nation but it is now a pleasure boat center. Here you enter civilization again with businesses, stores, motels and accommodations for cruising boats. Sanford is home to Riverwalk, a 2-mile paved walking and bike path that meanders along Lake Monroe. It is a great way to spend a day. Historic Sanford (1st Street) has a number of good restaurants that sponsor street parties and other public social events most weekends. The historic Sanford Welcome Center at 230 E. 1st St. is behind the public library. A Post Office is nearby and a grocery store is about 1.5 miles south of the waterfront. Connections from here are good including Orlando-Sanford (SFB) and Orlando International (MCO) airports. Stations with the Auto Train and commuter trains to Orlando are only a few miles from the marina.

Lake Monroe is broad and shallow and can vary greatly in depth with summer rainfall or winter drought. The charted values are correct for a low-water season but upstream runoff from a wet summer or a hurricane may raise the water level more than 5 feet.

Beyond Sanford Boat Works & Marina, Inc. (Mile 166.8), the St. Johns River system is wild, natural and unimproved and cruising is restricted to small skiffs with shallow drafts and airboats. Numerous cattle ranches are here and the area is excellent for bird watching.

The municipal Monroe Harbour Marina can provide details on lake Monroe water depths and conditions.

NAVIGATION: Use NOAA Chart 11498. The St. Johns River continues to meander 6 miles from the Wekiva River to the three bridges before Lake Monroe. Just before the bridges is a power plant with multiple overhead cables crossing the river. The last two cable crossings are significantly lower than the others with vertical clearances of 48.9 feet, according to the latest NOAA Chart.

St. Johns River, FL

HONTOON LANDING AREA		Largest Vessel	VHF	Total Slips	Approach/ Dockside Depth	Floating Docks	Gas/ Diesel	Repairs/ Haulout	Min/Max Amps	Pump-Out Station
1. St. Johns Marina & KOA **WiFi**	(386) 736-6601	70	16	170	12.0 / 10.0		GD		30 / 50	P
2. St. Johns Marina South	(352) 589-8370	50		53	/		GD	R	30	
3. Holly Bluff Marina **WiFi**	(386) 822-9992		12	74	8.0 / 6.0		G	RH	30 / 50	P
4. Hontoon Landing Resort & Marina **WiFi**	(386) 734-2474	60	88	50	12.0 / 6.0		G		30 / 50	P
5. Hontoon Island State Park	(386) 736-5309	50		40	17.0 / 6.0	F			30 / 50	

WiFi Wireless Internet Access **onSpot** Dockside WiFi Facility
Visit www.waterwayguide.com for current rates, fuel prices, website addresses and other up-to-the-minute information.
(Information in the table is provided by the facilities.)

Scan here for more details:

Lake Monroe

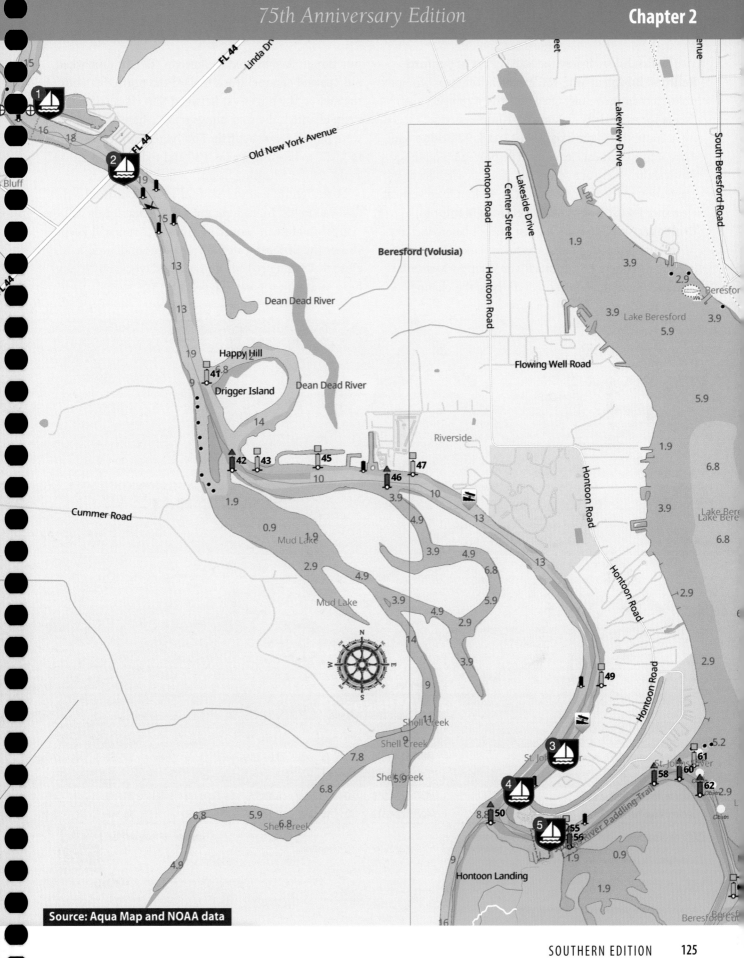

The first bridge before the lake is **Port of Sanford Railroad Bridge** at Mile 156.2, which will open promptly unless a train is coming. On weekends, it remains open except for twice daily closures for Amtrak service. Adjacent to that is the fixed **U.S. 17/U.S. 92 Bridge** with 45-foot fixed vertical clearance. The boat ramp on the south shore is very active and can generate significant congestion in the river channel. The 45-foot fixed vertical clearance **I-4 (St. Johns River Veterans Memorial) Bridges** at Mile 156.6 are the last bridges before the lake.

Be sure to use the latest charts for Lake Monroe buoyage. From the St. Johns River Veterans Memorial Bridges follow the markers carefully to the channel junction at flashing red daybeacon "8." An unmarked old charted channel leads toward the north. Stay out of the area to the northeast between that channel and the main channel; the spar buoys mark where sunken trees were placed to attract fish. Follow red daybeacon "10" to "12" to flashing green "13" and red daybeacon "14" at the Sanford turning basin.

A straight line at the Sanford waterfront from red daybeacon "6" to flashing red "2" at what locals call the "Government Cut" south of Mothers Arms will keep you in the deepest water to Indian Mound Slough. Stay close to flashing red "2" and to red daybeacon "4" and head straight for green daybeacon "5."

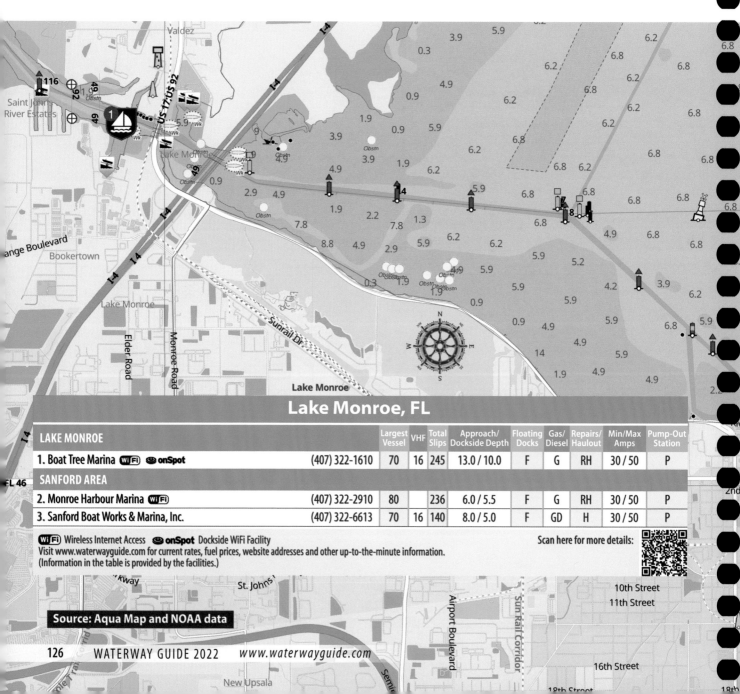

Lake Monroe, FL

LAKE MONROE		Largest Vessel	VHF	Total Slips	Approach/ Dockside Depth	Floating Docks	Gas/ Diesel	Repairs/ Haulout	Min/Max Amps	Pump-Out Station
1. Boat Tree Marina (WiFi) onSpot	(407) 322-1610	70	16	245	13.0 / 10.0	F	G	RH	30 / 50	P
SANFORD AREA										
2. Monroe Harbour Marina (WiFi)	(407) 322-2910	80		236	6.0 / 5.5	F	G	RH	30 / 50	P
3. Sanford Boat Works & Marina, Inc.	(407) 322-6613	70	16	140	8.0 / 5.0	F	GD	H	30 / 50	P

(WiFi) Wireless Internet Access **onSpot** Dockside WiFi Facility
Visit www.waterwayguide.com for current rates, fuel prices, website addresses and other up-to-the-minute information.
(Information in the table is provided by the facilities.)

Scan here for more details:

Source: Aqua Map and NOAA data

To continue up to the headwaters of the St. Johns River go from the unnumbered red daybeacon directly to flashing red daybeacon "2" south of Grassy Point. Depths of at least 5 feet MLW hold to Sanford Boat Works & Marina, Inc. if you stay quite close to the west shore once you have passed through the cut.

Dockage: Lake Monroe carries 7-foot MLW depths outside the channel and there is no wind or wake protection. We recommend taking a slip.

The full-service Boat Tree Marina on the north side of Lake Monroe offers slip-side pump-out service, a pool and restaurant and offers some repairs. To reach the east entrance to Sanford's municipal Monroe Harbour Marina, turn to port to red daybeacon "4" and red daybeacon "6." The marina places short-term transients in either the east or west basin. You will not see the entrance to the west basin until you are almost on it. They do not monitor VHF so call 407-322-2910 to get docking instructions. This is just two blocks from downtown.

Sanford Boat Works & Marina, Inc. in Indian River Slough has some transient dockage and Gator's Riverside Grille (407-688-9700) may be able to accommodate you as well. Note that pets are not allowed due to Seminole County code. Call ahead to be sure there is space for you.

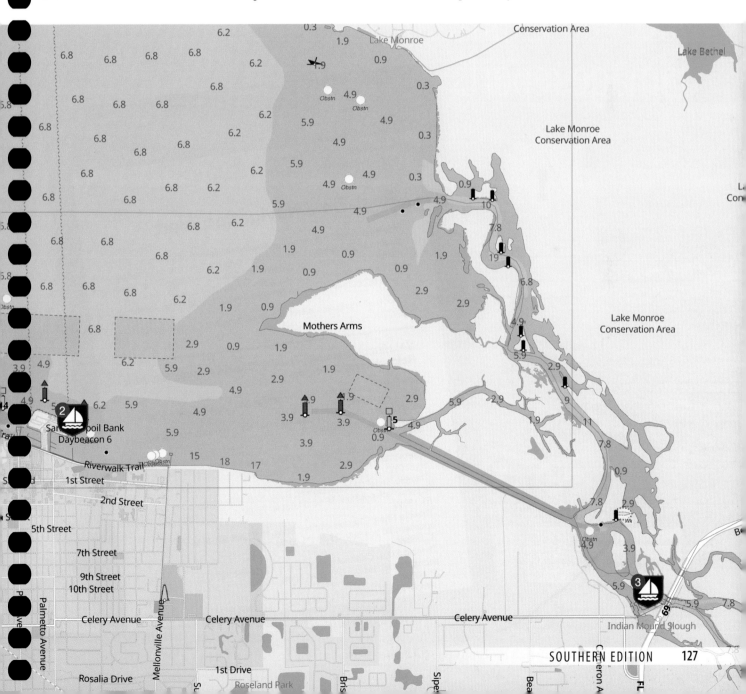

ICW Mile 741-Mile 847

TO ST. AUGUSTINE

The beach regions running south from Jacksonville are collectively referred to as the "First Coast" because this is the location of Florida's first European settlements. It vigorously competes with the Gold Coast, the Sun Coast and the Treasure Coast for developer and tourist dollars. The area begins a parade of shoreside communities such as Atlantic Beach, Neptune Beach, Jacksonville Beach and Ponte Vedra Beach.

NO WAKE ZONE

No Wake Zones, Idle Speed Zones and various Speed Limit restrictions are in effect throughout the waterways included in this chapter. Exercise diligence in knowing the regulations by observing signs and other markers. Enforcement is always present. As always, be courteous to other vessels and avoid manatees and other marine life.

Pablo Creek to Jacksonville Beach–ICW Mile 741 to Mile 748

Ponce de Leon landed in Jacksonville Beach in the 1500s in his search for the Fountain of Youth and it has been a lively community ever since. This popular stopover has beautiful beaches and offers a full range of services, stores and restaurants. It is also a convenient central base for road trips to Fernandina Beach, Fort Clinch, Fort Caroline, the Kingsley Plantation and the City of Jacksonville. Many mariners cruise south to this point in the fall, leave their boats and fly home from Jacksonville or Daytona Beach.

NAVIGATION: Use NOAA Chart 11489. After crossing the St. Johns River at Mile 740 the ICW enters Pablo Creek and continues south toward Jacksonville Beach. Keep red markers to starboard heading south. Follow the markers carefully to stay on the dredged channel's centerline and be prepared to squeeze over for tugs with barges. The strong currents make "going slow" difficult here so be sure to occasionally look behind for markers to verify that you are staying in the narrow channel.

Eddies between red nun buoy "2" and flashing green buoy "1" at the entrance to Pablo Creek require close attention to the helm. Passing close to flashing green buoy "1" take a heading for green daybeacon "5." Persistent shoaling at the entrance to Pablo Creek near Mile Point at Mile 740 has resulted in a realignment of the ICW by the Coast Guard. Flashing green "5" and flashing red "6" have been relocated and new aids added south of red nun buoy "2." The spoil island west of the ICW (red side) has been enlarged and concrete bulkheads added.

Follow the markers closely as positioned noting that the new buoys are small and hard to see but must pass them by at least 50 feet off. A new dredged channel holding at 20 feet MLW follows the bulkheads along the spoil islands. For safe passage cruisers can split the distance between the green markers and the bulkheads. However, it is generally deeper closer to the bulkheads.

Jacksonville Beach, FL

JACKSONVILLE BEACH AREA		Largest Vessel	VHF	Total Slips	Approach/ Dockside Depth	Floating Docks	Gas/ Diesel	Repairs/ Haulout	Min/Max Amps	Pump-Out Station
1. Palm Cove Marina (WiFi) MM 747.4	(904) 223-4757	90	16	221	6.0 / 6.0	F	GD	RH	30 / 50	P
2. Beach Marine (WiFi) MM 747.6	(904) 249-8200	125	16	350	6.0 / 6.0	F	GD		30 / 100	P
3. MarineMax Jacksonville	(904) 338-9970				/		GD	R		

(WiFi) Wireless Internet Access ⬤onSpot Dockside WiFi Facility
Visit www.waterwayguide.com for current rates, fuel prices, website addresses and other up-to-the-minute information.
(Information in the table is provided by the facilities.)

Scan here for more details:

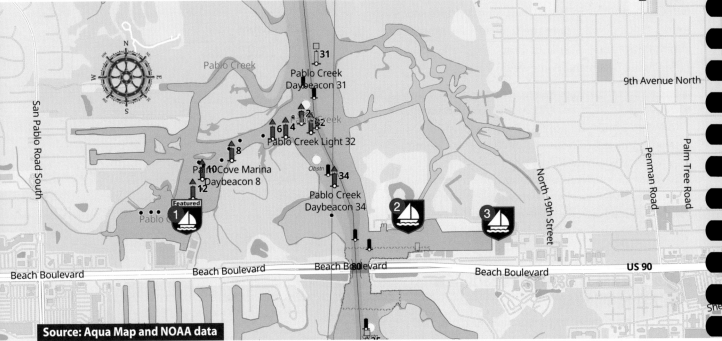

Source: Aqua Map and NOAA data

The channel widens from red daybeacon "8" to flashing red "10" past the high-rise **Wonderwood Drive (SR 116) Bridges** (65-foot fixed vertical clearance) at Mile 742.1. Note that NOAA Chart 11489 shows few soundings here. It's best to stay in the center of the marked channel.

The fixed **Atlantic Blvd. Twin Bridges** (Mile 744.7) mark the gateway to the Jacksonville Beach region. The bridges have a charted 65-foot vertical clearance but expect slightly less on higher tides.

⚠

The islands and partial causeway under the Atlantic Blvd. Twin Bridges help create strong currents here and eddies form above, under and below the bridges. It is easy to lose control here and there is not much horizontal clearance. Also watch for fishermen who work this area in small boats.

Near the high-rise **B. B. McCormick (U.S. 90) Bridge** at Mile 747.5 watch for strong currents, especially on the ebb (although they are not as strong as the currents through the Atlantic Blvd. Twin Bridges).

Dockage: North of the B. B. McCormick (US 90) Bridge flashing red "32" marks the entrance to a small creek leading to Lake Cusic (unnamed on the chart) to the west. Stay to the middle of the privately marked channel (with 6 feet at MLW) into the lake to access Palm Cove Marina. This marina offers wet and dry storage as well as transient dockage for boats up to 90 feet. There are nine other businesses on site ranging from boat sales and service to Marker 32 Restaurant (904-223-1534), which provides great views and first class dining.

On the east side of the ICW is the family-owned and operated Beach Marine with transient slips and a repair yard in a large enclosed basin. In the same basin is MarineMax Jacksonville, a full-service repair yard with no transient slips.

Anchorage: To the east of the ICW at Mile 744.2 and south of flashing green "17" at Pablo Creek lies a wide and surprisingly deep channel. If you choose to anchor behind the island here enter only from the north with an eye out for shoaling to the south. Leftover mooring anchors may still be on the bottom so be wary of snags and set the hook well against the swift current. The current should keep you away from the shore unless there is a strong crosswind at slack tide. This is not a great anchorage but will do in a pinch.

Palm Valley Cut to St. Augustine Inlet–ICW Mile 749 to Mile 776

NAVIGATION: Use NOAA Charts 11489 and 11485. South from the B. B. McCormick (US 90) Bridge the channel is well marked and the tidal range is about 4 feet. Passing under the high-rise **Butler Blvd. (SR 202) Bridge** at Mile 749.5, the ICW enters a narrow dredged channel. Just south of Mile 750 at the intersection of Pablo and Cabbage Creeks, strong cross-currents are possible

depending of tidal phase and recent rainfall. Watch for shoals encroaching from the west side here. Immediately south of this intersection the route enters 10-mile-long Palm Valley Cut with a charted depth of 10 feet MLW.

There are numerous pot markers along the cut that appear to be near the centerline. The deeper water is to the east of these floats. The only marker in Palm Valley Cut–red daybeacon "2"–marks shoaling on the west side along the 0.5-mile approach to the Palm Valley (SR 210) Bridge. Stay in the middle of the channel or favor the east side if depths start to decrease suddenly. Also watch for small craft entering from the paddling launch and launch ramp north of the bridge.

> As always, skippers are responsible for their own wakes. The east side of Palm Valley Cut is residential. Watch for debris, manatees and alligators through this popular fishing area and mind the depth sounder.

Near the end of the cut is the high-rise **Palm Valley (SR 210) Bridge** at Mile 758.8. At Mile 760, the ICW enters the headwaters of the Tolomato River, which flows

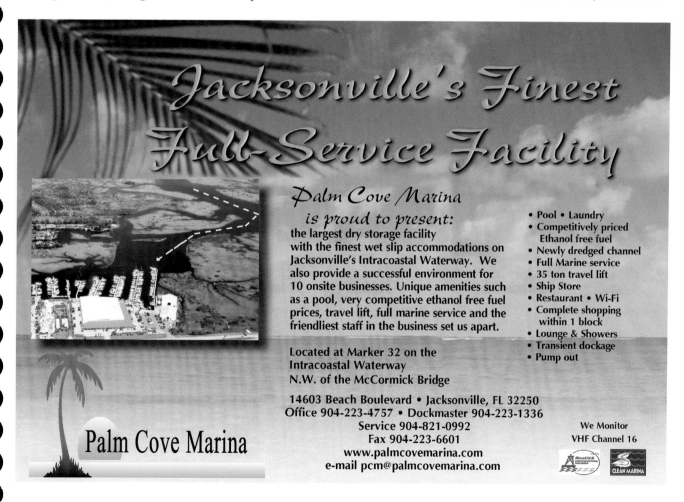

Palm Cove Marina

Jacksonville Beach

Isle of Palms

ICW

© Mapbox, © OpenStreetMap

south to meet the Matanzas River at the St. Augustine Inlet. The dredged channel between Mile 760 and Mile 765 provides a deep water route through the marshes and side waters but there are shoals near the channel edge on both sides. Avoid corner cutting through this stretch. Watch in particular between red daybeacons "16" and "18" for shoaling created by a small creek to the west.

The natural river channel begins to deepen below green daybeacon "19" at Mile 763.5 north of the cut across the Pine Island Loop (Mile 765). Note that the north arm of Pine Island Loop has filled in and is no longer navigable. The ICW follows this natural deep channel all the way to St. Augustine. Despite this depth there are several dangerous shoals along the upper stretch of the Tolomato River from Mile 765 to Mile 770. Pay close attention to the chart and your depth and observe navigation aids.

The first of these shoals extends into the channel from the east at flashing green "27." This shoal may be dry at low tide. Give this marker a wide berth and stay close to the west bank then take a straight line from green daybeacon "29" to flashing red "32" to avoid shoaling on both sides. Favor the west side from flashing red "32" to flashing green "35." Then switch to the east side to avoid a very dangerous shoal created by Stokes Creek that extends into the channel from the west bank at flashing red "36."

Take a wide turn around green daybeacons "37" and "39" and also flashing green "41" to avoid a shoal that is awash at low tide on the inside of this gentle curve. There is better depth closer to the western side through to red daybeacon "42" then turn wide eastward around red daybeacon "42," flashing red "44" and red daybeacon "44A" to avoid shoaling on the inside just before Mile 770. Center up south of red daybeacon "44A" (Mile 770) to avoid the shoal to the north of the Guana River mouth, which extends south from flashing green "45" into the river opening. Be alert for strong cross-currents at the junction of the Guana River and the ICW, which also may drag pot markers underwater. You will see an airport about 1 mile south of the Guana River to the west.

Heading south the river deepens considerably but take flashing green "49" wide at Mile 772.5 as shoaling to the east extends into the channel. Switch to the east side of the channel from red daybeacon "52" to flashing red "54" to avoid active shoaling. Keep a sharp eye out for markers through this stretch as they tend to blend in with the buildings and docks along the shoreline.

It is safe to follow the river's mid-line approaching the high-rise **Francis and Mary Usina (SR A1A/Vilano) Bridge** (Mile 775.8) (locally known as the Usina Bridge). There may be strong currents at an angle at the bridge and some cruisers report that the clearance may be less than the posted 65 feet at high tide. (Tidal range is about 4 feet here.) A dredged private basin at a condominium development south of flashing red "54" on the Tolomato River has two entrances on the east side of the river adding to boat traffic.

St. Augustine Inlet can be confusing; this is good time to review charts and to prepare yourself for the transit of this busy inlet.

Dockage: Several restaurants with dockage for patrons are north of the Francis and Mary Usina (SR A1A/Vilano) Bridge on the east side of the ICW. Tying up at Cap's on the Water, a popular restaurant in the vicinity of flashing green "51," can be very rough, especially on busy summer weekends. Call ahead (904-824-8794) to check on the approach

and dockside depths as well as dockage availability. Pass this area with no wake as there are usually boats at the dock sometimes rafted several deep.

Anchorage: At Mile 765 is the entrance to the Pine Island Loop anchorage, which is a fine place to drop the hook and enjoy a pleasant evening or two. Enter south of green daybeacon "25" giving it some berth then favor the north bank where it is deeper as there is a shoal extending out from the south bank of the loop. A line of crab pot markers indicates the shoal line on the southern edge of the anchorage. Mind the depth and allow for the full range of tide through your entire swing circle. The current is minimal but will affect your set. Holding and

protection are excellent; however, it can be very buggy when there is no wind. Shoals and submerged obstructions make the entrance to the loop north of the island between green daybeacon "21" and flashing green "23" impassable.

Another anchorage is at AIWW Mile 769. When abeam of red daybeacon "42" turn northeast toward shore. Be sure to avoid the southern tip of the charted shoal. Go about halfway between mid-channel and shore and turn northwest into the pocket behind the charted shoal until roughly abeam of green daybeacon "41." You should have 10 feet MLW. The farther you anchor from the ICW the less you will be affected by wakes of passing boats. This is a beautiful natural area to explore with your dinghy before the waterway becomes more developed to the south. You can see alligators, dolphins and a huge variety of birds and other wildlife.

Side Trip: St. Augustine Inlet

The St. Augustine Inlet opens to the east splitting Vilano Beach from Conch Island. The dead-end Salt Run is to the south between Conch Island and Anastasia Island.

NAVIGATION: Use NOAA Chart 11485. St. Augustine Inlet is frequently dredged and is well marked and wide. It is highly recommended that you only attempt passage with good visibility and in light wind conditions. Avoid this channel when the substantial tidal flow (particularly on ebb) is opposed by medium to strong winds. Breakers can often be seen in the shallow waters bordering the channel even in clam conditions. Charts do not show depth details nor

Usina Bridge

St. Augustine Inlet, St. Augustine, FL

TOLOMATO RIVER		Largest Vessel	VHF	Total Slips	Approach/ Dockside Depth	Floating Docks	Gas/ Diesel	Repairs/ Haulout	Min/Max Amps	Pump-Out Station
1. Camachee Island Marina Village (WiFi) MM 775.0	(904) 829-5676	135	16	260	6.0 / 7.0	F	GD	RH	30 / 100	P
2. Camachee Yacht Yard, Inc. (WiFi) MM 775.7	(904) 823-3641	65	16		/	F		RH	30 / 50	P

(WiFi) Wireless Internet Access onSpot Dockside WiFi Facility
Visit www.waterwayguide.com for current rates, fuel prices, website addresses and other up-to-the-minute information. (Information in the table is provided by the facilities.)

Scan here for more details:

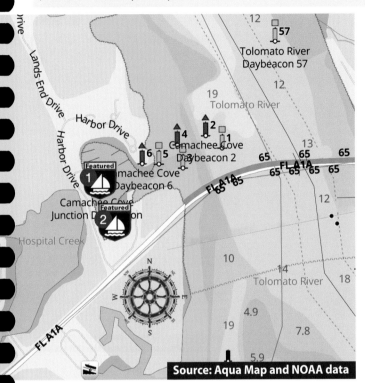

Source: Aqua Map and NOAA data

the position of navigational aids as this inlet is prone to frequent change. This is considered a "fair weather" inlet and local knowledge is recommended.

When preparing to enter the St. Augustine Inlet orient yourself as you approach the red and white sea buoy offshore. The large cross near the "Castillo" can serve as a shore reference. The inlet is frequently dredged and surveyed with typical depths of 12 to 15 feet MLW at the outside bar; however, remember that a single storm can affect depths at any time. Shoaling is continual and the markers are frequently moved and have no set position.

While markers positions cannot be anticipated, typically the north edge of the channel is marked by a series of red buoys and the south side is unmarked. Vessels headed in both directions tend to keep close to (and south of) the red markers. On flood and ebb in particular currents can run up to 3 knots or more; these currents often run cross-channel presenting additional

challenges at the helm.

Be sure to have a plan before attempting St. Augustine Inlet. Keep in mind that heavy wave action can cause engine failure. Although commercial and sportfishing boats use the inlet regularly, get local information before entering and avoid this entrance in rough conditions.

If intending to head northbound on the ICW from St. Augustine Inlet, it is important to run a sufficient distance past the tip of the beach to the north of the inlet channel before turning north into the ICW channel. Keep flashing green buoy "59" (an ICW marker) to starboard turning.

If heading southbound on the ICW from St. Augustine Inlet, the approach is roughly southwest toward the "Castillo," a large stone fort south of the cross on the mainland. To add to the confusion the numbering of ICW markers restarts where the Tolomato and Matanzas Rivers meet at the inshore-end of the inlet. Passing south of flashing green ICW marker "59" and keeping north of the entrance to the dead-end Salt Run, continue southwest splitting flashing green "1" and red nun "2" to enter the ICW then round the prominent thumb of Anastasia Island towards the **Bridge of Lions (SR A1A)**.

Camachee Island Marina Village and the local towing services (SeaTow and TowBoat U.S.) have updated information on possible shoaling and will be very accommodating if called on for "local knowledge."

St. Augustine–ICW Mile 776 to 779

St. Augustine ranks as one of America's finest visitor destinations. One draw is the battlements and dungeons of Castillo de San Marcos National Monument built in 1672. This is a place to relax, explore and enjoy. See more at "Goin' Ashore: St. Augustine, FL" in this chapter.

NAVIGATION: Use NOAA Chart 11485. The ICW traverses the inner reach of St. Augustine Inlet, exposing this area to surge in harsh weather conditions. There is also continual shoaling between Mile 776 and Mile 780,

St. Augustine Inlet, St. Augustine, FL

MATANZAS RIVER AREA		Largest Vessel	VHF	Total Slips	Approach/ Dockside Depth	Floating Docks	Gas/ Diesel	Repairs/ Haulout	Min/Max Amps	Pump-Out Station
1. Conch House Marina (WiFi) 0.65 mi. W of MM 776.7	(904) 824-4347	200	16	200	8.5 / 8.5	F	GD	R	30 / 100	P
2. St. Augustine Municipal Marina (WiFi) ⊙onSpot MM 777.7	(904) 825-1026	280	16	100	20.0 / 15.0	F	GD		30 / 100	P
3. Marker 8 Hotel & Marina (WiFi) MM 777.7	(904) 829-9042	103	16	24	9.0 / 7.0	F			30 / 100	

(WiFi) Wireless Internet Access　⊙onSpot Dockside WiFi Facility
Visit www.waterwayguide.com for current rates, fuel prices, website addresses and other up-to-the-minute information.
(Information in the table is provided by the facilities.)

Scan here for more details:

Source: Aqua Map and NOAA data

near constant dredging and frequent repositioning of aids to navigation making passage of the ICW through St. Augustine complex. Study the chart before arrival but realize that even the most recent charts may not be up to date and you may have to adapt.

In addition, there are numerous marked channels, significant marine traffic (both recreational and commercial), strong currents and a strict schedule for the Bridge of Lions (SR A1A). All of these factors suggest you should slow down and navigate this area with extreme care.

The ICW channel south of the Francis and Mary Usina (SR A1A/Vilano) Bridge tracks deceptively close to the beach to the east approaching the St. Augustine Inlet. Honor all markers in place south of the bridge at the time of your arrival. A pair of markers define the ICW channel heading south from the bridge: flashing green daybeacon "57A" and red nun buoy "58." Once centered between this pair head for flashing green buoy "59" (an east-side ICW marker), which is just off the southern tip of

Vilano Beach. Depths are more reliable on the green side along Vilano Beach.

Take a minute to orient yourself here. Looking southwest towards the mainland you should see a tall white cross and then the fort Castillo de San Marcos (both charted) on the shore of St Augustine. Farther south is the ornate bascule Bridge of Lions (SR A1A). The St. Augustine Inlet opens to the east splitting Vilano Beach from Conch Island. The dead-ended Salt Run is straight ahead lying between Conch Island and Anastasia Island. At flashing green buoy "59" the ICW turns southwest towards the Castillo.

Leaving flashing green buoy "59" to port and flashing red buoy "60" to starboard the ICW channel turns sharply southwest into the Matanzas River. The first set of Matanzas River markers are flashing green "1" located just off the northwest tip of Conch Island and red nun buoy "2," which should be lined up with the Castillo. The ICW markers can get lost in the jumble of markers here. Use flashing red "2A" if red nun "2" is not visible.

Green daybeacon "5" starts a gentle turn around Davis Shores thumb-like point (Anastasia Island's northern tip). Upon reaching green daybeacon "7," Bridge of Lions should be due south. Observe the ICW markers around the turn keeping about 100 yards off Davis Shores. This is a high traffic area. Call one of the local towing services for advice if you are unable to sort out the numerous markers. Always remember that the ICW markers have either a yellow square or a yellow triangle.

Check your speed approaching Bridge of Lions at Mile 777.9. Vertical clearance is 18 feet at the center when closed and you will likely need to wait for an opening. This bridge, one of the most attractive on the ICW, was originally completed in 1927. The bridge has been rebuilt in recent years with the goal to improve the bridge's safety while preserving its historic value.

Normal flood currents of 1 knot and ebb currents of 1.5 knots may be expected under the Bridge of Lions so exercise caution when approaching the bridge. The bridge opens on signal except between 7:00 a.m. and 6:00 p.m., when the draw only opens on the hour and half-hour; however, the draw need not open at 8:00 a.m., 12:00 p.m. or 5:00 p.m., Monday through Friday (except federal holidays). On weekends and holidays it opens only on the hour and half-hour between 7:00 a.m. and 6:00 p.m. Be aware that the bridge sometimes closes for special events (e.g., Blessing of the Fleet, 4th of July celebrations and various 5K walk/run events). These closures are usually well publicized and reasonably short in duration.

Dockage: The number of berths available to transients in St. Augustine reflects its long-standing popularity as a port of call. Several elaborate marine complexes cater to cruising boats. Immediately north of the Vilano Bridge on the west side of the ICW is Camachee Cove Yacht Harbor, the center of the huge Camachee Island Marina Village complex. Bulkheads and jetties on both sides of Camachee Cove's entrance help prevent shoaling and protect the outside slips. The entrance channel provides adequate depths for cruising boats of all sizes and the enclosed basin offers excellent protection. Camachee Cove Yacht

Bridge of Lions

GOIN' ASHORE

ST. AUGUSTINE, FL

Founded in 1565 as a Spanish military outpost, the restored buildings and narrow streets (mostly pedestrian) of the 40-acre Spanish Quarter depict Spanish Colonial life in St. Augustine. St. George Street's 3-block pedestrian walkway is lined with shops, restaurants and bars (many featuring live entertainment) and a series of museums, including the oldest wooden schoolhouse in the U.S. (according to 1716 records). Superb examples of 19th-century Spanish Renaissance architecture can be seen throughout St. Augustine.

SERVICES

1. St. Augustine Post Office
99 King St. (800-275-8777)

2. Visitor Information Center
10 San Marco Ave. (904-825-1000)

ATTRACTIONS

3. Castillo de San Marcos
This remarkable feat of engineering was built in 1672 and is the oldest and largest masonry fort in the continental U.S. Call 904-829-6506 for hours and admission fee.

4. Flagler College/Old Ponce de Leon Hotel
Tours of the beautifully restored building at 74 King St. are scheduled at 10:00 a.m. and 2:00 p.m. (for a fee). The old hotel now serves as the Flagler College offices and main dormitory but it maintains the original Tiffany stained glass windows, fountains, mosaics and sculpture (904-829-6481).

5. Lightner Museum
Built by Henry Flagler in 1887, this museum of antiquities are housed within the historic Hotel Alcazar at 75 King St. (904-824-2874).

6. Villa Zorayda Museum
Displays an eclectic collection of artifacts from the near and far east in a circa 1883 building based on a Moorish palace in Spain (83 King St., 904-829-9887).

7. St. Augustine Pirate & Treasure Museum
Transports you back in time over 300 years to Port Royal, Jamaica, at the height of the Golden Age of Piracy at 12 S. Castillo Dr. Call ahead for hours and fees (877-467-5863).

MARINA

8. St. Augustine Municipal Marina
111-E Avenida Menendez (904-825-1026)

Harbor has six fueling stations and some fueling can be done from individual slips. The marina is surrounded by 20 businesses offering every imaginable service for boaters including Camachee Yacht Yard, where trained on-site technicians can handle most any repair. First Mate Yacht Services is also on site offering full-service maintenance and repairs.

South of St. Augustine Inlet on Salt Run is Conch House Marina. The marina has a tropical motif and offers full amenities. It is easy to get to from the inlet or the ICW. The popular [Conch House Restaurant is on site offering seafood and Caribbean fare (800-940-6256). Every Sunday at 3:00 p.m. (seasonal) is Reggae Sunday. It can get crowded.

Dockage is also available south of the Bridge of Lions and these facilities are convenient to the city's many restaurants and historic attractions. St. Augustine Municipal Marina on the west side close to the tourist district offers transient dockage and moorings, laundry facilities and pump-out service. Consider the direction of the current when docking here and time arrival for slack tide. Their slips are popular so call ahead to reserve. A city dock is just to the south for free dockage with no amenities.

Across the river on the east shore is Marker 8 Hotel & Marina with 24 transient slips. They also offer a complimentary breakfast and an afternoon social hour. They do not monitor the VHF radio so you will need to contact them by phone (904-829-9042).

The San Sebastian River, which branches off the Matanzas River at Mile 780, is a better spot for provisioning and has a number of marine businesses and associated docks. You should exercise caution when docking anywhere on this river as the current can be swift.

Cat's Paw Marina is located past red daybeacon "8" on the west shore of the San Sebastian River. This is a dry storage facility. (No transient slips.) St. Augustine Marine Center is located near green daybeacon "13." This is a full-service yard with a cat crawler capable of hauling catamarans with up to 35-foot beam. This 23-acre yard has long and short-term storage and welcomes DIY boaters. What they do not offer, however, is transient slips.

Continuing upriver is the family-owned and -operated Xynides Boat Yard and next door is Oasis Boatyard & Marina. These are strictly repair/service facilities and do not offer overnight dockage to transients. On the other side of the river is the St. Augustine Shipyard, another full-service yard with a dry storage facility. (No transient slips.)

English Landing Marina at green daybeacon "29" does not have reserved transient slips but will not turn you away if they have an empty slip. (Call ahead.) This facility is followed by Rivers Edge Marina at green daybeacon "33." This full-service marina has the usual cruiser amenities plus an on-site restaurant (Hurricane Patty's). It is a short walk from here to Sailor's Exchange (www.sailors-exchange.com) at 222 W. King St., which buys-sells-trades new and used boating equipment.

The Marine Supply & Oil Company is less than 2 miles away (on the opposite shore) with diesel. Call for delivery options.

Moorings: The City of St. Augustine-owned mooring field consists of approximately 175 moorings, which are managed by St. Augustine Municipal Marina. There are four different mooring fields: Salt Run Mooring Field has two fields (north and south with a total of 80 moorings), while the downtown area has two additional fields–St. Augustine South (Menendez) Mooring Field with 70 moorings and St. Augustine North (San Marcos) Mooring Field with 28 moorings. There is a dinghy dock at the municipal marina.

The Salt Run Mooring Field can be reached by following the private channel markers of Conch House Marina. Once past the marina you will see the mooring fields (north and south). Both mooring areas have access to a pump-out boat and dinghy dock; however, if you want to be close to the City of St. Augustine, Salt Run Mooring Field is a poor choice. It would be a very long dinghy ride and a very long walk just to get there. This area is used primarily for long-term mooring.

The St. Augustine South (Menendez) Mooring Field is south of the Bridge of Lions and the St. Augustine North (San Marcos) Mooring Field is north of the Bridge of Lions. Both moorings fields have access to a free pump-out boat that operates daily between the hours of 9:00 a.m. and 12:00 p.m., a dinghy dock, a launch service (no need to "launch" your dinghy) and use of all of the facilities at the municipal marina. The moorings can accommodate vessels to 120 feet.

Enter the St. Augustine South (Menendez) Mooring Field just west of red daybeacon "8" on the ICW. Do not enter the field between daybeacons "8" and

St. Augustine Inlet, St. Augustine, FL

SAN SEBASTIAN RIVER		Largest Vessel	VHF	Total Slips	Approach/ Dockside Depth	Floating Docks	Gas/ Diesel	Repairs/ Haulout	Min/Max Amps	Pump-Out Station
1. Cat's Paw Marina **WiFi** 5	(904) 829-8040	40	16		20.0 / 15.0	F	GD	R		
2. St. Augustine Marine Center **WiFi** 0.8 mi. NW of MM 780.0	(904) 824-4394	150	16	50	10.0 / 6.0	F		RH	30 / 100	P
3. Xynides Boat Yard	(904) 824-3446	55		20	16.0 / 10.0	F		RH		
4. Oasis Boatyard & Marina **WiFi** 1.2 mi. NW of MM 780	(904) 824-2520	65		45	16.0 / 16.0	F		RH	30 / 50	
5. St. Augustine Shipyard	(904) 342-5159	120		300	/ 10.0	F	GD	R		P
6. English Landing Marina **WiFi**	(904) 669-7363	55		44	20.0 / 15.0	F			30	
7. Rivers Edge Marina **WiFi** 1.7 mi. NW of MM 780.0	(904) 827-0520	150	16	100	12.0 / 10.0	F	GD	R	30 / 100	P
8. The Marine Supply & Oil Company 1.8 mi. NW of MM 780.0	(904) 829-2271	200			/ 12.0		D			

WiFi Wireless Internet Access **onSpot** Dockside WiFi Facility
Visit www.waterwayguide.com for current rates, fuel prices, website addresses and other up-to-the-minute information.
(Information in the table is provided by the facilities.)

Scan here for more details:

"10A" as it had shoaled and has less than 4 feet MLW. Shoaling to 3 feet MLW has also been observed near and below some of the moorings. Ask the marina when you call for a mooring and get advice on where to enter the mooring field. This can be a little lumpy during the day on a weekend as it is not in a designated "no wake/minimum wake" zone and traffic on the Matanzas River can get heavy.

Anchorage: Anchoring is permitted but not within 100 feet of the mooring field boundaries and not within 50 feet of any other marine structure (such as private docks along the waterway). Local knowledge suggest anchoring north of the Francis and Mary Usina (SR A1A/Vilano) Bridge. Permits for dinghy dockage at the municipal marina grants the permit holder access to the secured restrooms, showers, laundry and lounge. Pump-out at anchor is available for $5 and must be arranged before 9:00 a.m. on the day of requested service. Water tender service is not available to anchored vessels.

St. Augustine

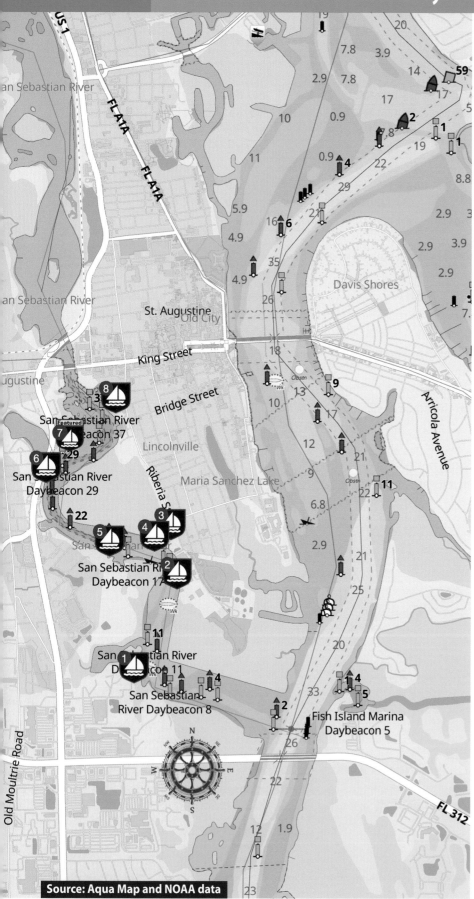

Source: Aqua Map and NOAA data

■ TO DAYTONA BEACH

Matanzas River to Palm Coast– ICW Mile 780 to Mile 803

Marshland alternates with forests along the banks of the Matanzas River as you pass through a part of the Guana-Tolomato-Matanzas National Estuarine Research Reserve south of Marineland Marina on the east side of the ICW. You will likely encounter kayak tour groups here during warmer weather. Give them a slow, no-wake pass out of courtesy. This cut seems eerie and almost desolate in places so it comes as a surprise when farther down several wide, rip-rapped channels appear on the west side. This is part of the community of Palm Coast, which is accessible via three canals.

NAVIGATION: Use NOAA Chart 11485. The Matanzas River channel is deep but narrow so follow markers carefully until the dredged cut takes over south of Matanzas Inlet (closed to navigation). Shoals are encroaching on the channel from both sides through this stretch so holding the magenta line is advised. Expect heavy small-craft traffic on this stretch, especially on weekends. Also watch for wake-wash in the narrow channel.

The river narrows south of St. Augustine at Mile 780.3 at the high-rise **SR 312 Bridges** and the current is swift here. This area is dredged regularly but shoals are constantly forming on the east side of the channel south of the bridge. Just upstream a large shoal that dries at low tide has formed between flashing red "18" and flashing red "24." To avoid this, split flashing red "16" and green daybeacon "17" while

Palm Coast, FL

PALM COAST AREA		Largest Vessel	VHF	Total Slips	Approach/ Dockside Depth	Floating Docks	Gas/ Diesel	Repairs/ Haulout	Min/Max Amps	Pump-Out Station
1. Marineland Marina **(WiFi)** MM 796.0	(904) 814-9886	100	16	41	6.5 / 6.0	F			30 / 100	P
2. Palm Coast Marina **(WiFi)** ⊜onSpot MM 803.0	(386) 446-6370	165	16	80	8.0 / 8.0		GD		30 / 50	P

(WiFi) Wireless Internet Access ⊜onSpot Dockside WiFi Facility
Visit www.waterwayguide.com for current rates, fuel prices, website addresses and other up-to-the-minute information.
(Information in the table is provided by the facilities.)

Scan here for more details:

rounding east; a shoal is extending into the channel from the east shore. Once past flashing red "16," switch over to favoring the green side around the curve until past flashing red "24."

Take a direct route between red daybeacon "28" and green daybeacon "31," passing within 100 feet of the red daybeacon. This route avoids a small shoal along the ICW channel between flashing green "29" and green daybeacon "31." Note that red daybeacon "30" may be obscured by boathouses. Ignore small craft that may cut the corner here.

The navigable channel narrows considerably at flashing red "50" at Mile 787. Stay close to the magenta line all the way south to the Matanzas Inlet (closed to navigation).

At Crescent Beach you will encounter the **Crescent Beach (SR 206) Bridge** (Mile 788.6) with 25-foot closed vertical clearance. The bridge opens on signal and the bridgetender is particularly helpful and accommodating. On both sides of the bridge for approximately 200 feet is an enforced No-Wake Zone. Traffic starts to increase again along this stretch due to numerous boat ramps along the east shore.

Just south of Mile 792 the waters from the Matanzas Inlet (closed to navigation) meet the ICW resulting in constant shoaling. This is one of the shallowest sections of the ICW in eastern Florida. To make matters worse the beach here is a popular swimming spot with locals and boat traffic is often quite busy. Slow down and exercise extreme caution between flashing green "81" and flashing red "82."

Buoys here are constantly being moved, added or removed. Follow the channel "as marked" during passage. The deepest water is surprisingly close to the beach around the outside of the curve on the west. The newly added bulkheads on the west bank seem to be improving depths. The channel holds a measured depth of 7 feet MLW. Honor the buoys. This area is always evolving and filling in. Check the Waterway Explorer (www.

waterwayguide.com) before transiting the area.

The current between the ICW crossing of Matanzas River (Mile 792) and Marineland Marina (Mile 796) can be strong enough to pull pot markers underwater but it decreases as you proceed toward Palm Coast. South from flashing red "82" there is shoaling on both sides of the narrow dredged channel so mind the depth sounder and keep to the center of the channel through this stretch.

There is some shoaling where the channel narrows from red daybeacon "92" to red daybeacon "104." Best to follow the channel center closely through Mile 800 where the cut to the Halifax River begins. The fixed, high-level **Hammock Dunes Bridge** is at Mile 803.0 just south of the entrance to Palm Coast Marina.

Dockage: If you are looking to stop for the night, Marineland Marina at Mile 796 can accommodate boats up to 100 feet in one of their 20 transient slips. After an extensive renovation the marina has a new restrooms, showers and laundry and offers pump-out service at each slip. They also accept catamarans on bulkhead tie-ups.

> Marineland Dolphin Adventure (www.marineland.net) is directly across the street with hands-on exhibits and educational programs with Atlantic bottlenose dolphins (for a fee). Call 407-563-4701 for details.

At Mile 803 a canal leads westward to the Palm Coast Marina. Once inside, favor the south side of the channel. The marina welcomes transients and is known for its friendly and attentive service. Within walking distance from the marina (approximately 0.5 mile) is European Village with numerous shops and dining.

Anchorage: An anchorage west of the ICW protected by a shoal can be found at Mile 781.2 on the Matanzas River. Enter from the north keeping flashing red "18" to the east. This anchorage offers deep water (at least 7 feet MLW). Tide can be up to 5 feet. There are several derelict and semi-submerged boats here so exercise caution.

South at Butler Beach at Mile 786.2 there is good holding in 6 to 7 feet MLW south of flashing green "43"

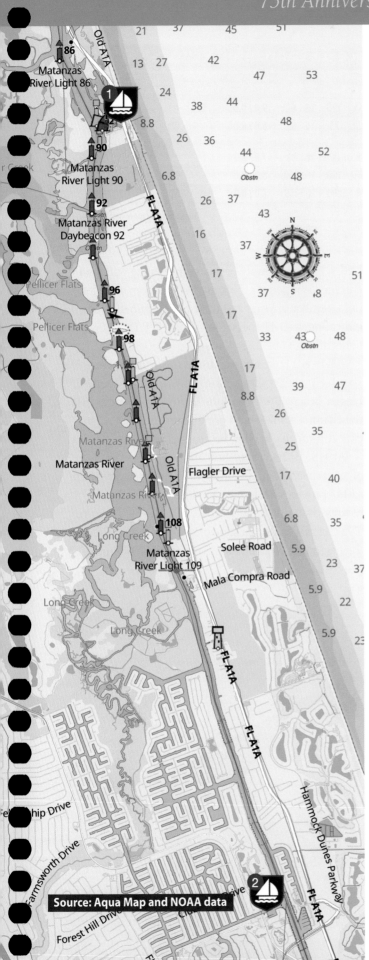

Source: Aqua Map and NOAA data

behind the spoil area. There are boat ramps nearby so this may get busy during the day.

At the north end of Rattlesnake Island (Mile 792) you will see the stark remains of Fort Matanzas, once a Spanish outpost and now a national monument. Like its larger cousin, Castillo de San Marcos in St. Augustine, this fort was built of coquina, a rock made of fused tiny shells. A small National Park Service ferry runs between Anastasia Island and Rattlesnake Island. Its terminal is just north of the Matanzas Inlet (closed to navigation). You can drop the hook in 8 to 10 feet MLW in front of Fort Matanzas by green can "81A." To enter the anchorage, turn between cans "80A" and "80B" and stay close to the north shore. Use extra caution at low tide. This is open to the north through southeast and you may experience strong currents.

Palm Coast to Daytona Beach–ICW Mile 804 to Mile 830

If you leave the Palm Coast area marinas on a slower boat (less than 10-knot speed) at the start of the ebb tide you can ride the current all the way south to Ponce De Leon (New Smyrna) Inlet. For several miles south of Palm Coast Marina condominiums with community docks and boat lifts, golf courses and private homes line both sides of the ICW.

As a point of interest, a narrow interconnecting canal intersects the east side of the ICW at Mile 804. This was part of the original ICW and gives an idea of the size of some earlier sections. A low clearance fixed bridge prevents passage through the older channel.

You will pass Tomoka State Park (www.floridastateparks.org/Tomoka) at Mile 819, which was once home to the Timucua Indians. Today you can walk beneath the same ancient oaks that shaded their villages nearly 400 years ago or explore the marshes and tidal creeks by dinghy.

NAVIGATION: Use NOAA Chart 11485. Stay in the center of the channel, especially south of the high-rise **SR 100 (Moody Blvd./Flagler Beach) Bridge** near the long series of docks on the west side. Be aware that the presence of residential docks is not an indication of deep water and should keep some distance off shore. If you see boats in the water at these docks, slow down out of courtesy and give them a "no-wake" pass. This area of the waterway is locally known as Smiths Creek.

Daytona Beach to Ponce de Leon Inlet, FL

DAYTONA BEACH		Largest Vessel	VHF	Total Slips	Approach/ Dockside Depth	Floating Docks	Gas/ Diesel	Repairs/ Haulout	Min/Max Amps	Pump-Out Station
1. Coquina Marina **WiFi** MM 829.4	(386) 317-0555	120	16	62	9.0 / 9.0	F			30 / 200+	
2. Loggerhead Marina - Daytona Beach Marina **WiFi** MM 829.6	(386) 523-3100	75	16	85	6.0 / 6.0		GD		30 / 100	P
3. Halifax River Yacht Club **WiFi** MM 830.7	(386) 255-7459	80	16	39	7.0 / 7.0	F			30 / 50	P
4. Halifax Harbor Marina **WiFi** MM 830.7	(386) 671-3601	100	16	550	8.0 / 8.0	F	GD		30 / 100	P
5. Daytona Marina & Boat Works **WiFi** **onSpot** MM 831.0	(386) 252-6421	200	16	159	8.0 / 8.0		GD	RH	30 / 100	P

WiFi Wireless Internet Access   **onSpot** Dockside WiFi Facility
Visit www.waterwayguide.com for current rates, fuel prices, website addresses and other up-to-the-minute information.
(Information in the table is provided by the facilities.)

Scan here for more details:

From Mile 805 exposed rocks line both sides of Fox Cut from green daybeacon "1" to green daybeacon "5." Red daybeacons "2" and "4" and flashing green "3" mark rocks that extend to the edge of the channel. A ramp, dock and launch facility have been dug out of the west side of the ICW opposite flashing green "3."

Stay to the center of the channel from Mile 805 to Mile 809 as rocks intermittently line the west side of the ICW close to shore.

The high-rise SR 100 (Moody Blvd./Flagler Beach) Bridge crosses the ICW at Mile 810.6. Watch for shoals near the bridge along the edges of the channel. A dock development on the east side of the ICW just north of the bridge has been empty of boats since being built and the entrance is roped off. This marina has been abandoned for a number of years and there are prominent signs indicating "NO TRESPASSING/PRIVATE DOCKS." (This means you!)

There is a busy ramp south of the bridge; pass at idle speed. For the 5 miles between the SR 100 (Moody Blvd, Flagler Beach) Bridge and the **Bulow (L.B. Knox) Bridge**, the channel is lined with pot markers on both sides; expect some markers in the channel itself.

At Mile 812.4 red daybeacon "20" marks the start of an eastward bend in Smith Creek and red daybeacon "20A" provides a reference to align cruisers in the narrow, dredged channel. At Mile 814 a small, marked side channel leads to a state park and a ramp. This is the beginning of a Manatee Zone with a 30-mph speed

Bulow (L.B. Knox) Bridge

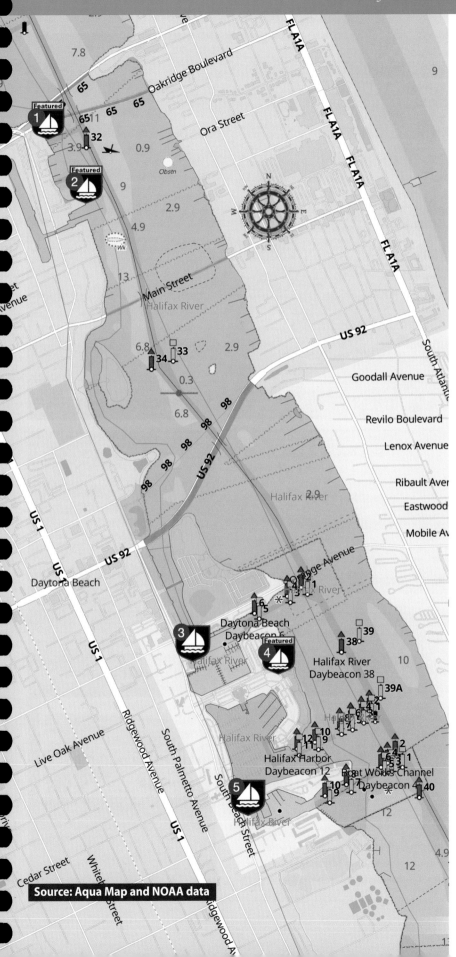

Source: Aqua Map and NOAA data

limit in the channel (25 mph at night) and slow speed required outside the ICW channel.

At Mile 816 expect congestion at the boat ramp next to the Bulow (L.B. Knox) Bridge. Vertical clearance is only 15 feet but the bridge opens on signal. South of the bridge shoals encroach the channel from both sides through to red daybeacon "30," particularly where small creeks enter the ICW. Mind your depth through this section and center yourself between the crab pots.

The ICW enters the headwaters of the Halifax River at Mile 816 and gradually widens on its run to Daytona Beach. The channel is straight and well marked and follows closely along the eastern bank as it passes a series of attractive homes. There is a negligible tidal range here.

For deeper-draft boats the 5-mile-long passage hugging the east shore of the Halifax River from the Tomoka Basin at ICW Mile 819 to the high-rise **SR 40 Bridge** (Ormond Beach Bridge) at Mile 824.9 calls for close attention. Stick to the middle on the marked channel along this stretch because both edges shoal quickly and it is very shallow outside. Markers are well spaced along this stretch but it can be difficult to maintain the channel close to the edge of what sometimes appears to be a wide basin particularly in strong crosswinds. Check behind occasionally to check your alignment. Depths are generally 8 feet MLW at mid-channel in this area. Just north of the Ormond Beach Bridge the channel gradually angles toward the middle of the river.

The open water of the Halifax River here is a popular windsurfing area. On a blustery day expect to see several windsurfers crisscrossing the channel.

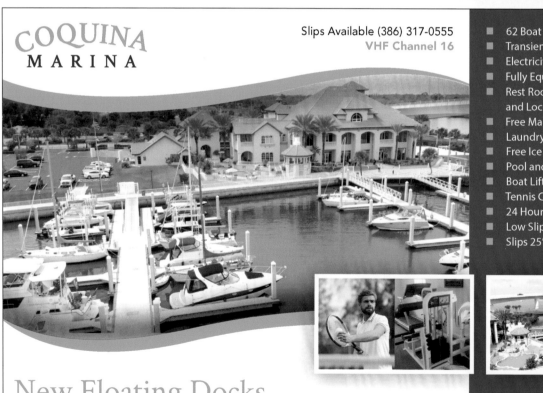

The SR 40 Bridge at Mile 824.9 has 65-foot fixed vertical clearance. There is a dangerous shoal on the east side opposite red daybeacon "20" just south of the bridge at Mile 825.6. Favor the west (red) side of the channel between green daybeacons "19" and "21." Heading south to Daytona Beach the ICW follows a narrow, dredged channel that runs roughly down the center of the Halifax River. Markers are spaced approximately 0.50 miles apart; take care to observe them carefully as depths shallow quickly at the channel edges.

Dockage: There are 14 complimentary floating slips and a restroom at Cassen Park City Docks at the foot of the SR 40 Bridge but no other amenities. Note that two busy boat launches are nearby so stay alert.

Note that the old Cement Plant basin at Mile 809 is no longer a viable anchorage due to new construction.

Daytona Beach–ICW Mile 830

The official tourist season for this northern Florida "summer resort" runs from Memorial Day to Labor Day but Daytona Beach is a popular destination year round. In spring and fall boats on the north–south run stop here and skippers often come to have work done at one of the area's excellent repair yards. See more at "Goin' Ashore: Daytona Beach, FL" in this chapter.

NAVIGATION: Use NOAA Chart 11485. It's a straight 5-mile shot from Ormond Beach to the series of closely packed bridges that welcome you to Daytona Beach. The ICW channel opens up slightly as you reach these bridges:

- **Seabreeze Bridges** (65-foot fixed vertical clearance)
- **Main Street Bridge** (22-foot closed vertical clearance). Opens on signal. (Also known as **Daytona Beach Bridge**.)
- **International Speedway Blvd. Bridge** (65-foot fixed vertical clearance)
- **Memorial Bridge** (65-foot vertical clearance)

Take care to follow the "hockey stick" alignment of the ICW channel between the Main Street Bridge and International Speedway Boulevard Bridge to avoid the dangerous shoal areas noted on the charts. If you take a direct line between bridge openings you will run aground!

Dockage: Marinas and boatyards line the shore on the west side of the ICW from north of the city all the way to Ponce De Leon (New Smyrna) Inlet. Just south of the Seabreeze Bridges at Mile 829 is the 62-slip Coquina Marina, which offers transient dockage for vessels to 120 feet and many amenities such as a fitness facility, a large pool and a tennis court. Groceries are available within 1 mile.

Just to the south, Loggerhead Marina–Daytona Beach Marina offers transient dockage with resort-like amenities. The on-site Caribbean Jack's (386-523-3000) is open daily. (We recommend snagging a swinging glider table on the waterfront deck.) First-rate Halifax River Yacht Club will rent slips to transients and has a nice restaurant. It is located at Mile 830.7 in a basin just south of Memorial Bridge.

The municipal Halifax Harbor Marina is in a separate enclosed basin just to the south. Enter the marina through the marked entrance channel just west of ICW green daybeacon "39A." The marina has 550 slips on a 60-acre property with excellent amenities, a free pump-out

GOIN' ASHORE

DAYTONA BEACH, FL

Daytona's Riverfront Park is bordered by shops and eateries on one side and the Halifax River on the other. The park's 0.5-mile walkway starts just north of the city's main yacht basins and is a great place for water-weary boaters to stretch their legs. A moving stop in the park is the gravesite of Brownie the Town Dog who was "owned by no one but loved by all." Should you need more exercise, 23 miles of white sand beaches are nearby.

SERVICES

1. Daytona Beach Area Convention & Visitor Bureau
126 Orange Ave. (386-255-0981)

2. Daytona Beach Post Office
220 N. Beach St. (386-258-9352)

3. Daytona Beach Regional Library (City Island)
105 E. Magnolia Ave. (386-257-6036)

4. Rawls Veterinary Hospital
127 Mason Ave. (386-253-2525)

ATTRACTIONS

5. Halifax Historical Museum
Experience Daytona Beach from a historical perspective at 252 S. Beach St. (386-255-6976).

6. Jackie Robinson Memorial Baseball Park
Fans can take in some minor league baseball at this historic ballpark (105 E. Orange Ave., 386-257-3172).

MARINAS

7. Coquina Marina
841 Ballough Rd. (386-317-0555)

8. Halifax River Yacht Club
331 S. Beach St. (386-255-7459)

9. Halifax Harbor Marina
450 Basin St. (386-671-3601)

10. Loggerhead (Daytona Beach) Marina
721 Ballough Rd. (386-523-3100)

service and a well-stocked marine store. The marina is convenient to downtown Daytona and the city bus stop is an easy walk away.

In that same channel is the well-regarded Daytona Marina & Boat Works, open 24/7 for fuel (both gas and diesel) and offering dockage and repairs. The gold dome you see is the on-site Chart House Restaurant (386-255-9022).

Anchorage: There are anchorages both above and below the Seabreeze Bridges. The anchorage south of the bridges is deeper but there is scattered debris on the bottom.

The Seabreeze anchorage north of the Seabreeze Bridges shallows up quickly and is in an area with submerged cables. Signs on each shore mark the location of the cables but the signs are difficult to pick out from the water. The sign on the western shore is just south of the twin condos. This entire anchorage area seems to be

generally shoaling but it is still handy when you arrive late in the day from St. Augustine.

There is a cozy anchorage east of the ICW in the vicinity of the charted 11-foot depths at Mile 830.7. To reach this anchorage, turn east off the ICW immediately south of Memorial Bridge. Using the yacht club's green daybeacons "3" and "5" as a back range, proceed east to within 100 to 150 feet of shore. If you stay on the range you should find at least 6 feet of water over the bar. At this point, turn south along the shore to find a slot of water 9 to 13 feet deep about 100 feet from shore. The shoal between the ICW and the anchorage is less than 3 feet MLW.

The Bethune Park anchorage at Mile 831 has lots of room and near-shore access for dog relief at a sandy beach. You must approach the anchorage from red daybeacon "44" to the south for at least 7 feet MLW. (Do not try to approach from red daybeacon "40.")

Daytona Beach to Ponce de Leon Inlet, FL

PORT ORANGE		Largest Vessel	VHF	Total Slips	Approach/ Dockside Depth	Floating Docks	Gas/ Diesel	Repairs/ Haulout	Min/Max Amps	Pump-Out Station
1. Seven Seas Marina & Boatyard MM 835.2	(386) 761-3221	44	16	30	6.0 / 9.0		GD	RH	30 / 50	
2. Windward Adventure Yacht Harbor **WiFi** MM 836.8	(386) 756-2180	65	16	137	4.5 / 7.0		GD		30 / 50	P
PONCE DE LEON INLET AREA										
3. Loggerhead Marina - Inlet Harbor Marina **WiFi** 0.8 mi. SE of MM 839.5	(386) 767-3266	180	6	84	9.0 / 15.0	F	GD		30 / 100	P
4. Sea Love Boat Works Inc. **WiFi** 1.3 mi. SE of MM 839.5	(386) 761-5434	90	16	10	12.0 / 12.0	F	GD	RH	30 / 100	

WiFi Wireless Internet Access **onSpot** Dockside WiFi Facility
Visit www.waterwayguide.com for current rates, fuel prices, website addresses and other up-to-the-minute information.
(Information in the table is provided by the facilities.)

Scan here for more details:

TO NEW SMYRNA BEACH

Daytona Beach to Ponce De Leon Cut– ICW Mile 831 to Mile 840

NAVIGATION: Use NOAA Chart 11485. South of Daytona Beach the ICW channel briefly opens up but narrows again at Mile 833.5 (near red daybeacon "50") and numerous shoals flank the channel to Mile 838.5. Channel markers are closely spaced through this section and must be closely observed.

The **A1A Port Orange Relief Bridge** is charted with a 65-foot fixed vertical clearance but tide boards at a full-moon high tide sometimes show a center span clearance of 63 feet. The channel under the bridge is constrained by a causeway and some small islands causing swift currents here. Avoid the shoals outside the narrow channel and watch for heavy boat traffic, especially on weekends. Watch your wake.

Just below the A1A Port Orange Relief Bridge, a small mangrove island on the west side of the ICW channel is a nesting ground for pelicans, egrets and cormorants during the spring. Confine your activity to watching only and do not disturb the nests.

A shoal extending from the east side at Mile 837 has entered the channel between green daybeacons "61" and "63." Take a wide line around the corner here. There is another shoal in the channel on the west side between red daybeacons "68" and "70" in the vicinity of Tenmile Creek, which drains a large marsh to the west. There is shoaling by red nun "68A" so pass green daybeacon "69" by 100 feet off at Mile 838.5. Note that flashing green "71," which appears on older charts, was removed to make room for a boat house.

The entrance channel for the private Harbour Village Marina between green daybeacon "71" and red daybeacon "72" is marked with a rather large red nun buoy and green can buoy on the east side of the ICW south of Daggett island. Do not confuse these for the floating ICW markers marking the beginning of the Ponce de Leon Cut just to the south of flashing green "1."

Dockage: Seven Seas Marina & Boatyard is located above the A1A Port Orange Relief Bridge on the east side at Mile 835.2. They have transient slips and a DIY boatyard. Pat's Riverfront Café (386-756-8070) is on the premises with breakfast all day (plus other options).

A short distance below the A1A Port Orange Relief Bridge on the east side of the ICW south of flashing green "59" is Windward Adventure Yacht Harbor with slips. They mostly cater to sportfishing boats but are close to amenities and provisioning supplies. Look for the marked entry channel. Note that there is a tidal range here of 2.5 feet and the channel can be as low as 5 feet MLW. Call ahead for more exact depths.

Ponce de Leon Cut–ICW Mile 840 to Mile 843

At about Mile 840, the ICW leaves the Halifax River and enters the Ponce de Leon Cut, bypassing the Ponce De Leon (New Smyrna) Inlet. The main ICW channel passes 2 miles west of the inlet through the Ponce de Leon Cut. The cut is protected from ocean surge but subject to extreme shoaling, especially at its north and south ends. The Ponce de Leon Cut ends at Mile 843.5 where it meets the Indian River North.

NAVIGATION: Use NOAA Chart 11485. This is a traditional shoaling

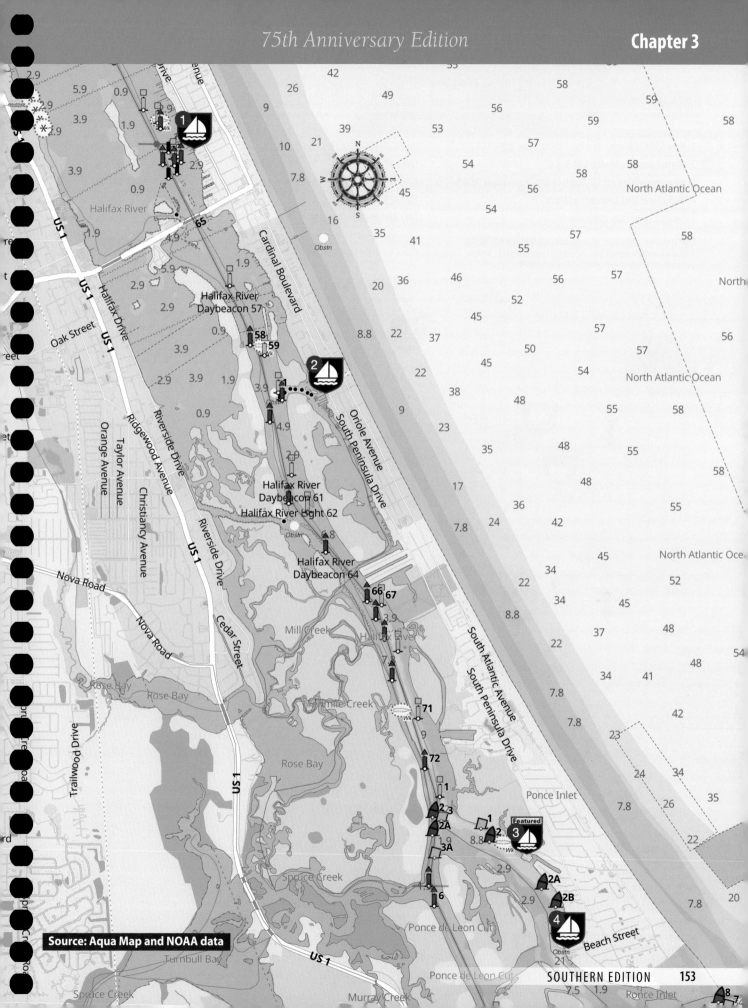

Source: Aqua Map and NOAA data

New Smyrna Beach, FL

NEW SMYRNA BEACH AREA		Largest Vessel	VHF	Total Slips	Approach/ Dockside Depth	Floating Docks	Gas/ Diesel	Repairs/ Haulout	Min/Max Amps	Pump-Out Station
1. New Smyrna Marina dba The Fishing Store **WiFi** MM 846.0	(386) 427-4514	125	16	31	12.0 / 10.0	F	GD		30 / 100	
2. North Causeway Marine MM 846.0	(386) 427-5267	60	16	35	8.0 / 10.0		G	RH	30 / 50	
3. New Smyrna Beach City Marina WiFi ● onSpot MM 846.5	**(386) 409-2042**	**65**	**16**	**43**	**8.0 / 10.0**	**F**			**30 / 100**	**P**
4. Night Swan Bed & Breakfast MM 847.0	(386) 423-4940	40		6	12.0 / 9.0	F			30 / 50	
5. Smyrna Yacht Club **WiFi** MM 847.0	(386) 427-4040	65	16	77	/ 4.0	F			30 / 50	P

WiFi Wireless Internet Access   **● onSpot** Dockside WiFi Facility
Visit www.waterwayguide.com for current rates, fuel prices, website addresses and other up-to-the-minute information.
(Information in the table is provided by the facilities.)

Scan here for more details:

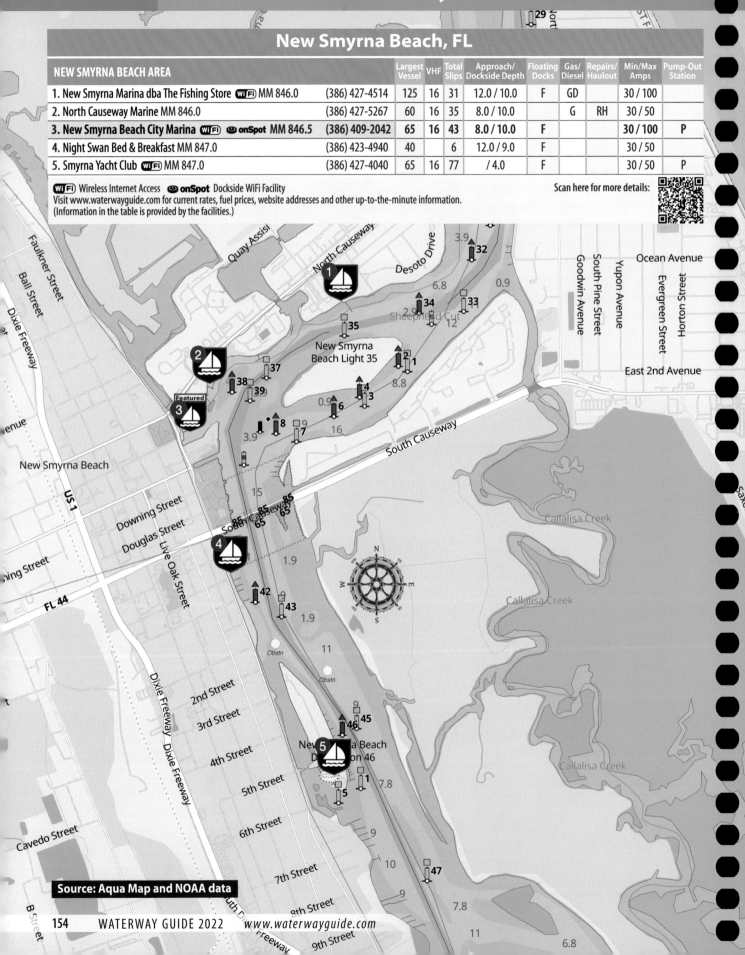

Source: Aqua Map and NOAA data

New Smyrna Beach

area that is frequently dredged. Flashing green "1" is permanent but red nuns "2" and "2A" and green cans "3" and "3A" are temporary and moved on a regular basis. Pass red "2" and red "2A" by 50 feet for 10 feet MLW. The depth and alignment of all the channels in this area change constantly and even the most recent charts are often outdated so up-to-date soundings are essential.

Shoaling has been reported between red daybeacon "16" and the green-over-red buoy "C," which marks the junction of the Ponce de Leon Cut and the Ponce De Leon (New Smyrna) Inlet channels. Do not hug either flashing green "17" or red nun "18A," just go down the middle. Make sure you are well past this marker pair before making a turn either north or south. Note: this area is an active shoaling area and may be shallower than the chart.

When heading northbound on the ICW from New Smyrna, watch carefully for the turn into the Ponce de Leon Cut at Mile 843.5. The cut's opening is marked by a green-over-red buoy "C" to the north and red nun "18A" to the south. These markers are less obvious than the larger set marking the Ponce De Leon (New Smyrna) Inlet and can be missed.

Anchorage: Note that all the side creeks in this area have approximately 7 to 9 feet MLW but are not included in the periodic dredging because they are not authorized federal channels. Rockhouse Creek at Mile 842.2 is a popular weekend anchorage and a congested small boat passage. Enter along the centerline of the cut from the ICW as shoals are building from both the north and south shores. Once inside 8- to 10-foot MLW depths are easy to find and holding is good. Provisioning opportunities are nearby.

Ponce de Leon Light

Side Trip: Ponce de Leon (New Smyrna) Inlet

The historic Ponce de Leon Lighthouse located north of the Ponce De Leon (New Smyrna) Inlet is open to the public (daily except Thanksgiving and Christmas) and provides a stunning panoramic view of the area.

Note that it is safer to access the Ponce De Leon (New Smyrna) Inlet from the south, which is used extensively by locals and sportfishing boats and is a convenient point to enter or leave the ICW between Daytona and Cape Canaveral. This is a fair weather inlet only. The next opportunity going south to leave the ICW and go offshore is the Canaveral Barge Canal at Mile 894 then east to Port Canaveral Inlet.

NAVIGATION: Use NOAA Chart 11485. The north approach channel to Ponce De Leon (New Smyrna) Inlet branches eastward from flashing green "1." To access the marine facilities on the east bank of the north approach channel to the Ponce de Leon Inlet enter the channel from the ICW at the north end of the Ponce de Leon Cut at Mile 839.6 near green can buoy "3."

Initially the Halifax River channel is well marked with good water on the eastern shore but it shallows radically before the inlet, and south of red nun buoy "4"

the channel is unmarked. The deeper water is close to the beach on the west side. Skippers of deeper draft boats should avoid this route unless they have local knowledge.

When approaching the Ponce De Leon (New Smyrna) Inlet from the ocean, aids to navigation may not match what is charted but the channel should be well marked. The inlet is considered a fair weather route; shoaling is continuous and dredging is frequent here. The shoaling is particularly bad extending from the beach along the inlet's south shore. Deeper water is generally found closer the inlet's north jetty, which unfortunately has suffered hurricane damage.

> ⚠️
>
> The Ponce de Leon North Jetty Light is missing its foundation and the outer 100 feet of the north jetty was destroyed by Hurricane Matthew. Long-planned repairs by the U.S. Army Corps of Engineers are expected to take well into 2022. The area surrounding the remains of the shifted structure and the ongoing construction will be a hazard to navigation. Mariners are advised to use extreme caution while transiting the area. Stay to the center of the channel (or closer to the green side).

A US Coast Guard station is located on the south channel of the Ponce De Leon (New Smyrna) Inlet and will respond to calls for inlet conditions and the local TowBoat U.S. is up to date on local conditions. Both can be hailed on VHF Channel 16.

Dockage: The first facility on the Halifax River approaching Ponce De Leon (New Smyrna) Inlet is Loggerhead Marina–Inlet Harbor Marina, which offers transient dockage and has dry storage facilities. The on-site restaurant, Off the Hook, offers good food, live music and brilliant sunsets (386-202-4490). Opposite red nun buoy "4" to the south is Sea Love Boat Works Inc. They offer transient berths and full repair services.

Anchorage: Anchorage space may be available along the shores of the North Approach Channel. This is a restricted manatee zone. Nevertheless, you may experience wakes and expect some strong currents. Piddler Island north of Sea Love Boat Works Inc. has depths to 9 feet MLW and good holding in sand. There are several restaurants where you can dock or dinghy up to. This is a protected and quiet location.

Ponce de Leon Inlet to New Smyrna Beach– ICW Mile 843 to Mile 847

New Smyrna Beach is known for its beaches including nearby Canaveral National Seashore and Smyrna Dunes Park, which has incredible views of the inlet and its lighthouse. For details on the attractions and shopping along the downtown's palm-lined Canal Street Historic District, see "Goin' Ashore: New Smyrna Beach, FL" in this chapter.

NAVIGATION: Use NOAA Chart 11485. The South Channel from Ponce De Leon (New Smyrna) Inlet is well marked with floating markers and the channel is always active with mostly recreational boat traffic. The inlet markers are repositioned occasionally and it is best to use up-to-date charts.

The **George E. Musson/Coronado Beach (SR 44) Bridge** at Mile 845.0 has 24-foot closed vertical clearance and its hydraulic mechanism is relatively slow in opening; expect a swift-moving current that can complicate the approach to the bridge. The bridge opens on signal except from 7:00 a.m. to 7:00 p.m. daily, when the draw opens only on the hour and half-hour.

South of the George E. Musson Bridge, continue to favor the eastern shore until the channel begins to swing west at flashing red "30." The area around red daybeacon "34" (Mile 845.5) always seems to be shoaling even when recently dredged. It is much easier and less stressful to just use the Sheephead Cut for 11.9 MLLW and bypass the shoaling.

Sheephead Cut runs south of Chicken Island and is a more direct, well-marked channel. It's entrance is indicated by a green-over-red daybeacon at the island's eastern tip. The channel carries 9 to 12-foot MLW depths and re-joins the ICW at another green-over-red daybeacon at the western end of Chicken Island. Stay centered in the marked channel to avoid shoals and watch for anchor lines as the cut is a popular anchorage.

If following the ICW channel north of Chicken Island, split red daybeacon "34" and the green-over-red daybeacon off the island's east tip to maintain 8 feet MLW. The ICW channel initially parallels the island's north shore. Approaching flashing green "35," depths tend to increase towards the docks along the north edge of the channel, away from Chicken Island. Do not cut the corner turning around green daybeacons "37" and "39" and a white "Danger" daybeacon to avoid a shoal.

New Smyrna Beach's harbor comes up suddenly beyond flashing red "38," which marks the turn toward the high-rise **Harris Saxon (South Causeway) Bridge** at Mile 846.6. Note that south of the Harris Saxon Bridge the ICW channel only has 10-foot MLW depths just off the Smyrna Yacht Club close to flashing green "45." As a courtesy, slow down and give the Yacht Club a "no-wake" pass.

The City of New Smyrna's attractive Riverside Park runs north of the bridge along the west bank of the Indian River North. The park has a boardwalk, fishing pier and three small docking areas. Overnight docking is not allowed at the park docks but you may tie up for up to 10 hours if an event is not being held at the nearby community center. The park bulkhead takes up the entire area between the condominiums at the nearby marina and the bridge. This can be a great stop for provisions.

Dockage: Located just 2.5 miles from Ponce De Leon Inlet, New Smyrna Marina dba The Fishing Store offers transient dockage on floating docks. A fleet of offshore and inshore fishing charters and daily pontoon boat rentals are based here. The on-site Outriggers Tiki Bar & Grille (386-428-6888) offers lunch, dinner and Sunday brunch. North Causeway Marine to the south has limited space (two slips) reserved for transients and offers repairs.

GOIN' ASHORE

NEW SMYRNA BEACH, FL

The downtown area of New Smyrna Beach begins only 1 block away from the municipal marina where a variety of restaurants and shops line the streets for local shoppers and visitors. The fort-like coquina ruins in Old Fort Park lead some historians to believe New Smyrna was originally the site of St. Augustine and that it could be even 500 years older. Across the Musson Bridge and 2 miles to the east is an extraordinarily wide, sandy ocean beach.

SERVICES

1. **AdventHealth New Smyrna Beach**
   401 Palmetto St. (386-424-5000)

2. **New Smyrna Beach Regional Library**
   1001 S. Dixie Fwy. (386-424-2910)

ATTRACTIONS

3. **Marine Discovery Center**
   This nonprofit educational center focuses on the Indian River Lagoon and coastal waters through live aquariums, interactive exhibits and a gift shop at 520 Barracuda Blvd. (386-428-4828).

4. New Smyrna Museum of History
Interpretive exhibits of local culture and history, including Native American artifacts, railroad memorabilia and Civil War displays (120 Sams Ave., 386-478-0052).

5. Old Fort Park
Home of the historic Turnbull Ruins and site of summer concerts and the annual Art Fiesta in February (115 Julia St., 386-424-2175).

SHOPPING

6. Little Drug Company
Full-service pharmacy with old-timey malts and burgers at 412 Canal St. (386-428-9041).

7. New Smyrna Outfitters
Brand name clothing is sold alongside fishing tackle and gear at 223A Canal St. (386-402-8853).

8. Save-A-Lot
Discount supermarket chain with some organic products and great produce at 720 S. Dixie Fwy. (386-847-8815).

MARINAS

9. New Smyrna Marina
200 Boatyard St. (386-427-4514)

10. New Smyrna Beach City Marina
201 N. Riverside Dr. (386-409-2042)

11. Night Swan Bed & Breakfast
512 S. Riverside Dr. (386-423-4940)

12. North Causeway Marina
4 N. Causeway (386-427-5267)

13. River Deck Marina
111 N. Riverside Dr. (386-428-7827)

14. Smyrna Yacht Club
1201 S. Riverside Dr. (386-427-4040)

New Smyrna Beach City Marina at Mile 846.5 offers slips on a first-come, first-served basis with a full suite of amenities. This is a well-run establishment that goes out of their way to accommodate visitors. Call ahead to reserve a slip. It is close to the Canal Street Historic District, where you can find arts, history, shopping and dining. It is also across the street from the Old Fort Park historical site, which hosts a weekly Farmers' Market every Saturday.

Want to get off the boat? Night Swan Bed & Breakfast just south of the Harris Saxon (South Causeway) Bridge offers dockage if you stay with them. Further south on an island west of the ICW, the Smyrna Yacht Club welcomes members of clubs that are listed in the American Registry of Yacht Clubs. (They do not offer reciprocity to Florida Council of Yacht Club members).

> New Smyrna Beach's FLEX is a "call first" curb-to-curb, flexible transportation service that can ferry cruisers from the downtown district to the beach or larger grocery stores further inland for a nominal fee. To use this service call 386-424-6810 at least 2 hours before you wish to travel.

Anchorage: The free dock in New Smyrna Beach no longer allows overnight stays. There is a 5-hour limit and it is enforced. There is room for two 40-foot boats and easy access to downtown should you need to go ashore.

There is space in Sheephead Cut for three or four boats to anchor on the south side of the channel between green daybeacon "1" and just beyond green daybeacon "3" (between the markers and the condominium docks on Bouchelle Island). Show an anchor light and make sure that you will not swing into the channel or the docks at the tidal change; this is a very small, tight anchorage. The depths are 8 to 10 feet MLW and the holding is good but local boats use the channel at all hours.

It is possible to anchor south of the Harris Saxon Bridge at Mile 846.5 in 12 feet MLW with good holding in mud. (Best water is found about 500 feet north of green daybeacon "45.") This anchorage provides easy access to the Riverside Park dinghy dock and the town; however, it is exposed to the south and passing boat wakes. There is a lot of debris on the bottom so a trip line on your anchor is recommended in case of snags.

■ NEXT STOP

South of New Smyrna Beach the ICW joins the Indian River North, which leads to the Space Coast. This is a delightful stop worthy of a few days off the boat.

ICW Mile 848-Mile 953

■ TO MELBOURNE

In what has come to be known as the Space Coast Area the coastal topography changes from a slender barrier strip to a broad stretch of land forming Cape Canaveral. Inside the Cape area, the waters divide around Merritt Island separating Indian River on the mainland side from Banana River to the east.

Indian River: Cruising Conditions

The Indian River starts at the Haulover Canal as a wide and shallow basin and the ICW follows a narrow dredged channel. Boaters in this basin are vulnerable to chop in any strong wind conditions. Note also that the nearest ocean inlets are some distance in either direction and rainfall or wind conditions can affect water levels by as much as 2 feet here.

Boaters headed south should take note as elevated water levels will reduce bridge clearances from their charted minimums. While most of the bridges that cross the Indian River are fixed, high-rise bridges with a charted 65-foot clearance elevated water levels can still be an important factor if your air-draft is near the limit.

South of Titusville the shorelines close in and the river deepens creating a wider navigable channel. This section of the Indian River is a pleasure to navigate, although strong winds can still kick up an uncomfortable chop in either north or south winds. Sailors often unfurl their sails along here if winds allow.

Currents are typically modest in the upper stretches of the river and strengthen as you head south but consider that elevated water levels can affect currents as well.

Wider channels also provide extra maneuvering space should you have to wait for a bridge opening. Extra space also allows you to drop anchor either to wait for an opening or overnight in the deeper waters outside the marked channel. Anchoring is preferable to navigating into a strange harbor at night.

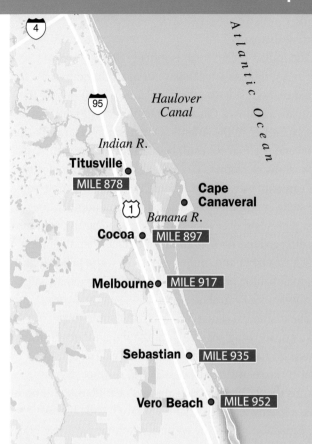

No Wake Zones, Idle Speed Zones and various Speed Limit restrictions are in effect throughout the waterways included in this chapter. Exercise diligence in knowing the regulations by observing signs and other markers. Enforcement is always present. As always, be courteous to other vessels and avoid manatees and other marine life.

Indian River North to Haulover Canal–ICW Mile 848 to Mile 869

Heading south from New Smyrna the waterway follows the Indian River North and traverses Mosquito Lagoon to the Haulover Canal. For the most part this is a beautiful journey through the wild Canaveral National Seashore, which is managed by the National Park Service. Note that access to and use of some areas within the park are restricted.

The river is rich in seafood so watch for crab pots and fish traps along this route as commercial fishermen work the area north of the park boundary at Mile 961. Numerous fishing camps also dot the shores north of the park.

The Indian River North is initially flanked to the east by a jumble of small islets but in truth the river is bound on both sides by the mainland. Were it not for the manmade Haulover Canal the narrow strip of land that forms a barrier to the Atlantic Ocean to the east (and Cape Canaveral itself) would still be a natural peninsula.

Mosquito Lagoon is an open, shallow expanse of water that can only be explored by dinghy or shallow-draft boat. The same conditions that make this water popular for mosquitoes and deer flies also create an ideal feeding and breeding ground for sport and commercial fish including redfish, sea trout and mullet. Flocks of white pelicans and the small fishing boats that fill Mosquito Lagoon attest to the abundance of fresh seafood.

The manmade Haulover Canal is a 1-mile-long rocky cut allowing passage from the Indian River North (Mosquito Lagoon) into the Indian River. Though the canal connects the headwaters of two distinct river systems the ICW's approach appears near identical at both ends–a narrow dredged channel through wide basins. The canal also marks the western extent of the Canaveral National Seashore. Look for increased activity by both commercial and recreational fishermen to the south.

NAVIGATION: Use NOAA Chart 11485. For about the next 10 miles the ICW runs down a straight, dredged channel between the mainland and a group of small islets. Staying in the center of the channel you will see 11- to 14-foot MLW depths and markers are closely placed. It shoals very quickly on the edges of the channel so extra care is required especially in a strong crosswind.

Markers are closely spaced in Mosquito Lagoon and boaters can see spots with 8-foot MLW depths in the marked channel but expect depths to decrease suddenly outside the marked channel, particularly to the west. Uncharted spoil banks flank the dredged Mosquito Lagoon channel and deeper draft boats should monitor the depth. Favor the green side but don't hug the markers too closely as the channel shallows near the edges. Shoals have been reported between green daybeacons "25" and "29." There is also shoaling through the gentle turn between green daybeacon "35" and flashing green "41." Give green daybeacon "37" a wide berth.

The sharp approach corner at Mile 869.2 should be taken wide. If you attempt to hug the red markers on the inside of the curve you will find shallow water. Follow the magenta line and give the red markers considerable berth.

Maintaining channel alignment can be difficult, especially in a strong crosswind. Strong winds can also cause an uncomfortable chop on the lagoon. Several fishing camps and the usual Florida waterfront housing run along on the west side above the park boundary at green daybeacon "19" (Mile 961). Keep an eye out for kayaks and small fishing boats here. They frequently anchor in the channel or too close to the edge. Reduce your wake as you pass.

As you reach the middle of Mosquito Lagoon you may be able to see a large building in the distance to the south. This is NASA's Vehicle Assembly Building (VAB) at Kennedy Space Center. In clear weather the giant VAB is visible for distances of 20 miles or more. In the past, the southern end of Mosquito Lagoon (from Haulover Canal east to 3 miles out in the Atlantic Ocean, excluding the ICW) was off limits to all watercraft 72 hours before any launches. Pay attention and ask local marinas for updates.

Passing through the Haulover Canal the ICW enters the upper stretch of the Indian River and exits the Canaveral National Seashore. Watch for an increase in both recreational and commercial fishermen here. Initially the route traverses a broad, shallow basin before the river narrows and the Indian River becomes better defined.

Beyond the marked channel edges the basin is extremely shallow with visible and submerged spoil islands. Deeper draft boats should carefully maintain channel alignment and proceed through this section with caution.

The **Allenhurst (Haulover Canal) Bridge** (27-foot closed vertical clearance) crosses the canal at Mile 869.2 and opens promptly on signal. If the bridgetender does not respond on VHF Channel 09 use a horn signal (one long, one short) to request an opening or call 321-867-4859.

The ramp in the small basin off the middle of the canal southeast of the Haulover Canal Bridge is always busy (particularly on weekends) and the Haulover Canal is often congested with small boats of every type and description. These small boats may have as many as three people standing up to cast at the edge of the channel or under the bridge.

This is one of the best spots to observe manatees on the ICW. Wildlife also abounds on shore, which is overgrown with vegetation. Heed the slow speed signs and keep a lookout for herons, alligators, stingrays and manatees.

Haulover Canal Bridge

Anchorage: If you are transiting the Mosquito Lagoon, there are few good anchorages off the ICW in good water between Haulover Canal and New Smyrna. Mosquito Lagoon does offer some deeper sections but wind protection is minimal. Be sure to exit the channel at minimum speed so that release from a possible grounding will be easier. Expect a mud bottom and beware that snags are possible so use of a trip line is advised.

The area east of green daybeacon "19" at Mile 861.3 at Mosquito Lagoon has 6- to 7-foot MLW depths. Enter south of the maker. This has good holding in sand but can be bumpy if the winds are up from almost any direction due to the long fetch. There is good fishing on the bar to the northeast. With a dinghy you can explore many of the islands in the lagoon from here.

A small area just outside the channel southeast of red daybeacon "24" (Mile 862.8) has charted 10-foot MLW depths. Exit the channel at the marker. There is deeper water to the south. As with other anchorages in Mosquito Lagoon, chop forms quickly in all but west winds due to the fetch between the ICW and land.

Upper Indian River—ICW Mile 869 to Mile 878

After exiting the Haulover Canal the ICW enters the upper stretch of the Indian River and exits the Canaveral National Seashore. Watch for an increase in both recreational and commercial fishermen here. Initially the route traverses a broad, shallow basin before the river narrows and the Indian River becomes better defined.

Beyond the marked channel edges the basin is extremely shallow, with visible and submerged spoil islands. Deeper draft boats should carefully maintain channel alignment and proceed through this section with caution. This is one of the best spots to observe manatees (often visible) on the ICW. Wildlife abounds on shore, which is overgrown with vegetation.

NAVIGATION: Use NOAA Chart 11485. Note that depths are shallower in the Indian River immediately past the Haulover Canal. Entrance jetties at both ends reduce chop and control shoaling in the canal but watch for shoaling outside the jetty at the south exit. Be advised the current in the canal can be swift. The tidal range is minimal but heavy rainfall or strong winds may raise or lower water levels here by as much as 2 feet.

Indian River, FL

TITUSVILLE		Largest Vessel	VHF	Total Slips	Approach/ Dockside Depth	Floating Docks	Gas/ Diesel	Repairs/ Haulout	Min/Max Amps	Pump-Out Station
1. Titusville Marina **WiFi** MM 878.3	(321) 383-5600	130	16	197	8.0 / 8.0	F	GD		30 / 100	P
2. Westland Marina **WiFi** **onSpot** MM 878.3	(321) 267-1667	55	16	70	7.0 / 8.0			RH	30 / 50	P
INDIAN RIVER CITY										
3. Kennedy Point Yacht Club & Marina **WiFi** MM 883.0	(321) 383-0280	70	16	80	6.0 / 4.5				30 / 50	P

WiFi Wireless Internet Access   **onSpot** Dockside WiFi Facility
Visit www.waterwayguide.com for current rates, fuel prices, website addresses and other up-to-the-minute information.
(Information in the table is provided by the facilities.)

Scan here for more details:

A straight, dredged channel extends from Haulover Canal's western mouth across the flats of the upper Indian River. This channel tends to shoal along both sides, although depths are usually well maintained in the center and in the 10-foot MLW range (remembering water levels fluctuate under certain conditions here). Navigate cautiously and avoid being pushed out of the channel by beam winds.

Flashing green "1" and red daybeacon "2" are the first two markers you will encounter as you head southwest out of the Haulover Canal. After reaching these markers two huge white tanks on the Indian River's west bank line

up with the less visible red markers lining the channel's northern edge and may be used as a forward navigation target. These tanks are charted as "TANK (NW OF TWO)." When steering for the tanks keep an eye on the markers ahead and astern watching for leeway. You do not want to stray out of the channel in this area as it shoals quickly.

After the turn south at green daybeacon "11" the channel begins to widen and the riverbed deepens. To avoid shoaling just outside the channel stay within the markers until reaching the **NASA (Jay-Jay) Railroad Bridge** at Mile 876.6. The bridge is normally left in the open position unless a train is approaching, which is infrequent.

Train operators control bridge closures. When approaching trains stop before the bridge and the operator issues a command to lower the bridge. The indicator lights go to flashing red and the draw lowers and locks if scanning equipment detects nothing under the draw. The draw remains down until a manual raise command is issued by the operator or will raise automatically after the track circuit over the bridge has been clear of rail cars for 5 minutes. After the draw fully opens the lights return to flashing green.

Titusville to Canaveral Barge Canal–ICW Mile 878 to Mile 894

Titusville is an important agricultural center for the Florida citrus industry. It is also good port from which to visit Disney World and the Orlando area theme parks. It is also conveniently located for a visit to Kennedy Space Center (an excursion not to be missed). To read more, see "Goin' Ashore: Titusville, FL" in this chapter.

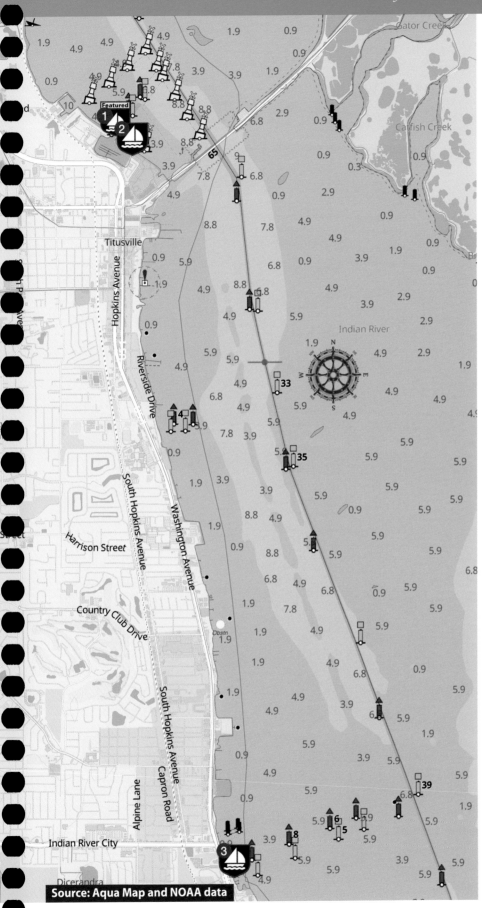

Source: Aqua Map and NOAA data

Check the Kennedy Space Center launch schedule if you're passing through and you may be rewarded; the small deck at the center of the high-rise A. Max Brewer (SR 406) Bridge provides an excellent view.

For most of the next 120 miles southward to the St. Lucie River, the Indian River is wide and deep. In many places the navigable channel is much wider than the marked channel. Several stretches allow sailboats to hoist their canvas and all boaters to temporarily relax at the helm. Beware though that much of the ICW to Cocoa is a dredged channel, there are numerous shoal areas and depths outside the marked may be less than charted.

NAVIGATION: Use NOAA Chart 11485. South of the NASA (Jay-Jay) Railroad Bridge the navigable channel in the Indian River widens significantly. Continue to observe channel markers in this area as many indicate shoal positions. Just south of Titusville's municipal marina, the high-rise **A. Max Brewer (SR 406) Bridge** crosses the ICW at Mile 878.9.

About 6 miles below Titusville at Addison Point (Mile 885.0), the **NASA Causeway Bridge** (27-foot closed vertical clearance) crosses the channel. The bridges open on signal except from 6:30 a.m. to 8:00 a.m. and from 3:30 p.m. to 5:00 p.m., Monday through Friday (except federal holidays), when the draws need not open. Note a closed vertical clearance as low as 21 feet has been reported. There's room to anchor if you have an extended wait here.

Stay well inside the marked channel from the Max Brewer Bridge to the NASA Causeway Bridge. There

GOIN' ASHORE

TITUSVILLE, FL

Titusville lives up to its slogan "Gateway to Nature and Space." Kennedy Space Center is within 20 minutes of the Titusville basin. The Merritt Island National Wildlife Refuge and Canaveral National Seashore are also close by and provide many opportunities to enjoy natural Florida, including horseback riding, kayaking, nature walks and pristine beaches. And, for those who love to fish, Titusville is also known as the "Redfish Capitol of the World."

SERVICES

1. Garden Street Animal Hospital
2220 Garden St. (321-267-4615)

2. Parrish Medical Center
951 N. Washington Ave. (321-268-6111)

3. Titusville Welcome Center
419 S. Hopkins Ave. (321-607-6216)

ATTRACTIONS

4. American Space Museum & Walk of Fame
Working consoles from Launch Pad 36A and a Model 4 Sequencer from Launch Pad 16 are among the attractions. Open Monday through Saturday from 10:00 a.m. to 5:00 p.m. at 308 Pine St. (321-264-0434.)

5. Pritchard House
Tours available of this restored circa-1891 Queen Anne mansion with period furnishings at 424 S. Washington Ave. (321-607-0203).

SHOPPING

6. The Downtown Art Gallery
Five showrooms feature local art and photography of the Indian River Lagoon area (335 S. Washington Ave., 321-268-0122).

7. Save A Lot Grocery Store
Discount supermarket chain at 120 S. Hopkins Ave. (321-269-4919).

MARINAS

8. Titusville Marina
451 Marina Rd. (321-385-5600)

9. Westland Boatyard & Marina
419 N. Washington Ave. (321-267-1667)

is shoaling to depths as shallow as 7.5 feet MLW at the edge of the channel, especially from green daybeacon "33" to south of red daybeacon "34" where the channel narrows. If you leave the marked channel proceed carefully and monitor your depth sounder.

Heading south from the NASA Causeway Bridge, markers are closely spaced and navigation is fairly straightforward. It is possible to stray "outside" in some stretches to anchor for lunch or for minor repairs but watch for spoil areas that flank the ICW on both sides. Note red daybeacon "52" has been replaced with a red nun. Maintain the center of the dredged channel from flashing red "64" to red daybeacon "66" as the channel shallows quickly at the edges.

At about Mile 888.5 there is a large power plant on the west side of the ICW from which power cables cross the ICW in a northeasterly direction. These cables have an authorized clearance of 85 feet over the main channel but only 45 feet elsewhere. If you have a tall mast be sure that you will have sufficient room when passing under power lines to avoid arcing.

At Mile 894.0 the **Bennett Causeway Bridges** with 65-foot fixed vertical clearance cross the ICW. Just south of the entrance to the Canaveral Barge Canal. There are spoil areas here close to the channel on both sides of the bridge.

Dockage/Moorings: The protected harbor at Titusville (north of the Max Brewer Bridge) has a well-marked entry channel that normally carries 7-foot MLW depths. Depths increase as soon as you enter the harbor. Two marinas and a mooring field are located in the basin.

The first is the well-regarded municipal Titusville Marina, which welcomes transients on both fixed and floating docks and can accommodate boats up to 130 feet. Security gates are on the entrance to each dock with a badge lock so no sharing of combinations. They also have a mooring field (normally tranquil but can be bouncy in a north wind) for vessels up to 60 feet. The mooring fee includes the use of the marina facilities along with a pump-out boat that will come out to you.

The second facility in the Titusville basin is Westland Marina with an over 6-acre yard and all types of services and repairs. This facility is also popular with DIY boaters. Groceries, a pharmacy and other amenities are a short

Side Trip: Kennedy Space Center

You will need a full day to tour the Kennedy Space Center Visitor Complex. "Must sees" include the U.S. Astronaut Hall of Fame, Astronaut Encounter (have lunch with a real astronaut), Shuttle Launch Simulator and Control Center tour. You will also want to visit the aptly named rocket garden as well as the final resting place of the Space Shuttle Atlantis. Complete your visit by visiting the inspiring tribute to America's fallen astronauts, The Astronaut Memorial.

Admission includes a bus tour to the launch sites and two 3-D IMAX movies. For more information, contact the Visitors Center at 866-737-5235.

Because the launch site itself is in a secured area, visitors must board buses for the 2-hour tour. The Visitor Complex opens daily at 9:00 a.m. daily except on Christmas Day (closed). For updated launch information, check the schedule at www. kennedyspacecenter.com.

walking distance from the basin.

A few miles south of Titusville off charted "Indian River City" a marked channel branches to the west at green daybeacon "39." This channel, with reported 6-foot MLW depths, leads to the newly refurbished and expanded Kennedy Point Yacht Club & Marina. This facility welcomes transients (yacht club affiliation is not required), has reasonable rates and offers long-term discounts. Some shopping and restaurants are within an easy walk. Call in advance for a reservation and to confirm dockside depths.

Anchorage: Anchoring is restricted north of the Max Brewer Bridge due to the proliferation of moorings. Be aware that your swing arc must maintain at least 150 feet from the mooring field. Boaters anchored nearby (outside the mooring field) may tie up at the Titusville Marina dinghy dock and use showers for a nominal fee.

There is some space to anchor in Titusville in 8 feet MLW just west of red daybeacon "30" but it can get bouncy here. Note that some spoil areas and shoals shown on the chart seem to be expanding in this area and mind the charted "Cable Area" under the bridge. It is a short

dinghy ride from here to the Titusville Marina.

Just south of Titusville at about Mile 883 (opposite Indian River City on the mainland) you will see a large charted area of deeper water with depths of 7 to 8 feet MLW to the east of the ICW (another excellent spot to watch launches). The holding is good in from red daybeacons "38" and "40" but there is little protection from wind or chop. To avoid the charted spoil areas, enter at the mid-point between flashing greens "41" and "43." If you sound your way in far enough (a mile or more from the ICW) wakes from channel traffic are almost entirely eliminated, although boats moving around in the anchorage may cause some rolling.

The NASA Causeway Bridge at Addison Point at Mile 885.0 (and subsequent causeway bridges) provides the best overnight anchorages and wind protection along the Indian River. Holding is fair in mud. Simply choose the side that will be best sheltered from the wind north or south of the bridge. Anytime you leave the channel to seek out protection behind a causeway, proceed slowly and keep an eye on your depth sounder.

◼ SIDE TRIP: CANAVERAL BARGE CANAL & BANANA RIVER

The 8-mile journey on the Canaveral Barge Canal leads from the ICW to the Atlantic Ocean at the Port Canaveral Inlet, a well-marked, deep ship inlet. The route includes a 3-mile cut through Merritt Island. The cut is very scenic with beautiful natural flora and an abundance of marine and wildlife. If you have some time this interesting side trip leads right into the Canaveral launch facilities and is worth the effort.

NAVIGATION: Use NOAA Chart 11485 (Banana River) and NOAA Chart 11478 (Cape Canaveral Lock and Inlet). Just north of the high-rise Bennett Causeway Bridges at ICW Mile 894, look for markers to the east indicating the entrance to the Canaveral Barge Canal, which cuts through Merritt Island to the Banana River.

Persistent northerly winds and low water levels in the Indian River Lagoon at the junction of the ICW and Canaveral Barge Canal have built up a sandbar from the western shore of the spoils island southward across the Canaveral Barge Canal between markers flashing red "12" and green daybeacon "11." Line up for the dredged canal well before entering and don't attempt to cut the corners.

If entering the canal from the south, give green daybeacons "13," "11A" and "11" a wide berth while turning to avoid severe shoaling.

Use caution transiting through here; it sets the minimum controlling depth for the route to the Atlantic. Note there is a slight jog in the course set by red flashing "10" and green daybeacon "9." These can be hard to pick out against the shoreline. The shallowest area observed was about 100 yards west of red flashing "10" at 7 to 8 feet MLW (center channel with a typical river level). The canal cut itself is deeper at 9 to 13 feet MLW.

> The spoils island north of the canal and closest to Merritt Island is a rookery for egrets, herons and roseate spoonbills. Please use binoculars and keep your distance from this active nesting site.

The **Christa McAuliffe Drawbridge** with 21.6-foot closed vertical clearance opens on the hour and half hour from 6:00 a.m. to 10:00 p.m. daily but is closed between 6:15 a.m. and 8:15 a.m. and from 3:10 p.m. to 6:00 p.m., Monday through Friday (except federal holidays). The bridge requires a 3-hour advance notice to open between 10:00 p.m. and 5:59 a.m. Call 321-452-5220 (daytime) or 321-213-2694 (after 10:00 p.m.).

Once you have transited Merritt Island via the Barge Canal, maintain the same course through the fairly narrow but well-marked channel across the Banana River carrying about 10-foot MLW depths. It is very shallow outside the channel to red daybeacon "6." Glance behind occasionally to check for lateral displacement by wind or current. The channel leading from red daybeacon "6" to the lock is wider.

A north–south channel intersects this route prior to the Cape Canaveral Lock. To the north green daybeacon "13" and red daybeacon "14" define the entrance to the Saturn Barge Channel (as noted on NOAA

Chart 11481). These waters are the backyard of Kennedy Space Center and provide unique views of the spaceport, cruise ship terminals and Canaveral National Seashore.

Vessels fitted with a propeller (even stowed) are not allowed into the Sanctuary.

The Bennett Causeway Bridges to the south has a fixed vertical clearance of 36 feet.

Continue easterly to the **Cape Canaveral Lock** (321-783-5421). Hours of operation are from 6:00 a.m. to 9:30 p.m. year-round. If locking through the lockmasters request arrival no later than 9:15 p.m. It is the largest lock in Florida and is designed to reduce tidal currents and prevent hurricane storm surge from entering the Banana River. The lift of the lock ranges from negligible to 3 to 4 feet depending on the ocean tide stage and Banana River water level.

Contact the Cape Canaveral lockmaster on VHF Channel 13 for instructions. Provide vessel name and direction of travel. Report that you will stand by until next green light. Set your fenders in place before entering the lock and fix your own lines to your boat fore and aft (lines are not provided in the lock). Line handlers (or anyone on deck) are required to wear a PFD while locking through. Be prepared. The lockmaster will typically remind you if you are not in compliance.

There are synthetic rub rails with cleats spaced every 10 feet making line control simple when locking through. Once in the Cape Canaveral Lock, loop (don't tie) to cleats as you will have to adjust these lines as

Canaveral Barge Canal & Banana River, FL

CANAVERAL BARGE CANAL		Largest Vessel	VHF	Total Slips	Approach/ Dockside Depth	Floating Docks	Gas/ Diesel	Repairs/ Haulout	Min/Max Amps	Pump-Out Station
1. Harbortown Marina - Canaveral (WiFi) onSpot E of MM 893.6	(321) 453-0160		16	274	6.0 / 6.0		GD	H	30 / 50	P

(WiFi) Wireless Internet Access onSpot Dockside WiFi Facility
Visit www.waterwayguide.com for current rates, fuel prices, website addresses and other up-to-the-minute information.
(Information in the table is provided by the facilities.)

Scan here for more details:

Source: Aqua Map and NOAA data

the lock's water level changes. Passing through a lock is a two-person effort. Each line must be tended by a crew member. There is not much of a raise/drop but lines must be tended during the flood and drain, which is done by cracking open the doors.

Dolphins will occasionally share the lock chamber with you and you may see manatee so be ready to put your engine in neutral as you glide past them. Expect congestion around the two sets of boat ramps near the east exit of the lock.

East of the Cape Canaveral Lock, the **SR 401 Drawbridge** with 25-foot closed vertical clearance has restricted openings. The bridge opens on signal, except from 6:30 a.m. to 8:00 a.m. and 3:30 p.m. to 5:15 p.m., Monday through Friday (except federal holidays) and from 11:00 a.m. to 2:00 p.m. on Saturdays and Sundays, when the draw need not open for the passage of vessels. From 10:00 p.m. to 6:00 a.m. the draws will open on signal only if at least a 3-hour notice is given.

Dockage: Harbortown Marina-Canaveral is located in the Canaveral Barge Canal and is considered a "hurricane hole" by the locals as the lock prevents any major tidal surge. has exceptionally good wind protection and is located in a basin 1 mile west of the Banana River. The marina offers resort-style amenities along with a fenced-in dog play area.

On the east side of the Cape Canaveral Lock is a protected basin containing several marinas and boatyards. Ocean Club Marina at Port Canaveral has floating transient slips and offers repairs. Their 110-ton lift is wide enough for large catamarans. The 50-slip Port Canaveral Yacht Club is in the same basin. They welcome transient boaters and reciprocating yacht club vessels and offer a full range of amenities.

The family-owned Cape Marina, Port Canaveral is a full-service marina and boatyard with a DIY area. They have high-speed fuel pumps on a 150-foot dock and a complete Ship's Store that carries everything from "bait to batteries." Relax in poolside lounge chairs or enjoy the on-site game room. In the same basin is Scorpion Marine/Port Canaveral Marine, which offers storage, service and sales but no transient slips. To the east on the canal is Bluepoints Marina with dry storage and boat lift slips primarily for fishing boats.

Sunrise Marina is closer to the inlet and provides easy ocean access. They cater to sport fisherman and welcome transients (with advance reservations). They also have an on-site waterfront restaurant (Grills Seafood & Tiki Bar, 321-868-2226) and a well-stocked tackle and gift shop.

Anchorage: It is possible to anchor south of the Bennett Causeway Bridges. Enter on the southwest side and anchor behind the causeway in 7- to 8-foot MLW depths with good holding. The overhead cables make anchoring north of the bridges dangerous.

A short run north in the Saturn Barge Channel offers access to anchorage possibilities near the spoil islands just off the eastern side with 6 to 7 foot MLW depths. If the winds are from the west or northwest this anchorage will be rocky. These islands are outside the "No-Motor Zone," which begins to their north and east.

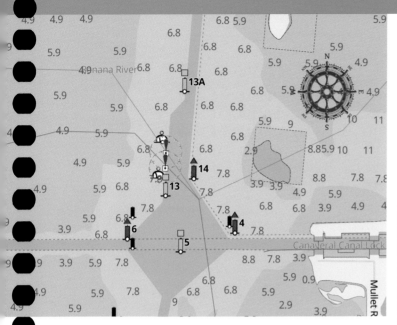

Side Trip: South on the Banana River

NAVIGATION: Use NOAA Charts 11481 and 11476. While this route has reasonable depths at its north end, it shallows quickly. This is not a dredged channel and there are some challenges on this route. The air-draft restriction is 36 feet. Local knowledge is recommended.

If heading south on the Banana River is your intention approach flashing green "5" at the junction of the barge canals and then turn south for the center of the high span of the **Bennett Memorial Causeway (SR A1A) Bridge** with a fixed vertical clearance of 36 feet.

The first marker on the Banana River route south is red daybeacon "28," which is a straight shot 2.5 miles south of the Bennett Memorial Causeway Bridge and just north of the **Willard Peebles Bridge** (fixed 36-foot vertical clearance). Expect depths as low as 5 to 6 feet MLW for this stretch to the Willard Peebles Bridge and depths to shallow further to the south of the bridge. Proceed with caution keeping an eye on your sounder and chartplotter.

NOTE: When proceeding southbound on the Banana River, keep red to port. The channel begins some 18 miles south at green daybeacon "1" off Dragon Point (ICW Mile 914.5) where the Banana River drains into the Indian River

Dockage: Island Time Marina is on the east bank just south of the Willard Peebles Bridge and may have space for you. (They report just three reserved transient slips so call ahead.) It is a 15-minute walk to Cocoa Beach amenities. Across the river is the recently upgraded Marker 24 Marina with covered and open slips. Transients are welcome (to 50 feet). The entry to the marina is well marked.

Canaveral Barge Canal & Banana River, FL

CAPE CANAVERAL LOCK		Largest Vessel	VHF	Total Slips	Approach/ Dockside Depth	Floating Docks	Gas/ Diesel	Repairs/ Haulout	Min/Max Amps	Pump-Out Station
1. Ocean Club Marina at Port Canaveral **WiFi** E of MM 893.6	(321) 783-9001	110	16	73	14.0 / 12.0	F	GD		30 / 100	P
2. Scorpion Marine/Port Canaveral Marine **WiFi** E of MM 893.6	(321) 784-5788	110	16		15.0 / 15.0	F		RH	30 / 100	P
3. Cape Marina, Port Canaveral **WiFi** 7.0 mi. E of MM 893.6	(321) 783-8410	130	16	115	12.0 / 12.0	F	GD	H	30 / 50	P
4. Port Canaveral Yacht Club **WiFi** 6.9 mi. E of MM 893.6	(321) 482-0167	60		50	40.0 / 10.0	F		H	30 / 50	P
5. Bluepoints Marina	(321) 799-2860	47	16	26	40.0 / 15.0	F	GD	H		P
6. Sunrise Marina **WiFi**	(321) 783-9535	98	16	21	20.0 / 8.0	F	GD	H	30 / 50	

WiFi Wireless Internet Access   **onSpot** Dockside WiFi Facility
Visit www.waterwayguide.com for current rates, fuel prices, website addresses and other up-to-the-minute information.
(Information in the table is provided by the facilities.)

Scan here for more details:

Source: Aqua Map and NOAA data

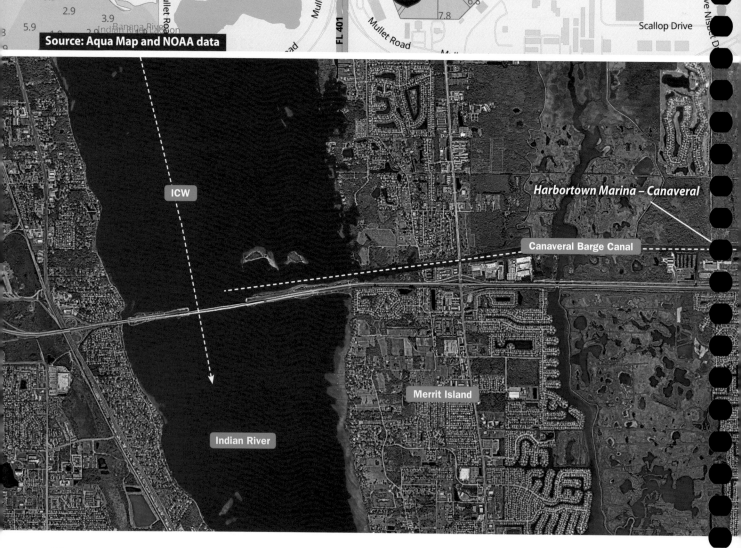

ICW

Harbortown Marina – Canaveral

Canaveral Barge Canal

Merrit Island

Indian River

Container Road

Cargo Road

Dolphin Road

33

38

37

1.9

33

4.9 2.9
Obstn *Obstn*

Hercules Road

Perigee Road

Sprint Road

Indian River Lagoon

East Basin Light 5

5

3.9

6.8

14A

44

42 33 34 32 33 38

15

Canaveral Harbor
Entrance Channel
Lighted Buoy 15

42 42

8.8 38 38

43 39 40

Herring Street

39

6

Featured

Mullet Road

Flounder

Herring Street

Jetty Park Road

Jetty Park Road

Interm

Sunrise Marina

Cape Marina, Port Canaveral

Banana River

© Mapbox © OpenStreetMap

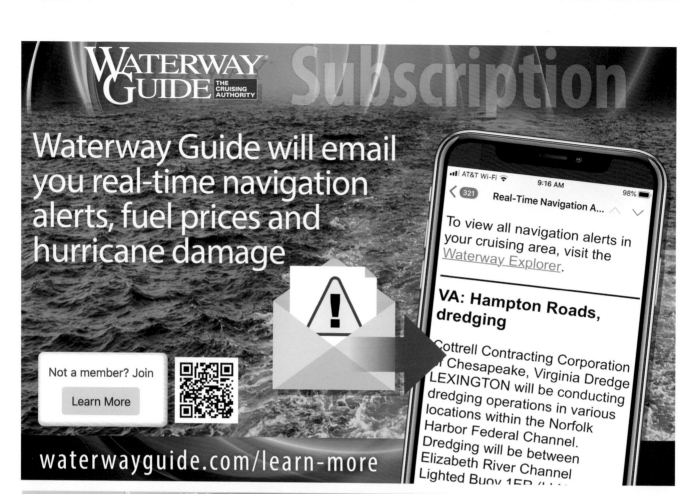

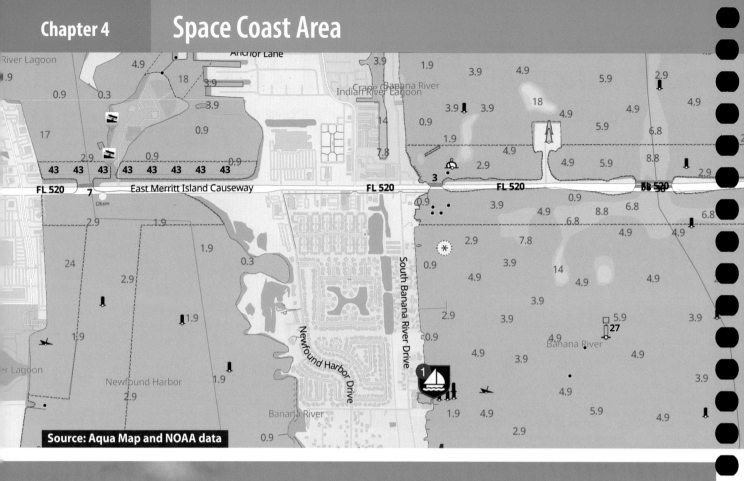

Source: Aqua Map and NOAA data

Boats anchored near Port Canaveral

Canaveral Barge Canal & Banana River, FL

BANANA RIVER		Largest Vessel	VHF	Total Slips	Approach/ Dockside Depth	Floating Docks	Gas/ Diesel	Repairs/ Haulout	Min/Max Amps	Pump-Out Station
1. Marker 24 Marina (WiFi)	(321) 453-7888	60		63	5.5 / 5.5		GD	RH	30 / 50	P
2. Island Time Marina (WiFi)	(321) 613-4852			30	6.0 / 6.0				30	P

(WiFi) Wireless Internet Access ⬤onSpot Dockside WiFi Facility
Visit www.waterwayguide.com for current rates, fuel prices, website addresses and other up-to-the-minute information.
(Information in the table is provided by the facilities.)

Scan here for more details:

■ TO MELBOURNE

Cocoa Village–ICW Mile 897

Cocoa Village is on the western shore and Merritt Island is on the eastern shore of the Indian River. Both offer numerous cruiser amenities. For details, see "Goin' Ashore: Cocoa Village, FL" in this chapter.

NAVIGATION: Use NOAA Chart 11485. The high-rise **Hubert Humphrey (FL 520) Bridge** (which is also known as Merritt Island or Cocoa Twin Bridges) crosses the ICW at Mile 897.4 at Cocoa. There is essentially zero lunar tide range in Cocoa since the ocean inlets are far distant. However, strong currents and some variation in level are possible as the river responds to wind load and other factors. Check tide boards for clearance if you are close to the limit.

While the high voltage overhead cables that cross the Indian River just south of the Hubert Humphrey (FL 520) Bridge are charted at 88 feet, they progressively descend towards shore and vertical clearance is substantially reduced (charted at 38 feet at landfall). This poses a serious risk for vessels operating or anchoring near the cables, not just from physical contact but open-air arcing from the power lines to a mast. We recommend a minimum mast-to-wire distance of 12 feet.

Dockage: The ever-popular Cocoa Village Marina is a fully modern, clean facility with an exceptionally friendly and helpful staff. This is a good place to stay or leave your boat. The well-marked approach channel is about a 0.25 mile north of the Cocoa Twin

Bridges. Enter north of the marina's wave attenuation fence. This marina is convenient to the attractions, shops and restaurants of Historic Cocoa Village.

A major cleanup and enhancement to the marine facilities of Lee Wenner Park, the city's boat ramp and docking venue that serves Cocoa Yacht Basin, has been completed. The project includes all new floating docks with a 250-foot-long T-dock for visiting ICW cruisers (with a 48-consecutive hours of free dockage limit), day slips and a provision for dinghies. For current information contact Historic Cocoa Village (321-631-9075).

Anchorage: You can anchor west of the ICW and south of the Cocoa Twin Bridges just off Cocoa Village in Cocoa Yacht Basin. (Note that the Cocoa Village Marina on the north side of the bridges does not offer dinghy dockage.) Sound your way in to a suitable depth avoiding the charted cable and pipeline area south

Indian River, FL

COCOA VILLAGE			Largest Vessel	VHF	Total Slips	Approach/ Dockside Depth	Floating Docks	Gas/ Diesel	Repairs/ Haulout	Min/Max Amps	Pump-Out Station
1. Cocoa Village Marina WiFi MM 897.0		(321) 632-5445	100	16	117	6.5 / 6.5				30 / 100	P

WiFi Wireless Internet Access onSpot Dockside WiFi Facility
Visit www.waterwayguide.com for current rates, fuel prices, website addresses and other up-to-the-minute information.
(Information in the table is provided by the facilities.)

Scan here for more details:

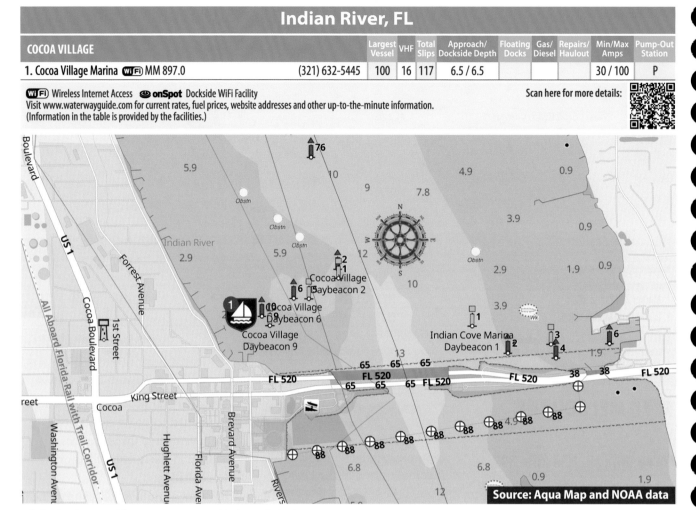

Source: Aqua Map and NOAA data

of the bridges and be sure to stay well clear of the low power lines (charted 38 feet).

The anchorage extends for 0.50 mile down river, along which you should find 6 to 9 feet MLW. Expect lots of crab pots. A particularly popular spot is west of the ICW at flashing green "77." Drop the hook in the lee of Rockledge in west wind.

The Merritt Island (east) side of the river offers the closest major provisioning. To anchor north of the Cocoa Twin Bridges, head easterly off the ICW paralleling the Causeway and hold about 7-foot MLW depths all the way to the daybeacons "1" and "2" for the Griffis Park anchorage. Griffis Landing at Blue Crab Cove county park has six finger docks for small boats, a ramp and a pump-out station; however, the approach/dockside depth is only 2 to 3 feet MLW precluding use by most cruisers. This is a 10-minute walk to businesses along SR 520.

To anchor on the east side of the ICW and south of the Cocoa Twin Bridges carefully sound your way in to the Cocoa Yacht Basin and be sure to avoid the charted (but now submerged) small spoil island. Also be aware there is a recently sunk vessel adjacent to the nearby manatee speed zone sign. Easy access to Griffis Landing via dinghy is available by passing under the feeder bridge on the eastern end of the causeway.

Should you choose to visit Cocoa Village on the mainland you can walk across the bridge. Note that walkways are narrow and exposed; exercise caution. The south bridge walkway is wider. It is easier/safer to access Cocoa Village via dinghy by going to the floating docks at Lee Wenner Park.

Cocoa Village to Eau Gallie—ICW Mile 898 to Mile 914

NAVIGATION: Use NOAA Charts 11485 and 11472. The stretch from Cocoa to Palm Shores presents few problems but watch for the ever-present pot markers that sometimes stray into the channel. Most spoil areas are well outside

GOIN' ASHORE

COCOA VILLAGE, FL

Cocoa Village is renowned for a multitude of truly unique shopping opportunities: art galleries, antique shops, art studios, boutiques and more. As you walk around, look for "Cocoa Village Loves ICW Cruisers" anchor logos in store windows. Those establishments will offer some type of perk for cruisers!

SERVICES

1. Brevard Veterinary Hospital
329 N. Cocoa Blvd. (321-632-0445)

2. Cocoa Post Office
600 Florida Ave. (321-632-6846)

3. Historic Cocoa Village Association
600 Florida Ave., Ste. 104
(321-631-9075)

4. Omni Healthcare (Service)
505 Delannoy Ave. (321-633-0988)

ATTRACTIONS

5. Cocoa Village Playhouse
Highly acclaimed playhouse with productions throughout the year at 300 Brevard Ave. (321-636-5050).

6. Library of Florida History
Housed at the The Florida Historical Society (425 Brevard Ave., 321-690-1971).

SHOPPING

7. S.F. Travis & Co. Hardware
Multi-building, old-style hardware store (circa 1885) with extensive inventory. Open weekdays only (300 Delannoy Ave., 321-636-1441).

8. Village Cycle Shoppe
Bicycle services, rentals and new/ used sales at 4 Harrison St. (321-806-3917).

MARINA

9. Cocoa Village Marina
90 Delannoy Ave. (321-632-5445)

Indian River & Banana River, FL

PALM SHORES		Largest Vessel	VHF	Total Slips	Approach/ Dockside Depth	Floating Docks	Gas/ Diesel	Repairs/ Haulout	Min/Max Amps	Pump-Out Station
1. Grills Riverside MM 908.5	(321) 242-8999			12	5.0 / 5.0		G		30	P
EAU GALLIE										
2. Eau Gallie Yacht Basin (WiFi) MM 915.0	(321) 242-6577	60	16	60	8.0 / 7.0				30 / 50	P
3. Waterline Marina (WiFi)	(321) 254-0452	80	16	92	8.0 / 8.0			R	30 / 50	P
INDIAN HARBOR										
4. Anchorage Yacht Basin MM 914.5	(321) 773-3620	60		80	6.0 / 10.0		G	RH	30 / 50	
5. Telemar Bay Marina (WiFi) 1.8 mi E of MM 914.0	(321) 773-2468	120	16	205	9.0 / 7.0		GD	H	30 / 50	P

(WiFi) Wireless Internet Access ⬤ onSpot Dockside WiFi Facility
Visit www.waterwayguide.com for current rates, fuel prices, website addresses and other up-to-the-minute information.
(Information in the table is provided by the facilities.)

Scan here for more details:

the marked channel and to the east. The only craft that may have problems are sailboats attempting to tack back and forth across the river.

At Mile 909 the high-rise **Pineda Causeway Bridge** crosses the ICW. As with other bridges built on causeways, be aware of increased currents under the bridge. Although the charted fixed vertical clearance is 65 feet, clearances may be closer to 64 feet.

Dockage: The very popular Grills Riverside has 5-foot MLW depths on approach and dockside. Call ahead to check slip availability. This full-service restaurant will even cook your catch!

Anchorage: At Mile 904.5 on the east shore of the Indian River is The Point. Just north is a pleasant spot off a residential strip bordering Honeymoon Lake that provides protection from northeast to southeast winds but chop is possible in other winds. Holding is good in 8- to 11-foot MLW depths but avoid nearby shoals. You may experience some wakes here.

> Don't be alarmed if you hear the cry of peacocks on shore. (It can sound like someone yelling "help.")

Eau Gallie–ICW Mile 914 to 915

On the mainland side of the ICW two once distinct towns, Eau Gallie and Melbourne, have merged under the name of Melbourne to form a "metropolis." Each town has its own harbor and facilities. To the east the Banana River meets the Indian River at Rocky Dragon Point where there are additional facilities. Many skippers leave their boats in this area for extended periods, catch a plane from Orlando Melbourne International Airport and then return later. For details see "Goin' Ashore: Eau Gallie, FL" in this chapter.

NAVIGATION: Use NOAA Chart 11472. Although the NOAA chart doesn't mention it by name, Eau Gallie at Mile 914 is on the west side of the Indian River. Just south of the high-rise **Eau Gallie Causeway (SR 518) Bridge** at Mile 914.4 the numbering sequence for ICW markers resets at Mile 915 with flashing red "2." (There is no green "1.") Avoid confusion at this point with the closely spaced markers for the channel to Eau Gallie's protected harbor to the west with a marker sequence in the same range. Just off the ICW are green daybeacons "1," "3" and "5" and then flashing red "6" closer to shore.

The controlling depth for Eau Gallie's entrance channel is reported as 6 feet MLW but deeper draft vessels use it. Beware of shoaling extending to the southeast of flashing red "6." Stay mid-channel or favor the green for the best water. Entering the narrows the channel bends to the northwest and continues into the harbor on the Eau Gallie River. Favor the seawalled north shoreline through this narrow passage and be alert to increased traffic from a launch ramp at Ballard Park to the south.

Dockage: Eau Gallie's harbor has good protection and an easy-to-enter, well-maintained entrance. Eau Gallie Yacht Basin operates a DIY yard and offers just two transient slips. It's a short walk to the quaint streets of Eau Gallie's restored historical downtown. Karen's Canvas is on site for all your marine canvas needs. Waterline Marina, part of a condominium development at the head of the harbor, has transient slips and offers some repairs.

Anchorage: Boats can anchor on either side of Eau Gallie Causeway (SR 518) Bridge depending on wind direction. (Avoid the charted cable areas and shoals.) Anchorages on both side of the bridge offer at least 9 feet MLW but are exposed to wakes.

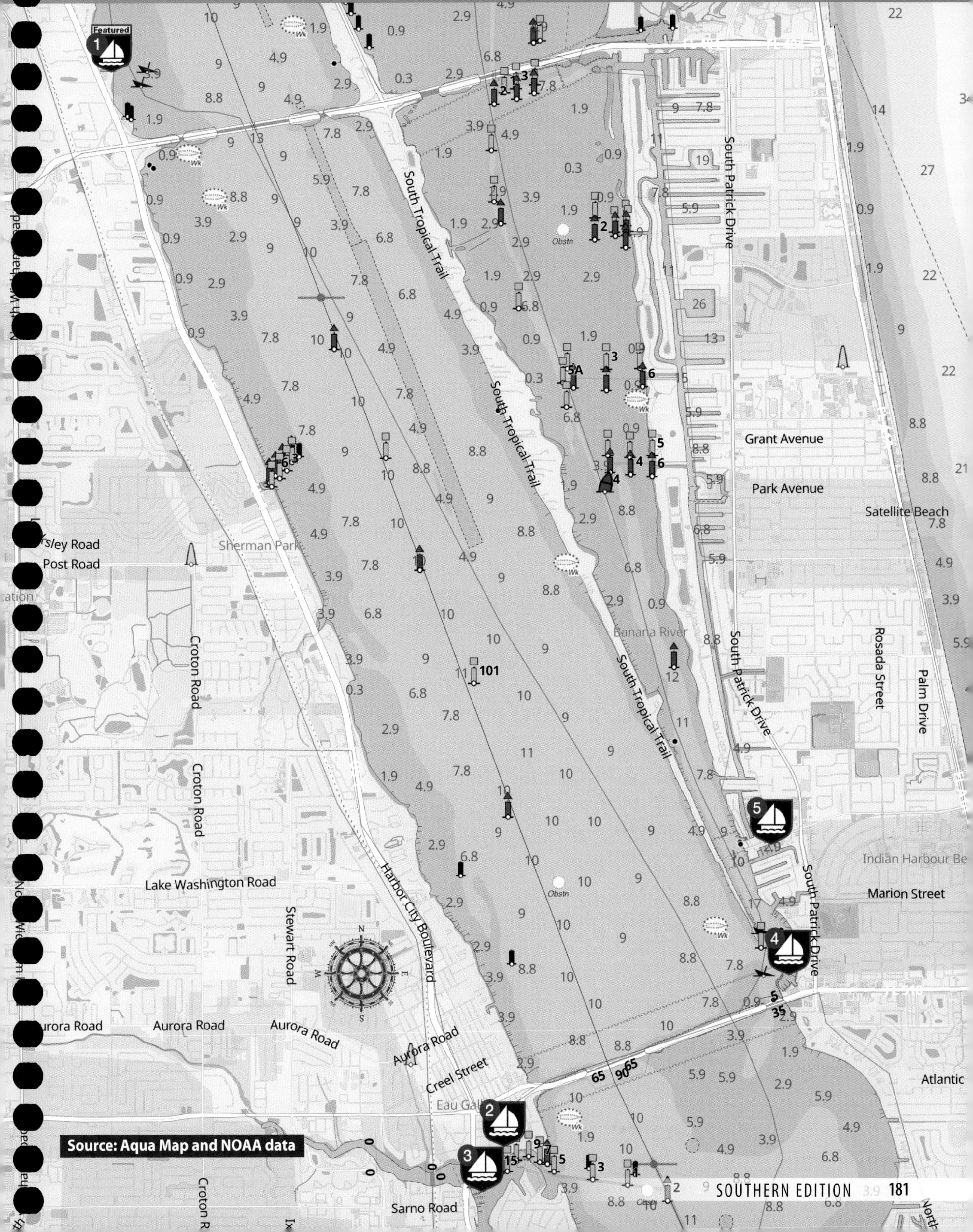

South Tropical Trail

South Patrick Drive

Grant Avenue

Park Avenue

Satellite Beach

Rosada Street

Palm Drive

Banana River

South Tropical Trail

Indian Harbour Be

Marion Street

Atlantic

Sherman Park

s/ey Road

Post Road

Croton Road

Lake Washington Road

Stewart Road

Harbor City Boulevard

Croton Road

Aurora Road

Aurora Road

Aurora Road

Creel Street

Eau Gall

Sarno Road

Obstn

Wk

101

Featured

Source: Aqua Map and NOAA data

GOIN' ASHORE

EAU GALLIE, FL

Eau Gallie began as a small coastal town along the Indian River Lagoon in 1860 and quickly became a busy thoroughfare as steamers, riverboats and freighters transported residents, cargo and tourists. Now merged into the City of Melbourne, Eau Gallie retains a quaint, historical district that strives to retain its cultural heritage and distinct early Floridian flavor. Many historic buildings remain in and around the downtown area, some dating back to the early 1900s.

SERVICES

1. Eau Gallie Medical Center
  1403 Highland Ave. (321-751-1414)

2. Eau Gallie Post Office
  681 St. Clair St. (321-259-5574)

3. Eau Gallie Public Library
  1521 Pineapple Ave. (321-255-4304)

4. Florida Aid to Animals (Vet)
  741 Creel St. (321-242-9826)

ATTRACTIONS

5. Foosaner Art Museum
  Art exhibits, classes and workshops offered Wednesday through Saturday from 10:00 a.m. to 4:00 p.m. at 1463 Highland Ave. (321-674-8916).

6. Intracoastal Brewing Company
  This neighborhood taproom features a rotating menu of original brews. "Namaste for one more" yoga and beer Sundays at 11:30 a.m. (for a fee) at 652 W. Eau Gallie Blvd. (321-872-7395).

SHOPPING

7. Boathouse Discount Marine
  A large selection of boat parts and accessories at 557 N. Harbor City Blvd. (321-254-2535).

8. Eau Gallie Ace Hardware
  Full-service hardware store at 590 Eau Gallie Blvd. (321-254-3261).

MARINAS

9. Eau Gallie Yacht Basin
  587 Young St. (321-242-6577)

10. Waterline Marina
  911 N. Harbor City Blvd. (321 254-0452)

Side Trip: North on the Banana River– ICW Mile 914.5

The Banana River continues north up to Cape Canaveral and intersects the Canaveral Barge Canal near the Cape Canaveral Lock in about 18 miles. While this route has reasonable depths at its south end, it shallows quickly. This is not a dredged channel and there are some challenges on this route. The air-draft restriction is 36 feet. Local knowledge is desirable.

NAVIGATION: Use NOAA Chart 11472 (also NOAA 11476 and 11481). North of the Eau Gallie Causeway (SR 518) Bridge and across the Indian River to the east, the narrow mouth of the Banana River turns to the northeast around Dragon Point. To enter keep at least 100 feet south of green daybeacon "1" marking rocky shoals off Dragon Point. Continue to maintain 100 feet off of this daybeacon as you turn northward.

⚠️

Stay in the channel to avoid Dragon Point's rocky rim. Reports are that the charted shoal extending up from the bridge causeway to the south ends well clear of green daybeacon "1." This is a sandy shoal and it would be better to ground there than on Dragon Point's rocks. If you do hit the rocks, edge off backwards; do not try to go over them!

The Banana River continues north up to Cape Canaveral and intersects the Canaveral Barge Canal near the Cape Canaveral Lock about 18 miles from Dragon Point. One-half mile north of Dragon Point, **Mathers (SR A1A) Swing Bridge** has 7-foot vertical clearance and opens on signal except from 10:00 p.m. to 6:00 a.m., Sunday through Thursday (except federal holidays) when the draw opens on signal if at least a 2-hour notice is given. This is a schedule change and the status is "until further notice." Contact the bridgetender at 321-779-4019 for further information.

Four miles north of Dragon Point is the Banana River span of the fixed **Pineda Causeway (East) Bridge** with a fixed vertical clearance of 36 feet. (Note that the span of the same bridge has a vertical clearance of 65 feet where it crosses the Indian River.)

The route north from here can be tricky due to widely spaced markers and skinny water. The controlling depth is 5 to 6 feet MLW but it is typically deeper. Follow the

channel up to red daybeacon "8A" and green daybeacon "9" and proceed west being careful to avoid the charted "Subm Piles" as shown. This cut-across provides about 7-foot MLW depths into the adjacent deeper water. (This deeper water is the result of dredging for fill to extend the landmass for the runways of adjacent Patrick Air Force Base.)

Once into the deep water and around the submerged pilings head north for 4.25 miles to pick up the marked channel at green daybeacon "11" and red daybeacon "12." (Note that there is no daybeacon "10.")

Willard Peebles Bridge is about 8 miles beyond that and **Bennett Memorial Causeway (SR A1A) Bridge** is just south of the Canaveral Barge Canal. Both have a fixed vertical clearance of 36 feet.

Dockage: Two marinas are available in the mouth of the Banana River. Just inside the river mouth on the south shore is Anchorage Yacht Basin, which is a repair and dry stack facility. They do, however, have some transient space and can also provide a diver to help you if you snag while anchoring. Telemar Bay Marina is located in a well-protected and quiet basin to the east (just south of the Mathers (SR A1A) Swing Bridge). Their helpful staff will help you tie up or haul out.

Anchorage: Between Dragon Point and the Mathers Swing Bridge on the Banana River you can anchor in at least 10-foot MLW depths with good holding. You will find the most room north of the bridge. Depths and current vary with wind and rain and wakes can be considerable (although numerous "No-Wake" signs have resulted in some improvement). Be careful not to interfere with the entrances to the yacht club or the marinas.

Melbourne–ICW Mile 915 to 918

The quiet, pleasant town of Melbourne sits midway between Jacksonville Beach and Florida's Gold Coast. It is home port to the Florida Institute of Technology's big research vessels, which are docked on the port side of the harbor entrance. There is much to see and do here as described in "Goin' Ashore: Melbourne, FL" in this chapter.

NAVIGATION: Use NOAA Chart 11472. The high-rise Melbourne Causeway (SR 516) Bridge crosses the ICW at Mile 918.2. Melbourne's harbor is easily approached just south of the bridges. To enter the basin from the ICW turn west at red daybeacon "6" and follow the markers until

Indian River, FL

MELBOURNE		Largest Vessel	VHF	Total Slips	Approach/ Dockside Depth	Floating Docks	Gas/ Diesel	Repairs/ Haulout	Min/Max Amps	Pump-Out Station
1. Melbourne Harbor Marina (WiFi) MM 918.5	(321) 725-9054	100	16	85	8.0 / 8.0		GD	R	30 / 100	
PALM BAY										
2. Palm Bay Marina MM 921.2	(321) 723-0851	40	74	60	3.0 / 3.0			RH	30	

(WiFi) Wireless Internet Access ⬤ onSpot Dockside WiFi Facility
Visit www.waterwayguide.com for current rates, fuel prices, website addresses and other up-to-the-minute information.
(Information in the table is provided by the facilities.)

Scan here for more details:

you are close to shore. Here the channel turns sharply to starboard and leads to the enclosed basin.

The harbor and channel are dredged to a controlling depth of 8 feet MLW, although the depth is reported to be closer to 6 or 7 feet MLW between red daybeacon "6" and flashing green "7." Local knowledge advises favoring the red side. The fixed 14-foot vertical clearance railroad bridge that follows the 65-foot vertical clearance highway bridge plus low water depths makes the northern reaches of Crane Creek inaccessible to most vessels.

Dockage: Melbourne Harbor Marina is to starboard at the head of the basin. The marina offers accommodates vessels to 130 feet. It has two restaurants on site and is a short walk from the quaint restored historical area with additional restaurants, shopping and art galleries.

Anchorage: Boats anchor on both sides of the high-rise Melbourne Causeway Bridge. Pick a spot that offers the best wind protection but avoid the charted cable area. You can tie your dinghy up at a park to the east on the south side of the causeway and walk one-half mile to a beach. You will find restaurants but no groceries here.

■ TO VERO BEACH

Melbourne to Sebastian–ICW Mile 919 to Mile 937

The Sebastian area includes the town of Micco, north of the St. Sebastian River, and the City of Sebastian to the south as well as the Sebastian Inlet. The scenery becomes a bit more natural from here to Vero Beach making this stretch of the ICW very pleasant for cruisers. There are also a few interesting stops along the way, which justify a slower passage. Ocean beaches are accessible by dinghy at

Melbourne, FL

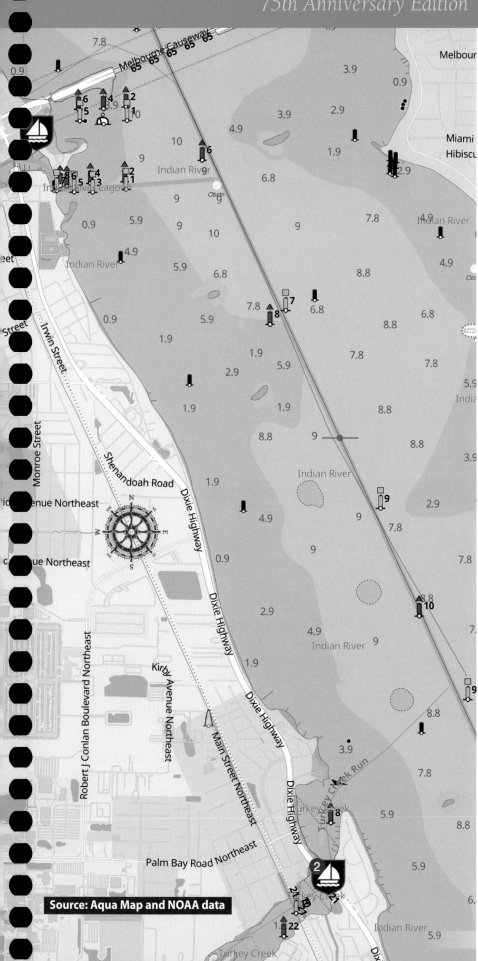

Source: Aqua Map and NOAA data

the inlet near the state park and the Environmental Learning Center in Wabasso is worth a gander.

While the Indian River appears to widen over this stretch, the ICW is confined to a narrow, dredged channel with shoaling just at the edges. Mariners must take precautions to stay inside the marked ICW channel, even in the open lagoons.

NAVIGATION: Use NOAA Chart 11472. The channel is wide along this stretch, although there is a string of shoals (many just below the surface) and spoil islands outside the ICW channel to the west. Exercise particular care south of red daybeacon "8" where depths of 7 feet MLW have been observed. Boats with deeper draft may want to pass east of the marked channel to find deeper water.

Shoals border the western edge of the channel off Cape Malabar (western shore between green daybeacon "15" and red daybeacon "16"). The channel also shallows quickly off both sides through the small cut near red daybeacon "18." The spoils island between red daybeacons "18" and "20" (Mile 925) is now very small but has a long sandy spit extending to the west.

Just past ICW Mile 925 the channel slants a bit toward the west and narrows considerably. You will enter a dredged channel at red daybeacon "20" with less than 6 feet MLW on both sides and on the spoils islands that are close in so take care to maintain channel alignment. Note that the spoils islands in this area are spreading, mostly on their north and west sides.

With frequent bends the ICW channel passes west of Grant Farm

GOIN' ASHORE
MELBOURNE, FL

Historic Downtown Melbourne surrounds Crane Creek, the authentic site of the city's historical beginning. Downtown Melbourne is ripe with opportunities to engage in the arts. In fact, you can't stroll the historic district without noticing the vibrant murals that illustrate Melbourne's history.

SERVICES

1. Brevard County Public Library
540 E. Fee Ave. (321-952-4514)

2. Melbourne Post Office
640 E. New Haven Ave. (321-723-6164)

3. Melbourne Chamber of Commerce
1005 E. Strawbridge Ave. #4740 (321-724-5400)

ATTRACTIONS

4. Strawbridge Art League Gallery
Interesting selection of artwork, each with a uniquely Floridian flavor at 819 E. Strawbridge Ave. (321-952-3070).

SHOPPING

5. CVS Pharmacy
Drugstore chain with health and beauty products plus prescriptions at 15 E. New Haven Ave. (321-409-3941).

MARINA

6. Melbourne Harbor Marina
2210 S. Front St. (321-725-9054)

Indian River Inlet, FL

SEBASTIAN AREA		Largest Vessel	VHF	Total Slips	Approach/ Dockside Depth	Floating Docks	Gas/ Diesel	Repairs/ Haulout	Min/Max Amps	Pump-Out Station
1. Sebastian River Marina & Boatyard **WiFi** MM 934.0	(772) 664-3029	70	16	60	5.0 / 5.0			RH	30 / 50	
2. Sebastian Inlet Marina **WiFi** MM 934.3	(772) 664-8500	45	16	25	5.0 / 5.0	F	GD	RH	30 / 50	P
3. Capt'n Butchers Marina **WiFi** MM 937.2	(772) 589-2552	60		25	5.0 / 5.0		GD		20 / 50	P
4. Fins Marina MM 937.5	(772) 589-4843	65	16	78	6.0 / 6.0				30 / 50	
5. Capt. Hiram's Sebastian Marina **WiFi** MM 937.7	(772) 589-4345	50	16	46	5.0 / 5.0				30 / 50	P

WiFi Wireless Internet Access **onSpot** Dockside WiFi Facility
Visit www.waterwayguide.com for current rates, fuel prices, website addresses and other up-to-the-minute information.
(Information in the table is provided by the facilities.)

Scan here for more details:

Island at green daybeacon "39" (Mile 930), the only inhabited spoils island in the Indian River and accessible only by boat. The lower part of Grant Farm Island is a rookery used mainly by ibis and egrets.

From here on proceed cautiously and be careful not to stray outside the channel where the MLW may only be a few feet deep. You may have to strain to make out the markers, which seem to blend into the shoreline. Also be alert for uncharted oyster beds and pot markers on both sides of the ICW. From flashing green buoy "49" (formerly a daybeacon) to flashing green "51" be sure to favor the red side of the channel in 10 to 12 feet MLW as opposed

to 6 feet MLW or less on the green side.

Sebastian Inlet is accessed from a marked channel that proceeds eastward from flashing green "63." This a local knowledge, fair-weather inlet used largely by smaller recreational fishing boats. The inlet is crossed by the fixed **A1A Bridge** (37-foot vertical clearance). Constant shoaling necessitates careful piloting and up-to-date local knowledge. Swift crosscurrents and the resulting shifting channel make navigation difficult in Sebastian Inlet, even with up-to-date local information.

Dockage: To the south at Mile 920 Palm Bay Marina is located in a basin between two fixed bridges (15-

Sebastian Inlet

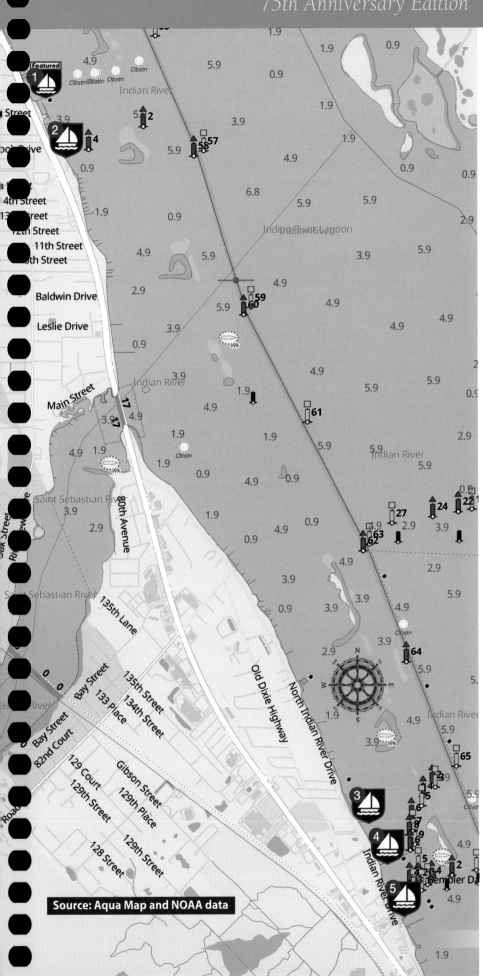

foot and 10-foot vertical clearance, respectively) on Turkey Creek. The marina accepts transients to 40 feet and offers some repairs. Call ahead for approach directions and depths.

Several marinas welcome cruising boats in the small community of Micco, north of Sebastian. At Mile 934 is the well-regarded Sebastian River Marina & Boatyard, a full-service facility offering slips, dry storage, service and repairs. The facility is in a seawall-protected basin close to a grocery store and restaurants. Sebastian Inlet Marina is just to the south with four reserved transient slips and repairs. Both marinas report 5-foot MLW dockside and approach depths. Call ahead for exact depths.

At Mile 937.5 in Sebastian two entrance channels on the west side give access to three facilities located in a small basin behind spoils islands. The northern channel (at green daybeacon "65") has shoaled in and is reported to carry somewhat less than the charted 6-foot MLW depths from the ICW to the marinas; therefore, we recommend the southern entrance channel at red daybeacon "66" for approaching. There are a number of permanently moored vessels here and with the attraction of Sebastian's active pubs and restaurants, it can get crowded.

The northernmost facility is Capt'n Butchers Marina followed by Fins Marina, both with some transient slips. The southernmost facility is Capt. Hiram's Sebastian Marina, which can be identified by its colorful rooftops. The resort features an inn, restaurant and popular tiki-style bar where you can relax with your feet in the sand and a drink in

Vero Beach Area, FL

WABASSO			Largest Vessel	VHF	Total Slips	Approach/ Dockside Depth	Floating Docks	Gas/ Diesel	Repairs/ Haulout	Min/Max Amps	Pump-Out Station
1. Loggerhead Marina - Vero Beach Marina **WiFi** MM 948.5		(772) 770-4470	120	16	161	6.0 / 6.5	F	GD		30 / 100	P
VERO BEACH											
2. Vero Beach City Marina **WiFi** MM 952.0		(772) 231-2819	160	16	88	8.0 / 10.0	F	GD		30 / 100	P

WiFi Wireless Internet Access   **onSpot** Dockside WiFi Facility
Visit www.waterwayguide.com for current rates, fuel prices, website addresses and other up-to-the-minute information. (Information in the table is provided by the facilities.)

Scan here for more details:

your hand. Between the two is Fins Marina with slips to 65 feet. Before attempting to dock at any of these it would be highly advisable to call and ask for depth information as this area is continually changing.

Anchorage: Because of the beach on the west side, the spoil island accessed by heading west off the ICW just north of red daybeacon "20" at Mile 925 has become a favorite local anchoring spot. On less crowded weekdays ICW travelers often use this area for overnight anchorage. (It will be too crowded and noisy during "peak" season.) Depths are slightly less than shown on the chart (5 to 8 feet MLW). Shoals extend westward from these islands and are usually marked with pipes or stakes. Passing boats on the ICW create wakes here.

In an eastern blow it may be more comfortable snugged in closer to the barrier island to the east. Just follow one of the deeper lobes off the ICW between Mile 920 and Mile 925. Note there are few anchorage opportunities between here and Sebastian Inlet at Mile 936. Consider that operation in darkness in this area is not advised.

Shallow-draft vessels can anchor off Capt. Hiram's Sebastian Marina in approximately 5-foot MLW depths. There are a number of permanently moored vessels here. This is close to several active pubs and restaurants and can get crowded, even through the marked channel. This basin has minimal protection and is very congested. There are better anchorages in Sebastian Inlet.

It is possible to anchor near the northeast side of Sebastian Inlet in 8 to 10 feet MLW opposite Sebastian Inlet State Park. There is only a 6-inch tide at this spot but a strong current. Only anchor here on a low wind day as it is exposed in all directions. It is a short dinghy ride to the basin to the north side of the inlet near the fixed bridge for snorkeling and swimming. Beach the dinghy on the sand beach prior to the "lagoon." Visibility for snorkeling is fair and the beach is perfect for a picnic or a dog run. You will be joined by a lot of fishermen and small boats.

In north through southeast winds shoal-draft boats can find protection about a mile off the ICW towards Campbell Pocket in 5 to 6 feet MLW. Ease east from the ICW south of green daybeacon "61" watching your depth. The bottom is irregular here and holding is fair in mud.

Sebastian to Vero Beach—ICW Mile 938 to Mile 952

The heavily congested areas are temporarily behind you as you enter one of the Indian River's most natural and attractive stretches. South from Wabasso small wooded islands suddenly crowd the narrowing river and create a maze through which the ICW channel twists and turns. This is a good place to spot manatees and other wildlife. Many islands here are bird rookeries.

> The Environmental Learning Center at Mile 943.4 is a 64-acre habitat for birds, fish, crustaceans and mammals of many kinds. Museum exhibits include a 145-gallon touch tank, several aquariums and hands-on activities. They also have 2 miles of elevated boardwalk and nature trails. Note the campus is a "no pet zone."

Vero Beach is a major boating center and stopover with all the amenities a cruiser would ever need. Read more at "Goin' Ashore: Vero Beach, FL" in this chapter.

NAVIGATION: Use NOAA Chart 11472. The dredged ICW channel runs straight for 6 miles to Wabasso. Be aware that numerous dangerous shoals flank the channel's edge. Observe the closely spaced markers through this section.

At Mile 938 near red daybeacon "66B" be aware of shoaling into the east side of the ICW that extends out to mid-channel from a small spoils island. Mean low water depths as low as 4 feet have been reported on the east side of the channel.

North Atlantic Ocean

Grand Harbor Marina
Daybeacon 1

Stingaree Point

Indian River

Indian River

Mc Cullers Cove

Indian River (South
Section) Daybeacon 125

McCullers Cove

Obstn

Gifford Cut

Indian River Gifford Cut

South Harbor Drive

South Harbor Drive

45th Street

Bethel Creek Drive

Sunset Drive

Indian River

Bethel Creek

Live Oak Road

Conn Way

Conn Way

Eugenia Road

37th Place

10th Court

Indian River Drive East

Phoenix Palm Drive

Obstn

Vero Beach Channel
Turning Basin
Daybeacon 7

Vossinbury Creek

Banyan Road

Acacia Road

33rd Street

Vero Marine Center

GOIN' ASHORE

VERO BEACH, FL

Vero Beach is a favorite with cruisers. Many who plan to leave, never do; hence the nickname "Velcro Beach." This affluent resort community is known for its immaculate ocean and riverfront amenities. The city's excellent free bus system, the GoLine (772-569-0903), is convenient for boaters making Vero a perfect stop to get off the boat and get things done.

SERVICES

1. Cleveland Clinic Indian River Hospital
1000 36th St. (772-567-4311)

2. Divine Animal Hospital
654 21st St. (772-299-3665)

3. Vero Beach Post Office
3320 Cardinal Dr. (772-231-4070)

4. Vero Beach Veterinary Hospital
498 22nd Place (772-562-0200)

ATTRACTIONS

5. Riverside Theater
Performing arts campus with live theater, children's programs and lectures (3250 Riverside Park, 772-231-6990).

6. Vero Beach Museum of Art
American and international art collections and programs in art education (3001 Riverside Park Dr., 772-231-0707).

SHOPPING

7. Publix Super Market
Supermarket chain with grcoeries, deli and bakery at 415 21st St. (772-562-0391).

8. The Fresh Market
Upscale grocery store with local produce, prepared eats, wine and more at 526A 21st St. (772-794-2216).

9. Ocseola Home Care Pharmacy
Medicines and medical supplies at 777 37th St. #C100 (772-567-5297).

10. West Marine
Chain specializing in boating accessories and parts, plus apparel and fishing supplies at 474 21st St. (772-562-2166).

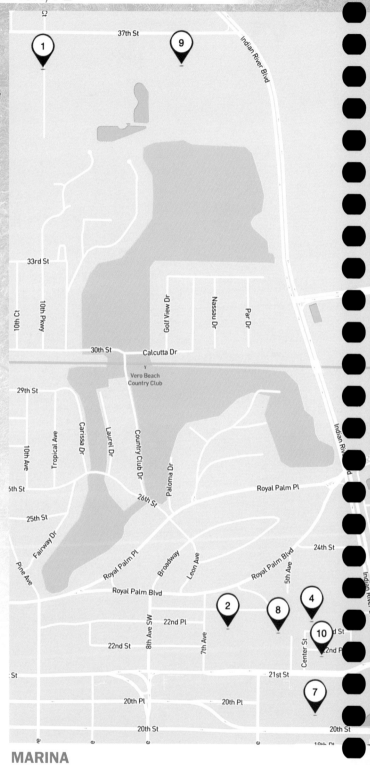

MARINA

11. Vero Beach City Marina
3611 Rio Vista Blvd. (772-231-2819)

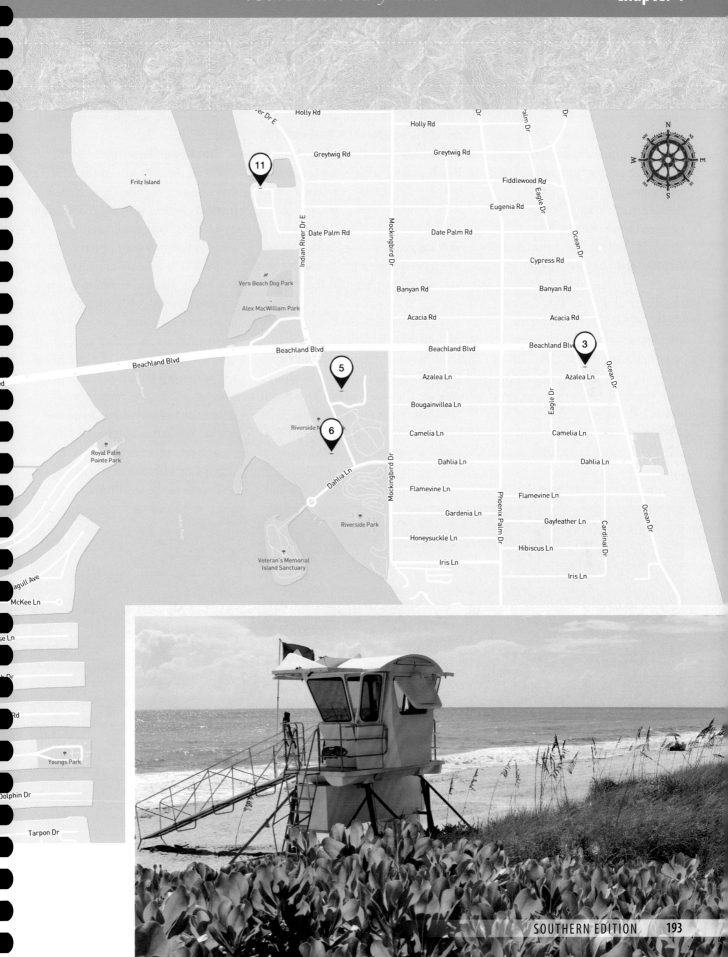

The high-rise **Wabasso Bridge** crosses the ICW at Mile 943.3. The bridge has a charted 65-foot fixed vertical clearance; however, a 64-foot vertical clearance has been observed on the tide boards.

Observe markers carefully and do not cut corners through this tight and winding stretch; dangerous shoals are immediately outside the marked channel. There is sporadic shoaling through this entire section. At Mile 944.6 be alert for green can "91" marking the end of a shoal extending from the adjacent spoils island. There is additional shoaling into the channel between red daybeacons "128" and "130" at Mile 950. Red daybeacon "128A" has been placed to help guide mariners through this area; keep to the center. (Note that red daybeacon "108" shown on the NOAA chart has been replaced with a red nun.)

After weaving past some sizable islands Vero Beach appears at Mile 952. This is a boating center and favorite cruiser stopover with a variety of facilities lining both sides of the Indian River above and below the high-rise **Merrill P. Barber (SR 60) Bridge** (also known as the Vero Beach Bridge). This is the beginning of the more densely populated areas along Florida's East Coast and boat traffic increases accordingly. Keep well inside the marked channel when passing through the bridge and maintain a firm hand on the helm, as winds and current can be strong here.

Depths outside the channel are extremely shallow through this entire stretch to the high-rise **Alma Lee Loy (SR 656/17th Street) Bridge** crossing the south end of Vero Beach. Shoaling inside the ICW channel extends from flashing green "139" to red daybeacon "142" and again from green daybeacon "149" to flashing green "153" reducing water

depths to 8 or 10 feet MLW in spots along the edges. Watch the depth sounder and stay in the middle of the channel to avoid shallow water and the spoil banks outside the channel through these segments.

Dockage/Moorings: At Mile 948.5 on the west side of the ICW and north of Vero Beach, a charted, marked channel with observed depths of 6 foot MLW at the centerline leads to the docks of Loggerhead Marina–Vero Beach Marina, located in a pretty planned community with condominiums, golf, tennis and handsome waterfront homes. The marina can accommodate transients (including catamarans) up to 120 feet with a 6.5-foot dockside depths. There is a shopping center about 1 mile away for provisioning and the marina has loaner bikes available.

The entrance channel to Vero Beach City Marina exits the ICW just north of the Merrill P. Barber

ICW

Indian River

(SR 60) Bridge. Markers to the east lead up the old ICW route past a city park to the marina. Call ahead for approach directions and depths. The marina is situated in a park-like setting and is protected from ICW wakes with transient dockage and free pump-out boat service (twice weekly). Located just south of the marina is a large dog park where your pet can get ashore and stretch its legs. There is also a free shuttle to town and to the beach district, both only 1 mile away. From town you can access the city's free public transit system GoLine (www.golineirt.com), making Vero Beach an excellent provisioning and repair stop for cruisers.

Inexpensive and well-maintained city-owned moorings are available above and below the Vero Beach City Marina. These moorings are very popular and it can get quite crowded in the busy season. Expect to raft up. Moorings are assigned by the dockmaster of the municipal marina (reservations recommended). Be aware that even if moorings are reserved boaters may still be expected to share them; boats traveling together are encouraged to make arrangements to raft together. Otherwise, the first boat at a mooring is asked to put out fenders and accept whatever raft is assigned. It is well protected in this area and rafting is rarely a problem. Crews of moored boats enjoy all the marina amenities including showers, a lounge, trash disposal and use of the dinghy dock.

Anchorage: Vessels have been observed anchored in a small pocket between the Wabasso Bridge and the Environmental Learning Center to the west of the ICW at Mile 943.4 with 10- to 12-foot MLW depths. Beware of charted underwater cables close to the bridge. Dinghy dockage is available at the Environmental Learning Center dock or at a small beach to the north. Depth at the dock is approximately 5 feet MLW. These are public docks but you must stay clear of the center's pontoon boat, which operates inside the "T" on both sides.

Shoal-draft boats have been observed at anchor behind the spoils island (charted as Hole in the Wall Island) near Mile 946.4, south of Pine Island. The entrance is from the south between the island and flashing red "112." Enter from the south and proceed in a northwesterly direction to anchor between the spoils island and Hole in the Wall Island. This anchorage provides some protection from ICW wakes.

> You can dinghy ashore but beware the live oysters that may cut your inflatable and your dog's feet! This may be your last secluded anchorage when southbound.

Most of the areas outside the ICW channel and near the mangrove islands above and below Vero Beach are shallow. Boats can anchor between the little islands but need to stay clear of the moorings and watch for shoals, which can be difficult in this area. Anchored boats are allowed to use the facilities at Vero Beach City Marina but must register at the office and pay a fee on a daily basis.

■ NEXT STOP

Boaters proceeding south will next encounter Fort Pierce. It has a number of marine facilities and its deep ocean inlet provides access to run outside to points south.

Mile 954-Mile 988

TO THE CROSSROADS

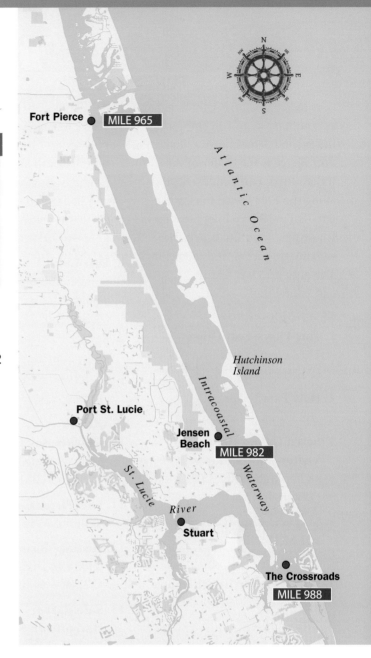

NO WAKE ZONE

No Wake Zones, Idle Speed Zones and various Speed Limit restrictions are in effect throughout the waterways included in this chapter. Exercise diligence in knowing the regulations by observing signs and other markers. Enforcement is always present. As always, be courteous to other vessels and avoid manatees and other marine life.

Some of the spoils islands scattered along this stretch are blanketed in the spring by nesting pelicans, cormorants, herons and egrets. Enjoy watching them but do not disturb their nests. In winter the stretch from the Merrill P. Barber (SR 60) Bridge for the 1.3 miles south to the Alma Lee Loy (SR-656, 17th Street) Bridge becomes a protected zone for manatees. They like the warm water discharged by the power plant on the west bank just before the Alma Lee Loy Bridge. Watch for the plant's three stacks.

Also keep a lookout for manatees farther south at the Peter B. Cobb Memorial (SR A1A) Bridge, which is another favorite lounging area for the gentle creatures. If staying in Fort Pierce you may also find manatees visiting the docks and walkways of the Fort Pierce City Marina.

Vero Beach to Fort Pierce Inlet–ICW Mile 954 to Mile 965

NAVIGATION: Use NOAA Chart 11472. South of Vero Beach the Indian River widens and the dredged ICW channel begins to straighten out for the 13 miles to Fort Pierce. The river's expanded width is deceptive; the actual navigable channel remains narrow. The project depth along this stretch is 12 feet MLW but the actual controlling depth is 8 feet MLW or less. Just beyond the edges of the marked channel depths in many places are 2 feet or less MLW. The tidal range on the Indian River at Vero Beach is 1 foot. Another factor is that with the river's increased width there is also increased fetch in crosswinds, which can produce some chop. Take care to stay in the channel through this section by occasionally looking behind to make sure you are maintaining course alignment.

GOIN' ASHORE

FORT PIERCE, FL

Fort Pierce was originally founded as a military supply depot during the Second Seminole War. Today Fort Pierce is the center of the Indian River citrus industry. Just along the Fort Pierce Inlet north jetty is Fort Pierce Inlet State Park, featuring a beautiful beach with swimming, surfing and picnicking. The park also has hiking and biking trails.

SERVICES

1. Fort Pierce Post Office
1717 Orange Ave.
(772-460-0835).

2. Holy Family Vet
709 US 1 (772-242-8320).

3. Seven Gables House/ Visitor Information
482 N. Indian River Dr.
(772-468-9152).

4. St. Lucie County Library
101 Melody Ln.
(772-462-1615).

5. Whole Family Health Center
725 US 1 (772-468-9900).

ATTRACTIONS

6. Manatee Observations and Education Center
Hands-on exhibits and boat tours to explore manatees, dolphins, pelicans and terns. The on-site Vanishing Mermaid Gift Shop is worth a look (480 N. Indian River Dr., 772-429-6266).

SHOPPING

7. CVS Pharmacy
Full-service drugstore chain selling health and beauty products plus some groceries and household items at 1891 Old US Hwy. 1 (772-461-7049).

8. East Coast Lumber & Supply
Lumber and building materials along with hardware and tools (308 Ave. A, 772-461-5950).

9. Publix
Full-service chain grocery store at 1851 N. US Hwy 1 (772-595-5321).

MARINAS

10. Cracker Boy Boat Works
1602 N. 2nd St.
(772-465-7031).

11. Fort Pierce City Marina
1 Marina Way (772-464-1245).

12. Heritage Boat Yard
2350 Old Dixie Hwy.
(772-464-5720).

13. Safe Harbor Harbortown Marina
1936 Harbortown Dr.
(772-466-7300).

14. Taylor Creek Marina
1600 N. 2nd St.
(772-465-2663).

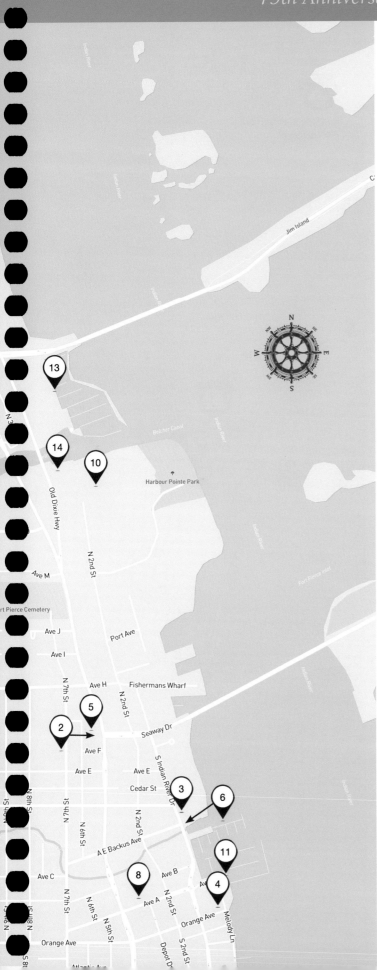

At Mile 951.9 you will pass under the high rise **Merrill P. Barber (SR 60) Bridge** (fixed 65-foot vertical clearance), which is also known as the Vero Beach Bridge. A little more than 1 mile south is another high rise bridge, the **Alma Lee Loy (SR-656/17th Street) Bridge** with a 65-foot fixed vertical clearance. The warm discharge of the power plant to the west along this segment attracts manatees and you must maintain a posted slow speed from November 15 through April 30.

Between the Merrill P. Barber (SR 60) Bridge and the Alma Lee Loy (SR-656/17th Street) Bridge you may see some shoals awash close to the channel. There is also shoaling inside the channel between flashing green "139" and red daybeacon "142" and again from green daybeacon "149" to flashing green "153," reducing water depths in spots near the edges to 8 feet MLW. Watch the depth sounder and stay in the middle of the channel to avoid shallow water and the spoils banks outside the channel through this area.

⚠️

From green daybeacon "155" (Mile 955.5) to green daybeacon "173" (Mile 961), the Manatee Speed Zone varies from seasonal to year-round. Observe the posted speeds through each of these zones. This is a good place to slow down anyway as shoaling has been observed in spots from flashing green "157" to green daybeacon "165" with depths of less than 8 feet MLW.

You will pass through a busy section starting with the **SR A1A North Causeway (Banty Saunders) Bridge** with 26-foot closed vertical clearance at Mile 964.8. The restricted bridge only opens on signal on the hour and half hour. This is sometimes referred to as North Pierce Bridge. Watch for current and boat traffic here. This can be an awkward place to wait for an opening. Note depths are less than charted northeast of the bridge span despite the marked, small-boat channel to the east.

South of the entrance to Taylor Creek at Mile 965.1 the ICW intersects the Fort Pierce Inlet at Mile 965.6. Shoaling has been reported along the eastern edge of the channel from the SR A1A North Causeway (Banty Saunders) Bridge to the inlet and, in particular, for the segment from red nun "184" to red daybeacon "186."

Just south of the intersection with the Fort Pierce Inlet at Mile 965.8 is the high-level **Peter B. Cobb Memorial (SR A1A) Bridge**, which is sometimes referred to as the

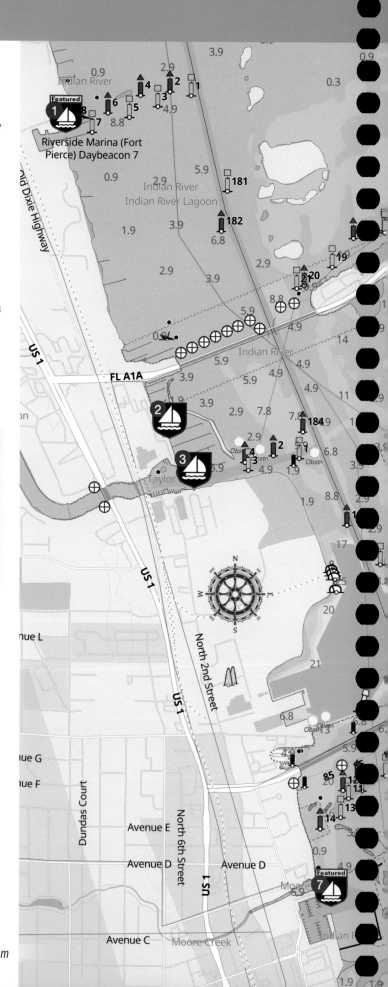

Riverside Marina (Fort Pierce) Daybeacon 7

Indian River, FL

FORT PIERCE AREA

	Phone	Largest Vessel	VHF	Total Slips	Approach/ Dockside Depth	Floating Docks	Gas/ Diesel	Repairs/ Haulout	Min/Max Amps	Pump-Out Station
1. Heritage Boat Yard & Marina (WiFi) MM 964.1	(772) 464-5720	105	16	70	6.0 / 6.0			RH	30 / 50	P
2. Safe Harbor Harbortown (WiFi) MM 965.0	(772) 466-7300	160	16	344	7.5 / 6.5	F	GD	RH	30 / 100	P
3. Cracker Boy Boat Works- Fort Pierce (WiFi) MM 965.1	(772) 465-7031		16		8.0 / 7.0			RH		
4. Dockside Marina & Resort (WiFi)	(772) 201-5773	175	16	57	16.0 / 12.0				20 / 200+	P
5. Pelican Yacht Club (WiFi) ⊙ onSpot 1.0 mi. E of MM 965.6	(772) 464-1734	95	16	93	6.0 / 6.0		GD		30 / 50	P
6. Fort Pierce Inlet Marina 0.8 mi. E of MM 965.6	(772) 236-3675	90		39	12.0 / 12.0				30	P
7. Fort Pierce City Marina (WiFi) ⊙ onSpot MM 966.5	(772) 464-1245	140	16	247	7.6 / 8.0	F	GD		15 / 200+	P
8. Causeway Cove Marina & RV Park (WiFi) ⊙ onSpot MM 966.3	(772) 242-3552	60	16	198	5.6 / 6.0				30 / 50	P
9. Harbour Isle Marina (WiFi) ⊙ onSpot 0.8 mi. E of MM 966.2	(772) 461-9049	120	16	63	9.0 / 9.0	F			30 / 100	P

(WiFi) Wireless Internet Access ⊙ onSpot Dockside WiFi Facility
Visit www.waterwayguide.com for current rates, fuel prices, website addresses and other up-to-the-minute information.
(Information in the table is provided by the facilities.)

Scan here for more details:

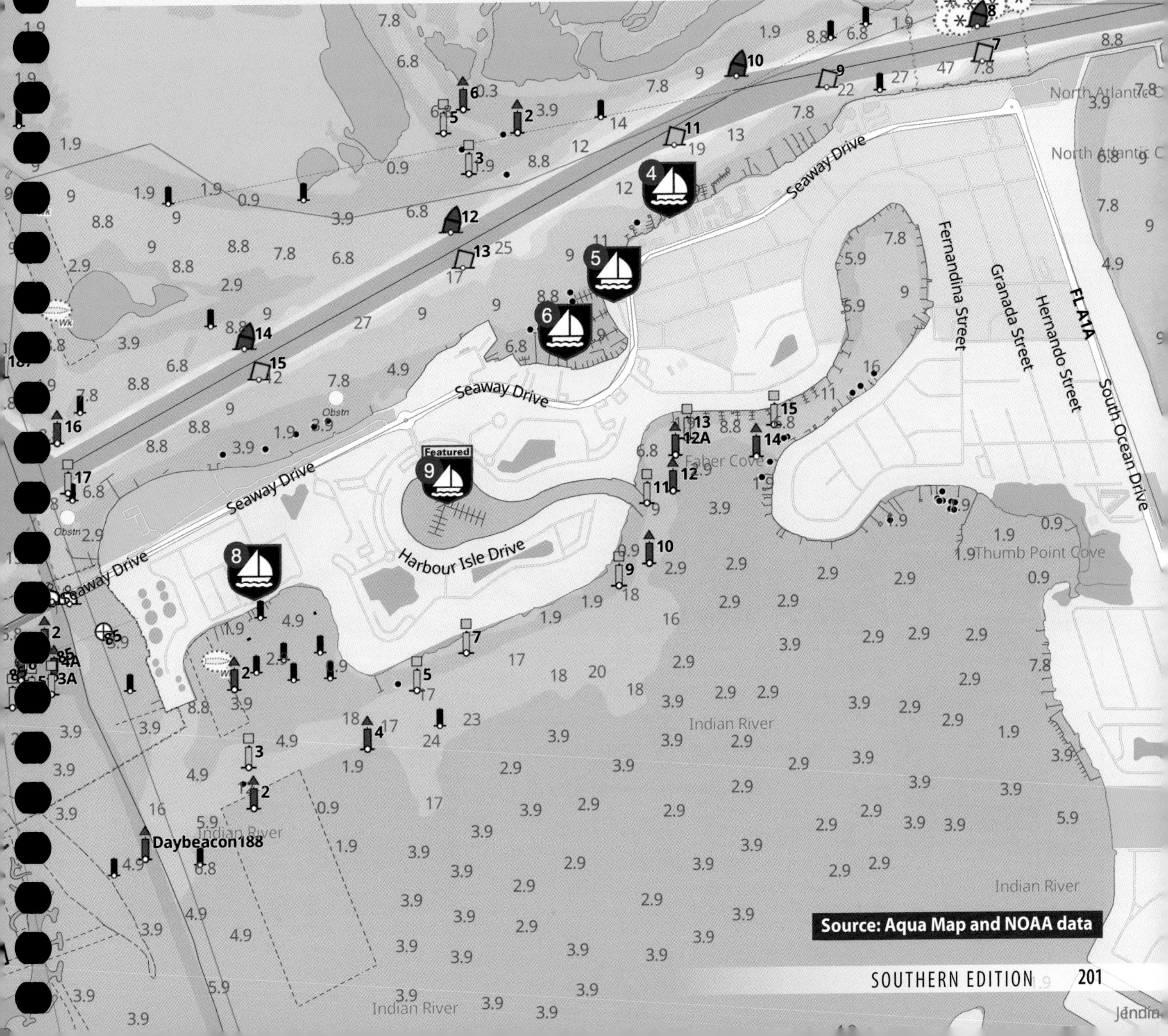

Source: Aqua Map and NOAA data

"South Bridge." Use caution and follow navigation aids closely in this area. Shoaling has been reported here on the west side of the ICW from just north of the bridge to the south limit of the turning basin.

Dockage: Heritage Boat Yard & Marina is just north of the Banty Saunders Bridge at Mile 964.1. Access is provided via a well-marked channel west from the ICW with reported 6-foot MLW depths. The marina has a large yard with a lift capable of hauling vessels with up to a 22-foot beam and offers many services (including DIY) as well as limited transient dockage. Call ahead to check slip availability. The remarkably well-stocked Marine Connection Liquidators (772-465-6460) is just a short walk north.

Immediately south of the Banty Saunders Bridge, a well-marked channel to the west leads to Taylor Creek where several facilities are located. The entrance channel holds 8 to 9 feet MLW but shoaling is reported nearby. Verify depths when calling for reservations.

The well-regarded Safe Harbor Harbortown is a large full-service marina and boatyard with a tropical atmosphere. The island-themed Harbor Cove Bar & Grill (772-429-5303) is located here as is Sunnyland Canvas (772-489-4850), specializing in marine canvas and upholstery. On the opposite (south) shore of Taylor Creek is Cracker Boy Boat Works-Fort Pierce with a DIY yard or you can let them fill your maintenance and service needs.

Anchorage: There is an anchorage convenient to Fort Pierce between the Banty Saunders Bridge and the Peter B. Cobb Memorial (SR A1A) Bridge at Mile 964.8. Turn westward just north of red nun "184" to find slightly less than the charted 8 feet MLW off Safe Harbor Harbortown. Watch for strong currents! Depths shallow near the bascule bridge where there is a charted Cable Area. From here you can dinghy to the marina and if you pay for dinghy dockage the fee may be applied towards marina services or ice.

Fort Pierce Inlet–ICW Mile 965

Fort Pierce Inlet is the only break in the barrier islands between the Sebastian Inlet and the St. Lucie Inlet. The 22-mile long Hutchinson Island lies to the south and 28-mile long Orchid Island (also known as North Hutchinson Island) lies to the north. These great distances help create strong tidal currents is the inlet. It is best to pass through with the tide or at slack tide as standing waves are possible.

NAVIGATION: Use NOAA Chart 11472. Fort Pierce Inlet is wide and deep with two stone jetties, an inner channel (30-foot MLW depths) and a turning basin (28-foot MLW depths). This is a big ship inlet and one of the best and easiest on Florida's east coast. The channel is marked with ranges and buoys (both lighted and unlighted). Tidal currents in the inlet are strong averaging 3 to 4 knots.

Where the inlet channel crosses the ICW down to the Peter B. Cobb Memorial (SR A1A) Bridge (Mile 965.8), strong crosscurrents exist with a set to the south on the flood and to the north on the ebb. Currents are strongest through the narrow neck of the channel inside the barrier islands near flashing green buoy "9." In strong east winds swells can create rough conditions inside the jetties (especially on ebb tides).

In the Fort Pierce Inlet entrance channel there is an area of shallow shoals along the north jetty near flashing red buoy "8." These shoals are a popular weekend hangout for local boaters and fishermen. Be aware of traffic in this area.

Many cruisers make Fort Pierce Inlet their exit or entry point for an outside run. It's a 65-nm north run to Cape Canaveral Inlet and 45-nm south run to Lake Worth Inlet. The proximity of the Gulf Stream to this safe, deep inlet makes it an attractive area for deep-sea fishing.

Fort Pierce is also a popular inlet when making landfall returning from West End Point on Grand Bahama Island. (The Gulf Stream gives a boost to cruisers heading north.) To read more about the Fort Pierce area see "Goin' Ashore: Fort Pierce, FL" in this chapter.

Dockage: Several dockage options line the south shore of Fort Pierce Inlet. Near green buoy "11" is Dockside Marina & Resort with ample deep-water slips. You have to approach into the current and sailboats are tied to the end of the piers. These are fixed docks and a tidal difference of 3 feet can make it a bit of a climb on low tide.

In the small basin near green buoy "13" (Faber Point) are Pelican Yacht Club and Fort Pierce Inlet Marina. Both have some transient space and primarily cater to large sportfishing vessels.

South of the Peter B. Cobb Memorial (SR A1A) Bridge at ICW Mile 966.5 (west shore) is the popular Fort Pierce City Marina with ample transient space on floating docks for vessels to 150 feet. To approach the marina turn west into the well-marked, dredged entry channel just south of the high-rise bridge. (Note the entry channel has been relocated from where it appears on older charts.) Contact the marina on VHF Channel 16 for information and docking and fueling instructions. Large yachts use this facility so keep

the radio on to check for Sécurité warnings. The channel is narrow and cross-currents can be significant. Four manmade rock islands protect the basin from ocean surge and wakes.

A privately marked channel east of red daybeacon "188" leads to additional marinas along the south shore of Causeway Island. This channel is initially shallow at the entry where the chart shows 7- to 8-foot MLW depths but it quickly deepens. The first facility is Causeway Cove Marina & RV Park with slips on fixed docks for boats up to 60 feet.

Further east along this channel in a protected basin is Harbour Isle Marina at Hutchinson Island, which has floating slips (with full finger piers) surrounded by luxury condos and resort amenities include a pool, fitness center and tennis courts.

Anchorage: There are several anchoring options off Causeway Island's south shore. These are accessed using the same privately marked channel that serves the marinas here. One is south of the marked channel just east of red daybeacon "4" and another is just south of green daybeacon "9." Both anchorages offer at least 6 feet MLW with excellent holding and protection from northwest to east winds.

If these anchorages are crowded, sound around the edges carefully with the dinghy as the boundary of deep water to the south is different than shown on the chart. Anchored boats may use the Fort Pierce City Marina dinghy dock, which is long and roomy.

For a peaceful anchorage with excellent all-round wind protection shoal-draft boats can proceed into beautiful Faber Cove with room for 3 to 4 boats. There is no place to land

Harbour Isle Marina

Fort Pierce City Marina

a dinghy and shore access is not permitted due to the private homes surrounding the cove. Going in proceed with caution as you round green "13" where you will only have 5 to 6 feet MLW. Note that charted green daybeacon "15" has been removed to make room for new docks; swing wide here towards red daybeacon "14" to avoid shoaling to the north.

Fort Pierce to St. Lucie Inlet–ICW Mile 965 to Mile 988

Below Fort Pierce the Indian River is deceptively wide. For the most part the ICW follows a deep, natural channel but the navigable channel narrows in many sections where you will see birds walking atop the shoals just outside of the dredged channel. Keep markers lined up ahead and astern through these narrow sections.This is also a good stretch to keep a watch out for wildlife. You may see rays, dolphin and sea turtles along this section of the Indian River.

NAVIGATION: Use NOAA Chart 11472. At Mile 966.3 there is an active shoaling area that is periodically dredged but even when dredged, the red side of the channel is often shallow. Shoaling to 7.5 feet MLW has been observed in the channel along this stretch. Immediately after leaving Fort Pierce southward expect shoaling into the channel on the red side between red daybeacons "188" and "190." Keep to the green side of the channel for deeper water.

The natural channel opens up south of green daybeacon "191" allowing some additional maneuvering space but watch for a series spoils shoals to the east of the ICW that run the entire length of Hutchinson Island. Watch again for shoaling south from red daybeacon "198" to the area past the overhead power cables for the St. Lucie Power Plant, which stands on Herman Bay Point at Big Mud Creek (90-foot authorized overhead clearance at the main channel) just north of red daybeacon "206."

Exercise particular care between green daybeacons "203" and "205" at about Mile 973.5, where private markers to Big Mud Creek head off to the east. (Do not mistake private green daybeacon "1" located in shallow water up Big Mud Creek for an ICW marker.) Safer water may be found to the west here.

Farther south at Mile 979 lies the residential development and marina at Nettles Island. Expect a depth of 5 to 6 feet MLW at the edges of the ICW along the shallow, unmarked spoils banks.

The channel appears to open up as you approach the high-rise **Jensen Beach Causeway (Frank A.**

Heritage Boat
Yard & Marina

Fort Pierce Inlet

Wacha/SR 707A) Bridge at Mile 981.4 but shoaling is a chronic problem heading south from the bridge to past red daybeacon "220." South of the high-rise **Ernest Lyons (SR A1A) Bridge** at Mile 984.9 there is dangerous shoaling on either side of the channel from north of red daybeacon "228" to red daybeacon "230." Stay in the middle for 7 feet MLW.

> This area is popular with windsurfers and small powerboats, so best to pay attention for traffic from here to The Crossroads.

Dockage/Moorings: Nettles Island Marina is located near the southeast corner of Nettles Island. An access channel carrying 8 to 10 feet MLW leads east from the ICW at Mile 979.2 between flashing red "214" and green daybeacon "215." The channel's start is marked by private green daybeacon "1." (Note some of these private markers are difficult to see.) There is a restaurant, grocery store, boutique and more in this gated community. The dockmaster doesn't always monitor the VHF so call ahead (772-229-2811).

Around the Jensen Beach Causeway Bridge, the first of the the moorings and waterfront facilities of Stuart start to appear. Sun Dance Marine Jensen Beach/Stuart on the mainland (Mile 982.2) can be approached from the body of deeper water extending south from the bridge. It is

best to pass well south of red daybeacon "220" to avoid shoaling before turning for the marina. Facilities include floating docks and some repairs.

Directly to the south at Mile 982.8 a marked channel (8 feet MLW reported) exits the ICW west from red daybeacon "222" and leads to the Four Fish Inn & Marina with transient slips in a park-like setting. On-site accommodations are available should you choose to get off the boat for a night.

Anchorage: Between the mainland and the ICW, you will find good anchorages north and south of the Jensen Beach Causeway Bridge. Pick your spot to maximize wind

Indian River, FL

HUTCHINSON ISLAND		Largest Vessel	VHF	Total Slips	Approach/ Dockside Depth	Floating Docks	Gas/ Diesel	Repairs/ Haulout	Min/Max Amps	Pump-Out Station
1. Nettles Island Marina (WiFi) MM 979.5	(772) 229-2811	115	16	65	7.0 / 10.0		G	RH	30 / 100	P
JENSEN BEACH										
2. Jensen Beach Mooring Field (WiFi)	**(772) 320-3184**				/	F				P
3. Sun Dance Marine Jensen Beach/Stuart MM 982.2	(772) 675-1913	45	16	10	8.0 / 4.0		G	RH	30	
4. Four Fish Inn & Marina MM 982.8	(772) 334-0936	90	16	35	8.0 / 6.0	F	GD	RH	30 / 50	P
5. Hutchinson Island Marriott Beach Resort & Marina (WiFi) MM 985.0	(772) 225-3700	125	16	77	7.0 / 6.0		GD		30 / 50	P

(WiFi) Wireless Internet Access (onSpot) Dockside WiFi Facility
Visit www.waterwayguide.com for current rates, fuel prices, website addresses and other up-to-the-minute information. (Information in the table is provided by the facilities.)

Scan here for more details:

protection but avoid the charted pipeline and cable areas. The tidal range here is only 1 foot, although currents can be significant. Expect wakes. The area of deep water north of the bridge is fairly small as depths are less than charted. The anchorage to the south is larger with depths of 7 feet MLW but it is often crowded with boats, some of which are permanent residents. To avoid shoals blocking the top of the south anchorage you must enter from a point midway between red daybeacon "220" and green daybeacon "221" and proceed west and then north towards the causeway.

There are dinghy landing options on both the south and north sides of the Jensen Beach Causeway Bridge. Shore access is also available at the thatched-roof Conchy Joe's Seafood Restaurant (772-334-1130), which is just north of the bridge. Dining patrons in dinghies and boats drawing less than 2 feet are welcome at their dinghy dock but call ahead to check availability. Follow the shallow approach channel carefully.

There are additional anchorages outside the charted Cable Areas that follow alongside the Ernest Lyons Bridge. You can anchor in 6 feet MLW north or south of the east causeway. Ease your way in as depths may be less than charted. To approach the south anchorage pass through the first pair of private channel markers and exit south to anchor.

Side Trip: Hutchinson Island

Hutchinson Island is a 22-mile long barrier island protecting the ICW between the Fort Pierce Inlet and the St. Lucie Inlet. Visitors from the mainland can reach Hutchinson Island and its gorgeous beaches via three long causeways. At the west end of the Jensen Beach Causeway a park with a large pier has restrooms, a picnic area and a playground. Currents at the north end of the island will be more affected by the Fort Pierce Inlet tides and at the south end by the St. Lucie Inlet tides.

Dockage: Just southeast of the high-rise Ernest Lyons Bridge, Hutchinson Island Marriott Beach Resort & Marina offers short and long-term transient dockage with resort amenities. Visiting boaters may visit the laundry, three pools, tennis courts, golf course, restaurant and two tiki bars. It is a short dinghy ride to the beach access on Indian River where coral surrounds an area that is great for swimming or snorkeling. Access is through a public access dock to the southeast of the marina. It is just a 1-mile walk to the ocean beach and 2 miles to St. Lucie Inlet, making this a convenient jumping off spot for a trip to the Bahamas.

The Crossroads—ICW Mile 988

At Mile 988 the ICW intersects the St. Lucie River. To the east, the St. Lucie Inlet opens into the Atlantic Ocean and to the west, the Okeechobee Waterway follows St. Lucie River upstream. Locally this intersection is known as "The Crossroads." This point defines Mile Zero on the Okeechobee Waterway's route to Florida's Gulf Coast. Here mariners have a choice of three routes:

1. Follow the ICW south to the resort areas on Florida's southeast coast and the Florida Keys.

2. Follow the St. Lucie Inlet to the Atlantic Ocean for crossing to the Bahamas (or to take "outside" routes north or south in the Gulf Stream).

3. Travel upstream along the St. Lucie River, down the South Fork, traverse the Okeechobee Waterway across Lake Okeechobee and on to Fort Myers and Florida's Gulf Coast.

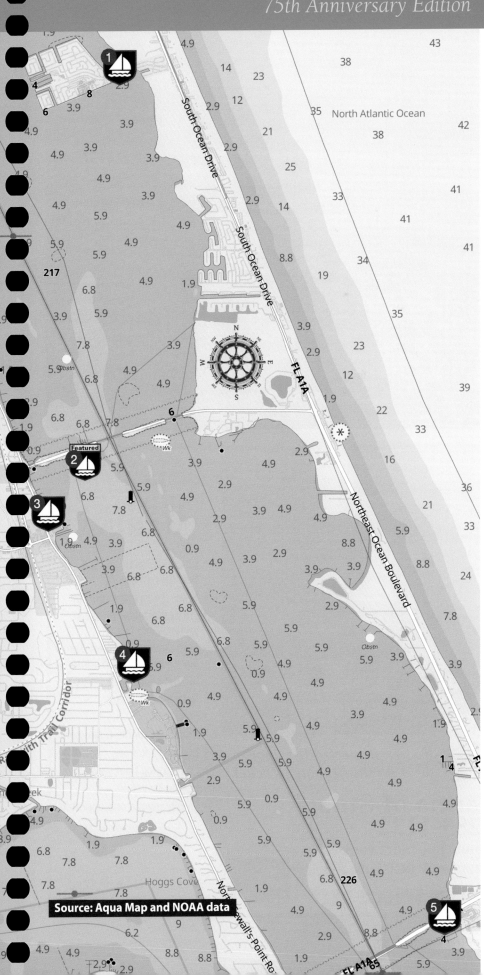

Source: Aqua Map and NOAA data

Note that you can only navigate the Okeechobee Waterway if your draft is shallow enough to do so and you have an airdraft of less than 49 feet. This is detailed in the "Side Trip on the Okeechobee" chapter.

NAVIGATION: Use NOAA Chart 11472 (inset) or NOAA Chart 11428 (inset). Boaters on the ICW may experience strong crosscurrents at the St. Lucie River. The set depends on tidal phase–westerly on flood or easterly on ebb. Also allow for the crosscurrents when making a turn at The Crossroads. Pay close attention to boat traffic in this area. You will most likely encounter fast-moving fishing boats heading to and from the St. Lucie Inlet, particularly between Manatee Pocket and the ocean.

The 16-foot-high flashing red buoy "240" (ICW marker) at The Crossroads marks the beginning of the Okeechobee Waterway westward. The westbound channel is prone to shoaling here and its markers are often repositioned to indicate the deepest water. Consult The St. Lucie River section for details on this route.

Southbound ICW traffic should note that the marker numbering sequence resets here and continues with red markers to starboard (if southbound).

Look up the natural channel to the south for red daybeacon "2" and flashing green "3" located 0.25 miles south of red buoy "240" and split these markers to proceed south. You will find them past a white sign ("DANGER–SHOAL") on the west side of the ICW, which should be kept well to starboard when southbound.

St. Lucie Inlet

ICW

To Manatee Pocket

St. Lucie River

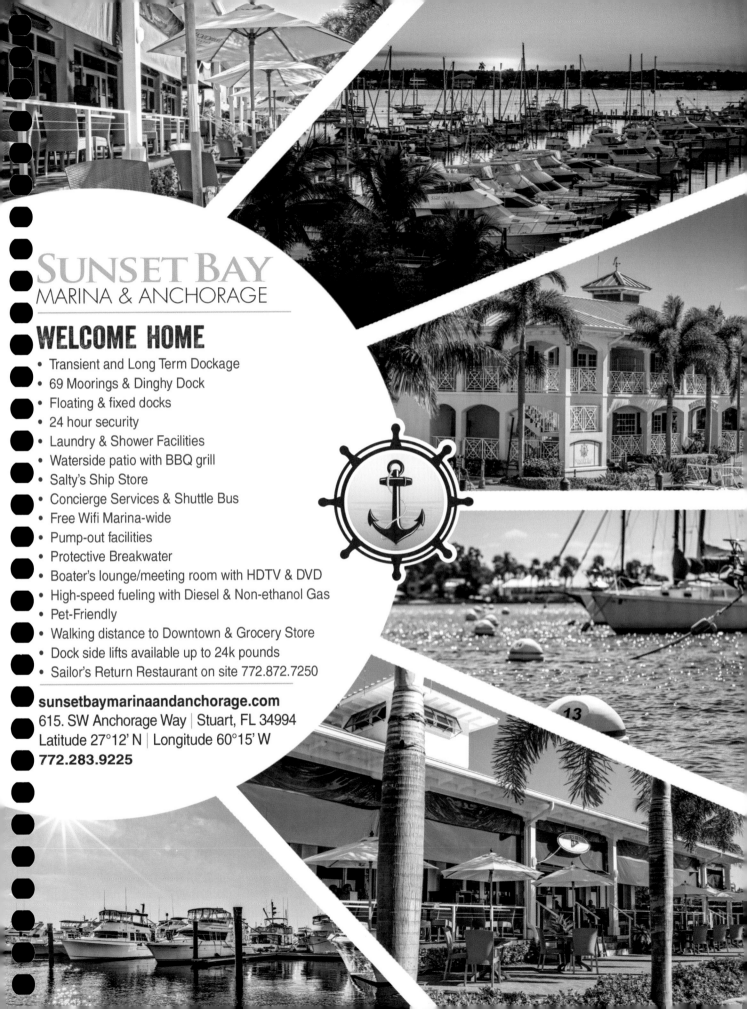

SUNSET BAY
MARINA & ANCHORAGE

WELCOME HOME

- Transient and Long Term Dockage
- 69 Moorings & Dinghy Dock
- Floating & fixed docks
- 24 hour security
- Laundry & Shower Facilities
- Waterside patio with BBQ grill
- Salty's Ship Store
- Concierge Services & Shuttle Bus
- Free Wifi Marina-wide
- Pump-out facilities
- Protective Breakwater
- Boater's lounge/meeting room with HDTV & DVD
- High-speed fueling with Diesel & Non-ethanol Gas
- Pet-Friendly
- Walking distance to Downtown & Grocery Store
- Dock side lifts available up to 24k pounds
- Sailor's Return Restaurant on site 772.872.7250

sunsetbaymarinaandanchorage.com
615. SW Anchorage Way | Stuart, FL 34994
Latitude 27°12' N | Longitude 60°15' W
772.283.9225

Manatee Pocket, FL

MANATEE POCKET AREA		Largest Vessel	VHF	Total Slips	Approach/ Dockside Depth	Floating Docks	Gas/ Diesel	Repairs/ Haulout	Min/Max Amps	Pump-Out Station
1. Whiticar Boat Works Inc. W of MM 987.8	(772) 287-2883	70	9	15	6.0 / 6.0		D	RH	15 / 50	
2. Sailfish Marina of Stuart (WiFi) onSpot 0.8 mi. W of MM 987.8	(772) 283-1122	85	16	55	12.0 / 10.0		GD	RH	30 / 100	
3. Mariner Cay Marina (WiFi) 1.1 mi. W of MM 987.8	(772) 287-2900	80	16	48	6.0 / 6.0		GD		30 / 50	P
4. Pirate's Cove Resort & Marina (WiFi) 1.8 mi. W of MM 987.8	(772) 287-2500	100	68	50	7.0 / 6.0		GD		30 / 100	P
5. Hinckley Yacht Services Stuart (WiFi) onSpot MM 989.0	(772) 287-0923	115	16	80	10.0 / 6.5	F	GD	RH	30 / 100	P
6. Stuart Corinthian Yacht Club MM 989.0	(772) 221-1900	45	16	25	8.0 / 5.0				50	
7. A & J Boat Works 2.2 mi. E of MM 987.8	(772) 286-5339	60		13	/ 6.0	F		RH	30 / 50	
8. Manatee Marina (WiFi) 2.2 mi. E of MM 987.8	(772) 283-6714	53		40	7.0 / 5.0		GD	RH	30 / 50	
9. Port Salerno Marine	(772) 223-5022		16	19	6.0 / 6.0			H	30 / 50	

(WiFi) Wireless Internet Access   onSpot Dockside WiFi Facility
Visit www.waterwayguide.com for current rates, fuel prices, website addresses and other up-to-the-minute information.
(Information in the table is provided by the facilities.)

Scan here for more details:

Mind your set as you pass through The Crossroads to maintain a straight course. This route picks up in the next chapter. Shoaling is less of a problem for mariners turning into the St. Lucie Inlet towards the Atlantic. To find the start of this channel look for green daybeacon "17."

Whichever route you take through The Crossroads expect heavy boat traffic, particularly along the St. Lucie River. Channels are narrow and many boats pass closely at high speed. This is not an area known for boater etiquette.

St. Lucie Inlet–ICW Mile 988

NAVIGATION: Use NOAA Chart 11428 (inset) or 11472 (inset). St. Lucie Inlet is a fair-weather inlet that is primarily used by the local sport fishermen. The 2-mile run from the ICW to the ocean is subject to continuous shoaling, currents may be strong and markers may be off station. Most markers are unlit; therefore, nighttime navigation is not recommended. Use of this inlet is not advised without considerable local knowledge. Use of the Fort Pierce Inlet or Lake Worth (Palm Beach) Inlet is advised.

To find the start of this channel look for green daybeacon "17." The channel maintains reasonable depth to flashing green "9" where charting of the channel ends with a warning of "constant shifting conditions." St. Lucie Inlet is frequently dredged and markers are frequently moved to mark shifting shoals. We recommend you obtain local knowledge before using this inlet. Depths between the ocean inlet and the ICW typically vary from 7 to 20 feet MLW but may be less.

Martin County begins just north of the Jensen Beach Causeway. Zoning laws restrict most buildings to a maximum of four stories so local captains returning from the Bahamas are said to locate St. Lucie Inlet by merely aiming for the "valley" midway between the high rise buildings of St. Lucie County to the north and Palm Beach County to the south.

■ SIDE TRIP: THE ST. LUCIE RIVER

From its intersection with the Atlantic ICW at The Crossroads (Mile 0 of the Okeechobee Waterway) the channel heads initially westward and then curves northward starting at Okeechobee Mile 0.5 (near the opening to Manatee Pocket).

Aids to navigation are often relocated and additional markers established to indicate the best water in this area. Keep red markers to starboard when heading upstream. Take time to observe all aids and don't be surprised if their positions or sequence differ from what's on your chart. Tidal range is only about 1 foot here but currents can be strong. These weaken proceeding up the St. Lucie River. Expect heavy boat traffic until you are through Hell Gate.

Manatee Pocket

Manatee Pocket is about 0.6 miles from The Crossroads and comes up quickly in the busy channel. It is often visited by cruisers traveling north and south on the ICW. Considered an all-weather anchorage this is a delightful basin where you can usually find dockage in a lake-like

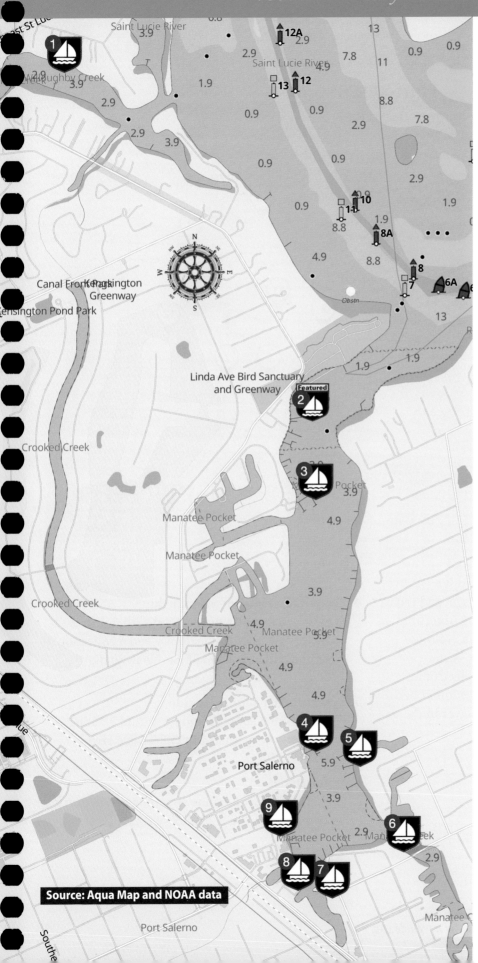

Source: Aqua Map and NOAA data

setting. Port Salerno, a small town at the head of Manatee Pocket, features several restaurants and also has a marine electronics store and grocery store. Manatee Pocket is also home to the Chapman School of Seamanship (www.chapman.org), which has courses and programs for recreational boaters and also offers vocational programs for careers in various maritime fields. See more on this salty port town at "Goin' Ashore: Port Salerno, FL" in this chapter.

NAVIGATION: Use NOAA Chart 11428 (inset) or NOAA Chart 11472 (inset). Heading west from The Crossroads toward Stuart and the Okeechobee Waterway flashing red buoy "2" and green can buoy "3" (located just southwest of flashing red "240") mark the channel entrance. Shoaling between 5 to 7 feet MLW has been observed over a bar between these two markers. Favor the green side of the channel to flashing green "7." There is a channel straight up the middle of Manatee Pocket approximately 100 feet wide with a depth of 10 to 12 feet MLW.

Be particularly alert for large wakes when traveling between The Crossroads area and the entrance to Manatee Pocket where the channel starts to deepen. This short but narrow stretch is often crowded with powerboats speeding to or from the ocean via the St. Lucie Inlet.

Dockage: The family-owned and -operated Sailfish Marina of Stuart is the first marina on the right upon entering Manatee Pocket and is the closest marina to the St. Lucie Inlet. This well-maintained facility offers transient dockage and a full-service boatyard. It is home to several businesses including a well-stocked bait and tackle shop, mobile yacht

GOIN' ASHORE
PORT SALERNO, FL

Founded in the 1920s, Port Salerno had its beginning as a commercial fishing village, and today the town still has a designated working waterfront dock area where commercial fishermen continue to work. Carpentry shops, prop shops, metal fabricators, fiberglass repairs, marine electronics and hardware, and canvas shops can be found here, making Port Salerno a major league player in the marine industry.

SERVICES

1. Port Salerno Animal Hospital
4515 SE Dixie Hwy. (772-286-3833)

2. Port Salerno Post Office
4755 SE Dixie Hwy. (772-463-8307)

3. Treasure Coast Hospital
3257 SE Salerno Rd. (772-249-5256)

SHOPPING

4. Chapman School of Seamanship
World-class boat training school with donated boats for sale, a maritime library and a collection of maritime artifacts (4343 SE St. Lucie Blvd., 772-283-8130).

5. Stuart Angler Bait & Tackle
Carries fishing supplies and ice within walking distance of the marinas (4695 SE Dixie Hwy., 772-288-1219).

6. Winn-Dixie
Grocery chain with online shopping and delivery at 3320 SE Salerno Rd. (772-283-2511).

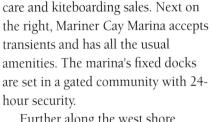

MARINAS

7. A&J Boatworks
4800 SE Anchor Ave.
(772-286-5339)

8. Hinkley Yacht Services Stuart
4550 SE Boatyard Dr.
(772-287-0923)

9. Manatee Marina
4905 SE Dixie Hwy.
(772-283-6714)

10. Pirates Cove Resort & Marina
4307 SE Bayview St.
(772-287-2500)

11. Port Salerno Marine
4715 SE Desoto Ave.
(772-223-5022)

12. Stuart Corinthian Yacht Club
4725 SE Capstan Ave.
(772-221-1900)

care and kiteboarding sales. Next on the right, Mariner Cay Marina accepts transients and has all the usual amenities. The marina's fixed docks are set in a gated community with 24-hour security.

Further along the west shore is Pirate's Cove Resort & Marina offering slips with resort amenities and engine repair services. On the opposite shore Hinckley Yacht Services Stuart offers just four reserved transient slips and specialize in repair services. They have on-site experts in painting, fiberglass, electronics, rigging, and canvas and upholstery. Call ahead for assistance docking.

At the split in the pocket is the friendly Stuart Corinthian Yacht Club (on the eastern branch), which accepts transients if space is available. A & J Boat Works and Port Salerno Marine (on the western shore) are repair/service yards and do not accept transients. Manatee Marina has a seawall for transients.

The full-service Whiticar Boat Works Inc. is located on the western shore on Willoughby Creek at Port Sewall (before Hell Gate). This is a "one stop shop" for service needs, parts and yacht sales. They will make room for you if you need them.

Anchorage: A 10-foot MLW channel is well marked to the south end of Manatee Pocket. Anchor in 5.5 to 6 feet MLW in the wide area between Mariner Cay and Pirates Cove Marina or in 5 feet MLW beyond Pirates Cove. You can tie up the dinghy at the small park dock south of Pirates Cove. Anchoring in Manatee Pocket is limited to 72 hours and the restriction is enforced. This can be a very crowded anchorage so be sure to have an alternate plan.

Stuart & the St. Lucie Canal

The City of Stuart, tucked back along the south shore of the St. Lucie River, is as well equipped as almost any port city on the Atlantic coast and supports a sizable winter boat colony. (See details at "Goin' Ashore: Stuart, FL" in this chapter. While the quaint city has some modern development, it retains an "Old Florida" feel and offers some respite from the high-rise development along the Florida coastline. Marine facilities and shore activities are a vital part of the community.

Beyond Stuart the Okeechobee Waterway follows the South Fork and then turns westward into the St. Lucie Canal and Lock and, ultimately, the Gulf of Mexico.

NAVIGATION: Use NOAA Chart 11428. Proceeding upstream on the St. Lucie River from the entrance to Manatee Pocket a close pack of makers line the channel on both sides as it gradually curves north towards the "Hell Gate" narrows (as noted on the NOAA chart). The shallowest spots are between red daybeacons "8" and "10." Turn wide around these marks.

Shoaling is continual through the curve to "Hell Gate," particularly on the red side, and navigation aids are regularly being added and moved in an effort to better mark the natural channel and the ever-encroaching shoals. (Some markers may not be shown on older charts.)

> ⚠️ Starting at Hell Gate Point marked by flashing green "15" the channel completes the turn northward around flashing green "17" and green can "17A." Keep all three of these markers well to port as you turn as there are shoals west of them. Favor the natural channel along Sewalls Point as the charted channel west of flashing green "17" has shoaled. You should end the curve halfway between green can "17A" and river's east shore.

Once through Hell Gate, the St. Lucie River opens up and the long finger of Sewall Point stretches along on the east shore. Parallel the shore of Sewalls Point keeping at least 100 yards off. The high ground is heavily wooded with estates and landscaped terrain. The western shore is equally attractive and is fronted by many private docks.

After approaching flashing green "19" the waterway heads northward on a straight-line course and passes

under the high-rise **Evans Crary (SR A1A) Bridge** at Okeechobee Mile 3.4. This area was dredged in 2021 and maintains good depths. Continue on the straight-line course towards flashing green "21" keeping it to port. Once past this marker (located off Hoggs Cove) turn west towards flashing red "22." It's another straight-line course to the next turn at flashing green "23A." Give green "23A" a wide berth and head southwest for the highest span of the 65-foot fixed vertical clearance **Roosevelt (U.S. 1) Bridge**.

This is one of three bridges that are clustered together within a distance of 800 feet. The other two are the **Florida East Coast Railroad Bridge-Stuart** (with a 7-foot closed vertical clearance) and the **Old Roosevelt (Dixie Highway) Bridge** (with a 14-foot closed vertical clearance).

The Florida East Coast Railroad Bridge is normally open but closes when a train approaches. It is an unmanned automated bridge that works in concert with the Old Roosevelt (Dixie Highway) Bridge, which opens on signal. (Note: This schedule was provided to us by the bridgetender and is different than the published schedule.) If you have concerns, call ahead to 772-692-0321. The railroad bridge will signal via a flashing light and repeating five blast siren for 8 to 10 minutes prior to lowering. It takes about 10 minutes for a train crossing.

The Florida East Coast Railroad Bridge has a horizontal clearance (width) of only 50 feet compared to the Old Roosevelt (Dixie Highway) Bridge with a horizontal clearance of 80 feet. With little in the way of a turning basin prior to the bridge and with marine traffic and currents running, passage through the two bridges can be tricky, especially from the wider Old Roosevelt (Dixie Highway) Bridge to the narrower railroad bridge. Exercise care.

Vessels with a wider beam may want to issue a Sécurité call on VHF Channels 9 and 16.

A turn to the north after passing through the Old Roosevelt (Dixie Highway) Bridge takes you off the Okeechobee Waterway and up the North Fork of the St. Lucie River. This can be a very pleasant side trip if your cruising schedule allows you the time.

Turn south to continue on the waterway toward Lake Okeechobee. At the opening to the South Fork the channel weaves around Arbeau Point and then Bessy Point. The waterway narrows into a dredged channel south of green daybeacon "25A."

At Okeechobee Mile 9.5 the 54-foot fixed vertical clearance Palm City (SR 714) Bridge crosses the waterway setting the air draft for the Okeechobee Waterway to Indian Town.

Manatee Pocket

Sailfish Marina

GOIN' ASHORE

STUART, FL

Stuart's claim to being the "Sailfish Capital of the World" is sometimes disputed by other Florida cities, but no one would deny that both its outside and inside waters offer outstanding fishing grounds. Along with fishing Stuart is famed for its historic and pedestrian-friendly downtown. A fountain in the shape of a sailfish marks the start of a group of unique galleries, cafés, restaurants, and shops along Flagler and Osceola Streets. One street over is the two-mile-long wooden Riverwalk, where you can enjoy free concerts on the weekends, fishing off the pier and check out the waterfront's restaurants and shopping.

SERVICES

1. Blake Library
2351 SE Monterey Rd. (772-288-5702)

2. Claunch Animal Hospital
665 SW Pine Ave. (772-221-1680)

3. Cleveland Clinic Martin Health
200 SE Hospital Ave. (772-287-5200)

4. Stuart Post Office
801 SE Johnson Ave. (772-288-0846)

5. Surfside Pet Hospital
812 SE Osceola St. (772-219-8022)

6. Tourist Information Center
101 SW Flagler Ave. (772-288-5451)

ATTRACTIONS

7. Lyric Theatre
Restored theater offering performance art, concerts and art cinema (films, documentaries, independent films and international cinema) at 59 SW Flagler Ave. (772-286-7827).

8. Stuart Heritage Museum
More than 10,000 artifacts from the 1880s located in the Stuart Feed Store (circa 1901). Open daily from 10:00 a.m. to 3:00 p.m. at 161 SW Flagler Ave. Call ahead for hours and fees (772-220-4600).

SHOPPING

9. Fresh Market

Grocery chain at 2300 SE Ocean Blvd.
(772-223-5240)

10. Publix Super Market

Supermarket chain with groceries, deli and
bakery at 746 SW Federal Hwy. (772-221-3922).

11. Stuart Ace Hardware

Chain hardware retailer selling household tools,
supplies and more at 975 SE Federal Hwy.
(772-287-3664).

12. Walgreens

Drugstore chain with health and beauty aids and
a pharmacy at 2110 SE Ocean Blvd.
(772-283-1045).

MARINA

13. Sunset Bay Marina & Anchorage

615 SW Anchorage Way (772-283-9225)

Stuart, FL

St. Lucie River, FL

ST. LUCIE RIVER AREA		Largest Vessel	VHF	Total Slips	Approach/ Dockside Depth	Floating Docks	Gas/ Diesel	Repairs/ Haulout	Min/Max Amps	Pump-Out Station
1. Central Marine Stuart MM 7.0	(772) 692-2000	50		20	6.0 / 5.0			RH	30 / 50	
2. Harborage Yacht Club & Marina (WiFi) onSpot NW of MM 987.8	(772) 692-4000	90	16	300	8.0 / 6.0	F	GD		30 / 100	P
3. Apex Marine-Stuart (WiFi) MM 7.5	(772) 692-7577	120		53	7.0 / 7.0			RH	30 / 100	
4. Waterway Marina MM 7.7	(772) 220-2185	65		51	7.0 / 6.0				30 / 50	P
5. Sunset Bay Marina & Anchorage (WiFi) MM 8.0	(772) 283-9225	120	16	198	8.0 / 8.0	F	GD		30 / 50	P
6. Meridian Marina & Yacht Club MM 9.6	(772) 221-8198	40	5	2	6.0 / 5.0	F	G	RH	30	
7. Loggerhead Marina - Riverwatch Marina MM 9.6	(772) 286-3456	80		28	6.0 / 5.0	F	GD	RH	30 / 50	

(WiFi) Wireless Internet Access onSpot Dockside WiFi Facility
Visit www.waterwayguide.com for current rates, fuel prices, website addresses and other up-to-the-minute information.
(Information in the table is provided by the facilities.)

Scan here for more details:

South Fork

Sunset Bay Marina & Anchorage

North Fork

St. Lucie River

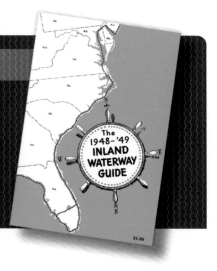

Back in the **Day** *1947*

Ilt's been 75 years since the first Inland Waterway Guide was introduced to the public. Boating, travel and adventure on America's waterways remain important ingredients to the success of communities and businesses of those waterfronts and harbors. Waterway Guide Media remains just as committed to accuracy today as the original publishers did in 1947. Thanks for coming along and staying onboard all these years. See you on the water!

The 1948-'49 INLAND WATERWAY GUIDE

$1.00

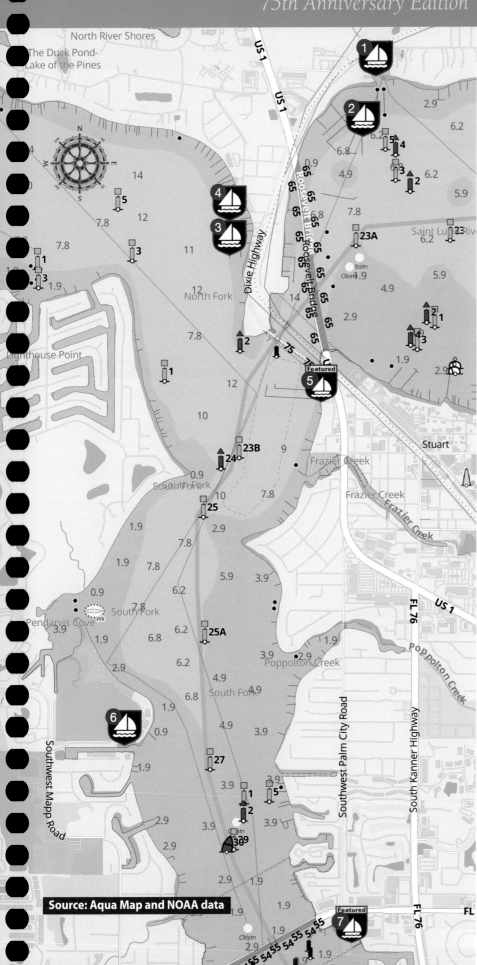

Source: Aqua Map and NOAA data

After entering the St. Lucie Canal, the Southwest Martin Highway Bridge (with 55-foot fixed vertical clearance) crosses at Okeechobee Mile 10.9. From here you can opt to continue on to the Okeechobee Waterway or backtrack to the ICW and points south.

Dockage/Moorings: Just before the Roosevelt Bridge on the north shore are Central Marine Stuart (a boat dealership and service yard) and Harborage Yacht Club & Marina. The 300-slip marina has space for transients on their floating docks with resort-style amenities. They also offer complimentary transportation downtown. Past the Stuart bridges at the start of the North Fork along Britt Point are Apex Marine–Stuart (a no-frills working boatyard) and the 51-slip Waterway Marina. Call to check for slip availability.

Immediately past the Old Roosevelt Bridge on the south shore is Sunset Bay Marina & Anchorage with 60 transient slips and 69 moorings. There is a popular restaurant on the premises called Sailor's Return (772-872-7250) serving seafood, steaks and spirits. Dine inside or out. The marina also offers loaner bikes and shuttle service.

Before reaching the Palm City (SR 714) Bridge (54-foot fixed vertical clearance) on the South Fork, a channel on the western shore marked by private daybeacons leads to Meridian Marina & Yacht Club. It is primarily a repair and storage facility with extremely limited dockage (two slips).

On the east shore just south of the Palm City (SR 714) Bridge a marked channel leads into Loggerhead Marina-Riverwatch Marina, which reports 5-foot MLW depths in the

St. Lucie River, FL

ST. LUCIE RIVER AREA		Largest Vessel	VHF	Total Slips	Approach/ Dockside Depth	Floating Docks	Gas/ Diesel	Repairs/ Haulout	Min/Max Amps	Pump-Out Station
1. Sandpiper Bay Marina (WiFi)	(772) 335-7875	150	16	65	8.0 / 8.0		GD	R	15 / 50	P

(WiFi) Wireless Internet Access   (●) onSpot Dockside WiFi Facility
Visit www.waterwayguide.com for current rates, fuel prices, website addresses and other up-to-the-minute information. (Information in the table is provided by the facilities.)

Scan here for more details:

Source: Aqua Map and NOAA data

docking basin. Limited transient dockage is available but be sure to call in advance.

Located 3.7 miles northwest of the Old Roosevelt (Dixie Highway) Bridge up the North Fork is the Sandpiper Bay Marina & Anchorage. They offer some supplies and can accommodate vessels to 150 feet. Visitors (including those who anchor off and dinghy in) can purchase discounted daily entrance passes from the co-located Club Med Sandpiper Bay all-inclusive resort that include access to all services. The resort has several restaurants and bars, swimming pools, a golf course (green fees extra) and a spa plus numerous water activities. For travel weary cruisers this can be a vacation within a vacation.

Anchorage: Boats anchor on the southwest side of Sewall Point at Hooker Cove near green daybeacon "19" in 7- to 8-foot MLW depths. Make sure that your anchor is set. Currents tend to run swiftly here. Expect lot of boat traffic early and late in day.

North of the Evans Crary (SR A1A) Bridge in Hoggs Cove holding is good in thick mud opposite flashing green "21" and there is protection from north and east winds. Watch the charted rocky shoal off Pisgah Hill and set the anchor in 7 to 9 feet MLW.

For short visits to Stuart or for dinghy access, Stuart Riverside Pier offers free dockage for up to 4 hours with 5-to 6-foot MLW depths. Beyond the bridges at Stuart it is possible to anchor almost anywhere in the North Fork but the best anchorage is by red daybeacon "6A." Kitching Cove, located past Sandpiper Bay Marina, is a fine anchorage in 6 to 7 feet MLW. At the north end of the anchorage you can take a scenic dinghy trip to the headwaters of the river where you reach groceries and other needs.

On the South Fork of the St. Lucie River you will find very good holding in thick mud at Pendarvis Cove. This is a popular anchorage with both cruisers and liveaboards. Across the river there is an excellent dinghy dock just inside Frazier Creek that is a 0.5-mile walk to a grocery

store, a laundry, restaurants and a hardware store. You can tie your dinghy to the wall at Frazier Creek Park and walk the dogs. There is water at the fish cleaning station and a dumpster in the park.

While in Stuart the pump-out boat M.S. Poop will come to your boat. Service is available Tuesday through Saturday from 8:00 a.m. to 3:00 p.m. Call 772-260-8326 or use VHF Channel 16 to arrange a time to receive your free pump-out service. We encourage you to take advantage of this service. Not only does it benefit the waterways but the Martin County Sheriff's Department conducts surprise inspections and can levy hefty fines for noncompliance.

■ NEXT STOP

Those wishing to continue their journey on the Okeechobee Waterway should continue to Chapter 6: "Side Trip on the Okeechobee Waterway." If you plan to return to the Atlantic ICW for the trip south, skip to next next section, Florida's Lower East Coast.

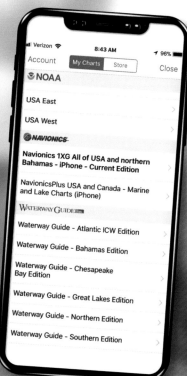

NAVIGATION NOTES

The Okeechobee Waterway (OCWW) provides a shortcut from the Atlantic Ocean to the Gulf or Mexico and divides central and south Florida. It starts at the ICW in the mouth of the St. Lucie River at Mile 0 and ends 154 miles later at Mile 0 on the Gulf ICW (GIWW) at San Carlos Bay south of Cape Coral. This efficient route allows boats to pass across the state from the ocean to the Gulf without having to make the long trip down around the Keys and up across Florida Bay.

The OCWW offers a chance to see rural Florida with small towns preserved much as they were early in the last century. Along the waterway ranches and big commercial farms alternate with moss-hung wilderness, while bustling boom towns coexist alongside sleepy villages that have been around since way before Miami.

The Caloosahatchee River was once the only way to get from the Gulf of Mexico to Central Florida via small steamers and freighters. Some still consider the 76.6-mile-long Caloosahatchee to be the most scenic part of the OCWW. For the boater the OCWW and Lake Okeechobee provide a stark transition from the busy coastal cities.

The OCWW is described here according to its three distinct sections:

1. From Mile Zero (the intersection of the OCWW and the ICW at St. Lucie Inlet down the South Fork of the St. Lucie River to the St. Lucie Canal to Lake Okeechobee.

2. Lake Okeechobee (either the "open-water route" directly across the lake or the "rim route" along the lake's south shore).

3. The Caloosahatchee River to the end of the OCWW in San Carlos Bay at Mile 0 of the GIWW heading north.

Cruising Conditions

Lake Okeechobee can be likened to a saucer full of water. It is shallow with normal depths from 7 to 11 feet MLW depending on the season and annual rainfall onto the drainage area to the north and the lake itself. The Army Corps of Engineers and the South Florida Water Management District manage the level of the lake.

The depths charted in Lake Okeechobee are based on a datum of 11.50 feet. If skippers know the lake level they can determine the difference between the datum and the current level and modify the charted depths accordingly. Depths in the sections between dams on either side of the lake vary slightly with lake level changes but the differences are seldom enough to affect navigation.

Note that water levels vary dramatically from season to season, month to month, and sometimes even day to

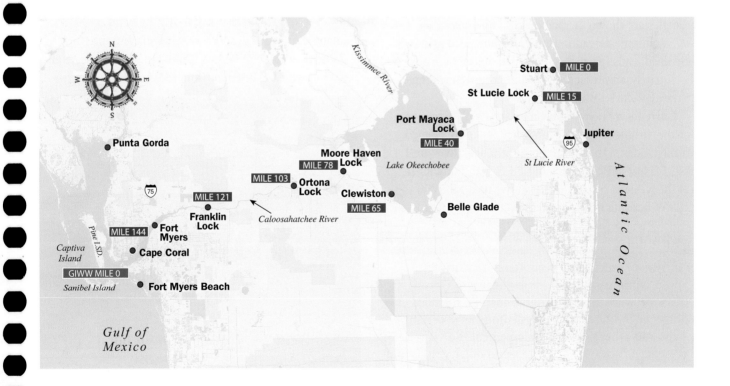

day. Rainfall is the driving force behind the water level fluctuations but lake levels can also be affected by strong southerly winds, which will lower the water level.

> ⚠️
>
> During a drought, lockage may be restricted depending on water supply. You can also call the Army Corps of Engineers in Clewiston (863-983-8101) for the latest updates.

Check during your pre-cruise planning and again at the first lock to make sure the entire OCWW is open before proceeding. Maintenance on the locks is normally conducted each summer and through-passage from the East Coast to the Gulf Coast may not be possible for as long as several months. During such times Lake Okeechobee may be accessible from one side or the other (but not both).

With the exception of a lake crossing in less than perfect weather passage along the OCWW is easy, piloting is simple and navigational aids are adequate for daytime running. Aids to navigation are numbered in several sequences from east to west all the way across. Even-numbered red aids are on the starboard side (as they are southbound along the Atlantic ICW). Conversely, leave red aids to port eastbound on the OCWW as you would when northbound on the ICW. Yellow squares and triangles are shown on daybeacons and buoys.

Nighttime navigation is not recommended as shoals and deadheads (partially submerged objects) are obscured. Fortunately, ample facilities and occasional anchorages make after-dark travel unnecessary.

Currents are not a problem on the OCWW except for the turbulence that occurs when locks are opened. Average tides at the mouth of the St. Lucie River are 1.1 feet, 1.3 feet at Fort Myers and 2.4 feet at Punta Rassa (at the western end of the waterway) near Mile 0 of the GIWW heading north. There is no tide in the lake itself.

> **NO WAKE ZONE**
>
> No Wake Zones, Idle Speed Zones and various Speed Limit restrictions are in effect throughout the waterways included in this chapter. Exercise diligence in knowing the regulations by observing signs and other markers. Enforcement is always present. As always, be courteous to other vessels and avoid manatees and other marine life.

Weather

Central Florida weather is generally mild. In winter the prevailing wind on Lake Okeechobee is north to northeast as opposed to summer, when wind is normally east to southeast with very little rain except when cold fronts from the north pass through.

Summer days are calm in the mornings with occasional patchy fog. Winds pick up at about 10:00 a.m. Afternoons often bring showers and thunderstorms, particularly late in the day, so it is a good idea to plan on getting in early. Hurricanes do occur in season–June through November–as well as other times and can affect the lake.

Lake Okeechobee is the second largest freshwater lake located wholly in the continental U.S. (Lake Michigan is the largest) and it can get nasty. You should know the forecast before you leave port. The continuous NOAA marine weather comes from West Palm Beach and Fort Myers on VHF Channel WX-3 and from Belle Glade on WX-2.

Using NOAA Charts

NOAA Chart 11428 covers the area from the intersection with the Atlantic ICW to Fort Myers, while NOAA Chart 11427 continues down the Caloosahatchee River to the GIWW and the Gulf of Mexico. From that point cruisers have the option of moving north on the GIWW to the Sun Coast, outside in the Gulf to the Big Bend or the Panhandle or south to southwest Florida and the Keys.

Note that much of NOAA Chart 11428 is at a scale of 1:80,000, which is different from the charts adjoining at

St. Lucie Lock

either end–NOAA Charts 11472 and 11427–both of which are at 1:40,000 or the usual ICW scale. NOAA Chart 11428 has two insets at its eastern end and one where it reaches Lake Okeechobee plus an extension at its western end; all of these are at various larger scales.

OCWW Bridges & Locks

The OCWW has five modern, spacious and well-handled locks and more than 20 bridges ranging from electronic controlled to hand operated. Some of the OCWW bridges operate daily from 6:00 a.m. to 10:00 p.m. and require a minimum of 3 hours notice to open at any other time. Phone numbers are posted on each bridge; calls are best made during normal office hours. You can use adjacent dolphins for tie-ups. Note that tying up to the dolphins can be tricky and the dolphins are there for commercial boats and tugs with barges to use in case of any delays. They always have priority.

The **Florida East Coast Railroad Bridge** at Mile 38 sets the 49-foot controlling vertical clearance (when open) of the OCWW. If you have any questions about clearance call the Army Corps of Engineers at Clewiston (863-983-8101).

Sailboaters can have their mast unstepped at Stuart or wait and have it done at Indiantown Marina, which is closer to the Florida East Coast Railroad Bridge (also known as Port Mayaca Bridge).

The water level in Lake Okeechobee is higher than anywhere on the Atlantic Ocean or Gulf ICW. Whether you are headed east or west you ascend through the locks to Lake Okeechobee and then descend after you leave. Typically locks operate between 7:00 a.m. and 5:00 p.m. with the last lockage beginning at 4:30 p.m. Note that the lockage schedule varies depending on lake levels. Allow approximately 15 minutes once inside a lock.

Note that the Army Corps of Engineers requires boat operators to turn off radar units during lockage to avoid exposing lock personnel to possible radiation risks. It is recommended, however, that engines be left running.

The OCWW locks are easier to transit when you are the only boat locking through and the lock attendant will give you the windward dock line first when winds are strong. Gusty winds can set up a surge in the locks so

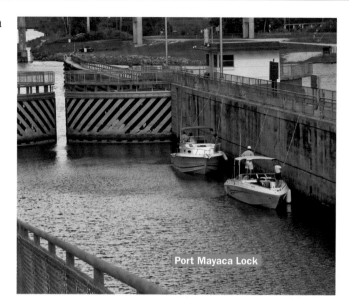
Port Mayaca Lock

use caution. The attendant also might warn you that you could be locking through with a manatee or an alligator.

When you reach the mooring dolphins and the sign Arrival Point before each lock contact the lockmaster on VHF Channel 13. If you receive no response on the VHF sound two long and two short blasts of your horn.

Give your vessel's name and direction and request lockage. At that time they will inform you of the current lockage status and your estimated wait time. The lockmaster will instruct you "port-to" or "starboard-to" indicating which side of the lock to steer to and how to arrange your fenders. The lockmaster will then indicate for you to enter when the traffic light is green.

Unlike in other locks the lockmasters will hand or drop down to you (depending on the water level) a bow line and a stern line, or the lines may be hanging down from the top of the lock's sidewall in which case you will have to steer to them and pick them up. (Keep a boathook handy.)

The locks of the OCWW are different from all other locks in North America in that they do not use valves to let water in to the lock. Instead, the front gates on the high side of the canal are opened about a foot and the water pours into the lock. In actuality it is not much worse than locks with valves; however, it can be a little disconcerting the first time you experience this.

Two people can safely handle a small or medium-sized boat but an extra pair of hands is always useful on larger boats. Single-handing through the locks is not safe and is strongly discouraged. Remember that the first boat into the lock should be the first boat out of the lock.

St. Lucie Canal, FL

ST. LUCIE CANAL		Largest Vessel	VHF	Total Slips	Approach/ Dockside Depth	Floating Docks	Gas/ Diesel	Repairs/ Haulout	Min/Max Amps	Pump-Out Station
1. American Custom Yachts Inc. WiFi MM 14.5	(772) 221-9100	135	16	25	8.0 / 8.0		GD	RH	50 / 100	
2. St. Lucie South Campground & Marina	(772) 287-1382	38		6	/				30 / 50	P
3. River Forest Yachting Center - Stuart WiFi MM 16.0	(772) 287-4131	150	16		10.0 / 9.0			RH	30 / 100	P

WiFi Wireless Internet Access   onSpot Dockside WiFi Facility
Visit www.waterwayguide.com for current rates, fuel prices, website addresses and other up-to-the-minute information.
(Information in the table is provided by the facilities.)

Scan here for more details:

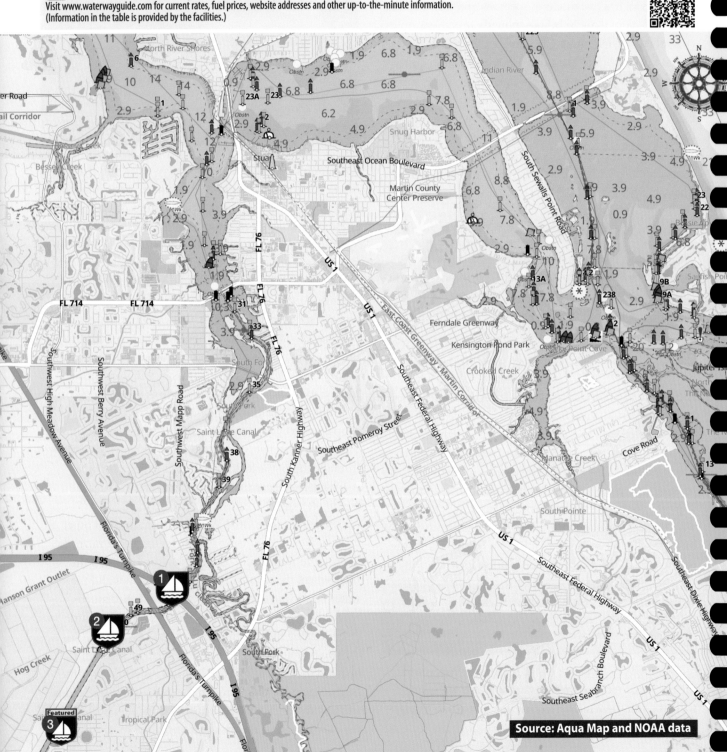

Source: Aqua Map and NOAA data

St. Lucie Canal, FL

INDIANTOWN		Largest Vessel	VHF	Total Slips	Approach/ Dockside Depth	Floating Docks	Gas/ Diesel	Repairs/ Haulout	Min/Max Amps	Pump-Out Station
1. Indiantown Marina (WiFi) MM 29.0	(772) 597-2455	120	16	34	8.0 / 8.0	F	GD	RH	30 / 50	P

(WiFi) Wireless Internet Access **onSpot** Dockside WiFi Facility
Visit www.waterwayguide.com for current rates, fuel prices, website addresses and other up-to-the-minute information.
(Information in the table is provided by the facilities.)

Scan here for more details:

Source: Aqua Map and NOAA data

Anchoring in approach areas to some of the locks is possible and the lockmasters can provide local knowledge concerning depths and conditions. Reservations are recommended at any marina on the OCWW.

⚠️

Anchoring anywhere along the waterway is limited to 24 hours in any one location. This is enforced by the Army Corps of Engineers and applies to the OCWW between the St. Lucie Lock and the W.P. Franklin Lock including all of Lake Okeechobee (OCWW miles 15 to 121.4).

■ ST. LUCIE CANAL

St. Lucie Canal to Indiantown–OCWW Mile 15 to Mile 28

The OCWW departs the South Fork and continues as the start of the St. Lucie Canal with the St. Lucie Lock at Mile 15 of the OCWW. The small community of Indiantown, located less than 1 mile north of the river, has some lots of citrus groves and some amenities including The Seminole Inn and Restaurant built in 1925 by S. Davis Warfield, a railroad executive. If you want to eat at The Seminole you need to make reservations ahead of time (772-597-3777). Ask at the Indiantown Marina for other dining options and suggestions on transportation.

NAVIGATION: Use NOAA Chart 11428. The canal carrying the OCWW up to Lake Okeechobee itself is deep and easy to traverse and was dredged in spring 2021. On the way to the St. Lucie Lock you will pass under the **Southwest Martin Highway Bridge** at Mile 10.9, the **I-95 Twin Bridges** at Mile 14 and the **Florida Turnpike Bridges** at Mile 14.5. All of these fixed bridges have at least 55-foot vertical clearance.

The **St. Lucie Lock** at Mile 15.1 operates on request from 7:00 a.m. to 5:00 p.m. (Last lockage is at 4:30 p.m.) Radio ahead or call the lock (772-287-2665) prior to your departure for current schedules. This first lock of the system lifts you approximately 13 feet. When approaching the No-Wake Zone entrance area check the light system. If the light is red and a call on VHF Channel 13 or 16 does not get a response give two long and then two short blasts then wait well downstream in the standby area to avoid the discharge from the dam and lock.

Many boats arrive at the lower side of this lock and then turn around and go back without locking through so the lockmaster does not assume, even if he sees you arrive, that you wish to lock through. You must call him via VHF or horn. On each side of each lock of the St. Lucie Lock system there is a sign marked "Arrival Point." Enter slowly on the green signal and be prepared to accept lines fore and aft from the lockmaster. Have fenders ready on the south side of your boat for locking. As the water level rises maintain your position with care.

> The OCWW plays host not only to many varieties of fish but also to manatees (an endangered species), alligators and turtles of all sizes. The manatees frequently are "locked through" so take extra care if they are reported in the area.

Approaching Indiantown from the east you will first pass under the **SR 76A Bridge** at Mile 17.1 then the **Indiantown (SR 710) Bridge** at Mile 28.1. Both of these fixed bridges have at least 55-feet of vertical clearance. Just past the Indiantown Bridge is the **Seaboard System Railroad Bridge** with a 7-foot closed vertical clearance. The railroad bridge opens on signal except between 10:00 p.m. and 6:00 a.m., when a 3-hour notice is required. (Call 772-597-3822.) The operator may anticipate you but if it is closed call on VHF Channel 09. If a train is approaching you may be delayed as the train always has the right-of-way.

Dockage: American Custom Yachts Inc. has a 63-acre marine facility that accommodates the construction of custom sportfishing vessels and provides a full range of marine services on site. They report six reserved transient slips. St. Lucie South Campground & Marina is at the St. Lucie Lock with short docks and fairly shallow slips for vessels less than 40 feet. Call ahead for slip availability.

Port Mayaca Lock

Florida East Coast Railroad Bridge

River Forest Yachting Center-Stuart is located in a protected basin west of the St. Lucie Lock and offers a full range of on-site repair, maintenance and installation services. Be sure to call well in advance for availability of transient dockage. This is one of two freshwater locations (the other is in LaBelle) with climate-controlled indoor storage buildings. The marina also offers a members-only Hurricane Club to offer boat owners safe harbor during hurricane conditions in both Stuart and LaBelle.

A short distance beyond the Seaboard System Railroad Bridge in Indiantown is the 34-slip Indiantown Marina. For those intending to cross Lake Okeechobee via the direct route, this is the last marina until Clewiston, which is 35 miles away. This is a well-protected hurricane hole offering transient slips as well as long-term boat storage with a DIY and full-service boat yard. As with any of the marinas on the OCWW skippers planning to overnight here should call ahead for availability.

Anchorage: To reach the anchorage at Four Rivers Loop, leave the channel at green daybeacon "37" (Mile 11.2) and tuck behind the unnamed island in 5 to 7 feet MLW. Directly across the OCWW from the Army Corps of Engineers slips at Mile 15 at the entrance to a narrow bay is a quiet overnight anchorage for one boat with 8 feet and good holding in mud on the north side of the St. Lucie Lock. If in Indiantown, it is best to take a slip as there is no viable anchorage.

Indiantown to Port Mayaca–OCWW Mile 28 to Mile 38

NAVIGATION: Use NOAA Chart 11428. At Mile 38.0 the **Florida East Coast (Port Mayaca) Railroad Bridge** with 49-foot open vertical clearance sets the controlling overhead clearance for the OCWW. Elsewhere, at least 54 feet of overhead clearance can be carried. The bridge has 7-foot closed vertical clearance but is usually open displaying flashing green lights to indicate that vessels may pass (unless a train is coming).

Be sure to stay south of red daybeacon "52" as a ledge of rocks and submerged pilings runs from the marker to the northern bank of the canal. The high-rise **U.S. 98/441 Bridge** at Mile 38.8 and the **Port Mayaca Lock** just a short distance ahead serve as the entrance to the lake. Mooring dolphins provide the only place to make fast before reaching the lock but they may be in use by barges.

At certain water levels the Port Mayaca Lock is open at both ends and on the flashing (or steady) green (or yellow) light you may proceed through cautiously. You should contact the lockmaster on VHF Channel 16 or 13 before entering or if you have any questions. Operating hours are 7:00 a.m. to 5:00 p.m. with a last lock opening at 4:30 p.m. (561-924-2858).

Eastbound boats may experience some difficulty with adverse winds and resulting seas. Under these conditions

entering the Port Mayaca Lock and making fast can be tricky. Until the lock is closed waves tend to ricochet from wall to wall. Heading westbound is considerably easier but if the winds are brisk be prepared for a choppy exit.

Anchorage: Be warned that anchoring beyond the Port Mayaca Lock is precarious. A layover elsewhere would be a better plan. It might be possible to anchor in the Port Mayaca Overflow Canal before the lock at OCWW Mile 36.6. You will find 7 feet MLW here and all-around protection; however, there is only room for one to two boats.

The Port Mayaca mooring dolphins before the lock are a possibility for tie-up if not occupied by barges. The east side is reportedly better. This is exposed to wind but if tied properly this won't be an issue: Tie a very long bow line to forward piling cluster, back down to aft piling cluster and tie long line to it. Then take in slack on forward line and your boat will be tied between the two dolphins with no drift, drag or swing. There is no current or tide here. There is also no shoreside access.

LAKE OKEECHOBEE

- The U.S. Army Corps of Engineers advises the public, marinas and those operating commercial and recreational vessels through the Okeechobee Waterway that there is the potential of encountering Blue Green Algae. Visitors should be aware that water from areas with blue-green algae can make animals and people sick and should be avoided. This algae may be blue, bright green, brown or red and can have a strong odor like rotting plants. People who are very sensitive to smells may have respiratory irritation. If you come into contact with blue-green algae, get out of the area and wash off with soap and water. See your doctor if you think blue-green algae has made you sick. The following precautions should be taken if you see algae:

* Do not swim at this location.
* Avoid getting water in your eyes, nose or mouth.
* Do not eat shellfish from affected area.
* Rinse fish fillets with tap or bottled water. Cook fish well.
* Keep pets and livestock away from affected location

Lake Okeechobee is completely enclosed by an impressive levee system, officially named the Herbert Hoover Dike. The dike's construction began during the Hoover administration as a result of two disastrous hurricanes in the 1920s when the lake was literally blown out of its banks. During periods of strong winds the lake becomes choppy and turbulent with short, steep seas typical of shallow water.

> The OCWW is 154 or 165 statute miles from the Atlantic Ocean to the Gulf of Mexico depending on whether you cross Lake Okeechobee (Route 1) or take the Rim Route (Route 2) along the lake's southern shore.

Route 1 is a 34-mile open-water crossing of the lake. Be sure you have all needed provisions with you before you start the trek across the lake as you will have few options once on the lake. The controlling depth varies but can be as little as 5 feet. The depth on this route is shallowest just after leaving the Port Mayaca Lock for about 0.5 mile then you will encounter 10 to 14 feet across the lake. At daybeacon "9" approaching Clewiston the depth will come up to 8 feet and remain there until you turn into the channel heading toward Moore Haven. Although 10 miles shorter, note that this route can get nasty in strong winds.

The more scenic Rim Route (Route 2) is 44 miles and follows the shoreline south from Port Mayaca Lock on the eastern shore. This route is subject to extensive shoaling and becomes impassable during periods of low water. The shallowest water is at the beginning of the route when heading west. After about 1.5 miles the water gets deeper (10-plus feet).

A low-hanging fiber optic cable at the Torrey Island is estimated to be 35 feet above the water. High-masted vessels are encouraged to use Route 1 until the cable is raised to 52 feet. Recreational and commercial boaters are asked to use caution when navigating through these sections of waterway.

Occasionally, the Rim Route will be closed to navigation because of vegetation in the water. These closures will be announced in the Local Notice to Mariners (www.navcen.uscg.gov).

Use the Rim Route (Route 2) at your own risk due to commonly present debris and low water depths (as low as 3 feet). Conditions can change rapidly, especially if tropical storms or hurricanes pass over Lake Okeechobee. Call the Army Corps of Engineers in Clewiston (863-983-8101) for the latest conditions.

Route 1: Crossing Lake Okeechobee to Clewiston

The open water crossing is normally an enjoyable run and Clewiston (at Mile 65) is a worthwhile stopover point. If the lake level and season are right expect to see hundreds of beautiful white pelicans bunched together on the half-dozen offshore spoil islands that line the Clewiston approach channel. Unlike brown pelicans, which plunge-dive from high above the water for their meals, white pelicans scoop up fish by merely submerging their heads and necks while swimming.

NAVIGATION: Use NOAA Chart 11428. Crossing the southern

portion of Lake Okeechobee entails a 25-mile-long passage after departing from the Port Mayaca channel in a southwesterly direction. The first run of 15 miles has just one aid to navigation, flashing red "6," which is located about 7 miles out. This will help you compensate for a slight magnetic anomaly in this area, which might affect your compass. About 3 miles out from the Port Mayaca Lock there is a visible wreck to starboard. Do not be led off course. Your GPS chartplotter or radar could be useful on this stretch if visibility is compromised.

As you approach flashing green "7" on the eastern edge of Rocky Reef note what appears to be a cluster of markers and the remains of a platform. Sort things out beforehand and follow the chart's magenta line carefully. After clearing the cut through the reef stick to the charted course. The apparent shortcut due west, a charted auxiliary floodway channel, is shoaled in and obstructed with large boulders (particularly noticeable at low lake levels). This cut should not be attempted by cruising boats.

Entering the Clewiston approach channel, marked by a private concrete cylinder and numerous lights and daybeacons, is simple. Westbound green daybeacon "1" is difficult to spot. If the water level is low or the winds are brisk pay strict attention to course keeping. This is where the controlling depth (5 feet) for Route 1 applies. The channel is lined on both sides with rocks and spoil areas. Exercise special care in the area between red daybeacons "4" and "6." This is another area in which the use of your GPS chartplotter will come in handy.

Lake Okeechobee, FL

CLEWISTON			Largest Vessel	VHF	Total Slips	Approach/ Dockside Depth	Floating Docks	Gas/ Diesel	Repairs/ Haulout	Min/Max Amps	Pump-Out Station
1. Roland and Mary Ann Martins Marina & Resort (WiFi) MM 75.6		(800) 473-6766	130	16	15	8.0 / 7.0	F	GD	R	30 / 50	

(WiFi) Wireless Internet Access ● onSpot Dockside WiFi Facility
Visit www.waterwayguide.com for current rates, fuel prices, website addresses and other up-to-the-minute information.
(Information in the table is provided by the facilities.)

Scan here for more details:

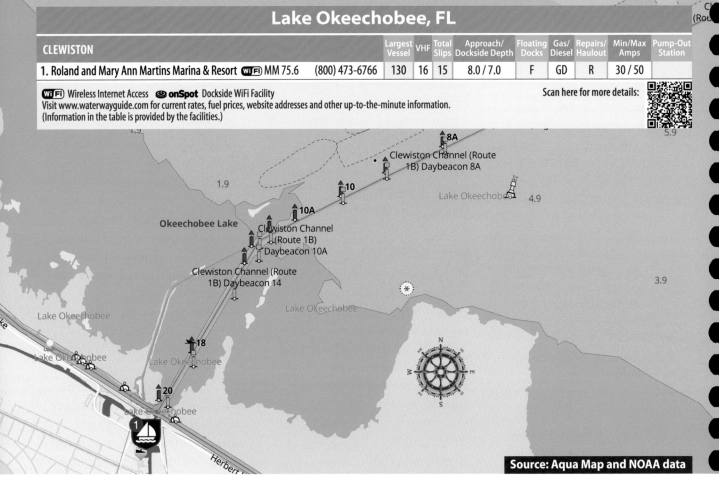

Source: Aqua Map and NOAA data

Close to Clewiston be aware that fishnets and traps are a way of life here and their small markers are sometimes difficult to see. Some of the fishermen in high-speed bass boats or skiffs also add to the obstacles.

Directly before reaching the Clewiston Lock the channel makes a hard 90-degree turn to the northwest. There are no nearby channel markers on this northwesterly stretch and a sign on the levee pointing to Moore Haven is difficult to read. The intersection can be confusing but don't go through the lock unless you wish to visit Clewiston.

The Clewiston Lock is not technically part of the OCWW and is not equipped with a VHF radio but if lake levels are not unusual the lock is left open. If the traffic light is green proceed through. If you wish passage and the lockmaster does not wave to you use two long and two short blasts of your horn or whistle. The Army Corps of Engineers in Clewiston (863-983-8101) has information on scheduled maintenance and lock operations at either route.

Route 2: The Rim Route to Clewiston

If you are not pressed for time or if the lake crossing is questionable due to weather the Rim Route (10 miles longer) can be an interesting alternative if the water level allows it. While open to Lake Okeechobee for about 15 miles the exposure is from west through north. Unless winds are from this quadrant (and in the small craft advisory category) this part of the passage should be pleasant.

NAVIGATION: Use NOAA Chart 11428. From Mile 55 on to Clewiston (where it joins Route 1) and on to the Caloosahatchee Canal entrance the course stays between the mainland levees surrounding Lake Okeechobee and the regular and spoil islands lining the rim. Depths vary according to lake levels and wind conditions. The shallowest stretch has been observed in the easternmost 4 miles; depths increase significantly beyond that.

The local harbor at Pahokee (OCWW Mile 50.6) can be reached from red entrance daybeacon "2," which is opposite red channel daybeacon "62." If the wind is strong from the northwest or north waves from Lake Okeechobee

will be reflected back from the breakwater and, when combined with the incoming waves, can result in an uncomfortable or even dangerous situation for boats in the channel as they pass the breakwater.

Near red daybeacon "78" (Mile 54) there is a charted, straight, well-marked channel that leads out through the shallows bordering the Rim Route to the deeper lake water (charted at 7 feet). The section of the OCWW from Mile 55 to Mile 75.7 (Clewiston) has always been one of the more interesting stretches on the trip. However, hyacinths and water lettuce grow in profusion, sometimes even clogging the channel. If you must pass through them do it slowly. Should you clog your prop and rudder, back down and then push ahead.

The **Belle Glade Dike (CR 717) Bridge** has only an 11-foot closed vertical clearance at normal lake levels. The fixed span just west of the swing span has a vertical clearance of 13 feet, which may be an advantage if you only require 12 feet of clearance. This bridge is hand-operated and it takes awhile for the operator to get in place to open the span so be sure to call ahead on VHF Channel 09 and give the operator an estimate as to the time of your arrival. Hours are from 7:00 a.m. to 6:00 p.m.

Monday through Thursday, and from 7:00 a.m. to 7:00 p.m. Friday through Sunday (fishing days). The bridge remains closed at night. It also need not open if winds are in excess of 20 mph.

From Belle Glade the OCWW first heads south for several miles then angles northwest past such communities as Bean City and Lake Harbor. A road parallels the OCWW most of the way but you will not see it since it is behind the ubiquitous levee.

Hurricane Gate 3 at about Mile 67 (behind Ritta Island) is usually closed. Continue to follow the markers along the way. At red daybeacon "94" (Mile 70), the channel is narrow and straightforward. As you approach Clewiston (Mile 75.7) be alert for small fishing boats anchored off and in the channel.

Anchorage: Marinas along this route are for small boats only. Some anchoring room is west of the Torrry Island Swing Bridge (with 8-foot depths). This anchorage is good if you want an early start, but note that early risers also include many small boat fishermen who may not show concern for anchored craft.

See navigation alert above about low-hanging (35-feet above the water) fiber optic cable at the Route 2 Bridge at Torry Island.

Caloosahatchee Canal & River, FL

MOORE HAVEN AREA		Largest Vessel	VHF	Total Slips	Approach/ Dockside Depth	Floating Docks	Gas/ Diesel	Repairs/ Haulout	Min/Max Amps	Pump-Out Station
1. Moore Haven City Docks MM 78.4	(863) 946-0711				6.0 / 6.0				30 / 50	
2. River House Marina MM 78.5	(863) 946-0466			6	5.0 / 5.0				30 / 50	

WiFi Wireless Internet Access **onSpot** Dockside WiFi Facility
Visit www.waterwayguide.com for current rates, fuel prices, website addresses and other up-to-the-minute information.
(Information in the table is provided by the facilities.)

Scan here for more details:

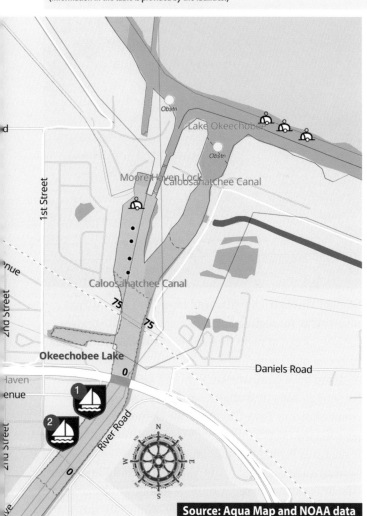

Source: Aqua Map and NOAA data

A better bet is to anchor in South Bay Basin at Mile 63. To reach this leave the OWW just west of the launch ramp and head north into the kidney-shaped basin. Here you will find over 8 feet at the entrance and 10 to 25 feet in the basin.

Islands, both natural and spoil, offer protection from winds off the lake along this route, although if the water level is high, it can get a bit unpleasant. There is room for several boats (plus lots of birds, alligators and bugs). From here you can easily dinghy back to the boat ramp.

Clewiston–OCWW Mile 75.7

Route 1 (open water route) joins Route 2 (rim route) at Clewiston, a point about halfway between Stuart and Fort Myers. Clewiston bills itself as the "Sweetest Town in America" due to its role in sugarcane production. Mileage from this point on is based on the lesser "cross lake" figure of Mile 65. The rim mileage of 75.7 stops here.

NAVIGATION: Use NOAA Chart 11428. On an eastbound trip from Clewiston heading toward Indiantown the Port Mayaca entrance markers may be hard to pick out. Power company stacks are clearly visible at the port from many miles out and a heading directly toward them will bring you almost directly to the channel entrance.

A hurricane gate and the 50 feet wide by 60 feet long **Clewiston Lock** allows access through the levee into Clewiston Harbor. This lock is not equipped with a VHF radio so contact with the lockmaster must be made visually (waving is the method of choice) or by whistle signals–two long and two short. The schedule calls for an open lock if the water level is low and the Clewiston Lock is usually open for direct passage. Otherwise, the hours are 7:00 a.m. to 5:00 p.m. Check the traffic light to see if it is green or red.

After entering the lock grab the lines hanging from the top of the chamber and hold on. Lock personnel may help with the lines but the change in water level as the lock opens and closes usually will not result in excessive turbulence.

Dockage: Roland and Mary Ann Martins Marina & Resort at Clewiston is a popular spot for transients and boat clubs (particularly bass fishing groups) to spend a weekend or more. Reservations are a must. The channel is very narrow and can be difficult to maneuver but the helpful staff will be glad to give you a hand.

Several of the dolphins on the channel's edge northwest of Clewiston can be used for making fast. The main street of this town is only 3 blocks away and includes a small grocery store, a hardware store, an auto parts store and a pharmacy.

Clewiston to Moore Haven–ICM Mile 78

From Clewiston to Moore Haven and the entrance to the Caloosahatchee Canal the OCWW is fairly wide and deep. Fast boats frequent this route and small-boat fishermen anchor or drift fish in the cuts and channel. Several facilities for small fishing boats are along the way and, at times, fishing activity is intense. If it is a sunny day, have your camera ready because this canal is probably one of the best places to see alligators sunning themselves on shore.

Be aware that strong southern winds can significantly lower water depths between Clewiston and Moore Haven. This is more severe during droughts. As noted previously hyacinths and water lettuce can clog the channel as well as your prop and rudder here.

NAVIGATION: Use NOAA Chart 11428. After transiting the 13-mile Caloosahatchee Canal the entrance to the **Moore Haven Lock** at Mile 78 is directly to port and easy to see and negotiate. Because it is in a protected canal it is even easier to pass through than the St. Lucie Lock with equally capable locktenders. If Hurricane Gate 1 is in use during discharge of high water turbulence on the "down" side of the lock can be considerable.

Stay well back from Moore Haven Lock until the green light comes on and enter carefully. Remember that you are now being lowered with the water level so do not tie off your bow or stern lines and be prepared for some surge as you drop. Wait for the gates to open completely before releasing the lines and then proceed slowly out of the lock. The lock operates from 7:00 a.m. to 5:00 p.m. with a last lock opening at 4:30 p.m. Call ahead to find out on which side to place fenders (863-946-0414). Information about conditions farther on can also be obtained from the lockmaster.

Immediately beyond Moore Haven Lock are two bridges. The first is the **Seaboard System Railroad Bridge** at Mile 78.3, which has 5-foot closed vertical clearance but is usually open. If closed it will open on signal except from 10:00 p.m. to 6:00 a.m., when it need not open. Signal before you leave the lock. The bridge is hand-operated and the delay can be considerable. Use the eastern draw. The **Moore Haven (U.S. 27) Bridges** have a fixed vertical clearance charted at 55 feet but there are no clearance gauges or fendering system.

Dockage: On the west side of the Caloosahatchee Canal (where the OCWW runs nearly north to south) the Moore Haven City Docks provides alongside dockage for 3 or 4 (depending on size) visiting yachts. Normally space is available but during peak travel seasons the early bird scores. Use minimum space for tie-up so that the next boat will have room. This is a well-constructed dock with vertical rubber bumpers on the pilings. Dockage fees may be paid at City Hall across the street or to the dockmaster who calls in the early evening (and is a good source of local information). Restrooms/showers are available behind City Hall during regular operating hours. You can get a key from the dockmaster.

Just beyond the City Dock is the River House Marina with 400 feet of alongside dockage. Dockage fees are collected on the "honor system" (with an envelope dropbox). At the far edge of these docks there is an overhead telephone or television cable (not a power line) crossing. Clearance seems quite adequate but specific height is not charted or known.

Anchorage: If you arrive at the east side of the Moore Haven Lock late in the day and would prefer not to lock through until morning you can proceed past the turn into the lock and anchor in the canal northwest of the lock or you can make fast for the night between the mooring dolphins located on the lake side of the OCWW just before the canal turns into the lock. Be sure to show an anchor light and also be aware of the limited swing room.

■ CALOOSAHATCHEE CANAL & RIVER

Moore Haven to Ortona Lock– OCWW Mile 78 to Mile 94

Early morning fog and mist sometime curtail an early departure but normally the Caloosahatchee Canal is straightforward, wide and deep, with no surprises. At about Mile 82.5 the channel passes through shallow Lake Hicpochee where again you may encounter small fishing boats anchored along the shore. Watch your wake as a matter of both prudence and courtesy.

NAVIGATION: Use NOAA Chart 11428. Like the Moore Haven Lock, the smooth concrete walls of the **Ortona Lock** are a vast improvement over timbered sides that invariably catch fenders and rub rails. Tie-up dolphins are located outside both ends of the lock; boats normally make fast to the south wall. The lock operates the same as the others.

Caloosahatchee Canal & River, FL

LA BELLE AREA		Largest Vessel	VHF	Total Slips	Approach/ Dockside Depth	Floating Docks	Gas/ Diesel	Repairs/ Haulout	Min/Max Amps	Pump-Out Station
1. The Glades Marina (WiFi) MM 89.0	(863) 673-5653	90		23	8.0 / 8.0	F			30 / 50	P
2. Glades Boat Storage, Inc.	(863) 983-3040		16		/			H		
3. River Forest Yachting Center - LaBelle (WiFi) MM 92.8	(863) 612-0003	150	16	20	9.0 / 8.0	F		RH	30 / 100	P
4. Port LaBelle Marina (WiFi)	(863) 675-2261	80		100	6.0 / 6.0	F	GD		30	P

(WiFi) Wireless Internet Access   onSpot Dockside WiFi Facility
Visit www.waterwayguide.com for current rates, fuel prices, website addresses and other up-to-the-minute information.
(Information in the table is provided by the facilities.)

Scan here for more details:

Source: Aqua Map and NOAA data

Be prepared for some surge as the water is let out. The change in level varies but 8 to 10 feet is normal depending on lake level. The lock operates from 7:00 a.m. to 5:00 p.m. with a last lock opening at 4:30 p.m. (863-675-0616). Call ahead to find out on which side to place fenders.

Before you get to Ortona Lock several small canals lead off to the north into the Turkey Creek community. Most of its residents are boaters and their docks usually are full of cruising boats of all descriptions.

Dockage: Just past Lake Hicpochee and the bend in the Caloosahatchee Canal is The Glades Marina on the southern bank at Mile 89. The basin is small and dockage is limited (just four transient slips). Glades Boat Storage, Inc. is nearby. (No transient slips.)

At approximately Mile 93 is River Forest Yachting Center-LaBelle, which is owned by the same people who own the River Forest Yachting Center-Stuart. This facility is very similar to the one on the eastern side of the lake except it is twice as large (at over 100,000 square feet). The marina has been constructed to withstand hurricane winds. Transients are welcome but be sure to call in advance for dockage availability.

Anchorage: At Mile 92.5 just before Turkey Creek there is a narrow canal that leads into Lollipop Lake. It is small but if you go all the way into the lake you will find ample room for anchoring in very protected water. The water in the canal is 8 to 9 feet and much deeper (30-plus feet) once inside the basin. This is a nice, out-of-the-way spot to spend an evening on the hook. Chirping birds, mooing cows and the occasional alligator will keep you company.

Ortona Lock to La Belle–OCWW Mile 90 to Mile 103

The quiet river town of La Belle dates back to the early 1800s. The Swamp Cabbage Festival is held in La Belle during the last full weekend in February. The festival includes live music, a parade, a rodeo, a fishing tournament and a Swamp Queen & Princess Pageant. Swamp cabbage (also known as hearts of palm) is the growing part of the sable palm and joins alligator as a local delicacy.

La Belle is also known as the "Honey Capital." The Harold P. Curtis Honey Company (863-675-2187) is located directly across from the LaBelle Heritage Museum

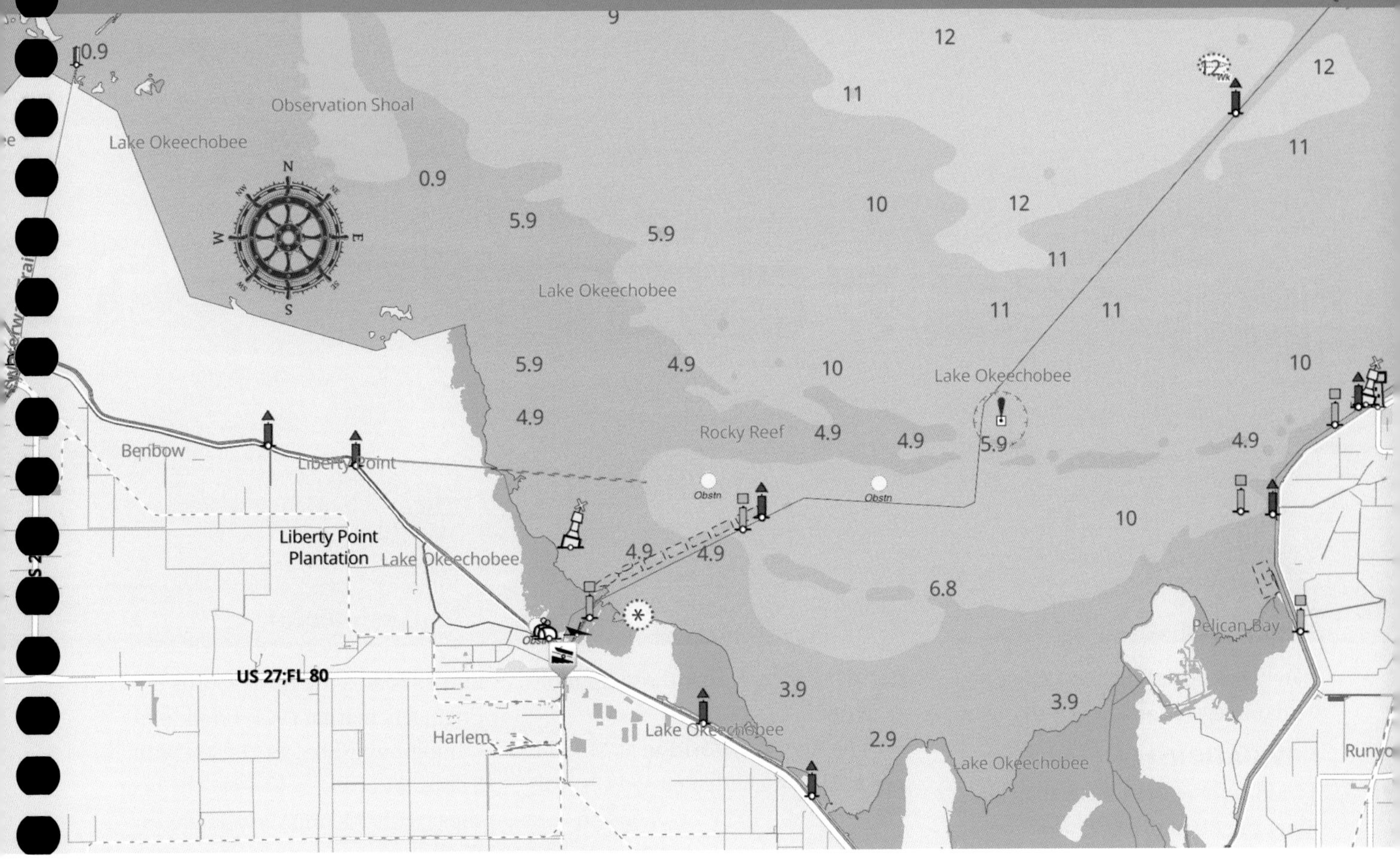

(863-674-0034) on the south side of the bridge. The company maintains about 1,000 beehives and will permit you to sample different types of honey (including Orange Blossom, Palmetto, Wildflower, Seagrape, and Mangrove) in the store, which also carries honey candy and candles.

NAVIGATION: Use NOAA Chart 11428. The **La Belle (SR 29) Bridge** at Mile 103.0 with 28-foot closed vertical clearance opens on signal except from 7:00 a.m. to 9:00 a.m. and 4:00 p.m. to 6:00 p.m., Monday through Friday (except federal holidays), when the bridge need not open. The bridge will open on signal between 10:00 p.m. and 6:00 a.m. if at least a 3-hour notice is given. Call 866-335-9696 for an opening during these hours.

Dockage: At Mile 100 an entry channel leads off to the south into the Port LaBelle Marina with limited transient slips and some amenities. Just to the east there is another cove (sometimes called Tranquility Cove) that is an extension of the marina.

Just beyond the La Belle (SR 29) Bridge on the south side, LaBelle City Dock has free dockage with electric and water. There is a 3-day limit and room for just 8 boats. These docks are usually full on the weekends and are on a first-come, first-served basis. They have mooring posts making it more difficult to off-board for smaller boats. Expect bridge noise. Provisioning needs are within walking distance.

The municipal Bob Mason Waterfront Park is on the north side of the canal and offers free dockage alongside a 50-foot aluminum dock with 7-foot MLW approach and dockside depths. Fender carefully to avoid errant shards of metal. There are no amenities or services.

Anchorage: There is a fair anchorage at Mile 103 just east of the dock at Bob Mason Waterfront Park. The La Belle anchorage is deep (15 to 20 feet at MLW) but open to wakes.

La Belle to Franklin Lock–OCWW Mile 103 to Mile 121.4

These are the scenic headwaters of the Caloosahatchee River, once a major transportation artery for the Calusa Indians and other early settlers to Fort Myers. Today powerboats and sailboats traverse the 67-mile-long river, which is an important link the OCWW. The river is wide enough to accommodate everyone including the abundant wildlife. The Caloosahatchee River and its meandering tributaries are bordered by lush, towering leather ferns,

Ortona Lock

stately oaks dripping with moss and verdant vegetation along every shore.

NAVIGATION: Use NOAA Chart 11428. Where the Caloosahatchee River once wandered is now a series of straight sections punctuated by gentle turns and numerous intriguing oxbows and streams. The water runs quite deep to the banks. Swinging room on the river, even at its widest points, is limited and anchoring is not recommended unless you can keep your vessel from swinging into the channel.

Some of the oxbows are deep enough if you feel adventurous but snags or shoals and even low-hanging power cables are prevalent. Well out from the northern bank at about Mile 106.6, red daybeacon "2" marks a shoal.

Two bridges cross this section of the Caloosahatchee River. **Fort Denaud Bridge** at Mile 108.2 has a 9-foot closed vertical clearance. The bridge opens on request and arrows indicate which side of the draw to use. It is closed from 10:00 p.m. until 6:00 a.m. and requires a 3-hour

notice to open during those hours (call 866-335-9696).

The **Alva Drawbridge** at Mile 116 has a 23-foot charted closed vertical clearance and likewise opens on signal except from 10:00 p.m. until 6:00 a.m. when a 3-hour notice is required. Use VHF Channel 09 or call 866-335-9696.

The final lock on the Okeechobee Waterway is at Olga. The **W.P. Franklin Lock** normally operates on request from 7:00 a.m. to 5:00 p.m. daily. (Last lockage at 4:30 p.m.) Enter on the green light and remember not to tie off your lines tightly as the level will drop about 3 feet. Wait until the lock is fully open before casting off and exit slowly. Sometimes eastbound boats are waiting nearby to enter. Please note that low water levels in Lake Okeechobee may result in schedule changes at the W.P. Franklin Lock. Be sure to call in advance to check schedules (239-694-5451 or VHF Channel 13).

Dockage: Immediately east of the W.P. Franklin Lock on the

north shore is the Army Corps of Engineers marina (W.P. Franklin Campground-Boat-In Docks) with 8 slips for boats to 40 feet. The boat slips (with 30-amp service) are in the lesser-populated RV area with picnic tables, shelter, a beautiful grass lawn and palm trees. Call ahead for reservations. You can also tie up to the dolphins (24-hour limit) in 6 feet MLW and dinghy to the nearby launch ramp. Trash disposal and water are available.

C-10 Caloosa Marina (formerly Calusa Jacks Marina) offers side tie only (no slips). Sweetwater Landing Marina is a dry-service storage facility that has 10 reserved transient slips. Call ahead for slip availability.

Owl Creek Boat Boat Works at Mile 125.5 has 48 slips for vessels of all sizes and offers a full range of repair and maintenance services including fine yacht refinishing. If you need to re-step a mast, this is a good time to do so although this can also be done in Fort Myers.

Anchorage: You can drop the hook in Hickey Creek at Mile 119.5

behind an unnamed island, where you will find all-around protection from wakes in 7 feet MLW. Another protected anchorage is just west of the W.P. Franklin Lock next to the Army Corps of Engineers campground where there is enough room for a couple of small boats to anchor.

Franklin Lock to Fort Myers–OCWW Mile 121.4 to Mile 135

While Fort Myers is not actually the western end of the OCWW, most cruisers consider it to be. Like most of Florida the city boasts a growing population, especially if you include the Cape Coral area, which is across the river on the north shore. To read more see "Goin' Ashore: Fort Myers, FL" in this chapter.

NAVIGATION: Use NOAA Chart 11428.

> ⚠
>
> Although the Caloosahatchee River is a navigable river coming in from the Gulf of Mexico, it is not marked with the conventional "red-right-returning" system with numbers increasing as one proceeds inland. The daybeacons, lights and such are a continuing part of the OCWW system; therefore, numbers increase as you cruise westward and the "reds" are on your right side even though you are going downriver. This can be confusing if you do not understand the system.

The Caloosahatchee River has many aids to navigation beginning with red daybeacon "2" just downriver from the W.P. Franklin Lock. From here to Fort Myers there are several bridges to consider. The first is the **Wilson Pigott Drawbridge** at Mile 126.3 with a 27-foot closed vertical clearance. The bridge opens on signal except between 10:00 p.m. and 6:00 a.m., when it requires at least a 3-hour notice to open.

> At Mile 127.5, the scale of Chart 11428 changes to 1:40,000 for its final section, an inset marked "Fort Myers Extension."

The I-75 Bridges cross the OCWW at Mile 128.9 with a 55-foot fixed vertical clearance. The **SCL Railroad Bridge** at Mile 129.9 at Beautiful Island is normally open unless a train is due. The closed vertical clearance is only 5 feet so signal or call on VHF Channel 9 for an opening and then hold well off until the train has passed and the bridge is fully opened. (Note that the overhang is 55 feet when the bridge is open.)

Beautiful Island lives up to its name but do not get too close due to depth concerns. There are some areas, particularly on the south side, where you can leave the channel but do so very cautiously after examining your chart.

There are two high-level bridges in Fort Myers–the **Edison Bridges** at Mile 134.6 in North Fort Myers and the **U.S. 41/Caloosahatchee River Bridge** at Mile 135. These bridges have at least 55-foot fixed vertical clearance.

Dockage: Before the Edison Bridges on the north bank of the river is Prosperity Pointe Marina, which is primarily a liveaboard marina with few amenities. Call ahead for approach directions and slip availability.

On the north bank at Mile 135 beside flashing red "52" look for the flashing green "1" and red daybeacon "2" of the well-marked channel to Hancock Creek, where you will find 5- to 7-foot MLW depths. Be aware of shoaling in the section of the channel that parallels the shore between green daybeacons "17" and "21" where

Did You Know?

Manatees only breathe through their nostrils since while they are underwater their mouths are occupied with eating! A manatee's lungs are two-thirds the length of its body. Manatees take up residence primarily in Florida's coastal waters during winter but some individuals migrate as far north as the Carolinas or as far west as Louisiana in summer. Manatees have swum as far north as Cape Cod, MA, in recent years.

Caloosahatchee River, FL

OLGA AREA		Largest Vessel	VHF	Total Slips	Approach/ Dockside Depth	Floating Docks	Gas/ Diesel	Repairs/ Haulout	Min/Max Amps	Pump-Out Station
1. W.P. Franklin Campground-Boat-In Docks MM 122.0	(239) 694-8770	40		8	/				30 / 50	
2. C-10 Caloosa Marina **WiFi** 124.2	(239) 694-2708	200	16	15	23.0 / 8.0		GD		30 / 50	
3. Owl Creek Boat Works MM 125.5	**(239) 543-2100**	125		48	7.0 / 7.0			RH	50	
4. Sweetwater Landing Marina **WiFi** MM 126.0	(239) 694-3850	200	16	65	9.0 / 5.0		G	R	30 / 50	P

WiFi Wireless Internet Access   **onSpot** Dockside WiFi Facility
Visit www.waterwayguide.com for current rates, fuel prices, website addresses and other up-to-the-minute information.
(Information in the table is provided by the facilities.)

Scan here for more details:

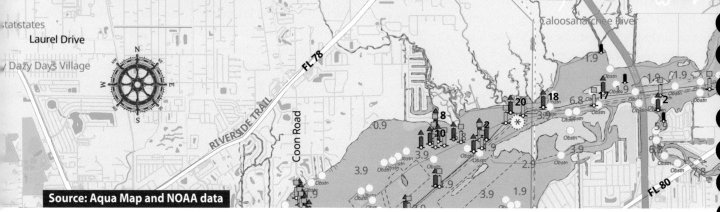

Source: Aqua Map and NOAA data

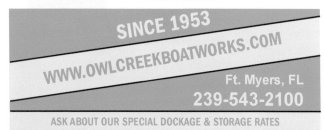

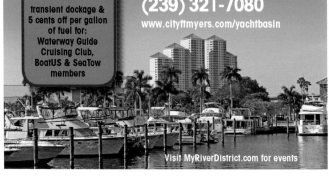

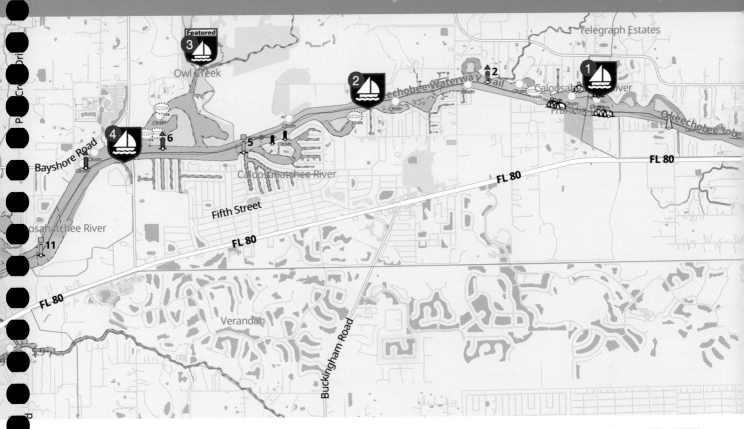

GOIN' ASHORE
FORT MYERS, FL

Strolling through the downtown area of Fort Myers is a great way to spend an afternoon or evening. Art lovers are sure to find events of interest throughout the year, including an Art Walk held on the first Friday of each month all year long. Theatre fans will find the plays, shows, and performances at the Florida Repertory Company at the Arcade, located right on the waterfront, to be greatly entertaining.

SERVICES

1. Edison Park Animal Hospital
2035 McGregor Blvd.
(239-689-3525)

2. Fort Myers Regional Library
2450 First St.
(239-533-4600)

3. Fort Myers Post Office
1350 Monroe St.
(239-332-3696)

4. Lee County Visitor & Convention Bureau
2201 Second St.
(239-338-3500)

5. Lee Memorial Hospital
2776 Cleveland Ave.
(239-343-2000)

ATTRACTIONS

6. Burroughs Home & Gardens

This Georgian Revival Mansion (circa 1901) overlooks the Edison Bridge at 2505 First St. and is open for guided tours. Reservations required (239-337-9505).

7. Edison & Ford Winter Estates

These side-by-side estates have been restored to their original grandeur and are open to the public. Edison's 14-acre riverfront estate is lined for 15 miles with 2,000 royal palms (2350 McGregor Blvd., 239-334-7419).

SHOPPING

8. Publix Super Market

Full-service grocery (groceries, deli and bakery items) at First Street Village shopping center at 2160 McGregor Blvd. (239-332-2403).

MARINAS

9. City of Fort Myers Yacht Basin

1300 Lee St. (239-321-7080)

10. Legacy Harbour Marina

2044 West 1st St. (239-461-0775)

11. The Marina at Edison Ford

2360 West 1st St.(239-245-7049)

Caloosahatchee River, FL

FORT MYERS AREA		Largest Vessel	VHF	Total Slips	Approach/ Dockside Depth	Floating Docks	Gas/ Diesel	Repairs/ Haulout	Min/Max Amps	Pump-Out Station
1. Prosperity Pointe Marina (WiFi) MM 134.0	(239) 995-2155	56	16	53	6.0 / 4.5	F			30 / 50	P
2. Marinatown Yacht Harbour (WiFi) MM 135.0	(239) 997-7711	68		135	6.0 / 5.0			R	30 / 100	P
3. City of Fort Myers Yacht Basin (WiFi) onSpot MM 134.5	(239) 321-7080	300	16	241	10.0 / 7.0		GD		30 / 100	P
4. Legacy Harbour Marina (WiFi) onSpot MM 135.5	(239) 461-0775	120	16	131	7.0 / 7.0	F			30 / 50	P
5. The Marina at Edison Ford (WiFi) onSpot MM 136.5	(239) 895-7703	80	16	45	7.0 / 5.0				30 / 50	P

(WiFi) Wireless Internet Access   onSpot Dockside WiFi Facility
Visit www.waterwayguide.com for current rates, fuel prices, website addresses and other up-to-the-minute information.
(Information in the table is provided by the facilities.)

Scan here for more details:

the channel carries only 4 to 4.5 feet MLW with a soft mud bottom. Marinatown Yacht Harbour is around the first bend above green daybeacon "25." They also cater to liveaboards but may have some transient space. Call in advance. There are four restaurants on site and kayak and paddleboard rentals.

City of Fort Myers Yacht Basin is situated on the south shore of the Caloosahatchee River between the westernmost span of the Edison Bridges and the US 41/ Caloosahatchee River Bridge. This facility is within walking distance of a large grocery store, a library, multiple restaurants and other amenities. The full-service marina can accommodate vessels both large and small but reserve your slip ahead to make sure space is available when you arrive.

The entrance to Legacy Harbour Marina is on the east side of the marina. Look for the piling with a white marina flag by the OCWW. Turn at that piling leaving it to starboard and head for the south shore. You will be headed toward a restaurant with a green roof (Joe's Crab Shack). Make a right into the marina basin. Legacy Harbour Marina has concrete floating docks that can accommodate vessels up to 120 feet with resort-style amenities. One of the largest floating breakwaters in the Gulf of Mexico protects the marina from the wakes of the river traffic. Grocery, shops and restaurants are within walking distance in the Historic Downtown River District.

The family-owned and -operated The Marina at Edison Ford is located about 1 mile beyond the US 41/ Caloosahatchee River Bridge. The marina maintains a well-marked channel on the south shore and is adjacent to the Edison Ford Winter Retreat. It is only a short walk to groceries and plenty of shopping and dining.

Anchorage: Because the Caloosahatchee River is more than 1 mile wide it can get rough in nasty weather so anchoring, although possible, could be unpleasant. At Mile 124.3 an oxbow on the south side of the waterway offers 5 feet MLW and some protection. Leave the OWW west of the oxbow and head southeast into loop.

Across from flashing green "13" at Mile 128 is the last good anchorage before Fort Myers. Locally known as Power Plant Slough, the western channel is reached by entering southwest of the manatee sign about halfway between the sign and shore. Continuing in the deepest water (at least 8 feet MLW) is about 100 feet off the western shore. The eastern channel of the slough is narrower, shallow and more difficult to follow. Manatees love it here too so be mindful that you will likely be sharing this space.

A former mooring field that has fallen into disrepair at Mile 134.8 offers 7 to 8 feet MLW. Ft. Myers–Lofton Island is between the Edison Bridges and the US 41/ Caloosahatchee River Bridge. These bridges have at least 55-foot fixed vertical clearance.

Fort Myers to Cape Coral–OCWW Mile 135 to Mile 142

Southwest of Fort Myers the Caloosahatchee River continues somewhat circuitously for another 15 miles to San Carlos Bay (Mile 149). On the way it passes Cape Coral, the second largest city in Florida, which was once swampland known as Redfish Point. Cape Coral is 114 square miles and its numerous canals total more mileage than those of Venice, Italy. This is a boating-oriented area and the traffic is reminiscent of downtown Fort Lauderdale.

NAVIGATION: Use NOAA Charts 11428 and 11427. At Mile 138.6 is the Midpoint Memorial Bridge followed by the Cape Coral Bridge at Mile 142. Both are charted at 55 feet. Note that water levels in the lake will affect bridge heights.

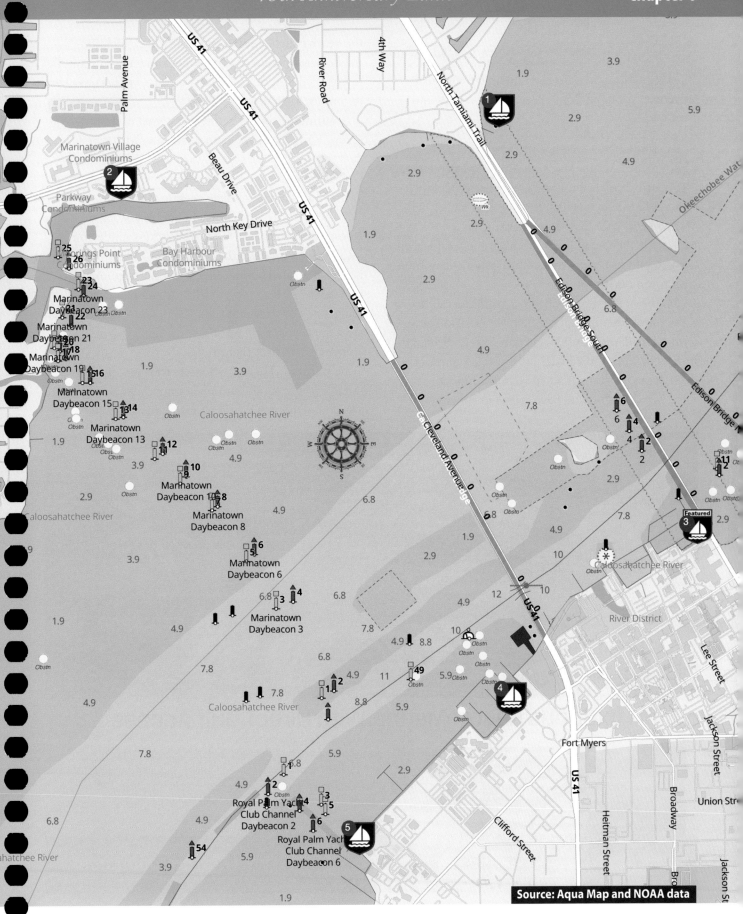

⚠️

Frequent groundings occur in the Caloosahatchee River west of Cape Coral. Be sure to use front and rear ranges.

Dockage: On a channel off Deep Lagoon the well-regarded MarineMax Fort Myers at Deep Lagoon is primarily a yacht brokerage and charter facility. Call ahead for slip availability. Nearby The Landings Marina is private. Near quick-flashing green "73" a well-marked channel leads southward to Gulf Harbour Marina, part of a yacht and country club community with resort amenities.

On the north shore at Redfish Point the municipal Cape Coral Yacht Basin/The Boat House Tiki Bar & Grill offers daily, monthly and annual rentals on a first-come, first-served basis. It is located north of red daybeacon "78" off a marked channel. Individuals who rent slips in the marina have access to amenities at the nearby Yacht Club Community Park including a public beach, tennis courts, a pool and a restaurant. Be forewarned that this is an active place. It's best to plan to join the rush or move along.

Continuing on the south shore, east of flashing green "85" a marked channel (starting with green daybeacon "1") leads southward to St. Charles Yacht Club. This club is a member of the Florida Council of Yacht Clubs and recognizes reciprocity.

At red daybeacon "92" a channel leads behind Cattle Dock Point to the north, where markers guide you into the well-appointed Tarpon Point Marina, which is part of a gated community. They can accommodate vessels to 120 feet and offer kayak and paddleboard rentals as well as sight-seeing excursions. Reservations are a must. Just past Tarpon Point signs will guide you to a small lock that provides access to Safe Harbor Cape Harbour. The marina offers transient dockage to 60 feet in a condominium setting. A laundry, pool and competitive fuel pricing make this a popular

Luxurious Resort Marina With Direct Gulf Access

Tarpon Point Marina is just a few miles from the Gulf of Mexico and some of the best cruising and fishing grounds in Florida. Our sheltered deepwater harbor accommodates vessels to 120 feet and is accented with luxurious resort amenities, fine dining, spas, and boutiques. Come for a day and you may just stay for a lifetime!

www.tarponpoint.com

stop. Be sure to call well in advance as this marina is usually full.

Anchorage: At red daybeacon "84A" there is a well-marked channel off to starboard that will lead you into the well-protected Bimini Basin. You need to stay in this channel and make a 90-degree turn to port when you get to green daybeacon "25." Then keep the red markers on your port side (we know that this is different but it is very important) until you come to the canal that will lead you into the anchorage. This is a handy spot to get to a couple of supermarkets and West Marine plus a very large hardware store as well as a variety of other services. There is a dinghy dock at Four Freedom's Park but no overnight dockage. You must register your boat with the harbormaster (239-574-0809).

Glover Bight, just behind Cattle Dock Point at Mile 147, is another excellent, all-weather anchorage. You will find good protection from all points with 10 to 12 feet at MLW with good holding in mud.

Tarpon Point Marina will let you tie up at the restaurant dock for 2 hours and charges a mandatory landing fee for skiffs and dinghies that are used to ferry passengers from vessels that are not tenants of the marina. The landing fee is refundable with proof of purchase from the nearby Marina Village Shops.

■ NEXT STOP

Should you choose to continue your journey westward to the Gulf, our coverage continues in Chapter 12: "Fort Myers Beach to Sarasota Bay." Otherwise, we will return to the ICW traveling south in Chapter 7: "St. Lucie to Pompano Beach."

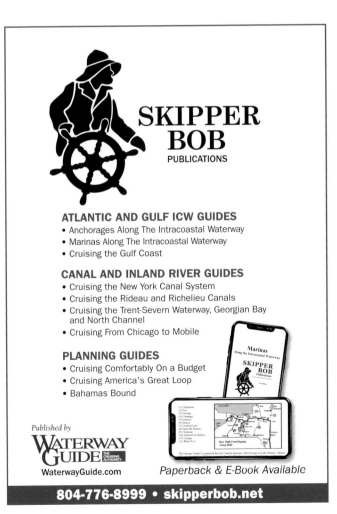

Source: Aqua Map and NOAA data

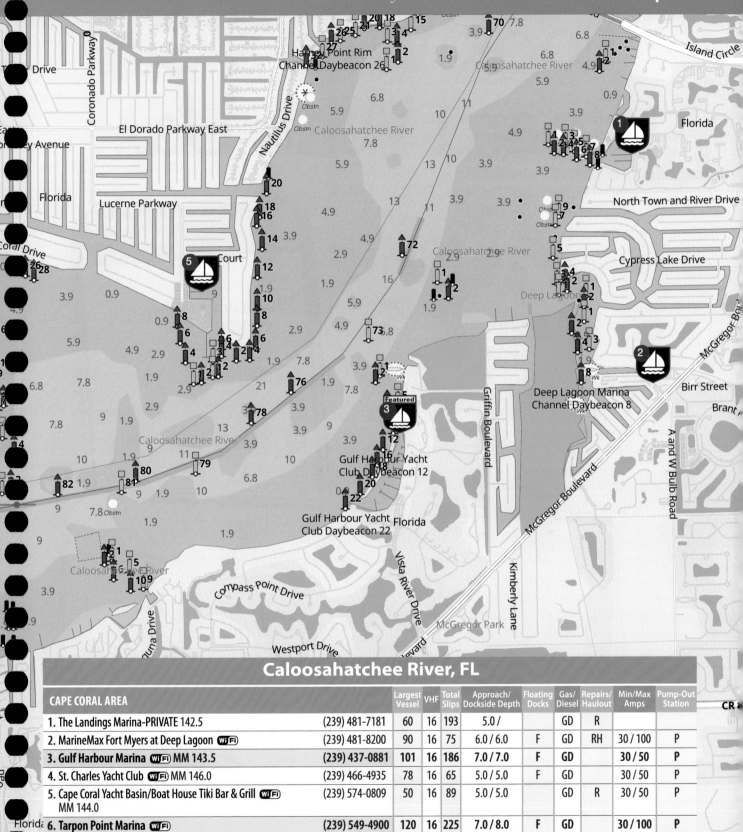

Caloosahatchee River, FL

CAPE CORAL AREA		Largest Vessel	VHF	Total Slips	Approach/ Dockside Depth	Floating Docks	Gas/ Diesel	Repairs/ Haulout	Min/Max Amps	Pump-Out Station
1. The Landings Marina-PRIVATE 142.5	(239) 481-7181	60	16	193	5.0 /		GD	R		
2. MarineMax Fort Myers at Deep Lagoon (WiFi)	(239) 481-8200	90	16	75	6.0 / 6.0	F	GD	RH	30 / 100	P
3. Gulf Harbour Marina (WiFi) MM 143.5	(239) 437-0881	101	16	186	7.0 / 7.0	F	GD		30 / 50	P
4. St. Charles Yacht Club (WiFi) MM 146.0	(239) 466-4935	78	16	65	5.0 / 5.0	F	GD		30 / 50	P
5. Cape Coral Yacht Basin/Boat House Tiki Bar & Grill (WiFi) MM 144.0	(239) 574-0809	50	16	89	5.0 / 5.0		GD	R	30 / 50	P
6. Tarpon Point Marina (WiFi)	(239) 549-4900	120	16	225	7.0 / 8.0	F	GD		30 / 100	P
7. Safe Harbor Cape Harbour (WiFi) MM 147.0	(239) 945-4330	60	16	76	6.0 / 6.0		GD	H	30 / 50	P

(WiFi) Wireless Internet Access　(onSpot) Dockside WiFi Facility
Visit www.waterwayguide.com for current rates, fuel prices, website addresses and other up-to-the-minute information. (Information in the table is provided by the facilities.)

Scan here for more details:

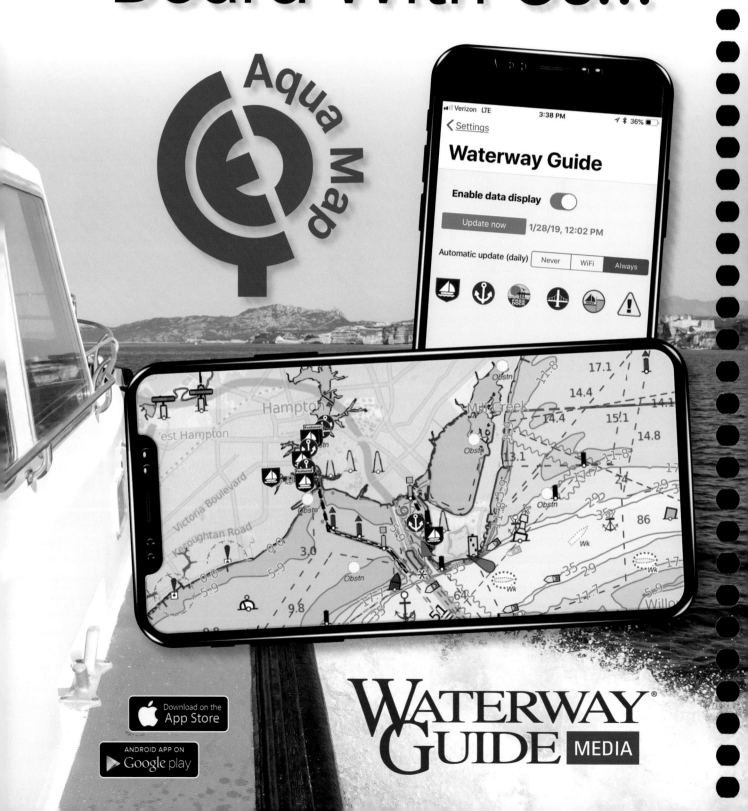

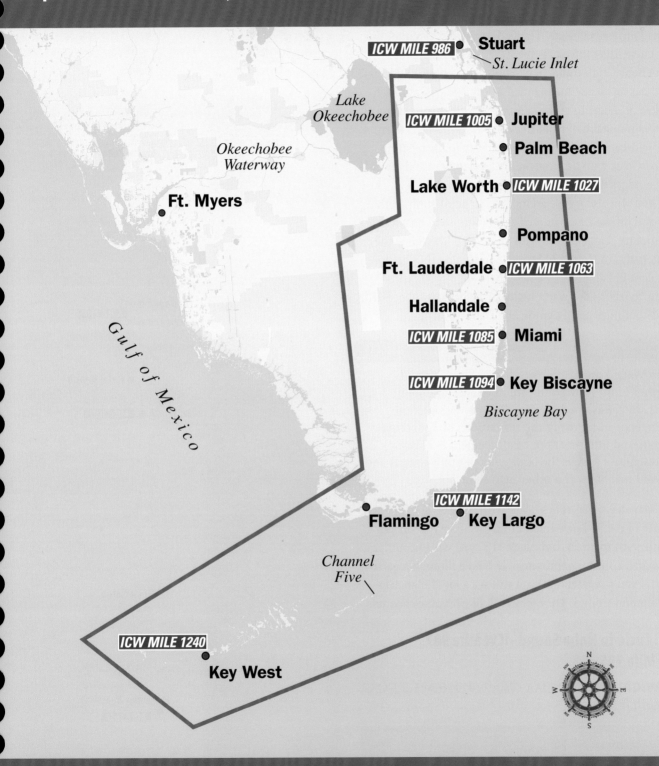

Mile 987-Mile 1057

■ ST. LUCIE TO POMPANO BEACH

This journey begins at "The Crossroads," where the St. Lucie River intersects the ICW. All the waterways experience high-traffic here. Study your charts in advance and have a courseline planned before you pass through. Below St. Lucie Inlet the coastline becomes truly tropical with a profusion of palm trees and exotic flowers. Here the laid-back Treasure Coast gives way to the bustling Gold Coast with its burgeoning development and fewer anchorages than you might wish.

You will also notice an increase in population–both on and off the water–as well as an increase in boat and home size. Large estates with manicured lawns line the waterways in Hobe and Jupiter Sounds and they get more opulent in Palm Beach, where there are more "yachts" than "boats." The "water highway" widens at Lake Worth and continues past Boynton and Delray Beaches.

NO WAKE ZONE

No Wake Zones, Idle Speed Zones and various Speed Limit restrictions are in effect throughout the waterways included in this chapter. Exercise diligence in knowing the regulations by observing signs and other markers. Enforcement is always present. As always, be courteous to other vessels and avoid manatees and other marine life.

Manatee speed zones occur with increasing frequency south of the St. Lucie Inlet. From green daybeacon "13" (Mile 990) to green daybeacon "15" you will encounter a Manatee Zone for approximately 1 mile through a narrow cut. If you pay attention, you will see a lot of manatees swimming around. They may look like floating coconuts.

St. Lucie to Hobe Sound–ICW Mile 987 to Mile 995

NAVIGATION: Use NOAA Chart 11472 (inset) or NOAA Chart 11428 (inset).

Southbound ICW traffic should note that the marker numbering sequence resets here but stay consistent with the rest of the ICW and continue to keep red markers to starboard when heading south.

Hobe Sound, Jupiter Inlet, FL

PECK LAKE		Largest Vessel	VHF	Total Slips	Approach/ Dockside Depth	Floating Docks	Gas/ Diesel	Repairs/ Haulout	Min/Max Amps	Pump-Out Station
1. Loblolly Marina (WiFi) MM 992.2	(772) 546-3136	110	16	74	7.0 / 7.0				30 / 100	

(WiFi) Wireless Internet Access   ◉onSpot Dockside WiFi Facility
Visit www.waterwayguide.com for current rates, fuel prices, website addresses and other up-to-the-minute information.
(Information in the table is provided by the facilities.)

Scan here for more details:

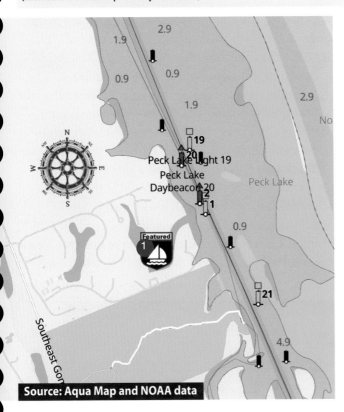

Source: Aqua Map and NOAA data

The 16-foot-high flashing red buoy "240" (ICW marker) at The Crossroads marks the beginning of the Okeechobee Waterway westward. Look for channel entry markers red daybeacon "2" and flashing green "3," located 0.25 mile south of flashing red "240" inside Rocky Point. Split these markers proceeding south. The course is approximately 160° magnetic from flashing red "240." You will find these markers past a white sign on the west side of the ICW reading, "DANGER–SHOAL." Favor the green side through to green daybeacon "5" when southbound as a series of dangerous shoals flank the east shore of Rocky Point.

When traversing Great Pocket south from Horseshoe Point watch for shoaling and use caution; it is quite shallow outside the marked channel. In particular watch for extreme shoaling at the west edge of the channel between red daybeacon "12" and flashing red "14." Leaving Great Pocket the ICW enters a cut just south

of paired green daybeacon "13" and flashing red "14." (Note that long docks and piers are on both sides of Great Pocket and are not shown on the chart.) The cut ends at paired flashing green "15" and red daybeacon "16" and enters Peck Lake.

There is shoaling on the west (red) side at flashing red "16" to red daybeacon "18" to 5 feet MLW. Favor the green side of the channel for 7 feet MLW. Peck Lake has depths throughout of 6 to 12 feet MLW from the ICW channel to close to shore. Depths are extremely shallow outside the marked channel through most of the lake.

The ICW between Peck Lake and Hobe Sound is a pleasant run through a series of dredged channels and cuts. The ICW channel is sparsely marked on this stretch but fairly obvious. South from Peck Lake favor the west side of the channel for better water. Consistent with Martin County's bylaws, buildings are restricted to four stories here. While development is less imposing, there are a number of side channels so expect increased boat traffic.

Dockage: On the mainland side of Peck Lake near the south end is Loblolly Marina. Don't be scared off by the two "Private" signs. Transient and long-term dockage is available in this gated golf course community in a very protected and pretty basin. Note that Loblolly Marina offers basic amenities and is not a resort but it is quiet and surrounded by lush mangroves and offers easy access to the beach on Jupiter Island. You can easily dinghy, kayak or paddle from the marina across Peck Lake to the Hobe Sound National Wildlife Refuge.

Anchorage: Low dunes, uninhabited beaches and sparkling ocean waters beckon and dredging of Peck Lake and lake access has made anchoring less of a challenge than in the past. Deep water access into Peck Lake is found to the south of flashing green "19." The anchorage is very close to the ICW channel and can be subject to large wakes. Take it slow and head toward the "Danger" sign. Watch for shoaling south of the sign. You will find 6 to 12 feet MLW in a narrow strip with room for half a dozen boats or more. There is the possibility of debris on the bottom so exercise caution when choosing an anchoring spot and we recommend use of a trip-line.

Even though Peck Lake is well protected on all sides and a no wake zone you will still encounter wakes from some passing boats. The anchorage is often busy during the week and becomes even more crowded on weekends. Once anchored a dinghy ride to shore brings you to within a short distance over the dunes to a beautiful, unspoiled ocean beach that is part of Hobe Sound National Wildlife Refuge.

Side Trip: St. Lucie Inlet Preserve State Park

A bit of natural wilderness is preserved just south of the inlet in the St. Lucie Inlet Preserve State Park and adjoining Hobe Sound National Wildlife Refuge (officially the Nathanial P. Reed National Wildlife Refuge). The two reserves combined run for 5 miles starting at the north tip of Jupiter Island from Mile 988.5 to Mile 993.5. The state park ends and the wilderness seashore begins at the south end of the cut between Great Pocket and Peck Lake. The reserves are known for their fine beaches, kayaking, trails and boardwalks.

The reserves can be accessed from a dock on Great Pocket or a beach on the east shore of the ICW in Peck Lake. An elevated boardwalk with restrooms and picnic pavilions at either end takes visitors from the Great Pocket docks at Mile 989.3 through mangrove forests and hammocks of live oaks, cabbage palms, paradise trees and wild limes to a neatly preserved Atlantic beach.

A portion north of the crossover path is closed in the spring and early summer months to protect nesting Least Terns (sterna antillarum, the smallest of the American terns). South of this path the beach is available for walking and swimming. Note that dogs are allowed on the walkway but not on the beach. Also, when temperatures are above 60 degrees, with little or no wind, sand gnats (commonly called "no-see-ums") can be a problem.

Dockage: A floating dock and a long pier with slips for smaller boats are near the north end of the St. Lucie Inlet Preserve State Park, which is accessible only by boat. Watch for shoaling between the dock and the ICW channel. There is a lot of shallow water in this area. Come out of the channel right by the big dock sign that reads "St. Lucie Inlet Preserve Park" for the deepest water. On

LOBLOLLY MARINA

Peck Lake

the way back out be sure to turn into the channel right away. If you venture too far west, you will find shoaling.

There is an unmarked, shallow channel (4-foot MLW depths) that is best accessed by dinghy. Don't anchor near the docks as they lie in a charted Pipeline Area. It's best to anchor in Peck Lake, farther south through the cut. Tie off carefully as powerboats often pass without slowing causing heavy wakes. A small fee is collected on the honor system for use of the park.

Peck Lake to Jupiter Inlet–ICW Mile 996 to Mile 1004

The Native American Jove tribe (pronounced "Ho-bay") gave Hobe Sound its name. This highly exclusive area is sometimes compared with Palm Beach due to its grand mansions and manicured lawns along the eastern shore of the channel. The natural wilderness of Hobe Sound National Wildlife Refuge on the western shore at about Mile 997 provides a striking contrast with the sculptured lawns on the opposite shore.

NAVIGATION: Use NOAA Chart 11472. The **Hobe Sound (CR 708) Bridge** crosses the ICW at the northern end of Hobe Sound (Mile 995.9). The bridge has a closed vertical clearance of 21 feet at the center and opens on

signal. For the most part both sides of the well-marked channel through Hobe Sound have good depths but it's best not to stray too far from the centerline as there are some dangerous shoals. In particular watch for bars that extend from the points jutting from the west shore. Give red markers a wide berth as most mark shoals at the edge of the channel and carefully watch depths near red daybeacons "40" and "44."

A Slow-Speed/Minimum-Wake zone is in effect year-round for all vessels between red daybeacon "44" and green daybeacon "49."

The ICW leads into Jupiter Sound at Mile 1002, where the estates of Hobe Sound give way to only slightly more modest homes. Nearby spoil areas and shoals demand careful attention; stay in the channel! Jupiter Inlet at Mile 1004 marks the confluence of Jupiter Sound to the north, Lake Worth Creek to the south and the Loxahatchee River to the west. The inlet is known for its red brick lighthouse and aquamarine-colored waters.

Jupiter Inlet fights a constant battle with shifting sand. Despite frequent dredging, the inlet is cited by the Coast Guard as "not navigable without current local knowledge." The inlet channel is unsafe for all but small boats with local knowledge and very shallow draft. A

Hobe Sound, Jupiter Inlet, FL

JUPITER AREA		Largest Vessel	VHF	Total Slips	Approach/ Dockside Depth	Floating Docks	Gas/ Diesel	Repairs/ Haulout	Min/Max Amps	Pump-Out Station
1. Blowing Rocks Marina (WiFi) MM 1002.2	(561) 746-3312	70	16	60	6.0 / 5.0	F	GD	RH	30 / 50	P
2. Black Pearl Marina and Gilbane Boatworks	(561) 744-2223	65		41	8.0 / 8.0			R	20 / 50	
3. JIB Yacht Club Marina (WiFi) MM 1004.2	(561) 746-4300	70	16	30	8.0 / 8.0		GD		30 / 50	P

(WiFi) Wireless Internet Access   onSpot Dockside WiFi Facility
Visit www.waterwayguide.com for current rates, fuel prices, website addresses and other up-to-the-minute information.
(Information in the table is provided by the facilities.)

Scan here for more details:

short jetty protects the inlet entrance to the north and a steel barricade extends halfway into the inlet from the south bank. The mouth of the inlet has strong currents, eddies, turbulence and breaking seas over sandbars that extend from the south side of the inlet offshore towards the northeast. The average tidal range is 2.5 feet.

Shoals also flank the east edge of the channel south from green daybeacon "57" to the Jupiter Island (CR 707) Bridge (hail as the "707 Bridge") at Mile 1004.1. The bridge has a 25-foot closed vertical clearance and opens on signal. If your vessel is lightly powered, mind the swift current here while waiting for the bridge. Contact the bridgetender prior to your arrival and allow for the set of the current passing through.

Dockage: At Mile 1002 Blowing Rocks Marina has limited space for transients (two slips). Black Pearl Marina and Gilbane Boatworks just on the opposite side of Hell Gate is a repair/service facility that does not offer transient dockage. The JIB Yacht Club Marina is just south of the Jupiter Island (CR 707) Bridge on the east side of the ICW with five transient slips. Call ahead for slip availability.

Anchorage: Because there is a 25-mph speed limit in the Hobe Sound channel almost all anchorages here are susceptible to annoying boat wakes. There are numerous anchorages with 8 to 9 feet MLW west of the ICW channel between red daybeacon "38" and green daybeacon "49." Shore access to the wildlife refuge is easy at several sandy beaches and the sunrises are outstanding.

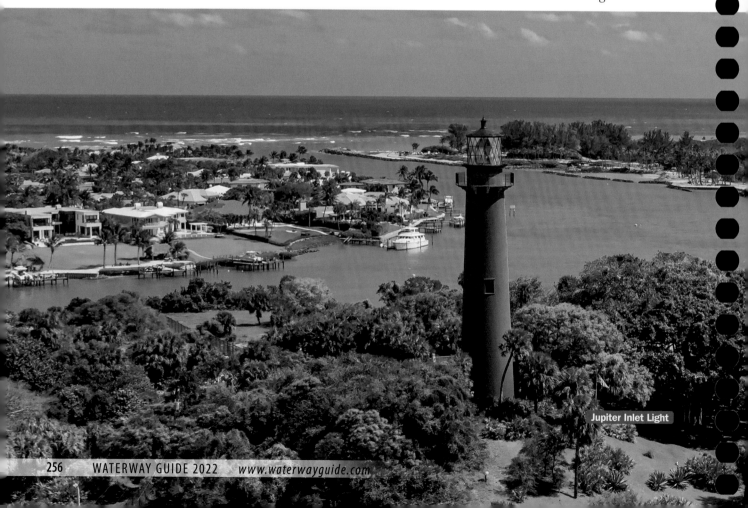

Jupiter Inlet Light

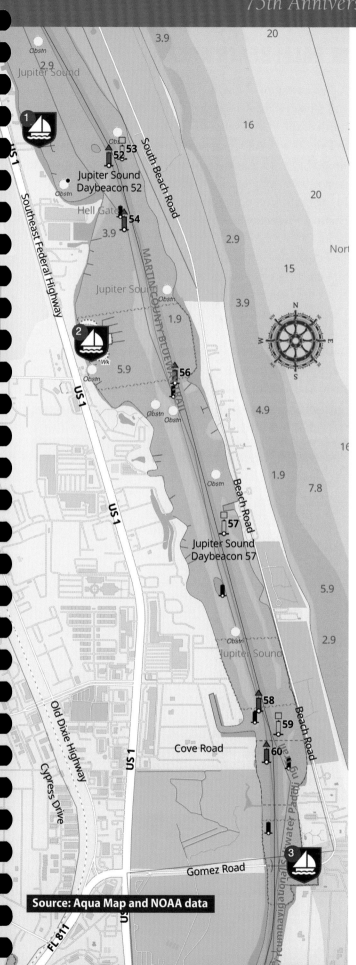

Source: Aqua Map and NOAA data

A favorite spot is the large lobe of deep water north of Mile 999 on the west side of the channel between red daybeacon "38" and "40" and others north or south of red daybeacon "44" where the speed restrictions apply. Be careful here as shoaling extends from shore to red daybeacon "44." Mind your depth as you leave the channel. Passing vessels and water skiers may throw some wake your way in the daytime but nights are generally peaceful. Do not be surprised by a routine boarding from local marine police and be sure to show an anchor light.

A fair anchorage is by green daybeacon "49" in Home Sound. This anchorage is in front of large homes in an expensive Jupiter golf community with docks and quite a few large motor yachts. There's room for three boats in 10 to 12 feet MLW. Anchor as far north as possible.

Lake Worth Creek–ICW Mile 1004 to Mile 1012

The ICW intersects the Loxahatchee River at Mile 1004.5. The Jupiter Inlet runs to the east and the ICW continues to the west. The ICW route south begins a sharp reverse S-curve, first to starboard (west) up the Loxahatchee River passing under the **U.S. 1 (Jupiter) Bridge** at Mile 1004.8, then to port (south) out of the Loxahatchee River and into Lake Worth Creek. The bridge has 26-foot closed vertical clearance and opens on signal. This is a high-traffic area and obstructions come up quickly so slow down! Large vessels may want to issue a Sécurité call on VHF Channels 09 and 16. Watch currents through the entire S-curve and make the blind turn into Lake Worth Creek cautiously.

The route appears to dead end shortly after in a false lead created by the **Old Dixie Hwy. Bridge** with a 25-foot fixed vertical clearance and the **Loxahatchee Railroad Bridge**, both on the Loxahatchee River. The railroad bridge is normally open except during train traffic and was under construction at press time. The ICW actually turns south before the bridges, starting a long sweeping curve at green daybeacon "7" where the ICW leaves the Loxahatchee River and enters Lake Worth Creek. Note that you will not see the opening southbound into Lake Worth Creek until you are almost in it, and boats coming from the south will not be visible until after you are well in to the turn. A slow, wide turn is advised.

Lake Worth Creek bustles with boats of all sizes and the shore gleams with condominiums and houses set among beautifully manicured lawns. But do not let your eye stray too far from mid-channel and check the depth and boat speed frequently.

Indiantown (SR 706) Bridge crosses the ICW at Mile 1006.2. The bridge has 35-foot closed vertical clearance and opens on the hour and half-hour, 24 hours a day, 7 days a week. This is an enforced No-Wake Zone. **Donald Ross Bridge** (35-foot closed vertical clearance) at Mile 1009.3 opens on the hour and half-hour.

Dockage: On the west side of the waterway at Mile 1006.8 is Loggerhead Marina–Jupiter Marina offering secure wet or dry storage. Amenities include a pool and a well-stocked Ship's Store. Call ahead.

Admirals Cove Marina offers slips and resort-style amenities at Mile 1007.8 The marina can accommodate boats up to 170 feet and is considered a natural weather refuge for yachts. The Bluffs Marina at Mile 1008 is primarily a "dockominium" marina with limited transient slips; call ahead.

Anchorage: There is a shallow anchorage north of Indiantown Bridge on the east side past flashing green "11." This area is full of small boats permanently moored, along with a public boat ramp and a floating hot dog stand on weekends (in season). There are not a lot of anchoring opportunities on Lake Worth Creek due to the number of private docks lining both shores.

■ PALM BEACH AREA

A concentration of marinas offering all kinds of services and repairs is located on the ICW stretch from just north of the PGA Boulevard Bridge in North Palm Beach to Palm Beach. All are convenient to the area's famous shopping. With this increase in services expect an increase boat activity. While Lake Worth seems expansive, most to the traffic is confined to the narrow, dredged ICW channel. Expect wakes to be high and boater etiquette to be low on the lake.

For those waiting for a weather window for a Gulf Stream crossing or an "outside run" the Lake Worth area offers some excellent anchorage opportunities. Unfortunately, there are few dockage facilities for dinghies and a provisioning run may necessitate a marina stay. Boat traffic on Lake Worth can be extremely heavy. It's best to anchor in an area with speed restrictions. Noise can be an issue near Peanut Island, particularly on weekends.

> Remember to always stay up to date on the most current Florida anchoring laws. They are challenged almost every year in the state legislature.

Loxahatchee River

North Palm Beach–ICW Mile 1012 to Mile 1016

NAVIGATION: Use NOAA Chart 11472. The ICW continues south on an easy run through a wide cut to Lake Worth. There are no aids to navigation in the cut and few hazards. The North Palm Beach Waterway forks off the ICW to the southwest at the apex of the curve between the **PGA Boulevard Bridge** and **Parker (U.S. 1) Bridge**. The PGA Boulevard Bridge at Mile 1012.6 has 24-foot closed vertical clearance and opens on the hour and half-hour. Just over 1 mile south and around a blind curve the Parker (US 1) Bridge at Mile 1013.7 has 25-foot closed vertical clearance and opens on the quarter and three-quarter hour.

This waterway serves a heavily developed area so expect increased boat traffic here. The extra traffic justifies a Slow-Speed/Minimum-Wake Zone that continues to the opening into Lake Worth at Mile 1014.2.

At Mile 1014 just south of the Parker (US 1) Bridge the ICW enters the open waters of Lake Worth. The lake is long and broad but shallow outside the ICW channel. Do not confuse the ICW markers leading south with those splitting off to the east and then north to Safe Harbor Old Port Cove and the upper end of Lake Worth (and on to Little Lake Worth, a separate body of water). Lake Worth is crowded with boats, marinas and private docks so damage from wakes can be severe.

Popular Peanut Island

Peanut Island was originally created in 1918 as a result of material excavated when the Lake Worth Inlet was created. Originally called Inlet Island, Peanut Island amounted to only 10 acres. Today, as a result of continued maintenance dredging of the inlet and the ICW, Peanut Island comprises approximately 80 acres.

Peanut Island is a public park that is popular with small powerboaters who anchor around its perimeter and party in the shallow, sandy-bottom water that extends out into the ICW. (There are also 18 boat slips available for day use only.)

Swimming areas, kayaking lagoons and terrific snorkeling are among the draws of Peanut Island. There are paved walkways with scenic outlooks. Island facilities include picnic shelters and restrooms, and a dredged boat basin on its northwest side for dinghy tie-up.

The former Coast Guard Station and JFK Bomb Shelter on the south side of Peanut Island are part of the Palm Beach Maritime Museum and open for tours. The shelter, about 1,500 square feet in all, was abandoned after JFK's assassination in 1963 and was close to ruin when the Palm Beach Maritime Museum took over in the 1990s.

Water taxi service is available from Palm Beach Water Taxi (561-683-8294) and Peanut Island Shuttle Boat (561-723-2028). Call the water taxi on VHF Channel 16.

Hobe Sound, Jupiter Inlet, FL

JUPITER AREA		Largest Vessel	VHF	Total Slips	Approach/ Dockside Depth	Floating Docks	Gas/ Diesel	Repairs/ Haulout	Min/Max Amps	Pump-Out Station
1. Jupiter Yacht Club & Marina-PRIVATE MM 1006.5	(561) 741-3407	65		79	5.0 / 5.0				30 / 50	
2. Loggerhead Marina - Jupiter Marina MM 1006.8	(561) 747-8980	100	16		7.0 / 6.0	F	G	R		P
3. Admirals Cove Marina WiFi onSpot MM 1007.8	(561) 745-5930	170	16	65	11.0 / 10.0	F	GD		30 / 100	P

WiFi Wireless Internet Access **onSpot** Dockside WiFi Facility
Visit www.waterwayguide.com for current rates, fuel prices, website addresses and other up-to-the-minute information.
(Information in the table is provided by the facilities.)

Scan here for more details:

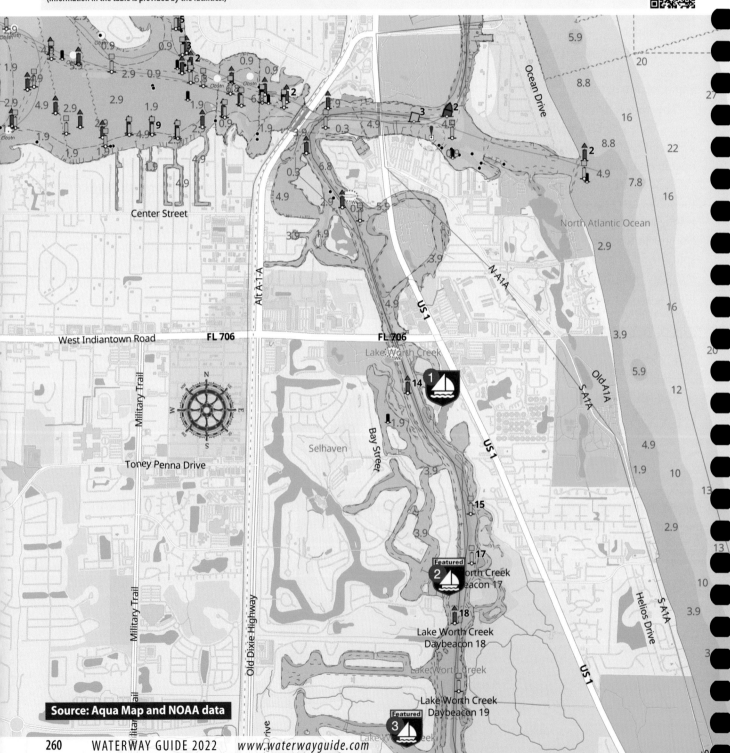

Source: Aqua Map and NOAA data

Hobe Sound, Jupiter Inlet, FL

JUPITER AREA		Largest Vessel	VHF	Total Slips	Approach/ Dockside Depth	Floating Docks	Gas/ Diesel	Repairs/ Haulout	Min/Max Amps	Pump-Out Station
1. The Bluffs Marina (WiFi) ☺ onSpot MM 1008.0	(561) 408-3993	130	16	102	/	F	GD		50 / 100	P
2. Loggerhead Marina - Palm Beach Gardens (WiFi) ☺ onSpot	(561) 627-6358	120	16	136	8.0 / 8.0		GD		30 / 100	P

(WiFi) Wireless Internet Access ☺ onSpot Dockside WiFi Facility
Visit www.waterwayguide.com for current rates, fuel prices, website addresses and other up-to-the-minute information.
(Information in the table is provided by the facilities.)

Scan here for more details:

Dockage: Loggerhead Marina–Palm Beach Gardens at Mile 1009 is just south of the Donald Ross Bridge in a well-protected basin off the ICW. Loggerhead can accommodate transient boats up to 120 feet plus offers resort-like amenities and easy access to restaurants, shopping, golf, tennis and other activities.

Hemingway's Boatyard and Seminole Marine Maintenance are both full-service boatyards located north of the PGA Boulevard Bridge. Call ahead to check for slip availability.

Soverel Harbour Marina is tucked away in a protected basin and welcomes transients on its floating docks. This well-known "hurricane hole" is close to dining, shopping and entertainment. PGA Marina & Boating Center to the south has dry slips, wet dockage and commercial marine sales. They have just five reserved transient slips so call ahead.

Just south of the Parker (US 1) Bridge is Safe Harbor North Palm Beach. This facility is located in a secluded, sheltered keyhole-shaped harbor and can accommodate vessels to 150 feet. The marina features a fully stocked Ship's Store and pump-out service at every slip in addition to the usual amenities.

At flashing green "27" turn east into a privately marked channel leading into the north lobe of Lake Worth for Safe Harbor Old Port Cove. Hail "Old Port Cove" on VHF Channel 16 to be directed to a slip. This marina offers resort amenities including a restaurant, a fitness room and indoor laundry facilities. A West Marine and provisioning options are nearby. Call in advance.

Anchorage: Some cruisers have reported adequate depths for anchoring in the lagoons off the North Palm Beach Waterway. They are reached by turning to starboard at the bend just before Parker (US 1) Bridge. The canal is charted at 7 feet MLW with 6-foot MLW depths in the first basin and 8 feet MLW in the second, both of which will be to starboard. This is a high-end residential community; dinghy landings are not permitted.

Another well-protected anchorage is located in the north lobe of Lake Worth opposite Safe Harbor Old Port Cove in Turtle Cove. Continue north past the marina into the lake's deeper basin. You can drop the hook in 9- to 14-foot MLW depths and have plenty of swinging room. This anchorage is surrounded by a residential neighborhood and the only potential dinghy landing is a small patch of sand north of the Little Lake Worth (A1A) Bridge. A Publix and a microbrewery are a few hundred yards west along PGA Boulevard but be aware that attempts have been made to close this landing in recent years.

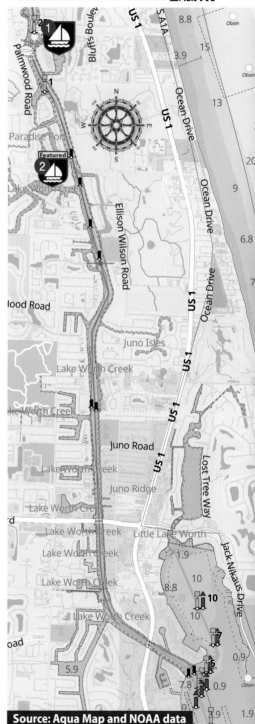

Source: Aqua Map and NOAA data

Lake Worth, FL

NORTH PALM BEACH		Largest Vessel	VHF	Total Slips	Approach/ Dockside Depth	Floating Docks	Gas/ Diesel	Repairs/ Haulout	Min/Max Amps	Pump-Out Station
1. Hemingway's Boatyard MM 1012.0	(561) 622-8550	80	16	10	10.0 / 5.0			RH	30 / 50	
2. Seminole Marine Maintenance MM 1011.9	(561) 622-7600	100		9	6.0 / 6.0			RH	50 / 100	
3. Soverel Harbour Marina (WiFi) ◉ onSpot MM 1011.9	(561) 691-9554	100	16	146	12.0 / 8.0	F	GD		30 / 50	P
4. PGA Marina & Boating Center (WiFi) MM 1011.9	(561) 626-0200	120	16	30	8.0 / 8.0		GD	RH	30 / 50	
5. Safe Harbor North Palm Beach (WiFi) ◉ onSpot MM 1013.7	(561) 626-4919	150	16	107	10.0 / 8.0	F	GD	R	30 / 100	P
6. Safe Harbor Old Port Cove (WiFi) ◉ onSpot MM 1014.0	(561) 626-1760	250	16	203	12.0 / 15.0	F	D	R	30 / 200+	P

(WiFi) Wireless Internet Access ◉ onSpot Dockside WiFi Facility
Visit www.waterwayguide.com for current rates, fuel prices, website addresses and other up-to-the-minute information.
(Information in the table is provided by the facilities.)

Scan here for more details:

⚠️

Turtle Cove can be a problem anchorage based on local law enforcement's interpretation of the regulations and where vessels choose to anchor. The cautionary note is vessels must know where navigation channels are and anchor well out of those channels. Some homeowners is the area complain about boats being anchored near their docks, which can lead to a visit from law enforcement.

Riviera Beach Area–ICW Mile 1016 to Mile 1018

NAVIGATION: Use NOAA Chart 11472. Lake Worth is broad in the first stretch leading to the high-rise Blue Heron (SR A1A) Bridge (65-foot fixed vertical clearance) at Mile 1017.2 but depths outside the dredged channel are shallow. Stay in the marked channel even if you see small craft taking other routes. The City of Riviera Beach has two bodies of land split by the waters of Lake Worth and the ICW. Parts of the city lie at each end of this bridge.

⚠️

While the **Blue Heron (SR A1A) Bridge** is charted at 65-foot fixed vertical clearance, actual clearance at high tide will be lower. Check the clearance boards on the bridge.

The channel is narrow and a Slow-Speed/Minimum-Wake applies from the Blue Heron (SR A1A) Bridge to the turning basin. Considerable chop can build in Lake Worth and watch the set of your course in a strong crosswind.

Just through the Blue Heron (SR A1A) Bridge you must make a decision. Directly ahead is Peanut Island and one of the most congested areas on the ICW. If you plan to continue south on the ICW, alter course to starboard following the ICW around Peanut Island on the west side. On weekends it can be difficult to discern the channel markers from the mayhem surrounding Peanut Island. Reduce speed here.

There are two channels leading to Lake Worth (Palm Beach) Inlet. The most direct route is via a channel that hugs the shore of Singer Island. After passing under the Blue Heron (SR A1A) Bridge, turn east and follow the marked channel, which ends at the Lake Worth (Palm Beach) Inlet. Keep green markers to starboard while

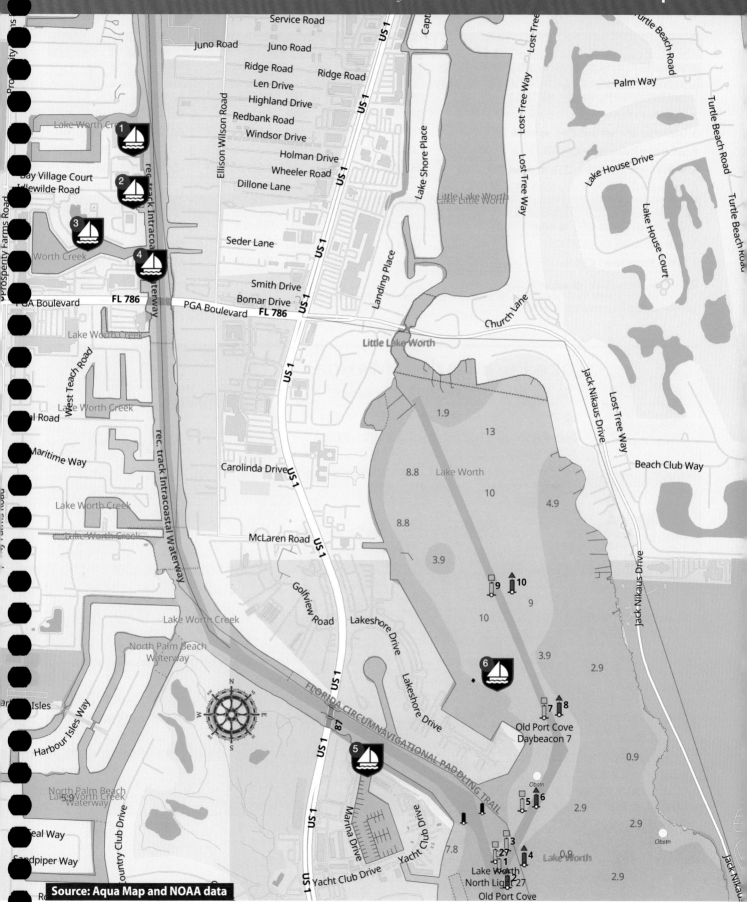

Source: Aqua Map and NOAA data

Lake Worth, FL

RIVIERA BEACH		Largest Vessel	VHF	Total Slips	Approach/ Dockside Depth	Floating Docks	Gas/ Diesel	Repairs/ Haulout	Min/Max Amps	Pump-Out Station
1. Lake Park Harbor Marina **WiFi** MM 1016.2	(561) 881-3353	80	16	112	6.0 / 5.5	F	GD		30 / 50	P
2. Loggerhead Marina - Riviera Beach Marina MM 1017.0	(561) 840-6868	47		300	6.0 / 6.0		GD		30 / 50	P
3. Safe Harbor New Port Cove **WiFi** ◉ onSpot MM 1017.4	(561) 844-2504	80	16	49	5.0 / 5.0	F	GD	R	30 / 50	P
4. Safe Harbor Riviera Beach **WiFi** MM 1017.8	(561) 863-4126	300	16	10	15.0 / 17.0	F		RH	30 / 200+	P
5. Riviera Beach City Marina **WiFi** ◉ onSpot MM 1018.0	(561) 842-7806	270	16	164	8.0 / 7.0	F	GD		30 / 200+	P
6. Cracker Boy Boat Works - Riviera Beach **WiFi** MM 1018.1	(561) 845-0357	110	16		19.0 / 19.0			RH	30 / 100	
SINGER ISLAND										
7. Cannonsport Marina **WiFi** ◉ onSpot MM 1017.5	(800) 627-8328	130	16	54	10.0 / 8.0		GD		30 / 100	P
8. Buccaneer Marina **WiFi** MM 1017.6	(561) 842-1620	85	16	16	12.0 / 12.0		GD		30 / 50	
9. Sailfish Marina Resort **WiFi** MM 1017.7	(561) 844-1724	110	16	94	8.0 / 8.0	F	GD		30 / 200+	

WiFi Wireless Internet Access ◉ **onSpot** Dockside WiFi Facility
Visit www.waterwayguide.com for current rates, fuel prices, website addresses and other up-to-the-minute information.
(Information in the table is provided by the facilities.)

Scan here for more details:

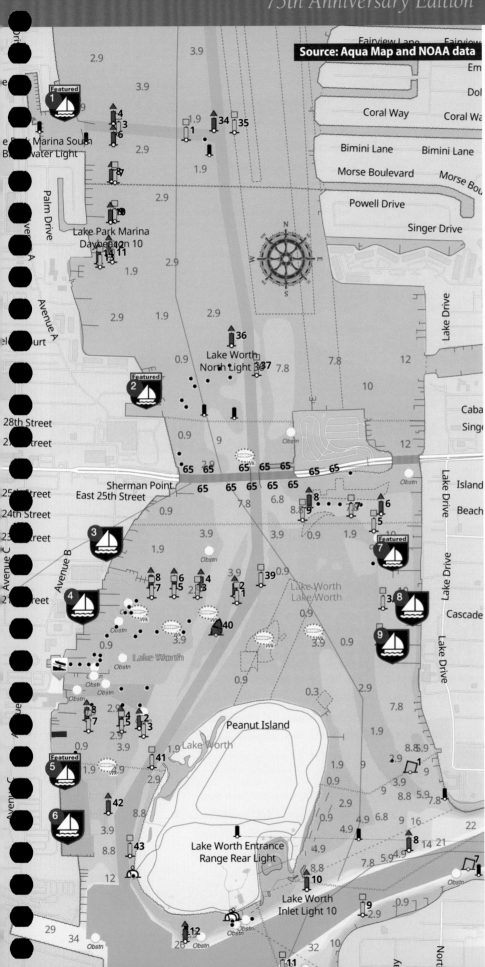

Source: Aqua Map and NOAA data

traveling southbound on this channel and out of the inlet. Be sure to stay to the north (red) side of the channel as that is where you will find the deeper water. You will pass close to the marinas on the shore of Singer Island so watch your wake. Also note the charted large bar extending east from Peanut Island towards the inlet.

A deeper and wider route passes around the west side of Peanut Island and enters the deepwater Turning Basin at the shipping wharves. From here you follow the Main Ship Channel through to the ocean or continue south on the ICW.

Dockage: Above the Blue Heron (SR A1A) Bridge on the west shore at Mile 1016.2 is the park-like Lake Park Harbor Marina. This well-maintained marina can accommodate vessels to 80 feet on floating docks. The staff is friendly and knowledgeable and dog friendly too.

The 300-slip Loggerhead Marina–Riviera Beach Marina is also on the west shore just north of the Blue Heron (SR A1A) Bridge (Mile 1017). It's easy to spot its two towers and huge (hurricane-rated) dry storage facility. The marina offers club-type amenities with close proximity to waterfront restaurants, shopping, golf, beaches, tennis and nightlife. Call ahead for slip availability.

South of the Blue Heron (SR A1A) Bridge marine facilities are abundant both north and south of Lake Worth (Palm Beach) Inlet. On the west shore beginning at Riviera Beach are repair yards capable of handling boats of any size. Safe Harbor New Port Cove has a state-of-the-art dry stack storage system, wet slips and gas and diesel with high-speed pumps. They also have a well-stocked Ship's Store. Call ahead for slip availability.

Cannonsport Marina

Riviera Beach City Marina

ICW

Lake Worth Inlet

Peanut Island

The next facility heading south is Safe Harbor Riviera Beach, a superyacht marina. Their in-house tug can escort you to dry dock or floating slips and provide most any service or refit. Complimentary shuttles are available to transport crew between Safe Harbor Riviera Beach and West Palm Beach facilities as well as Downtown West Palm Beach and the surrounding area.

Continuing south is the Riviera Beach City Marina at Mile 1018 (across from Peanut Island), which offers dockage including catamaran slips. This is a busy marina with fishing charters and pump-out service at every slip. Crosscurrents can be strong here and maneuvering space gets tight so take some care while docking. Cracker Boy Boat Works-Riviera Beach is nearby for repairs and maintenance. They allow DIY and also have on-site contractors should you need a hand.

On the east shore the resort area of Singer Island is crowded with houses, motels, docks and restaurants. There is a strong current at all the marinas on Singer Island so exercise care while docking. The 54-slip Cannonsport Marina is the northernmost facility. It caters to sportfishing vessels but all transients are welcome. They have a fully stocked Ship's Store, in-slip diesel fuel and pump-out service.

The iconic Buccaneer Marina at Mile 1017.6 may have space for you. This is billed as a "fisherman's paradise" and has been around well over 50 years. Sailfish Marina Resort located just north of the Lake Worth (Palm Beach) Inlet on Singer Island also caters to sportfishing vessels but welcomes all. They have a popular on-site restaurant.

Anchorage: Just northeast of Blue Heron Bridge you can drop the hook in 8 to 13-foot MLW depths over the "Discontinued Spoil Area." There are a number of derelict boats and a few sunken ones here. Beware of wreckage on the bottom. It is best to wait to anchor in Lake Worth. Note that anchor lights must be used in all Lake Worth anchorages.

Lake Worth (Palm Beach) Inlet—ICW Mile 1018

Wide, well-marked and protected by jetties, Lake Worth (Palm Beach) Inlet boasts a deep straightforward big ship channel that is one of the easiest to enter on the Atlantic coast. The meandering Gulf Stream is closer here than at any point in the U.S. (sometimes as close as 1 mile offshore but usually out about 8 to 12 miles) and both commercial and recreational craft give the Lake Worth (Palm Beach) Inlet heavy use. It is located approximately midway between Fort Pierce Inlet (45 nm north) and Lake Worth (Palm Beach) Inlet (40 nm south) making it popular with boaters who prefer to travel offshore.

> Lake Worth (Palm Beach) Inlet is a favorite point of departure for boats bound to and from the Bahamas Islands. It's the closest U.S. point to the West End on Grand Bahama Island and boats returning from Bimini can enjoy a boost from the Gulf Stream door-to-door.

NAVIGATION: Use NOAA Chart 11472. To access the ocean continue on the ICW around the west side of Peanut Island to the Turning Basin and then pick up the main Lake Worth (Palm Beach) Inlet channel and follow it to the ocean. It is deep and well marked.

The Coast Guard establishes fixed and moving security zones at the Port of Palm Beach for the protection of passenger vessels (cruise ships), vessels carrying cargoes of a particular hazard and vessels carrying hazardous gases. A moving security zone activates when such a vessel passes red and white buoy "LW" when entering the port and becomes a fixed zone when the ship is docked. These zones cover the waters within 100 yards all around the subject vessels and no craft can enter without prior permission. Patrol craft may be contacted on VHF Channel 16 for the status of these security zones.

Anchorage: There are several anchorages in the vicinity of Lake Worth (Palm Beach) Inlet. This is a high-traffic area and anchor lights should be used in all Lake Worth anchorages. When entering any anchorages pay strict attention to your depth sounder as there are several areas of shallow water and measured depths may not be as charted.

Just southeast of the turning basin marked by flashing green "11" and "13," you will find 9 to 13 feet MLW. Avoid the charted Cable Areas. Note that the bottom is irregular here and some shoals as shallow is 4 feet MLW may be present. Proceed with caution. This area is subject to strong tidal currents from the Lake Worth (Palm Beach) Inlet so pay-out extra scope and observe the proximity of other anchored vessels and their anchor set.

West Palm Beach to Palm Beach–ICW Mile 1018 to Mile 1026

Before entering the ICW south from the Lake Worth (Palm Beach) Inlet cruisers should consider their passage options and the dimensions of their vessel.

> Between the Fort Worth Inlet and the Port Everglades (Fort Lauderdale) Inlet there are 23 bascule bridges, many with restricted schedules. One of these bridges has a reported air draft of 64 feet at MLW and shoaling restricts water draft to 6 feet MLW in some spots.

Comfort can also be an issue. Ocean waves may prove less irritating than the wakes from power boats when confined in the narrow, 30-mile-long canal below Lake Worth. Because of this, many choose to take the 40-nm "outside passage" to Ft. Lauderdale. Both the Lake Worth (Palm Beach) Inlet and the Port Everglades (Fort Lauderdale) Inlet are all-weather channels with fully lighted aids to navigation.

The main drawback to the outside route south is the close proximity of the Gulf Stream to shore off Palm Beach, although this factor goes in the plus column if making a northbound passage. Weather conditions and tides are also important factors. There are no intermediate ports of call between the two main inlets. Favorable weather and an early start should be considered essential conditions to making this passage in either direction.

Lake Worth is open south of the Lake Worth (Palm Beach) Inlet and Peanut Island and the ICW channel follows the lake's western shore. The waterway is well marked and maintained and the lake bed is pocked with patches of deep water mainly along the eastern shore with Palm Beach, as well as some shoals and spoils areas. Palm Beach remains a winter ocean resort-town of elegance and charm.

The West Palm Beach shore is mostly given over to marinas, boatyards and yachting amenities. In other places any one of these would be outstanding in size, quality of work and service; here, however, mariners can be overwhelmed by the choices. Not all the services available are confined to the waterfront. A phone call or a short walk can put you in touch with just about every known kind of nautical specialist–sailmakers, electronic sales and services, boat designers, boat maintenance and cleaning and diving services. Supplies of all kinds are also close at hand.

Downtown West Palm Beach and Rosemary Square, an upscale outdoor mall surrounding an open-air plaza, are near the marinas. In this festive commercial and cultural district you will find live entertainment, shopping, theaters, restaurants, groceries and art galleries. A free trolley runs from Clematis St. in West Palm Beach to the downtown area.

West Palm is the home of the Palm Beach International Boat Show held in March. The event includes hundreds of boats from inflatables to megayachts, plus tents full of the latest electronics and accessories, seminars and fishing clinics for kids.

West Palm Beach

NAVIGATION: Use NOAA Charts 11472 and 11467. There are three bridges connecting the mainland and Palm Beach. At Mile 1021.8 is the Flagler Memorial (SR A1A) Bridge with 21-foot closed vertical clearance. The bridge opens on the quarter and three-quarter hour. The second crossing is the Royal Park (SR 704) Bridge at Mile 1022.6, which has a 21-foot closed vertical clearance and opens on the hour and half-hour. (These schedules are subject to change if the Coast Guard establishes a security zone.) The third bridge is the Southern Boulevard (SR 700/80) Bridge at Mile 1024.7, which is under construction.

> Construction of a replacement 21-foot vertical clearance Southern Boulevard (SR 700/80) Bridge is proceeding with an expected completion date of fall 2021. The temporary bridge (north of the existing bridge) has a vertical clearance of 14-feet in the closed position and a reported clearance of 64 at low tide in the open position with a 125-foot navigable channel. The tidal range is 3 feet. Boats with an airdraft exceeding 60 feet are advised to consider the outside route to avoid this restriction.

Dockage: On the mainland side just before Mile 1020 privately maintained green daybeacon "1" and red daybeacon "2" flank the entrance to Safe Harbor West Palm Beach, a full-service superyacht marina and service facility. They can accommodate vessels to 330 feet.

North of the Flagler Memorial (SR A1A) Bridge at Mile 1022.9 is Palm Beach Yacht Club & Marina, which is open to the public on a "first-come first-served" basis with resort-style amenities for vessels ranging up to 150 feet. Just south of the bridge on the mainland side is Palm Harbor Marina, which has transient berths and all the usual amenities.

Palm Beach Town Docks on the ocean side below the Royal Park (SR 704) Bridge at Mile 1024.5 can accommodate power and sailing vessels up to 260 feet in length. Transient slips may be reserved with a 48-hour advance notice of arrival. An online form makes this easy (www.townofpalmbeach.com).

Anchorage: Between the ICW and the channel flanking Palm Beach a popular anchorage extends about 3 miles south from red daybeacon "6" (off Palm Beach) at Mile 1019. If coming from the south, enter between the two charted spoil areas directly across from Rybovich Marina. Avoid the charted cable areas and the numerous permanently moored vessels in this area.

At Mile 1022 there are two municipal free docks located north of the Royal Park (SR 704) Bridge (on western side). The docks offer complimentary dockage for visits during the daytime hours of 8:00 a.m. to 5:00 p.m. There is no overnight dockage but you can drop the hook between the docks. Free shuttles are available for provisioning and getting the dog off the boat is easy.

Lake Worth, FL

WEST PALM BEACH		Largest Vessel	VHF	Total Slips	Approach/ Dockside Depth	Floating Docks	Gas/ Diesel	Repairs/ Haulout	Min/Max Amps	Pump-Out Station
1. Safe Harbor West Palm Beach **WiFi** MM 1019.5	(561) 840-8308	330	16	60	18.0 / 18.0	F	GD	RH	30 / 200+	P
2. Palm Beach Yacht Club & Marina **WiFi** **onSpot** MM 1022.9	(561) 655-1944	150	16	47	13.0 / 13.0		GD	H	30 / 100	
3. Palm Harbor Marina **WiFi** MM 1022.0	(561) 655-4757	250	16	200	11.0 / 11.0	F	GD		30 / 200+	P
PALM BEACH										
4. Palm Beach Town Docks **WiFi** MM 1024.5	(561) 838-5463	262	16	83	9.0 / 12.0				50 / 100	P

WiFi Wireless Internet Access **onSpot** Dockside WiFi Facility
Visit www.waterwayguide.com for current rates, fuel prices, website addresses and other up-to-the-minute information.
(Information in the table is provided by the facilities.)

Scan here for more details:

Palm Beach to Lantana–ICW Mile 1026 to Mile 1034

Lake Worth may be wide in this area but south of Palm Beach the water is shallow outside the ICW channel. Small islands (many of them originating as spoils banks) break the open expanses and are overgrown with foliage. Estates border most of the eastern shore and tall condominiums appear with increasing frequency on both banks. Even though the Atlantic Ocean is barely 0.5 mile away in places you will find it hard to see among the proliferation of houses, motels, high-rise apartments and condominiums that line the route.

NAVIGATION: Use NOAA Chart 11467. Starting from Mile 1027 (just south of red daybeacon "24") the ICW route is confined to a dredged channel south to Boynton Beach where the waterway enters a cut and Lake Worth ends. There is some shoaling along the edges so stay centered and watch your channel alignment in strong crosswinds.

The **Lake Ave. (SR 802) Bridge** with 35-foot closed vertical clearance is at Mile 1028.8 and opens on signal. Continuing south over the next 30 miles the ICW alters its configuration and becomes a narrow land cut in the vicinity of Boynton Beach. Lined with residences and spanned by numerous bridges the ICW truly looks like a "water highway" here. The numerous bridges slow

Downtown West Palm Beach

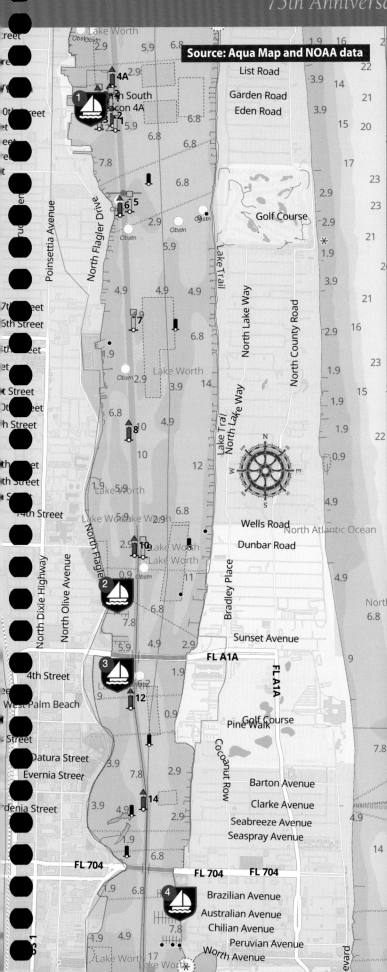

Source: Aqua Map and NOAA data

Options from Lake Worth Inlet

Before entering the ICW south from the Lake Worth Inlet, cruisers should consider their passage options and the dimensions of their vessel. Between the Fort Worth Inlet and the Port Everglades Inlet at Fort Lauderdale, there are 23 bascule bridges, many with restricted schedules. One of these bridges has a reported air draft of 64 feet at MLW and shoaling restricts water draft to 6 feet MLW in some spots. Comfort can also be an issue; ocean waves may prove less irritating than the wakes from power boats when confined in the narrow, 30-mile-long canal below Lake Worth.

Many choose to take the 40 nm "outside passage" to Fort Lauderdale. For some their vessel's dimensions necessitate this choice, but for many others it's just a decision to save time. Both the Fort Worth Inlet and the Port Everglades Inlet are all-weather channels with fully lighted aids to navigation. The main drawback to the outside route south is the close proximity of the Gulf Stream to shore off Palm Beach, although this factor goes in the plus column if making a northbound passage. Weather conditions and tides are also important factors.

Finally, there are no intermediate ports of call between the two main inlets. Favorable weather and an early start should be considered essential conditions to making this passage in either direction.

Boynton Inlet Area, FL

LANTANA		Largest Vessel	VHF	Total Slips	Approach/ Dockside Depth	Floating Docks	Gas/ Diesel	Repairs/ Haulout	Min/Max Amps	Pump-Out Station
1. Loggerhead Marina - Lantana Marina (WiFi) ⊜onSpot MM 1030.2	(561) 582-4422	100	16	83	6.0 / 8.0		G	R	30 / 50	
2. Murrelle Marine (WiFi) MM 1030.4	(561) 582-3213	55	16	36	4.5 / 5.0			RH	30 / 50	
3. Loggerhead Marina - South Lantana (WiFi) ⊜onSpot MM 1030.5	(561) 582-4422	120	16	80	5.0 / 7.0		G		30 / 50	

(WiFi) Wireless Internet Access   ⊜onSpot Dockside WiFi Facility
Visit www.waterwayguide.com for current rates, fuel prices, website addresses and other up-to-the-minute information.
(Information in the table is provided by the facilities.)

Scan here for more details:

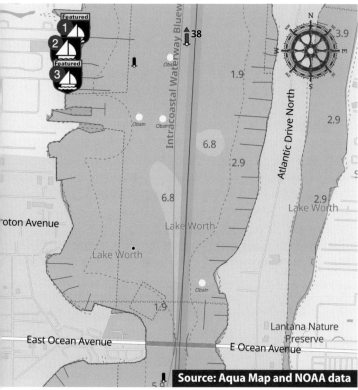

Source: Aqua Map and NOAA data

Lantana to Boynton Inlet–ICW Mile 1031 to Mile 1034

NAVIGATION: Use NOAA Chart 11467. Lantana is the next town southbound on Lake Worth. The **E. Ocean Avenue (Lantana) Bridge** (21-foot closed vertical clearance) at Mile 1031 connects Lantana on the mainland with Hypoluxo Island and South Palm Beach on the ocean side. The bridge has scheduled openings on the hour and half-hour. South from the E. Ocean Avenue (Lantana) Bridge the route enters the Boynton Inlet approach area. Past the inlet at Mile 1035 is **E. Ocean Avenue (Boynton Beach) Bridge** with 21-foot closed vertical clearance, which opens on the hour and half-hour. Bridge restrictions apply 24 hours a day, 7 days a week. Less than 1 mile further south, the **E. Woolbright Road (SE 15th Street) Bridge** (25-foot closed vertical clearance) crosses the ICW at Mile 1035.8 and opens on signal.

The ICW is narrow where it passes Boynton Inlet and depths are shallow, both inside and outside the channel.

Shoaling is a continuing problem where the ICW intersects with the flow from Boynton Inlet. Depths can be as shallow as 6 feet MLW in the vicinity of red nun buoy "46." Favor the green side from just north of red nun "46" to flashing green "49" to avoid shoaling on the red side.

Watch your course carefully as groundings are frequent here, often resulting from the current at Boynton Inlet pushing vessels out of the channel. Deeper draft vessels should seek local knowledge. Do not be confused by green can "1" to the east or the green buoys marking a channel leading in to the western shore; these are not ICW markers.

progress and anchorages are in short supply. Passage south will require some planning.

Dockage: In Bryant Park on the west shore just north of the Lake Ave. (SR 802) Bridge, the municipality provides five slips for free day-use dockage at Snook Islands. No published project depth is available. The park also has a public launch ramp with dock south of the bridge that can accommodate dinghy landings.

Anchorage: At Mile 1031.1 there is room for a half dozen boats in 8 to 10 feet MLW. This anchorage is best for winds out of the north, it's rocky with a south wind. There is shore access at the public dock by the anchorage. The nearby restaurant, The Old Key Lime House, has a dinghy dock if you eat there (561-582-1889). Pets are not allowed at the restaurant.

Boynton Inlet Area, FL

BOYNTON BEACH		Largest Vessel	VHF	Total Slips	Approach/Dockside Depth	Floating Docks	Gas/Diesel	Repairs/Haulout	Min/Max Amps	Pump-Out Station
1. Palm Beach Yacht Center (WiFi) MM 1032.7	(561) 588-9911	80	16	100	6.0 / 6.0		GD	RH	30 / 50	P
2. Gateway Marina MM 1033.1	(561) 588-1211	35	68	211	6.0 / 6.0	F	G	RH		
3. Boynton Harbor Marina (WiFi) MM 1035.0	(561) 735-7955	40	16	23	12.0 / 6.0		GD		30 / 100	

(WiFi) Wireless Internet Access onSpot Dockside WiFi Facility
Visit www.waterwayguide.com for current rates, fuel prices, website addresses and other up-to-the-minute information. (Information in the table is provided by the facilities.)

Scan here for more details:

There is some charted shoaling on both sides from just north of red daybeacon "52A" to just south of green daybeacon "53." Hold the channel center and monitor depths through this stretch.

Boynton Inlet (also known as South Lake Worth Inlet) at Mile 1034 is popular with local fishermen but it is narrow, shallow and crossed by the fixed **Boynton Inlet Bridge** with an 18-foot vertical clearance. The Coast Guard does not recommend passage through the inlet without complete local knowledge of all the hazardous conditions that exist. A seawall helps stabilize Boynton Inlet's shoreline but currents run swiftly and bad tidal rips develop in strong easterly winds.

Dockage: Three marinas are clustered on the mainland side just north of the E. Ocean Avenue (Lantana) Bridge. Loggerhead Marina–Lantana Marina is at Mile 1030.2 with dry rack storage and wet slips (including catamaran slips) for vessels up to 100 feet. Nestled in what was once a tiny fishing village this facility reflects the quiet pace of Old Florida. Just to the south is Loggerhead Marina–South Lantana, which has transient dockage to 120 feet, a pool and a health club. This location is convenient to groceries and restaurants. Located between the two Loggerhead facilities is Murrelle Marine, which is a DIY boatyard with an index of specialist contractors that can help you with your boat maintenance.

Further south along the mainland is Palm Beach Yacht Center in a basin at Mile 1032.7. This facility has both in-and-out rack storage (to 38 feet) and wet slips (to 80 feet). They also have a 5-acre paved full service repair yard. Nearby Gateway Marina is primarily a "dry stack" marina. They have just two reserved transient slips (no shore power) so call in advance.

Just north of the E. Ocean Avenue (Lantana) Bridge in Boynton Beach on the mainland the friendly Boynton Harbor Marina (Mile 1035) may have a slip on a face

dock for you and offers easy access to their fuel pumps. They offer a multitude of water activities including fishing charters, drift fishing, scuba diving charters, jet-ski rentals, boat rentals and waterfront dining. A shopping center and supermarket are within walking distance of the waterfront.

Anchorage: Just to the southwest of the E. Ocean Avenue (Lantana) Bridge is a good anchorage with 6 to 8-foot MLW depths and room for many boats. Watch the charted Cable Area. This anchorage is best for winds out of the north and can be rocky with a south wind. Anchoring here is limited to 18 hours. Commercial fishing boats operate from a nearby pier.

■ TO POMPANO BEACH

Lake Worth ends just south of the Boynton Canal at Mile 1034. South from here the ICW becomes a canal with concrete bulkheads lining its borders. Two small, shallow lakes–Wyman and Boca Raton–and a brief stretch of the Hillsboro River are the only naturally formed bodies of water along this route. This area is well-developed with town following town and beautiful homes surrounded by subtropical growth provide the scenery. Even though the Atlantic Ocean is barely 0.5 mile away in places, you will find it hard to see among the proliferation of houses, motels, high-rise apartments and condominiums that line the route.

NO WAKE ZONE

Traveling south from Lake Worth keep an eye out for the many Slow-Speed/Minimum-Wake Zones. They increase with greater frequency the closer you get to Fort Lauderdale.

Be ready to call on VHF Channel 09 or whistle signal (two blasts: one prolonged, one short) for the opening of many of the 28 bridges that span the

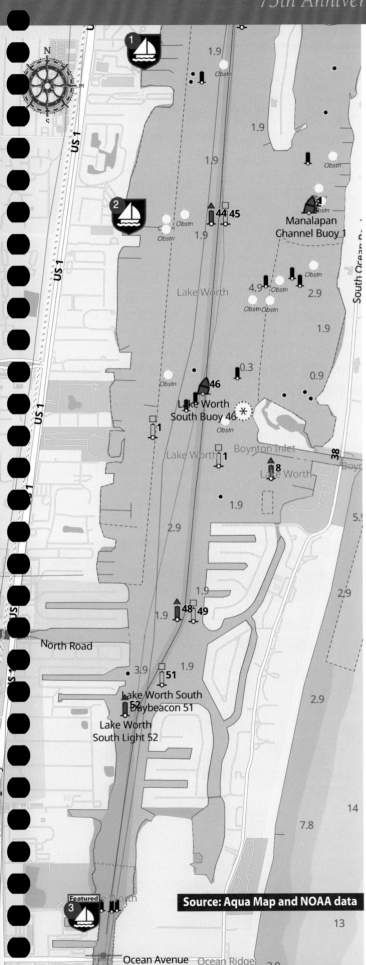

channel between Lake Worth and Government Cut at Miami Beach. Schedule a little extra time to allow for restricted openings, occasional bridge malfunctions and No-Wake Zones.

Boynton Inlet to Delray Beach–ICW Mile 1034 to Mile 1044

Delray Beach is a first-class resort destination and a diverse, vibrant, community situated on the Atlantic Ocean between Boca Raton and West Palm Beach. The area has diverse restaurants, a great art museum housed in a 1913 schoolhouse (Cornell Art Museum) and the quirky Silverball Museum, which is dedicated to the preservation of the vintage arcade. In this arcade you pay by the hour, not with tokens or quarters. They also sell food at this marvelous rainy day diversion.

From Delray Beach a confined 25-mile-long canal runs south to Fort Lauderdale. Smaller boats and those bothered by the constant buffeting of the irregular chop caused by wakes might consider traveling on weekdays when traffic is lighter. Wakes on this narrow channel retain their energy between opposing cement bulkheads bouncing back and forth for some time after the passing of a vessel. If weather permits you may just want to make the outside run from Lake Worth (Palm Beach) Inlet to avoid the numerous bridges and boat wakes.

NAVIGATION: Use NOAA Chart 11467. The first Delray Beach bridge you will encounter is the **George Bush Boulevard Bridge** (Mile 1038.7, 9-foot closed vertical clearance). This bridge opens on signal. The second bridge in Delray Beach is the **Atlantic Avenue (SR 806) Bridge** (Mile 1039.6, 12-foot closed vertical clearance), which opens on the quarter and three-quarter hour. The **Linton Boulevard Bridge** (Mile 1041.0, charted 30-foot closed vertical clearance) opens on the hour and half-hour at all times. Our Cruising Editors have observed an actual clearance of 27 feet. Call ahead (561-278-1980).

Approximately 0.6 miles south of the Linton Boulevard Bridge at Mile 1041.7, steer well clear of the white buoy marked "Rocks" well out from the western shore of the ICW.

Dockage: Boating amenities at Delray Beach range from restaurants with dockage to full-service marinas and repair shops. Just south of the George Bush Boulevard Bridge is Marina del Ray, which is primarily a yacht brokerage with only one reserved transient slip and 5-foot MLW approach and dockside depths.

Hillsboro River, FL

DELRAY BEACH		Largest Vessel	VHF	Total Slips	Approach/ Dockside Depth	Floating Docks	Gas/ Diesel	Repairs/ Haulout	Min/Max Amps	Pump-Out Station
1. Marina Delray MM 1038.0	(561) 276-7666		16	9	5.0 / 5.0		GD	RH	30 / 50	
2. The Seagate Yacht Club (WiFi) ⊙ onSpot MM 1039.9	(877) 673-6564	120	16	44	6.5 / 6.5		D		30 / 100	
3. Delray Beach City Marina MM 1039.8	(561) 243-7250	55		24	/ 10.0				30 / 50	P
4. Delray Harbor Club Marina (WiFi) MM 1040.5	(561) 276-0376	200	16	44	8.0 / 8.0	F	GD	RH	30 / 100	

(WiFi) Wireless Internet Access ⊙ onSpot Dockside WiFi Facility
Visit www.waterwayguide.com for current rates, fuel prices, website addresses and other up-to-the-minute information.
(Information in the table is provided by the facilities.)

Scan here for more details:

Continuing south past the Atlantic Avenue (SR 806) Bridge are Delray Beach City Marina (mainland side) and The Seagate Yacht Club directly across the waterway. The Delray Beach City Marina provides 24 rental slips for boats to 55 feet in a nicely landscaped environment with restrooms, showers, washer and dryer, and an ice machine. The upscale The Seagate Yacht Club has slips for vessels to 140 feet with resort accommodations. In a basin to the south (Mile 1040.5) is the gated Delray Harbor Club Marina with dockage and various services.

Just north of the Atlantic Avenue (SR 806) Bridge is the municipal Veterans Park at Mile 1039.5 (mainland side). Park amenities include lawn bowling, shuffleboard and complimentary daytime dockage along the seawall for visitors (2-hour limit, no overnight docking).

Anchorage: At about Mile 1042 the round basin to the west of the ICW, which is locally known as Pelican Harbor, is a 24-hour only anchorage (by order of the town of Delray Beach). The basin has 5-foot MLW depths at the entrance and 6-foot MLW depths inside. Poor holding has been reported due to a very soft bottom.

Delray Beach to Boca Raton–ICW Mile 1044 to Mile 1050

The area now known as Boca Raton is shown on old Spanish navigational maps charts as Boca de Ratones, meaning "mouth of the harbor of the hidden rocks." It appears that the name was originally applied to Biscayne Bay near Miami Beach, but early mapmakers moved the name to the present location. The construction of the Florida East Coast Canal (today's ICW) and the Florida

Boca Raton Inlet

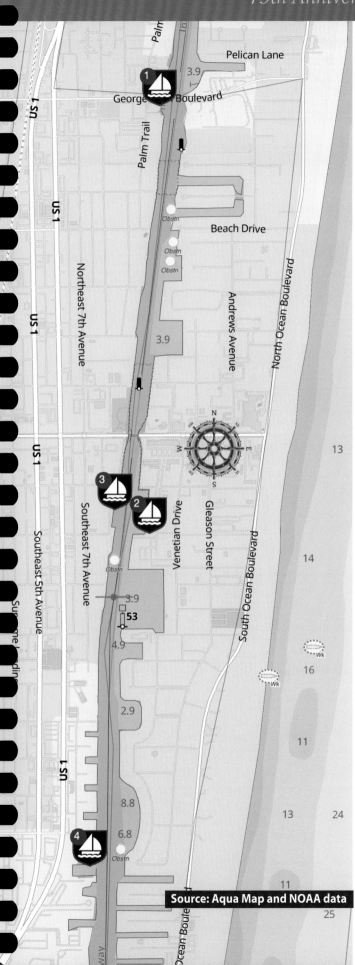

Source: Aqua Map and NOAA data

East Coast Railway in the 1890s brought pioneers and farmers to the area. In 1925, eccentric architect Addison Mizner was hired to design a world-class resort community. His exclusive hotel, known as the Cloister Inn, was completed in 1926, and remains a landmark as the Boca Raton Resort and Club.

NAVIGATION: Use NOAA Chart 11467. The **Spanish River Boulevard Bridge** at Mile 1044.9 has 25-foot closed vertical clearance and opens on the hour and half-hour, 24 hours a day. There are some spots of shoaling along the channel's edges between red daybeacon "54" through Lake Wyman to flashing green "61." Stay to the well-marked channel's center for this stretch. Lake Wyman is a broad, shallow lake with numerous, unmarked shoals. Exercise caution and stay in the marked channel. Be on the lookout for water skiers and swimmers in the water.

Leaving Lake Wyman southward the ICW route leads into Lake Boca Raton through a cut bordered by beautiful homes. Before entering the lake the ICW passes under **Palmetto Park Bridge** (19-foot closed vertical clearance) at Mile 1047.5. The bridge opens on the hour and half-hour. The opening under the bridge is extremely narrow so expect strong currents. When running with the current in a lightly powered vessel be sure to avoid being carried into the bridge or being carried by eddies into the concrete walls and docks along the sides.

During weekends (particularly in season), many small boats mill around the boat ramp next to the southwestern bridge abutment at Silver Palm Park, adding to the confusion. This is usually a very busy area and extra caution should be taken.

The ICW traverses Lake Boca Raton along its western shore and continues south through the **Camino Real Bridge** (Mile 1048.2, 9-foot closed vertical clearance). It opens on the hour, and at 20 and 40 minutes past the hour, 24 hours daily. This is the only restricted bridge in Palm Beach County that opens more than twice an hour attesting to the large number of boats passing through. This is also the southernmost bridge in Palm Beach County.

When heading south through the Palmetto Park Bridge and Camino Real Bridge, keep in mind that the current usually reverses in the ICW as it passes the Boca Raton Inlet. The current is not particularly strong and poses little difficulty even for lightly powered vessels but be aware of it, particularly on an incoming tide. Traffic can be quite busy, particularly on weekends in season.

Hillsboro River, FL

BOCA RATON AREA		Largest Vessel	VHF	Total Slips	Approach/ Dockside Depth	Floating Docks	Gas/ Diesel	Repairs/ Haulout	Min/Max Amps	Pump-Out Station
1. Boca Raton Resort & Club MM 1048.2	(561) 447-3000	170	16	32	12.0 / 10.0				50 / 100	
2. Two Georges at the Cove Waterfront Restaurant & Marina MM 1050.1	(954) 427-0353	65	16	31	7.0 / 7.0		GD		30 / 50	
HILLSBORO CANAL										
3. Pennell's Marina	(954) 426-2628				/		GD	R		

WiFi Wireless Internet Access **onSpot** Dockside WiFi Facility

Visit www.waterwayguide.com for current rates, fuel prices, website addresses and other up-to-the-minute information. (Information in the table is provided by the facilities.)

Scan here for more details:

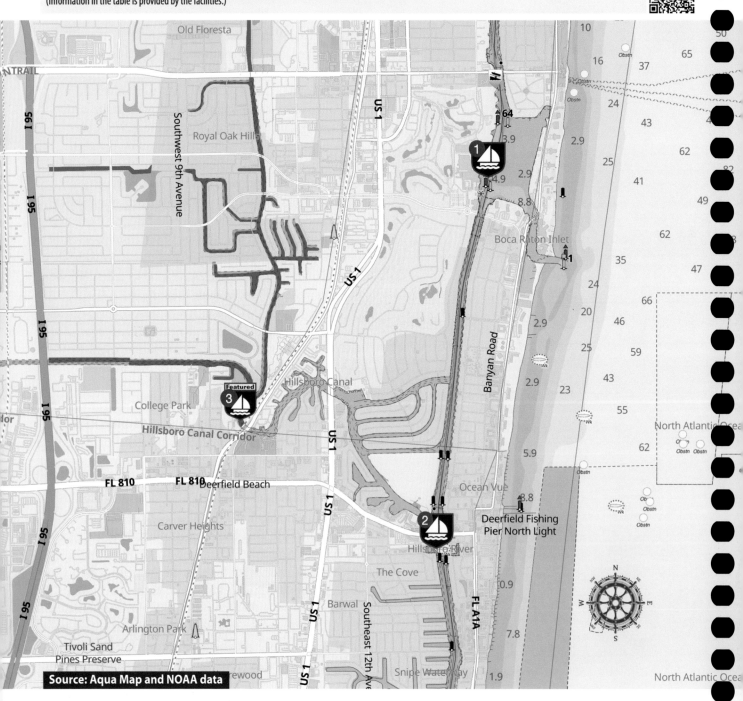

Source: Aqua Map and NOAA data

The ICW channel through Lake Boca Raton is an Idle-Speed/No-Wake Zone and the local marine police make a point to strictly enforce it. It is busy with tour boats and water taxis ferrying passengers between the Boca Raton Resort & Club and its private beach.

The Boca Raton Inlet is not recommended for passage without local knowledge due to shoaling to 4 feet MLW. The inlet's entrance has short jetties marked by private lights and the continuous shoaling and shifting sandbars make depths unreliable. The inlet channel and markers are not charted and transit is considered dangerous. The **Haven Ashe (SR A1A) Bridge** (locally known as the Boca Inlet Bridge) crosses the inlet with 23-foot closed vertical clearance. It opens on signal.

Dockage: Boca Raton Resort & Club is located at Mile 1048.2 on Lake Boca Raton. The pink hotel is a local landmark and offers dockage with a 50-foot minimum. They have a private beach, a FlowRider wave simulator (surf on land) and various watersport rentals.

Triangle-shaped Deerfield Island Park (charted) is on the west side of the ICW where the Hillsboro Drainage Canal intersects the ICW route. The park has picnic areas and nature walks. A short distance up the Hillsboro Drainage Canal the park boat dock can accommodate dinghies and small runabouts up to about 16 feet. Marina One is located 0.6 mile to the north on the canal. It is a boat storage and rental facility (no overnight dockage).

Hillsboro River, FL

HILLSBORO INLET AREA		Largest Vessel	VHF	Total Slips	Approach/ Dockside Depth	Floating Docks	Gas/ Diesel	Repairs/ Haulout	Min/Max Amps	Pump-Out Station
1. Lighthouse Point Yacht Club [WiFi] MM 1052.2	(954) 942-7244	100	16	78	10.0 / 8.0				30 / 100	P
2. Lighthouse Point Marina Inc. [WiFi] MM 1053.7	(954) 941-0227	80	16	100	7.0 / 7.0		GD		30 / 50	P
3. Yacht Management Marina [WiFi] MM 1054.0	(954) 941-6447	130	16	24	12.0 / 5.0			RH	30 / 50	P
POMPANO BEACH										
4. Merritt's Boat & Engine Works MM 1054.8	(954) 941-5207	100			10.0 / 8.0			RH	30	
5. Loggerhead Marina - Hidden Harbour Marina [WiFi] MM 1054.8	(954) 941-0498	43		3	/	F	GD	RH	15 / 30	P
6. Sands Harbor Resort & Marina [WiFi] MM 1056.2	(954) 942-9100	120	16	50	10.0 / 10.0		GD	R	30 / 100	P
7. Taha Marine Center	(954) 785-4737			25	10.0 / 10.0		GD			P

[WiFi] Wireless Internet Access ◉ **onSpot** Dockside WiFi Facility
Visit www.waterwayguide.com for current rates, fuel prices, website addresses and other up-to-the-minute information.
(Information in the table is provided by the facilities.)

Scan here for more details:

Two Georges at the Cove Waterfront Restaurant and Marina is just south of the Hillsboro Boulevard (SR 810) Bridge on the ICW. They have five reserved transient slips with 7-foot-MLW approach depths. Call ahead for reservations. The restaurant has a fun seafood, steak and pasta menu and a popular Friday Night Happy Hour.

Anchorage: Just south of the Palmetto Park Bridge (Mile 1047.5) a small anchorage is located at the northeastern end of Lake Boca Raton. Enter north of flashing green "65" and anchor in 8-foot MLW depths north and east of the charted shoal areas. An unmarked channel runs through the anchorage area and along the eastern shore to the Boca Raton Inlet. For southbound cruisers it's 10 miles and four bridges to the next anchorage at Lake Santa Barbara.

Boca Raton to Hillsboro Inlet–ICW Mile 1050 to Mile 1053

NAVIGATION: Use NOAA Chart 11467. The ICW leaves Lake Boca Raton through the Camino Real Bridge at Mile 1048.2 (described above) and then enters a straight cut with some side canals. At Mile 1050 the ICW enters the Hillsboro River with its many bridges and speed restrictions.

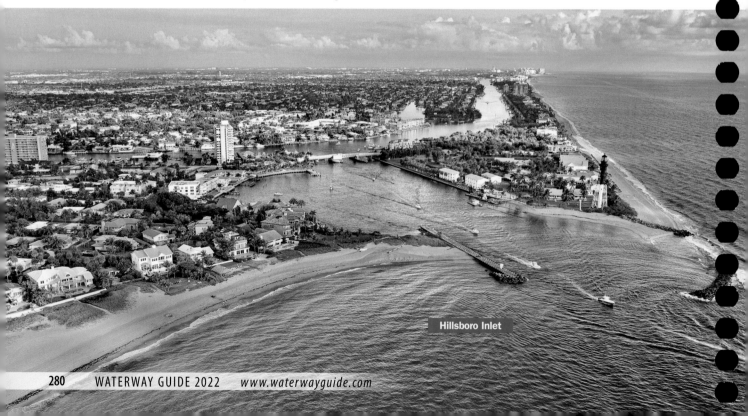

Hillsboro Inlet

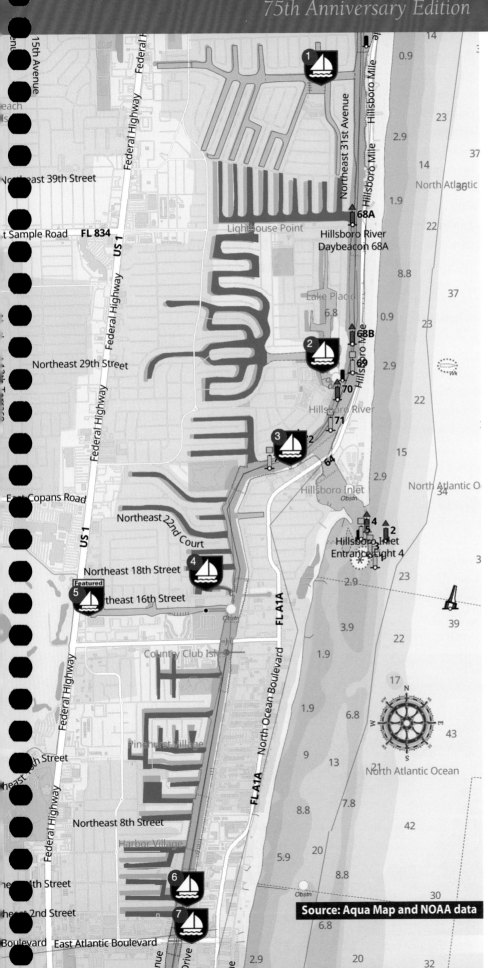

Source: Aqua Map and NOAA data

NO WAKE ZONE

Along this stretch Manatee Zones and Boating Safety Zones are frequent and often overlap. Where they do the more restrictive limitation applies. Some are seasonal (November 15 through March 31), some are year-round, some are weekends only, some are for the full width of the water and some are more restrictive within a specified distance from the shore. The official signs are well placed and repeated at intervals and may vary in only small details. You must keep a sharp lookout and read each sign carefully. The speed and wake limits are enforced by state, county and municipal police boats.

Deerfield Beach is the next city, closely followed by the Lighthouse Point area, Hillsboro Inlet and Pompano Beach proper. A maze of manmade canals shoots off the ICW in all directions and from here southward consider that each of these canals contributes to ICW traffic.

Near Deerfield Beach the Hillsboro Drainage Canal enters the ICW from the west at Mile 1049.9. During times of high flow (recent heavy rainfall) from the canal strong currents are created only 100 yards from the **Hillsboro Boulevard (SR 810) Bridge** at Mile 1050. The bridge (21-foot closed vertical clearance) opens on the hour and half-hour at all times. Southbound boats approaching the bridge should not proceed past the canal until the bridge is fully open and should maintain adequate headway to avoid being pushed into the east bridge fender by the canal crosscurrents.

At Hillsboro Inlet the 136-foot-tall lighthouse for which the area is named has one of the most powerful beacons on the coast (visible from 28 miles at sea). The fast-operating **SR A1A (Hillsboro Inlet) Bridge** (13-foot closed vertical clearance) spanning the inlet approach from the ICW opens on signal except from 7:00 a.m. to 6:00 p.m., when it need only open on the hour and at 15, 30 and 45 minutes past the hour. (Note that this bridge is not on the ICW proper.) If you are planning on using the Hillsboro Inlet be sure to get up-to-date information regarding the status of the bridge. The current runs swiftly beneath the bridge. Wait for the bridge to open completely before approaching.

Although shoals at Hillsboro Inlet shift rapidly, dredging is frequent and local boats and the large fleet of charter fishing and head boats heavily travel the passage here. Swells and/or tidal rip on the ebb against an easterly wind will decrease the available depth. Under good weather conditions, boats with 5-foot drafts or less can run Hillsboro Inlet safely by observing the constant flow of local boats going in and out. With any swell from the east, passage becomes hazardous.

Proceed all the way to the red-and-white sea buoy "HI" before turning south to avoid shoals. A rock jetty extends southeast from the north side of the inlet and is submerged at the outer end. It is wise to seek local knowledge before running this inlet.

Just south of Hillsboro Inlet the ICW swings wide around a projecting point that builds out from the eastern shore. For 1.5 miles south from the inlet spots of shoaling occur along the edges of the ICW channel. The speed limit is Slow-Speed/Minimum-Wake to just before the NE 14th Street Bridge where an Idle-Speed/No-Wake Zone begins. Beyond that bridge a sign lists the complex speed restrictions that prevail for the next 2.5 miles.

Dockage: Lighthouse Point Yacht Club at Mile 1052.2 can accommodate vessels to 100 feet, while Lighthouse Point Marina Inc. to the south has slips for vessels to 80 feet. Just past Hillsboro Inlet (Mile 1054) is Yacht Management Marina, which is a boatyard with yacht care services. Call ahead for docking availability and details.

Hillsboro Inlet to Pompano Beach– ICW Mile 1053 to Mile 1056

Pompano Beach equates to "fishing." Even its name was inspired by one of the more popular species found in its waters. When some native folks served the local game fish to a group of surveyors who were mapping the area, the name of the pompano fish was added to the map and the name has stuck to the spot ever since.

Every April the Pompano Beach Seafood Festival brings together arts and crafts, non-stop live entertainment and great seafood. During the summer "Music Under the Stars" sponsors a variety of free concerts throughout the city.

NAVIGATION: Use NOAA Chart 11467. Two bascule bridges cross the ICW in Pompano Beach, both with 15-foot closed vertical clearance. The northernmost, the **NE 14th Street Bridge**, crosses the ICW at Mile 1055. The bridge opens on the quarter hour and three-quarter hour. The **Atlantic Boulevard (SR 814) Bridge** at Mile 1056 opens on the hour and half-hour. Both bridges monitor VHF Channel 09.

Pompano Beach

Dockage: Pompano Beach has abundant boating services on protected side canals or in enclosed basins along the ICW. Almost anything the yachtsman might want in the way of service, supplies, convenience or outright luxury is available in the immediate area.

Merritt's Boat & Engine Works is a major yacht yard located just north of the NE 14th Street Bridge. Transient dockage is not available but they offer all types of repairs. Loggerhead Marina– Hidden Harbour Marina (located at the end of a well-protected canal off the ICW) also does repair work and offers some services but they do not offer transient dockage.

Two side-by-side facilities are just north of the Atlantic Boulevard (SR 814) Bridge on the ocean side. Sands Harbor Resort & Marina (Mile 1056.2) is part of a large complex and provides transient dockage with resort amenities. Taha Marine Center has easy dockage. Call ahead for slip availability.

Anchorage: Anchoring is possible in Lettuce Lake across the ICW on the east. This anchorage has 7 to 12-foot MLW depths but is also not recommended due to notoriously poor holding in very soft mud and an abundance of debris on the bottom. The lake (actually just a wide spot in the ICW) is also exposed to the wakes of the heavy and fast moving ICW traffic. For northbound cruisers it's 10 miles and four bridges to the next anchorage at Lake Boca Raton.

■ NEXT STOP

Just to the south lies a world-class yachting center, Fort Lauderdale. If you're Bahamas bound, check out "Crossing to the Bahamas" at the end of Chapter 9 of this guide for headings from either Hillsboro Inlet or Port Everglades Inlet to Grand Bahama or Bimini.

Florida Clean Marina Program

The Florida Clean Marina Program is designed to bring awareness to marine facilities and boaters regarding environmentally friendly practices intended to protect and preserve Florida's natural environment. Marinas, boatyards and marine retailers receive clean designations by demonstrating a commitment implementing and maintaining a host of best management practices.

The Florida Clean Boater Program, in turn, encourages boaters to use the designated clean marinas, boatyards and marine retailers. Boaters are also encouraged to adopt their own environmentally friendly efforts such as practicing proper trash management, using bilge socks and fueling collars and recycling.

Visitwww. dep.state.fl.us/cleanmarina for more information and to sign the clean boater pledge.

Source: Florida Dept. of Environmental Protection

Mile 1058-Mile 1080

FORT LAUDERDALE & PORT EVERGLADES

Nearly 300 miles of mostly navigable inland waterways carve through the Fort Lauderdale area making it the "Venice of America." With the Atlantic Ocean surf to the east and the traffic-laden ICW running north and south the city is conspicuously water-oriented. The New River and its tributaries cut through the center of town and manmade side canals sprout in all directions.

Well known as a yachting center Fort Lauderdale harbors more recreational boats than any other port in Florida. Not surprisingly the marine industry ranks second only to tourism. The city boasts more than 800 marine-related businesses—including a collection of marinas, yacht services, sailmakers, boatyards, yacht brokers, dinghy manufacturers and marine supply stores—and the craftspeople here are some of the best in the business.

Although the entire city of Fort Lauderdale has the look of a huge yachting center, most boating amenities and services are concentrated in three main areas: the main ICW channel, the New River and the Dania Cut-Off Canal.

NO WAKE ZONE

No Wake Zones, Idle Speed Zones and various Speed Limit restrictions are in effect throughout the waterways included in this chapter. Exercise diligence in knowing the regulations by observing signs and other markers. Enforcement is always present. As always, be courteous to other vessels and avoid manatees and other marine life.

Lauderdale-By-The-Sea to New River Sound—ICW Mile 1058 to Mile 1064

This section of the ICW runs through a manmade canal to the junction with Middle River in Fort Lauderdale. Mostly residential development lines the sides of the canal with the exception of the wilderness of Hugh Taylor Birch State Park opposite Sunrise Bay. While some areas along this stretch look like potential anchorages, local bylaws restrict

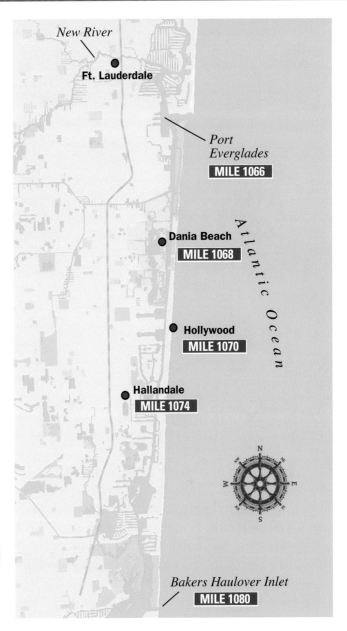

overnight stops for most. Keep in mind these restrictions are updated constantly and you may want to check with local authorities before planning a stop.

NAVIGATION: Use NOAA Charts 11467 and 11470. Between Mile 1058 and Mile 1064 are four bridges, all with restricted schedules (i.e., do not open on signal):

- Mile 1059: **Commercial Boulevard (SR 870) Bridge** has 15-foot closed vertical clearance and opens on the hour and half-hour (not on signal).

- Mile 1060.5: **Oakland Park Boulevard Bridge** has 22-foot closed vertical clearance and opens on the quarter-hour and three-quarter hour.

GOIN' ASHORE

FORT LAUDERDALE (PORT EVERGLADES), FL

Fort Lauderdale is known for its beautiful beaches and extensive canal system. A vibrant yachting center, some skippers travel only on weekdays to avoid the heavy weekend traffic between Pompano Beach and Miami. But there isn't another harbor like it, and it would be a shame to pass through without stopping or a visit. Skippers can tie up at on-the-water restaurants and shopping centers for shore-side dining, shopping or strolling.

SERVICES

1. Broward Medical & Urgent Care
103 SE 20th St. (954-462-7558)

2. Fort Lauderdale Post Office (Causeway)
1515 SE 17th St. (954-525-2031)

3. Fort Lauderdale Veterinary Clinic
1493 SE 17th St. (954-463-1616)

SHOPPING

4. Publix Super Market
Full-service grocery store (groceries, deli and bakery items) located in the Harbor Shops at 1940 Cordova Rd. (954-847-2844).

5. Winn Dixie
Full-service grocery store chain at the end of the 15th St. Canal (1625 Cordova Rd., 954-763-2275).

MARINAS

6. 17th Street Yacht Basin at the Hilton Marina Hotel
1881 SE 17th St. (954-527-6766)

7. Cable Marine East
1517 SE 16th St. (954-462-2822)

8. Lauderdale Marina/15th Street Fisheries
1900 SE 15th St. (954-523-8507)

9. Lauderdale Yacht Club
1725 SE 12th St. (954-524-5500)

10. Marina Boathouse of Fort Lauderdale
1601 SE 16th St. (866-397-9993)

11. Pier Sixty-Six Hotel & Marina
2301 SE 17th St. (954-728-3578)

12. Pier Sixty-Six South
2150 SE 17th St. (954-525-3484)

- Mile 1062.6: **East Sunrise Boulevard (SR 838) Bridge** has 25-foot closed vertical clearance and opens on the hour and half-hour.

- Mile 1064: **East Las Olas Boulevard Bridge** has 24-foot closed vertical clearance and opens on the quarter and three-quarter hour.

From Mile 1057 to Mile 1063 the ICW runs through a cut and its course is straight and obvious (with no need for aids to navigation). The shores are densely populated and the waterway is heavily traveled. At Mile 1061.5 residential development is broken by the 180-acre Hugh Taylor Birch State Park, which stretches for about 1 mile along the east side of the ICW opposite the yacht club and marina in Sunrise Bay. The park is a pleasant, wooded oasis that offers rental canoes on a quiet lagoon and a swimming beach for a tropical picnic. Unfortunately, the park has no docks

on the ICW. The Fort Lauderdale Water Taxi does stop at the park. Local marine police frequently patrol the ICW here and vigorously enforce the speed limit.

North of the East Sunrise Boulevard (SR 838) Bridge near Mile 1062 the channel starts to zigzag past the private Coral Ridge Yacht Club and Sunrise Harbor Marina and associated condominiums to the west. Stay close to the western bank from here until you reach the first aid to navigation, flashing green "3" where the channel heads southeast.

At flashing green "5" the channel turns back southwest. Make a gentle turn giving the mainland point opposite flashing green "5" a wide berth. The next marker, flashing red "8," can be hard to find in the seemingly large pond here. It is just off the western shoreline located just north of the East Las Olas Boulevard Bridge. There is an area of privately rented slips from here to the bridge.

Dockage: Numerous restaurants just above and below the Oakland Park Boulevard Bridge have docks for their customers. On weekends several of the livelier drinking and dining spots on the east side have boats rafted out six or more deep.

Just north of the East Sunrise Boulevard (SR 838) Bridge (Mile 1062.6) are Coral Ridge Yacht Club followed by Sunrise Harbor Marina. The Yacht Club is private but accepts reciprocals from Florida Council of Yacht Clubs and Yacht Clubs of America if there is space. Sunrise Harbor Marina caters to megayachts (up to 200 feet) and has upscale amenities including a health and fitness center, spa, tennis courts and two heated pools.

To reach the long-term dockage areas at Isle of Venice and Hendricks Isle, turn west off of the ICW at Middle River between flashing green "3" and "5." These canals are the last three straight, north-south canals in

Fort Lauderdale

Yes, You can have it all...only in Fort Lauderdale

Two Great Downtown Locations in One Great City!

The City of Fort Lauderdale's Downtown New River Docks offer secure dockage and ample power for all sizes including mega-yachts, while Cooley's Landing caters to vessels up to 50 feet.

The Downtown Docks are located on the New River in the heart of the City. Renowned Las Olas Boulevard offers upscale shopping, boutiques, restaurants and clubs which are just one block away from the north side of the New River. Groceries are just two blocks away.

Cooley's Landing Is a quaint park tucked away in the City's historic Sailboat Bend District and offers tree-lined walks along the New River to the Museum of Discovery and Science, restaurants, clubs and the Broward Center of the Performing Arts/Florida Grand Opera.

Cooley's Landing

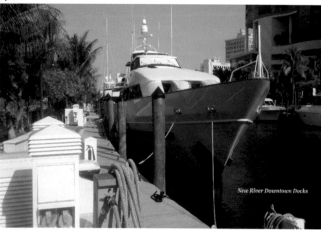
New River Downtown Docks

CITY OF FORT LAUDERDALE

marine facilities

City Of Fort Lauderdale Marine Facilities
2 South New River Drive East, Suite 103
Fort Lauderdale, Florida 33301
954-828-5423   VHF Channels 9 &16

Amenities Include:

On-Spot Wi-Fi   Free Pumpout   Boat U.S. Participating Marina   Florida Clean Marinas   Showers   Laundry   Security   Lounge

Prompt and Courteous Staff

Fort Lauderdale, FL

FORT LAUDERDALE AREA		Largest Vessel	VHF	Total Slips	Approach/ Dockside Depth	Floating Docks	Gas/ Diesel	Repairs/ Haulout	Min/Max Amps	Pump-Out Station
1. Coral Ridge Yacht Club-PRIVATE **WiFi** MM 1062.3	(954) 566-7886	100		58	10.0 / 8.0				30 / 50	P
2. Sunrise Harbor Marina **WiFi** MM 1062.3	(954) 667-6720	200	16	22	10.0 / 8.5	F			50 / 200+	
3. Las Olas Marina **WiFi** ⊙onSpot MM 1063.4	(954) 828-7200	200	16	60	10.0 / 10.0	F			30 / 200+	
4. Hall of Fame Marina **WiFi** MM 1063.8	(954) 764-3975	150	16	40	9.0 / 9.0				30 / 200+	P
5. Bahia Mar Yachting Center **WiFi** MM 1064.4	(954) 627-6309	300	16	240	16.0 / 16.0	F	GD		30 / 200+	P

WiFi Wireless Internet Access   ⊙onSpot Dockside WiFi Facility
Visit www.waterwayguide.com for current rates, fuel prices, website addresses and other up-to-the-minute information.
(Information in the table is provided by the facilities.)

Scan here for more details:

the Nurmi Isles section. Many properties rent private slips on these two islands. Most are long-term rentals but some are rented out on a daily basis. The docks are various sizes with unique shoreside amenities and are priced accordingly. The best way to find a slip here is to stop elsewhere temporarily and then visit the area to check availability. Slips are hard to find during the winter season.

Florida legislation bans overnight anchoring in the section of the Middle River at Mile 1063.4 from NE 21st Street to the ICW. It is illegal to anchor at any time during the period between one-half hour after sunset and one-half hour before sunrise. Revisions to the anchoring laws in Florida have continued to include this restriction, despite widespread opposition by boaters.

East Las Olas Boulevard Bridge to Port Everglades–ICW Mile 1064 to Mile 1066

Between the East Las Olas Boulevard Bridge and the **SE 17th Street (Brooks Memorial) Bridge** there is a concentration of marinas close to the bridges. Canals branch off in all directions and are lined by spectacular homes with yachts docked in their back yards. Many of these residences have been "remodeled" and expanded in size numerous times.

The Fort Lauderdale oceanfront between Bahia Mar and Sunrise Blvd. is limited to one-way north-bound traffic and features bike trails, sidewalks and landscaping, all creating an attractive setting. A large number of high-rise luxury condominium resorts, quite conspicuous from offshore, line the strip between Sunrise and Las Olas Boulevards. Many of these offer upscale shopping

and dining experiences on their lower floors. Read more at "Goin' Ashore: Fort Lauderdale (Port Everglades), FL" in this chapter.

NAVIGATION: Use NOAA Charts 11470 and 11472. East Las Olas Boulevard Bridge has 24-foot closed vertical clearance and opens on the quarter and three-quarter hour. SE 17th Street (Brooks Memorial) Bridge at Mile 1065.9 has a vertical clearance of 55 feet and opens on the hour and half-hour as needed for sailboats and large motor yachts. Northbound vessels waiting for a bridge opening should stay clear of the turning basin and cruise ship berths as well as any government patrol boats.

> Marine Police boats are active here and it is necessary to maintain the slowest possible speed through this area to avoid a warning or ticket. Do not be tempted to speed up to make a bridge opening.

For those with the time to spend a few days in Fort Lauderdale a side trip up New River is strongly recommended. You will pass directly through the city's vast Historic District and find easy dockage right next to Fort Lauderdale's active Arts & Museum district with premier dining and shopping areas nearby.

Dockage/Moorings: Although jam-packed with permanent year-round or seasonal boats most marinas reserve some space for transients so the visiting cruiser is almost certain to find a berth at one place or another. At the height of the season you must reserve a berth in advance of arrival.

The first concentration of marine facilities southbound begins at the East Las Olas Boulevard Bridge on the eastern side of the ICW. (The western side is residential except for the small anchorage and mooring area just south of the bridge.) The first is the municipal Las Olas Marina with floating dock slips north and south of the bridge. They offer the usual amenities for vessels to 200

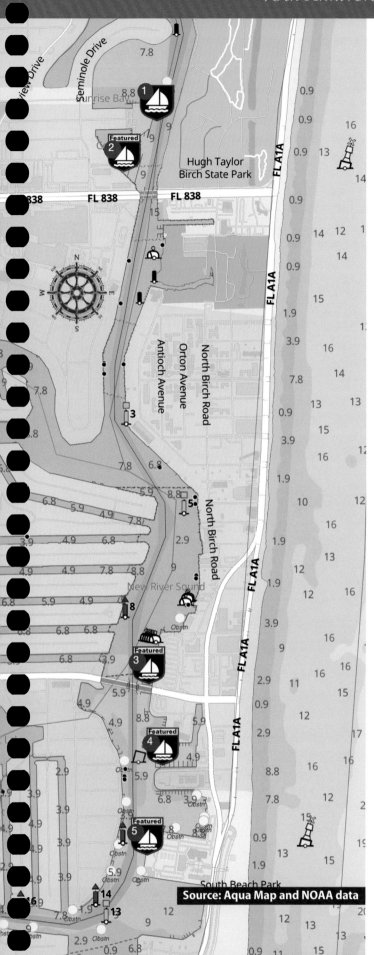

feet and are just steps from the beach.

Las Olas Moorings & Anchorage is on the opposite (west) side of the waterway and contains 10 city-owned moorings available on a first-come, first-served basis (for up to 30 days). The city dockmaster, whose office stands by on VHF Channels 09 and 16, will come by to collect fees. Dinghy landing is at the Las Olas Marina on the opposite (east) side of the ICW from the anchorage where showers, laundry and trash disposal are available for moored boats.

Hall of Fame Marina to the south offers slips and full amenities plus car rentals, beach access and three adjacent restaurants. The marina is named for the on-site International Swimming Hall of Fame, a tribute to competitive swimming, diving, water polo and synchronized swimming. The Hall of Fame hosts the world's largest outdoor swimming complex plus a museum and art gallery making this a fascinating place to visit.

Bahia Mar Yachting Center has dockage for vessels up to 250 feet and sells gas and diesel (high-speed fueling) and some supplies. The marina features restaurants, shops, pool and tennis directly across the street from a pristine sand beach. Bahia Mar Yachting Center is home to the world-renowned Fort Lauderdale International Boat Show.

The second concentration of marinas begins just north of the SE 17th Street (Brooks Memorial) Bridge. Heading south on the ICW the 65-slip Lauderdale Yacht Club welcomes guests from other yacht clubs and individuals sponsored by their members. (Call ahead for availability.)

Next on the western side is the Lauderdale Marina/15th Street Fisheries offering boat sales, service and parts. The award-winning Fifteenth Street Fisheries Restaurant is here as well as a 365-foot fuel dock. Boaters should try to come in against the current, take up as short a space as possible and fuel up quickly. There is often a line of boats waiting, especially on weekends.

17th Street Yacht Basin at the Hilton Marina Hotel accommodates megayachts up to 300 feet (10-foot dockside depths at MLW) along a facewall directly on the ICW but accommodates smaller vessels in a quiet basin off the canal. Guests of the marina have access to the Hilton Hotel amenities including a waterfront cocktail bar, restaurant, pool and fitness center. Further west along the same canal is Marina Boathouse of Fort Lauderdale, which offers traditional slips but also has a unique fully

Fort Lauderdale, FL

FORT LAUDERDALE AREA		Largest Vessel	VHF	Total Slips	Approach/ Dockside Depth	Floating Docks	Gas/ Diesel	Repairs/ Haulout	Min/Max Amps	Pump-Out Station
1. Lauderdale Yacht Club MM 1066.0	(954) 527-2209		16	64	5.0 / 5.0				30	
2. Lauderdale Marina/15th Street Fisheries **WiFi** MM 1065.0	(954) 523-8507	100	16	60	10.0 / 8.0	F	GD	RH	50 / 200+	P
3. 17th Street Yacht Basin at the Hilton Marina Hotel **WiFi**	(954) 527-6766	300	16	35	20.0 / 10.0				30 / 200+	
4. Marina Boathouse of Fort Lauderdale **WiFi** MM 1065.0	(954) 306-1056	200		10	14.0 / 12.0			R	50 / 100	P
5. Cable Marine East MM 1065.0	(954) 462-2822	120	16	12	20.0 / 15.0			RH	50	
6. Pier Sixty-Six Marina **WiFi** MM 1065.0	(954) 728-3578	400	16	157	16.0 / 25.0		GD		30 / 200+	P
7. Pier Sixty-Six South **WiFi** MM 1065.9	(954) 728-3578	500	16	20	45.0 / 24.0	F	GD		30 / 200+	

WiFi Wireless Internet Access   **onSpot** Dockside WiFi Facility
Visit www.waterwayguide.com for current rates, fuel prices, website addresses and other up-to-the-minute information.
(Information in the table is provided by the facilities.)

Scan here for more details:

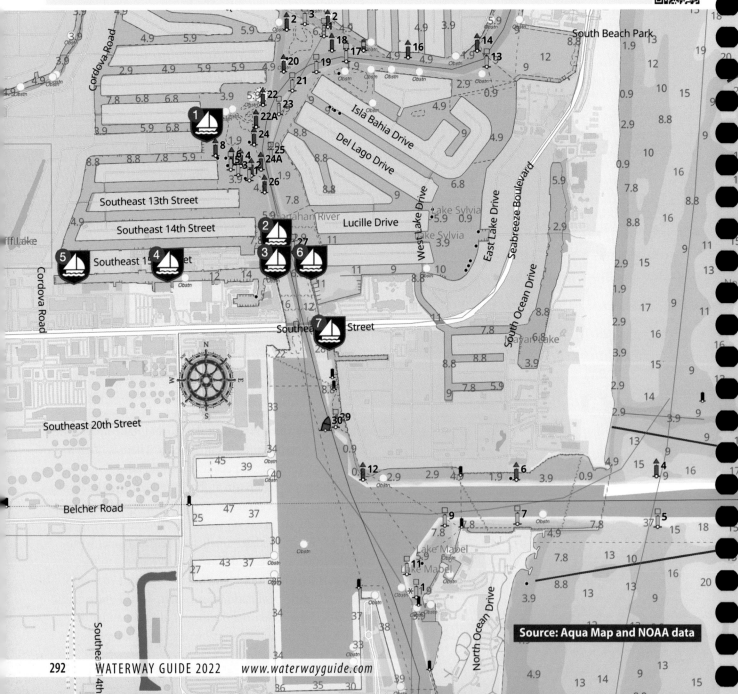

BAHIA MAR
A SUNTEX EXPERIENCE

Extraordinary Luxury

Who wouldn't want to spend their days enjoying first-class amenities at this spectacular waterfront destination? Featuring a DoubleTree by Hilton hotel, you can relax with an array of amenities, including tennis, shops, restaurants and lounge, live music, pool, the beach, and activities for the whole family! Bahia Mar is also the home to the world-renowned Fort Lauderdale International Boat Show.

Whether you stay for a day, a week, or longer, we will make sure that you have a great time along with a safe, comfortable and stress-free experience.

---

250 slips for vessels up to 300' • 3,000 foot parallel dock • Over 5,000' of floating docks • High speed fueling Free WiFi • Cable TV • In slip sanitary pump-out • Marine Store • Dive shop • Marine maintenance provider

GOIN' ASHORE

FORT LAUDERDALE (NEW RIVER), FL

The New River area of Fort Lauderdale is an extraordinary visitor destination. Spanning the north and south banks of the river is the Riverwalk Park, a waterfront park in the heart of downtown. The lush tropical landscape and winding walkways link attractions, restaurants and shops and is the epicenter for special events, including a Jazz Brunch, held the first Sunday of every month in the Bubier Park area of Riverwalk.

SERVICES

1. Broward County Main Library
100 S. Andrews Ave. (954-357-7444)

2. Fort Lauderdale Post Office
1404 E. Las Olas Blvd. Ste. B (954-523-0327)

3. Greater Fort Lauderdale Convention & Visitors Bureau
101 NE 3rd Ave #100 (954-765-4466)

4. Quik Clinic Medical Center
900 NW 6th St. (954-530-9591)

5. Victoria Park Animal Hospital
626 N. Federal Hwy. (954-617-8724)

ATTRACTION

6. Broward Center for the Performing Arts

The center is home of the Florida Grand Opera, plus ballet and dance performances, music and theater at 201 SW 5th Ave. (954-462-0222)

7. History Fort Lauderdale Museum

The museum displays history of the area with exhibits and artifacts housed in Broward County's oldest standing hotel at 231 SW 2nd Ave. (954-463-4431).

8. Museum of Discovery and Science

The museum includes hands-on exhibits and an IMAX 3D Theater (401 SW 2nd St., 954-467-6637) and has a floating dock for those who wish to arrive by boat (for day use only).

MARINAS

9. Cooley's Landing Marina

450 SW 7th Ave. (954-828-4626)

10. New River Downtown Docks

2 S. New River Dr. East (954-828-5423)

11. Riverfront Marina

420 SW 3rd Ave. (954-527-1829)

covered, megayacht dockominium and can accommodate vessels to 200 feet. Cable Marine East at the head of the canal is a full-service boatyard with on-site mechanics, specialists and craftsmen.

Just north of the SE 17th Street (Brooks Memorial) Bridge on the east side of the ICW is the 157-slip Pier Sixty-Six Marina with dockage for vessels to 400 feet and just south of the bridge is Pier Sixty-Six South with 20 slips to 500 feet. The marina offers resort amenities including concierge service.

Anchorage: There is little space near the Las Olas Moorings & Anchorage but you must stay at least 500 feet from the moorings. Boats anchored on the outside close to the channel are subject to the effects of the current. Anchored vessels are requested not to block access to the docks at private residences adjacent to the mooring area. The dinghy dock is under the SE 17th Street (Brooks Memorial) Bridge.

Lake Sylvia south of Bahia Mar Yachting Center is your best bet now for anchoring in this area. Leave the intracoastal headed east at flashing green "13." Hug the east shore for 6-foot MLW depths into lake. Once in the lake alter course west-southwest to avoid a shallow area

and anchor in 8 to 9 feet MLW where space permits. Luxurious homes surround the anchorage. On weekends Lake Sylvia is full of local boats, many rafted for the night. It is also a favorite spot for water skiers.

There is not a dinghy landing in Lake Sylvia but water taxis stand by on VHF Channel 68 and will pick up or drop off passengers at locations throughout Fort Lauderdale along both the ICW and the New River. A pass provides the passenger with unlimited stops and rides for the whole day.

Side Trip: New River–ICW Mile 1065

The gently curving, meandering New River bisects the heart of Fort Lauderdale and serves as another major waterway and yacht service area. The New River is Fort Lauderdale's yachting center with some of the finest facilities for building, repair, haul-out and storage on the entire East Coast. Even if you don't need anything it is worth taking a trip–by boat, dinghy or one of the regularly scheduled sightseeing craft–just to see the contrast of the old and new Fort Lauderdale. See details on attractions and amenities at "Goin' Ashore: Fort Lauderdale (New River), FL" in this chapter.

Just beyond its mouth the New River wanders lazily through a short stretch edged by fine lawns and some of the area's older, grander and more gracious homes. Entering the commercial area you pass over south Florida's only traffic tunnel, which carries U.S. Hwy. 1 beneath the river. This area was Fort Lauderdale's original business district and its original marine-services center. Attesting to Fort Lauderdale's long-standing prominence in the marine industry, New River's wooded riverbanks were lined with docks long before World War II much as they are today.

Riverwalk Fort Lauderdale lines both the north and south banks of the New River. The extraordinary waterfront park lies in the heart of downtown and offers lush tropical landscaping and winding brick walkways that link attractions, restaurants and shops. Most cruisers thoroughly enjoy this stretch of river frontage and find this a pleasant place to tie up for a day or two.

Water traffic is heavy on weekends and extra fenders are desirable, although wake action is not nearly as noticeable as you might expect. Every manner of watercraft will pass by and the sights and sounds of this traffic are fascinating. You may also spot the broad back of a manatee or the bulging eyes of an alligator. Nearby Las Olas Blvd. offers excellent restaurants, gourmet food shops, fashionable boutiques and specialty shops. Fort Lauderdale's well-preserved historic districts are all within an easy walk.

The New River forks beyond the William H. Marshall (7th Avenue) Bridge into the North Fork and the South Fork of the New River. The North Fork is residential while the South Fork serves as the principal channel that leads to the heart of Fort Lauderdale's marine-services hub and additional marinas.

NAVIGATION: Use NOAA Charts 11470 and 11467. Entrance to the New River from the ICW has two approaches and entry instructions depend on whether you are southbound or northbound. Southbound ICW traffic enters New River via the approach at Mile 1065 near flashing red "16." The New River approach channel follows a northwesterly course, while the ICW turns southwest. Care should be taken to keep the red-over-green junction daybeacon "A" to port on entry. The water is very shallow immediately behind this daybeacon and you will run aground if you pass it on the wrong side.

Continuing northwest observe daybeacons "1" through "4," which clearly mark the channel. Just inside the approach entry, a white-and-orange DANGER daybeacon marks a shoal. Keep that well to port as you pass.

Northbound ICW traffic enters New River via the south approach at Mile 1065.5 between two red ICW markers. Take red daybeacon "22" to port and keep flashing red "20" to starboard for the New River approach channel, which follows a northerly course. (The ICW turns northeast at this junction). Beware of a rock just outside the channel at red daybeacon "22." Favor the bulkhead-lined western shore from flashing red "20" to green daybeacon "5" in the river's mouth. Northbound vessels should study the chart closely and sort out the confusing transposition of buoys and colors before trying this entrance.

> ⚠️
> Tarpon River Bend is a blind S-turn at the river's mouth at green daybeacon "11." To make matters worse the last New River marker, red daybeacon "12," marks a hard shoal extending into the channel at Tarpon Bend. We suggest signaling with a horn when approaching this area so oncoming traffic knows you are coming.

Deep-draft vessels should not hug red daybeacon "12" too closely and make a long and wide turn around it. After red daybeacon "12" it's best to keep to the middle of the river. Minimum depths are around 8 feet MLW but there are ongoing plans to dredge it to accommodate the megayachts needing to reach the facilities upriver.

The strong tidal current should be considered when transiting the New River because there is always congestion, especially at the bridges and along the Las Olas Riverfront dining and entertainment area. All of the bridges open on signal with some restrictions.

> ⚠️
> Be alert in "Danger Bend" just before the SE 3rd Avenue Bridge where there is a blind corner in a narrow section of the river.

- **SE 3rd Avenue Bridge** (16-foot closed vertical clearance): Opens on signal except from 7:30 a.m. to 9:00 a.m. and from 4:30 p.m. to 6:00 p.m., Monday through Friday (except federal holidays), when the draw need not open.

Fort Lauderdale (New River), FL

NEW RIVER		Largest Vessel	VHF	Total Slips	Approach/ Dockside Depth	Floating Docks	Gas/ Diesel	Repairs/ Haulout	Min/Max Amps	Pump-Out Station
1. New River Downtown Docks **WiFi** ⊙onSpot	(954) 828-5423	170	16	100	15.0 / 8.0				30 / 100	P
2. Riverfront Marina	(954) 527-1829	40	16		10.0 / 6.0		G	RH	30	
3. Cooley's Landing Marina **WiFi** ⊙onSpot	(954) 828-4626	50	9	30	10.0 / 6.0				30 / 50	P

WiFi Wireless Internet Access ⊙onSpot Dockside WiFi Facility
Visit www.waterwayguide.com for current rates, fuel prices, website addresses and other up-to-the-minute information.
(Information in the table is provided by the facilities.)

Scan here for more details:

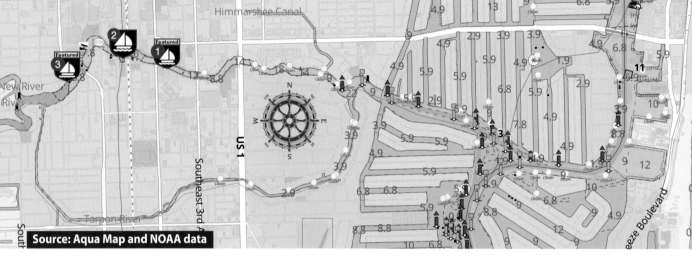

Source: Aqua Map and NOAA data

- **Andrews Avenue Bridge** (21-foot closed vertical clearance): Opens on signal except from 7:30 a.m. to 9:00 a.m. and from 4:30 p.m. to 6:00 p.m., Monday through Friday (except federal holidays), when the draw need not open. The bridge will not open if the FEC Railroad Bridge is closed.

- **Florida East Coast Railroad Bridge-New River** (4-foot closed vertical clearance): Usually open unless train approaching. It is remotely operated.

- **William H. Marshall (7th Avenue) Bridge** (20-foot closed vertical clearance at center): The draw opens on signal except from 7:30 a.m. to 9:00 a.m. and from 4:30 p.m. to 6:00 p.m., Monday through Friday (except federal holidays), when the draw need not open.

Where the New River forks beyond the William H. Marshall (7th Avenue) Bridge, the narrow and shallow North Fork is residential and has only one bridge (**11th Avenue Bridge**). The hand-operated swing has 3-foot closed vertical clearance and opens on signal. This branch is best explored by dinghy.

The stretch between the William H. Marshall (7th Avenue) Bridge and the South Fork is a good place to wait for coming around the S-curve from the south ("Little Florida"), which can be difficult in a strong current. A Sécurité call may be in order here.

New River's South Fork continues from the junction as a wide channel with 8-foot MLW controlling depths. Development flanking the South Fork is residential for a distance but the waterway serves as the principal channel that leads to the heart of Fort Lauderdale's marine-services hub and additional marinas. A 2-mile stretch of boatyards, service shops and freshwater storage begins less than 1 mile above the **Davie Boulevard Bridge**. The bridge has 21-foot closed vertical clearance and opens on signal except Monday through Friday from 7:30 a.m. to 9:00 a.m. and from 4:30 p.m. to 6:00 p.m. (except federal holidays), when the draw need not open. Exercise caution at the 90-degree turn past the bridge as there is not room for two vessels to pass in the turn.

The service and storage yards for deep-draft vessels continue up to the **I-95 Twin Bridges** (55-foot fixed vertical clearance) where there the air-draft limitation will block many larger vessels. (There is a fixed 55-foot vertical clearance railroad bridge for Tri-Rail passenger trains running alongside the I-95 Twin Bridges.) The water is brown and murky, tinted by the Everglades' cypress swamps that drain into the river upstream. Floating water hyacinths, coconuts and other debris is often seen here. You may spot the broad back of a manatee or the bulging eyes of an alligator. Another Idle-Speed/No-Wake Zone extends about 500 yards on either side of the I-95 Twin Bridges.

Next is the **SCL Railroad Bridge** with 2-foot closed vertical clearance, which is open except when trains are approaching. You may encounter strong currents near the twin bridges and around the railroad bridge and turning room is limited. Call the bridgetender ahead of time on VHF Channel 09 to see if you will need to wait for a train. Do not attempt to wait for a bridge opening under the I-95 Twin Bridges. Wait in front of the Lauderdale Marine Center boat sheds instead.

The South New River Canal continues to the southwest. Although narrow, it holds good depths but a 50-foot-high cable south of the boatyards restricts vertical clearance here. This is as far as most cruising boats go. The South New River Canal passes under the **SR 84 Bridge** with 21-foot closed vertical clearance (opens only with 24-hour advance notice). This unmanned bridge is one of the few in Fort Lauderdale not equipped with a VHF radio. Note that the bridge is undergoing maintenance and openings are restricted through January 2021. Call the bridge at 954-776-4300 or check Waterway Explorer (www.waterwayguide.com) for updates. The final bridge before joining the Dania Cut-Off Canal (located 2 miles south) is the 40-foot fixed vertical clearance **I-595 Bridge**.

NOAA Chart 11467 notes that the latest reported depths for the Dania Cut-Off Canal is just 2 feet MLW west of the I-595 Bridge. This passage is surrounded by wilderness and swamp and is suited for small boat exploration only. East of this junction is a water-controlled gate that rises like a guillotine to allow vessels with less than 10-foot vertical clearance to pass beneath. For this reason the Dania Cut-Off Canal is typically entered from the ICW south of Port Everglades. There are several large yards at Port Laudania, where small freighters and cargo ships dock. This is discussed in more detail in the Port Everglades section below.

Dockage: Be aware that the current along New River can be swift so take care in docking and ensure mooring lines are secure. Dockage at the municipal New River Downtown Docks are available on a first-come-first-served basis or by advance reservation. The docks (linear docking along the seawall) are located in the heart of downtown beginning a short distance upriver from the SE 3rd Avenue Bridge and extending intermittently to the William H. Marshall (7th Avenue) Bridge near Cooley's Landing.

The dockmaster's office is on the south bank just east of the Andrews Avenue Bridge. New River Downtown Docks has ample deep-water dockage, pump-out stations and grassy picnic areas and is within walking distance of grocery stores and the famous Las Olas Blvd., known for its shops, galleries, fine restaurants and cafés.

Cooley's Landing Marina is another municipal marina with slips with the usual amenities. This facility is located on the north

Offshore Buoys for Divers

Broward County has placed buoys at locations of interest in the offshore waters for divers and snorkelers. To protect the coral from damage caused by anchoring, the buoys should be used as moorings. Buoy locations are:

Pompano Drop-Off:
N 26° 13.034'/W 80° 05.028'

Hall of Fame:
N 26° 11.581'/W 80° 05.000'

Anglin's Ledge:
N 26° 11.338'/W 80° 05.246'

Oakland Ridges:
N 26° 09.276'/W 80° 05.072'

The Caves:
N 26° 07.631'/W 80° 05.354'

Barracuda Reef:
N 26° 04.575'/W 80° 05.505

The mooring buoys are maintained by the Natural Resources Planning and Management Division. For more information or to report a problem, call 954-519-1270.

Fort Lauderdale (New River), FL

NEW RIVER - SOUTH FORK		Largest Vessel	VHF	Total Slips	Approach/ Dockside Depth	Floating Docks	Gas/ Diesel	Repairs/ Haulout	Min/Max Amps	Pump-Out Station
1. Safe Harbor Lauderdale Marine Center (WiFi)	(954) 713-0333	80		89	12.0 / 10.0	F	GD	RH	30 / 100	P
2. Safe Harbor South Fork (WiFi)	(954) 713-0333	200	16	180	10.0 / 12.0	F		RH	30 / 100	P
3. Marina Mile Yachting Center (WiFi)	(954) 583-0053	150		35	12.0 / 10.0	F		RH	50 / 100	
4. Marina Bay Yachting Center (WiFi)	(954) 791-7600	150		168	12.0 / 45.0	F			30 / 200+	
5. Yacht Haven Park & Marina (WiFi)	(954) 583-2322	120			10.0 / 6.0				30 / 100	
6. Cable Marine West Yard (WiFi)	(954) 587-4000	120	16	75	12.0 / 12.0			RH	50	
7. Rolly Marine Service, Inc. (WiFi)	(954) 583-5300	150			9.0 / 9.0			RH	50 / 100	
8. Billfish Marina	(954) 587-6226	130	16	45	14.0 / 9.0	F		RH	30 / 100	
9. Yacht Management South Florida (WiFi)	(954) 941-6447	140	16	25	13.0 / 7.0	F	D	RH	30 / 100	P
10. Bradford Marine (WiFi)	(954) 791-3800	180	78	105	10.0 / 8.0	F		RH	20 / 100	
11. Roscioli Yachting Center (WiFi)	(954) 581-9200	150		75	10.0 / 10.0			RH	30 / 200+	P
12. Aquamarina Marina Road Boat Yard	(954) 793-4214	65		4	/			RH	30	

(WiFi) Wireless Internet Access (onSpot) **onSpot** Dockside WiFi Facility
Visit www.waterwayguide.com for current rates, fuel prices, website addresses and other up-to-the-minute information.
(Information in the table is provided by the facilities.)

Scan here for more details:

bank and is adjacent to the arts and science district featuring the Broward Center for the Performing Arts, the Museum of Discovery and Science and Esplanade Park.

Between the two municipal marinas on the south side of the river (just above the Florida East Coast Railroad Bridge) is Riverfront Marina, which offers small boat storage (up to 40 feet) but does not have transient dockage. They do, however, have an on-site convenience store and sell gas (no diesel).

Most of the facilities on the South Fork of the New River are oriented towards providing repair services but some offer transient and long-term dockage. On the north side of the I-95 Twin Bridges is the well-regarded Safe Harbor Lauderdale Marine Center and in a basin to the north, Safe Harbor South Fork. Both specialize in repairs and refits and Safe Harbor South Fork can accommodate large catamarans. Lauderdale Marine Center is outfitted for major repairs. Port 32 Fort

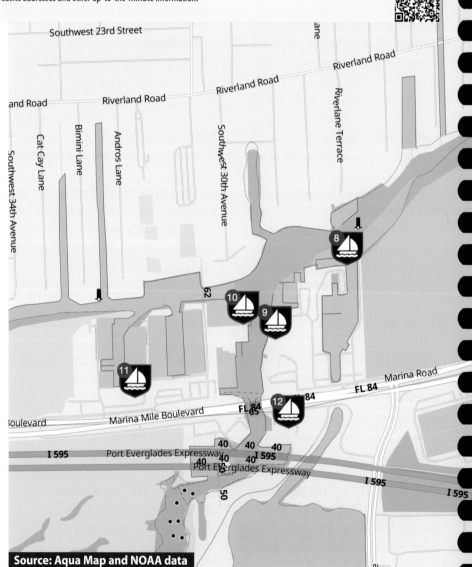

Source: Aqua Map and NOAA data

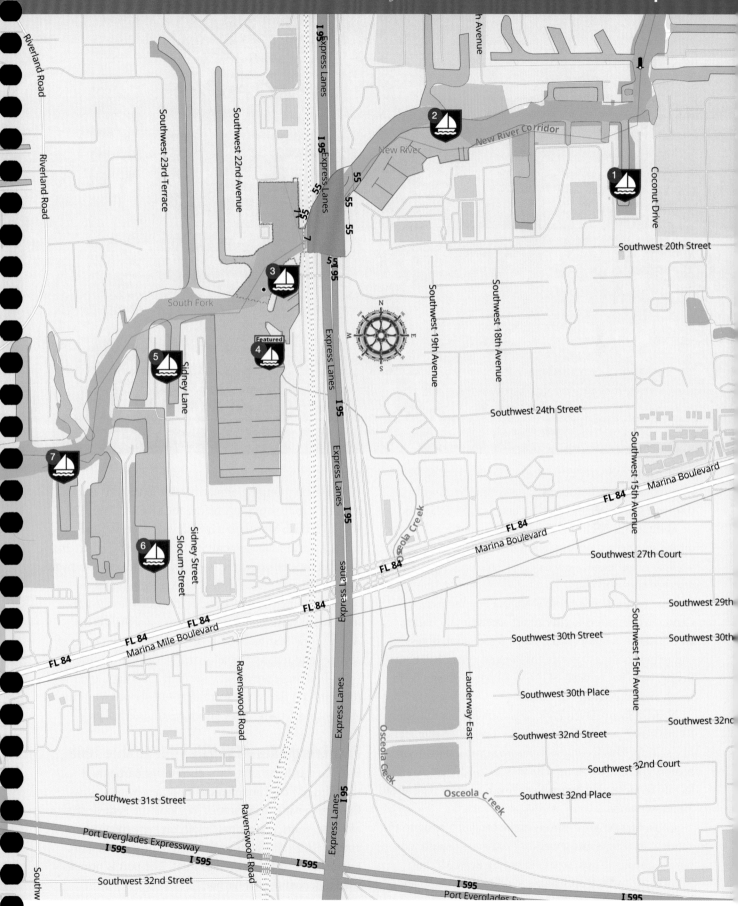

Marina Bay Yachting Center

New River

© Mapbox, © OpenStreetMap

Lauderdale (formerly Fort Lauderdale Boatyard & Marina) was undergoing renovations at press time but may have transient slips available. Call for details (954-895-8360).

Marina Mile Yachting Center is located across the river on the southern shore and is a full-service boatyard with a 6-acre repair facility and dry dockage. They maintain 10 reserved transient slips.

Next on the south shore is Marina Bay Yachting Center, which offers luxury resort amenities including an expansive activity center with a resort pool, fitness and tennis facilities, private theater and a handball court. Rendezvous Bar & Grill (954-797-0054) is on site with lunch and an evening bar menu.

Nearby Yacht Haven Park & Marina is a combination RV park and marina. It is located in a gated 20-acre, park-like setting. This facility welcomes long and short-term boaters and can accommodate vessels to 120 feet. The facility requests that larger boats (over 100 feet) call ahead for a reservation.

Cable Marine West Yard is in the back of a basin to the south with repairs and a well-stocked parts department but no transient slips. It is followed by Rolly Marine Service, Inc., which specializes in refits, extensions and

re-powers but does not have transient space.

The next grouping of marinas and boatyards is located about 0.5 mile south just before the SR 84 Bridge. The 45-slip Billfish Marina is a full-service boatyard and marina. Yacht Management South Florida specializes in yacht maintenance, while Bradford Marine offers shipyard services and repairs as well as brokerage services.

In the same basin just under the SR 84 Bridge (21-foot closed vertical clearance, opens on signal) is the Aquamarina Marina Road Boat Yard offering all types of services and repairs and allowing DIY. A canvas shop and yacht brokerage are on site. Roscioli Yachting Center to the south on the New River offers full-service renovations, storage and repairs. They also have transient slips.

Port Everglades–ICW Mile 1066 to Mile 1068

Port Everglades is a modern deep water harbor and the third of Fort Lauderdale's important boating areas. Expensive waterfront homes overlook the endless stream of cruise ships, recreational craft, tankers, freighters and warships that constantly parade through the Port Everglades (Fort Lauderdale) Inlet. The port is primarily used as a commercial harbor.

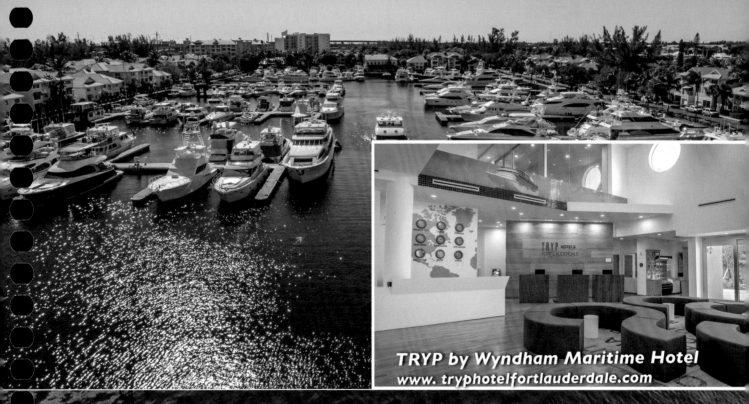

The straight, deep Port Everglades (Fort Lauderdale) Inlet forms an excellent big-ship terminal and commercial port that handles millions of tons of ocean cargo each year. The ship terminals in the port often accommodate cruise ships, tankers, freighters and military vessels. Nearly 150 warships, both domestic and foreign, visit the port every year. When military vessels are in port a security cordon is set up for which entry by private craft is prohibited.

Keep clear of large-vessel traffic in the busy inlets, especially Port Everglades (Fort Lauderdale) Inlet, Government Cut (Miami) Inlet and Lake Worth (Palm Beach) Inlet. The Coast Guard establishes a moving security zone for the protection of passenger vessels (cruise ships), vessels carrying cargoes of particular hazard and vessels carrying liquefied hazardous gas when such a vessel passes buoy "PE" to enter the port. Approaching closer than 100 yards to such a vessel is prohibited without prior permission.

When large vessels are docked and secured in the port boat traffic may still proceed along the ICW provided that they stay to the east of law enforcement craft and cruise ship tenders being used to mark the transit lane. When such vessels are not docked boats may use the ICW without restriction. Occasionally all traffic may be halted temporarily while ships are docking or leaving. Patrol craft may be contacted on VHF Channel 16 for the status of these security zones. The Coast Guard-established and well enforced Slow-Speed Zone in the Port Everglades Entrance Channel.

NAVIGATION: Use NOAA Charts 11470 and 11467. The entire Port Everglades area has deep water with the exception of the northeastern corner alongside the marked ICW channel near flashing green "29." Deep water vessel dockage extends to the south along the ship channel that includes the ICW route to the Dania Cut-Off Canal at flashing green "35" (Mile 1068.5) where the ICW marker sequence resumes. (Note there are no ICW markers in the between these two flashing greens.)

At the point where the ICW crosses the ship channel keep the Port Everglades (Fort Lauderdale) Inlet and ICW buoys sorted out in your mind. The southbound ICW route takes a straight-line course across the Turning Basin and enters a large ship channel to the south. Once across the Main Turning Basin vessels southbound on the ICW pass to the west of flashing green "11" (not an ICW marker) and proceed with a close pass of the Fort Lauderdale Coast Guard Station.

South of the Coast Guard Station be careful to avoid the mangroves and partially submerged rocks outside of the channel on the eastern side of the ICW, while keeping the required distance from the cruise ships usually berthed on the mainland side. The ICW route follows the east side of the ship channel as you continue south towards the Dania Cut-Off Canal (Mile 1068.5).

> Keep in mind the continuing ICW makers can't be seen from the Main Turning Basin and pick up 1.75 miles south at the Dania Cut-Off Canal. Remember that ICW markers have a yellow triangle or square above the numerals.

One of the best and safest big ship inlets in Florida, Port Everglades (Fort Lauderdale) Inlet is well marked with flashing buoys along the entrance channel. Currents average 0.7 knots with a tidal range of 3.1 feet in the Turning Basin. The port and inlet may be crowded with both commercial and recreational traffic. This is a popular take-off point for cruisers heading to and from the Bahamas, fishermen heading out to the nearby Gulf Stream and skippers cruising north and south along the coast to escape the bridges and speed restrictions. It is also popular with ICW boaters hankering for different scenery.

Vessels with mast heights over 56 feet that are headed south of Miami's Julia Tuttle Causeway Bridge at Mile 1087.2 have no choice but to go outside at Port Everglades. These vessels can then rejoin the ICW via Miami's Government Cut at Dodge Island.

When approaching the port from offshore the RACON sea buoy will be your best offshore waypoint. However, the air traffic to and from Fort Lauderdale airport provides a visual aid from miles out to sea. If heading north from Port Everglades you must follow the marked shipping channel offshore for at least 1 nm before turning northwards to avoid the dangerous shoals extending out from shore at the channel's north edge. Also note that the channel markers are spaced at approximately 0.5 nm apart and the jetty ends are not marked. Be sure to maintain a compass courseline and maintain alignment on exit or entry.

Port Everglades Inlet

Dania Beach & Dania Cut-Off Canal–ICW Mile 1068 to Mile 1070

Named for its early Danish settlers the city of Dania Beach was once the "Tomato Capital of the World." Visitors today can enjoy the beach, the 800-foot-long fishing pier and a remarkable collection of antiques shops. The Dania Marine Flea Market is billed as the largest marine flea market in the world. It is held annually in March. Check online at www.daniamarinefleamarket.com for general information, dates and location as it moves from year to year. Just about anything for a boat can be found at the event. If you love garage sales, this is the largest one of all and is worth visiting if you are passing through in March.

NAVIGATION: Use NOAA Chart 11467. Leaving Port Everglades observe the buoys and, if in doubt, favor the mainland. The eastern side of the ICW is shallow and marshy with rocks outside the channel. Observe the ICW markers. The first in the continuing sequence south of the Port Everglades (Fort Lauderdale) Inlet is flashing green "35" located directly adjacent the Dania Cut-Off Canal at Mile 1068.5. Favor the west side of the marked channel to Mile 1070.

The Dania Cut-Off Canal, which branches to the west at Mile 1068.5, is a busy marine service area. Businesses here include well-equipped yards, modern marinas, boat builders and marine service specialists. Expect heavy marine traffic as you past the canal entrance. When approaching the canal from either direction along the ICW keep a sharp lookout for unexpected high-speed traffic swinging out of the canal into the ICW. Also expect traffic entering from Whiskey Creek to the east at Mile 1069.2. Just south of Whiskey Creek is the **Dania Beach Boulevard (SR A1A) Bridge** (22-foot closed vertical clearance). This restricted bridge opens on the hour and half-hour (not on signal).

Dockage: First on the Dania Cut-Off Canal is the 165-slip Harbour Towne Marina with a compliment of over 20 businesses and a wide range of amenities. The marina offers wet and dry storage, can accommodate transient vessels to 200 feet and offers marine services and repairs. Sun Power Diesel is in the next basin to the west with a staff of factory-certified technicians selling and servicing premium brands of marine diesel engines and generators.

Next on the north bank is Playboy Marine Center, a DIY boat repair facility that also has highly qualified independent contractors should you decide to seek professional services. Each visiting boat receives a clean, spacious work space equipped with water and electrical hook-ups. The on-site marine store is stocked with a full line of antifouling paints, primers, painting supplies and

Outside Run to Miami

The Gulf Stream is like a giant moving sidewalk. Slower vessels can travel against the Gulf Stream showing speed through the water while making minimal progress over ground. Coastal cruisers must factor in the Gulf Stream in East Florida.

In ordinary weather an outside run to or from Miami is safe, comfortable and provides some beautiful views of the coastline. With a Gulf Stream boost and by avoiding bridges transit times are generally faster on the outside. Plan your departure and arrival times and wait for a weather window. For most this is an easy and enjoyable passage.

⚠️

Southbound vessels with an air draft in excess of 56 feet must take the outside route to Miami's Government Cut. The Julia Tuttle Causeway Bridge (Mile 1087.2, 56-foot fixed vertical clearance) crosses the ICW between Miami and Miami Beach.

Be sure to plan for your passage and remember to check maintenance issues and tie down deck gear in advance. You are committing to a 20-mile passage south or a 40-mile passage north to the next reliable inlet. Plan to leave early in the day to insure you arrive before nightfall.

While these inlets can accommodate large commercial ships and are marked with lighted aids to navigation, nighttime arrivals can be difficult and add unnecessary risk. At least 30 minutes before you leave monitor VHF Channel 16 for a Sécurité from large vessels either entering or exiting. Wait until these vessels are safely clear and secure before you enter the inlet channel from either end.

Proceeding out the wide, straight ship channel of the Port Everglades (Fort Lauderdale) Inlet you will find good water depths in the channel and beyond the entrance buoys. (The last cruise ship through has checked it for you.) But there are submerged hazards beyond the channel's edges north and south. To the south good water extends well inshore and many boaters turn south just beyond flashing green buoy "5."

The Gulf Stream is not a hazard but it does require a strategy. Heading north is simple; angle out passing flashing red entrance buoy "2" until you detect a course deflection and then turn north to enjoy the ride. Southbound boats want to stay inside the Gulf Stream to avoid the retarding current but also stay well outside the dangerous breakers along the beach. In offshore winds you can travel safely keeping 0.5 mile off the beach; in onshore winds it's best to double that distance. This route keeps you inshore of the Gulf Stream and its approximately 2-knot northerly set. You may even find gentle southward counter-current close to shore but remember to maintain a safe distance from the beach.

The NOAA Weather Stations (Miami, WX-1, serves this area) broadcast the location of the inshore edge of the Gulf Stream from 4:00 p.m. to 8:00 p.m. on Monday, Wednesday and Friday and from 4:00 a.m. to 8:00 a.m. on Tuesday, Thursday and Saturday in the fall and winter. The western edge of the Gulf Stream ranges from as close as 1 nm offshore to more than 10 nm; the width of the Gulf Stream is also stated in the WX broadcasts. NOAA Weather also advises on expected wind conditions and wave height, which can help with finding your weather window.

Using your knowledge of the Gulf Stream direction and speed can make your passage both enjoyable and safe.

Dania Cut-Off Canal

Source: Aqua Map and NOAA data

stainless steel fasteners. Their 93-ton lift can handle sail or powerboats up to 80 feet in length (maximum beam of 20 feet).

Opposite on the south bank is Royale Palm Yacht Basin specializing in all aspects of yacht refinishing and with ample transient dockage. Derecktor Shipyards is a megayacht repair, storage and refit facility and can handle most any large (or small) job. This is one of four Derecktor yards. MarineMax East Florida Yacht Center is primarily a yacht sales and service facility. They also host raft-ups and getaways as well as seminars and boating classes.

Seahaven Superyacht Marina on the south shore is specifically designed to cater to superyacht clientele. They can accommodate vessels to 250 feet in deep water slips with all the expected amenities plus a fitness center and concierge service. The last facility east of the US 1 Bridge is Cozy Cove Marina with boat sales, dockage and services. They offer covered and uncovered slips to 48 feet but can accommodate boats to 100 feet. (Call ahead.)

The well-regarded Thunderboat Marine Service Center-Dania Beach is west of the US 1 Bridge (with 12.1-foot fixed vertical clearance) with storage and dockage for boats to 44 feet. They also offer boat rentals. To the west past the 17.7-foot fixed vertical clearance Dania Cut-Off Canal Bridge (carrying FL 818) and the 15-foot fixed vertical clearance I-95 Bridge is Nautical Ventures Marine Center, a full-service yard that allows DIY. Call ahead for approach depths and slip availability.

Dania Canal, FL

DANIA CUT-OFF CANAL		Largest Vessel	VHF	Total Slips	Approach/ Dockside Depth	Floating Docks	Gas/ Diesel	Repairs/ Haulout	Min/Max Amps	Pump-Out Station
1. Harbour Towne Marina 1.0 mi. W of MM 1068.6	(954) 926-0300	200	16	165	17.0 / 7.0		GD	RH	30 / 200+	P
2. Sun Power Diesel 1.0 mi. W of MM 1068.6	(954) 237-2200	100		13	20.0 / 10.0	F		RH	50	
3. Playboy Marine Center (WiFi) 1.0 mi. W of MM 1068.6	(954) 920-0533	86	16	3	17.0 / 15.0			H	30 / 50	
4. Royale Palm Yacht Basin (WiFi) 1.0 mi. W of MM 1068.6	(954) 923-5900	80	78	60	7.0 / 7.0			RH	50	
5. Derecktor Shipyards (WiFi) 1.0 mi. W of MM 1068.6	(954) 920-5756	210		49	17.0 / 14.0	F		RH	30 / 200+	
6. MarineMax East Florida Yacht Center 1.0 mi. W of MM 1068.6	(954) 926-0308	112	16	11	6.0 / 6.0			RH	30 / 50	
7. Seahaven Superyacht Marina (WiFi) onSpot	(954) 416-1860	250	16	30	16.0 / 16.0	F			50 / 200+	P
8. Cozy Cove Marina	(954) 921-8800	100		59	/	F		RH	30	
9. Thunderboat Marine Service Center-Dania Beach	(954) 924-9444	44		60	5.0 / 5.0	F	G	R		
10. Nautical Ventures Marine Center	(954) 962-8702	70		65	8.0 / 8.0			RH	30	
WHISKEY RIVER										
11. Dania Beach Marina (WiFi)	(954) 647-8655		16	92	4.0 / 4.0	F			30 / 50	P

(WiFi) Wireless Internet Access   onSpot Dockside WiFi Facility
Visit www.waterwayguide.com for current rates, fuel prices, website addresses and other up-to-the-minute information.
(Information in the table is provided by the facilities.)

Scan here for more details:

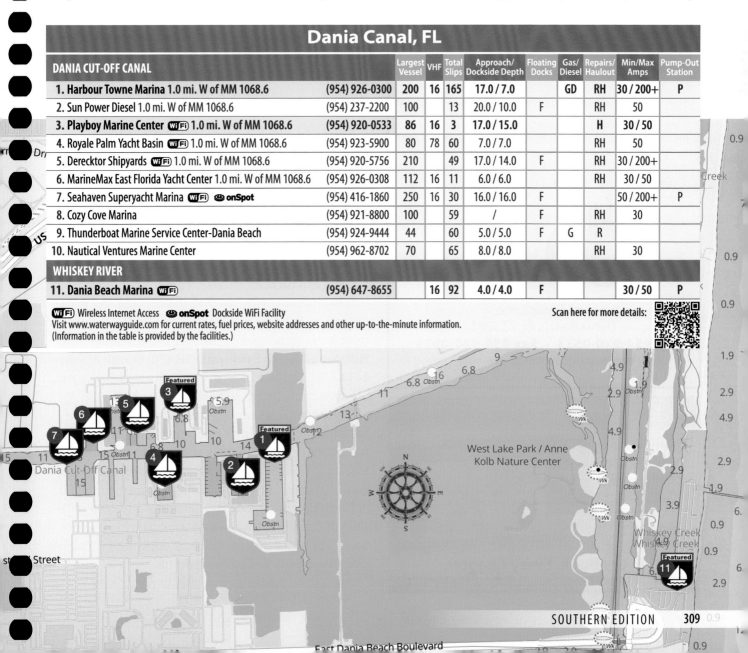

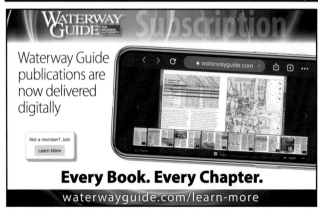
Back on the ICW the gated Dania Beach Marina is across from the Dania Cut-Off Canal at Mile 1069.2 on Whiskey Creek. The creek's entrance crossed by the 18-foot fixed vertical clearance Whiskey Creek Bridge. The marina offers transient dockage and is adjacent to the Dania Beach Pier and the beach as well as numerous restaurants.

◼ TO BAKERS HAULOVER INLET

Hollywood Area–ICW Mile 1070 to 1073

South of Dania Beach is an area that has become almost a suburb of Fort Lauderdale and Miami. Hollywood Beach's proximity to Fort Lauderdale makes it a fine alternative when berths are hard to find. Just a short walk from the Hollywood Marina across the Hollywood Beach Boulevard (SR 820) Bridge is beautiful Hollywood Beach and Oceanwalk, a 2-mile-long, brick-lined pedestrian promenade with lots of outdoor dining options. A few miles west in downtown Hollywood you will find extensive shopping and a historic recreated old town with a family-oriented park in the center of Hollywood Circle.

NAVIGATION: Use NOAA Chart 11467. South of Dania Beach the ICW cuts through several broad natural lagoons where the water is spread thinly and the dredged channel is narrow. Pay careful attention to navigation markers and your depth sounder. The **Sheridan Street Bridge** at Mile 1070.5 has 22-foot closed vertical clearance and opens on the quarter and three-quarter hour (not on signal) and has a dogleg approach.

The channel cuts across from the east close to the western shore before passing under the bridge. Be sure not to stray out of the marked channel. The next bridge is the **Hollywood Beach Boulevard (SR 820) Bridge** at Mile 1072.2, which has a 25-foot closed vertical clearance and opens on the hour and half-hour (not on demand).

Dockage: South of the Sheridan Street Bridge the eastern shore is lined with casual restaurants complete with tie-up locations on the bulkhead for dining customers. The municipal Hollywood Marina maintains transient slips and may have space for you. Controlling depths in the middle of North Lake are reportedly as little as 1.5 to 2.5 feet MLW. If docking at Hollywood Marina, stay close to the docks and follow the contour of the docks. Call ahead to check availability and approach depths.

Hollywood Beach, FL

HOLLYWOOD BEACH AREA		Largest Vessel	VHF	Total Slips	Approach/ Dockside Depth	Floating Docks	Gas/ Diesel	Repairs/ Haulout	Min/Max Amps	Pump-Out Station
1. Hollywood Marina **WiFi** MM 1072.1	(954) 921-3035	115	16	55	6.0 / 7.0		GD		30 / 50	P
2. Loggerhead Marina - Hollywood Marina **WiFi** ⊙ onSpot	(954) 457-8557	120	16	190	15.0 / 8.0			H	30 / 100	P

WiFi Wireless Internet Access ⊙ **onSpot** Dockside WiFi Facility
Visit www.waterwayguide.com for current rates, fuel prices, website addresses and other up-to-the-minute information.
(Information in the table is provided by the facilities.)

Scan here for more details:

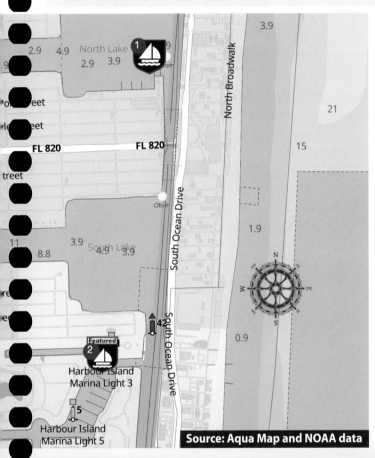

Source: Aqua Map and NOAA data

Loggerhead Marina–Hollywood Marina offers 190 slips for vessels to 120 feet at red daybeacon "42," just south of the Hollywood Beach Boulevard (SR 820) Bridge. They offer professional concierge service and access to restaurants, shopping, golf and tennis courts. The Hollywood Beach boardwalk is just minutes away.

Anchorage: Anchorages are available both north and south of the Sheridan Street Bridge, along the east shore. The little cove with the beach north of the Sheridan Street Bridge is within the boundaries of a park where anchoring is prohibited so be sure you drop your anchor a bit north of the cove for 7-foot MLW depths. There is a snug anchorage for one or two boats north of the line of docks along the edge of the ICW in 9- to 11-foot MLW depths. Dinghy access to the adjacent park is prohibited.

A short distance south of the Hollywood Beach Boulevard Bridge is South Lake. Although the chart still shows depths of 4 and 5 feet MLW, dredging has increased controlling depths to 13 feet MLW but investigate with caution. There is room for a number of boats and the holding is good but it may be rolly from wakes.

Hollywood, FL

North Miami Beach, FL

NORTH MIAMI BEACH AREA		Largest Vessel	VHF	Total Slips	Approach/Dockside Depth	Floating Docks	Gas/Diesel	Repairs/Haulout	Min/Max Amps	Pump-Out Station
1. Hallandale Beach City Marina (WiFi)	(954) 457-1653	60		26	/				30	P
2. Loggerhead Marina - Aventura Marina (WiFi) MM 1075.2	(305) 935-4295	120	16	99	20.0 / 10.0				30 / 100	P
3. Turnberry Marina (WiFi) MM 1075.5	(305) 933-6934	225	16	68	30.0 / 20.0	F			50 / 200+	P
4. Loggerhead Marina - Hi-Lift Marina MM 1077.3	(305) 931-2550	40		9	/	F	G	RH	30	
5. Williams Island Marina (WiFi) MM 1076.6	(305) 937-7813	160	16	106	10.0 / 8.0	F			30 / 100	P
6. Marina Palms Yacht Club (WiFi)	(786) 707-2629	100	16	112	/ 9.0	F	GD		30 / 100	P

(WiFi) Wireless Internet Access **onSpot** Dockside WiFi Facility
Visit www.waterwayguide.com for current rates, fuel prices, website addresses and other up-to-the-minute information.
(Information in the table is provided by the facilities.)

Scan here for more details:

Hallandale to Bakers Haulover Inlet—ICW Mile 1074 to Mile 1080

When you observe the tidal current speeding up along the ICW route you are nearing Bakers Haulover (North Miami Beach) Inlet. This inlet is the northernmost of Miami's inlets from the Atlantic Ocean and is heavily used by recreational fishermen and local boats.

NAVIGATION: Use NOAA Chart 11467. The **Hallandale Beach Boulevard (SR 858) Bridge** at Mile 1074.0 has 26-foot closed vertical clearance and, like other bridges along this stretch, has restricted openings (in this case on the quarter hour and three-quarter hour). The high-rise **William Lehman Causeway (SR 856) Bridge** crosses the ICW at Mile 1076.3 with 65-foot fixed vertical clearance. South of Golden Beach the ICW leaves the cut channels and returns to dredged channels through interconnected lagoons beginning with Dumbfoundling Bay.

The lagoon adjoining Dumfoundling Bay is a broad, open and generally shallow body of water with a few deeper patches along its eastern shore. At the lagoon's southern end the marked route crosses over to the western shore. To the north of the Maule Lake entrance, which is popular for anchoring and has dockage facilities, there is a shoal marked by a privately maintained white daybeacon. Give it a wide berth.

Heading south the ICW enters Biscayne Creek, which borders the community of Sunny Isles to the east. At Mile

Williams Island Marina

Atlantic Ocean

ICW

Bakers Haulover Inlet

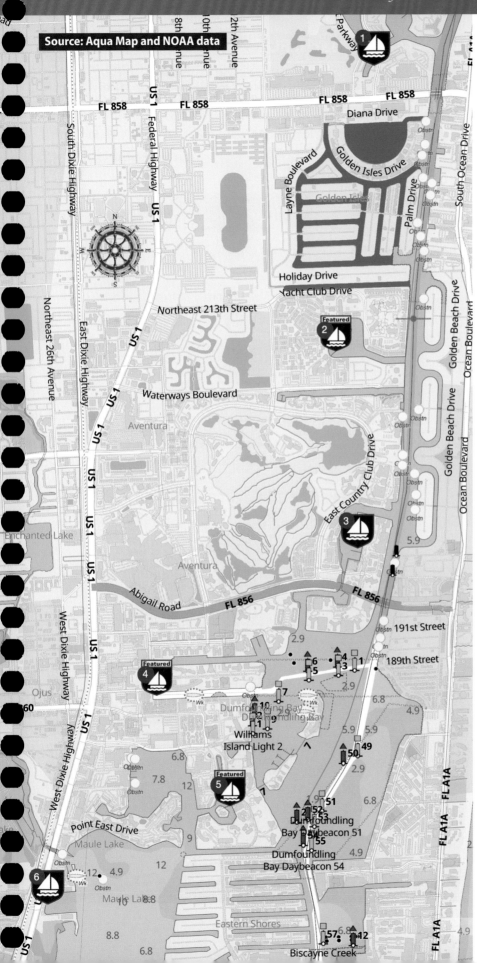

Source: Aqua Map and NOAA data

1078.0 the **NE 163rd Street (SR 826) Bridge** links that community to the mainland. This 30-foot closed vertical clearance bridge opens on signal, except from 7:00 a.m. to 6:00 p.m., Monday through Friday (except federal holidays), and from 10:00 a.m. to 6:00 p.m., on weekends and federal holidays when the draw need only open on the quarter hour and three-quarter hour.

Bakers Haulover (North Miami Beach) Inlet is spanned by the **Bakers Haulover Inlet Bridge** with 32-foot fixed vertical clearance. Jetties are short here and currents are strong (2.0 to 3.0 knots). The inlet can become especially nasty when wind and current oppose. Because of this it is best to head just 8.3 miles south to Government Cut (Miami) Inlet, a clear, well-marked large ship inlet.

The shoaling problem on the ICW channel west of Bakers Haulover (North Miami Beach) Inlet at Mile 1080 is legendary. Periodically the area south of red daybeacon "6A" is dredged and, inevitably, it fills back in. Follow buoys "7," "7A," "7B" and "7C," even if it appears that they are leading you to one side of the normal channel. Markers are moved or added regularly here to indicate the deepest channel; follow the markers as positioned.

If the sun is at the proper angle you can see the path through the shoal area. Watch for a strong set to the west with flood tide and to the east with the ebb. This is a very busy area of the ICW. Proceed with caution.

North Miami Beach, FL

BAKERS HAULOVER INLET AREA		Largest Vessel	VHF	Total Slips	Approach/ Dockside Depth	Floating Docks	Gas/ Diesel	Repairs/ Haulout	Min/Max Amps	Pump-Out Station
1. Bill Bird Marina at Haulover Park MM 1079.7	(305) 947-3525	120	16	150	8.0 / 8.5		GD		30 / 100	P
2. Bal Harbour Yacht Club-PRIVATE (Wifi)	(305) 865-6048	140		35	8.0 / 8.0		GD			
3. Keystone Point Marina 1.3 mi. W of MM 1080.8	(305) 940-6236	110	16	26	8.0 / 8.0	F	GD	RH	30 / 50	P

(Wifi) Wireless Internet Access ◉ onSpot Dockside WiFi Facility
Visit www.waterwayguide.com for current rates, fuel prices, website addresses and other up-to-the-minute information.
(Information in the table is provided by the facilities.)

Scan here for more details:

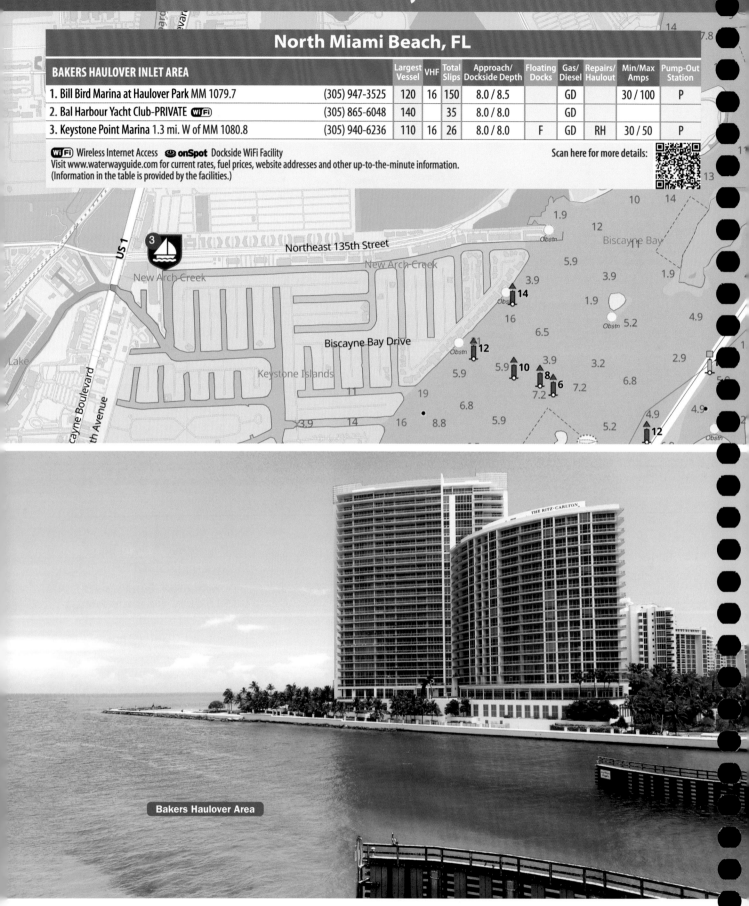

Bakers Haulover Area

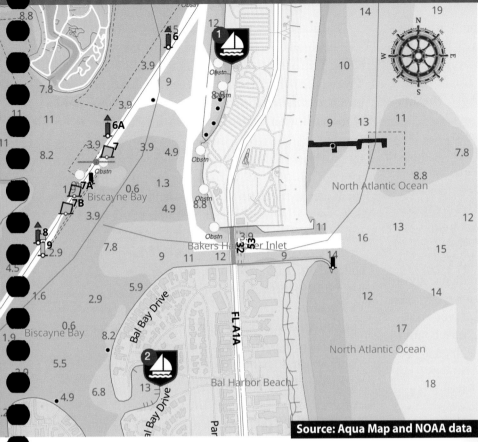

Source: Aqua Map and NOAA data

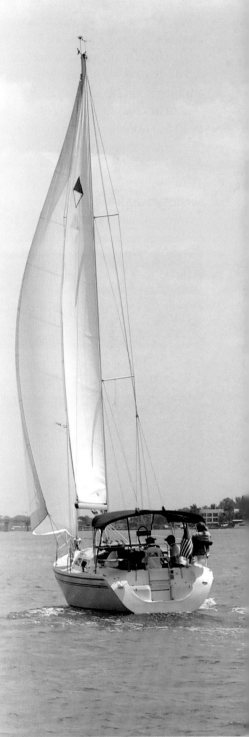

Dockage: Hallandale Beach City Marina is located at Mile 1074 on the west side of the ICW in the canal just north of the Hallandale Beach Boulevard (SR 858) Bridge. The marina has just three reserved transient slips. Be aware that there is a fixed bridge (**Three Islands Boulevard Bridge**) with 17-foot vertical clearance prior to reaching the marina. Call the marina for approach details.

Loggerhead Marina–Aventura Marina across from Golden Beach (Mile 1075.2) accepts vessels to 120 feet in their large, protected harbor. This marina offers many upscale amenities including valet shuttle service and is located within the Waterway Shoppes with open-air shopping (including groceries), dining and entertainment. To the south at Mile 1075.5, Turnberry Marina is located at the JW Marriott Miami Turnberry Resort & Spa. The marina offers full amenities including in-slip pump-out service and access to an on-site fitness center.

At Mile 1076 a straight, narrow and deep canal cuts westward off the ICW to Maule Lake and Williams Island Marina, which offers dockage in a well-protected harbor with resort amenities. Nestled on 84 lush acres, this facility offers multiple pools, a spa, 16 tennis courts and several restaurants. Loggerhead Marina–Hi-Lift Marina is to the north with lift slips and storage for vessels to 40 feet plus some repairs.

Marina Palms Yacht Club is in a condominium complex on the western shore of Maule Lake with slips to 100 feet and an on-site Boat Club, which offers a full range of activities from jet skiing to kayaking and snorkeling. Reservations should be made in advance.

North of Bakers Haulover (North Miami Beach) Inlet on the east side of the ICW is the full-service Bill Bird Marina at Haulover Park, home to the largest charter/drift fishing fleet in South Florida with on-site bait & tackle stores, boat and jet-ski rentals and a dive boat. This facility has 152 slips for vessels to 120 feet.

The mainland opposite Bakers Haulover (North Miami Beach) Inlet is the start of North Miami. Here, in protected New Arch Creek, are a number of boating amenities, repair yards and stores that are eager to serve transient mariners including Keystone Point Marina. There is a well-marked approach channel leading west from ICW red daybeacon "12." The marina is usually full so call in advance to check on the availability of a slip.

Anchorage: It is possible to anchor in Maule Lake in 8 to 20 feet MLW by exiting the ICW west of red daybeacon "54." Even though this provides all-around protection, the holding is just fair due to the mud and rock bottom. There is shore access at the launch ramp with plenty of shopping within walking distance. (Note that we do not recommend anchoring in Dumfoundling Bay as it is a cable crossing area.)

One of the finest overnight anchorages along this section of the ICW is in the basin across the ICW from Bakers Haulover (North Miami Beach) Inlet at Mile 1080. The only drawback is its entrance. At high tide you should turn northwest off the ICW (approximately 75 feet north of red daybeacon "6A") and then slowly head directly toward the large, green, rounded roof of the Florida International University athletic building. Proceed slowly between the 3-foot MLW bar to port and the 4-foot-deep spoils area to the north. If you encounter depths of less than 8 feet MLW within the first couple of hundred feet, you are beginning to stray out of the channel.

Once you pass over the bar (soft mud and sand), you will find 8 to 12-foot MLW depths inside Bakers Haulover Basin. Inside this virtually undeveloped deep-water basin are serene anchorages protected from all wind directions. The bottom is quite soft and there may be debris in some places. Make sure that your anchor is set well. Visiting boaters are not permitted ashore on the Florida International University's property.

■ NEXT STOP

Next we take you to the Greater Miami area including North Miami, Miami Beach, the Miami River, Key Biscayne, Coconut Grove and Coral Gables. Florida's tropical waters truly begin in Biscayne Bay. A boater's paradise, the bay's shallow, turquoise waters are protected by the accessible barrier islands of Biscayne National Park and are not only a destination themselves, but serve as a gateway to the Florida Keys.

ICW Mile 1080-Mile 1111

▪ BISCAYNE BAY

Navigating Biscayne Bay

At 35 miles long and up to 8 miles wide Biscayne Bay ranks as one of North America's great inland waters. Over it's great size the bay also undergoes great variation of scenery, color and development. While not shown on charts, the bay is generally divided into three distinct segments: North, Central and South.

North Biscayne Bay stretches from Bakers Haulover (North Miami Beach) Inlet to Government Cut (Miami) Inlet, the main entrance to the Port of Miami. This segment starts very narrow adjacent to North Miami and gradually widens as it fills the gap between Miami Beach's barrier islands and the mainland. The appearance changes as well. The murky green water and mud bottom of its upper reaches gradually change to a turquoise color with a sandy bottom farther south, just as low-rise development gives way to high-rise on its shores. This segment provides access to Miami Beach, which is a worthy side trip.

Starting south of Dodge Island, Central Biscayne Bay is a boater's paradise. From here south to Cutter Bank, the bay's central segment is wider and its beautiful turquoise waters are deeper. The breadth of the bay here provides boats with room to maneuver but it's barrier islands still create excellent protected anchorages. The high-rise development that flanked the lower reaches of the north segment slowly give way to wilderness and parkland as you enter Biscayne National Park. This land and sea reserve is a treasure and well worth a stop for a walk or snorkel.

From Card Sound south to Jewfish Creek, South Biscayne Bay is squeezed between Key Largo and the Everglades. The waters here darken as they are fed by the swamps to the

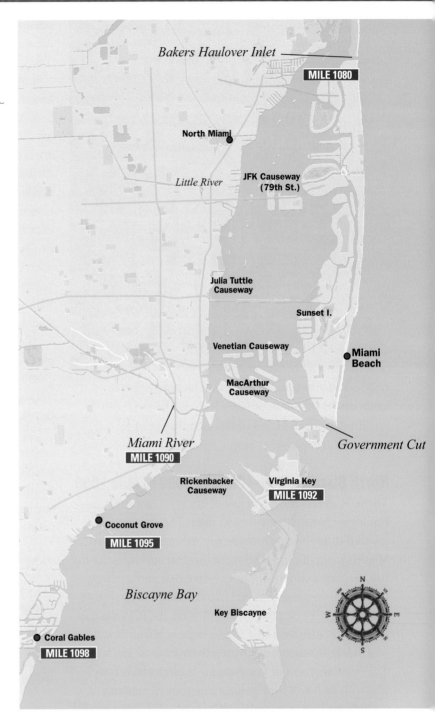

No Wake Zones, Idle Speed Zones and various Speed Limit restrictions are in effect throughout the waterways included in this chapter. Exercise diligence in knowing the regulations by observing signs and other markers. Enforcement is always present. As always, be courteous to other vessels and avoid manatees and other marine life.

Sunset Islands

Sunset Harbour Yacht Club

© Mapbox, © OpenStreetMap

north. These sounds still provide tacking room for sailboats but shallow progressively as the southern terminus is reached. All of Biscayne Bay is well protected and provides ample opportunities to anchor.

North Biscayne Bay–ICW Mile 1080 to Mile 1090

The ICW enters the north end of Biscayne Bay at Bakers Haulover (North Miami Beach) Inlet. The area generally referred to as "North Biscayne Bay" stretches from here to Miami's main inlet, Government Cut (Miami) Inlet. As the bay deepens a variety of routes weave past and amongst the manmade causeways and islands. Cruisers can opt to stay in the ICW closer to Miami or leave the ICW via any of several routes for a side trip to explore Miami Beach.

Greater Miami bustles with activity on land and water. The north segment of Biscayne Bay is particularly busy and with its heavy boat traffic, numerous islands and shallow pockets of water, it can be confusing to navigate. Study your charts carefully before attempting to transit this sometimes confusing area.

NAVIGATION: Use NOAA Chart 11467. South from Bakers Haulover (North Miami Beach) Inlet, the ICW maintains a straight course as it angles diagonally across North Biscayne Bay, reaching the western shore just before the **West 79th Street Bridge**. The narrow but well-marked channel parallels the eastern shore until it

passes Broad Causeway Bridge with 16-foot closed vertical clearance. This is the first of five restricted Miami spans. The span opens on signal except from 8:00 a.m. and 6:00 p.m. when the draw need only open on the quarter hour and three-quarter hour (year-round).

Continuing south from Broad Causeway follow your chart carefully. Starting from green daybeacon "17" there are numerous hazards just outside the marked channel. At flashing red "26" the ICW channel changes course and heads for West 79th Street Bridge at Mile 1084.6 (25-foot closed vertical clearance). The bridge opens on signal except from 7:00 a.m. to 7:00 p.m., Monday through Friday (except federal holidays), when the draw need only open on the hour and half-hour. Be sure to indicate that you want the "western" span when calling the bridge on VHF Channel 09, rather than the East 79th Street Bridge span for the Miami Beach Channel.

If your intention is to "diverge" from the ICW to explore Miami Beach, you should exit the marked ICW channel just past green daybeacon "15" turning southeast toward Normandy Isle. The relatively well-marked Miami Beach Channel route is described in detail below.

Just south of the West 79th Street Bridge on the western shore is the marked entrance to Little River, which has facilities with various services for transients. South of Little River, the ICW–now narrow and surrounded by shoals–continues on a relatively straight course to the **Julia Tuttle Causeway Bridge**.

⚠️

The Julia Tuttle Causeway Bridge (charted 56-foot fixed vertical clearance) at Mile 1087.2 sets the limiting overhead clearance for the inside passage from Fort Lauderdale to Miami. A few extra feet may be gained at low tide but study the tide gauge before starting through as there is only a 2-foot tidal range.

South from the Julia Tuttle Causeway Bridge the water outside the channel is slightly deeper but still too shallow for most cruising vessels. Take a moment to consult the charts before approaching the next series of closely packed bridges and channels. The short stretch from Mile 1088.5 to Mile 1089.5 is one of the most complex along the ICW. Over the 1-mile stretch you will pass four bridges, cross the turning basin of Miami's Main Ship Channel and make an abrupt course adjustment.

Sunset Harbour Yacht Club

Sunset Harbour Yacht Club offers a unique equity club membership program where owners and shareholders share a piece of the prime waterfront real estate in Miami Beach. In addition, to their berths and a gated covered parking space, new buyers are granted membership privileges including private access to the equity members lounge, use of a private fitness centre, heated Olympic-size pool, high power electrical service, fresh water, phone, extremely fast internet, digital satellite TV and a personal dock box.

LOCAL POINTS OF INTEREST

- Ocean Drive and South Beach 1 mile away with Bal Harbour shoppes
- Le Gorce Golf Course, The Forge and Nobu Restaurant
- Art Basel International Art Show
- Annual Miami International Boat Show
- Located In Sunset Harbour Shops with 17 restaurants, 10 retail shops, 4 salons, 6 fitness/spa just across the street

Slip into South Beach

Slide into the lifestyle

TECHNICAL SERVICES

- Extremely fast hard wire internet and Wifi
- Private gym
- Olympic-size heated pool
- In-slip fueling and pump-out
- 24-hour security with CCTV and access control
- Private equity membership clubhouse
- Assigned private parking space
- Up to 480v 3 phase 200 amps

BERTHING DETAILS:

- 125 slips ranging in size from 40' up to 310'
- 8 slips over 120 feet
- Controlling draft at Mean Low Tide is 8 feet

Sunset Harbour Yacht Club

dmason@sunsetharbouryc.com

305-398-6800

www.sunsetharbouryc.com

1928 Sunset Harbour Dr.
Miami Beach, Fl 33139
USA

Did You Know?

Sunset Harbour Yacht Club is Miami Beach's only private yacht club that sells equity memberships with berths in perpetuity. The values of these berths have more than doubled in the past four years.

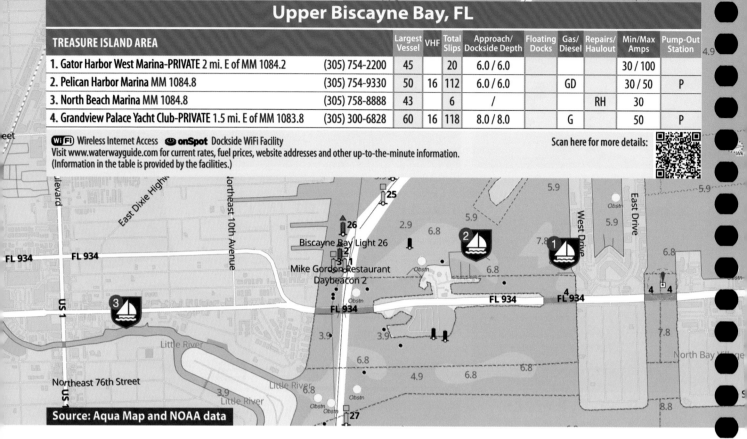

Upper Biscayne Bay, FL

TREASURE ISLAND AREA		Largest Vessel	VHF	Total Slips	Approach/ Dockside Depth	Floating Docks	Gas/ Diesel	Repairs/ Haulout	Min/Max Amps	Pump-Out Station
1. Gator Harbor West Marina-PRIVATE 2 mi. E of MM 1084.2	(305) 754-2200	45		20	6.0 / 6.0				30 / 100	
2. Pelican Harbor Marina MM 1084.8	(305) 754-9330	50	16	112	6.0 / 6.0		GD		30 / 50	P
3. North Beach Marina MM 1084.8	(305) 758-8888	43		6	/			RH	30	
4. Grandview Palace Yacht Club-PRIVATE 1.5 mi. E of MM 1083.8	(305) 300-6828	60	16	118	8.0 / 8.0		G		50	P

WiFi Wireless Internet Access **onSpot** Dockside WiFi Facility
Visit www.waterwayguide.com for current rates, fuel prices, website addresses and other up-to-the-minute information.
(Information in the table is provided by the facilities.)

Scan here for more details:

Source: Aqua Map and NOAA data

Note that this segment or the ICW is sparsely marked. Be sure to get aligned from the start to simplify navigation. When centered between green daybeacon "47" and flashing red "48" adjust your heading to thread through the next two bridge openings. This straight-line course continues across the Main Ship Channel's turning basin.

The **Venetian Causeway Bridge (West)** at Mile 1088.6 is first. This bridge has a 12-foot closed vertical clearance and opens on signal except from 7:00 a.m. to 7:00 p.m., Monday through Friday, when the draw need only open on the hour and half-hour. Next are the high-rise **MacArthur Causeway Bridges** (65-foot fixed vertical clearance) at Mile 1088.8. Once clear of the bridges you should be headed across the charted turning basin for flashing red "50" (ICW marker) located just west of Dodge Island.

To continue south on the ICW keep flashing red "50" to starboard. Off to port you will see flashing red "20" (Main Channel marker). If your intent is to follow the Main Ship Channel towards Government Cut (Miami) Inlet, keep this marker to port and turn east and out the channel. (No small boat traffic is allowed in the Main Ship Channel when the cruise ships are in and marine police

diligently patrol the entrance. Monitor VHF Channel 16 for possible Sécurité warnings.) If the Main Channel is blocked proceed south on the ICW and turn east once past Dodge Island for an alternate route through the Dodge Island Cut.

If continuing south on the ICW, the course changes at flashing red "50." Adjust course to parallel the west wall of Dodge Island as you line up to pass through the next two bridge openings. The closely spaced **Dodge Island Bridge** and **Dodge Island Railroad Bridge** cross the ICW at Mile 1089.3. The fixed Dodge Island Bridge has a 65-foot vertical clearance, while the Dodge Island Railroad Bridge has a 22-foot closed vertical clearance. The railroad bridge is usually in the open position unless a train is approaching.

Once you pass these bridges keep flashing green "53" on you port side. The ICW intersects with two other channels at Mile 1089.8. To the east is Fishermans Channel, which is the alternate route to reach Government Cut (Miami) Inlet (as well as Miami Beach Marina) when the Main Ship Channel is closed. To the west is the entrance to the Miami River. Passage of these routes is described in later sections.

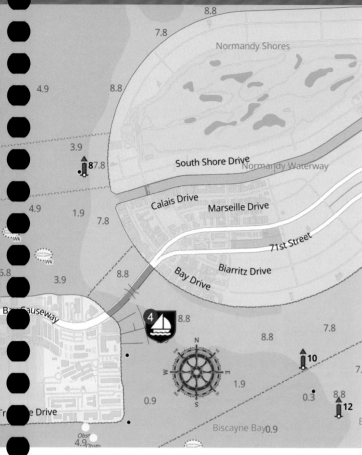

■ SIDE TRIP: MIAMI BEACH

This short diversion from the ICW takes you along the western shore of Miami Beach by way of the Miami Beach Channel and eventually rejoins the ICW at the Julia Tuttle Causeway Bridge. Whether you take the ICW or the Miami Beach Channel to Miami Beach be sure to allow ample time for sightseeing once you get there. If you travel with a pet aboard, you will find that virtually all the sidewalk restaurants here are extremely pet friendly.

The resort potential of Miami Beach's beautiful 9-mile oceanfront was recognized early on. After filling wetlands and taming the barrier island's mangroves, Miami Beach's first hotel was built in 1915, the same year the city was incorporated. Essentially a creation of the tourism industry, Miami Beach and its islands are mostly manmade and were literally "made for tourists." Today its hip, vibrant image thrives in the Art Deco District with numerous hotels and acclaimed restaurants, as well as the trendy South Beach area. So many people in the entertainment industry have moved here that it has been dubbed "Hollywood East" including the exclusive neighborhood of Indian Creek Village (on Indian Creek Island), home to Miami Beach's rich and famous.

NAVIGATION: Use NOAA Chart 11467. The relatively well-marked Miami Beach Channel runs south along the eastern shore of Biscayne Bay (which is also the western shore of Miami Beach) all the way to Government Cut (Miami) Inlet. Land for homes was created by pumping sand up from Biscayne Bay's bottom and depositing it behind bulkheads. As a consequence, depths of 6 to 7 feet MLW lie almost anywhere near the shore except where indicated on the chart. The open bay outside marked channels, on the other hand, only has depths of 1 to 3 feet MLW.

There are several options for crossing Biscayne Bay to the Miami Beach Channel. The northernmost crossover from the ICW for cruising-size boats is just south of the Broad Causeway Bridge. Southbound vessels should exit the marked ICW channel between green daybeacon "15" and red daybeacon "16," turning southeast toward Normandy Isle. This route is sparsely marked but follow the charted deeper water, keeping red markers

To continue south on the ICW into Central Biscayne Bay, keep green daybeacon "57" and quick-flashing green "59" to port while preparing to skirt the east shore of Claughton Island.

Dockage/Moorings: The private Grandview Palace Yacht Club at the east end of Treasure Island, immediately south of the East 79th Street Bridge, has mostly privately owned slips. Transient slips for vessels to 60 feet may be available; call in advance to check availability. The municipal Pelican Harbor Marina is on the north side of the 79th Street Causeway with transient slips (for boats to 50 feet), a sailboat mooring field and a dinghy dock. Call to check for slip availability and approach instructions. The 27 moorings for boats up to 35 feet are available by reservation only.

Anchorage: It is possible to anchor near the West 79th Street Boat Basin at North Bay Island (south side) in 6 to 8 feet MLW with good holding in mud but watch the charted Cable and Pipeline Area. This is open to the south through west and to wakes. You can also drop the hook in 14 feet at MLW north or south of the Julia Tuttle Causeway. This provides minimal protection and is open to ICW wakes.

Miami

to starboard. Start with a wide turn southward around flashing red "2" where there is a charted obstruction with no precise location. When approaching Biscayne Point steer to split green daybeacon "3" and red daybeacon "4."

Proceed through the narrow channel splitting green daybeacon "5" and red daybeacon "6" and then hug the shore of Normandy Isle gradually turning southward towards the East 79th Street Bridge with 25-foot vertical clearance (opens on signal). Be sure to indicate that you want the "East" span when calling the bridge on VHF Channel 09; there is another span (West 79th Street Bridge) for the Miami Beach Channel to the west.

Once past the **East 79th Street Bridge** continue to skirt the shoreline of Normandy Isle turning eastward until abeam of red daybeacon

"10." Here you begin a wide turn southward splitting quick-flashing green "11" and red daybeacon "12," both off La Gorce Island. It is extremely shallow behind the red daybeacons inside this turn. Pass close to red daybeacon "16" to avoid shoaling in the channel to the east where the Biscayne Waterway discharges into the channel.

Vessels with an airdraft of 35 feet or less can continue south of the Julia Tuttle Causeway following the Miami Beach Channel to Government Cut (Miami) Inlet. Turning southwest at red daybeacon "22" head towards green daybeacon "25." Keeping this daybeacon to port enter the narrow channel to pass under the **Julia Tuttle Causeway Bridge (East)** (35-foot fixed vertical clearance) and take a heading to keep red daybeacon "26" just to starboard.

Once clear of the channel parallel the Sunset Islands chain south towards Bell Isle, keeping combined green-over-red daybeacon "S"/red daybeacon "30" to starboard. Turn west just before reaching Belle Isle drawing close to shore and keeping the green daybeacons to starboard and avoiding the charted submerged pilings. The route skirts the north shore of Belle Isle.

There are two more bridges en route to Government Cut. The first bridge is at the **Venetian Causeway Bridge (East)**, which is formed by a chain of manmade islands crossing Biscayne Bay. Belle Isle is the oldest island in Biscayne Bay and is the closest to Miami Beach in the causeway chain. The Venetian Causeway Bridge (East) is located midway between Belle Isle and Rivo Alto Island. This bridge has a 5-foot closed vertical clearance and opens on signal except from 7:00 a.m. to 7:00 p.m., when the draw need only open on the hour and half-hour. Be sure to specifically request the "East" bridge on VHF Channel 09, as a bridge with a similar name crosses the ICW to the west.

The channel enters deeper water south of Belle Isle. Swing eastward around the isle and then parallel Miami Beach's main island southward. Keep well east of red daybeacon "2" to avoid shoaling southeast of the Flagler Monument. The final bridge on this route is south of Star Island and connects the east end of the MacArthur Causeway to Miami Beach. The channel runs under the MacArthur Causeway Bridges (35-foot fixed vertical clearance) near the U.S. Coast Guard base. After passing under the bridge follow the Meloy Channel to the inner end of Government Cut.

Note some of the dockage and anchorages described in this section can be reached by vessels requiring a higher airdraft by following the marked channel just north of the Venetian Causeway and passing through the Venetian Causeway Bridge (East).

Dockage: In Miami Beach you will find many excellent, upscale marinas with substantial amenities alongside less fancy but somewhat more economical ones. All are convenient to provisioning options, fine dining and shopping.

The Miami Beach Channel leads directly to Sunset Harbour Yacht Club on Biscayne Bay, which offers slips for long-term lease or sale and offers non-members use of available slips on a transient basis. This full-service marina is located on 2 acres and features 125 slips accommodating vessels from 45 to 200-plus feet. Be sure to call ahead to check availability. Membership privileges including use of a private fitness center and heated Olympic-size pool. The 16-slip Bentley Bay Marina is just north of the MacArthur Causeway Bridges (East) with transient slips for vessels to 65 feet.

Farther south on Meloy Channel (the southern end of Miami Beach Channel), just opposite the Coast Guard base, the 400-slip Miami Beach Marina can accommodate vessels up to 250 feet. They also have a professional service team for repair, maintenance and restoration. One Island Park–Miami Beach (IGY) is located adjacent to the Coast Guard station. The smallest yacht that is permitted to dock is 100 feet (with 800 feet being the largest) in their eight superyacht berths. Crew activities and fitness classes, transportation

to a local market and complimentary use of bicycles are among the amenities.

Anchorage: There are several local restrictions on overnight anchoring in effect for North Biscayne Bay but also lots of available spots close to Miami Beach that provide excellent protection from the prevailing southeast winds.

Note that Florida legislation bans overnight anchoring in Sunset Lake and in sections of Biscayne Bay including between Rivo Alto Island and Di Lido Island, San Marino Island and San Marco Island, and San Marco Island and Biscayne Island. It is illegal to anchor at any time during the period between one-half hour after sunset and one-half hour before sunrise. Exemptions include cases of mechanical failure, weather conditions or during certain events. Miami Beach also enforces an ordinance that limits anchoring to 7 days.

On the Miami Beach Channel you can drop the hook at Tuttle Causeway Bight south of the east span of the bridge. Here you will find 8 to 9 feet MLW with excellent holding and protection from all directions except west. You can also anchor just off the Sunset Harbour Channel (privately maintained daybeacons and lights) on the northeast side of Belle Isle in 7- to 11-foot MLW depths. Wakes from passing vessels, particularly on weekends, can be disturbing.

A good anchorage is southwest of the small island with the Flagler Monument Island (south of the eastern span of the Venetian Causeway). Approach via the Miami Beach Channel or the cross-bay route south of the Venetian Causeway (on the northern side of the entrance channel) with 6-foot MLW depths.

Finding a place to dock your dinghy to go ashore at Miami Beach can be difficult and rules are constantly changing. You can try the Publix Super Market On the Bay dinghy dock north of Venetian Causeway, the Marine Patrol dock or the city-owned dinghy dock up the Collins Canal. We suggest you check with locals or the Marine Patrol (305-673-7959) before using any of the docks.

It is unlawful to tie a dinghy to a canal wall to visit the City of Miami Beach. The city also strictly enforces the 20-minute limit for the dinghy dock at the end of 17th Street. These restrictions carry stiff civil fines.

Upper Biscayne Bay, FL

MIAMI BEACH		Largest Vessel	VHF	Total Slips	Approach/ Dockside Depth	Floating Docks	Gas/ Diesel	Repairs/ Haulout	Min/Max Amps	Pump-Out Station
1. Sunset Harbour Yacht Club WiFi onSpot	(305) 398-6800	210	16	125	8.0 / 8.0				30 / 100	P
2. Bentley Bay Marina	(305) 674-0686	65	16	16	10.0 / 8.0				30 / 100	P
3. Miami Beach Marina WiFi 3.0 mi. E of MM 1089.0	(305) 673-6000	250	16	400	13.0 / 12.0		GD		30 / 200+	P
4. One Island Park - Miami Beach (IGY) WiFi MM 1089.0	(305) 299-3997	800	16	8	/ 40.0		GD		100 / 200+	
GOVERNMENT CUT										
5. Sea Isle Marina & Yachting Center WiFi MM 1089.0	(305) 377-3625	132	16	220	13.0 / 10.0		GD		30 / 100	P
6. Island Gardens Deep Harbour Marina WiFi	(305) 531-3747	550	16	50	13.0 / 22.0	F			50 / 200+	P
7. Miamarina at Bayside WiFi MM 1089.5	(305) 960-5180	165	16	130	14.0 / 10.0	F			30 / 100	P
8. Miami Yacht Club WiFi MM 1089.0	(305) 377-9877	65		48	7.0 / 6.0			H	30	

WiFi Wireless Internet Access   onSpot Dockside WiFi Facility
Visit www.waterwayguide.com for current rates, fuel prices, website addresses and other up-to-the-minute information.
(Information in the table is provided by the facilities.)

Scan here for more details:

Source: Aqua Map and NOAA data

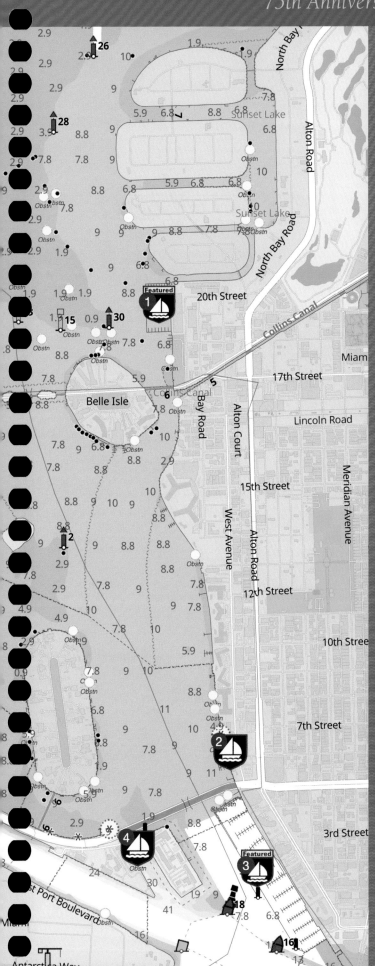

Outside Run From Miami

Coming up on the outside from the south, northbound boats that want to enter inshore waters can take either Cape Florida Channel or Biscayne Channel once they have passed Fowey Rocks Light, or they can continue on to Government Cut. The Miami GPS Differential Beacon (nominal range 75 miles) is located on Virginia Key near the west end of the fixed bridge across Bear Cut.

Coming down along the ocean side of Key Biscayne, southbound boats should stand offshore on the run from Miami. Take a heading due south from the entrance buoys off Government Cut's Outer Bar Cut to pick up Biscayne Channel Light (better known locally as Bug Light), the 37-foot-high spidery pipe structure (flashing white every four seconds) marking the seaward entrance of Cape Florida and Biscayne Channels. Coming in at flashing red "6," you have a choice of two channels leading to Biscayne Bay. Depths in the shared entrance channel to the Cape Florida Channel and the Biscayne Channel are charted at 7 feet at MLW over the bar.

From the sea the right-hand, northern fork is the Cape Florida Channel leading past the prominent lighthouse and the lovely palm-fringed beach. The chart clearly identifies the deep-water passage along the curving shoreline and indicates two shoal spots situated between 0.1 and 0.2 mile southwest of the shore. Hug the shore along the curving concrete bulkhead of the park property to clear the charted shoals, marked by green daybeacon "1." At the inner end bear off to leave red daybeacon "2" and flashing red "4" to starboard. From the outside this is the easiest route to No Name Harbor, the area's most popular jump-off point for mariners awaiting favorable weather for a Bahamas passage.

The southern route, which is better marked and deeper than the unmarked Cape Florida Channel, is known as Biscayne Channel. It is wide, straight, well marked and easy to run. Depths in the channel range from 11 to 16 feet MLW. Even so, the entrance depth from the ocean sometimes limits the channel. At its western end the channel produces good fishing during flood tide.

MIAMI BEACH MARINA
A SUNTEX EXPERIENCE

Your Premiere Destination

- Dock attendants, security patrol, & surveillance cameras
- Wireless Internet
- Heated swimming pool
- Air conditioned restrooms & laundry facilities
- Lighted, covered parking
- Gasoline, diesel & high speed diesel

- 30/50/100 amp single phase/ 100 amp three phase, 480 volt
- 1000+' of floating pier, easy access for small vessels
- Marine Store open 7 days a week
- Boat lifts for vessels to 40,000 lbs.
- In-slip pump-out on most piers
- Taxi service, auto rentals available

- Provisioning from the on-site deli
- On-site casual dining,
- Adjacent to world famous beaches, Ocean Drive & SoBe Night Life

SUNTEX MARINAS®
YOUR PLACE IN THE SUN

300 Alton Road
Miami Beach, FL 33139
(305) 673-6000

miamibeachmarina.com
VHF: Hail on 16,
Working Channel: 68

Marina

Marina

Berths within a Protected Harbour
10 foot Deep-Water Approaching
Monitored VHF Channel 16/10
106 Yacht Berths | Max 160 Ft/8 Ft Draft
Parallel Docking for Larger Yachts
Floating Docks for Smaller Yachts
Three Phase Electric Dockage
North Marina Slips with Pump Out
Wi Fi Internet & Cable
24 Hour Monitored Security

Marina Office

Staffed with over 37 Years of Experience
Richly Appointed Lobby & Reception
Fully Equipped Business Center
Spacious Conference Room
Boaters Lounge with Smart TV
Top-of-the-line Laundry Facility
Modern Showers and Lockers
Convenient Fitness Center

Club Amenities

27,000 Sq. Ft. Spa & Fitness Center
    with personalized programs
Grand Slam Tennis Center
    16 Hard & HAR-TRU Courts
    Tennis Center with Pro Shop
Island Club - Social Events
Dining
    Island Grille | Overlooking Tennis
    Island Pool Bar | Casual Open Air

Welcome to Williams Island, nestled on 84 acres in Aventura, Florida, mid-way between Miami and Fort Lauderdale. Close to both airports and seaports. Williams Island offers an exclusive, private way of life to those accustomed to the finest of things at one of South Florida's most prestigious addresses. This magnificent Marina enjoys a protected harbour with berth's up to 135 feet and depths of 10 feet approaching the marina and 8 feet within the marina itself, plus a Marine Basin area to help assure a calm, restful environment. Our 106 berths are as comfortable and convenient for our boaters as they are for their vessels.

Marina guests will be treated to an amenity-rich lifestyle that encompasses a luxurious Marina office with richly appointed conveniences: boater lounge, conference room, gym, business center and laundry. A complimentary Williams Island Social Club membership is included in your stay and includes: the 27,000 sq ft Spa and Fitness Center. The Grand Slam-inspired Tennis Center with 16 tennis courts and pro shop that is expertly staffed. Exquisite fine dining and weekly specials are enjoyed at the Island Grille overlooking Center Court. Enjoy a lighter fare at the Island Club Pool Bar your destination for outdoor casual dining and relaxed pool side favorites. Entertainment, Social Events as well as Private Parties are offered at the Island Club.

The Marina is conveniently open daily from 9 am to 6 pm.

4100 Island Boulevard, Aventura, Florida 33160 | 305.937.7813 office | 305.936.5713 fax
WilliamsIslandMarina.com | dockmaster@WilliamsIslandMarina.com

Upper Biscayne Bay, FL

INDIAN CREEK		Largest Vessel	VHF	Total Slips	Approach/ Dockside Depth	Floating Docks	Gas/ Diesel	Repairs/ Haulout	Min/Max Amps	Pump-Out Station
1. Miami Beach Resort & Spa (WiFi)	(305) 532-3600	200	16	20	7.0 / 7.0				30 / 50	
2. Fontainebleau Marina Indian Creek	(305) 538-2022	140		23	7.0 / 7.0				30 / 100	

(WiFi) Wireless Internet Access onSpot Dockside WiFi Facility
Visit www.waterwayguide.com for current rates, fuel prices, website addresses and other up-to-the-minute information. (Information in the table is provided by the facilities.)

Scan here for more details:

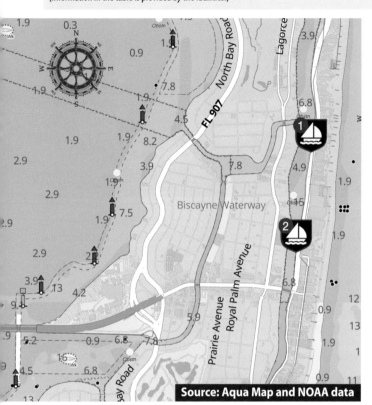

Source: Aqua Map and NOAA data

Alternate Route: Miami Beach Downtown to Indian Creek

Indian Creek is a waterway that runs between Miami Beach's main island and the jumble of manmade islands immediately to the west. The primary access to Indian Creek is from the channel between Normandy Isle and La Gorce Island. The route northward inside Normandy Isle is restricted to small craft by a series of fixed, low-clearance bridges. The lowest is the fixed 71st Street Bridge with a 5-foot vertical clearance, which connects Normandy Isle to the ocean beach. This can be a pleasant route by dinghy to have a "gander at the grandeur" of the mega-mansions in exclusive Indian Creek Village.

NAVIGATION: Use NOAA Chart 11467. The route south on Indian Creek from La Gorce Island is navigable by larger vessels and leads into the heart of downtown Miami Beach. The controlling depth is charted as 7 feet MLW but check with one of the Indian Creek marinas for local knowledge before entering. There is transient dockage but no anchorage on this route.

Leave the Miami Beach Channel at red daybeacon "10" and hug the shore of Normandy Isle eastward into the opening of Indian Creek. Be sure to stay in the charted deep water to avoid the shoaling closer to La Gorce Island. Continuing south Indian Creek skirts the area's downtown across the road from many of the lavish hotels in Miami Beach's Bar Harbor district. Favor the eastern shore in Indian Creek; shoaling occurs along parts of the western bank of the creek.

Do not try to circumnavigate Normandy Isle unless you do so in a dinghy. The fixed **71st Street Bridge** with a 5-foot vertical clearance connects the island to the ocean beach.

To access the Indian Creek marinas head south on the eastern side of Allison Island through the **63rd Street Bridge**, which connects Allison Island with the beach island. This bridge has 11-foot vertical clearance and opens on signal, except from 7:00 a.m. to 7:00 p.m., Monday through Friday (except federal holidays), when the draw need only open on the hour and half-hour. Additionally, from 7:10 a.m. to 9:55 a.m. and 4:05 p.m. to 6:59 p.m., Monday through Friday (except federal holidays), the draw need not open for the passage of vessels.

Dockage: Indian Creek is chock-full of hotel and condominium docks as well as Miami Beach Resort & Spa with space for vessels to 200 feet and full amenities. To the south is the world-class Fontainebleau Marina. Tie up for a day or overnight to enjoy Fontainebleau's distinctive restaurants and neon nightlife or relax with friends around the bowtie pool (requires pool chair or cabana rental). This facility provides easy access to the bustling Collins Avenue.

Government Cut & Fishermans Channel

Government Cut (Miami) Inlet is the primary inlet for the port of Miami. This is a deep-water channel flanked by lighted markers. At its west terminus Government Cut (Miami) Inlet forks into Miami's Main Ship Channel, often clogged with cruise ships, and also Fishermans Channel, which also serves large ships but is generally less congested. If a cruise ship is in port a security zone is established and the Main Ship Channel will be closed requiring you to take Fishermans Channel to get to the ICW. No small boat traffic is allowed in the Main Ship Channel when the cruise ships are in and marine police diligently patrol the entrance. Monitor VHF Channel 16 for possible Sécurité warnings. On either route you must yield to large vessels and ferries.

NAVIGATION: Use NOAA Chart 11467. Government Cut (Miami) Inlet is a big ship inlet that is wide, deep and free of hazards. It runs between Miami Beach (to the north) and Fisher Island (to the south). The Main Ship Channel extends past the end of the Government Cut between Dodge Island and Watson Island to the Turning Basin.

The Main Ship Channel (where cruise ships dock) is often closed for security reasons including when cruise ships are at the Main Ship Channel docks. Closures are announced on VHF Channel 16. Cruisers then must use a route combining Fishermans Channel and the Dodge Channel Cut to skirt the south shore of Dodge Island as an alternative. A short connector channel runs from the west terminus of the Dodge Island Cut to the ICW. The controlling depth is about 12 feet MLW but make sure you identify the markers carefully. Watch for frequent dredging operations in this area and for the numerous ferries headed to and from Fisher Island.

Fishermans Channel and the Dodge Island Cut are similarly free of hazards. When entering the west end of this route from the ICW keep green daybeacon "53A" and flashing green "55" well to port before turning in to the channel due to shoaling extending into the channel. To reach the Dodge Island Cut first split flashing red "18" and green daybeacon "57" (an ICW marker) and then split red daybeacon "16" and flashing green "17." Stay as close to the wharf as is safe as it is quite shallow south of the marked channel. This route is particularly difficult in darkness and it's best to pass at reduced speed. This also serves as the main access to the Miami River and there are several marinas nearby so traffic can be heavy.

Commercial traffic is generally busy here as well and there is a car ferry that runs between Dodge Island and Fisher Island with frequent crossings. You must pay attention in this area and always give the ferry the right of way.

Dockage: The 220-slip Sea Isle Marina & Yachting Center (north of the Venetian Causeway) is located in the heart of downtown Miami. They can accommodate yachts up to 110 feet. Call ahead for transient space. Island Gardens Deep Harbour Marina is located on the west side of Watson Island just south of the MacArthur Causeway. They have an outdoor lounge (The Deck), laundry service and courtesy cars. Miami Yacht Club is on the east side of Watson Island with just two reserved transient slips. The marina has store, restaurant, pool and bar.

The municipal Miamarina at Bayside is south of the Dodge Island bridges at Bayfront Park and may have transient space for vessels to 100 feet on their floating docks; call ahead. Miamarina is situated within the Bayside Marketplace with an assortment of over 100 stores, shops, restaurants and cafés representing multiple nationalities.

Anchorage: It is also possible to anchor on the east side of Watson Island (7 to 8 feet MLW). This also falls under the local 7-day anchorage limit. Long-passage cruisers sometimes follow Fishermans Channel as far as Fisher Island and anchor off its southwestern side (clear of traffic) to get an early start crossing the Gulf Stream. The holding is good here in sand and you should have at least 10 feet MLW. This is open and exposed to the northwest and southeast.

◼ SIDE TRIP: MIAMI RIVER

One of Miami's principal yacht service areas is along the Miami River, which flows out from the Everglades and divides the city. From its mouth at Mile 1090 on the ICW the navigable section of the Miami River extends upstream 4 miles to its head of navigation at 36th Street. Most of the operations along the river are primarily repair facilities. Marine services along its banks include custom builders, yacht brokers and boat dealers, sales and service agents, propeller specialists and sailmakers. Along with these are full-service haul-out, repair and storage yards.

NAVIGATION: Use NOAA Chart 11467. The mouth of the Miami River meets the ICW about 0.5 miles south of the Dodge Island Bridges between Bay Front Park and Claughton Island. The ICW follows the shore of Bay Front Park for this stretch and you must execute a sharp turn to starboard (west) to enter the river's mouth at the south end of the park. Give green daybeacons "1" and "3" (the river's only markers) a wide berth and favor the river's north shore (Bay Front Park) upon entry. Shoals extend off the north side of Claughton Island and are at the edge of the marked channel.

Miami River's controlling depth is 14 feet MLW up to the NW 27th Avenue Bridge and then 9 feet MLW up to the 36th Street Dam. Boats proceeding upriver should lower outriggers and antennas for bridge clearance. If land traffic is heavy (and it usually is) bridgetenders will enforce this law.

The stated controlling depths hold for Miami River's more important side branches–South Fork (3 miles from the river's mouth) and Tamiami Canal (1 mile farther on). Both shoot obliquely off to the southwest and, like the main river, each has its own series of boatyards and marine installations. Tamiami Canal is a drainage ditch that parallels the Tamiami Trail Highway to the northwest most of the way across the Florida Peninsula. It is navigable for vessels with up to 6-foot draft (8 feet at high tide) as far as a low-limiting fixed bridge over NW 37th Avenue.

In addition to a wide variety of recreational craft, the Miami River carries considerable commercial traffic. Tugs working in pairs maneuver to place the large oceangoing vessels that line the last mile or so of the river. Give these ships plenty of room.

All lift bridges on the Miami River follow the same restricted schedule (with a few exceptions) and open on signal year-round, except Monday through Friday (not including holidays) from 7:35 a.m. to 8:59 a.m., 12:05 p.m. to 12:59 p.m. and 4:45 p.m. to 5:59 p.m., when the draw need not open. The SW 1st Street Bridge (Mile 0.9) up to and including the NW 27th Avenue Bridge (Mile 3.7) follow the same schedule with one change–they remain operational between 12:05 p.m. to 12:59 p.m. Bridge schedules are always subject to change. If you plan to go upriver, check ahead of time for bridge restrictions.

Most Miami River clearance gauges show the clearance at the fenders instead of the center of the span. There

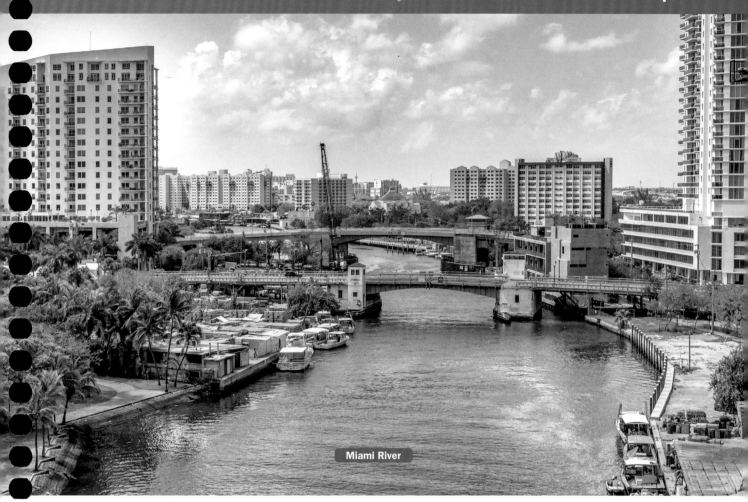

Miami River

may be a sign indicating the additional clearance available at the center. Charted closed vertical clearances for the bridges in sequence up the Miami River are:

- **Brickell Avenue Bridge** (23-foot clearance)
- **Metro Train Bridge** (75-foot fixed clearance)
- **South Miami Avenue Bridge** (21-foot clearance)
- **Metro Rail/M Path Bridge** (75-foot fixed clearance)
- **SW Second Avenue Bridge** (11-foot clearance)
- **I-95 Twin Bridges** (75-foot fixed clearance)
- **SW 1st Street Bridge** (18-foot clearance)

New SW 1st Street Bridge is under construction. Expect delays.

- **West Flagler Street Bridge** (35-foot clearance)
- **NW 5th Street Bridge** (12-foot clearance)
- **NW 12th Avenue Bridge** (22-foot clearance)
- **Dolphin Expy. Bridge** (75-foot fixed clearance)
- **NW 17th Avenue Bridge** (17-foot clearance)
- **NW 22nd Avenue Bridge** (25-foot clearance)
- **NW 27th Avenue Bridge** (21-foot clearance)

There is one fixed bridge (8-foot vertical clearance) over the South Fork and a swing bridge (erroneously charted as bascule) with 6-foot vertical clearance crossing the Tamiami Canal.

Whenever a big event takes place at Orange Bowl Stadium, home of the University of Miami Hurricanes football team, extra closures are usually imposed. All closures for the regularly scheduled events at the Orange Bowl from August through January are posted online in the *Local Notice to Mariners* starting in late July; they are repeated a week or two before the event dates. These closures usually last only about 2 hours.

Dockage: Behind Claughton Island is the full-service Vice City Marina, a wet storage facility with transient space (30-foot minimum) convenient to the shopping, art and entertainment of Brickell in downtown Miami.

There are many repair facilities for the cruising boater on the Miami River but few transient slips. Always call ahead for space availability. Epic Marina is a luxury destination directly on the Miami River with full amenities and two on-site restaurants (Area 31 and ZUMA). The 20-slip marina can accommodate yachts over 300 feet in deep-water slips.

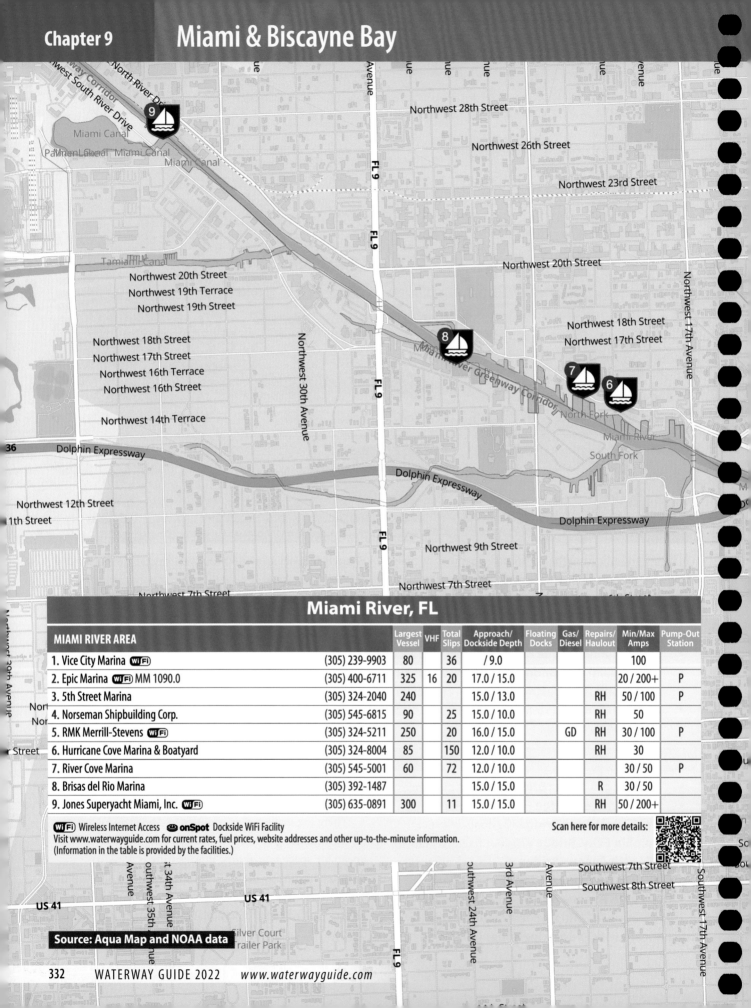

Miami River, FL

MIAMI RIVER AREA		Largest Vessel	VHF	Total Slips	Approach/ Dockside Depth	Floating Docks	Gas/ Diesel	Repairs/ Haulout	Min/Max Amps	Pump-Out Station
1. Vice City Marina WiFi	(305) 239-9903	80		36	/ 9.0				100	
2. Epic Marina WiFi MM 1090.0	(305) 400-6711	325	16	20	17.0 / 15.0				20 / 200+	P
3. 5th Street Marina	(305) 324-2040	240			15.0 / 13.0			RH	50 / 100	P
4. Norseman Shipbuilding Corp.	(305) 545-6815	90		25	15.0 / 10.0			RH	50	
5. RMK Merrill-Stevens WiFi	(305) 324-5211	250		20	16.0 / 15.0		GD	RH	30 / 100	P
6. Hurricane Cove Marina & Boatyard	(305) 324-8004	85		150	12.0 / 10.0			RH	30	
7. River Cove Marina	(305) 545-5001	60		72	12.0 / 10.0				30 / 50	P
8. Brisas del Rio Marina	(305) 392-1487				15.0 / 15.0			R	30 / 50	
9. Jones Superyacht Miami, Inc. WiFi	(305) 635-0891	300		11	15.0 / 15.0			RH	50 / 200+	

WiFi Wireless Internet Access   onSpot Dockside WiFi Facility
Visit www.waterwayguide.com for current rates, fuel prices, website addresses and other up-to-the-minute information.
(Information in the table is provided by the facilities.)

Scan here for more details:

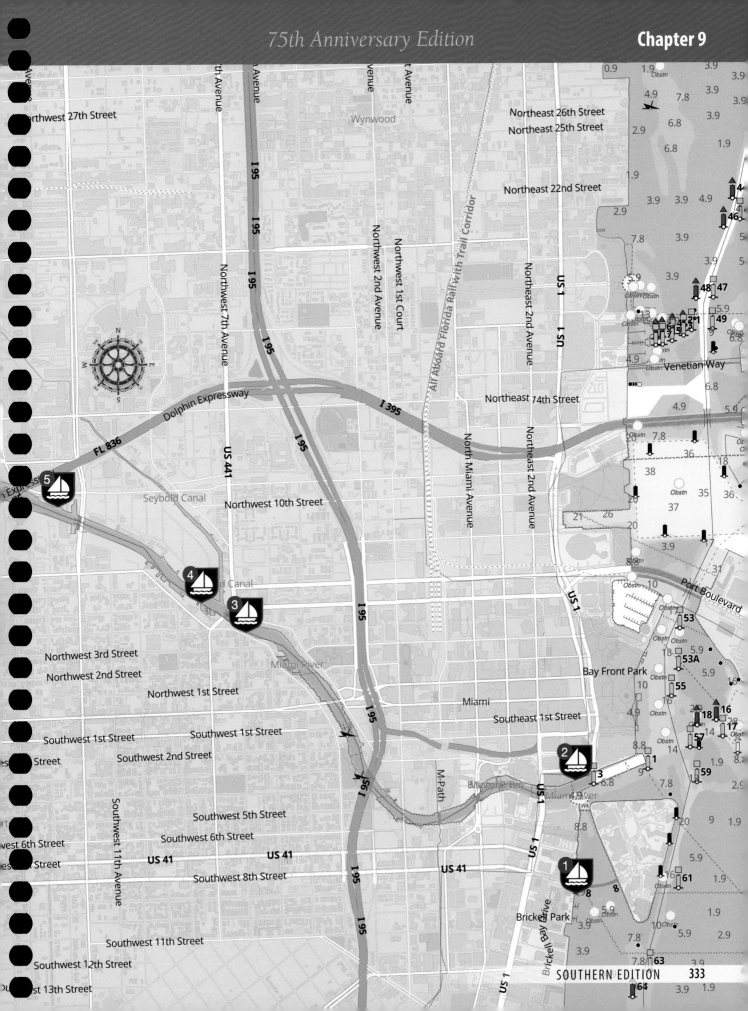

Continuing upriver 5th Street Marina has a seawall with limited dockage and is co-located with a full-service boatyard, Norseman Shipbuilding Corp. RMK Merrill-Stevens (north of NW 12th Avenue Bridge) is a large shipyard dedicated to yacht refit and repair. They maintain 10 transient slips.

The next group of facilities includes Hurricane Cove Marina & Boatyard, a 150-slip marina, boatyard and yacht repair facility (both DIY and full service). River Cove Marina has boat slips (to 45 feet) and wet slips (to 60 feet) and while they do not keep designated transient slips, they do lease empty slips. Brisas del Rio Marina offers repairs (no transient slips).

Several other facilities in the area offer varying levels of repairs and services (but few transient slips)

including Jones Superyacht Miami, Inc. (located north on the Miami Canal), which caters to vessels to 300 feet and offers large-yacht repairs.

■ CENTRAL BISCAYNE BAY

When entering Central Biscayne Bay, cruisers will finally feel they have arrived in the tropics. The beautiful turquoise waters and surrounding sand beaches give this area a "postcard" feel. The bay widens and deepens in this segment and provides a protected passage to multiple destinations. Just below Key Biscayne the Cape Florida and Biscayne Channels provide ocean access for either a Gulf Stream crossing east to the Bahamas or a southwest (deep water) route to the Florida Keys along the Hawk Channel.

At the bay's extreme south end are smaller channels to the ocean on the east and the ICW route to the south through Jewfish Creek to Florida Bay and the Upper Florida Keys. On the Bay's western shore are the laid-back communities of South Miami including Coconut Grove, a destination in itself. And, finally, there is Biscayne National Park, encompassing both land and sea in all its natural wonder.

> Those intending to follow the "Inside Route" to the Florida Keys on the ICW through Jewfish Creek should be warned that this route has an air-draft of 65 feet and minimum water depths of 5 feet MLW. This route is not recommended for vessels drawing more than 4.5 feet. Additional information on this route is provided in "The Florida Keys" chapter. We suggest you consult this section in advance.

Biscayne Bay

Dodge Island to Virginia Key– ICW Mile 1090 to Mile 1092

This section continues the route south on the ICW from the Dodge Island Cut and into Central Biscayne Bay. Navigation on the ICW north from the Dodge Island Cut is particularly complex. Over the first 1.5-mile stretch you will pass four bridges and cross the turning basin of Miami's Main Ship Channel. Review the appropriate section in this guide before reaching Dodge Island.

NAVIGATION: Use NOAA Chart 11467. Flashing green "55" is the final ICW marker before the entrance into the Dodge Island Cut and flashing red "18" is the cut's final marker. To the south the ICW enters a narrow, dredged channel. Observe markers carefully; this section can be particularly confusing in darkness. Starting with green daybeacon "57" and quick-flashing green "59" keep the green markers to port.

When approaching Claughton Island, gradually turn to parallel the island's east shore. The location of the channel is not precisely marked and vessels should proceed at slow speed and use the depth sounder to find and maintain alignment. Depths hold up quite close to shore. If you are reading less than 9 feet MLW, you may have strayed out of the channel.

South of Claughton Island the channel appears to open up but depths at the channel's edge are actually more shallow. You should maintain 9 feet MLW by passing close to quick-flashing green "63," green daybeacon "65" and flashing green "67." For nighttime passage be sure to locate green daybeacon "65" with a searchlight. South from flashing green "67" it's a straight run to the span of the **Rickenbacker Causeway Bridge** (65-foot fixed vertical clearance), which is sometimes referred to as "the Powell-Rickenbacker Bridge." The older structure is dwarfed alongside its modern replacement and remains in use as a fishing pier that abuts the channel.

> Marine Stadium on Virginia Key (northeast of the Rickenbacker Causeway Bridge) was originally built in 1963 to promote powerboat racing. It was considered a modernist icon because of its cantilevered, fold-plate roof and construction of lightweight, poured-in-place concrete, popular in mid-century stadiums. At 326 feet in length (longer than a football field) it was the longest span of cantilevered concrete in the world when it was built. Its eight big slanted columns are anchored in the ground. It has served as the home of the Miami International Boat Show since 2016.

Dockage: Rickenbacker Marina Inc. is located on Virginia Key with 100 slips but only 2 reserved for transients. Marine Stadium Marina is a dry storage facility. There are restaurants and shopping within walking distance. Just south of the Rickenbacker Causeway (on the mainland side) is an emergency dock belonging to Mercy Hospital. It has depths of 4 feet MLW and is restricted to emergency use only.

Anchorage: You can anchor at the Marine Stadium for 24 hours only. The anchoring provides good protection in 8- to 12-foot MLW depths with a mud and sand bottom. This anchorage offers a beautiful view of downtown Miami. Jet-skis and wakeboarders use this area on the weekends. There are signs that indicate no dinghy landing and the Miami-Dade Police strictly enforce dinghy landing rules.

> Please note: The Marine Stadium anchorage is closed from mid-January until after the Miami Boat Show (February) each year.

A popular anchorage is just southeast of Virgina Key in at least 7 feet MLW with good holding in sandy mud. This is open and exposed to the south. Or drop the hook outside the basin north of the Miami Seaquarium at Virginia Key (marked on NOAA chart as DOME.)

Shore access to the beach on Virgina Key is difficult. There are signs that indicate no dinghy landing. The Miami-Dade Police strictly enforce dinghy landing rules but drop-offs are possible.

To Biscayne National Park– ICW Mile 1092 to Mile 1107

Biscayne Bay changes character south of the Rickenbacker Causeway, becoming broad, relatively deep (average 10 feet MLW) and natural. Sailing regattas are held in these waters nearly every weekend, while fishing, swimming, water skiing and cruising are everyday activities, year-round. Cruisers will find this part of Biscayne Bay especially inviting. The deep, open water makes a pleasant change from the narrow, dredged sections of the ICW to the north and the sand bottom and clear, turquoise water gives a tropical feel.

While the ICW leads south from here, Key Biscayne lies to the east and the Cape Florida Channel, leading to the Atlantic Ocean, skirts its south end. This is a popular staging area for cruisers waiting for a weather-window to make a "Bahama's Run" across the Gulf Stream. This area offers some well-

Key Biscayne, FL

KEY BISCAYNE AREA		Largest Vessel	VHF	Total Slips	Approach/ Dockside Depth	Floating Docks	Gas/ Diesel	Repairs/ Haulout	Min/Max Amps	Pump-Out Station
1. Rickenbacker Marina Inc. (WiFi) MM 1091.5	(305) 361-1900	100	16	200	8.0 / 9.0		G	RH	30 / 50	P
2. Marine Stadium Marina MM 1091.5	(305) 960-5140	43	16		8.0 / 10.0		G	RH		
3. Crandon Park Marina MM 1094.0	(305) 361-1281	80	16	294	6.0 / 5.0	F	GD		30 / 50	P
4. Key Biscayne Yacht Club	(305) 361-8229	60		100	/		GD	H		P

(WiFi) Wireless Internet Access **onSpot** Dockside WiFi Facility
Visit www.waterwayguide.com for current rates, fuel prices, website addresses and other up-to-the-minute information.
(Information in the table is provided by the facilities.)

Scan here for more details:

protected anchorages, access to South Miami and some beautiful barrier islands to explore.

This section describes the "Inside Route" on the ICW towards the Florida Keys. The route to the Keys running outside the barrier islands and a side-trip to the barrier islands for shoal-draft boat is described in Outside (Hawk Channel) Route.

NAVIGATION: Use NOAA Chart 11467 and 11465. Cruising south of the Rickenbacker Causeway is easier if you use NOAA Chart 11465 (ICW–Miami to Elliot Key). Although the scale is the same on both charts, NOAA Chart 11465 covers a larger area (as far as Elliot Key) and makes tracing longer courselines simpler.

Bear Cut is flanked by Virginia Key on the west and Key Biscayne to the east. It is unmarked at its northeastern end except for red daybeacon "2," which provides an outlet to the ocean for smaller boats that can pass under the **Bear Cut Bridge** (16-foot fixed vertical clearance).

Skippers headed southbound on the ICW should consult their charts and take time to plan their route. Navigation markers are sparse here and can get lost in the expanse of Central Biscayne Bay. While the bay is open and relatively deep, there are some shoals and route planning is

essential. Compass headings should be planned and followed for each passage segment. After clearing the Rickenbacker Causeway Bridge, steer toward flashing green "69" (an ICW marker). From here adjust to 199° magnetic for the 13.5 nm run to Featherbed Bank (off Sand Key). It is 7 miles south to the next ICW marker, flashing green "1." The route enters Biscayne National Park at Mile 1102.

Key Biscayne–Cape Florida Channel to Outside Route

Key Biscayne, site of southern Florida's first town, was founded in 1839. It was also headquarters for a band of renegades who lured ships onto the reefs and "salvaged" their cargo. Today the key is made up of two parks. Crandon Park occupies the northern end of Key Biscayne. This county park boasts a marina (Crandon Park Marina), boat ramp, two miles of ocean beach and excellent picnic grounds. Nearby is the International Tennis Center and an excellent golf course. Bus service is available to the city. Bill Baggs Cape Florida State Park is at Key Biscayne's southern end featuring the restored Cape Florida Lighthouse, the keeper's house with tours, walking trails and another beautiful beach.

This is also the route to the Cape Florida Channel (7 feet MLW), perhaps the easiest route from Central Biscayne Bay to the Atlantic Ocean. Follow the route to the No Name Harbor anchorage to take this route.

NAVIGATION: Use NOAA Charts 11467 and 11451. After clearing the Rickenbacker Causeway Bridge at Mile 1091.6 and keeping Virginia Key to the east, you will enter Central Biscayne Bay. Flashing green "69" lies south of the bridge and is the last ICW marker for some distance. There are three approaches to Key Biscayne: (1) Bear Cut, (2) Hurricane Harbor and (3) Cape Florida Channel to "No Name Harbor." The entrance to Bear Cut is framed by quick-flashing green "1" and flashing red "2" at Mile 1094. Most of the markers for the cut are not lighted so use caution in darkness. The channel leading to Hurricane Harbor is at Mile 1095 just past flashing green "1." And the first marker for the Cape Florida Channel is flashing red "4" at Mile 1096. This channel hugs Key Biscayne's southwestern shore.

Just below Key Biscayne to the east are the remaining houses of Stiltsville, an eclectic group of homes on stilts that now belong to the National Park Service. Stiltsville has a colorful history that dates back to the 1930s. The few remaining structures are visible along the reef.

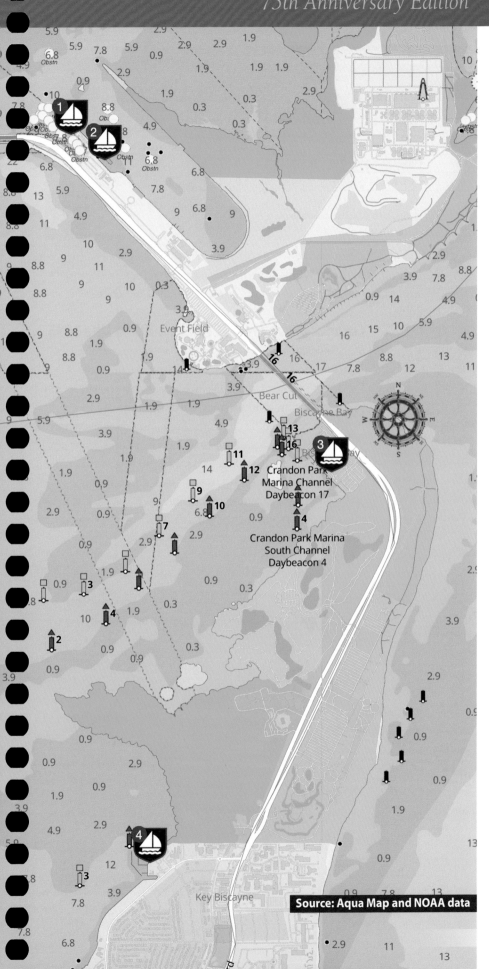

Dockage/Moorings: Crandon Park Marina at Key Biscayne is best approached from Biscayne Bay by a privately marked natural channel that leads northeastward from the shoal light (flashing white, 4 sec.) off West Point. The marina has slips and moorings (available to sailboats only) in its protected cove with easy access to marina amenities. (Note that the showers are cold water only.) If you have to do any type of shopping, you will need to arrange for ground transportation as there are no shops or restaurants for several miles.

The use of the facilities at the private Key Biscayne Yacht Club are extended to Members of the Florida Council of Yacht Clubs and Reciprocal associations only.

Anchorage: Two of the most popular harbors among boaters waiting for favorable weather to cross over to the Bahamas are Hurricane Harbor near the southwest corner of Key Biscayne and No Name Harbor around the point from Hurricane Harbor (in the Bill Baggs State Park). Hurricane Harbor does not have shore access but is a sheltered spot for inclement weather. Favor the port side as you come in as the starboard side of the channel shoals to 4 feet MLW. Drop the anchor in 5 to 13 feet MLW with excellent holding and some exposure to the northwest.

No Name Harbor has shore access and a fee for overnight anchoring and use of the facilities ($20 at press time in summer 2021). Envelopes are provided for depositing the fees in an honor box ashore. There is room for about 25 boats. (Expect lots of company on weekends.) The bottom is hard mud in 11 to 12-foot MLW depths and holding is good with wind

Biscayne Bay – West Shore, FL

COCONUT GROVE AREA		Largest Vessel	VHF	Total Slips	Approach/ Dockside Depth	Floating Docks	Gas/ Diesel	Repairs/ Haulout	Min/Max Amps	Pump-Out Station
1. Coral Reef Yacht Club MM 1094.0	(305) 858-1733	65	71	104	7.0 / 7.0	F		H	30 / 100	P
2. Bayshore Landing (WiFi) MM 1094.0	(305) 854-7997	100	16	114	5.0 / 6.0	F		H	30 / 100	P
3. Grove Harbour Marina MM 1094.0	(305) 854-6444	150		58	18.0 / 8.0	F	GD	RH	30 / 100	P
4. Dinner Key Marina MM 1095.0	(305) 329-4755	110	16	582	8.0 / 7.0	F			30 / 100	P
5. Matheson Hammock Marina 3.6 mi. W of MM 1098.0	(305) 665-5475	55		243	5.5 / 5.0	F	GD		30 / 50	P

(WiFi) Wireless Internet Access onSpot Dockside WiFi Facility
Visit www.waterwayguide.com for current rates, fuel prices, website addresses and other up-to-the-minute information.
(Information in the table is provided by the facilities.)

Scan here for more details:

protection from all directions except due west (and that is actually not too bad).

There are clean restrooms, inexpensive showers and a laundry (although not always operational). Cleats along the seawall make going ashore much simpler. There is no protection along the raw concrete seawall so you should rig your own fenders in advance. A pump-out station is located on the southern side of the harbor near the entrance, but it's not always working. There is a small fee for daily tie-ups but overnight stays along the wall are prohibited.

When the wind is out of the east, another option is to simply anchor in the lee of the west side of Key Biscayne north of Hurricane Harbor in at least 8 feet MLW. Leave the ICW at Mile 1095 and head due east towards flashing green "3." Head into the small cove to the east located just south of a large (private) yacht club. You will have plenty of swinging room and a great view of the Miami skyline.

Do mind the shoals off West Point and stay well south of them. Winds from the west (rare) can set up choppy conditions due to long fetch from mainland coast.

Coconut Grove Area–ICW Mile 1095 to Mile 1098

Once a seaplane base–first for the Pan American clippers flying to the Caribbean and South America and later for the U.S. Coast Guard–Dinner Key is now the site of Miami's premier municipal marina and the old Pan American terminal has been restored and serves as Miami City Hall. The surrounding Coconut Grove area offers a cluster of friendly marine services including yacht clubs, marinas, a boatyard, restaurants, entertainment and shopping. The municipal Dinner Key Marina is a great place to stop for provisioning to get off the boat and stretch your legs. See more at "Goin' Ashore: Coconut Grove, FL" in this chapter.

No Name Harbor

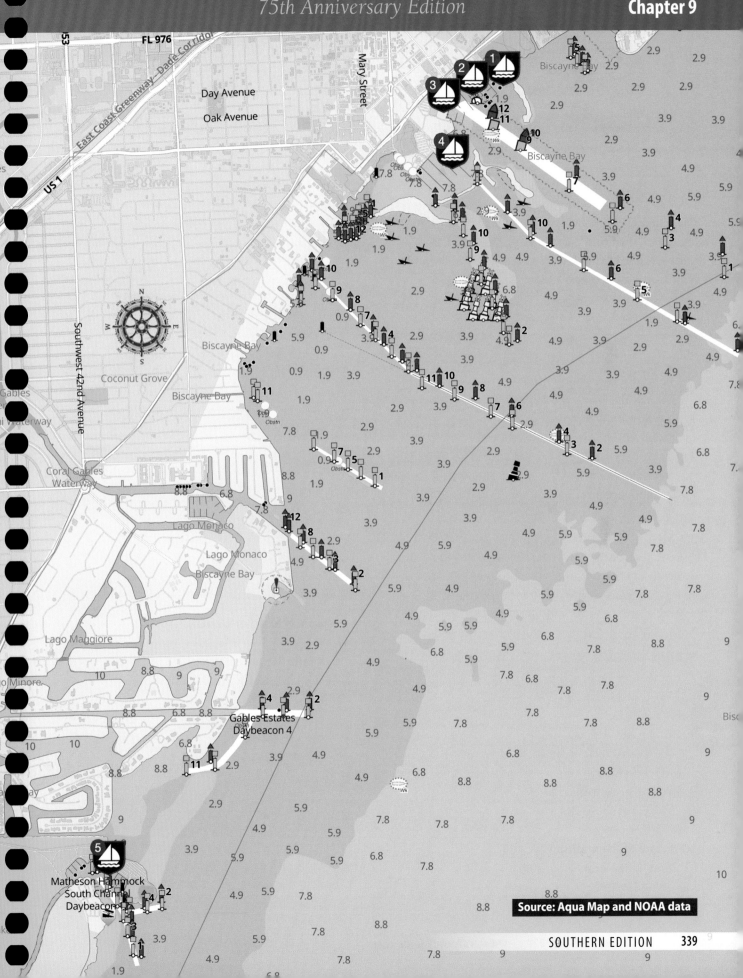

GOIN' ASHORE

COCONUT GROVE, FL

Part of the City of Miami, Coconut Grove is known to locals as "The Grove." Unlike the rest of Miami, low-key and restful Coconut Grove preserves much of the ambiance of traditional Florida. Coconut Grove was once a seaplane base for the enormous Pan American clippers flying to the Caribbean and South America. The airport complex took up all of Dinner Key and a large part of the adjacent mainland was designed to look like an airplane when viewed from above.

SERVICES

1. **Coconut Grove Branch Library**
   2875 McFarlane Rd. (305-442-8695)
2. **Coconut Grove Post Office**
   3191 Grand Ave. (305-529-6700)
3. **Grove Animal Hospital**
   2803 SW 27th Ave. (786-789-0660)
4. **Miami City Hall**
   Located in the original Pan Am complex on Dinner Key at 3500 Pan American Dr. (305-250-5300).

SHOPPING

5. **CVS**
   Drug store chain at 3215 Grand Ave. (305-569-1162).
6. **Fresh Market**
   Upscale grocery store with local produce, prepared eats, wine and more (2640 S. Bayshore Dr., 305-854-7202).

MARINAS

7. **Coral Reef Yacht Club**
   2484 S. Bayshore Dr.
   (305-858-1733)
8. **Dinner Key Marina**
   3400 Pan American Dr.
   (305-329-4755)
9. **Grove Harbour Marina**
   2640 S. Bayshore Dr.
   (305-854-6444)
10. **Prime Marina Miami**
    2550 S. Bayshore Dr.
    (305-854-7997)

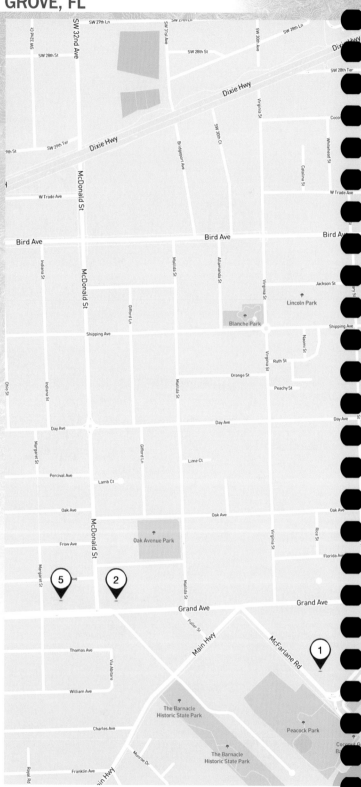

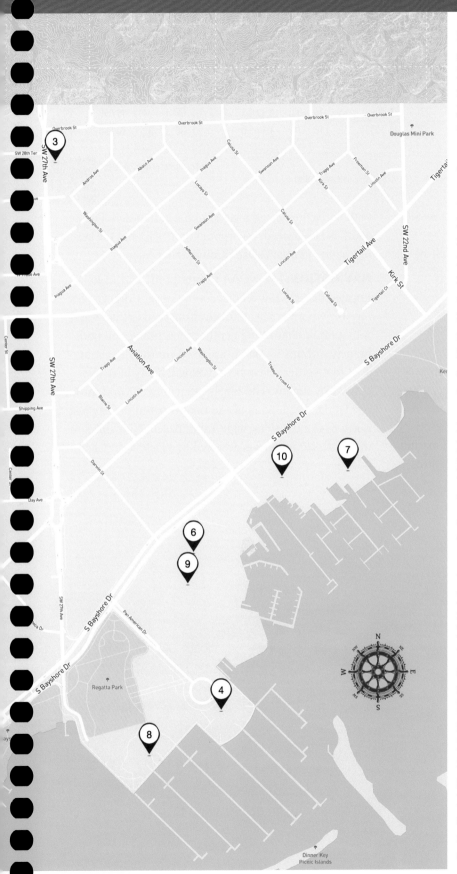

NAVIGATION: Use NOAA Charts 11467 and 11465. On the mainland opposite Key Biscayne lies distinctive Dinner Key, the major center of boating activity for Central Biscayne Bay. Dinner Key is accessed via the well-marked, 1.5-mile-long Dinner Key Channel. Expect 8-foot MLW approach depths to the marina.

Dockage/Moorings: Coral Reef Yacht Club uses the same entrance channel from Biscayne Bay as the nearby marinas. Like most of the private marinas and yacht clubs in the area, they offer reciprocal agreements for members of other recognized yacht clubs. Slips are available only by advance reservation with the dockmaster. Fuel is available via a pre-scheduled fuel truck only. Space is limited and it is suggested that you contact Coral Reef Yacht Club at least one day in advance.

Accessible by the same channel is Bayshore Landing, home to local favorite Monty's Raw Bar & Restaurant (305-856-3992) as well as a number of marine-related businesses including yacht sales and brokerage firms and commercial fishing charter companies. Grove Harbour Marina in the same basin has some transient space.

The municipal Dinner Key Marina to the south provides accommodations in a park-like setting to transients and long-term renters. The 582-slip marina is Florida's largest wet slip marine facility and offers transient, long-term, and commercial dockage at very reasonable rates. Dinner Key also offers a mooring field with 225 mooring balls. All of the moorings are available on a first-come, first-served basis. Call Dinner Key Marina for a mooring assignment. Included in the cost of the mooring are pump-out service and a dinghy dock next door at the launching ramp. A free launch service will shuttle you to and from the marina, which is very close to the attractions of Coconut Grove. You can also come in to take on

Biscayne Bay West Shore, FL

HOMESTEAD AREA		Largest Vessel	VHF	Total Slips	Approach/ Dockside Depth	Floating Docks	Gas/ Diesel	Repairs/ Haulout	Min/Max Amps	Pump-Out Station
1. Loggerhead Marina - South Miami Marina (WiFi) MM 1106.0	(305) 258-3500	38	13	234	5.0 / 9.0	F	GD	RH	15 / 30	
2. Black Point Park & Marina MM 1106.0	(305) 258-4092	55	16	200	4.9 / 5.5	F	GD		30 / 50	P
3. Herbert Hoover Marina at Homestead Bayfront Park (WiFi) MM 1111.0	(305) 230-3033	50	16	174	3.5 / 5.0		GD	H	30 / 50	P

(WiFi) Wireless Internet Access ●**onSpot** Dockside WiFi Facility
Visit www.waterwayguide.com for current rates, fuel prices, website addresses and other up-to-the-minute information. (Information in the table is provided by the facilities.)

Scan here for more details:

water. This is a popular spot to wait for favorable weather to cross to the Bahamas.

Anchorage: Anchoring is still possible outside of the mooring field to the north (on the opposite side of the channel) and to the east in 7 to 8 feet MLW. This is open and exposed to the east through southeast. The Dinner Key anchorage is usually crowded so study the area carefully before dropping your hook.

Coral Gables & Homestead– ICW Mile 1098 to 1111

About 2.5 miles south of Coconut Grove is Matheson Hammock Park, a county park, sandy beach and marina. It is one of South Florida's few remaining natural areas with native forest and a lagoon-type atoll beach. Further south is Homestead, incorporated in 1913 and the second oldest city in Miami-Dade County after Miami.

NAVIGATION: Use NOAA Charts 11467 and 11465. Located directly south of Coconut Grove, Coral Gables has its own waterway with a well-marked entrance and 5-foot MLW controlling depths. Since bridges on both branches of this waterway are fixed (most offer about a 12-foot vertical clearance), you will likely have to explore by dinghy. The canals interconnect, wind through residential developments and finally exit to the bay just north of Coral Gables' wide Tahiti Beach. Nine miles to the south Homestead is accessed by Black Point Channel.

Dinner Key Mooring Field

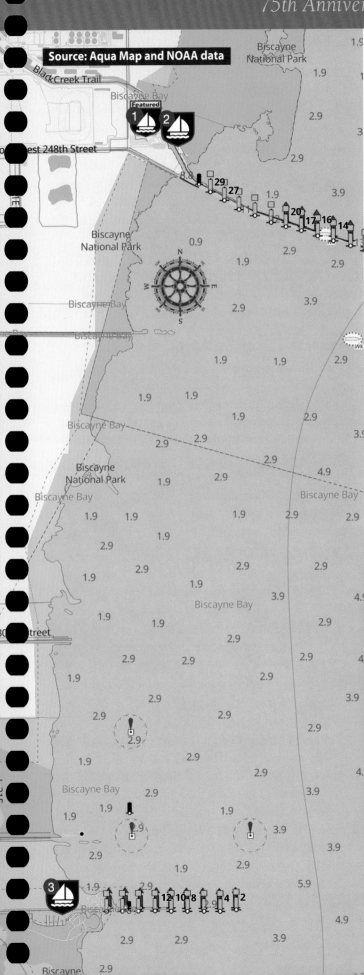

Source: Aqua Map and NOAA data

Dockage: Matheson Hammock Park has a full-service marina, snack bar and restaurant built into an historic coral rock building plus picnic pavilions and nature trails. Matheson Hammock Marina also contains a sailing and power boat school.

In the Homestead Area, Loggerhead Marina–South Miami Marina provides dry storage and one reserved transient slip. They have a well-stocked marine store. Located in the same protected basin is Black Point Park & Marina with transient dockage, bike trails and a dockside restaurant and bar.

Five miles south at Convoy Point next to the Biscayne National Park Headquarters (south side) is the 174-slip Herbert Hoover Marina at Homestead Bayfront Park. This facility is in a beautiful tropical setting with a natural atoll pool and a pristine beach. Depths, however, are reported by the facility as 3.5 feet MLW. Call ahead for approach and dockside depths.

■ NEXT STOP

You are now in an ideal position to head either east to the Bahamas or continue south to the Florida Keys and beyond. If you choose to run north outside from Government Cut, the Gulf Stream will provides a boost to Port Everglades and points north. This route also provides a spectacular view of the Miami Beach skyline.

PLANNING YOUR TRIP

One thing to consider when planning your trip to the Bahamas is the season. In the northern Bahamas, cold fronts with the northwest and northeast blows occur from December to April, and although late spring and summer bring calmer seas and the softer prevailing easterly and southeasterly winds, from mid-June to mid-November is the official hurricane season. This shouldn't deter you, as many have discovered, because ample warning is given and one can simply outrun storms and move away from their predicted path. A further thought is that, between mid-August to September or October, many resorts and restaurants close to renovate or take vacations–or simply because business is slow.

Several marinas and resorts are members of various Bahamian promotion boards that offer specials such as air travel and boating fuel credits, and dockage and lodging incentives. In your planning, make sure to visit The Association of Bahamas Marinas (www.bahamasmarinas.com) and the promotion boards: The Bahamas Out Islands (www.myoutislands.com), Nassau Paradise Island (www.nassauparadise.com) and Grand Bahama Island (www.grandbahamavacations.com).

Crossing Options

We offer three popular routes to enjoy the diverse islands of The Bahamas. The Northern Route comprises Grand Bahama and The Abacos; the Central Route covers Bimini, The Berry Islands, Harbour Island, Spanish Wells and Eleuthera; and the Southern Route begins in Nassau and covers the Exuma Cays. On these time-honored routes you'll encounter a mix of seclusion and modernity, a range of native authenticity and sophistication, and great beaches, snorkeling and fishing. All have fabulous destinations to satisfy a range of tastes and "activity speeds."

Route 1: The Northern Route

Our Northern Route starts at Old Bahama Bay & Yacht Harbour, a port of entry 55 nm due west of West Palm Beach. If you're coming via the north, such as Port St. Lucie Outlet or Fort Pierce, you can either cruise north of Grand Bahama or through the Little Bahama Bank to reach the northern Abaco Cays. Or you can stay in deep water and head straight for an Abaco port of entry at Little Grand Cay, where fishing is top notch. Head farther

south to check in at the popular Green Turtle Cay or Treasure Cay, which are both great for provisioning. "Turn the corner" southeast of Marsh Harbour for popular Hope Town & Elbow Cay or continue south to Little Harbour.

Route 2: The Central Route

The Central Route starts a mere 50 nm from Miami in Bimini, skips across the Great Bahama Bank to the sublime Berry Islands, and through the Northwest and Northeast Providence Channels to pass Nassau for history-rich Spanish Wells, Harbour Island, where you will find some of the best diving in the world, and Eleuthera, offering an exquisite resort marina and a stunning beach. To the south are numerous small, friendly settlements to explore.

Route 3: The Southern Route

The Southern Route heads to New Providence and Paradise Island, where you will find marinas and boatyards, anchorages, ample shopping and a ridiculous array of dining options. From Nassau Harbour you can head to the northern Exuma Cays, home of the Exuma Land and Sea Park, which stretches 23 nm and is the world's first natural undersea and land park. Farther south is George Town and Stocking Island, a well-known beach picnic and hang-out spot for cruisers.

THE GULF STREAM

For vessels crossing between the Florida east coast and the Bahamas, the Gulf Stream is the principal navigational consideration. It is a wide, deep and warm river of fast moving water flowing north, where sea conditions are deeply influenced by the wind. Crossing this river requires careful planning while considering the characteristics of your vessel and crew and the expected wind and weather.

The Gulf Stream current generally begins a few miles out from the Florida coast and extends for approximately 43 nm eastward. The current will gradually increase as you travel east reaching a maximum of roughly 3.6 knots about 8 to 11 miles from the western wall. The current gradually subsides to little or no current at the eastern edge of the Gulf Stream. The average northerly speed over the 43 mile width is 2.5 knots while the average direction of flow is 1° True when north of Lake Worth (Palm Beach) Inlet and about 2° True south of the inlet.

Cruising Conditions

The sea state in the Gulf Stream is largely a function of the prevailing ocean swell in the area, combined with local wind generated waves. The National Weather Service marine forecast provides the Significant Wave Height expected for the Gulf Stream, which is the average height of the highest one-third of the combined swells and wind waves. Be sure to check this when planning your departure. For a useful rule of thumb: south to southeast winds at 10 knots will develop 2-foot seas; 15 knots, 4- to 5-foot seas; 20 knots, 7-foot seas; and 25 knots, 9-foot seas.

For most cruising boats it is generally not advisable to cross the Gulf Stream in winds higher than 15 knots. And it is never a great idea to cross in winds with any significant northerly component as winds against the current cause a very steep, choppy sea. Winds of 10 knots or less offer a relatively comfortable ride for the typical semi-displacement recreational boat 35 to 45 feet in length, provided there are no significant swells in addition to the wind waves.

In winter the location of the Gulf Stream will sometimes be marked by mist rising from its warm waters, which are significantly warmer than the colder coastal water. In winter and whenever a northerly wind is blowing the horizon looking toward the Gulf Stream will often look jagged or saw-toothed. Sailors observing from inshore may say there are "elephants" out there—giant square topped waves kicked up by the Gulf Stream's determination to win its way north against the wind.

In bright sunlight the Gulf Stream is a deep cobalt blue and if the sun is right you may see light dancing in its depths. You will usually see blond-colored patches of Sargasso weed drifting in its waters. Fish will often congregate near and under these patches. You can be sure you have entered the Gulf Stream when the water temperature noticeably increases over a short distance from the near shore ocean temperature. If you are navigating using GPS, you will likely see the effects of the current quickly as your course and speed over ground change significantly.

Planning to Cross

Crossing the Gulf Stream is like traversing a wide, moving walkway–your boat is being steadily pushed northward. The longer you spend in the Gulf Stream, the further north you will be unless you compensate for that movement. Your best strategy is to take advantage of that push by starting as far south (or upstream) of your destination as possible. To the extent that it is possible careful planning and navigation can minimize the time it takes to cross.

NOAA weather broadcasts give daily information about the Gulf Stream including its width, speed, distance offshore at different locations along the Florida coast and its temperature. Many online sources also give daily, detailed maps of the Gulf Stream. For planning purposes a reasonable rule of thumb is to assume the entire distance you have to run from a Florida departure to a point lying along the W 79° 15.000' line of longitude will be subject to an average 2.5-knot, north-flowing current. For faster boats this may have relatively little effect on your course and time to cross but for slower boats, particularly those under sail, the effect is profound and must be taken into account. There are essentially three ways to navigate this challenge:

■ In the days before GPS and chartplotters, boats would compute a heading based on the average current and then steer that constant heading. The disadvantage to this approach is that it is based solely on averages, while the actual current and wind will vary from day to day and during the crossing. But it usually works because it generally gets the boat close enough to your destination that it can be recognized.

■ The boat can be steered to stay pointed at the destination waypoint. This works but is not the most efficient method and will take more time.

■ For boats equipped with GPS, a chartplotter and preferably autopilot, steer to constantly keep the boat on the route from starting point to destination. The actual heading will vary constantly; adjusting to the actual current and wind drift as you move along the route. This is the most efficient way to navigate the crossing.

Magnetic Heading & Time-To-Cross

Direction (M) Distance (nm)	From	To	Top Number = Heading to Steer (Magnetic) Bottom Number = Time Between Waypoints (Hours) Based on Boat Speed (Knots)								
			5 kn	6 kn	7 kn	8 kn	9 kn	10 kn	15 kn	20 kn	25 kn
312° 82.3 nm	West End	Fort Pierce	297° 14.5	299° 12.3	301° 10.6	302° 9.4	303° 8.4	304° 7.6	307° 5.2	308° 4.0	309° 3.2
302° 67.4 nm	West End	Saint Lucie	283° 12.4	286° 10.4	289° 9.0	290° 7.9	292° 7.1	293° 6.4	296° 4.3	297° 3.3	298° 2.6
282° 55.7 nm	West End	Lake Worth	259° 11.9	263° 9.7	266° 8.2	268° 7.1	269° 6.3	271° 5.6	274° 3.7	276° 2.8	277° 2.2
101° 55.7 nm	Lake Worth	West End	124° 12.3	120° 9.9	117° 8.4	115° 7.2	114° 6.4	113° 5.7	109° 3.8	107° 2.8	106° 2.2
65° 69.3 nm	Port Everglades	West End	83° 11.9	80° 10.1	78° 8.8	77° 7.8	75° 7.0	74° 6.3	71° 4.3	70° 3.3	69° 2.7
111° 69.0 nm	Lake Worth	Freeport	129° 15.6	126° 12.6	124° 10.6	122° 9.2	121° 8.1	120° 7.2	117° 4.7	115° 3.5	114° 2.8
78° 74.5 nm	Port Everglades	Freeport	95° 13.9	92° 11.7	90° 10.0	88° 8.8	87° 7.9	86° 7.1	84° 4.8	82° 3.6	81° 2.9
259° 74.5 nm	Freeport	Port Everglades	242° 17.6	245° 14.1	247° 11.8	248° 10.2	249° 8.9	250° 8.0	253° 5.2	254° 3.8	255° 3.1
291° 69.0 nm	Freeport	Lake Worth	273° 13.6	276° 11.3	278° 9.6	280° 8.4	281° 7.5	282° 6.8	285° 4.5	287° 3.4	288° 2.7
336° 74.6 nm	Bimini	Lake Worth	319° 10.7	322° 9.3	324° 8.2	325° 7.4	327° 6.7	328° 6.2	330° 4.4	332° 3.4	333° 2.7
306° 48.2 nm	Bimini	Port Everglades	279° 8.6	284° 7.2	287° 6.2	289° 5.5	291° 4.9	293° 4.4	297° 3.0	299° 2.3	301° 1.9
281° 43.8 nm	Bimini	Miami	251° 9.9	257° 7.9	260° 6.6	263° 5.7	265° 5.0	267° 4.5	272° 2.9	274° 2.2	275° 1.8
126° 48.2 nm	Port Everglades	Bimini	152° 14.3	147° 10.8	144° 8.7	142° 7.3	140° 6.3	138° 5.6	134° 3.5	132° 2.6	131° 2.0
101° 43.8 nm	Miami	Bimini	130° 10.2	125° 8.1	121° 6.7	119° 5.8	117° 5.1	115° 4.5	110° 3.0	108° 2.2	106° 1.8
87° 49.8 nm	Lake Worth	Memory Rock	113° 10.1	108° 8.3	105° 7.0	103° 6.1	101° 5.4	100° 4.9	96° 3.3	93° 2.5	92° 2.0
306° 70.2 nm	Memory Rock	Fort Pierce	288° 12.6	291° 10.6	293° 9.2	295° 8.1	296° 7.3	297° 6.6	300° 4.5	302° 3.4	303° 2.7
105° 61.7 nm	Fort Pierce	Matanilla Shoal	126° 13.8	122° 11.2	120° 9.4	118° 8.1	116° 7.2	115° 6.4	112° 4.2	110° 3.1	109° 2.5
286° 61.7 nm	Matantilla Shoal	Fort Pierce	265° 12.6	269° 10.4	271° 8.8	273° 7.7	274° 6.8	276° 6.1	279° 4.1	281° 3.1	282° 2.5

Corrected courses and estimated elapsed times at varying speeds under normal sea conditions

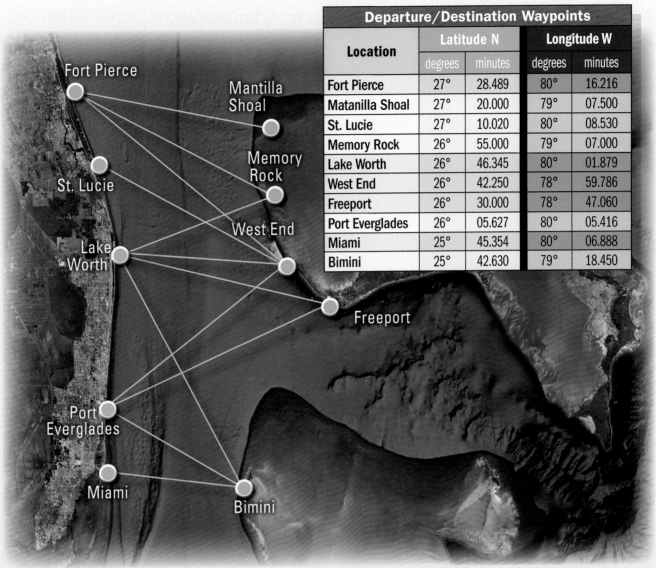

Departure/Destination Waypoints				
Location	**Latitude N**		**Longitude W**	
	degrees	minutes	degrees	minutes
Fort Pierce	27°	28.489	80°	16.216
Matanilla Shoal	27°	20.000	79°	07.500
St. Lucie	27°	10.020	80°	08.530
Memory Rock	26°	55.000	79°	07.000
Lake Worth	26°	46.345	80°	01.879
West End	26°	42.250	78°	59.786
Freeport	26°	30.000	78°	47.060
Port Everglades	26°	05.627	80°	05.416
Miami	25°	45.354	80°	06.888
Bimini	25°	42.630	79°	18.450

There are as many opinions on when to depart Florida and at what time to arrive at your Bahamian waypoint as there are vessels crossing the Gulf Stream. Night crossings are common but they do present the additional challenge of traveling amidst the ever-growing number of freighters and cruise ships in very busy shipping lanes to and from Florida.

Dawn departures provide easier travel in the shipping lanes and arrival in Bahamian waters with the sun behind you. And if you decide to continue across the Banks, night passage will be in many ways easier there than in the Gulf Stream. You should consider your speed of travel, destination and what conditions are expected when you arrive. A vessel departing for and planning to visit North Bimini will have a much different crossing schedule than one headed non-stop to Nassau.

Regardless, pay attention to the weather and don't develop forward-only vision.

Be vigilant about frequent checks for other vessels to starboard, port and aft! Don't become another victim rundown by an inattentive skipper traveling on autopilot. And don't forget to file a Float Plan. (A number of free iOS and Android apps allow you to create a Float Plan and email it to participants or emergency contacts.)

The Constant Heading Table

If you choose the constant heading approach to your passage, the Magnetic Heading & Time-to-Cross table provides for a given boat speed, the single heading to steer and the time to cross on that heading. This data will always be an approximation but is a good estimate for your constant heading and also a good tool for planning passage time if you will be steering to stay on a route line.

The tables are based on the WGS84 datum and 2019 magnetic variation from the National Centers for Environmental Data at NOAA. The results are accurate to within 1° True. The current was assumed to be the average current in the Gulf Stream, which is 2.5 knots. They do not consider wind drift or leeway; compensating for these for your vessel will improve accuracy. The from/to locations correspond to the waypoints identified in the Departure/Destination Waypoints table. They can be used regardless of your destination but you will have to adjust your total trip plan for additional distances to be run.

For example, assume you want to leave from Lake Worth (Palm Beach) Inlet and go to West End. The fourth entry in the table shows the distance traveled between these waypoints is 55.7 nm at a bearing of 101° magnetic. Also assume you plan to travel at 8 knots boat speed. The table shows that at 8 knots you must steer on average 115° magnetic to arrive near the destination waypoint. The time en route will be approximately 7.2 hours between the two waypoints. So if you plan to leave your anchorage or slip early and arrive at the departure waypoint at 7:00 a.m., you should arrive at the destination waypoint at approximately 2:12 p.m. Of course, you need to allow for the time required to get from there to your final overnight stop wherever that may be.

Remember that if you use GPS and remain on the route line between points your heading will vary with the current and wind conditions but you will average 115° magnetic over that time. On the other hand, if you steer a constant 115° magnetic, you will deviate from the route line but should end up at or near the destination.

Listen to the Forecast

The Gulf Stream is a relatively constant, predictable force. The weather is not. Listen to the forecasts. Believe the bad ones and don't trust the good ones. Go to the beach if you can and look out over the ocean. What is happening out there? As stated before the most difficult and dangerous time for any vessel to cross the Gulf Stream is when the wind is from the north, including the northeast and the northwest. Whether you are running a 180-foot motor yacht or skippering an 18-foot sailboat, northerly conditions are definitely not the ones in which to cross.

Remember that the Gulf Stream is flowing north at 2.5 knots. When the wind blows from the north, it is like rubbing a cat the wrong way; all the fur kicks up and the results are the "elephants" mentioned earlier. These are high, ugly waves as closely spaced as elephants holding each other's tails in a circus parade. In those conditions the Gulf Stream is not where you want to be.

Weather is available on the VHF NOAA weather channels from numerous online sources and with many weather apps. Pay close attention, plan carefully, pick your weather window and enjoy a pleasant crossing to the wonderful Bahamas.

■ NAVIGATION & ANCHORING NOTES

Extending in a sweeping southwesterly curve from Miami and the mainland the Florida Keys offer a cruising experience unlike any other waterway area. In many ways the Keys resemble the islands of the Bahamas except for the main highway and 42 bridges (a total of 18.94 miles of bridges) that tie them together. West of Marathon the Seven Mile (Moser Channel) Bridge–which is actually 6.77 miles long–is the longest in the Keys, while the Harris Gap Channel Bridge at 108 feet is the shortest. The highway runs from the tip of the Florida peninsula to Key West, the nation's southernmost city and one with a year-round carnival atmosphere.

Geologically the Florida Keys are mainly the exposed parts of coral reefs and weathered limestones. Some of the islands have been exposed for so long that sand has built up around them creating barrier islands, while other smaller islands remain as coral atolls. With outstanding natural and artificial underwater reefs, fishermen, snorkelers and divers have found a submarine paradise flanking the southeastern shores of the Keys. Beyond the Keys' northwestern shores lies Florida Bay: a fisherman's heaven and also the gateway to the Everglades National Park. This natural area offers its own unique beauty.

> See details on snorkeling and diving, kayaking and paddleboarding, hiking, biking, birding and sportfishing in the "Waterway Guide Florida Keys" edition.

Inside or Outside Route?

Cruisers continuing west from Miami to the Florida Keys have two options:

1. Inside Route: Stay on the ICW following Biscayne Bay and the sounds to their western ends then pass under the Card Sound Road Bridge and on into Florida Bay following the chain of the Keys along the bay side.

2. Outside Route: Enter the Atlantic Ocean from Biscayne Bay at either Cape Florida Channel or Angelfish Creek then follow the Hawk Channel westward around Key Largo and continue on along the ocean side of the Keys.

With either choice, cruisers can switch from one route to the other at Channel Five or Moser Channel, on each side of Marathon and west from Marathon.

This choice is not a simple one. Each skipper must evaluate conditions and make the appropriate decision. If taking the inside (ICW) route, slow down and keep a close watch on the depth sounder as depth changes of up the 1.5 feet are common in strong winds in Florida Bay and elsewhere in the Keys. Note that these changes

Sunset Key

are greater than tidal effects and must be taken into consideration in planning a passage along the ICW on the Inside Route. Obviously in depths of 4 to 5 feet MLW a reduction of 1.5 feet is significant.

Along the bay side stretch of the ICW from Tavernier Creek to Shell Key, you can expect some of the shallowest conditions you will see anywhere on the ICW system with charted depths of 4.5 to 5 feet MLW. To make matters worse the bottom conditions along this stretch are charted as "rocky." For boats that draw over 5 feet we recommend the Outside (Hawk Channel) Route (or "keep to the ocean side" as the locals might say).

Wind strength and direction are other critical considerations. Prevailing winds in the Keys generally have an easterly component. In the summer a southerly component is added, whereas a northerly component is more common in the winter. (Note this is based on probability and is not a prediction.) If winds have either an easterly or southerly component at more than 10 to 15 knots expect choppy conditions in the Hawk Channel (Outside Route). In northwest to north-northeast winds the Outside Route will be the more comfortable route as the westerly curve of the keys will provide more protection.

On the Inside (ICW) Route, cruisers can expect better protection, at least in the closed sounds and basins initially followed by the ICW until things open up north of the Matecumbe Keys. Here the fetch increases and cruisers will experience chop in north to southwest winds. Chop is of particular concern on the inside route as effective water depths will be reduced by the boat's bobbing motion. In east through south-southwest winds the Inside Route is well protected by the unbroken chain of the Florida Keys.

The final consideration, which is well known by seasoned Florida Keys mariners, is that the unbroken chain of the Florida Keys blocks the movement of water as well as waves. The water in the large expanse of the Florida Bay is landlocked on the north, east and south. Strong winds from any of these directions will push the waters of the shallow bay from one side to another creating "wind tide" conditions.

Some cruisers will opt to visit both "sides" of the Keys via a roundtrip. Be aware that depth and clearance restrictions will make some harbors and marinas inaccessible, particularly to sailboats. Careful planning of anchorages and provisioning stops can influence your routing decisions.

NO WAKE ZONE

No Wake Zones, Idle Speed Zones and various Speed Limit restrictions are in effect throughout the waterways included in this chapter. Exercise diligence in knowing the regulations by observing signs and other markers. Enforcement is always present. As always, be courteous to other vessels and avoid manatees and other marine life.

Connections Between the Inside & Outside Route

There are only three major channels between the ICW and Hawk Channel. The first is the Cape Florida (Biscayne Channel) at ICW Mile 1096, which is the northernmost crossover from Biscayne Bay to the Atlantic and also the best marked. The others–Channel Five at ICW Mile 1170 and Moser Channel at ICW Mile 1195–pass under fixed bridges with 65-foot vertical clearances along U.S. Route 1. Several other channels with various limitations exist (including Angelfish Creek) but these are not recommended.

Anchoring in the Keys

Anchoring in the Keys has some unique challenges but is well worth the effort. The bottom may be sand, rock or grass and generally offers good holding but, as in any cruising area, attention to depths, tides and general surroundings requires vigilance. The payoff is a night spent under the stars with the gentle lapping of waves on your boat's hull lulling you to sleep!

A few things to remember when anchoring in the Keys:

- Never anchor over coral.

- Anchor as far away from fellow boaters as possible.

- If the shore is covered in vegetation, scrub or mangroves, expect visitors–the kind that bite!

- Be prepared for 180- and 360-degree swings and strong tidal flows, both of which are common in anchorages in the islands.

- Never use two anchors when one will do. However, if you find yourself in a situation where nothing but two anchors will do, the easiest solution is to set your first anchor and either dinghy out your second anchor or drop back to put down the second anchor and then position yourself between them. Remember that current and tidal flow always win over wind.

- Always try to dive to check that your anchor has set or check it using a dive mask or a glass-bottom bucket from your dinghy. If the bottom is hard-packed sand or rocky, you may have to dive to set an anchor.

- If you run your generator, consider that noise travels better over water and better still at night. Keep use to a minimum and always avoid quiet times when others may not want to hear it such as during breakfast, sunset, dinner time and nighttime.

- Always set an anchor light. Local boats go about their business at all hours of the night often at high speeds. A conventional masthead light is just too high to warn off someone racing along at sea level. Mount an auxiliary anchor light about 10 feet above the water and see how that looks to you from your dinghy. It could be just the most sensible precaution you ever took.

- Take anchor bearings or get a GPS fix and keep them displayed at the helm station. Check them to ensure that you have not dragged. If the risk is high, make out a roster and keep checking through the night. Most modern chartplotters have a built-in anchor alarm feature that can alert you if you have moved more than a set amount of feet from your point of set. Always use these and consider a backup such as a phone app.

Best Ground Tackle

You need to carry two anchors while cruising in the islands (three if you count your tender's anchor). We recommend a plow or spade type and a Danforth. Fit your anchor to your boat length and go oversize if in doubt. When it comes to anchors, BIGGER is always better. In addition, make sure you know the safe working load and the breaking point of your ground tackle.

Depth & Scope

Scope is the length of anchor rode you put out measured from the bow roller into the water to the anchor and it helps determine how well your anchor will hold under most conditions. Generally the greater the scope, the better. With an all-chain rode 5:1 is sufficient in sheltered water. (That is about 5 feet of anchor chain for every 1 foot of depth at high tide.) With nylon and chain 7:1 scope is good. If you are working in meters, take that initial 5-foot figure and work it as 1.5 meters. It is simpler and errs on the side of safety. Don't forget to add your freeboard (the vertical distance from your bow roller to the water surface) to the depth of the water when calculating your scope.

Dive Site Mooring Buoys

There are almost 500 mooring buoys available on a first-come, first-served basis throughout the Everglades National Park Service. These are provided at no cost to the boater to help protect the coral reef. Boaters can tie off to the 18-inch diameter, blue-striped buoy markers to avoid anchoring on the reef. Run your boat's bow line through the loop of the yellow pick-up line. Cleat both ends of your bow line to the bow of your boat. Never tie the yellow pick-up line directly to your boat as it puts undue stress on the mooring anchor.

Buoys used for marking zones such as sanctuary preservation areas, ecological reserves and special-use research are 30 inches in diameter and yellow. Do not tie your boat to these!

Anchoring on living coral within the sanctuary is prohibited. If no mooring buoy is available and you are outside a no-anchor zone, you may anchor in sand; however, if a mooring buoy is available, you must use it.

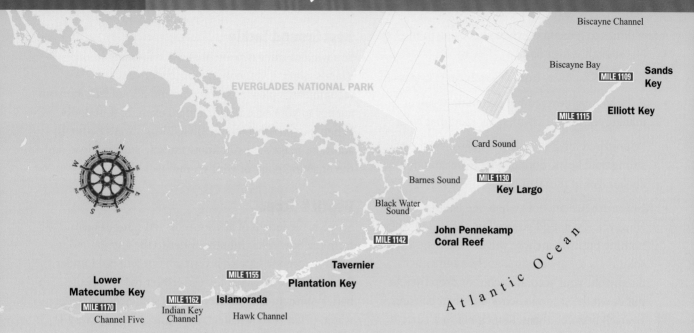

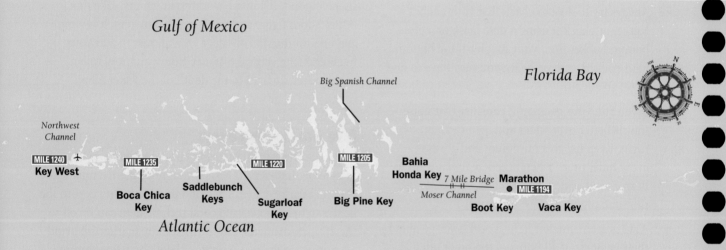

In Severe Storm Conditions

We all dream of idyllic, calm, isolated and uncrowded anchorages. You will definitely find them in the islands; however, you won't have perfection all the time. Your Bahamian anchorage may well turn out to be swept by reversing tidal currents, open to squalls or already crowded with other boats by the time you get there.

If you are unlucky and have to weather a severe storm at anchor, avoid exposed harbors and crowded anchorages. Try to find a hurricane hole or a channel in mangroves where you can secure lines to the sturdy trees. Use every line you have. Make a spider's web of lines allowing 10 feet of slack for tidal surge and use all your anchors fanned out at 90 to 120 degrees to complement your spider's web.

Use chafe protectors on your lines where they come on board. Reduce your windage. Take down any canvas including sails. Lower your antennas, deflate and store your inflatable below deck then lash down everything that must remain on deck. Make the hull as watertight as possible.

If you can't find a hurricane hole (and there are very few that are ideal), you can anchor out to face the wind. Set three anchors in a 120-degree fan. Ideally lead the three rodes to a swivel and then run line from the swivel to the boat. Try for a 10:1 scope. If you use all chain put a nylon snubber (equal to 10 percent of the chain length) on the chain to absorb shock.

Mile 1092–Mile 1243

■ INSIDE (ICW) ROUTE

Cruising Conditions

For boats that draw no more than 5 feet and can take the occasional short, hard chop of shallow water, the Inside (ICW) Route on the bay side provides a relatively well protected and interesting passage option to Islamorada, Marathon and beyond to Key West. This route is clearly marked; however, for certain stretches the markers are far apart and careful attention is required to stay in the controlled channel. In many places you do not have to stray too far out of the channel to find yourself hard aground. Many boats will leave "tracks" (usually just stirred-up, powdery sand) somewhere along this route.

Mariners need to be particularly aware of the wind conditions while navigating the Keys. The region's shallow waters make "wind tide" a serious problem. This is a phenomenon in which strong winds push water from one side of an enclosed basin to another. It is of particular concern on the bay side where operating depths can be a low as 5 feet MLW. In strong northwest winds dockside depths at the marinas can be increased by as much as 1.5 feet, while dockside depths can be reduced by 1.5 feet in strong southeasterly winds. Also the strong tidal flow in the channels between islands tends to move material from these natural channels and deposit it at the channel mouth, either on the bay side or the ocean side. Near these channels the charted depths are suspect and prudent boaters should reduce speed and keep a close watch on their depth sounder.

There are towing services available should you run hard aground and both the Coast Guard and its Auxiliary monitor VHF Channel 16 and have stations along the way. They are not permitted to tow except in a life-threatening situation but they can provide assistance with contacting a commercial towing service (e.g., BoatU.S. or SeaTow). In calm conditions it may be best to wait for a rising tide.

Obviously visual navigation techniques are imperative here and we do not recommend nighttime operation. Your passage plan must be for a series of "achievable daytime hops" allowing travel to end well before nightfall.

To Biscayne National Park–ICW Mile 1092 to Mile 1120

The central segment of Biscayne Bay is its largest and this extraordinary land-and-sea park covers much of it, as well as the adjacent barrier islands and a 3-mile swath of the Atlantic Ocean beyond. Biscayne National Park covers 270 square miles and the ICW runs its entire 20-mile length. Eight miles south of the park's northern boundary (at Mile 1097) a 100-mile-long island chain begins with the tiny Ragged Keys group. This island chain is a world-renowned tourist area known as the Florida Keys.

> SHHHH! Personal watercraft (jet skis) are prohibited in Biscayne National Park, as are generators (after 10:00 p.m.).

NAVIGATION: Use NOAA Charts 11451 and 11463. Central Biscayne Bay runs 25 miles south from Virginia Key to Card Sound. The bay is open and relatively deep. Despite its large size there are only a dozen ICW markers and only eight are visible from the channel. The ICW takes a straight 13.4 nm run at 199° magnetic from flashing green "69," just south of Virginia Key at Mile 1092, to flashing green "3" marking the cut through the Featherbed Bank at Mile 1107. Biscayne National Park boundary flashing yellow light "C" lies exactly on the ICW route at Mile 1102.5 and serves as a helpful intermediate checkpoint on this long run. The four ICW markers in between mark the shoals closest to the designated channel and most are at least 1 mile distant from the ICW.

A well-marked but narrow channel cuts through Featherbed Bank at Mile 1107. Split flashing green "3" and red daybeacon "4" when entering the channel from the north and maintain alignment to split green daybeacon "5" and flashing red "6" to exit south. South from here the ICW takes a straight 7-nm run at 193° magnetic from flashing red "6" to flashing red "8" at Mile 1116.

From flashing red "8" alter your course to split flashing green "9" and red daybeacon "8A." This marker pair frames the entrance to the straight cut through Cutter Bank. Through the cut split the two intermediate marker pairs and keep green daybeacon "13A" well to port to avoid a very shallow shoal behind. Exit the south end of the cut through paired flashing red "14" and green daybeacon "15" and enter Card Sound, the first section of South Biscayne Bay. Passing through the cut you will notice a change in water color from dark turquoise to a murky green.

FLORIDA BRIDGES MONITOR (VHF) CHANNEL 09

Mile	Height	Bridge
1091.6	65'	Rickenbacker Causeway Bridge: Fixed
1126.9	65'	Card Sound Road Bridge: Fixed
1134.1	65'	Jewfish Creek (US 1) Bridge: Fixed
1152.0	15'	Tavernier Creek Bridge: Fixed
1156.0	27'	Snake Creek Bridge: Opens on signal, except from 7:00 a.m. to 6:00 p.m., when the draw need open only on the hour.
1157.0	10'	Whale Harbor Channel Bridge: Fixed
1162.0	7'	Teatable Key Relief Bridge: Fixed
1162.1	10'	Teatable Key Channel Bridge: Fixed
1163.0	27'	Indian Key Channel Bridge: Fixed
1164.5	10'	Lignumvitae Channel Bridge: Fixed
1168.5	10'	Channel Two Bridge: Fixed
1170.0	65'	Channel Five Bridge: Fixed
1176.0	23'	Long Key Viaduct Bridge: Fixed
1179.0	8'	Toms Harbor Cut Bridge: Fixed
1180.0	7'	Toms Harbor Channel Bridge: Fixed
1188.0	13'	Vaca Cut Bridge: Fixed
1194.0	19'	Knight Key Bridge: Fixed
1197.0	65'	Seven Mile Bridge (also known as Moser Channel Bridge): Fixed
1205.0	20'	Bahia Honda Bridges: Fixed
1209.0	11'	Spanish Harbor Channel Bridge: Fixed
1215.0	15'	Pine Channel Bridge: Fixed
1215.0	40'	Niles Channel Bridge: Fixed

Anchorage: Anchoring is available anywhere in Biscayne National Park except over coral or sponge beds. Mooring buoys are available throughout the park but use is limited to 4 hours by any one boat for snorkeling and diving.

Side Trip: Boca Chita & Elliott Keys

Just south of the Ragged Keys lies historic Boca Chita Key followed by Sand Key and Elliott Key beyond. Vessels that draw 5 feet or less can leave the ICW and take a parallel route closer to these barrier islands and stop visit some of the park's wonderful land-based attractions. This side trip doesn't add much distance, offers some excellent anchorages and is well worth the time.

NAVIGATION: Use NOAA Charts 11465 and 11463. To reach the channel to Boca Chita Key southbound vessels should leave the ICW at Mile 1105 on a southeast heading to split green daybeacon "1" and flashing red "2" marking a passage through the northern extremity of the Featherbed Bank. Continue on this course into the center of the small sound to the west of Boca Chita Key and once there, adjust your course to head for the charted "TOWER" on Boca Chita Key. Follow the well-marked but shallow channel to the Key's small harbor, which starts with paired floating markers green "1" and red "2." As you approach shore turn with caution northward into the well-protected harbor. Tiny Boca Chita Key with its cozy harbor and elegant 65-foot lighthouse (circa 1937) is a popular stop.

> ⚠️ The route continuing south to Sands and Elliott Keys is only viable for shoal draft vessels. Be aware that these channels are prone to shoaling. Maintain low speed and a watchful eye on your depth sounder as you pass through this area.

About 1 mile west of Boca Chita Key another marked channel crosses the eastern extremity of Featherbed Bank. The entrance to this channel is about a 0.5 mile south of the entrance to the Boca Chita Key approach channel. Split flashing green "3" and red daybeacon "4" to cross the bank and access Sand Key and Elliot Key; the channel over the bank carries 5.5 feet MLW. Heading south the route inside Elliot Key is well protected and has better depths, although there are a few unmarked shoals.

Elliott Key, lying about 3 miles east of the ICW, is another popular attraction in Biscayne National Park and is open to the public. Graced with a hardwood jungle and a shell-laden ocean beach, Elliott Key is the largest of the 25 keys encompassed by the park.

South of Elliott Key there are a few navigable creeks that lead to Hawk Channel that are often used by cruisers to get access to the Outside Route or start a "Bahamas Run" across the Gulf Stream. See more in the BONUS: Crossing to the Bahamas section of this guide. The approaches to these creeks have charted depths of 4 feet MLW and we recommend you seek local knowledge before attempting passage.

Dockage: The entry channel to the Biscayne National Park facility at Boca Chita Key has charted depths of 4 feet MLW but minimum depths of 5 feet MLW have been observed. Proceed with caution and adjust for wind-tide or chop. The channel is marked with three pairs of floating buoys. Alongside dockage for 25 to 30 boats is available and there are restrooms ashore but no drinking water, showers or dock-side power.

> Boats with pets on board are not permitted to dock on Boca Chita Key, even if the animal remains on the boat.

While the Biscayne National Park service maintains docks for small boats (less than 20 feet) on Elliot Key, there is no marked approach channel to the boat basin and dockside depths may be as little as 2 feet MLW. This is strictly dinghy territory for most cruisers and there are two dinghy landings. Showers and restroom facilities are at the campground close to the docks but only non-potable water is provided. Potable water is available from a faucet nearby.

While ashore pets must be on an attended leash that is no longer than 6 feet in length. Be sure to bring lots of bug spray because you will encounter mosquitoes and no-see-ums. Visitors are requested not to (purposely) feed the wildlife.

Mangrove Shorelines

Nearly every inch of the Florida Keys natural shoreline is covered in mangrove trees. There are actually three types of mangrove that live in the Keys: red, black and white. The most commonly recognized is the red mangrove, which grows along the shoreline standing on a web of prop roots. Black mangroves are almost the opposite; their roots shoot straight up a few inches above the surface. White mangroves are inland trees that grow around tropical hardwood hammocks and are found on drier land.

Mangroves are extremely salt tolerant. Their roots absorb water from the sea and their waxy leaves excrete the excess salt. Mangroves grow all over the world but are sensitive to cold weather and are only found in tropical climates like those of Florida, Mexico and Central America.

Of course, mangroves encompass so much more than just species of trees. They thrive in conditions that other plants cannot and create entire ecosystems with their roots and structure. The biodiversity found in mangrove swamps is astounding, with hundreds of algae, crustacean, mollusk, fish, reptile and insect species present. Their roots provide shelter for smaller animals that live their entire lives there or that just visit for spawning. Mangroves are sometimes referred to as the nurseries of the coral reefs.

For the islands of the Florida Keys mangroves also provide shelter and protection. Mangroves form a natural barrier to erosion and especially to the damaging storm surge that comes with hurricanes. For this reason, mangroves are protected in Florida and especially in the Keys. Without mangroves the Florida Keys would be washed away.

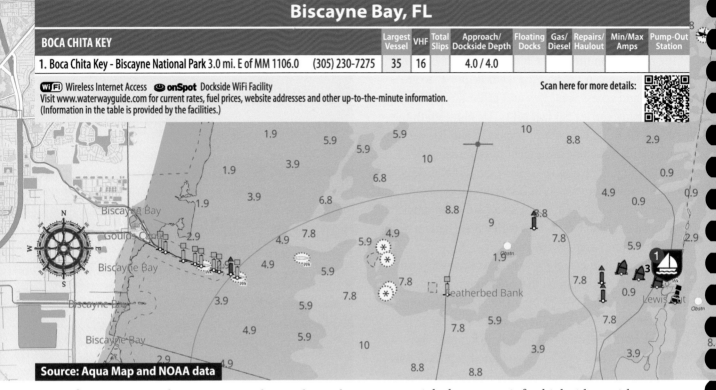

Biscayne Bay, FL

BOCA CHITA KEY		Largest Vessel	VHF	Total Slips	Approach/ Dockside Depth	Floating Docks	Gas/ Diesel	Repairs/ Haulout	Min/Max Amps	Pump-Out Station
1. Boca Chita Key - Biscayne National Park 3.0 mi. E of MM 1106.0	(305) 230-7275	35	16		4.0 / 4.0					

WiFi Wireless Internet Access   **onSpot** Dockside WiFi Facility   Scan here for more details:
Visit www.waterwayguide.com for current rates, fuel prices, website addresses and other up-to-the-minute information.
(Information in the table is provided by the facilities.)

Source: Aqua Map and NOAA data

Anchorage: An anchorage at Ragged Keys, located 3 miles east of Mile 1106, has 7 to 8 feet MLW with good holding in grass and mud. However, it's exposed to northwest through southwest winds.

Two miles south, the Sands Key inner anchorage has excellent holding in 6 to 7 feet MLW and all-around protection. The shallow approach (with spots as shallow as 4 feet MLW) restricts this spot to all but shoal draft boats. The approach is a little tricky, so you might have to wait for high tide to either enter or exit. There are a few rocks but you should find a place to drop your hook. If you can't manage the inner anchorage, you can anchor outside on the west side of Sands Key in 5 to 6 feet MLW, holding is good in grass and mud. It's exposed to north through southwest winds.

Cruising vessels typically anchor in deeper water well offshore at Elliott Key. During summer months with the prevailing winds from the southeast, this is a popular anchorage hosting hundreds of boats. Keep an eye out for storm systems during the summer. During the winter far fewer boats will visit this beautiful area because frequent northerlies can make anchoring here risky and downright uncomfortable. It is possible to anchor off Coon Point on the northwest side of Elliot Key in 4 to 6 feet MLW with good holding. This spot is protected from the east.

Caesar Creek winds around tiny Adams Key (7- to 12-foot MLW depths with facilities ashore for day use only) and has a southern spur leading to an anchorage between Rubicon and Reid Keys. The approach depths to this anchorage are only about 3 feet MLW; however, you should have up to 12 feet MLW once inside.

Distances
Inside Route: ICW (Miles from Miami)

LOCATION	STATUTE MILES	NAUTICAL MILES
Miami (Mile 1090)	0	0
Angelfish	30	26.1
Jewfish Creek	43	37.4
Tavernier	60	52.1
Islamorada	69	60.0
Channel Five	80	69.5
Marathon (Sisters Creek)	102	88.6
Moser Channel	107	93.0
Harbor Key Bank Light	128	111.2
Northwest Channel	147	127.7
Key West	154	133.8

(For comparison, Moser Channel to Key West on the Outside Route via Hawk Channel is 40 statute miles versus the 47 shown here.)

Card Sound–ICW Mile 1120 to Mile 1126

Card Sound marks the upper segment of South Biscayne Bay. South from here the water is a murky green and the bottom changes to mud and grass much like the sounds of Florida Bay. These sounds have shorter fetch and are less prone to chop than the larger segments to the north. Depths are good but expect some local shoaling at the ends of the cuts through the banks.

> The local weather station in this area is WCTH-FM 100.3, offering up-to-date local weather and music.

NAVIGATION: Use NOAA Charts 11451 and 11463. South from Cutter Bank it's a 4.6 nm run at 234° magnetic from flashing red "14" to marker pair flashing green "17" and red daybeacon "16" that frame the north entrance of the cut through Card Bank. Pass through the intermediate marker pair and then exit the cut splitting flashing red "20" and green daybeacon "21" and into Little Card Sound. It's just over 1 mile southwest to the next ICW marker (flashing red "22"), which sets alignment for the bridge immediately to the south.

From Card Sound there is a channel that runs between the adjacent keys east to the ocean that is popular with local fishermen. In favorable weather Angelfish Creek is a heavily used passage between the ICW and Hawk Channel. For vessels wanting to maximize the Gulf Stream's powerful boost for a transit to Bimini in the Bahamas, the 1.8-nm-long Angelfish Creek provides a more southerly approach than Miami, despite the added 14 nm distance

Boca Chita

(56 nm versus 42 nm) some argue a quicker passage time. Angelfish Creek is a fair-weather proposition only, with 4-foot MLW depths on both ends (although some cruisers report better depths).

Anchorage: In a north wind some protection can be found south of Long Arsenicker located between Biscayne Bay and the northeast corner of Card Sound near the south end of Midnight Pass (Mile 1120).

To the southeast just past Mile 1120 and the entrance to Angelfish Creek from Card Sound is a well-known rendezvous and anchoring spot in the lee of small Pumpkin Key. ICW cruisers frequently congregate here, some waiting to cross the Gulf Stream to the Bahamas by exiting

via Angelfish Creek and others just to enjoy a quiet stop en route. Drop the anchor in 7 to 9 feet MLW with excellent holding in grass and mud. (No shore access.) Little Pumpkin Creek, just below the mouth of Angelfish Creek, is another "locals spot" and can get busy on weekends. Locals also regard it as a hurricane hole.

The southernmost anchorage in Card Sound is off Jew Point near the very south pocket of the sound, about 1.5 miles east of the mouth of Steamboat Creek. The anchorage at Steamboat Creek–Jew Point (Mile 1125) has 7 to 9 feet MLW with good holding in grass and mud and protection from all but north winds.

It is possible to anchor in Little Card Sounds but because of its small size it's tough to get out of the wakes of boats passing on the ICW. Boat traffic can be busy here, even at night.

Barnes Sound–ICW Mile 1127 to Mile 1133

NAVIGATION: Use NOAA Charts 11451 and 11463. From Cutter Bank Pass set a course of 234° magnetic for about 4.6 nm to flashing green "17" (located just south of distinctive Card Point) marking the entrance to a narrow cut through Card Bank to Little Card Sound (Mile 1125). Watch for shoaling at the well-marked north entry of the cut.

The **Card Sound Road Bridge** (fixed 65-foot vertical clearance bridge) at Mile 1126.9 serves as the next landmark. This is the first of two highway bridges linking Key Largo with the mainland. The channel under the bridge is marked and dredged, but it shallows rapidly at its south exit into Barnes Sound so follow markers closely. Once you are through the channel and on to flashing red

"26" in Barnes Sound, minimum 8 foot MLW depths hold for the straight 4.5 nm run to the end of Barnes Sound where flashing green "29" marks the entrance to Jewfish Creek. Depending on wind direction the chop can build in Barnes Sound and it can get sloppy.

Jewfish Creek in the southeast corner of Barnes Sound leads to Blackwater Sound. This can be a high traffic area. During the winter season, you will likely encounter commercial stone crabbing or lobster boats, in addition to the usual menagerie of sport fishermen and ICW cruisers. There is good fishing in Barnes Sound and you can dinghy through the mangroves.

Dockage: SeaHunter Marina at Manatee Bay operates a working yard east of Mile 1130 inside Manatee Bay where Manatee Creek was dead-ended by construction of the Overseas Highway (US Route 1) decades ago. The facility normally reserves dockage for repair customers. Transients looking for dockage in this laid-back and out-of-the-way location may find it at one of the smaller marinas to the east.

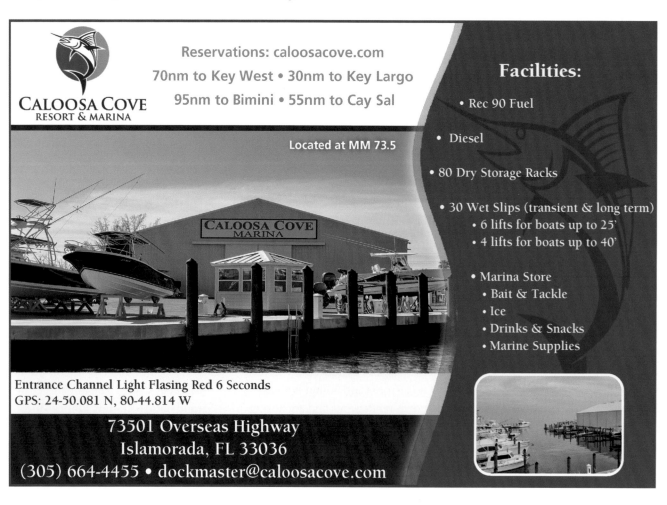

Transient Slips Available Year Round!

PIL T H USE

N 25° 05.250' / W 080° 26.470'

Email info@pilothousemarina.com
Marina (305) 747-4359
Restaurant (305) 451-3142

55 Slips
70 Dry Storage Racks
Diesel & Gasoline
Haul Out Service (25ft)
Pump Out
Laundry / Showers

Our bar & restaurant is open for lunch and dinner from 11:30 am to 9:00 pm from Wednesday to Sunday. Happy Hour is from 4:30 to 6:30 pm daily.

Pilot House Marina, located in Key Largo, is a full-service marina with 55 slips and 70 dry storage racks. Contact us to learn more or check availability. Welcome to Paradise!

Pilot House Restaurant & Marina
13 Seagate Blvd., Key Largo, FL 33037
www.pilothousemarina.com

Visit Us!
MM 99.6
The Keys

Upper Keys, FL

KEY LARGO AREA		Largest Vessel	VHF	Total Slips	Approach/ Dockside Depth	Floating Docks	Gas/ Diesel	Repairs/ Haulout	Min/Max Amps	Pump-Out Station
1. SeaHunter Marina at Manatee Bay 3.4 mi. NW of MM 1131.5	(305) 451-3332	50	16	45	4.5 / 5.0	F		RH	30	P

WiFi Wireless Internet Access **onSpot** Dockside WiFi Facility
Visit www.waterwayguide.com for current rates, fuel prices, website addresses and other up-to-the-minute information.
(Information in the table is provided by the facilities.)

Scan here for more details:

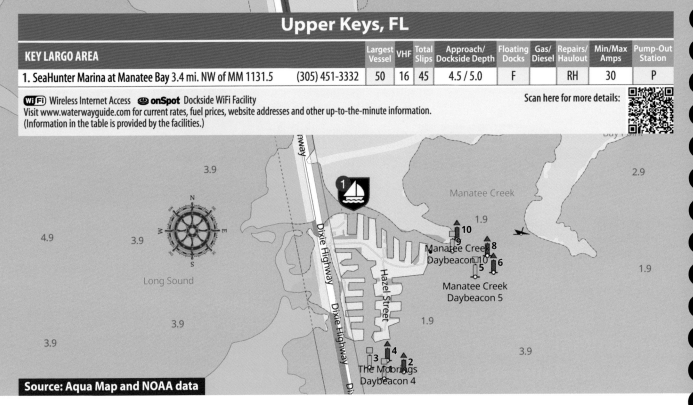

Source: Aqua Map and NOAA data

Anchorage: In the northeast corner of Barnes Sound near Steamboat Creek is a protected cove with 7 to 9 feet MLW. It offers protection from the north through east winds only. (Shoal-draft boats can ease in farther for 5-foot MLW depths and find better protection from northeast winds.) You can also drop the hook in Manatee Creek in 5-foot MLW depths.

Jewfish Creek–ICW Mile 1133 to Mile 1134

At about Mile 1133 you enter a well-marked, deep channel through Jewfish Creek. From here on you really are in the Keys. Key Largo lies to the east and offers many sites of historical, geological and romantic interest along its 30-mile length. Some sites are close to the marinas but if this is a first visit, it's best to arrange for land transportation so you can explore the area fully.

NAVIGATION: Use NOAA Charts 11451 and 11463. Jewfish Creek itself is a favorite fishing spot and small boats often congregate in the area. The numerous anchored or slow-trolling small fishing boats occupying this narrow channel require a close watch and it's best to throttle back Idle-Speed/No-Wake here. Be prepared to navigate carefully and defensively here. Also expect watercraft around the surprisingly active docks at the south end of the creek. The creek passes under the

Jewfish Creek (U.S. 1) Bridge at Mile 1134.1 (with 65-foot fixed vertical clearance).

Dockage: Immediately south of the Jewfish Creek (US 1) Bridge (on the western side) is the popular Gilbert's Resort and Marina with a long, wooden wharf along the channel for easy access to the fuel pumps. If you are coming through Jewfish Creek, keep going to red daybeacon "38" before turning to starboard. Water depths are less than 3 to 4 feet starboard of the channel. Steer to the northwest of the charted wreck before turning in towards Gilbert's Resort.

There is a Keys-style hotel with waterfront rooms on site as well as a tiki bar, restaurant, swimming pool and beach. Call ahead to reserve one of their 50 slips. Opposite on the east side is Anchorage Resort & Yacht Club, part of a condominium complex that has just six reserved slips for transients.

Anchorage: The anchorage near Gilbert's gives good wind protection from slightly northwest to east winds. Cell phone reception is excellent and you may be able to pick up free WiFi from Gilbert's Tiki Bar and Restaurant. Holding is excellent in sand/coral with sea grass. Try to find an area with little/no sea grass if visibility permits. You'll be rewarded with frequent dolphin visits next to your boat. Fishing is good in the sound as well as in the mangroves. Watch for manatee in the mangrove channels in cooler months.

Boats are often seen anchoring just to the south of the Jewfish Creek (US 1) Bridge near green daybeacon "37." Charted depths outside the channel south of the bridge at Jewfish Creek in the immediate vicinity 6 to 8 feet MLW. There is room to anchor on the west side; just pay attention to your depth sounder and feel your way in. This anchorage is exposed to wakes and winds with any westerly or southerly component. There can be noise from the nearby resort and be sure to have plenty of bug spray at all times of the year!

Blackwater Sound–ICW Mile 1135 to Mile 1038

Considered the upper reaches of Florida Bay by some, Blackwater Sound is a completely enclosed basin. The sound has considerable fetch and you may see some chop here.

After exiting Jewfish Creek, the ICW meets the southeast corner of Everglades National Park and skirts the park's southern boundary for the next 41 miles westward. In the past sporadic signs marked the park boundary that were useful for navigation but few of these signs remain. Be sure to check park regulations before entering. Everglades National Park is famous for its vast expanses of water, mangrove forests and marshy grasslands.

> The boundary for Everglades National Park is marked on charts as "PARTICULARLY SENSITIVE SEA AREA" (PSSA). Landings are not allowed at any of the Keys within the park except where specifically designated and charted by park authorities. .

NAVIGATION: Use NOAA Charts 11451 and 11464.

There is a shallow sandbar to the north side of the marked channel between red daybeacon "36" and flashing red "38" just before Mile 1135. This may not be shown on your charts.

Leaving Jewfish Creek at flashing red "38" set a course of 223° magnetic for 1.7 nm to the mouth of the creek with charted depths as low as 4 feet MLW. Throttle back here and monitor your sounder. Some cruisers have advised diverging east from the magenta line here to find deeper water. Mangrove-lined Dusenbury Creek enters Tarpon Basin at Mile 1138.5.

The fishing on the expansive shallow flats here is outstanding but catch and licensing regulations are in effect and enforcement is strict.

Dockage: The Marina Club at BlackWater Sound is located just north of a dredged canal that leads to Largo Sound on the ocean side. This facility is storage only (no transients) and the club concierge can provide Certified Service Technicians and a variety of other boat care services. The facility reports 4-foot MLW approach and dockside depths.

Anchorage: There are numerous anchorages on the eastern side of Blackwater Sound. Sexton Cove at the northeast end (Mile 1135) has 6- to 7-foot MLW depths and a grassy bottom with fair holding. (Lake Surprise to the north has a 3-foot MLW entrance channel and is not a viable anchorage for most cruising vessels).

Farther south you can snug up to the south of Stellrecht Point in 6 to 7 feet MLW with good holding in grass and mud. At the southeast end of Blackwater Sound you can drop the hook near Dusenbury Creek in 6 to 7 feet MLW with good holding and protection from south winds.

Tarpon Basin–ICW Mile 1139 to Mile 1140

NAVIGATION: Use NOAA Charts 11451 and 11464. From Blackwater Sound the ICW snakes through mangrove-lined Dusenbury Creek (Mile 1138) to Tarpon Basin. The narrow creek carries good depths but small powerboats pass through here full-throttle so slow down and proceed with caution around the blind corners.

The expanse of Tarpon Basin is deceptive. The basin is very shallow outside the dredged channel (charted at 5 to 6 foot MLW) and it is best to maintain a low speed around the tight curve in the channel. Dangerous shoals (with 2.5-foot MLW depths) line the channel's edge on the outside of the turn from red daybeacon "42" through flashing red "48." Favor the markers on the inside of this tight curve. Straighten up at flashing red "48" and head directly for red daybeacon "48A" and then on to flashing red "50." Westbound traffic should keep red daybeacon "52" to starboard at the entry to narrow Grouper Creek.

Depths are shallow at both ends of the creek so maintain channel alignment. After exiting the creek between green daybeacon "53" and red daybeacon "52A" head straight for flashing red "54," which leads into Buttonwood Sound.

Upper Keys, FL

KEY LARGO AREA		Largest Vessel	VHF	Total Slips	Approach/ Dockside Depth	Floating Docks	Gas/ Diesel	Repairs/ Haulout	Min/Max Amps	Pump-Out Station
1. Gilbert's Resort and Marina (WiFi) MM 1134.0	(305) 451-1133	105	16	50	6.0 / 15.0		GD		30 / 50	
2. Anchorage Resort & Yacht Club (WiFi) MM 1134.2	(305) 451-0500	180	16	20	6.0 / 8.0				30 / 50	
3. The Marina Club at BlackWater Sound (WiFi) MM 1136.5	(305) 453-0081	40	16		4.0 / 4.0	F	G	RH	30 / 50	

(WiFi) Wireless Internet Access   onSpot Dockside WiFi Facility
Visit www.waterwayguide.com for current rates, fuel prices, website addresses and other up-to-the-minute information.
(Information in the table is provided by the facilities.)

Scan here for more details:

Anchorage: Tarpon Basin offers good anchoring opportunities due to short fetch. Just be aware that holding is just fair due to the grassy bottom. (Some flat rock has also been reported.) The most popular area is just south of the large shoal in the center of the basin. To enter proceed all the way to red daybeacon "48A" and then head south from this marker to find the charted deeper water. Watch your depth and anchor with care. Some also anchor north of red daybeacon "48A" in the pocket with 7- to 8-foot MLW depths. Signs at the Nelson Government Building prohibit overnight parking without a county permit, tying up to the dock or trees or mooring within 25 feet of the dock.

> If you do drop a hook here be sure to seek local knowledge about the mangrove tunnels that you can explore from the comfort of your dinghy.

Buttonwood Sound & Baker Cut–ICW Mile 1141 to Mile 1144

Buttonwood Sound is not fully enclosed and once here you are officially in Florida Bay. Snook's Bayside Restaurant and the Grand Tiki are located in Buttonwood Sound with an excellent "happy hour" and great food. They also host a nightly sunset celebration. The Upper Keys Sailing Club is to the northeast at nearby Point Pleasant. This is a private sailing club but you can ask for permission to tie up for a short stop and wander down to town, which isn't more than a 0.5-mile walk. A liquor store, some good restaurants and Publix are nearby.

NAVIGATION: Use NOAA Charts 11451 and 11464. While Florida Bay is expansive and the fetch can be very long, the bay's shallow depths reduce chop, which is typically light even in moderate winds. But winds can cause other effects. Although the normal 1-foot tidal range is modest here strong winds can cause "wind tide" conditions raising or lowering normal water levels by up to 1.5 feet. Strong north to east winds reduce water levels in Florida Bay and strong west to south winds can raise them. If you detect depths below what is charted or expected, throttle back and consider postponing your passage. Winds can also affect course alignment and auto pilot settings.

The ICW markers are widely spaced for many sections along this route. Glance astern occasionally to check your actual course heading, which can differ significantly from your compass heading.

Depths are as shallow as 5 feet MLW in the stretch from flashing red "54" (Mile 1141) to flashing green "55" in the marked ICW channel. Some cruisers choose to diverge slightly east here and parallel the ICW channel in the charted 7-foot MLW depths.

The ICW leaves Buttonwood Sound through Baker Cut. Flashing green "55" marks the entrance to the cut at Mile 1143. Initially the ICW continues along this shallow stretch through a well-marked but narrow dredged channel, which carries 7 feet MLW initially but drops to 6 feet MLW at flashing red "58." Spots of shoaling flank both sides of the channel from the cut to flashing red "60." Maintain the center of the marked channel through here. Once past flashing red "60" some cruisers will diverge north into the charted deeper water adding some wiggle room but the markers are widely spaced and channel alignment is difficult.

Groundings are common. If your draft is above 5 feet, seek local knowledge. Another option may be to wait for a favorable wind tide; strong southwest winds can improve depths in upper Florida Bay.

Anchorage: To the east of Baker Cut lies Sunset Cove. The anchorage has minimal tide but is exposed in north and west winds. You will not be alone.

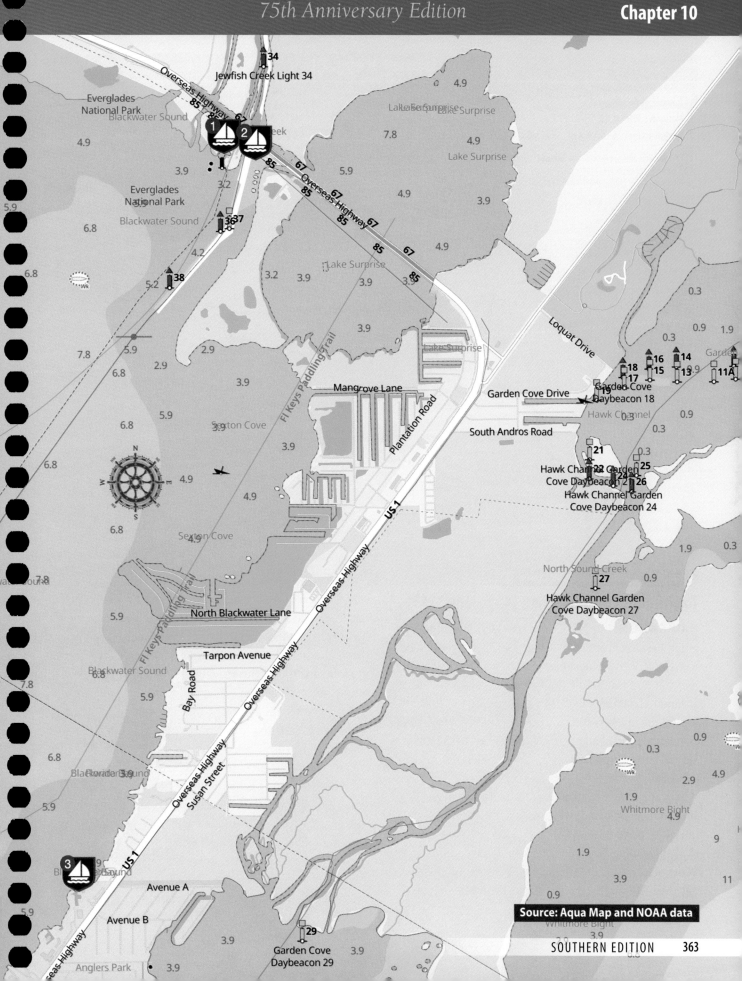

34
Jewfish Creek Light 34

Overseas Highway
85 67

Everglades
National Park
Blackwater Sound

4.9

Lake Surprise
Lake Surprise
Lake Surprise

4.9

7.8

4.9

Lake Surprise

3.9

1 **2**

85 67
Overseas Highway
85 67

5.9

4.9

85 67

5.9

Everglades
National Park
Blackwater Sound

36 37

6.8

4.2

38

5.2

85 67

85

4.9

0.3

Loquat Drive

0.9 1.9

0.3

16 14
18 15 13
17 **11A**
19
Garden Cove
Daybeacon 18

0.3

0.9

3.2

3.9

Lake Surprise

3.9

3.9

4.9

4.9

3.2

3.9

5.9

2.9

7.8

N

6.8

2.9

6.8

5.9

Fl Keys Paddling Trail

Sexton Cove

Mangrove Lane

Plantation Road

Garden Cove Drive

South Andros Road

0.9

0.3

21
Hawk Channel Garden
Cove Daybeacon 22

22 **25**
24 **26**

0.3

Hawk Channel Garden
Cove Daybeacon 24

Hawk Channel

3.9

3.9

4.9

5.9

Sexton Cove
4.9

6.8

US 1

North Blackwater Lane

Overseas Highway

North Sound Creek

27
Hawk Channel Garden
Cove Daybeacon 27

0.9

1.9

0.3

Tarpon Avenue

Bay Road

Overseas Highway

Susan Street

Blackwater Sound
6.8

5.9

Blackwater Sound
Florida Sound
3.9

5.9

US 1

3

Overseas Highway

Avenue A

Avenue B

Overseas Highway

29
Garden Cove
Daybeacon 29

3.9

3.9

0.9

0.3

2.9 4.9

1.9
Whitmore Bight
4.9

9

1.9

3.9

11

0.9

Whitmore Bight
3.9

Anglers Park 3.9

5.9

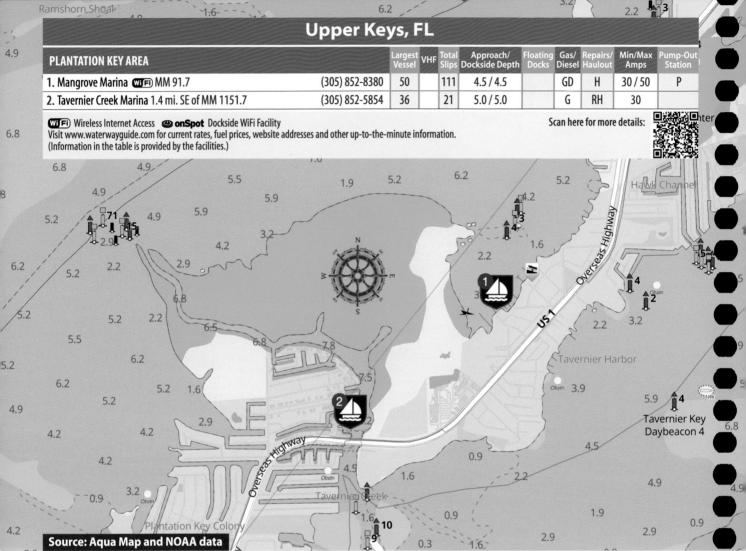

Upper Keys, FL

PLANTATION KEY AREA		Largest Vessel	VHF	Total Slips	Approach/ Dockside Depth	Floating Docks	Gas/ Diesel	Repairs/ Haulout	Min/Max Amps	Pump-Out Station
1. Mangrove Marina (WiFi) MM 91.7	(305) 852-8380	50		111	4.5 / 4.5		GD	H	30 / 50	P
2. Tavernier Creek Marina 1.4 mi. SE of MM 1151.7	(305) 852-5854	36		21	5.0 / 5.0		G	RH	30	

(WiFi) Wireless Internet Access (onSpot) Dockside WiFi Facility
Visit www.waterwayguide.com for current rates, fuel prices, website addresses and other up-to-the-minute information.
(Information in the table is provided by the facilities.)

Scan here for more details:

Source: Aqua Map and NOAA data

To Cowpens Cut–ICW Mile 1145 to Mile 1153

NAVIGATION: Use NOAA Charts 11451 and 11464. At quick-flashing green "61" (Mile 1147.5) just past Pigeon Key, the ICW turns abruptly south towards quick-flashing red "62" and Hammer Point beyond. Take a gentle turn around red daybeacons "62A," "64" and "64A" keeping 50 feet off the markers to maintain 7 feet MLW. Avoid a little (unnamed) island and surrounding shoals to the north. Several groundings have been reported here so don't cut the corner between markers and watch your depth. The ICW route continues westward past flashing green "65" and through well-marked Ramshorn Cut. Stay centered in the cut to carry 6 feet MLW as the edges shallow quickly.

Approaching Tavernier Creek things get confusing as the markers for the two channels are placed close together. Although the chart shows the magenta line passing between red daybeacon "18" and green daybeacon "17," note that these markers are for the Tavernier Creek channel. The ICW passes north of this marker pair, closer to the charted PSSA boundary of Everglades National Park. You pass the shallowest spot (5.5 feet MLW) near flashing green "71" but the exit of Tavernier Creek is prone to shoaling. Slow down and find your way carefully. There have been numerous groundings reported here. If it starts getting shallow, move north to gain better depth.

From Tavernier Creek proceed straight toward flashing green "73" at the opening of Cowpens Cut. Enter the cut with caution as its east entrance has a charted depth of 5 feet MLW. You will find deeper water closer to the green side of the entrance. Maintain center channel in the cut through the "Cross Bank" to flashing red "78."

Dockage: Popular Mangrove Marina hosts many liveaboard boaters, both transient and long term. Transient slips must be reserved in advance. Access is provided via a short, privately marked channel. Once past ICW red daybeacon "64A" look south and see a little bay (next to charted "Community Hbr") and private markers. The water depths just off the channel are 6 feet MLW and shallow to 4 feet as you get closer to shore. Call the marina for specific navigation directions. If you are in need of supplies, there is a shopping center with a supermarket close by. Tavernier Creek Marina north of the fixed **Tavernier Creek Bridge** (15-foot vertical clearance) is primarily a boat storage facility with numerous on-site services including marine detailing, engine repair and yacht sales as well as a bait and tackle shop, dive shop, fishing charters and a restaurant.

Anchorage: You can anchor on the south side of Butternut Key at Mile 1146 in 5 to 6 feet MLW. This provides fair holding with no protection from the south. At Mile 1150 the Community Harbor at Plantation Key offers a fair anchorage with 4 to 5 feet MLW. There is no protection here from the north.

To Islamorada–ICW Mile 1153 to Mile 1161

This leg of your trip will take you past popular Islamorada. The village of Islamorada is actually made up of five islands: Tea Table Key, Lower Matecumbe Key, Upper Matecumbe Key, Windley Key and Plantation Key. See details on things to see and do in this area at "Goin' Ashore: Islamorada, FL" in this chapter.

NAVIGATION: Use NOAA Charts 11451 and 11464. Southwest from flashing red "78" (Mile 1153.5) it can be difficult to find the ICW route. It appears as if the ICW ends here because the yellow squares and triangles no longer appear on aids to navigation and the daybeacons and lights appear in a different section of the Light List published by the USCG. Also the magenta line and mileage bars have been removed from the most recent NOAA charts. NOAA, however, considers the ICW to continue on to Key West and coverage in the Coast Pilot Vol 4 chapter on the ICW does, in fact, continue to Key West. From this point to Key West, this guide will provide either a compass heading and/or visual reference points for the ICW route.

From Cotton Key at ICW red daybeacon 80 (Mile 1158) to Steamboat Channel, the ICW passes through what is perhaps the shallowest part of the entire route.

Remember, touching a sandy bottom at slow speeds is rarely dangerous but at high speeds can do considerable damage to your props. There just isn't enough water here to take any chances. Care is recommended.

The ICW route parallels the charted PSSA boundary line for another 20 miles where the marker numbering sequence next resets at flashing green "1" (Mile 1173) located at the north end of Old Dan Bank. As previously mentioned, the PSSA line charts the Everglades National Park boundary and there may be some signage along this route reading "National Park Boundary."

Proceeding west floats for lobster and stone crab traps fill the ICW channel and surrounding water in season. Be careful not to foul your propeller. Traps and floats are usually removed during the off-season (May 15 to October 15) making navigation simpler but many stray traps remain requiring a sharp lookout.

The Cowpens Cut through Cross Bank (at Mile 1153) leads into Cotton Key Basin. As mentioned above the magenta line showing ICW channel centerline is not shown on recent NOAA charts. For this segment the ICW runs immediately south of the charted PSSA boundary line indicating the southern boundary of the Everglades National Park. From flashing red "78" at the exit from Cowpens Cut the ICW "channel" runs a straight-line course of 250° magnetic for 4.2 nm across the Cotton Key Basin to flashing green "81" northwest of Cotton Key. The only intermediate marker is red daybeacon "78A," positioned midway on the run.

The segment to Cotton Key is very shallow even though there is some evidence that Cotton Key Basin has been scoured-out by recent storms. The latest charts show an additional foot of depth along the designated ICW route, which was confirmed by our Cruising Editor. Caution through to flashing red "90" is suggested as minimum depths may be less than the charted 5 feet MLW in spots. Reduce speed, watch your course and monitor depth readings carefully.

Markers are spaced 2.1nm apart in Cotton Key Basin and course alignment can be a challenge. Glance behind occasionally to check for leeway traversing the shallow basin. Remember that wind-tide is a factor in Florida Bay and depths may be shallower than charted minimums. In a strong southeast breeze you may have to anchor and wait for a change in conditions.

At flashing green "81" adjust course to 235° magnetic and follow the straight-line defined by closely spaced red

GOIN' ASHORE

ISLAMORADA, FL

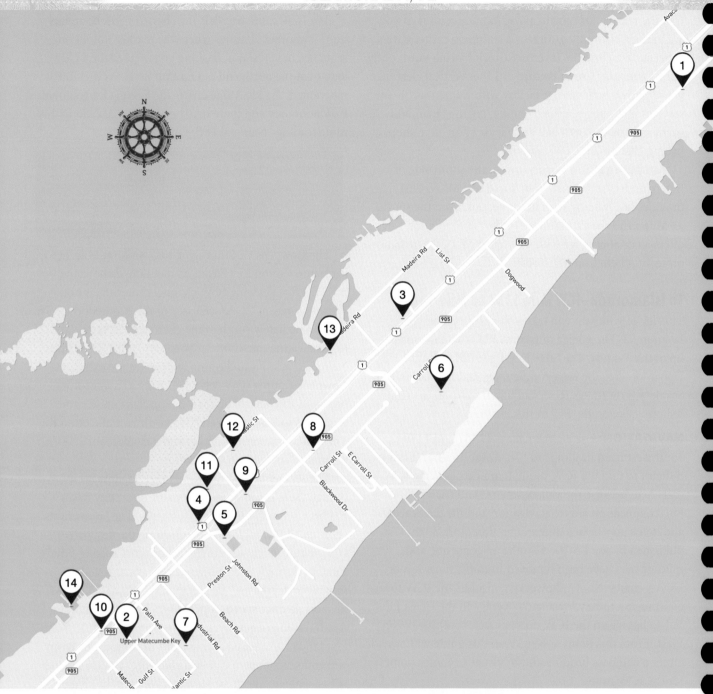

Islamorada (which translates as Purple Isle) is a flourishing village spread across five islands along the Overseas Highway. Arriving from the north are: Plantation Key, Windley Key, Upper Matecumbe Key and Lower Matecumbe Key. Teatable Key (or Tea Table Key) to some, lies south of the highway and can't quite decide on a name. Nearby Indian Key, Shell Key and Lignumvitae Key are only accessible by boat and are part of Florida's State Park System.

SERVICES

1. Islamorada Post Office
82801 Overseas Hwy. (305-664-4738)

2. Island Paws Veterinary Hospital
81581 Old Hwy. (305-664-0142)

3. Keys Medical Center
81990 Overseas Hwy. #101 (305-664-2488)

4. Monroe County Public Library
81830 Overseas Hwy.(305-664-4645)

5. 1935 Hurricane Monument
Memorializes the World War I veterans and civilians who perished in the 1935 hurricane (1831 Old Hwy.).

6. Keys History & Discovery Center
Located at Islander Resort with a model of Indian Key the way it looked in 1840, a "Legends of the Line" fishing exhibit and numerous historical photos of the area (82100 Overseas Hwy., 305-922-2237).

7. Redbone Gallery
Specializing in fine original angling and island art with portions of all original art sales benefiting The Cystic Fibrosis Foundation. Unique paintings, sculptures and jewelry (much related to saltwater fishing) are among the offerings at 200 Morada Way. Open daily except Sunday (305-664-2002).

SHOPPING

8. Hooked on Books
Small, independent bookseller with a collection of new and used books about the Keys, the Everglades and Florida, as well as an extensive fiction section at 81909 Overseas Hwy. (305-517-2602).

9. Trading Post Market and Deli
Small but well-stocked supermarket and deli open 24 hours at 81868 Overseas Hwy. (305-664-2571).

10. Worldwide Sportsman
Large destination owned by Bass Pro Shop with fishing tackle and some boating supplies (81576 Overseas Hwy., 305-664-4615). Be sure to check out the tarpon swimming in the pen alongside the dock.

11. Caribee Boat Sales & Marina
81500 Overseas Hwy. (305-664-3431)

MARINAS

12. Coral Bay Marina
601 Mastic St. (305-664-3111)

13. Islamorada Yacht Basin
96 Madeira Rd. (305-664-2692)

14. Worldwide Sportsman Marina
81576 Overseas Hwy. (305-664-3398)

Upper Keys, FL

PLANTATION KEY AREA		Largest Vessel	VHF	Total Slips	Approach/ Dockside Depth	Floating Docks	Gas/ Diesel	Repairs/ Haulout	Min/Max Amps	Pump-Out Station
1. Plantation Yacht Harbor Marina (WiFi) MM 1154.6	(305) 852-2381	80	16	85	5.0 / 5.0		GD		30 / 100	P
2. IslaMarina (WiFi) MM 1156.0	(305) 664-3636	60	16	12	5.0 / 6.0		GD		30 / 50	
3. Snake Creek Marina (WiFi)	(305) 396-7724	40	9	20	3.5 / 3.5	F	G	RH	30 / 50	P

(WiFi) Wireless Internet Access onSpot Dockside WiFi Facility
Visit www.waterwayguide.com for current rates, fuel prices, website addresses and other up-to-the-minute information. (Information in the table is provided by the facilities.)

Scan here for more details:

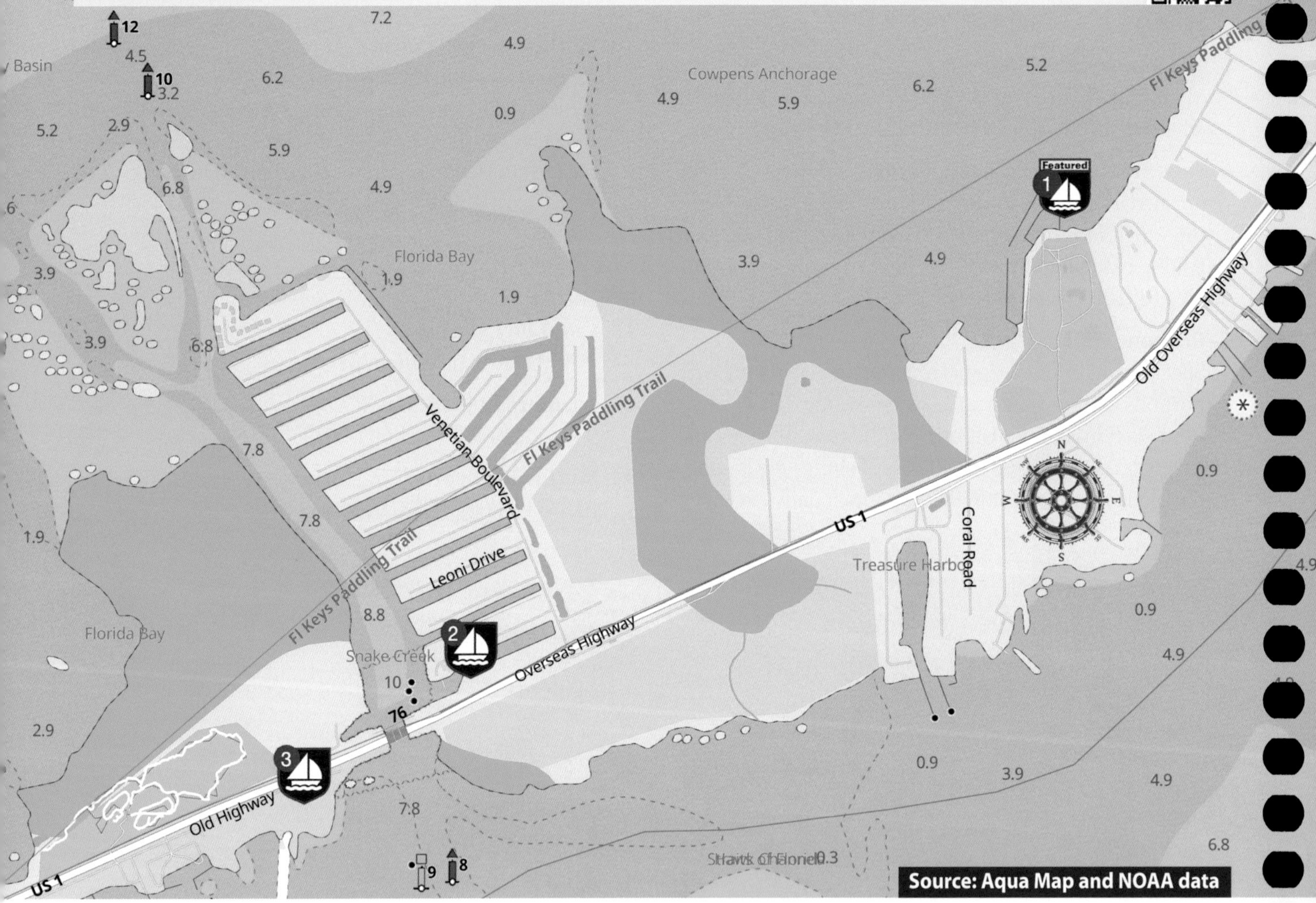

Source: Aqua Map and NOAA data

daybeacons "80" through "86" keeping them well to the north. While Barley Basin has deepened in recent years, measured depths in the channel were slightly less than charted (5.5 feet MLW). Also note there are still some extremely shallow shoals just north of the channel. The ICW continues to parallel the charted Everglades National Park PSSA boundary line along the National Park.

Enter the narrow Steamboat Channel at flashing green "87" and aim for flashing red "90" at the west end. Maintain center through the channel. Birds standing on the shallow shoals on each side will supervise your progress. Once in the Lignumvitae Basin the ICW channel deepens considerably westward and the shallowest depths are behind you. A course of 247° magnetic should keep you in the channel running parallel to the charted Everglades National Park PSSA boundary line.

South from red daybeacon "78A" a side channel leads to Snake Creek, which is a very shallow route to Hawk Channel on the ocean side. Local knowledge is advised before attempting passage. This poorly marked channel begins with flashing red "12" at its northern end. (Note that the aids on this channel are numbered from the ocean side.) The **Snake Creek Bridge** (27-foot closed vertical clearance) spans the creek with Plantation Key to the east and Windley Key to the west. The bridge opens on signal except from 8:00 a.m. to 6:00 p.m. when it need only open on the hour. South of the bridge the channel has shoaled on the ocean side and passage is not recommended.

Whale Harbor Channel separates Windley Key and Upper Matecumbe Key, both part of the village of Islamorada. The 10-foot fixed **Whale Harbor Channel Bridge** gives dinghy access to the ocean side. At Upper Matecumbe Key a second access channel off Barley Basin leads to the village of Islamorada. One nautical mile south of red daybeacon "84" the Shell Key Channel is flanked by green daybeacon "21" and red daybeacon "22." The channel has a charted controlling depth of 6 feet MLW but this area is prone to shoaling and it is best to check locally for more recent soundings. This well-marked channel connects with Teatable Key Channel, which offers a dinghy route to Islamorada's ocean-side.

At the south end of Upper Matecumbe Key, **Upper Matecumbe Key Bridge** (7-foot fixed vertical clearance) crosses a shallow (not navigable) channel. Just south is **Teatable Key Channel Bridge** (10-foot fixed vertical clearance) crossing Teatable Key Channel to the ocean side.

Dockage: On Plantation Key the well-regarded Plantation Yacht Harbor Marina offers protection

© Mapbox, © OpenStreetMap

Plantation Key

Plantation Yacht Harbor Marina

from all but hurricane-force winds. If westbound from flashing red "78" continue toward red daybeacon "78A" for 1 mile then alter course to about 150° magnetic and continue about 1 nm toward shore. You will spot a red and white horizontally striped lighthouse at the end of the marina's breakwater. Leaving it to starboard make a sharp starboard turn around the lighthouse and follow the marked channel. The village of Islamorada owns the 42-acre Founder's Park in which Plantation Yacht Harbor Marina is located. In addition to the slips and the regular cruiser amenities the park offers a swimming pool, a dog park, sandy beaches and walking trails.

IslaMarina is at the south end of Snake Creek with slips and a

well-stocked Ships Store. They also rent fishing gear and floatables. The facility is located north (bay side) of the Snake Creek Bridge (27-foot closed vertical clearance), which spans the creek with Plantation Key to the east and Windley Key to the west. The bridge opens on signal, except from 8:00 a.m. to 6:00 p.m., when it need only open on the hour. South of the bridge the channel has shoaled on the ocean side and passage is not recommended. Seek local knowledge before attempting. To the south of the bridge is Snake Creek Marina, which has slips to 40 feet.

From red daybeacon "84" steer a course of 150° magnetic cross through the middle the reasonably deep Barley Basin to Islamorada

Upper Keys, FL

MATECUMBE KEYS		Largest Vessel	VHF	Total Slips	Approach/ Dockside Depth	Floating Docks	Gas/ Diesel	Repairs/ Haulout	Min/Max Amps	Pump-Out Station
1. Islamorada Yacht Basin **WiFi** 2.2 mi. S of MM 1160.2	(305) 664-2692	45	16	15	4.5 / 4.5				30 / 50	P
2. Coral Bay Marina **WiFi** 2.2 mi. S of MM 1160.2	(305) 664-3111	62	16	35	5.0 / 6.0			RH	50	P
3. Caribee Boat Sales & Marina 2.2 mi. S of MM 1160.2	(305) 664-3431	32			5.5 / 5.5		G	RH	30	
4. World Wide Sportsman / Bayside Marina MM 1160.0	(305) 664-3398	40		43	3.0 / 5.0		GD		30 / 50	P

WiFi Wireless Internet Access   **onSpot** Dockside WiFi Facility
Visit www.waterwayguide.com for current rates, fuel prices, website addresses and other up-to-the-minute information.
(Information in the table is provided by the facilities.)

Scan here for more details:

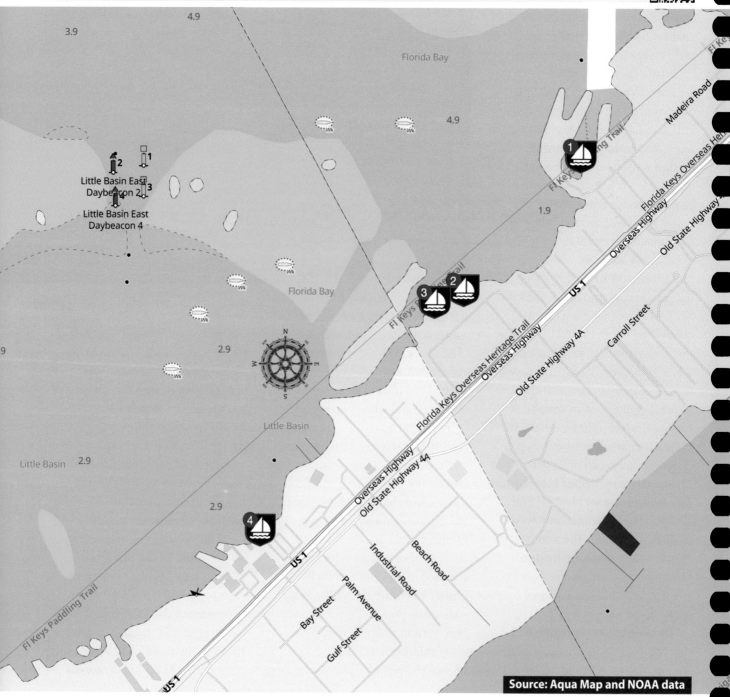

Yacht Basin (home to the well-regarded Lorelei Restaurant). This tight, well-protected yacht basin (4.5-foot MLW controlling depth) is beside the busy outdoor bar and restaurant. They only maintain three transient slips so call ahead.

To the south a set of white stakes mark the entrance to the full-service Coral Bay Marina, which has a full-time inboard mechanic and many subcontractors (including fiberglass repairs and bottom painting). Caribee Boat Sales & Marina is in the next basin to the south with boat sales and outboard repairs (no transient slips). Farther south in Little Basin is World Wide Sportsman/Bayside Marina located at the popular Bass Pro Shop sporting goods retailer. The marina can accommodate vessels to 40 feet.

Safe Harbor Islamorada on Yellow Shark Channel is primarily a dry storage facility. The marina also has a dive center, restaurant and service center. Located one channel to the south is Safe Harbor Angler House, which has charter fishing, floating villas and resort-style amenities. It is private but maintains two transient slips.

Anchorage: The charted Cowpens anchorage at Mile 1155 has 5- to 6-foot MLW depths with good holding in grass and mud. This anchorage is open and exposed to the west. From here you can dinghy to Marker 88 for lunch and dinner. You can also anchor in 5 to 6 feet MLW south of Cotton Key at Mile 1158 in Barley Basin. This provides protection from the east through southeast with excellent holding in at least 5-foot MLW depths.

A local anchorage area is located offshore from Lorelei Restaurant. Dinghies from anchored boats are welcome at the boat docks at World Wide Sportsman/Bayside Marina and Morada Bay Beach Café. The Lorelei dinghy dock is reserved for diners (and this is enforced). Coral Bay Marina does not have a dinghy dock. You can ask permission to tie up in front of the office for an hour or two when it's open.

Lignumvitae Basin to Channel Five–ICW Mile 1162 to Mile 1170

Lying between Steamboat Channel (Mile 1161) on the east and Bowlegys Cut (Mile 1165) to the west, the Lignumvitae Basin offers improved controlling

Upper Keys, FL

MATECUMBE KEYS		Largest Vessel	VHF	Total Slips	Approach/ Dockside Depth	Floating Docks	Gas/ Diesel	Repairs/ Haulout	Min/Max Amps	Pump-Out Station
1. Safe Harbor Islamorada **WiFi**	(305) 664-8884	50		14	5.0 / 4.5		GD	RH	30 / 50	
2. Safe Harbor Angler House	(305) 664-5247	45			8.0 / 4.0		GD		30 / 50	

WiFi Wireless Internet Access **onSpot** Dockside WiFi Facility
Visit www.waterwayguide.com for current rates, fuel prices, website addresses and other up-to-the-minute information. (Information in the table is provided by the facilities.)

Scan here for more details:

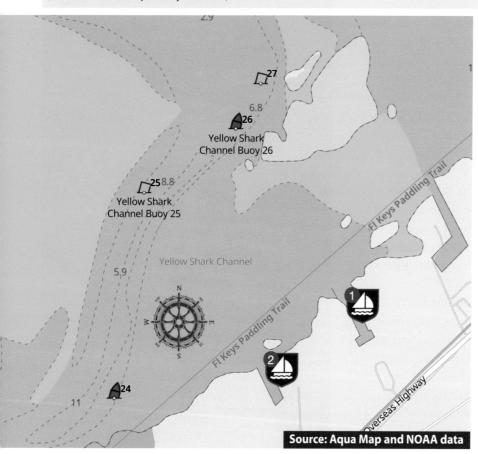

Source: Aqua Map and NOAA data

depths (7 foot MLW) reducing keel scuffs for sailors and saving props for power boaters. At just 18 feet above sea level Lignumvitae Key has the highest elevation of the Keys and is named for one of the hardest woods in the world.

Lignumvitae State Botanical State Park is a worthwhile visit. Park hours are Thursday through Monday, 8:00 a.m. to 5:00 p.m. and a ranger collects the $2.50 entry fee. The park has mooring balls and a dinghy dock but a strict "no pets" policy. The park suggests visitors bring shoes and mosquito repellent.

Three shallow channels weave through the islands that border the basin's southeast flank and connect Lignumvitae Basin to the ocean side. These channels are strictly dinghy territory as they are blocked by entry shoals and low clearance fixed bridges.

NAVIGATION: Use NOAA Charts 11451 and 11464. Once clear of the southwest end of Steamboat Channel (marked by flashing red "90") adjust to a course of 247° magnetic, once again paralleling the charted Everglades National Park PSSA boundary line. You should see some small signs marking the park's boundary with the basin on the north as you cross. Continue on this course for the 3 nm to the north end of Bowlegys Cut, which is marked by flashing green "93." Line up for the cut well before entry and stay center channel through to flashing red "98" at the south end. This is the last marker before the numbering sequence resets.

Cruisers have a choice of two viable routes at this point. To continue west through Florida Bay on the Inside Route (ICW) to Marathon steer a course of 247° magnetic for 6nm from flashing red "98" (at the south entrance to Bowlegys Cut) to flashing green "1" marking the north tip of Old Dan Bank (Mile 1173.8).

Alternately, turn southwest to a course of 214° magnetic for the 4-nm run to the **Channel Five Bridge** (fixed 65-foot vertical clearance) and then on to Hawk Channel ocean side for the Outside Route.

Of the three well-marked channels directly from Lignumvitae Basin to the ocean side only **Indian Key Channel Bridge** offers significant fixed vertical clearance (27 feet). The Teatable Key Channel Bridge at the end of the Race/Shell Key Channel has just 10 feet fixed vertical clearance, as does the **Lignumvitae Channel Bridge** to the south.

The shallow turtle grass flats in this area are clearly marked. The flats are all closed to boats with internal combustion engines (gas or diesel, inboard or outboard). State law enforcement officers police the area and violators (particularly those who have damaged the grass with their props) are subject to stiff fines.

Dockage/Moorings:

Lignumvitae Key Dock & Moorings can accommodate medium-size cruising craft (4-foot MLW depths), although no docking is permitted after 5:00 p.m. and pets are not allowed ashore. They also have complementary moorings off the northwest side of the island for stays of up to one week.

Anchorage: Matecumbe Bight at Mile 1167 in 6 to 7 feet MLW. This anchorage is large and wide and provides excellent holding and protection (unless the wind is out of the north).

Long Key to Moser Channel– ICW Mile 1168 to Mile 1196

This section covers the stretch between the Florida Key's two major crossovers: Channel Five and the Moser Channel. There are some shallow spots along this route. Most are shoals associated with one of the numerous sinewy banks that extend northward from the Keys. Shoals bordering the channel are marked and navigation is straightforward here. Remember to keep red markers to the right. Mariners straying from the designated route should exercise caution.

NAVIGATION: Use NOAA Charts 11449, 11451 and 11453. The ICW continues west flashing green "1" off Old Dan Bank on a course of 247° magnetic for about 4.8 nm with depths between 6 and 9 feet MLW to reach flashing green "5" off the Channel Key Banks, running north of Duck Key. These banks are extremely shallow where they cross the ICW. Deeper-draft boats should stay on the ICW route over this stretch. There are rocky shoals charted at 5 feet MLW just north of the course line about 1 mile west of flashing green "1" (at Mile 1174). These are unmarked as they are within the range of controlling depths, but they do pose a threat.

A more dangerous shoal at Mile 1178 is marked by red daybeacon "4." The course line passes well south here and this is a good place to verify your alignment. This shoal is the first in a series that make up the Channel Key Bank. It is essential that you follow the narrow Channel Key Pass through the banks. Be sure to split green daybeacon "7" and red daybeacon "8" to stay in the narrow dredged cut at Mile 1178.8. Favor red daybeacon "8" as you thread through this pass.

The **Long Key Viaduct Bridge** with 23-foot fixed vertical clearance lies southeast of the ICW at Mile 1176. Boats with lower airdraft can take this channel to reach Duck Key on the ocean side. Local knowledge is needed as the charted (and uncharted) shoals in this channel are not marked. Given the close proximity to the Channel Five Bridge, this channel poses unnecessary risks.

Once clear of the Channel Key Bank, the ICW follows a heading of 257° magnetic for a 6.5 nm straight-line run from red daybeacon "8" to flashing green "13." On this route you must pass north of flashing green "11" marking the north end of the Grassy Key Bank (Mile 1182), which projects northerly from long, low Grassy Key. Be aware that Grassy Key Bank has water depths below 1 foot MLW to the south of this marker. Also note some rocky shoals with 5 feet MLW in a patch north of Bamboo Key. These pose no threat if you are on the designated ICW course.

Some cruisers seeking bay-side services in Marathon often leave the designated ICW either at flashing green "11" or "13," passing north of Bamboo Key then skirting Stirrup Key for the first route, or south of the Rachel Bank towards Rachel Key for the second. There is sufficient depths for most cruising vessels in these waters but plan compass course lines that avoid the rocky shoals in this area. For those continuing to Moser Channel under the Seven Mile Bridge, the ICW route is shorter and the shoals are better marked.

Cruisers heading on to Moser Channel change course back to 247° magnetic at flashing green "13" for the 5.9-nm run to flashing red "20" marking Bethel Bank. This segment is well marked. Daybeacons "14" and "18" assist with course alignment and mark threats. Pass close to these markers to avoid the hazards to the south. In particular, when passing Rachel Bank we advise rounding north of the bank's charted shallows and a charted obstruction as a precaution.

Pass through flashing red "20" and green daybeacon "19" keeping south of Bethel Bank. If continuing to Key West on the inside route, adjust course to 259° magnetic at

Middle Keys, FL

MARATHON AREA		Largest Vessel	VHF	Total Slips	Approach/ Dockside Depth	Floating Docks	Gas/ Diesel	Repairs/ Haulout	Min/Max Amps	Pump-Out Station
1. Coconut Cay Resort and Marina (WiFi)	(305) 289-7672				5.0 /					
2. Blackfin Resort and Marina (WiFi)	(305) 743-2393	40		27	8.0 / 10.0				30	P
3. Banana Bay Resort & Marina (WiFi)	(305) 743-3500	56	16	34	5.0 / 7.0				30 / 50	P
4. Marlin Bay Resort & Marina (WiFi) (onSpot)	(305) 731-2207	80	16	99	7.0 / 15.0				30 / 100	P
5. Keys Fisheries Marina	(305) 743-4985				/		GD			

(WiFi) Wireless Internet Access　**(onSpot)** Dockside WiFi Facility

Visit www.waterwayguide.com for current rates, fuel prices, website addresses and other up-to-the-minute information. (Information in the table is provided by the facilities.)

Scan here for more details:

Source: Aqua Map and NOAA data

flashing red "20" for the 5.5 nm run to red daybeacon "26" at ICW Mile 1200. This route passes close to red daybeacons "22" and "24."

Dockage: The 2-mile stretch west from Rachel Key (Mile 1191) is packed with dockage options. Coconut Cay Resort and Marina may have space for you in a canal alongside the hotel. This resort dates from the 1950s and has an "old Florida" feel. Amenities include loaner bikes, paddle boats, kayaks and fishing rods plus an outdoor pool.

Blackfin Resort and Marina has 27 slips (20 transient) and good approach depths (8 feet MLW) and has a nice mix of liveaboards, seasonal slip holders, transients and fishing boats. Nearby Banana Bay Resort & Marina is a small marina (34 slips) with a great seasonal community of boaters. Restaurants, grocery stores and a Home Depot are all within easy walking distance. Nearby Keys Boat Works is a repair facility (no transient slips).

Marlin Bay Resort & Marina has a combination of wet and dry slips and boutique-style resort amenities including a clubhouse lounge and game room, fitness center, heated pool and hot tub, a pool bar and concierge service. This is a great place for a crew change or a visit with friends who can stay at the on-site accommodations (advance reservations required).

Keys Fisheries Marina accommodates vessels up to 55 feet in length and the restaurant provides fresh seafood on the days you simply don't feel like cooking your own catch.

Anchorage: At the start of this stretch there are some excellent anchorages near Fiesta Key (Mile 1172). You can find good protection in Jewfish Hole west of Fiesta Key (7- to 8-foot MLW depths) or in 6 feet MLW between Fiesta Key and Jewfish Bush Banks, which is protected by a causeway. Tiny Rachel Key at Mile 1191 offers some protection. Shoal-draft boats can snug in close to shore. Pick the side with best wind protection. There is good holding in sand and 6 to 7 feet MLW. The area just east of Pretty Joe Rock offers the best protection. Holding is only fair in sand and grass from here west along the bay side of the Vaca Key shoreline.

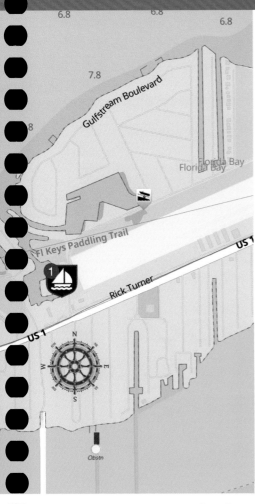

Boot Key Harbor (Marathon)

While many marine services and anchorages are located in the Marathon area, its principal harbor is Boot Key Harbor, which is entered south of the Seven Mile Bridge either from Moser or Hawk Channels. Marathon's bay-side facilities offer some great options but most visitors to Marathon choose to stay in the city's massive and well-protected Boot Key Harbor. (See "Goin' Ashore: Marathon, FL" in this chapter for more.)

Cruisers should note that the current is swift in both the Moser Channel and Knight Key Channel. If under sail this can have an extreme effect on your set. Also shoal areas are expanding along north-south lines with the current. Watch your

depth and give charted shoal areas a wide berth. Stay 1 mile south of the Seven Mile Bridge while passing the Pidgeon Key Banks then proceed to red daybeacon "2" in Moser Channel before turning for Boot Key.

NAVIGATION: Use NOAA Chart 11453. From the north shore of Marathon you can round Knight Key and head south under the **Knight Key Channel Bridge** (19-foot fixed vertical clearance) to flashing green "1" marking the entrance to Boot Key Channel. This route is impassible for most cruising-size boats and is not recommended. The route is poorly marked, currents run swiftly on either tide and the monofilament lines of multitudes of anglers dangle from the old bridge. Controlling depth is 8 feet MLW but a shallow shoal is evident before the bridge at low tide. Be careful. If you do choose this route, once through to the ocean side keep well clear of the shoal extending west from Knight Key.

The preferred entry route from the ICW is via the Moser Channel to the west, the primary passageway and the last major crossover between the inside (ICW) route and the outside (Hawk Channel) route. Simply maintain your designated course line until the gap in the **Old Seven Mile (Moser Channel) Bridge** is on your beam. Then turn 90° towards the center of this gap. This approach stays well clear of the charted shoals that flank Moser Channel but monitor your depth as shoaling in the channel is continual.

As you approach Seven Mile Bridge, adjust your course to take a straight-line course through the three sets of bridge pilings. Note that currents can be strong and boat traffic is often heavy in the passage. Check VHF Channel 16

for a Sécurité if large craft are present.

Once under the bridges and south of Moser Channel marker red daybeacon "2" turn east and head towards the distant red daybeacon "2" off Boot Key (2.5 nm east). This is a Boot Key Harbor entrance channel marker. If coming from the Hawk Channel, keep north of flashing green "49," which marks East Washerwoman Shoal. This is a dangerous shoal with only 2 feet MLW so keep well to the north.

To enter Boot Key Harbor use the Boot Key Channel, which starts between Knight and Boot Keys. Enter the Boot Key Channel centered between flashing green "1" and red daybeacon "2" and favor the green daybeacons in to green daybeacon "9." The shoaling to the south is awash at low tide but depth along this route should maintain 9 feet MLW. Keep a close watch. If you see shallower depths, you've turned too soon and must head further west around the shoals off Boot Key and then turn north. The channel narrows past green daybeacon "9" and depths increase to 10 feet MLW or more.

Continue in favoring the green side close to the mangroves along the channel's north edge until centering again after the turn towards the bridge opening. Note the draw of the old Boot Key Harbor Bridge and nearby charted overhead cables have been removed. The bridge opening is narrow. Be aware that incoming traffic has a bad visibility angle and you may not see outgoing boats on the other side (and vice versa); exercise caution.

None of the channel markers in Boot Key Harbor are lighted and while ambient light is usually sufficient, night entry is

GOIN' ASHORE
MARATHON, FL

Marathon's waterfront boasts fine restaurants, beautiful beaches and access to world-class diving and snorkeling. It is a cruiser's dream, with extraordinary marine services, comprehensive provisioning opportunities, fine dining and a wonderful community feel. The marina loans out bikes to visitors who can show evidence of a working lock, and that makes provisioning a breeze. You'll meet dozens who came here to visit and simply could not leave.

SERVICES

1. Fishermen's Community Hospital
3301 Overseas Hwy. (305-743-5533)

2. Marathon Post Office
82801 Overseas Hwy. (305-664-4738)

3. Marathon Veterinary Hospital
5001 Overseas Hwy. (305-743-7099)

4. Monroe County Public Library
81830 Overseas Hwy. (305-664-4645)

ATTRACTIONS

5. Crane Point Museum & Nature Center
Includes a natural history museum, marine touch tanks and a bird rescue center at 5550 Overseas Hwy. (305-743-3900). Several nature trails wind through the tropical palm forest.

6. Turtle Hospital
Located in a 1940s-era motel at 2396 Overseas Hwy. and committed to the rehabilitation of endangered sea turtles. Offers 90-minute guided tours and a chance to feed the permanent residents. Call for hours and fees (305-743-2552).

11. West Marine

Boating supplies located to the west of the dinghy dock at 2109 Overseas Hwy. (305-289-1009).

MARINAS

12. Burdines Waterfront Marina

1200 Oceanview Ave. (305-743-5317)

13. Banana Bay Resort & Marina

4590 Overseas Hwy. (305-743-3500)

14. Blackfin Resort and Marina

4650 Overseas Hwy. (305-743-2393)

15. Boot Key Harbor City Marina

800 35th St. (305-289-8877)

16. Capt. Pip's Marina & Hideaway

1480 Overseas Hwy. (305-743-4403)

17. Faro Blanco Resort & Yacht Club

1996 Overseas Hwy. (305-743-1234)

18. Marlin Bay Resort & Marina

3800 Gulfview Ave. (305-731-2207)

19. Marathon Marina

1021 11th St. Ocean (305-743-6575)

20. Marathon Boat Yard

2059 Overseas Hwy. (305-735-4594)

21. Pancho's Marina & Fuel Dock

1280 Oceanview Ave. (305-743-2281)

22. Skipjack Resort & Marina

19 Sombrero Blvd. (305-600-4281)

23. Sombrero Marina Dockside

35 Sombrero Blvd. (305-743-5663)

SHOPPING

7. Marathon Liquors & Deli

Local favorite with a huge selection of beers, wines and liquors and perhaps the best gourmet deli selection in the Keys at 5101 Overseas Hwy. (305-743-6350).

8. Publix

Grocery store for provisioning (groceries, deli and bakery items) at 5407 Overseas Hwy. (305-289-2920).

9. Seamark Electronics

Full range of marine electronics at 2994 Overseas Hwy. (305-743-6633).

10. Walgreens

Drugstore chain with health and beauty aids and prescriptions at 5271 Overseas Hwy. (305-359-3634).

Boot Key Harbor City Marina

not recommended for first-timers. Should you arrive after dark, an alternate anchorage is outside off the west end of Boot Key.

> ⚠️
>
> There is severe shoaling between red daybeacons "18" and "20" in Boot Key Harbor. The controlling depth has been reduced to 5 feet MLW and there are a few spots in the channel where depths are between 4.5 and 5.0 feet MLW.

The deepest water is on the green side of the channel about 50 feet to the south of the white shallow area markers that delineate grass flats. Vessels drawing more than 5 feet should pay close attention to the tides in this part of the channel.

> Note that Sister Creek, slicing between Vaca and Boot Keys, has shoaled at its south entrance and is no longer a viable entry into Boot Key Harbor. Local sportfishing boats that still use the shallow entry report 3-feet MLW depths in ideal conditions but use of this entrance to Boot Key Harbor is not recommended.

Dockage/Moorings: Boot Key Harbor, perhaps the best and most heavily populated harbor in the Keys, has an abundance of marine facilities along the channel and in the harbor beyond. Don't be surprised if a small boat cuts across traffic to get to the fuel docks along the channel's narrow section. Be sure to obey the strictly enforced "SLOW-SPEED/MINIMUM-WAKE ZONE" in effect for the entire harbor.

Boot Key Harbor is a busy place and first-time visitors are always surprised by the number of boats packed

Marathon Marina

Faro Blanco Resort & Yacht Club

Marathon Boat Yard Marine Center

Boot Key Harbor City Marina

Boot Key Harbor

Skipjack Resort Suites and Marina

Boot Key Harbor City Marina is a modest community of liveaboards, ranging from year-round residents to transient loopers to cruisers from all over the world. With the City Park located just next door, you can enjoy bocce ball, tennis, basketball, or one of the several events hosted there throughout the year...and walk back to your boat when you're done. We hope to welcome you soon!

Boot Key Harbor City Marina
(305) 289-8877

VHF Channel 16 for Dock or Mooring Assignment
www.cityofmarathonmarina.com

Side Trip: Sombrero Key Reef

If you are waiting around for a mooring in Boot Key Harbor, a trip to Sombrero Key is a good way to bide your time. Sombrero Key Reef is one of the Florida Key's prime snorkeling sites. Reef visitors will see all manner of reef fish, stingrays, lots of barracudas and the occasional nurse shark. Barracuda are particularly plentiful under the 142-foot Sombrero Key Lighthouse (circa 1858). Clearest conditions are found the day after calm weather. But get there early, as this popular snorkeling site can get busy.

The route to the reef is a straight line 4 miles due south from flashing green "1" in the Boot Key Channel entrance. Just aim for the big tower. Pick up a mooring ball to the south of the reef (offshore side). Mooring balls are plentiful, but anchoring is allowed only if all mooring balls are in use. You must anchor well clear of the reef, which can make a snorkeling visit difficult. It's better to wait for a mooring ball to free up.

Middle Keys, FL

MARATHON AREA		Largest Vessel	VHF	Total Slips	Approach/ Dockside Depth	Floating Docks	Gas/ Diesel	Repairs/ Haulout	Min/Max Amps	Pump-Out Station
1. Faro Blanco Resort & Yacht Club (WiFi)	(305) 743-9018	130	16	74	7.0 / 5.0		GD		30 / 100	P
2. Marathon Boat Yard (WiFi) MM 1193.0	(305) 735-4594	75		20	8.0 / 20.0	F		RH	30 / 50	
3. Burdines Waterfront Marina MM 1193.0	(305) 743-5317	120	16	21	10.0 / 7.0	F	GD		30 / 50	P
4. Pancho's Marina and Fuel Dock (WiFi) MM 1193.0	(305) 743-2281	90	16	20	8.0 / 6.5		GD		30 / 50	P
5. Safe Harbor Marathon Marina & Boatyard (WiFi) MM 1193.0	(305) 743-6575	125	16	123	9.0 / 11.0	F	GD	RH	30 / 100	P

(WiFi) Wireless Internet Access onSpot Dockside WiFi Facility
Visit www.waterwayguide.com for current rates, fuel prices, website addresses and other up-to-the-minute information.
(Information in the table is provided by the facilities.)

Scan here for more details:

Source: Aqua Map and NOAA data

inside. Before entering you should have arranged dockage or a mooring in advance. If you intend to anchor be warned you must be 100 feet outside a mooring field for your entire swing circle. Also be aware of several shoals in the harbor as well as many submerged and partially submerged boats. Caution should be exercised.

The well-regarded Faro Blanco Resort & Yacht Club is located on the bay side with state-of-the-art facilities and world-class amenities including 24-hour security, marine

concierge services, a marine store, pool and fitness center, and first-class accommodations on site. This is a fine location for a crew change or visit with friends and family.

Several other facilities are located on the north shore of Boot Key Channel. The first is located just before the channel narrows at green daybeacon "9." Marathon Marina is a premier marina with deep-water slips to 130 feet and a convenient fuel dock. This well-maintained marina and boat yard offers either DIY or full

service. Amenities include a fitness center, a saltwater pool, laundry facilities and a restaurant and tiki bar.

Just in past the mangrove "hedge" is Pancho's Marina and Fuel Dock. To the east is Burdines Waterfront Marina offering slips on floating docks and a large store selling snacks and professional fishing tackle. The Chiki Tiki Bar and Grille (305-743-9204) upstairs has a great menu and is the place to watch the continuous channel traffic below.

Just inside the remnants of the Boot Key Bridge is the long entry channel to the very well-regarded Marathon Boat Yard. The 20-slip facility handles every aspect of boat repairs and power for vessels to 75 feet and are known for quality workmanship. They maintain just five transient slips; call ahead. A large West Marine is next door.

The friendly municipal Boot Key Harbor City Marina can be hard to locate. The office is next to a thatched roof hut at the end of the channel between the two main mooring fields (or just watch where the dinghies are

Middle Keys, FL

MARATHON AREA		Largest Vessel	VHF	Total Slips	Approach/ Dockside Depth	Floating Docks	Gas/ Diesel	Repairs/ Haulout	Min/Max Amps	Pump-Out Station
1. Yacht Haven Marina	(305) 393-5073	120		42	/				30 / 100	P
2. Skipjack Resort Suites and Marina **WiFi** MM 1192.0	(305) 289-7662	65	16	54	10.0 / 15.0				30 / 50	P
3. Sombrero Marina Dockside **WiFi** MM 1193.0	(305) 743-5663	85		57	7.0 / 9.0				20 / 50	P
4. Boot Key Harbor City Marina **WiFi** MM 1193.0	(305) 289-8877	60	16	12	10.0 / 20.0	F			30 / 50	P

WiFi Wireless Internet Access **onSpot** Dockside WiFi Facility
Visit www.waterwayguide.com for current rates, fuel prices, website addresses and other up-to-the-minute information.
(Information in the table is provided by the facilities.)

Scan here for more details:

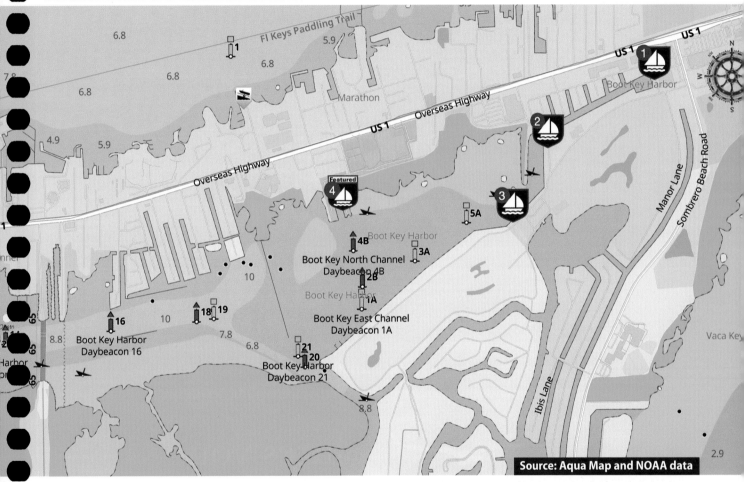

Source: Aqua Map and NOAA data

heading). The facility only has room for 12 boats dockside but manages 211 moorings for boats up to 45 feet and 15 more for boats to 60 feet. They do not take reservations but keep a waiting list when they're full. You must appear in person to get on the list.

A large dinghy dock is adjacent to their shoreside facilities. The mooring rates include showers, a weekly pump-out service and free loaner bikes (if you bring a secure lock). Cruiser's also take advantage of the beautiful park and sports complex next the city marina. Numerous provisioning options are nearby.

Boot Key Harbor City Marina is the hub of a thriving cruiser community with events and get-togethers organized weekly. To check out what's going on tune into the "Cruiser's Net " on VHF Channel 68 every morning at 9:00 a.m. or just hang out in the cruiser's lounge by the marina office.

Two additional marinas are located at the east end of the harbor. On the south shore where the harbor starts to narrow is Sombrero Marina Dockside. This marina has transient dockage and basic amenities plus there is a restaurant located on site. A golf course across the

street is open to the public. Further east up the narrows on the north shore is 54-slip Skipjack Resort Suites and Marina. Cruisers give this facility high marks for the wind protection and free weekly pump-out service. The facility can accommodate vessels to 60 feet. At the end of the protected canal adjacent to Skipjack Resort is the well-protected Yacht Haven Marina with slips to 120 feet. This facility is within walking distance to many area services and amenities.

Anchorage: If you arrive late, you can drop the hook outside in the lee of Boot Key's west shore in 8 to 9 feet MLW. Shoal-draft vessels can work closer in to the charted 5-foot MLW area. This anchorage is comfortable in northeast through southeast winds but you will want to move around to the north side of Vaca Key for strong winds out of the south or southwest. You will find excellent holding in sand and grass but the downside is that there are near constant wakes from powerboats taking a shortcut to nearby Sombrero Key.

Finding a place to anchor inside Boot Key Inner Harbor can be a challenge from Thanksgiving through March. Most cruisers anchor east of the Boot Key Harbor Bridge inside red day beacons "16" through "18" but you will have lots of company here; make sure you have swing room. Remember that by Florida law you must stay 100 feet from a designated mooring field. Also watch for shoal areas in the harbor.

Note that we do not recommend anchoring in Sister's Creek for various reasons including constant small boat traffic, shoaling and the array of 100,000-watt radio antennas that can interfere with your electronics.

> At the south end of Sister's Creek is Sombrero Park, which is accessible by dinghy via Sister Creek. This can be a lovely place to cool off on a hot day.

Boot Key Harbor City Marina will provide pump-out services for a nominal fee either at their dock or at your anchored boat in Boot Key Harbor. You can tie up at the marina (for a fee) for full access to their facilities. (Hint: If you are staying for awhile ask about the weekly rates, which are lower.)

Lower Keys, FL

BAHIA HONDA KEY AREA		Largest Vessel	VHF	Total Slips	Approach/ Dockside Depth	Floating Docks	Gas/ Diesel	Repairs/ Haulout	Min/Max Amps	Pump-Out Station
1. Bahia Honda State Park & Marina **WiFi** MM 1205.0	(305) 872-3210	50	16	19	3.5 / 4.5				30	P

WiFi Wireless Internet Access **onSpot** Dockside WiFi Facility
Visit www.waterwayguide.com for current rates, fuel prices, website addresses and other up-to-the-minute information.
(Information in the table is provided by the facilities.)

Scan here for more details:

Source: Aqua Map and NOAA data

Bahia Honda State Park

Side Trip: Bahia Honda

Two of the nicest beaches in the Keys are located at Bahia Honda State Park. The palm-rimmed Calusa Beach near the concession stand is sheltered and roped off for swimming and snorkeling. The park concession stand sells snacks and ice. There are also three nature trails.

NAVIGATION: Use NOAA Charts 11445, 11448, 1451 and 11453. The channel into Florida Bay is deep and wide from the gap in Old Seven Mile Bridge about 1 mile west of Pigeon Key. Once clear of the gap set a course of 310° magnetic for the 1.2-nm run to red daybeacon "24." After 0.7 nm adjust course to 253° magnetic on a course to take flashing green "25" to port. Continue on this heading to Bahia Honda Key keeping well off the shallows surrounding the north shore of the island. Once the Bahia Honda Light (flashing white) is on the beam adjust to a course of 235° magnetic towards the high-span of the **Bahia Honda Bridges**.

Note: For those that can clear the bridges Hawk Channel is 1.2 nm due south of the gap in the Old Seven Mile Bridge. Watch for unmarked shoals and the small island just southeast of the Old Bridge.

To rejoin the ICW route from the Bahia Honda Bridges via Big Spanish Channel on to Florida Bay head due north for flashing red "32," keeping west of the shoal extending south from Little Pine Key. Here the course picks up the route described below. Remember you are returning to Florida Bay so keep red navigational aids to starboard.

Dockage: The slowly disintegrating Old Bahia Honda Bridge (Mile 1207) located at Bahia Honda Key's western end is a national historic monument. The Old Bridge has a span removed so that sailboats can pass through into the cove between the Old Bridge and the newer Bahia Honda Bridges (20-foot fixed vertical clearance). Transients can find dockage in the well-protected boat basin at Bahia Honda State Park & Marina. Expect 8 to 10 feet MLW dockside but the entrance is shallow (as low as 3.5 feet MLW) with a tidal range of a little over 1 foot. Boat slips include fill use of the park facilities (bathhouse, trash disposal and pump-out service). This is a popular spot so call ahead.

Anchorage: The cove between the old and new bridges west of Bahia Honda State Park & Marina is a popular anchorage. Be warned that the holding is only fair in sand and grass and the currents are strong. (If you choose to swim off the boat, hang a grab-line off the back just in case you get caught in the current.) It is wise to check your position after a turning tide to avoid a closer look at one bridge or the other. This is a good place to let out extra scope. Once securely anchored you can go ashore to the park (short-term dinghy tie-ups allowed). If going ashore, bring shoes to hike the nature trails.

Moser Channel to Northwest Channel– Mile 1196 to Mile 1242

Once past the Seven Mile Bridge there are no air-draft restrictions all the way to Key West. However, the controlling depth for the Big Spanish Channel on this route has been reduced to 4.5 feet MLW in recent years.

NAVIGATION: Best shown on NOAA Charts 11448 and 11442; but also use NOAA Charts 11445, 11451 and 11453. Keep all red markers to starboard on this route. Starting at the gap in the Old Seven Mile Bridge set a course of 310° magnetic for the 1.2-nm run to red daybeacon "24" where you rejoin the ICW along its run from Bethel Bank. From red daybeacon "24" adjust course to 259° magnetic for the 2 nm to red daybeacon "26." Keeping south of red daybeacon "26" adjust course to 271° magnetic and continue for 4 nm to the southern entrance to Big Spanish Channel. On this leg pass just north of flashing green "27" then split green daybeacon "29" and red daybeacon "30." Keep well south of flashing red "32," which marks dangerous shoals (2 feet MLW) to the north.

The well-marked Big Spanish Channel stretches to the northwest from Mile 1205. Initially the channel is wide and deep (controlling depth 7 feet MLW). Once clear of flashing red "32" proceed 2 nm on a course of 303° magnetic towards red daybeacon "34" then adjust to 316° magnetic towards red daybeacon "36." Once clear of red daybeacon "36" proceed for 2 nm at a course of 326° magnetic towards red daybeacon "38" near Mile 1210. From here the course is 297° magnetic for the 1 nm to red daybeacon "40."

Beyond red daybeacon "40" the Big Spanish Channel narrows and shallows dramatically. Set a course of 305° magnetic for the 1.7 nm from red daybeacon "40" to red daybeacon "42." Continue with caution on this heading for the 0.8 nm onwards to green daybeacon "43." Over this segment expect depths as low as 4.5 feet MLW and shoals just off the designated route as shallow as 3 feet MLW. It is advised that you slow down through this stretch and closely monitor depths. The tidal range is up to 4 feet here; if depths appear too shallow, wait for a high tide.

Passing green daybeacon "43" the winding but well-marked channel narrows further but the controlling depth returns to 7 feet MLW. Continue to follow the closely packed markers as placed through this tight section to green daybeacon "53." (Markers are occasionally repositioned here to reflect the changing alignment of the natural channel.) Once past green daybeacon "53" the channel begins to widen again through to flashing green "57." The course is roughly 340° magnetic for this 2.3-nm leg but you should follow the deep, natural channel into the open Florida Bay.

From here to the Northwest Channel leading into Key West the designated ICW route traverses the open expanse of Florida Bay, paralleling the Lower Keys to the south. You can expect some chop in any winds lacking a southerly component. The course is 251° magnetic for this 28-nm run but it's easier to use the near straight-line alignment of the Keys as a reference. Initially the controlling depth is 8 feet MLW but deepens to 20 MLW beyond Mile 1222.

Note beyond Cudjoe Channel the route picks up on NOAA Chart 11442, which covers to flashing green bell buoy "1" marking the Northwest Channel to Key West (N 24° 38.880'/W 081° 53.960'). There is no reason to stray from your course as you must reach bell buoy "1" before turning south towards Key West. The semi-submerged east jetty and the adjacent shallow flats block any attempts to turn early. The Calda Channel and various other shortcuts are not recommended for use by cruising vessels.

Anchorage: About 8 miles west from green daybeacon "57" the Cudjoe Channel has a controlling depth of 7 feet MLW. This branching channel cuts back to the southeast through the flats of the National Key Deer Refuge. There are some nice options for anchoring here. One favorite is southwest of Crane Key; another is closer to Raccoon Key. Choose a spot that gives the best protection. Despite being open this can be a beautiful, quiet anchorage in the right conditions. You are off the beaten track but close enough to it to get underway again with no trouble. The fishing in the deeper channel is great.

Another popular spot is Tarpon Belly Keys. Anchor right up next to the western side of the island in charted tongue of water with at least 8-foot MLW depths.

There is good holding and fair protection. There aren't many other anchorage options along the route onward to Key West. Most channels are very shallow (4 to 4.5 feet MLW) and tucked between low-lying mangrove islands.

Northwest Channel to Key West– ICW Mile 1242 to Mile 1245

NAVIGATION: Use NOAA Chart 11441. Note that shoaling on the Frankfort Bank leaves no viable route directly leading from the Northwest Channel into Man of War Harbor. The recommended route is to follow the Northwest Channel south of Tank Island and round into the Main Ship Channel to enter Key West Harbor. The channel provides the only viable entry from the north that leads to Key West Harbor. Do not attempt any shortcuts as there are many submerged hazards here. A shorter but unmarked route may be possible via the shallow channel between Tank and Wisteria Islands but this route is not recommended.

The entry to the Northwest Channel can be quite sloppy in certain conditions. Avoid entry in strong winds in the northwest quadrant if possible. Many channel markers are not lighted and nighttime navigation of this channel is not recommended. To avoid the jetties you must pass green bell buoy "1" on entry or leaving. This is not a place to attempt shortcuts.

Northwest Channel begins at flashing green bell buoy "1." From this point steer a course for red nun buoy "2" and, leaving it to starboard, adjust to a course to split quick-flashing green "3" to port and red nun "4" to starboard. From this pair a course of approximately 132° magnetic should keep you centered to flashing red "10." This approach should keep you safely inside the two submerged (east and west) jetties. (Note that the east jetty is awash at low tide.)

From flashing red "10" a course of approximately 147° magnetic should maintain channel alignment for the 5 nm to Main Ship Channel marker flashing green buoy "15." Here the route turns northward up the Main Ship Channel and into the harbor.

To reach Key West's main yacht harbor in Key West Bight turn east at flashing red buoy "24" towards quick-flashing red "4" at the end of the seawall. Quick-flashing red "4" marks the Key West Bight harbor entrance.

Key West dockage options are detailed in the section "Key West & The Dry Tortugas."

■ OUTSIDE (HAWK CHANNEL) ROUTE

The deepest and only viable route for vessels with a draft of 5 feet or more is the Hawk Channel running from Biscayne Bay to Key West. Not "officially" part of the ICW system, Hawk Channel tracks southwest 1 to 3 nm off the ocean side of the Keys. Taking the form of a somewhat protected "channel," it runs over the flat banks (Florida Platform) between the Keys and Florida's barrier reef to the southeast. In ordinary weather it is a pleasant sail or an easy run for the entire length of the Keys.

The prevailing southeasterly winds can provide a nice boost for a long reach on an outside run under sail. However, with numerous breaks in the outer reef it can offer its share of rough water should the wind be strong from either the southern or southwestern quarter.

Navigating Hawk Channel

Hawk Channel is relatively wide; nevertheless, navigation should be precise as aids to navigation are typically spaced far apart and can be difficult to spot. Unlike on the ICW, NOAA charts show no magenta line or mile markers for the Hawk Channel so skippers must plan each passage segment. A compass heading for every course segment should be the rule, as should following prudent piloting practices. An autopilot can be very helpful on some of the long tedious runs (particularly under power) but this route is busy with recreational and commercial traffic so the helm must be attended at all times. A GPS will be extremely useful on this passage particularly during times of poor visibility as numerous shoals pose a hazard along this route.

Expect a controlling depth of 9 feet MLW (but generally closer to 20 feet MLW for most of the route) and all major shoals along the route are marked. The route is generally well protected from north through west wind conditions when the channel is in the lee of the Keys themselves. It is important to be aware that if you run aground in the Keys and hit coral heads, coral reefs or sea grass beds, you could be levied a large fine in addition to any towing or repair costs.

Anchor in designated areas only. Also avoid entering designated "Marine Sanctuaries." These are restricted areas and should never be considered "cruising grounds" or traversed as part of a planned passage route.

Boats destined for the Florida Keys that draw over 4.5 feet must stay on the ocean side at least as far as Channel Five (Mile 1170), which is just southwest of Lower Matecumbe Key. For a passage on the Outside Route, Hawk Channel is well marked and provides some protection in most winds. Eastbound vessels often make an ocean leg, riding the Gulf Stream outside the reefs, but most cruisers prefer the comfort and convenience of the Hawk Channel in both directions.

While nighttime operation is an option on the Hawk Channel many markers are not lighted and we recommend that a passage be broken into a series of "achievable daytime hops." Consider appropriate stops and plan to complete each day's run well before dark. Skippers who do plan for nighttime operation should be aware the Florida Keys are strewn with hazards to navigation and a well-developed set of nighttime operation skills are mandatory here. Fortunately both anchorages and marinas can be found at reasonable intervals throughout the Keys.

For nighttime operation, and if weather allows, many skippers will choose a run off the Florida Platform in the open ocean beyond the reefs. This puts cruisers further from hazards and can simplify navigation. Be warned: Once this choice is taken there are few viable places to switch to the Hawk Channel along this 44-mile route.

In heavy easterly weather beam seas are the rule amplified by current and counter-current in the stretches abeam the numerous gaps in the Florida reef. Sailboats might like this weather but powerboats may wish to sit it out or move inside to the ICW. Conditions quiet down when winds slacken and veer to the southeast and south. With slack winds sailboats may choose to motorsail or make short close-hauled runs. Powerboats may still roll a bit but the journey will be generally enjoyable.

Government Cut to Cape Florida Channel

This section describes the route to the Outside Route (Hawk Channel) leaving Miami harbor through Government Cut (Miami) Inlet. This route is advised for deep-draft vessels and is better suited for operation in darkness.

Departing from the Miami area remember that when there are cruise ships docked at the Port of Miami, the Main Channel is closed to recreational boats. This restriction is strictly enforced. You will have to access the cut through Fishermans Channel located south Dodge Island. To avoid a wait for commercial traffic in one of the shipping channels it may be quicker to proceed south via the Inside (ICW) Route, exiting Biscayne Bay south of Key Biscayne. The route through the Cape Florida Channel/Biscayne Channel is actually a shorter route for boats departing from south of Virginia Key.

NAVIGATION: Use NOAA Charts 11451, 11463, 11465 and 11468 (large-scale chart of Miami Harbor). To enter Hawk Channel from North Biscayne Bay you will depart through Government Cut (Miami) Inlet. Access to the in-shore end of the cut may be restricted. Check VHF Channel 16 to see if a security zone is in effect. Government Cut (Miami) Inlet exits the harbor between Miami Beach and Fisher Island, has lighted markers and is flanked by large jetties jutting into the ocean. About 0.5 mile off the north jetty, the ship channel takes a northward dog-leg and proceeds 2 nm seaward through Outer Bar Cut past the charted spoil areas.

An alternate route (weather permitting) is to turn south at flashing green sea buoy "11" once well clear of the south jetty. Pass (but stay clear of) the Miami entrance range markers and the nearby spoils areas and keep well east of the shallows off Virginia Key. From flashing green sea buoy "11" it is a 6.5-nm run southwards on a course of 185° magnetic to flashing red "2" off Cape Florida.

Distances
Outside Route: Hawk Channel
(Miles from Miami)

LOCATION	STATUTE MILES	NAUTICAL MILES
Miami (Government Cut)	0	0
Miami (Cape Florida)	8	6.9
Fowey Rocks Light	14	12.0
Angelfish Creek	28	24.0
South Sound Creek	51	44.0
Tavernier	63	54.7
Islamorada	70	60.8
Channel Five	82	71.0
Duck Key	92	79.9
Marathon (Sisters Creek)	102	88.6
Moser Channel	109	94.7
Key West	151	131.0

Angelfish Creek

Central Biscayne Bay to Cape Florida Channel

This section describes the route from Central Biscayne Bay through the Cape Florida Channel/Biscayne Channel and has a controlling depth of 7 feet MLW at the ocean-side entrance. This is the shorter route for boats departing from the Coconut Grove area south of Virginia Key. There is actually a choice of two channels: the Cape Florida Channel closer to Key Biscayne or the more southerly Biscayne Channel. The two channels converge at 12-foot flashing red "6" located south of Cape Florida's lighthouse. Current charts and local knowledge should be obtained before attempting these channels for the first time.

NAVIGATION: Use NOAA Charts 11451 and 11465.

Some variation in channel markers has resulted from frequent storms so navigate carefully using the latest charts.

Heading seaward in either channel remember that green markers are to starboard until past flashing green "1" on the ocean side. Ocean-bound vessels enter Biscayne Channel (7 feet MLW) through paired markers flashing red "20" and flashing green "21" located 1 nm east of the ICW (Mile 1097.8). Follow the well-marked channel and be sure to pass between the paired markers

green daybeacon "7" and red daybeacon "8" (positioned oddly). Turn northeastward through this pair toward flashing red "6" keeping green daybeacon "7" to starboard. This is a well-marked channel but watch for shallow spots.

Eastbound vessels taking Cape Florida Channel (6 to 7 feet MLW), leave the ICW at Mile 1095.8 and head east 0.7 nm to flashing red "4" off the southwest tip of Key Biscayne. While rounding red day beacon "2" gradually turn to the northeast, keeping green daybeacon "1" to starboard and head towards Key Biscayne. Turn east to follow the shoreline keeping at least 100 yards off (in 7 feet MLW) for approximately 1.5 nm until adjacent to the southernmost tip of Key Biscayne near the lighthouse then head towards flashing red "6" to avoid nearby shoals.

The merged channel follows a path from flashing red "6" to flashing green "3" to flashing green "1." When exiting hold course for 0.5 nm past flashing green "1" before turning south. It is 3 nm due south from here to the entry to the Hawk Channel.

Shoaling to 6 feet MLW have been reported along the entire merged channel from around flashing red "6" to flashing green "1." Proceed with caution and note depths can be less than charted in high wind or surge conditions.

Keeping 0.5 nm off flashing red "2" marking the entrance to Biscayne Channel head due south for 3 nm to the start of the Hawk Channel. The matched pair of daybeacons–red "2" and green "3"–mark the channel's entrance. The pair's center is about 1.5 nm west of the Fowey Rocks Light (flashing white every 10 seconds). From this point to Channel Five is approximately 74 miles south-southwest.

Note the Hawk Channel markers generally follow red-right-southbound (the same as the ICW).

Cape Florida to Angelfish Creek

This section continues the trip south from Cape Florida for vessels entering the ocean from either Government Cut (Miami) Inlet or the Cape Florida (Biscayne Bay) Inlet. Immediately south from Cape Florida and Key Biscayne the waters are open and depths should exceed 15 feet MLW. The first Hawk Channel markers are 3 nm south of the Cape Florida (Biscayne Bay) Inlet entry markers and the Florida Keys begin at the Ragged Keys another 3 nm south.

The Hawk Channel narrows considerably approaching the Ragged Keys with shoals flanking the channel's edges and depths shallow to 12 feet MLW in spots. Most of the markers on Hawk Channel are un-lit and cruisers should take particular care if operating in darkness. Many opt to move an additional 5 miles off the barrier islands through this stretch and operate in the deeper water (several hundred feet) beyond the edge of the Florida Platform. The drop-off is quite close

to the barrier islands here and the Hawk Channel can be re-entered 45 miles south at Mosquito Bank. This section passes Caesar Creek and Angelfish Creek, the last two crossovers (for shoal-draft vessels) between the Hawk Channel and Biscayne Bay. Below Angelfish Creek, Key Largo, the largest of the Florida Keys, extends 33 miles southwest to Tavernier Creek.

NAVIGATION: Use NOAA Charts 11451 or 11465, 11463, 11464 and 11449 heading southwards. This route will be described as a series of course segments, each with a compass heading. Starting just east of flashing green "1" marking the east entry of the Cape Florida (Biscayne Bay) Inlet run for 3 nm at a course of 180° magnetic to red daybeacon "2." Paired red daybeacon "2" and green daybeacon "3" frame the entry of the Hawk Channel (approximately 1.5 nm to the east you should see the Fowey Rocks Light). Continue 5.4 nm south at a course of 198° magnetic from red daybeacon "2" to flashing red "8" near Bowles Bank Light lying off Sands Key.

A series of dangerous shoals flanking both sides of Hawk Channel starts at Bowles Bank and continues 29.5 nm south to Mosquito Bank. Sailboats that are close-hauled will want to plan their course carefully in this area as there is little room to tack. At flashing red "8" adjust course to 205° magnetic and run 7.7 nm to flashing red "20" marking the opening to Caesar Creek. When passing the mouth of the creek continue on this heading for another 2.4 nm to flashing red "22" off the Old Rhoads Bank. There is a series of green daybeacons and one flashing green marking dangerous shoals to the east of the channel through this stretch. Operation is darkness here can be challenging and a close watch is required.

At flashing red "22" the channel bends to the south-southwest as the westward curve of the Florida Keys commences. (The northernmost point of Key Largo is about 2 nm west of the marker.) Adjust course to 219° magnetic and run 9.3 nm to flashing green "31." Continue to watch for un-lit daybeacons close to the channel on this stretch. At flashing green "31" make a slight course adjustment to 217° magnetic and continue 10.2 nm to flashing green "35" at Mosquito Bank. South of Mosquito Bank the Hawk Channel opens up and hazards are fewer and farther from the marked channel.

Upper Keys, FL

KEY LARGO AREA - OUTSIDE		Largest Vessel	VHF	Total Slips	Approach/ Dockside Depth	Floating Docks	Gas/ Diesel	Repairs/ Haulout	Min/Max Amps	Pump-Out Station
1. Garden Cove Marina 1006.5	(305) 451-4694	35	16		4.0 / 14.0		G	RH	30	
2. John Pennekamp Coral Reef State Park	(305) 451-6300	50	16	9	/				30	P

WiFi Wireless Internet Access **onSpot** Dockside WiFi Facility
Visit www.waterwayguide.com for current rates, fuel prices, website addresses and other up-to-the-minute information.
(Information in the table is provided by the facilities.)

Scan here for more details:

Source: Aqua Map and NOAA data

Caesar Creek at the southwest end of Elliott Key is the first crossover to the ICW. Flashing red "20" is at the entrance to the National Park Service's marked channel. It is open to shoal-draft vessels only due to the shallows on the western end of the cut. The channel is well marked but narrow and bounded by 1 to 2-foot MLW depths. Pay attention to the wind direction as it will affect depths. Pass in daylight to enable visual navigation. Use extreme caution when transiting this area. We suggest you obtain local knowledge before using this as a crossover.

Angelfish Creek to Largo Sound

For vessels wanting to take advantage of the Gulf Stream for a transit to Bimini Island in the Bahamas, Angelfish Creek provides a more southerly approach than Miami. Be aware that the 1.8-nm-long inlet adds 14 nm to the Bahamas trip making it 56 nm instead of 42 nm.

NAVIGATION: Use NOAA Charts 11451 and 11463. Local skippers often use well-marked Angelfish Creek (located about 3 nm south of Caesar Creek) to cross between Biscayne Bay and the ocean. (Study your chart carefully and avoid Broad Creek to the north, which is shoaled at the entrance.) There are shoals at both the east and west ends of Angelfish Creek but for boats that draw 5 feet or less it is a fairly simple

passage. Boats with drafts greater than 5 feet should use the channel on a rising tide. Note the tidal range in this area is approximately 1 foot. Stay well out from the entrance until the channel markers are lined up. Just inside the entrance from Hawk Channel is a rocky ledge with 5-foot MLW depths; avoid this area in rough conditions.

Keep dead center in Angelfish Creek at low tide and maintain enough speed to prevent leeway. Do not enter if another boat is coming out. You need to able to stay on the centerline. Once inside the controlling 5-foot MLW depth creates no problem and you can often find deeper water. Depths of at least 7 feet MLW along the creek are the rule rather than the exception. Side creeks offer anchorages but note that the bottom is rocky and currents are strong.

Dockage: South of the ocean side entrance to Angelfish Creek is the private Ocean Reef Resort & Yacht Club, which accepts only members and sponsored guests. Other facilities along the Hawk Channel cater to transients although many are oriented primarily to charters and sport fishermen. Average approach depths to many of these privately marked channels are 5 feet or less MLW. Be sure to call ahead for channel depths.

A little over 10 nm to the south Garden Cove Marina has a well-marked channel that begins at red daybeacon "32" (at Rattlesnake Key). Sound your way into their channel. The approach depth is about 4 feet MLW. There is plenty of water once you get into the basin where you will find slips and the Buzzard's Roost Restaurant (305-453-3746) serving lunch, dinner and Sunday brunch.

Side Trip: John Pennekamp Coral Reef State Park

The John Pennekamp Coral Reef State Park in Largo Sound offers glass-bottom boat tours, scuba gear rentals and instruction, boat rentals, a campground and a Visitor's Center with a 30,000-gallon saltwater aquarium. There are 50 miles of natural mangrove trails to explore by kayak or stand-up paddleboard (available for rent) and the underwater park contains 178 square miles of mangrove swamps, sea grass beds and coral reef including the larger of the two living reefs that lie in Florida waters. Abundant reef fish live around the coral and there are several shipwrecks creating an underwater paradise for divers and snorkelers. Only hook-and-line fishing is permitted in the park.

NAVIGATION: Use NOAA Charts 11451, 11463 and 11464. Hawk Channel crosses the John Pennekamp Coral Reef State Park north boundary at green daybeacon "23" (off Angelfish Creek). The park's land attractions are located 20 miles southwest in Largo Sound, which is about midway down Key Largo. To visit by boat enter through South Sound Creek southwest of Largo Sound and less than 2 nm north of Mosquito Bank, which is marked by flashing green "35." The entrance to South Sound Creek is marked by flashing red "2." Do not cut inside this marker. There are shoals to the north. The channel carries 6-foot MLW depths but 5-foot MLW depths have been reported inside Largo Sound. It is best to contact the park ranger in advance to confirm approach depths.

Dive and sightseeing boats use this channel frequently so be prepared to move but not too far as 3-foot MLW depths have been observed outside of the channel. Because of the narrow channel and blind turns commercial vessels will make a Sécurité call on VHF Channel 16 before entering. Listen for such calls and make your own if appropriate.

Vessels with drafts of 4 feet or less and airdrafts of 14 feet or less can cross over from Largo Sound to Blackwater Sound through a rock cut (charted as Marvin D. Adams Waterway). The cut runs between the southernmost corner of Blackwater Sound and the western shore of Largo Sound. (The shallowest water lies at the two ends of the cut.) If you cannot get your big boat through here, it still makes a worthwhile dinghy trip. Be advised that a strong current runs through the cut.

Dockage/Moorings: John Pennekamp Coral Reef State Park offers nine full-service slips accommodating boats up to 50 feet in length. It is highly recommended you call the dockmaster on VHF Channel 16 to check availability and approach/dockside depths before arrival. Slips can also be booked directly online through John Pennekamp Coral Reef State Park.

Although overnight anchoring is prohibited in Largo Sound, about a dozen white mooring balls are located near the park headquarters in the southwest corner of the sound. Simply tie up to a vacant ball and dinghy over to the dockmaster's office (in the Dive Center) to check in.

America's First Underwater Park

As early as the 1930s work had begun to protect the reefs of the Upper Florida Keys. When Everglades National Park was first proposed the intent was to protect all of the connected ecosystems found in South Florida, including the mangroves, seagrass beds and coral reefs off the Keys. Local property owners and business protested and when Everglades National Park was created in 1947, it did not include areas south of Florida Bay.

But by the late 1950s residents of the Keys were becoming more and more concerned about the future of the reefs. Coral, starfish, sea horses and many other living creatures were being harvested and sold as souvenirs. In 1960 President Dwight D. Eisenhower proclaimed the reefs off Key Largo as the Key Largo Coral Reef Preserve. Later when adjacent lands on Key Largo were acquired by the State of Florida, the present state park was formed absorbing responsibility for the underwater reefs as well. John D. Pennekamp, an editor for the *Miami Herald* and a supporter of the efforts to protect the Everglades and the reefs, helped lead the effort to create both Everglades National Park and the park that now bears his name in Key Largo.

The John D. Pennekamp Coral Reef State Park opened in 1963 as the first underwater park in the U.S. The park includes the visitor center and concessionaire complex at MM 103 in Key Largo, where several beaches, trails, a campground, a boat ramp and a marina are located. The park extends 3 miles offshore over the flats of the Florida Platform and covers 70 square nautical miles. It protects the unique ecosystems of the Upper Keys and is Florida's most visited state park.

Upper Keys, FL

KEY LARGO AREA		Largest Vessel	VHF	Total Slips	Approach/ Dockside Depth	Floating Docks	Gas/ Diesel	Repairs/ Haulout	Min/Max Amps	Pump-Out Station
1. Key Largo Harbor Marina (WiFi) 1.7 mi. E of MM 1141.3	(305) 451-0045	65	16	24	4.0 / 10.0		GD	RH	30 / 50	
2. Marina Del Mar Resort and Marina (WiFi)	(305) 453-7171	60	16	77	4.5 / 18.0				30 / 50	P
3. Pilot House Marina & Restaurant (WiFi) MM 1142.0	(305) 451-3142	85	16	55	4.5 / 10.0	F	GD	RH	30 / 100	P

(WiFi) Wireless Internet Access ⊙ onSpot Dockside WiFi Facility
Visit www.waterwayguide.com for current rates, fuel prices, website addresses and other up-to-the-minute information.
(Information in the table is provided by the facilities.)

Scan here for more details:

Source: Aqua Map and NOAA data

Largo Sound to Hens & Chicks

While Hawk Channel opens up on this stretch there are still a few dangerous shoals skirting the green side. This stretch passes Rodriguez Key off Rock Harbor and Tavernier Key off Tavernier Creek, where 33-mile long Key Largo ends and Plantation Key begins.

NAVIGATION: Use NOAA Charts 11451 and 11464. Continuing southwest in the Hawk Channel it is a 11.7-nm run at 230° magnetic from flashing green "35" at the Mosquito Bank to flashing red "40" marking the Hens and Chickens reef. The reef is designated as a Marine Sanctuary and is quite close to Hawk Channel. This can be a great place to stop for a snorkel but be sure to avoid passage through the marked prohibited area. Note the extremely shallow shoals (3 to 5 feet MLW) marked by "triangles" that flank the green side between green daybeacons "37" to "39."

To the south of Largo Sound is Port Largo Canal offering some dockage options. About 1 nm south from flashing green "35" along Hawk Channel turn northwest and continue 1 nm to flashing red "2." From here take a wide turn around red daybeacons "4" and "6" staying in the deeper water and keeping these to starboard. Once around red daybeacon "6" start your approach to the canal splitting flashing green "7" and red daybeacon "8." (Keep red to port here.)

Watch your depth as the approach channel is only around 5 feet MLW. Just to the south of Port Largo there is a large tower south of the entrance to the canal leading to Lake Largo. This canal is to port just before red daybeacon "8" for the entrance to Port Largo.

Dockage: The full-service Key Largo Harbor Marina is the first facility (to starboard) on Port Largo Canal with maintenance and repairs. They report 4-foot MLW approach depths. Call ahead for slip availability. A bit farther into the canal is the 77-slip Marina Del Mar Resort and Marina offering transient dockage and resort-style amenities. The marina also provides access to snorkeling and diving adventures.

Pilot House Marina & Restaurant is to the south on Lake Largo in the heart of downtown Key Largo. The marina has 55 slips available for transients and can accommodate power or sailboats up to 85 feet in length. They offer climate-controlled restrooms and showers, laundry facilities and have an on-site restaurant.

Anchorage: Rodriguez Key is directly northwest from Hawk Channel marker green daybeacon "37." This is a popular anchorage. Anchor in 5 to 8 feet MLW on whichever side of the island gives the best wind protection. Often the best protection in north winds is between Rodriguez Key and Key Largo closer to (outer) Rock Harbor. The holding is good in grass and sand in 6 feet MLW. Check the tide stage before anchoring as the range is 3 feet. There are several small marinas and a boat ramp in and around Rock Harbor where you might land your dinghy. Straight out from the anchorage is Molasses Reef with excellent snorkeling. This is a popular stop for boats preparing to cross to the Bahamas or heading on to Marathon.

Hens & Chicks to Channel Five

Over this stretch there are fewer shoals on the seaward side and several hazards between Hawk Channel and the Keys. The Hens and Chickens, Cheeca Rocks or a small shoal 1 mile south of Lower Matecumbe Key can make a pleasant stop for lunch and a snorkel. Passage through charted "Marine Sanctuaries" should be avoided.

NAVIGATION: Use NOAA Charts 11451 and 11464. South from the flashing red "40" marking the Hens and Chickens reef take a course of 236° magnetic for 4.2 nm southwest to green daybeacon "41" located 1 nm seaward from Cheeca Rocks Marine Sanctuary. If leaving Hawk Channel watch for an unmarked 3-foot MLW shoal known as "The Rocks" that is located northwest of the Hen and Chickens.

From green daybeacon "41" proceed 10.5 nm at 246° magnetic to the Channel Five entry marker flashing red

"2." Be aware of a shoal that extends 0.5 mile south of the channel entry marker. Continuing on the Hawk Channel proceed 0.7 nm on the same heading past Channel Five to reach flashing red "44" off Long Key. This marks the start of the Middle Keys.

The fixed Tavernier Creek Bridge (15-foot vertical clearance) crosses Tavernier Creek at ICW Mile 1151.5. The creek's entrance has charted 3-foot MLW depths but many cruisers anchor outside in the harbor protected by Tavernier Key and take a dinghy ride to visit the bay side.

Snake Creek is a limited crossover to the bay side. The creek is crossed by the Snake Creek Bridge with 27-foot closed vertical clearance. The bridge opens on signal, except from 8:00 a.m. to 6:00 p.m., when it need only open on the hour. The channel has shoaled (4 feet MLW reported) on the ocean side and passage is not recommended except by dinghy.

West of Snake Creek is Windley Key Fossil Reef Geological State Park, which has self-guided trails including one along an 8-foot high quarry wall revealing preserved fossilized specimens of a variety of ancient coral animals. Interpretive tours are offered in winter months. This interesting site is open Thursday through Monday from 8:00 a.m. to 5:00 p.m.

West of Windley Key is Whale Harbor Channel (5 feet MLW), which leads to Cotton Key Basin. The 10-foot fixed vertical clearance of the Whale Harbor Channel Bridge restricts vessels needing more clearance.

Next is tiny and picturesque Teatable Key on the ocean side off the south tip of Upper Matecumbe Key. This was once a Navy base and is now a private island. Between Teatable Key and Indian Key are two well-marked channels leading to the bay side. Teatable Key Channel's airdraft is restricted by the 10-foot fixed vertical clearance of the Teatable Key Channel Bridge. The airdraft restriction of the Indian Key Channel is set by the Indian Key Channel Bridge (27-foot fixed vertical clearance).

Lower Matecumbe Key is the midpoint in the run from Fowey Rocks to Key West. At its western tip Channel Two is another restricted crossover restricted by the 10-foot fixed vertical clearance of Channel Two Bridge.

Dockage/Moorings: Snake Creek Marina (west of Snake Creek Bridge) is shoal-draft territory with reported 3.5-foot MLW approach and dockside depths. In addition to 10 transient slips, they offer repairs.

Postcard Inn Marina at Holiday Isle, located at the north end of the Whale Harbor Channel Bridge, caters to

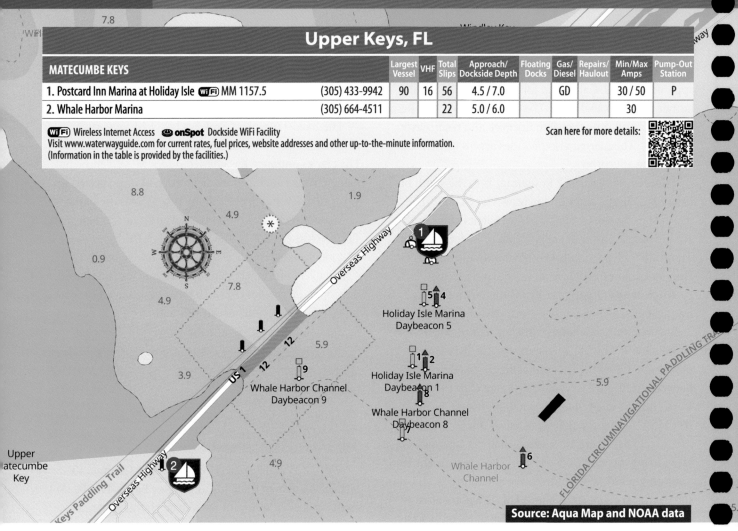

Upper Keys, FL

MATECUMBE KEYS		Largest Vessel	VHF	Total Slips	Approach/ Dockside Depth	Floating Docks	Gas/ Diesel	Repairs/ Haulout	Min/Max Amps	Pump-Out Station
1. Postcard Inn Marina at Holiday Isle **WiFi** MM 1157.5	(305) 433-9942	90	16	56	4.5 / 7.0		GD		30 / 50	P
2. Whale Harbor Marina	(305) 664-4511			22	5.0 / 6.0				30	

WiFi Wireless Internet Access **onSpot** Dockside WiFi Facility

Visit www.waterwayguide.com for current rates, fuel prices, website addresses and other up-to-the-minute information. (Information in the table is provided by the facilities.)

Scan here for more details:

Source: Aqua Map and NOAA data

sportfishing vessels and sells gas and diesel fuel. There are many fishing charters based here as well as shoreside accommodations, several restaurants and many bars including a well-known tiki bar. At the south end of the Whale Harbor Channel Bridge is Whale Harbor Marina, which also caters to sportfishing crews and has two on-site restaurants. Call ahead for slip availability.

On Upper Matecumbe Key a privately marked channel leads to La Siesta Resort & Marina. Call for instructions before entering this channel (reported 3.5-foot MLW approach depths). They have just five reserved transient slips along with rooms, cottages and houses for rent. Behind Teatable Key to the east a privately maintained channel (controlling depth of 4.5 feet MLW) leads to Bud'n Mary's Fishing Marina, one of the oldest and most active sportfishing/charter centers in the Keys. Rental skiffs and guided fishing charters are available along with transient dockage. Call ahead for reservations. There are a number of retail shops, art galleries and restaurants north of the marina.

Caloosa Cove Resort & Marina on Lower Matecumbe Key is in a protected basin with 4-foot MLW approach and dockside depths. They have 10 transient slips and a well-stocked hardware and Ship's Store. The resort also has shoreside accommodations and a restaurant with Cuban-inspired cuisine.

Indian Key has a small boat dock and three complementary moorings (for up to one week) off the southeast side. The Indian Key Moorings are exposed but provide easy access from Hawk Channel. One mooring ball is very close to the island's pretty beach area and wooden dock.

Anchorage: The harbor protected by Tavernier Key has 4 to 7 feet MLW with good holding in sand and grass. This is open and exposed from the northeast through the east. In calm conditions or with light winds from the west through to the north-northeast it is possible for vessels drawing up to 5 feet to anchor in the sand off Whale Harbor. This is not a particularly good or recommended

Upper Keys, FL

MATECUMBE KEYS		Largest Vessel	VHF	Total Slips	Approach/ Dockside Depth	Floating Docks	Gas/ Diesel	Repairs/ Haulout	Min/Max Amps	Pump-Out Station
1. La Siesta Resort & Marina **WiFi** MM 1162.5	(855) 335-1078	30		24	3.5 / 6.0		G			
2. Bud'n Mary's Fishing Marina MM 1162.1	(305) 664-2461	45	77	35	4.5 / 4.5		GD	RH	30 / 50	

WiFi Wireless Internet Access **onSpot** Dockside WiFi Facility
Visit www.waterwayguide.com for current rates, fuel prices, website addresses and other up-to-the-minute information.
(Information in the table is provided by the facilities.)

Scan here for more details:

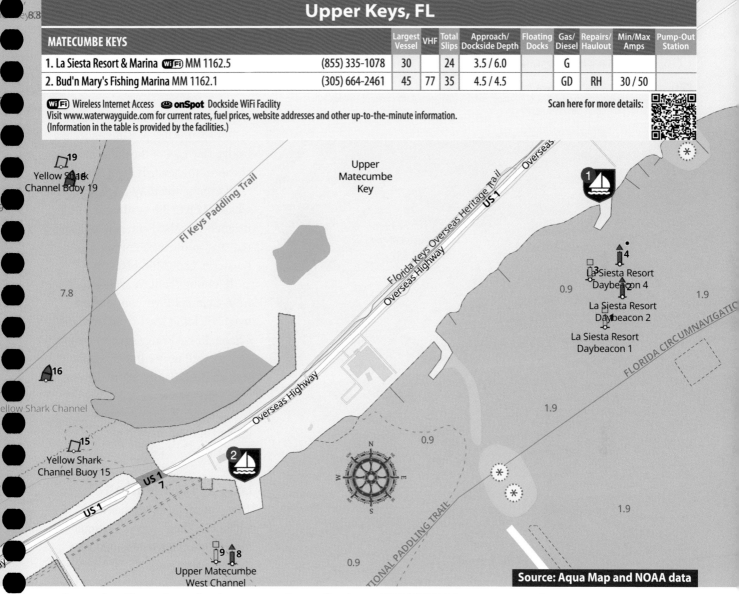

Source: Aqua Map and NOAA data

anchorage but if you do anchor here you and your dinghy are welcome at the Whale Harbor Inn, which boasts a huge seafood buffet and a fun rooftop bar (The Sandbar).

Channel Five Crossing (from ocean)

Channel Five is the first major crossover below Biscayne Bay. This channel allows cruisers to cross between the ocean side and bay side or perhaps just to switch sides to get away from weather and find an anchorage. While there are minimal markers, navigation of the wide channel is straightforward. It has a controlling depth of 8 feet MLW. The fixed Channel Five Bridge (65-foot vertical clearance) sets the channel's vertical clearance.

NAVIGATION: Use NOAA Chart 11451.

The dangerous shoals that flank both sides of Channel Five are poorly marked and growing. Do not cut close to markers or charted shoals while turning. Monitor depths through the active shoaling area and expect channel minimum 7 feet MLW near flashing red "2."

When entering from the ocean side westbound traffic should continue in the Hawk Channel until flashing red "2" is on the beam. At flashing red "2" turn due north keeping west of red daybeacon "4" and the shoals behind. After pass red daybeacon "4" slowly adjust your course to 025° magnetic to pass through the Channel Five Bridge

Upper Keys, FL

MATECUMBE KEYS		Largest Vessel	VHF	Total Slips	Approach/ Dockside Depth	Floating Docks	Gas/ Diesel	Repairs/ Haulout	Min/Max Amps	Pump-Out Station
1. Caloosa Cove Resort & Marina **WiFi** MM 1168.0	(305) 664-4455	60		40	4.0 / 4.0		GD	H	30 / 50	

WiFi Wireless Internet Access **onSpot** Dockside WiFi Facility
Visit www.waterwayguide.com for current rates, fuel prices, website addresses and other up-to-the-minute information.
(Information in the table is provided by the facilities.)

Scan here for more details:

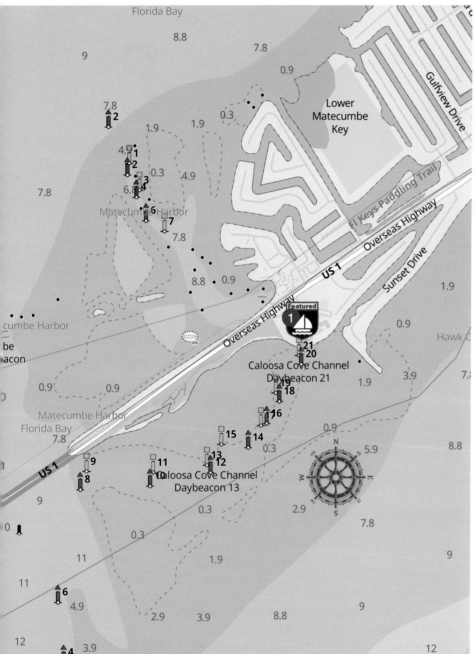

Source: Aqua Map and NOAA data

center span. After passing under the bridge stay east of the dangerous shoals of the Jewfish Bush Banks.

If joining the ICW eastbound from Channel Five, the heading is 034° magnetic for the 4-nm run to flashing red "98" at the west entrance to Bowlegys Cut (Mile 1165.6).

If joining the ICW westbound from Channel Five, continue on 025° magnetic for at least 1 nm from the Channel Five Bridge span to ensure you are well north of the dangerous Jewfish Bush Banks before turning westward to join the ICW. The first ICW marker is flashing green "1" located at the north tip of Old Dan Bank (Mile 1173.8).

Long Key to Marathon

This section picks up the Hawk Channel route just past Channel Five at flashing red "44" off Long Key. Dangerous shoals flank Channel Five and the southeast shore of Long Key. You must observe Channel Five markers carefully and stay at least 1 nm south of Long Key while operating in this area.

NAVIGATION: Use NOAA Charts 11449, 11451 and 11453. Southwest along the Hawk Channel keep red markers to starboard. From flashing red "44" (marking shoals off Long Key and the Channel Five entrance) set a course of 248° magnetic toward flashing green "45" located just north of East Turtle Shoal (with 5-foot MLW depths). Along this 9.2-nm run there are few hazards

Middle Keys, FL

MARATHON AREA	Largest Vessel	VHF	Total Slips	Approach/ Dockside Depth	Floating Docks	Gas/ Diesel	Repairs/ Haulout	Min/Max Amps	Pump-Out Station
1. Hawks Cay Resort Marina (WiFi) 3.0 mi. S of MM 1180.0 (888) 974-8469	110	16	85	5.0 / 5.0				30 / 50	P

(WiFi) Wireless Internet Access (onSpot) Dockside WiFi Facility
Visit www.waterwayguide.com for current rates, fuel prices, website addresses and other up-to-the-minute information.
(Information in the table is provided by the facilities.)

Scan here for more details:

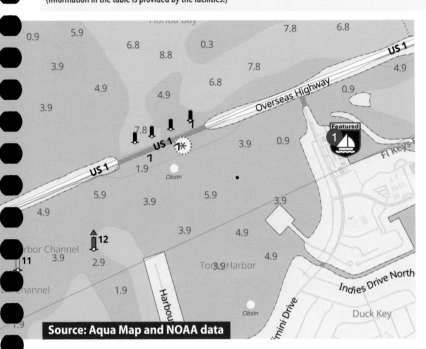

Source: Aqua Map and NOAA data

although some charted obstructions and an 8-foot MLW shoal lie off the designated courseline.

To avoid East Turtle Shoal head west from flashing green "45" on Hawk Channel at 253° magnetic for the 5.3-nm run toward red daybeacon "48." From this marker southwest the heading for the designated route swings further to the west to 259° magnetic. Hawk Channel continues southwest on this heading for 14.2 nm past Moser Channel and Bahia Honda Key. (Note the controlling depth on this stretch is only 8 feet MLW.) If diverging from the courseline, be wary of East Washerwoman Shoal marked by flashing green "49." This is a dangerous shoal (2 feet MLW) so keep well to the north.

Continuing southwest from Long Key you will begin to see the urban sprawl of Marathon to the north plus Grassy Key, Crawl Key, Fat Deer Key and Vaca Key. (There is a Sea Tow office on Grassy Key should you need it.) Boot Key lies at the end of this chain and is uninhabited and covered with mangroves and the occasional radio tower. Fronting Fat Deer Key is Coco Plum Beach, which is well marked by a 14-story-high condominium tower. This tower serves as an excellent landmark for cruisers on Hawk Channel (and is also the highest building in all of the Florida Keys).

Dockage: About 8 nm southwest along Hawk Channel from flashing red "44" is Hawks Cay Resort Marina on Duck Key. The entrance to the Duck Key canal system (known as the Duck Key "moat") is at the Key's southernmost point. Private markers guide you to the entry channel starting with a quick-flashing white and followed by a pair of daybeacons–green "1" and red "2." Once inside the Duck Key moat entrance take the right branch and enjoy deep water on your way to the marina at Hawks Cay Resort Marina. Observe Idle Speed/ No Wake signs.

The upscale Hawks Cay Resort Marina features 85 boat slips accommodating vessels up to 110 feet in length (35-foot minimum) and offers a boat-in/boat-out service as well as dockage for resort guests and liveaboard boaters. All overnight guests at the marina have access to its restaurants and attractions with a free shuttle service between the marina and the resort.

Driftwood Marina & Storage to the south on Fat Deer Key has haul-out and repair facilities and also offers boat storage in a protected basin with a well-marked channel. (The marina reports 4-foot MLW approach depths but with deeper water inside). Call ahead for slip availability.

The 14-story Bonefish Towers stands at the eastern edge of the deep channel leading to the Key Colony Beach Marina, which maintains some transient slips. The well-kept White Marlin Marina is located around a 2.5-acre private island on the same channel. It offers excellent weather protection and features a huge tiki area and a fire pit with amazing sunset views. Also nearby are Outta the Blue Marina and Shelter Bay Marine. Both offer repairs but no transient slips.

Middle Keys, FL

MARATHON AREA		Largest Vessel	VHF	Total Slips	Approach/ Dockside Depth	Floating Docks	Gas/ Diesel	Repairs/ Haulout	Min/Max Amps	Pump-Out Station
1. Driftwood Marina & Storage 3.2 mi. S of MM 1187.3	(305) 289-0432	60			4.0 / 18.0	F		RH		
2. Outta the Blue Marina MM 1187.3	(305) 289-0285	48		10	8.0 / 12.0			RH	30	P
3. White Marlin Marina-FL (WiFi) 53-54 MM	(866) 770-5454	82		27	6.5 / 5.2				20 / 50	P
4. Shelter Bay Marine	(305) 743-7008	38		20	8.0 / 12.0	F	G	RH		
5. Key Colony Beach Marina (WiFi) MM 1187.0	(305) 289-1310	120	16	35	12.0 / 8.0		GD		30 / 100	P

(WiFi) Wireless Internet Access onSpot Dockside WiFi Facility
Visit www.waterwayguide.com for current rates, fuel prices, website addresses and other up-to-the-minute information.
(Information in the table is provided by the facilities.)

Scan here for more details:

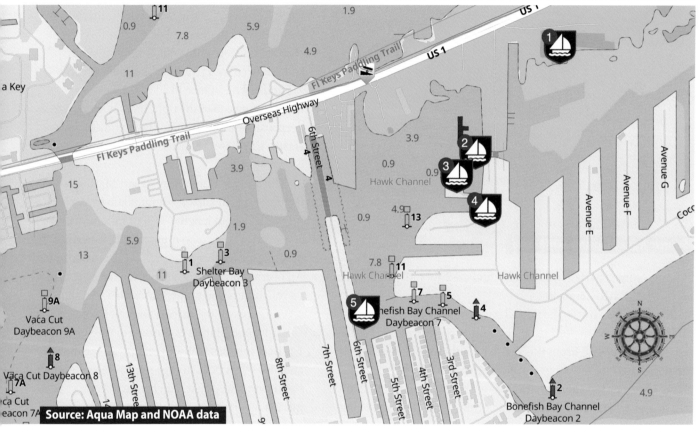

Source: Aqua Map and NOAA data

Captain Hook's Marina & Dive Center–Marathon is on the ocean side of the Vaca Cut Bridge (13-foot fixed vertical clearance). The family-owned business offers boat rentals and all types of charters and tours including scuba diving, snorkeling, fishing, paddle sports and sightseeing.

> Boot Key dockage options are detailed in the section are described in the Inside (ICW) Route section and in "Goin' Ashore: Marathon, FL" in this chapter.

Anchorage: Long Key is the home of Long Key State Park, a 300-acre wild area with a campground, numerous picnic tables and grills. You can drop the hook in Long Key Bight in 4 to 6-foot MLW depths with good holding

in sand and grass. It is open to the northeast but you can relocate south of the island to seek protection in these conditions.

Marathon to Stock Island

A great stop along the way is Bahia Honda State Park & Marina at Mile 1207. The slowly disintegrating Old Bahia Honda Bridge located at the island's western end is a national historic monument. The Old Bridge has a span removed so that sailboats can pass through into the cove between the Old Bridge and the newer Bahia Honda Bridges (20-foot fixed vertical clearance).

Two of the nicest beaches in the Keys are located at Bahia Honda State Park. The palm-rimmed Calusa Beach near the concession stand is sheltered and roped off for swimming and snorkeling. The park concession stand sells snacks and ice. There are also three nature trails. We like it so much, we cover it here and in the on Inside (ICW) Route section of this chapter.

NAVIGATION: Use NOAA Chart 11445. Leaving Marathon you will parallel the Seven Mile Bridge as you head southwest passing the 142-foot Sombrero Key Light to port. Leaving from the Boot Key Channel entrance adjust course to 247° magnetic for 9.5 nm passing south of the Molasses Keys and the nearby shoals. Once directly abeam of the west tip of Bahia Honda Key parallel the Keys at 261° magnetic for 5-nm run to Cook Island at Mile 1212. Tighten the course slightly here to 265° magnetic for the 10-nm run to the Ninefoot Shoal Light (18-foot, flashing white 2.5 sec) at Mile 1225. The shoal is actually charted at 10 feet MLW and is not a hazard for most cruising vessels.

Hawk Channel narrows past the marked lighted Ninefoot Shoal (Mile 1224.5) and passes safely north of West Washerwoman Shoal (Mile 1227). For the 10-nm run from Ninefoot Shoal to the Boca Chica Channel (Mile 1236) the heading changes slightly to 263° magnetic passing the western end of Sugarloaf, the Saddlebunch Keys and the Boca Chica Key air base. On Boca Chica Key

the hangers, control tower and radar dome of the Naval Air Station Key West make good landmarks.

Dockage: Transients can find dockage in the well-protected boat basin at Bahia Honda State Park & Marina. Expect 8 to 10 feet MLW dockside but the entrance is shallow (as low as 3.5 feet MLW) with a tidal range of a little over 1 foot. Boat slips include fill use of the park facilities (bathhouse, trash disposal and pump-out service). This is a popular spot so call ahead.

Anchorage: The cove between the old and new bridges west of the park at Bahia Honda Key is a popular anchorage. Be warned that the holding is only fair in sand and grass and the currents are strong. (If you choose to swim off the boat, hang a grab-line off the back just in case you get caught in the current.) It is wise to check your position after a turning tide to avoid a closer look at one bridge or the other. This is a good place to let out extra scope. Once securely anchored you can go ashore to the park (short-term dinghy tie-ups allowed). If going ashore, bring shoes or aqua socks to hike the nature trails and visit the two sandy beaches.

West of Bahia Honda Key at flashing red "50" lies the Newfound Harbor Channel, about 4.5 miles due north of the superb snorkeling sites of Looe Key National Marine Sanctuary (an excellent snorkeling site). The relatively well-marked and well-protected channel leads to what has become an increasingly popular anchorage area. The

Newfound Harbor anchorage has depths of 8 to 16 feet MLW but the approach is quite shallow, particularly in strong north winds when depths can be reduced by over 1 foot. In normal conditions you should have 7 to 8 feet MLW. On entry give flashing red "2" a wide berth to starboard to avoid shoaling that extends about 100 yards south and west of this marker but don't go too far west as the channel has shoaled there as well.

Shoal-draft boats can anchor in 5- to 6-foot MLW depths just east of the main channel or in 4-foot MLW depths near the channel entrance. Picnic Island to the south is a popular anchorage. Follow the channel for 5.2 feet MLW (at the shallowest spot). Once into the anchorage the depth deepens to 7 to 8 feet MLW. There is better weather protection from wave action than it appears due to the dampening action of the nearby shoals. The island is a local favorite for pet owners, it's like a dog park where pets can run free. It was devastated by the last hurricane but the island is still there.

About 2 nm to the west Niles Channel offers a reasonably well-protected anchorage between Ramrod Key and Summerland Key. Anchor between red daybeacons "4" and "6" in 7 to 10 feet MLW. Be careful to avoid a couple of 2 and 3-foot MLW shoals here. The area is also not well protected from southerlies.

Farther west before Loggerhead Keys and due north of flashing red "50A" a marked shoal-draft channel with the entrance by green daybeacon "1" leads to sheltered, although relatively shallow, Kemp Channel between Cudjoe and Summerland Keys. This channel only carries 4 to 5 feet MLW. Be sure to monitor your depth sounder.

Saddlebunch Harbor located just east of Boca Chica Key has fair holding in 7 to 8 feet MLW with a grassy and mud bottom. It offers good protection from the east but only limited protection from the south. In east winds snug-in close to shore just north of daybeacon red "8." The current is strong here but the depth holds quite close to land. This is usually a quiet spot.

Stock Island

NAVIGATION: Use NOAA Charts 11441, 11442 and 11446. Immediately west of Boca Chica Channel (located about 2 miles past flashing red "56") is the charted channel leading to the Stock Island service facilities. Several boat builders, boat storage and fishing docks are here. Provisioning from this location, however, requires

Oceans Edge Key West Resort Hotel & Marina

© Mapbox, © OpenStreetMap

ground transportation. Check with marinas as some offer a shuttle service into Key West. Public transit stops are also nearby.

An overhead power cable with an authorized vertical clearance of 60 feet restricts access to the basins for both Boca Chica and the Stock Island anchorage.

Dockage: Just 2.4 nm past flashing red "56" the deep, well-marked Boca Chica Channel leads into the basin and mooring area of the Boca Chica Naval Air Station. Boca Chica Marina is only open to retired and active-duty members of the armed forces. Rental moorings, ice, showers and limited snacks are available. An overhead power cable with an authorized vertical clearance of 60 feet sets the controlling vertical clearance for the basin.

The full-service Stock Island Yacht Club and Marina, which has transient slips, is in a protected basin off Boca Chica Channel (before the overhead power cable). There is an on-site restaurant with incredible views of the Atlantic Ocean (and a private beach).

The unnamed channel into Oceans Edge Key West Resort & Marina is east of the Stock Island Channel just after green daybeacon "5." They have slips for boats up to 140 feet. The marina caters to sportfishing vessels with well-maintained docks and secure dry-rack storage. They also have a great restaurant serving breakfast, lunch and dinner. Note that the entry channel has an S-shaped curve where it leaves the Stock Island Channel and there are rocks 50 feet off the dock so study your charts.

On the main Stock Island Channel is Robbie's of Key West LLC, which specializes in the repair and refurbishing of large commercial vessels as well as megayachts (no transient slips). Stock Island Marina Village at the head of the Stock Island Channel can accommodate vessels up to 450 feet. With 288 slips and state-of-the-art floating docks, every type of boat can be accommodated. They offer resort-style amenities and a boutique hotel and several restaurants are on site as well as a distillery. The marina also offers shuttle service to downtown Key West. There is a West Marine nearby at 5790 2nd Ave. (305-294-2025).

Stock Island to Key West

NAVIGATION: Use NOAA Charts 11441, 11442 and 11447. Following the Hawk Channel westward from Stock Island the towers and radar domes of Key West International Airport appear to starboard along with many waterfront hotels and condominiums. Hawk Channel ends at its intersection with Key West's Main Ship Channel.

The channel turns due west off Stock Island and runs 4.7 nm to flashing red buoy "12" (at Mile 1241.7) marking a corner of the Key West's Main Ship Channel. Stay offshore of the quick-flashing green range marker off Whitehead Spit (the southwesterly tip of Key West at Mile 1241) and turn north into the Main Ship Channel at flashing red "12." Keeping red markers to starboard as you enter the well-marked channel.

Continue to follow the Main Ship Channel northwards toward the harbor. Favor the east side of the channel (closer to the docked cruise ships) and keep well off Tank Island (locally known as Sunset Key) and Wisteria Island from flashing green buoy "23" to flashing green "29." There are 1-foot MLW shoals off Wisteria Island and throughout Man of War Harbor. If there is commercial traffic you can follow the markers outside the channel's eastern edge as there is plenty of depth. Pass the cruise ship docks with caution and also note that there is ferry traffic coming out of Margaritaville Harbor at all hours.

The channel has good width and depth but the current and wind can be significant factors here along with the vessel traffic. The abundance of buoys in the area can confuse a first-time visitor, particularly at night. We strongly recommend that first-timers do not attempt a night entry. Day or night, it's prudent to have a "Plan B" in case of traffic conflicts or possible breakdowns in this area.

It is important to monitor VHF Channel 16 in the Main Ship Channel. Larger vessels will issue a Sécurité call before they enter the channel. This is particularly important when the massive cruise ships are on the move (usually in the morning and early evening).

An alternate entry to the Main Ship Channel past the Stock Island Channel is well-marked but rarely used by recreational craft. The channel is marked by lighted red-and-white whistle buoy "KW" located at the reef-line 5 nm south of Key West. It initially follows a range (flashing green over quick-flashing green) aligned with the prominent (and lighted) red-and-white water tank on the western end of the island. The channel takes an abrupt dogleg to the northwest at quick-flashing red "8" and then another dogleg (about 1 nm farther) to the north between quick-flashing green "9" and quick-flashing red "12," which serves at as the entry point for boats southbound on Hawk Channel.

Stock Island Yacht Club & Marina

Stock Island, Key West, FL

STOCK ISLAND		Largest Vessel	VHF	Total Slips	Approach/ Dockside Depth	Floating Docks	Gas/ Diesel	Repairs/ Haulout	Min/Max Amps	Pump-Out Station
1. Stock Island Yacht Club and Marina (WiFi)	(305) 292-3121	110	16	100	8.0 / 10.0	F	GD	R	30 / 100	P
2. Oceans Edge Key West Resort & Marina (WiFi) MM 1237.0	(786) 862-6315	140	16	125	20.0 / 12.0		GD		30 / 50	P
3. Robbie's of Key West LLC (WiFi) MM 1237.0	(305) 294-1124	400			/ 15.0	F		RH	30 / 100	
4. Stock Island Marina Village (WiFi)	(305) 294-2288	450	16	288	15.0 / 20.0	F	GD		30 / 200+	P

(WiFi) Wireless Internet Access   (onSpot) Dockside WiFi Facility
Visit www.waterwayguide.com for current rates, fuel prices, website addresses and other up-to-the-minute information.
(Information in the table is provided by the facilities.)

Scan here for more details:

Source: Aqua Map and NOAA data

■ KEY WEST & THE DRY TORTUGAS

Key West is the sunny, end-of-the-line destination for tourists and travelers of all descriptions. Many are drawn down U.S. 1 and thousands more arrive by cruise ship, all landing at the Key West waterfront. However they get there, visitors quickly confirm to the laid-back local style where casual sailing duds substitute for more formal attire almost anywhere on this island. To read more, see "Goin' Ashore: Key West, FL" in this chapter.

Key West is difficult to categorize. It is a unique and irresistible magnet to yachtsmen, long-distance cruisers and sportfishers. The ready availability of amenities and attractions makes the city a great stop for recreation, repairs and provisioning.

NAVIGATION: Use NOAA Charts 11441. To reach Key West's main yacht harbor in Key West Bight turn east at flashing red buoy "24" towards quick-flashing red "4" at the end of the seawall. Quick-flashing red "4" marks the Key West Bight harbor entrance.

Continue north past flashing red buoy "24" and cross the Fleming Key Cut to access Man of War Harbor and Garrison Bight. The municipal mooring field, Garrison

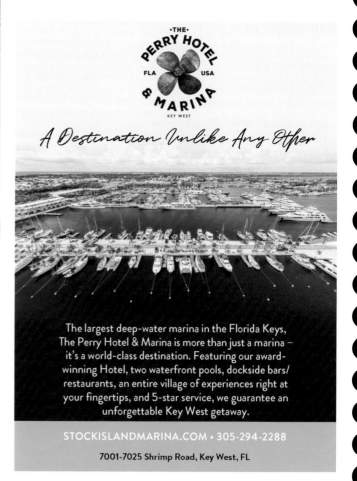

Bight Harbor and the north Stock Island facilities are east of Fleming Key and are accessed by the Garrison Bight Channel through its entry at the north end of Man of War Harbor. The well-marked channel rounds the north end of Fleming Key. Fleming Key Bridge at the south end of Fleming Key has 18-foot fixed vertical clearance. If you stay centered in the channel you should carry at least 7- to 8-foot MLW depths.

⚠

Before entering Garrison Bight, beware that the charted overhead cables crossing the entry channel have an authorized vertical clearance of 50 feet and only 34 feet elsewhere over the north basin. Some local businesses report a higher clearance but no precise measurements were provided. To be on the safe side respect the charted clearance, which effectively blocks all but small sailboats.

In addition, overnight anchoring in the Bight is prohibited for all vessels. Note also that the fixed Garrison Bight Bridge over the channel to the south basin has a charted vertical clearance of 19 feet.

Dockage: The 37-slip Opal Key Resort & Marina (formerly Margaritaville Resort & Marina) is located just off the east side of the Main Ship Channel opposite flashing green buoy "23" just south of the cruise ship wharf. The resort has multiple restaurants, a pool surrounded by tropical native plants and lush trees and a private spa. The marina is located just one block away from Old Town Key West.

Several facilities are located in Key West Bight. The entry is marked by quick-flashing red "4" at the east end of the protective seawall. These facilities are adjacent to the Historic Seaport Harbor Walk, which extends to the restaurants and shops on the southeast side of the Key West Bight. Key West Marine Hardware (818 Caroline St., 305-294-3425) is within easy walking distance from the bight and has a complete selection of marine paint and hardware.

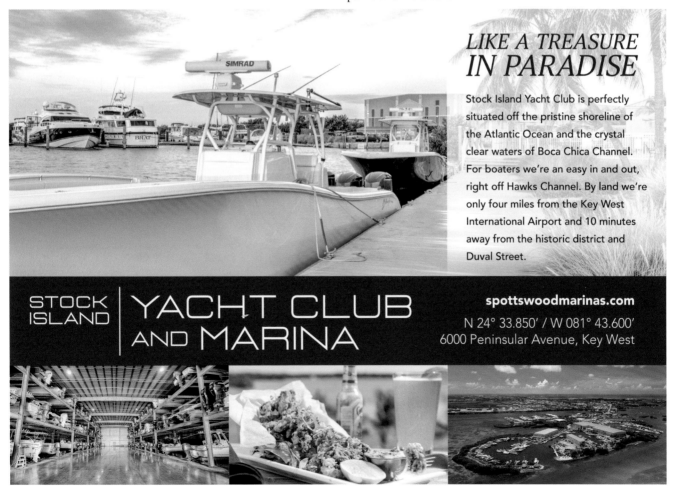

Stock Island, Key West, FL

KEY WEST		Largest Vessel	VHF	Total Slips	Approach/ Dockside Depth	Floating Docks	Gas/ Diesel	Repairs/ Haulout	Min/Max Amps	Pump-Out Station
1. Opal Key Resort and Marina WiFi MM 1243.0	(305) 292-4375	160	16	37	37.0 / 14.0	F			15 / 100	P
2. Galleon Marina WiFi MM 1243.0	**(305) 292-1292**	150	16	91	**12.0 / 9.0**	F			**30 / 100**	P
3. A & B Marina WiFi MM 1243.0	(305) 294-2535	217	16	50	14.0 / 12.0	F	D		30 / 100	P
4. Key West Bight Marina WiFi onSpot MM 1245.0	(305) 809-3984	140	16	145	20.0 / 12.0		GD		30 / 100	P
5. Conch Harbor Marina WiFi onSpot MM 1245.0	(305) 294-2933	195	16	40	30.0 / 9.0		GD		30 / 100	P
6. Spencer's Boat Yard MM 1243.0	(305) 296-8826	45			4.0 / 6.0			RH	30 / 50	P
7. Garrison Bight Marina MM 1243.0	(305) 294-3093	40		280	4.0 / 6.0		G	RH		
8. City Marina at Garrison Bight WiFi onSpot MM 1243.0	(305) 809-3981	70	16	245	7.0 / 6.0	F			30 / 50	P
9. Key West Yacht Club WiFi MM 1243.0	(305) 896-0426	58	16	68	6.0 / 9.0				30 / 50	

WiFi Wireless Internet Access   onSpot Dockside WiFi Facility
Visit www.waterwayguide.com for current rates, fuel prices, website addresses and other up-to-the-minute information.
(Information in the table is provided by the facilities.)

Scan here for more details:

Stock Island, Key West, FL

STOCK ISLAND		Largest Vessel	VHF	Total Slips	Approach/ Dockside Depth	Floating Docks	Gas/ Diesel	Repairs/ Haulout	Min/Max Amps	Pump-Out Station
1. Sunset Marina Key West MM 1239.0	(305) 296-7101	55	16	120	6.0 / 9.0	F	GD		30 / 50	P

WiFi Wireless Internet Access   onSpot Dockside WiFi Facility
Visit www.waterwayguide.com for current rates, fuel prices, website addresses and other up-to-the-minute information.
(Information in the table is provided by the facilities.)

Scan here for more details:

Cow Key Channel
Daybeacon 32

Cow Key Channel
Daybeacon 30

Source: Aqua Map and NOAA data

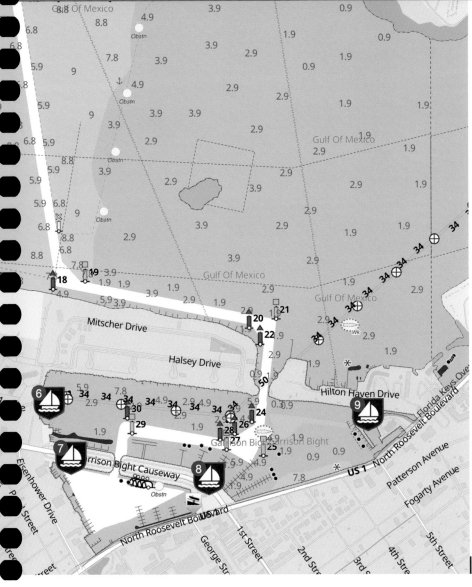

on site. Slips are reserved well in advance and reservations are required.

Additional transient dockage may be available at Garrison Bight. Access to Garrison Bight is restricted by the 50-foot authorized clearance power line at its entrance and reported 4-foot MLW approach depths. Garrison Bight Marina caters to local small-boat fishermen (boats to 40 feet) utilizing the marina's ample dry storage capability. Also in this inner harbor is City Marina at Garrison Bight with floating docks along both sides of the 19-foot vertical clearance fixed **Garrison Bight Bridge**. They can accommodate vessels to 70 feet.

Key West Yacht Club at the east end of Garrison Bight (before the bridge) has limited dockage for members of the Yachting Clubs of America (outside a 50-mile radius). They have a full-service dining room and bar. On the opposite (west side) of the basin is Spencer's Boat Yard with boat rentals and repairs (no transient space).

Sunset Marina Key West, located in a channel northeast of Sigsbee Island, offers acess to Stock Island and Key West and can accommodate vessels to 55 feet.

Moorings: The City of Key West has a mooring field east of Fleming Key with daily and monthly rates. City Marina at Garrison Bight administers these. For reservations call 305-809-3981. To the west of Fleming Key (north of the Key West Historic Harbor) is a second mooring field that is free but be advised that mooring integrity is questionable. The east side has significantly less traffic (and wakes) and is much less bumpy than the west side. It's a short dinghy ride under the **Fleming Key Bridge** (18-foot closed vertical clearance) to get to the tourist area of Key West.

The spacious floating docks (finger piers port and starboard) of the Galleon Marina lie at the far west end of the bight inside the seawall. Marina guests have access to all the resort's amenities including a pool, private beach and sauna and exercise room. Reservations are recommended far in advance during high season and especially for regatta weeks and Fantasy Fest.

A & B Marina is also located on the Historic Seaport Harbor Walk. The marina offers transient slips and free laundry facilities. They request that you tie up "stern to" and will help you arrange this. This is a hub for several fishing charter companies.

On the south side of the bight is Key West Bight Marina, easily identified by the easily accessible fuel dock and the cluster of schooners available for harbor cruises. This friendly and affordable marina can accommodate vessels to 140 feet in its deep-water transient slips with all the usual amenities.

In the southeast corner of the bight, Conch Harbor Marina offers slips for vessels to 200 feet on a monthly and transient basis. They have a large pool and two restaurants

GOIN' ASHORE

KEY WEST, FL

Key West's Old Town is the city's main attraction. Beyond the boutiques, wonderful eateries, seasoned drinking holes and countless T-shirt shops, this is a place to find a sitting spot and just watch as the throngs pass by. Be sure to get a few blocks off Duval St. and have a look at the city's beautifully preserved and restored buildings. Pick up a free Key West map before you start out, available at most marinas and many shops. The free "Duval Loop" bus is a great way to get around the downtown. Walk one way and take the bus back.

SERVICES

1. Advanced Urgent Care
   1980 N. Roosevelt Blvd. (305-294-0011)

2. Key West Chamber of Commerce
   510 Greene St. (305-294-2587)

3. Key West Post Office
   400 Whitehead St. (305-294-9539)

4. Key West Vets and Pets
   1118 White St., Ste. A (305-294-0099)

5. Monroe County Library
   700 Fleming St. (305-292-3595)

ATTRACTIONS

6. The Ernest Hemingway Home & Museum

Ernest Hemingway lived and wrote at 907 Whitehead St. for more than 10 years. Wander through the lush grounds and enjoy the whimsy of the more than 40 resident six-toed cats (305-294-1136).

7. Key West Aquarium

Interactive conservation talks and animal feedings are offered at 1 Whitehead St., home to alligators, jellyfish, sharks, turtles and stingrays (305-296-2051).

8. Key West Butterfly & Nature Conservatory

Glass-enclosed, plant-filled habitat for interactive walks among species of butterflies and birds at 1316 Duval St. (305-296-2988).

9. Key West Lighthouse Museum

Take the 88 steps to the top of the lighthouse for astounding views at 938 Whitehead St. (305-294-0012). The keepers quarters are also on site.

10. Mel Fisher Maritime Museum

This small museum and conservation lab displays artifacts from a 17th-century shipwreck at 200 Greene St. Open daily year-round (305-294-2633).

SHOPPING

11. Fausto's Food Palace

Convenient for provisioning with reasonable prices (522 Fleming St., 305-296-5663).

12. Key West Marine Hardware

Well-stocked chandlery at 818 Caroline St. (305-294-3425).

13. West Marine

Boating supply chain at 951 Caroline St. (305-296-0953).

MARINAS

14. A&B Marina

700 Front St. (305-294-2288)

15. City Marina at Garrison Bight

1801 N. Roosevelt Blvd. (305-809-3981)

16. Conch Harbor Marina

951 Caroline St. (305-294-2933)

17. Galleon Marina

619 Front St. (305-292-1292)

18. Garrison Bight Marina

711 Eisenhower Dr. (305-294-3093)

19. Key West Bight Marina

201 William St. (305-809-3984)

20. Key West Yacht Club

2315 N. Roosevelt Blvd. (305-896-0426)

21. Opal Key Resort and Marina

245 Front St. (305-294-4000)

22. Spencer's Boat Yard

701 Palm Ave. (305-296-8826)

The Conch Republic

On April 23, 1982 the U.S. Border Patrol established a military-style roadblock on U.S. 1 at Florida City. The Border Patrol stopped all northbound highway traffic at a place motorists know as The Last Chance Saloon and searched for illegal aliens and drugs. The ensuing well-publicized traffic jam–traffic stretched back for 19 miles–supposedly stymied the Key's tourism industry.

This spurred a movement in which citizens of the Keys (called "Conchs") elected to secede from the Upper 48. With tongue in cheek, but with a serious gleam in their eyes, they selected a flag, designated their boundaries and became the "Conch Republic." They proclaimed their independence, declared war on the U.S., immediately surrendered and then applied for foreign aid. The roadblock was discontinued after several days and the economy was saved.

Today the tradition of the Conch Republic revolution continues with a yearly celebration in April and appointment of various Conch Ambassadors. To many Key West locals, both natives and transplants alike, the event symbolizes both the intense individualism of the island's people and keen sense of humor that they enjoy.

Key West is a federal No-Discharge Zone meaning no waste, even that which has been treated, should be discharged overboard. A pump-out service for boats on moorings, anchored or in marinas is provided by PumpOut Florida Keys (305-809-3981 or VHF Channel 16) with service available Monday through Saturday, 8:00 a.m. to 4:00 p.m. They will visit marinas but anchored and moored boats take priority.

Anchorage: Key West abounds with anchorage possibilities but many locations afford only modest protection from fast-shifting winds and swift currents. Despite its popularity the holding around Wisteria Island (known locally as Christmas Tree Island) is poor. The exposure from north through east can be a problem in unsettled weather. Nevertheless, boats continue to anchor northwest and southeast of the island.

Nearby Sunset Key (identified on the NOAA chart as "Tank Island") is a 27-acre private residential neighborhood and resort island. This tiny island was a Navy fuel tank depot until 1994 (hence the label "Tank Island"). Do not attempt to go ashore.

West of Fleming Key there is a strong reversing current making careful watches during the first turn of the tide a virtual necessity. Remember to take into consideration the number of anchors, swinging radius and wind-age of surrounding vessels. You will find 7 to 10 feet MLW at Fleming Key Bight and lots of boat traffic.

Note that the charted Restricted Area (150-yard exclusion zone) around the military facilities on Fleming Island have expanded and patrol boats are issuing tickets to violators. Be careful where you anchor.

Both the Wisteria Island and Fleming Key anchorages are relatively close to Old Town and the City Marina at Garrison Bight dinghy dock. It's about a 1-mile walk from Garrison Bight to downtown. The dinghy dock is located immediately in front of Turtle Kraals Restaurant and allows vessels up to 13 feet. The fee for tying up your dinghy is payable to the City Marina. (Discounts are available for longer stays.) The dinghy dock has two sections–one with reserved spots with numbers (outer dock) and another (more chaotic inner dock) for everyone else. Expect shenanigans if you tie up in the wrong space.

An alternative anchorage is the area just to the north of the mooring field and Sigsbee Park where there are good depths of 7 to 10 feet MLW and good holding. Make sure you are outside of the mooring field buoys.

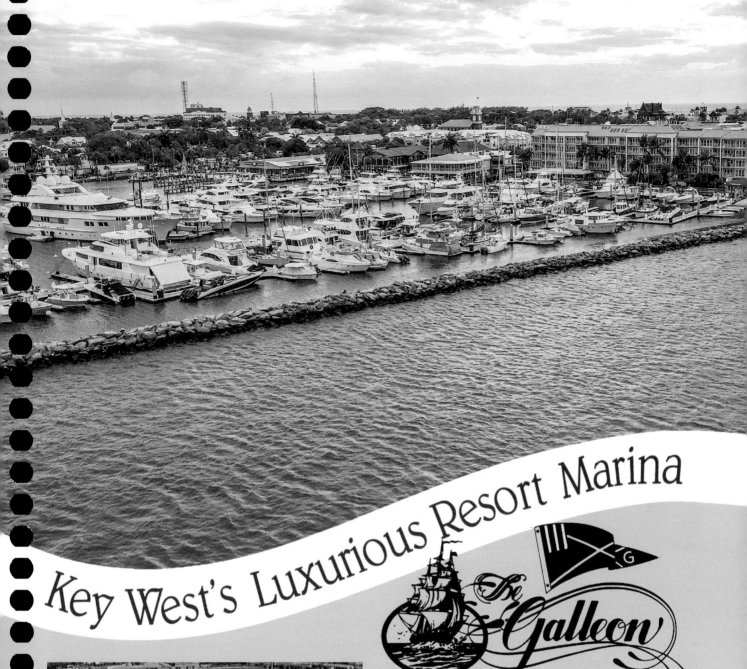

This anchorage is exposed to the north but has much less current and boat wakes than the others. Even in strong northerly winds the shallow water between here and the Gulf cuts down most of the swells leaving you with wind chop, which can be significant in a strong northerly. Some cruisers have been unable to dinghy back to this anchorage under harsh conditions. Be sure to monitor the weather when you plan to go ashore. If you happen to have access to military facilities, the dinghy dock at the Sigsbee Island Marina is a very short walk from showers at the campground and groceries at the commissary.

Side Trip: Sand Key

If you decide to explore the wonders of the underwater world, you can make the 6-mile trip southwest from Key West to the Sand Key Moorings. This is a great snorkeling site, especially in calm conditions. The nearby Marine Sanctuary sites also offer excellent snorkeling. Exercise caution when transiting this area. Sand Key Light has been extinguished because it was structurally unsound and a temporary light has been established in its place.

Anchorage/Moorings: There are 21 mooring balls for visitors to tie to next to this shallow reef. If a mooring buoy is not available and you are outside a no-anchor zone, you may anchor in sand but it is a long swim to the reef. It is best to wait for a mooring ball.

To the Dry Tortugas

Seventy nautical miles from the nearest settlement in Key West the Dry Tortugas are the westernmost of the Florida Keys, the most remote and, in some respects, the most fascinating and beautiful. With careful preparation a voyage to the Dry Tortugas can be most rewarding.

Before departure from Key West skippers should consult the most up-to-date *Local Notice to Mariners* (www.navcen.uscg.gov). In addition to changes in aids to navigation in the area, check on any military operations in the restricted area west of the Marquesas Keys. The

Coast Guard can be reached on VHF Channels 16 and 22A in Key West.

Because of erratic and sometimes severe weather in the area (unpredicted fronts packing high winds are not that unusual) passage to the Dry Tortugas requires planning for the unexpected. Weekend trippers, Caribbean-bound cruisers and fishermen alike often find themselves holed up for a week or more in the modestly protected harbor off Garden Key in persistent 25- to 35-knot winds from stalled fronts in the Gulf of Mexico or off the Cuban coast. If weather conditions are less than ideal a trip to the Dry Tortugas should be postponed. (Or opt for a seaplane ride!)

In all conditions boats bound for the Dry Tortugas should be equipped at a minimum with a VHF radio, depth sounder and GPS unit. Careful checking with NOAA radio forecasts before and during such a trip is essential for your safety. The National Park Service posts daily NOAA weather reports at the docks at Garden Key.

NAVIGATION: Use NOAA Charts 11420, 11434 and 11439. One route to the Dry Tortugas runs south of the Marquesas and the other to the north. The southern route permits easy access to the best anchorage in the Marquesas. Check your charts for shoal areas and stay clear of both keys. Boca Grande Key is approximately 12 nm west of Key West.

The southern route leaves Key West southbound via the Main Ship Channel and enters the Southwest Channel at flashing green "15." From flashing green "15" take a heading of 236° magnetic for the 5.3 nm run to point north of green daybeacon "3" marking shoal charted as Middle Ground. From this point adjust your course to 277° magnetic for 10.3 nm through West Channel to the southern terminus of the Boca Grande Channel, about 2.5 nm north of Coalbin Rock. This leg runs south of Man Key and Boca Grande Key and north of Parsonage Shoal. The route to the Dry Tortugas continues for another 42 nm to the Southeast Channel approach.

The Boca Grande Key anchorage is to the north. Watch for shoals off the key's west flank on approach. Continuing west it is about 4 nm from the Boca Grade Channel at 277° magnetic to the Marquesas Keys. Keep well north of Coalbin Rock. The passage to the Dry Tortugas continues at 277° magnetic for another 10 nm passing south of the Marquesas and The Quicksands.

The Elusive Green Flash

Some say it brings luck; others believe it's a bad omen. Everyone can agree, however, that the green flash is not an everyday occurrence. The green flash refers to the elusive (and often tiny) flash of green sometime seen at the beginning of a sunrise or end of a sunset, just above the disk of the sun. It is called a "flash" because it last only one to two seconds. It is caused by the refraction of the sun's rays at the horizon, or the Earth's atmosphere acting as a prism.

The momentary change in color is dependent on weather, latitude and season. The green flash is best seen after a cold front, when the water temperature is warmer than the air. A clear sky and flat horizon are essential. Because of this, your best bet for witnessing a green flash are in Hawaii, the Caribbean and Florida.

Key West, as the southernmost point in the U.S., is a great place to see the phenomena, but it can also be seen along the Gulf Coast. Seaman are most likely to see the green flash because they have the clearest view of the horizon. Remember: It is not safe to look directly at the sun until it is close to the horizon.

Anchorage: If you choose to take the southern route you can stop off and anchor to the northwest of Boca Grande Key near green daybeacon "17" in 10 to 16 feet at MLW. This site can accommodate boats with deeper drafts. Choose your location based on wind direction. There are no other intermediate anchorages, facilities or supplies of any kind after leaving Key West.

Stopover: The Marquesas Keys

The beautiful Marquesas Keys lie along the route to the Dry Tortugas and are only 21.6 nm west of Key West. An interesting stopover with a fairly well-sheltered but shallow lagoon the Marquesas are made up of numerous small keys arranged in the shape of a South Seas atoll. Use binoculars to locate a suitable entrance. If you have a shoal-draft boat, a high tide and an overhead sun, then you might want to try it; otherwise, don't risk it and anchor outside. You are likely beyond VHF range for assistance.

NAVIGATION: Use NOAA Chart 11439. The Marquesas atoll can be approached from either the northern route or the southern route. You can switch between these routes using the north-south Boca Grande Channel located approximately 2 nm west of Boca Grande Key and identified by green daybeacon "1" to the north and red daybeacon "2" to the south. There are some promising-looking entrances to the Marquesas Keys lagoon on the charts. Only extreme shoal-draft vessels should attempt entry and be prepared to get yourself off the bottom if you run aground. You are likely out of VHF range for assistance here.

Anchorage: At the Marquesas Keys try to figure out the winds and then anchor in the lee of the islands. The NOAA chart shows Mooney Harbor Key as having room for several boats but that is deceiving. Shallow draft boats can snug up due west of the island in at least 4 feet MLW with exposure from the south. It is shallow but you will find excellent holding here. An anchorage on the western side of the atoll is comfortable in winds from an easterly quadrant. Depths of 8 to 13 feet MLW can be found fairly close to shore.

Enjoy a dinghy ride through the maze of passages in the Marquesas atoll but also a marine sanctuary and signs on the shore prohibit you from landing. This area is known for the famous Spanish treasure ship, *The Atocha*, which sank just to the west of the Marquesas in the Quick Sands.

Marquesas Keys to the Dry Tortugas

Dry Tortugas National Park was dedicated in 1992. Its boundary now marked by an elliptical circuit of 10 large yellow buoys. Touring Fort Jefferson on your own is an option but a ranger-guided tour provides many interesting and unusual facts that will enhance your visit and understanding of life at the fort. It is the largest and best-preserved fort of the 19th-century U.S. coastal defense perimeter (8-foot-thick brick walls, standing 50 feet high and surrounding a 17-acre quad).

NAVIGATION: Use NOAA Charts 11420, 11438 (for harbor details) and 11439. Heading west from the Marquesas Keys the southern route continues at 277° magnetic for another 10 nm passing south of The Quicksands. At this point adjust to 290° magnetic for the 28-nm run to flashing red "2" that marks the entrance to Southeast Channel just east of Long Key in the Dry Tortugas.

Plot a course to pass well south of Halfmoon Shoal and Rebecca Shoal along this route. The flashing red lights on these shoals can be useful as waypoints.

Once 0.3 nm west of flashing red buoy "2" adjust course (approximately 315° magnetic) to split flashing green "3" marking Iowa Rock and red daybeacon "4" marking Hospital Key. Then turn due west passing flashing green "3" south of charted Middle Ground. Once west of Garden Key and the associated shoals turn southwest towards the harbor entry channel.

The northern route from the Marquesas starts at the Ellis Rock light located 2 nm northwest of the Marquesas atoll. It is a straight 35-nm run at 272° magnetic to flashing red "2" marking the Southeast Channel approach to the Dry Tortugas. There are some markers in the shallows south along this route. Pass south of the flashing white on the western edge of New Ground shoal (4 second, 19 feet high).

Pass north of the flashing red markers for Halfmoon Shoal and Rebecca Shoal. You should maintain 20 feet MLW on this segment. As you approach the eastern edge of the Dry Tortugas you can pick out Bush Key and Garden Key with Fort Jefferson dominating the island landscape. This route joins the southern route at flashing read "2."

The channel to the anchorage is entered by splitting red daybeacon "2" and green daybeacon "3." Visual navigation is required here and entry should not be attempted in darkness. The course swings southeast after passing the entry markers so keep south of green daybeacon "7." Rounding green daybeacon "7" turn east into the Garden Key anchorage.

Vessels approaching from the south are advised to use Southwest Channel running between Loggerhead Key and Garden Key. Keep green markers to port on this channel and enter east of green can buoy "1." At red daybeacon "6" take a wide turn to the southeast and follow the closely spaced markers on both sides of the deep channel into the Garden Key anchorage.

> ⚠️
> Note that a solid isthmus between Bush Key and Garden Key has formed in recent years. We suggest that you refer to print-on-demand charts to get the most recent published information on the channels in and out of the Garden Key anchorage at Fort Jefferson.

Keep in mind the shoals can change in a single storm so visual shallow water techniques will be required in and around the Dry Tortugas. Entry in good light is advised.

Anchorage: The best anchorage is found in front (to the east) of the deteriorated steamship docks at the southern end of Garden Key. There is variable holding in 15 to 20 feet MLW. Be careful outside the channel as charted depths are about 1 foot MLW. Find a sandy patch, power back, test the set and then perform a visual check or an anchor dive to make sure. In this relatively confined and exposed area there are almost always at least half a dozen boats and often more than twice that number during a blow.

> Park regulations restrict overnight anchoring to within 1 mile of Garden Key Harbor Light. During nesting season you may want to anchor away from Bush Key to avoid the nighttime noise of the Sooty Terns.

When visiting Garden Key by private boat you must check in at the National Park Service Visitor Center inside Fort Jefferson upon arrival. Rangers will provide a copy of the park's brochure with maps and regulations and the latest weather report. There are restrooms at the docks and beach space for dinghy landings.

The park is a No-Discharge Zone and park rangers may check your vessel's Y-valve. The park has picnic tables, a few charcoal grills and a beautiful designated swim beaches. No services or supplies are available and all trash must be carted back to your boat.

■ NEXT STOP

Next up is the eclectic West Coast of Florida where the alligators, fish camps and seagrass of the Everglades give way to the fast-paced urban life of the Tampa Bay area to the north. Take your time and consider a stop in Everglades National park on the way. The scenery and wildlife are spectacular.

KEYS ANCHORAGES

ICW ROUTE

Ragged Keys (Mile 1106). East of the ICW, 7-foot approach, 8 feet to shoal west of Keys. Holding fair to good in grassy mud. Limited protection from northeast through southeast.

Sand Key (Mile 1108). East of the ICW, 6.5-foot approach, 5 feet in area west of northern portion of the key. Holding fair to good in grassy mud. Protected from south to northeast.

Elliott Key (Mile 1109 to Mile 1114). East of the ICW, 5-foot approach, 5 feet to shoal anywhere along west side of the key. Holding fair to good depending on rocky to grassy mud bottom. Protection from northeast through southeast.

Caesar Creek (Mile 1115). East of the ICW, anchorage open to both routes. Four-foot approach from ICW; 12 feet in best area between Rubicon and Reid keys. Holding good; mud and some grass. Well protected.

Angelfish Creek (Mile 1120). East of the ICW, anchorage open to both routes. Five-foot approach from both ends. Anchorage in side creeks north of channel is 5 feet deep. Holding mixed: some rocky areas, some hard. Strong currents. Well protected.

Pumpkin Key (Mile 1122). East of the ICW, 9-foot approach, 7 feet to shoal anywhere in lee of key depending on winds. Holding fair to good in grassy mud with some rocks.

Steamboat Creek in Card Sound (Mile 1125). East of the ICW, 9-foot approach, 7 feet to shoal north and in mouth of creek off Jew Point. Holding good in grassy mud. Protection only from southwest to east.

Manatee Bay in Barnes Sound (Mile 1132). West of the ICW, 5-foot approach and 5 feet to shoal in area near marked channel leading into Manatee Creek. Holding good in hard bottom. Protection fair to good except in strong winds from north to northwest.

Thursday Cove, Barnes Sound (Mile 1133). East of the ICW, 7-foot approach, 5 to7 feet between Largo Point and Thursday Point. Holding good in grassy mud. Protection only from southwest to northeast.

Sexton Cove (Mile 1135). East of the ICW, 7-foot approach, 6-foot depth to shoaling close in. Holding fair in grass and hard bottom with some rocks. Protection from northwest through southeast.

Stellrecht Point (Mile 1136). Southeast of the ICW, 7-foot approach, 6 feet to shoal just south of the point. Holding fair to good in grassy mud. Protected from northeast through south.

Tarpon Basin (Mile 1139). Southeast of the ICW, 7-foot approach, anchor in 5-6 feet south of shoal in center of the basin. Holding fair to good in grassy mud over rock. All-round protection.

Sunset Cove, Buttonwood Sound (Mile 1143). Southeast of the ICW, 5-foot approach, 4 feet or less close in, 5 feet near Pelican Key and near Upper Keys Sailing Club docks. Holding fair to good. Protection depends on location.

Butternut Key (Mile 1146). Northwest of the ICW, 6-foot approach, 5 feet near eastern Butternut Key just north of marker "60." Holding fair in soft bottom. Protection only from northwest to north. (Note this anchorage is in Everglades National Park.)

Tavernier Community Harbor (Mile 1150). South of the ICW, 5-foot approach, 5 feet outside basin, 4 feet inside. Holding poor to fair in dense, grassy bottom. Protection fair to good in all but strongest north winds.

Cowpens Anchorage (Mile 1155). Southeast of the ICW, 5-foot approach and depth. Numerous spots to anchor in Cowpens Anchorage area. Fair to good holding in soft bottom, some grass. Protection from east through west, depending on exact anchoring spot.

Cotton Key (Mile 1157). South of the ICW, 7-foot approach and 5 feet in the anchorage. Leave ICW at red day-beacon "86." Protection from north through southeast. Holding fair in grassy mud bottom.

Upper Matecumbe Key (Mile 1160). South of the ICW, 6-foot approach and 5 feet in the anchorage off of the restaurant/bar. Protection from south through southeast. Holding fair in soft bottom.

Shell Key (Mile 1161). Southeast of the ICW, 7-foot approach from the west. Can drop anchor close to shore for good protection from east winds. Holding good in grass and sand.

Lignumvitae Key (Mile 1164). Southeast of the ICW, 7-foot approach to either side of key. DO NOT ANCHOR; use the heavy moorings provided. Protection is dependent on being in the lee of the key.

Long Key Bight (Mile 1170). On ocean side of Channel Five Bridge, 7-foot approach, shoaling to 5 feet at center. Anchor as far in as draft allows. Holding good in grassy mud. Protection from all but east winds.

Fiesta Key (Mile 1171). On bay-side of Channel Five Bridge, 9-foot approach, 6 feet at anchor. Anchor as close to causeway as draft allows. Holding good in sand and grass. Protection west through southeast.

Rachel Key (Mile 1190). Southwest of the ICW, south of Rachel Bank, 7-foot approach, 5 feet in area southwest of Rachel Key and southeast of charted shoal. Holding fair to good in sand and grass. Anchoring in the bight southeast of Rachel Key is also possible. Protection fair to good depending on exact location.

Boot Key Harbor (Mile 1195). East of the ICW, accessible through Knights Key Channel or Moser Channel, then east to Boot Key Channel. See details in anchorages for Hawk Channel route.

Bahia Honda Area (Mile 1205). Southwest of the ICW in charted cove, 7-foot approach, 7 feet to shoal inside 6-foot line. Holding fair in grassy mud. Protection from east through southwest only. You can, with care, anchor just outside the park basin in 8 feet if you can get under the 20-foot clearance at the bridge.

Crane Key (Mile 1225). Enter through Cudjoe Channel in good light. Eight-foot approach, 6 feet at anchor. Anchor as close to key as draft allows. Holding good in grassy mud. Protection from northeast through southeast.

HAWK CHANNEL ROUTE

Caesar Creek (Mile 1118). Anchorage open to both routes. Seven-foot approach from Hawk Channel, 4 feet from ICW. Anchorage best between Rubicon and Reid keys. Twelve-foot depth, holding good. Well protected.

Angelfish Creek (Mile 1122). Anchorage open to both routes. Five-foot approach from both channels. Anchorage in side creeks north of channel. Five-foot depth, holding mixed, some hard and some rocky areas. Strong currents, well protected.

Largo Sound (Mile 1141). Five-foot approach, some 5-foot depths near the channel, but 3 feet is the norm. Holding fair, some grass, well protected.

Rodriguez Key (Mile 1145). Seven-foot approach, 7 feet or less close in. Anchor in lee as required for protection. Holding good. Note wrecks north of key and shoal to the west.

Rock Harbor (Mile 1144). Seven-foot approach, anchor as close in as draft will permit. Protection from north to northeast. Mandalay Restaurant (cash only) has a dinghy beach.

Tavernier Key (Mile 1150). Six-foot approach, less close in. Anchor in Tavernier Harbor area. Holding good. Some protection from northwest to north, southwest through south.

Whale Harbor (Mile 1158). Five-foot approach, 5 feet in anchorage. Anchor in lee relative of keys to north and to small key to southwest near marker "5A." Holding fair, some grass. Protection fair northwest through east. Note shoals.

Indian Key (Mile 1165). Seven-foot approach, 7 feet or less at anchorage close in. Anchor on southeast side of key in lee. Holding good in sand and sea grass. Protection fair from northwest through northeast.

Long Key Bight (Mile 1172). Nine-foot approach, shoaling to 5 feet in center. You can anchor as far in as draft allows. Holding good in some sea grass. Good protection from all but due east.

Boot Key Harbor (Mile 1193). Seven-foot approach from Sister Creek, 7-foot approach from Boot Key Channel. Eleven feet to shoaling near head of harbor. Holding good. Good protection for 360° except in severe east-northeast winds. Little room to anchor outside of mooring field. Alternative is to harbor outside, just west of Boot Key in 5 to 8 feet.

Bahia Honda Key (Mile 1207). Ten-foot approach, 9 feet or less close in between bridges. Holding fair to good. Fair to good protection. Strong tidal currents. Anchor checks on tide swings are advised.

Newfound Harbor (Mile 1215). Seven-foot approach. Most anchor in the cross-bar of the "H" etched by the deeper channels in 7 to 8 feet. Or in 9 feet or less close in toward highway bridge. Holding good. Fair to good protection in all but worst southerly winds.

Niles Channel (Mile 1215). Seven-foot approach, depths of 7 to 21 feet in sand and grass. Holding fair to good in mud and grass. Fair to good protection in all but worst winds from the south.

Saddlebunch Harbor (Mile 1228). Six-foot approach through narrow channel between Saddlebunch Keys and Pelican Key. Anchor in 7 to 8 feet close to mangroves on east shore. Holding fair. Strong currents. Buoy your anchor. Fair to good protection.

Key West (Mile 1245). Anchoring is not permitted in Garrison Bight. Many of the best spots in Key West are taken by liveaboards. Also be wary of submerged wrecks. The anchorages north or east of Wisteria Island are popular but exposed in north and west winds. Holding is fair in a sand and grass with depths of 7 feet to shoal near shore. West of Fleming Key is another alternative but not within 150 yards of the military facilities on Fleming Island. This anchorage is adjacent and contiguous to the harbor and is exposed to the wash and wake of passing vessels. Holding is good with a fairly hard bottom with protection from east and south winds and partially by the shoals to the north. Alternately, proceed around the north end of Fleming Key and find limited protection north of the mooring field and off of Sigsbee Park.

Florida's West Coast

Chapter 11: Florida Keys to Fort Meyers Beach   **Chapter 13:** Tampa Bay to Tarpon Springs

Chapter 12: Fort Meyers Beach to Sarasota Bay

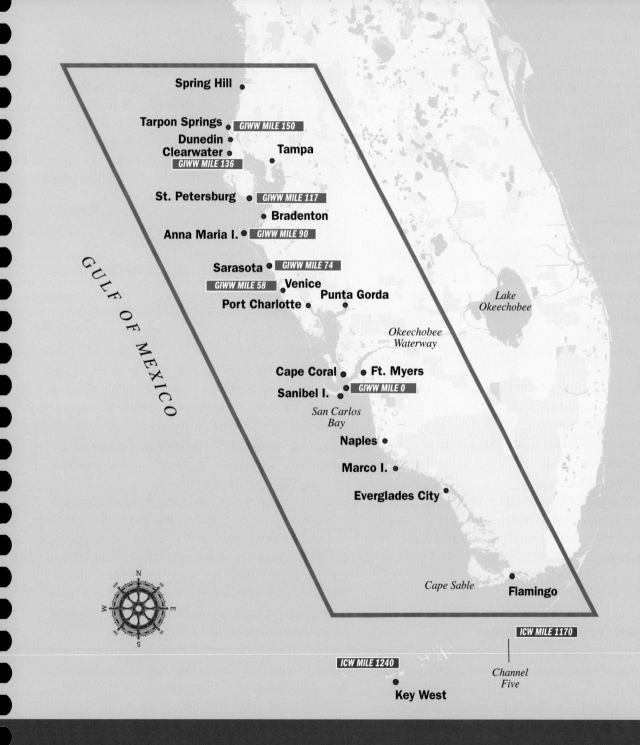

Spring Hill

Tarpon Springs   *GIWW MILE 150*

Dunedin

Clearwater   Tampa

GIWW MILE 136

St. Petersburg   *GIWW MILE 117*

Bradenton

Anna Maria I.   *GIWW MILE 90*

Sarasota   *GIWW MILE 74*

GIWW MILE 58   Venice

Port Charlotte   Punta Gorda

GULF OF MEXICO

Lake Okeechobee

Okeechobee Waterway

Cape Coral   Ft. Myers

Sanibel I.   *GIWW MILE 0*

San Carlos Bay

Naples

Marco I.

Everglades City

Cape Sable   Flamingo

ICW MILE 1170

Channel Five

ICW MILE 1240

Key West

■ NAVIGATION NOTES

With sugar sand beaches and seashells, tropical hardwoods and Everglades swampland, Florida's lower west coast provides a greater diversity of experiences than the east. Instead of being packed with crowds, cultural communities and glamour, cruising the west coast brings opportunities for relaxation and the kind of casual luxury that is experienced in isolated high-end resorts. The cruising, too, is entirely different as it is less confined by the waterway and offers more open water passages.

The amenities may be more limited and spaced farther apart but Florida's southwestern waters give access to the swampy wilderness of the Everglades, the long sweep of Sanibel and Captiva Islands, picturesque fishing villages, bustling Tampa Bay and the history- and restaurant-rich Greek sponge center of Tarpon Springs. Here cruisers think more about enjoying the ride and less about putting down miles.

The lower half of the coast is alternately wild and developed. At the bottom of the peninsula Cape Sable and the Ten Thousand Islands guard the swampland of the Everglades. Up the coast the shoreline transitions to sandy beaches backed by walls of pine and tropical hardwood jungle.

The tropical barrier islands emerge at San Carlos Bay. Deep water moves in closer toward shore and resort communities begin to appear. Mile 0 of the Gulf Intracoastal Waterway (GIWW) whets the appetite for travel at the mouth of the Caloosahatchee River, where the Okeechobee Waterway ends for westbound traffic and begins for those heading east.

From Marco Island northward the west coast sees increasing development, boat traffic, marinas and shore activity. The wilderness that defines the Everglades shoreline is relegated to protected pockets and south Florida's dominant mangroves increasingly give way to extensive shoreside development.

Gulf Coast Cruising Conditions

Much of the shoreline of the lower half of Florida's west coast remains undeveloped and natural. Most significant is the 65 nm of Everglades National Park shoreline from Flamingo to Everglades City. This navigable coastal area is uninhabited, is only accessible by boat and offers no services. This shoreline does, however, provide well-provisioned cruisers access to a natural paradise.

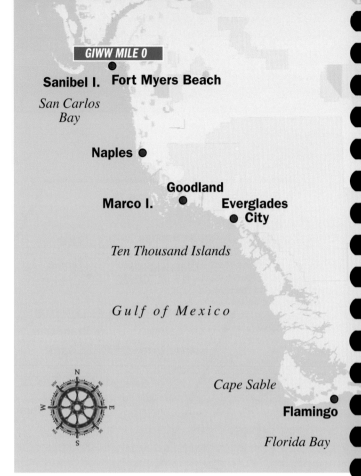

Farther north along the west coast there are 14 aquatic preserves, 40 state parks, 14 national wildlife refuges and the over 100,000-acre Rookery Bay National Estuarine Research Reserve–one of the few remaining undisturbed mangrove estuaries in North America. Florida's west coast is wonderful destination for cruisers hoping to explore some of Florida's natural habitat.

Unlike Florida's east coast there is not a continuous inland waterway running the full length of the Gulf Coast. For most cruising boats it will be an open ocean passage for the 125 nm from Marathon (in the Florida Keys) to the start of the GIWW at Cape Coral on San Carlos Bay. There are anchorages along the way that allow cruisers to break up the trip but cruisers will need to complete several ocean passages of 40 nm or more.

The GIWW leads north from Cape Coral and is either a dredged channel behind barrier islands or a passage through one of Florida's large Gulf Coast bays. This protected waterway begins at the mouth of the Caloosahatchee River and runs 150 statute miles north to Anclote Keys. Much of the waterway is constrained to a narrow, marked channel with shoals lurking outside similar to the ICW on Florida's east coast. While the option of an "inside route" is reassuring, many cruisers make the trip northward as a series of open ocean hops. Seas are generally manageable in the shallow off-shore waters and refuge can be sought at regular intervals. Be sure to check for a suitable weather window and plan your passage based on inlets with sufficient depth.

Although they might seem worse to the inexperienced, most tidal currents are less than 2 knots here. At 1 to 3 feet the tidal range is relatively small and water depths tend to be governed more by wind than by tide. When winds blow from the northeast the water is driven out of the bays, while strong winds from the southeast and southwest push water in. Under northeast wind conditions there is generally less water in the bays than the charted mean low water. Be especially wary when a spring low tide combines with a fresh northeast breeze.

From time to time your navigational skills will be tested as you follow the course offshore into the Gulf proper. The occasionally capricious weather may surprise you with a severe and sudden storm. Navigable inlets are few and far between and most are subject to severe shoaling. Be prepared with the latest charts and up-to-date weather advisories and make sure your boat and equipment are in top shape.

Navigating the GIWW

The GIWW begins at the mouth of the Caloosahatchee River and runs 150 statute miles north to Anclote Keys, much of it through a narrow channel. While there are fewer bridges on the GIWW than the ICW. Most are bascule or swing bridges and many operate on a fixed schedule. The air-draft for the GIWW is 65 feet and is set by fixed bridges. The minimum authorized overhead cable clearance is 85 feet.

Shoals flank much of the marked route similar to the ICW on Florida's east coast. The Army Corps of Engineers' project depth for the length of the 150-mile-long GIWW is purported to be 9 feet MLW but do not count on having that much water. Keep an eye on the depths here, especially in winter when northerly winds push the water out of bays and channels. Even under optimum conditions shoaling is so chronic in certain spots (noted in the text) that boats must slow down and gently ease their way through.

This west coast waterway provides the same type of protection from inclement weather as the Atlantic ICW

and like its East Coast counterpart the GIWW varies in nature with location. In some areas the GIWW is serpentine with many sharp bends and turns; in other places, it runs in open straightaways. No matter its course the GIWW still requires navigational vigilance so keep the following precautions in mind:

- Look astern as often as ahead and keep markers lined up fore and aft to maintain your course in-channel.

- Stay mid-channel if possible and be alert to side currents and crosswinds that may cause lightly powered or high-windage vessels to drift off course and out of the dredged channel.

- Slow down in any area where shoaling is likely, especially if your boat draws more than 3 feet. West coast bottoms tend to commonly consist of soft mud or sand. Grounding at slow speed will do less damage than barreling full-tilt onto a shoal.

Heading north on the GIWW leave red daybeacons to starboard and green to port. As with the Atlantic ICW, GIWW channel markers are green or red with small yellow triangles on red markers and squares on green markers (and an occasional yellow stripe) in addition to the numbers and/or letters. Another way to remember this is that the red marks delineate the mainland side of the GIWW channel.

NO WAKE ZONE

No Wake Zones, Idle Speed Zones and various Speed Limit restrictions are in effect throughout the waterways included in this chapter. Exercise diligence in knowing the regulations by observing signs and other markers. Enforcement is always present. As always, be courteous to other vessels and avoid manatees and other marine life.

Navigating the Everglades

Traveling through the wild and uninhabited expanse of the Everglades cruisers are enveloped in nature and learn to respect its power at the same time. There are no services between Marathon and Everglades City and you must plan the passage carefully. For most this will enhance the experience but this is true cruising and crews must be self-reliant and prepared.

Heading north through the natural beauty of the Everglades and the Ten Thousand Islands, you may wonder if you are still in Florida. The natural diversity and seclusion of Florida's west coast is a gunkholer's dream and makes cruising here a draw for the adventuresome.

■ FLORIDA KEYS TO EAST CAPE–INLAND PASSAGE

Two routes are available to leave the ICW in the Keys and traverse Florida Bay westward for Cape Sable to points north along Florida's west coast. If you have a vessel large enough to cruise offshore, a faster boat or are comfortable with a longer duration passage, then hugging the shore of Cape Sable is just adding extra miles to your trip. Routes that hug the Everglades coast eventually have to head westward to avoid the Cape Romano Shoals that extend south from Marco Island.

Basically if the weather is right and your objective is to reach Naples or points north, you may want to take a direct route passing well offshore of the Everglades. We describe "Offshore" and "Coastal" routes separately below.

Regardless of which route you choose, there are three practical departure points northward from the Keys. The most easterly is the Yacht Channel north from the Channel Five Bridge. The most central is via Moser Channel from the Marathon area. And many leave directly from Key West via the Northwest Channel (or from the Cudjoe Channel if an intermediate stop is planned).

Should you choose to try a side trip to Flamingo, realize this is small boat territory only. Call ahead for up-to-date information and conditions. Taking it slow and easy is recommended when exploring this area. Follow the buoys and daybeacons carefully; depths outside the channel are 1 to 2 feet MLW. Play the tides if your draft is over 3 feet.

■ FLORIDA KEYS TO EAST CAPE–OFFSHORE ROUTE

These are longer routes and slower craft will need longer than 12 hours to complete the passage necessitating nighttime operation for many. There are hazards on these routes and caution should be exercised for operation in darkness. Offshore depths are consistent but numerous fishing boats operate in these waters and there are typically a multitude of lobster pots in the area. Be sure that you have a sufficient weather window (with a 24-hour buffer) before attempting an overnight passage.

Route 1: From Long Key via Yacht Channel

NAVIGATION: Use NOAA Charts 11449, 11431, 11429 and 11452. This route is not recommended for vessels with drafts exceeding 5 feet or for passage in poor light. Expect depths to be shallower than the charted nominal depths of 5 to 6 feet MLW, especially if the wind has a strong easterly component. Particular caution should be exercised crossing the Arsenic Bank and the Sprigger Bank.

The route is the same as for the coastal route to flashing red "2" located south of East Cape. From here it's a heading of 321° magnetic north-westward for 60 nm to clear the Cape Romano shoals. Turning north at this point paralleling the shore of Marco Island for 11 nm to the Capri Pass entrance.

Route 2: From Vaca Key via Moser Channel

NAVIGATION: Use NOAA Charts 11442, 11453, 11431, 11429 and 11452. Depths on this route should maintain 7 to 8 feet MLW. From the Moser Channel gap in the Seven Mile Bridge the course is initially due north magnetic. Several shoals flank the route on both sides until clear of the Bullard Bank approximately 7 nm north of the bridge, and your course must be adjusted to keep red markers to starboard and green markers to port. From flashing green "17" off the Bullard Bank shoal it's a heading of 327° magnetic for 70 nm to clear the Cape Romano shoals. Turning north at this point paralleling the shore of Marco Island for 11 nm to the Capri Pass entrance.

Route 3: From Key West via Northwest Channel

NAVIGATION: Use NOAA Charts 11442, 11431, 11429 and 11452. It is a single 80-nm leg at 008° magnetic from flashing green "1" marking the northern terminus of Key West's Northwest Channel to flashing red "2" marking the entry to the Capri Pass south of Naples. The minimum depth is 14 feet MLW and is much deeper offshore. Despite being an offshore route, you must man the helm on this passage as numerous fishing boats operate in these waters and it is littered with lobster pots.

Side Trip: Flamingo & Cape Sable

The Flamingo Basin forms the northern reach of Florida Bay and its navigable waters allow cruisers to explore the bay's shallows and provides shore-access to the Everglades National Park. The Cape Sable structure is Florida's southernmost mainland feature and has some beautiful, isolated beaches that have been formed by costal storm action.

The cape's relatively high elevation (by Everglades standards) provides the dry land site of the Flamingo Visitors Center. The Visitor Center offers canoe, kayak and bike rentals in addition to daily tours and a small museum that highlights the park's unique plant and animal life. For activity schedules, trail guides, a backcountry trip planner, natural history and more, call 239-695-2945.

NAVIGATION: Use NOAA Charts 11433 or 11451. This is shoal-draft boat territory and "wind tide" can be significant. The dredged access channel to Flamingo has a charted design depth of 4.5 feet MLW but is unreliable. Before you venture into Flamingo we suggest that you call ahead for up-to-date information and conditions. Most larger cruising vessels anchor in Florida Bay at the end of the access channel north of Murray Key (close to red daybeacon "8") and dinghy in. Taking it slow and easy is recommended when exploring this area.

The turn to reach Flamingo either for a daytime visit or an anchorage is at flashing red "2," which is 1.95 nm on a bearing of 178° magnetic from East Cape on Cape Sable. From flashing red "2" keep red markers to starboard and green markers to port. The channel passes south of the Middle Ground shoals. It is 8.5 nm from East Cape to the Flamingo access channel marked by flashing green "9." The shallow access channel runs north-northeast for a little over 1 mile to the Flamingo harbor but is only passible by extreme shoal draft vessels.

Follow the buoys and daybeacons carefully. Depths outside the access channel are 1 to 2 feet MLW. Play the tides if your draft is over 3 feet. The chart shows 4.5 feet MLW in the entry channel but the date of the sounding data is quite old. Be sure to refer to the most up-to-date charts.

It's approximately 115 nm from Flamingo to Fort Myers Beach. Many skippers with faster craft choose to travel this distance offshore. From flashing red "2" located

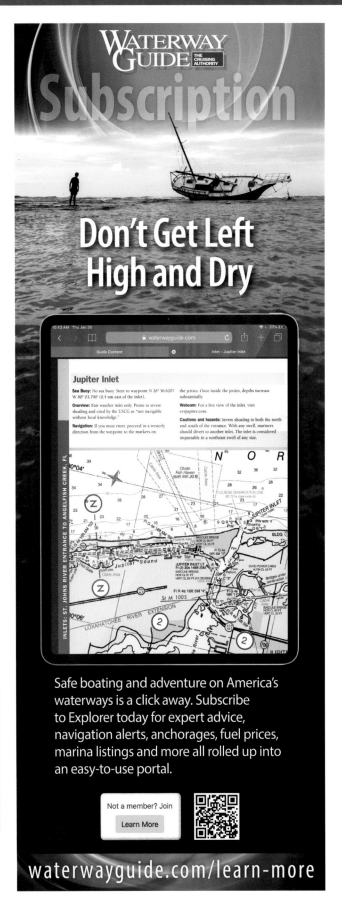

Flamingo, FL

FLAMINGO		Largest Vessel	VHF	Total Slips	Approach/ Dockside Depth	Floating Docks	Gas/ Diesel	Repairs/ Haulout	Min/Max Amps	Pump-Out Station
1. Flamingo Marina	(239) 695-2945	40	16	26	1.0 / 3.5		G	H	30	P

WiFi Wireless Internet Access   **onSpot** Dockside WiFi Facility
Visit www.waterwayguide.com for current rates, fuel prices, website addresses and other up-to-the-minute information.
(Information in the table is provided by the facilities.)

Scan here for more details:

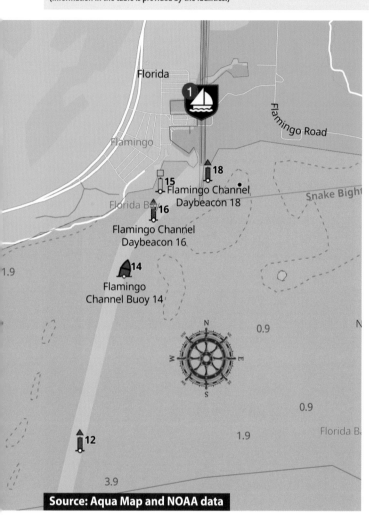

Source: Aqua Map and NOAA data

Anchorage: It is possible to anchor outside the breakwater immediately south of the Flamingo Visitors Center in 4 to 5 feet MLW with good holding in mud. Flamingo Basin provides all-around protection. Larger vessels must anchor in Florida Bay north of Murray Key at the end of the access channel. Depths drop off quickly on the Dan Foy Bank so anchor just outside the marked channel in 5 to 7 feet MLW. The protection is only fair but the chop is limited by the surrounding shallow waters. A mild breeze is welcome as it will reduce the mosquito annoyance.

■ NORTH FROM EAST CAPE– INLAND PASSAGE

The coastal (inland) route continues northward inside the 3-mile limit and parallels the Everglades National Park shoreline. First passing Cape Sable and then into the Ten Thousand Islands, which begin near the mouth of the Chatham River. It's about 16 nm from East Cape to Little Shark River and another 19 nm to Little Turkey Key at the start of the Ten Thousand Islands. This island group stretches for about 26 nm to Cape Romano. Primitive, remote and uninhabited, these islands form the northern shoreline of the Everglades National Park.

Cape Sable has three distinct prominences: East Cape, Middle Cape and Northwest Cape. The southernmost, East Cape, is also the most southerly point of mainland Florida. The cape's beautiful, pristine beaches make a wonderful stop for cruisers but don't expect complete solitude; they are inhabited by American Crocodiles.

NAVIGATION: Use NOAA Charts 11429, 11431, 11433 and 11451. To avoid the shoals extending from East Cape, keep south and west of green daybeacon "1A" as you turn north. (Note the charted submerged pile near the daybeacon.) You will encounter thousands of lobster and crab pot markers if you leave the marked boundaries of Everglades National Park. It's best to parallel the shoreline about 2 miles off.

south of East Cape a heading of 321° magnetic north-westward for 60 nm should allow you to clear the Cape Romano Shoals. Once north of Cape Romano adjust to 340° magnetic and parallel Florida's west coast for the 40-nm run to San Carlos Bay. From here you can pass under the Sanibel Causeway Boulevard 'B' Span Bridge and enter the Gulf Intracoastal Waterway (GIWW).

Dockage: Flamingo Marina is open year-round with electric and water hookups. There is a marina store with limited supplies. The access channel is only viable for vessels with a 4-foot draft maximum.

Pay close attention to your chart and the depth sounder while underway as several sandbars extend from shore. Enter waypoints or follow courselines on your chartplotter to keep a safe distance offshore and to avoid hazards. If you are planning to head for Cape Romano, Marco Island or Naples, set your course to remain well offshore of the Cape Romano Shoals some with depths below 1 foot MLW. These shoals begin 10 nm south of Cape Romano.

Heading north to round Cape Romano and its extensive shoal system courselines run offshore and you are exposed to winds from the entire northern sector. "Holing up" in a blow is recommended. Even in the summer squall lines or simply strong prevailing southeasterlies can stir things up. NOAA weather reports on VHF Channel WX2 or WX3 should keep you informed so you can make the passage safely.

Should you choose the offshore route it's approximately 115 nm from Flamingo to Fort Myers Beach. Many skippers with faster craft choose to travel this distance offshore. From flashing red "2" located south of East Cape a heading of 321° magnetic north-westward for 60 nm should allow you to clear the Cape Romano Shoals. Once north of Cape Romano adjust to 340° magnetic and parallel Florida's west coast for the 40-nm run to San Carlos Bay. From here you can pass under the Sanibel Causeway Boulevard 'B' Span Bridge and enter the Gulf Intracoastal Waterway (GIWW).

Anchorage: If the winds have an easterly component and are light you can anchor off the beautiful Cape Sable beaches that extend from East Cape to Northwest Cape. East Cape Sable north of Middle Cape is particularly pleasant. You can dinghy ashore but watch for the American Crocodiles that inhabit this area and keep pets on a leash. These animals are more aggressive than alligators but typically enter the ocean when humans approach. Everglades National Park rangers report that incidents with the crocodiles are rare but you may want to avoid swimming here.

Depths will depend on your chosen location. Be sure to test your hold in the sand and grass bottom as a wind shift could leave you awash on the beach. This is open northwest through south. The area provides excellent beach combing opportunities and you will have little competition as few people anchor here.

> The Middle Cape Canal just north of Middle Cape is reported to be a good fishing spot but you will need a freshwater license if you intend to dip the rod in Lake Ingraham.

Little Shark River

The well-protected Little Shark River anchorage a popular stop for cruisers in slower craft that are breaking up the journey from the Florida Keys to Naples. The river is also an access route to Everglades Wilderness Waterway, Oyster Bay and the park's inner regions.

NAVIGATION: Use NOAA Charts 11431 and 11432. About 6 miles above Northwest Cape pick up the marked entrance to the Little Shark River off the tip of Shark River Island just south of Ponce de Leon Bay. Note that some of Shark River Island has been eroded away in storms and may not appear exactly as charted.

Little Shark River is a gateway to the inner regions of the Everglades National Park and can provide access to the Everglades Wilderness Waterway connecting Flamingo and Everglades City. This route is not recommended for vessels requiring more than 18 feet of clearance nor those that have high cabins and/or windscreens because of the narrow channels and over-hanging foliage in some areas.

Marked channels lead into coffee-colored wide and shallow bays or up narrow rivers through hundreds of islands and winding waterways. Uncharted snags and bars are common in these waters so operate with caution here. Remember navigating this type of course requires knowing where you are at all times. It is easy to get lost in the numerous channels many of which seem to dead end.

The in-shore waters north of Little Shark River are riddled with shoals and spots of very shallow water (2 to 3 feet MLW). Your depth sounder and your chartplotter will be your friend. It's best to follow your "cookie crumbs" when reversing course in shallow waters.

Anchorage: If you are looking to wait out nasty northerly weather or just wanting to break up your passage into daylight hops, getting the hook down in Little Shark River and out of the waves is a good option. The water is deep (10 to 15 feet MLW) and the scenery is beautiful. Mariners have been waiting out bad weather here for many years. Many cruising boats anchor in the first mile or so of the Little Shark River, which is protected by a 60-foot-high mangrove forest.

Ten Thousand Islands, FL

EVERGLADES		Largest Vessel	VHF	Total Slips	Approach/ Dockside Depth	Floating Docks	Gas/ Diesel	Repairs/ Haulout	Min/Max Amps	Pump-Out Station
1. Everglades Rod & Gun Club	(239) 695-2101	100	16	17	5.5 / 6.0				50	
2. Everglades Isle Marina **WiFi**	(239) 695-2600	60		100	/	F	G		20 / 100	P

WiFi Wireless Internet Access **onSpot** Dockside WiFi Facility
Visit www.waterwayguide.com for current rates, fuel prices, website addresses and other up-to-the-minute information.
(Information in the table is provided by the facilities.)

Scan here for more details:

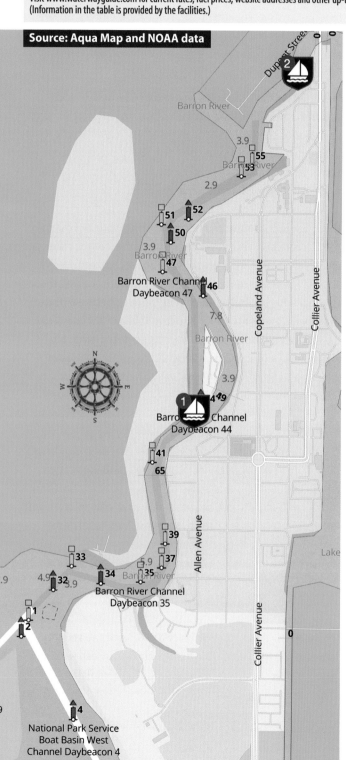

Source: Aqua Map and NOAA data

A popular spot to anchor is in the bend in the river north of red daybeacon "4." This area has shoaled in with mud/shell and may be more shallow than the charted depth of 4 to 12 feet MLW. Since the bottom is so soft you can slowly feel your way in to anchor but be sure to sound out your entire swing radius as tidal currents are strong. Snags are a potential problem here; use of a trip line is advised. If the wind has an easterly component, it is also possible to anchor in the mouth of the river along the south shore.

If your boat is not screened in, keep plenty of bug repellent handy. (On second thought, keep some handy even if you do have screens.) Those with keen eyes can spot alligators along the banks or in the water. At night a flashlight shone into the wilderness will usually reveal dozens of little red eyes that belong to alligators. This is a definite "no swimming" area!

The pelicans work this area quite often and are fun to watch. A crab line dropped overboard and carefully hauled in will supply the galley with a magnificent meal. Fishing is good but licenses are required and limits must be carefully observed. Leave the area as you found it. There are no shoreside facilities in this area.

If you don't want to go all the way to Everglades City for your next stop, you can anchor behind New Turkey Key in depths of 3 to 6 feet MLW (so only shoal draft boats can find refuge here). This anchorage is just south of the Chatham River and approximately 19 nm north of Ponce de Leon Bay. Make sure you set your anchor well as the currents are strong in this area.

Side Trip: Everglades City

Everglades City's history dates back more than 2,000 years to the age of the coastal Calusa mound dwellers, who had a major settlement on Chokoloskee Island. This island has one of the highest elevations in the Everglades achieving 20 feet above sea level. The island's abnormal elevation is artificial and the result of the discard of shells by the

Ten Thousand Islands, FL

TEN THOUSAND ISLANDS AREA		Largest Vessel	VHF	Total Slips	Approach/ Dockside Depth	Floating Docks	Gas/ Diesel	Repairs/ Haulout	Min/Max Amps	Pump-Out Station
1. Port of the Islands Marina **WiFi** **onSpot**	(239) 642-3133	65	16	175	5.0 / 6.0	F	G		30 / 50	P

WiFi Wireless Internet Access **onSpot** Dockside WiFi Facility
Visit www.waterwayguide.com for current rates, fuel prices, website addresses and other up-to-the-minute information.
(Information in the table is provided by the facilities.)

Scan here for more details:

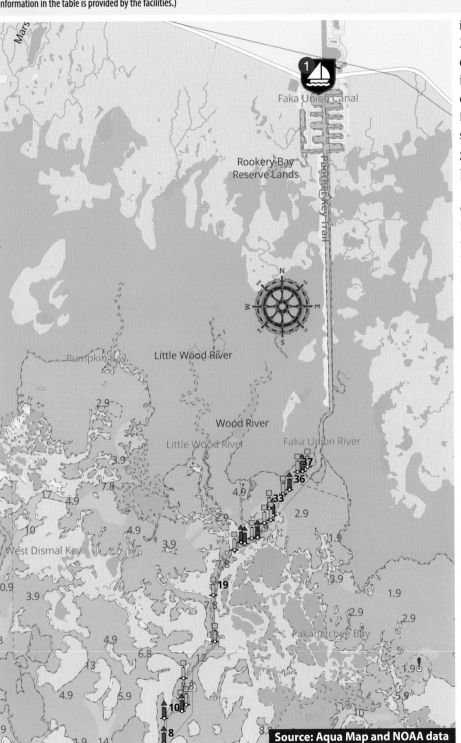

Source: Aqua Map and NOAA data

indigenous inhabitants over their 2000-year occupation. Europeans established a settlement here in the late 1800s and the local economy was based on trade, fishing and shellfishing. As more settlers arrived the community gradually evolved into a shipping port for produce and seafood.

Seafood is still a major economic factor in the area but is following the decline of the produce market and tourism has become the area's major economic driver. The city is the northern terminus of the Everglades Wilderness Waterway and offers water-based tours of all types including airboats, kayaks, canoes and swamp buggies. A bike ride to the ancient Calusa settlement site on nearby Chokoloskee Island can be an interesting experience.

Unique to Everglades City is The Everglades Rod and Gun Club (239-695-2101). Once a trading post that opened in the late 1800s the club has hosted many famous faces who come for the renowned hunting and fishing including former U.S. presidents, Mick Jagger and Ernest Hemingway. The rambling wood frame home is now a delightful marina, restaurant, with nearby cottages right on the Barron River. The old clubhouse, which was constructed in the early European period, is well worth a visit.

Ten Thousand Islands, FL

TEN THOUSAND ISLANDS AREA		Largest Vessel	VHF	Total Slips	Approach/ Dockside Depth	Floating Docks	Gas/ Diesel	Repairs/ Haulout	Min/Max Amps	Pump-Out Station
1. Walker's Coon Key Marina	(239) 394-2797	60	16	40	8.0 / 6.0	F	GD	RH	30	
2. Safe Harbor Calusa Island WiFi	(239) 394-3668	70	16	84	5.0 / 6.0	F	GD	RH	30 / 50	P

WiFi Wireless Internet Access **onSpot** Dockside WiFi Facility
Visit www.waterwayguide.com for current rates, fuel prices, website addresses and other up-to-the-minute information.
(Information in the table is provided by the facilities.)

Scan here for more details:

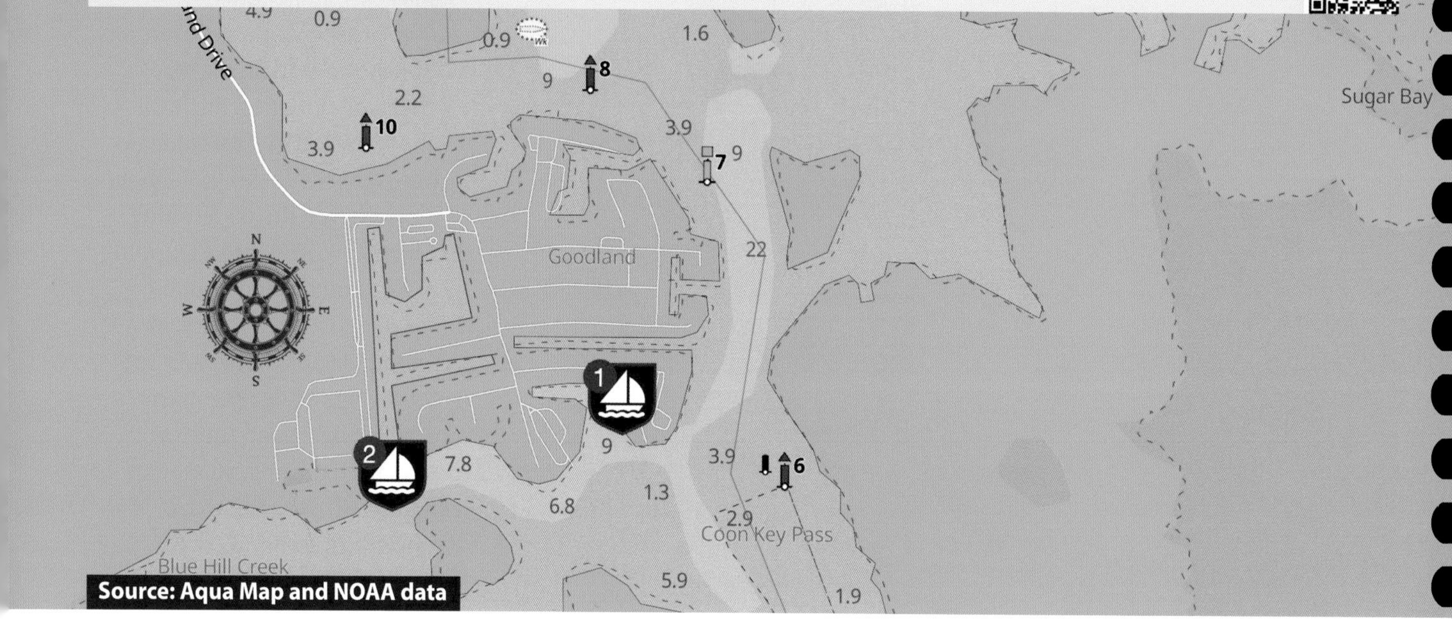

Source: Aqua Map and NOAA data

NAVIGATION: Use NOAA Charts 11429, 11430 and 11432. A sparse series of Everglades National Park boundary signs and flashing red markers parallel the coastline north from Little Shark River. Along this stretch it is advisable to roughly follow the Three Nautical Mile Line outside these markers to avoid the wide and shallow mouth of Ponce de Leon Bay and other obstructions closer to shore.

Several channels break the coastline. Some are deep enough to attract shoal-draft boats and skippers seeking more remote anchorages and good fishing. These passes and rivers have numerous sandbars and shoals and aside from Indian Key Pass are unmarked. Operation here requires careful, experienced navigation. Small-boat operators may be able to provide local knowledge for those adventuresome cruisers planning side trips and excursions off the main channels. No sign of civilization will be evident other than a remote ranger station.

The entrance to the Indian Key Pass (leading to Everglades City) is marked by 16-foot-high flashing white light "IK" located about 3.5 nm offshore of flashing green "1" at Indian Key. Flashing green "1" can be difficult to pick out from offshore. Use GPS coordinates to guide you in. Well-marked Indian Key Pass starts as a natural channel but quickly narrows into a dredged channel. You should maintain 6-foot MLW depths but be careful to maintain alignment as the channel is flanked by shoals on both sides. Some markers are lighted but entry in darkness is not recommended. Tidal range is approximately 3 feet and, in addition, "wind tide" can be a factor here in a strong northeast blow.

Between the flashing red "22" and the red "30" where the channel crosses the Chokoloskee Bay there is a strong lateral current from the south during the ebb and to the north during the flood. The channel is deep but narrow and you need to watch the marks ahead and behind as it is easy to drift out of the channel and into depths of 2 to 3 feet MLW.

In Everglades City between the red daybeacons "44" and "46" (past The Everglades Rod and Gun Club) the marked channel cuts off a natural bend in the river.

Depths at the bend are charted at 7 to 8 feet MLW but it has shoaled to less than 6 feet MLW. Be sure to stick to the marked channel.

Dockage: Up the Barron River, Everglades Rod & Gun Club has dockage with limited facilities. Water is available but is not potable. Everglades Isle Marina is 0.5 mile north on the Barron River. The marina is a combination marina/Class A RV resort. The grounds are beautiful and the high-end club house includes a movie theater and a spa. Golf cart rentals are available to explore the small town. Call ahead for slip availability. They have no reserved slips but may make room for you.

Anchorage: You can anchor shortly after entering Indian Key Pass just northwest of flashing green "7" in Russell Pass in at least 7 feet MLW. For more wind protection proceed farther up Russell Pass to where it opens up to the south for 7- to 8-foot MLW depths. Make sure you avoid the uncharted pocket or you could find yourself on the bottom at low tide.

Panther Key north of West Pass has 7 to 10 feet MLW with good holding in soft mud. This is somewhat exposed to the south. Anchor for best wind protection. This is wilderness. Don't expect amenities or even land access.

Side Trip: Faka Union River

NAVIGATION: Use NOAA Charts 11429 and 11430. Seven miles west of Everglades City as the crow flies lies the shallow Faka Union River, home of Port of the Islands Marina. Heading northwest from Indian Key proceed to green daybeacon "3" off Gomez Point at the tip of Panther Key. This marks the entrance to the 5-mile-long, mangrove-fringed channel on the Faka Union River to the marina. The straight channel to the marina is well marked by daybeacons beginning with green daybeacon "3" and red "4." Charted depths in the channel are 5 to 6 feet MLW. This is a year-round manatee zone so proceed at idle speed only.

Dockage: The remote Port of the Islands Marina located at the head of the Faka Union River provides "full immersion" in the Everglades. The marina offers transient boat slips, dry storage rentals, fishing charter services and a Ship's Store with convenience store items. Amenities are limited. Call ahead on VHF Channel 16 to verify available space and for advice on tide and channel conditions. (Tides in this area are from 1 to 3 feet MLW.)

◼ TO MARCO ISLAND

Two routes are available to travel from the Ten Thousand Islands area to Marco Island and beyond: the Outside Passage and the Inland Passage. The Inland Passage is only viable for extreme shoal-draft vessels with an air-draft of less than 55 feet. It's a long back-track to avoid the Cape Romano Shoals so it's best to plan your route before entering Gullivan Bay. Most cruising size vessels take the Outside Passage.

Ten Thousand Islands to Marco Island– Outside Passage

Most cruising size vessels take this route. Set course waypoints in advance to ensure you pass west of the dangerous Cape Romano Shoals.

NAVIGATION: Use NOAA Charts 11429 and 11430. To reach Marco Island from Everglades City or points farther north in the Gulf you must pass outside the Cape Romano Shoals and well offshore of the Cape itself. Charts record isolated spots with depths of as low as 1-foot MLW at the Three Nautical Mile Line. Your course should take you at least 3 to 4 miles west of Cape Romano, whether coming from the south or north. Use your GPS and enter a good standoff waypoint south of the finger shoals. If using radar Cape Romano will be prominently displayed as you run offshore to avoid it.

The shoals extend 9.5 nm south from Cape Romano where a flashing white light marks the southmost finger shoal. If approaching from Everglades City this light is 12 nm southwest of Indian Key. From Little Shark River it's a course of 310° magnetic to clear the light.

Once clear of the southern extremity of the finger shoals a course of 335° magnetic will lead past Marco Island to the Capri Pass. This is the main entrance to the Marco Island marinas and the inland channel to Naples. When approaching Capri Pass from the south, pass west of 16-foot-high flashing red buoy "2" before turning for entry to stay clear of the shoaling near Big Marco Pass. Coconut Island, once located in Capri Pass, just south of the green-over-red daybeacon is now submerged and has been removed from recent charts; however, it lies just under the surface.

>>>>>>>>>>>>>>>> ⚠ >>>>>>>>>>>>>>>>>

Big Marco Pass is too shallow for passage by most vessels. The viable route into Marco Island is via well-marked Capri Pass just to the north. To enter pass close to flashing red "2" offshore and align to the channel.

Follow the markers carefully through Capri Pass. Head from flashing red "6" to split quick flashing green "9" and red daybeacon "8" while favoring the green side. There is plenty of room but traffic can be heavy on weekends and the markers are confusing where the inside channel to Naples splits off northward at the green-over-red daybeacon.

Ten Thousand Islands to Goodland–Inland Passage

Situated on a small peninsula of a large island and marsh complex the village of Goodland is a laid-back fishing village with good but unpretentious restaurants, fishing supplies and limited groceries.

NAVIGATION: Use NOAA Charts 11429 and 11430. If your draft is 3 feet or less and your air-draft requirement is less than 55 feet, you may save some time by taking the protected inside route to Marco Island. Vessels with slightly deeper drafts may take this route, if they have the flexibility to schedule their passage at high tide.

The route begins about 6 miles west of Faka Union Bay at the head of Gullivan Bay off Coon Key where Coon Key Light, a 22-foot-high flashing white light, marks the entrance to Coon Key Pass. Stay 400 to 500 yards east of the light and head north up the east side of Coon Key towards red daybeacon "2" (on the west side of Tripod Key). Next proceed through well-marked Coon Key Pass (if heading north, leave red markers to starboard) to the village of Goodland, which is east of Marco Island. The route is quite shallow in spots and charted depths are unreliable. Fortunately, the bottom is reported to be soft mud.

Local boats frequently use this passage (some at high speed) so ask for latest channel conditions and then make your own decision. The fixed **Goodland Bridge** (55-foot vertical clearance) sets the bar as the lowest bridge for the rest of this route.

Dockage: Walker's Coon Key Marina south of Goodland Bridge is primarily a boat rental and dry storage facility with a few transient slips. They also offer some repairs. Safe Harbor Calusa Island (west of Coon Key Pass red daybeacon "6") is a members-only facility slips to 70 feet, dry storage and competitive fuel pricing. Call ahead for transient slip availability.

Anchorage: You can anchor at Blue Hill Creek to the west of Goodland in 7 to 10 feet MLW and dinghy to town. In the northeast corner of Goodland Bay there's a deep water hole (at least 8 feet MLW) northeast of green daybeacon "7." To the southeast at Tripod Key you can anchor at the intersection of Sugar Bay at Coon Key Pass in 5 feet MLW.

Goodland to Marco Island–Inland Passage

NAVIGATION: Use NOAA Chart 11430. The route through Goodland Bay to the Big Marco River requires considerable care even for those who have traveled it before. Seek local knowledge in Goodland or over the VHF radio. Markers are moved when necessary to reflect shifting shoals and may not be exactly where the chart shows them. Many prefer to pass through on a rising tide for obvious reasons.

Maintain a close watch on the depth sounder and use a pre-set alarm if possible. To get oriented it's a good idea to study your charts and GPS carefully after you have gathered some local knowledge. This is a scenic and viable route for some shoal-draft vessels. Refer to NOAA online charts for the most up-to-date information.

After you have passed Goodland at red daybeacon "10" you will need to make a sharp turn to the north, staying close to the marker and pass under the Goodland Bridge (55-foot fixed vertical clearance). After passing under the bridge you will find deeper water for a short time. Just beyond daybeacon "16" there is a very shallow area (as low as 3 feet MLW) when approaching daybeacon "18."

Once past "18" the water deepens again. When you pass green daybeacon "25" make sure you do not head straight for the bridge open span. You will need to veer further west and head for daybeacon "26." It will appear as if you are going completely off track because daybeacon "26" is almost to shore on the west side of the river. Don't be fooled by smaller boats that go straight to the bridge; it gets extremely shallow!

Just past the Marco Island Bridge the channel markers reverse. Northbound boats will now have green to starboard and red to port until you reach the Gulf of Mexico.

The next marker for the main channel is green daybeacon "15" not to be confused with nearby green daybeacon "1," which starts the northern channel into Factory Bay. Those heading directly to the Gulf continue north and then west through Capri Pass. When passing through Capri Pass be warned that the markers in the pass can be confusing and there are several sand bars. Check the notes on the Outside Passage for a description of Capri Pass.

Dockage: If you approach Marco Island from the Isle of Capri Pass, Collier Bay will be to starboard, which leads to the 77-slip Esplanade Marina. The marina is tucked inside Smokehouse Bay, which is tricky to get

into but once inside is well protected (360°). Between red daybeacons "12" and "14," turn south and follow the shallow but well-marked channel to Collier Bay. Continue southwest to red daybeacon "6" and make a sharp eastward turn leaving green daybeacon "7" to the north and heading into Smokehouse Bay. Esplanade Marina has 6-foot MLW approach and dockside depths alongside their floating docks. Two great restaurants are on site and a grocery store is across street.

Continue north on Isle of Capri Pass for Pelican Bend Restaurant & Marina, which has three reserved transient slips. The Tarpon Club Marina looks to be adjacent to Pelican Bend at first glimpse but a closer look at the chart reveals that it is located on Tarpon Bay, accessible from the Big Marco River (not Isle of Capri Pass). They sell some marine supplies and may have space for you; call ahead.

Snook Inn on the Big Marco River has been a landmark for more than 30 years and offers dockage for patrons and waterfront dining inside or out at the tiki bar. They

Marco Island, FL

MARCO ISLAND AREA		Largest Vessel	VHF	Total Slips	Approach/ Dockside Depth	Floating Docks	Gas/ Diesel	Repairs/ Haulout	Min/Max Amps	Pump-Out Station
1. The Tarpon Club Marina	(239) 417-6802	36	16	140	4.0 / 5.0	F	G		50	
2. Pelican Bend Restaurant & Marina	(239) 394-3452	60	16	18	5.0 / 7.0		GD		30	
3. Snook Inn	(239) 394-3313	60		20	15.0 / 6.0					
4. Pelican Pier Marina **WiFi**	(239) 389-2628	55	16	5	10.0 / 10.0	F	G			
5. Marina at Factory Bay **WiFi** Marker 3A	(239) 389-2929	107	6	72	10.0 / 15.0	F			30 / 100	P

WiFi Wireless Internet Access   **onSpot** Dockside WiFi Facility
Visit www.waterwayguide.com for current rates, fuel prices, website addresses and other up-to-the-minute information.
(Information in the table is provided by the facilities.)

Scan here for more details:

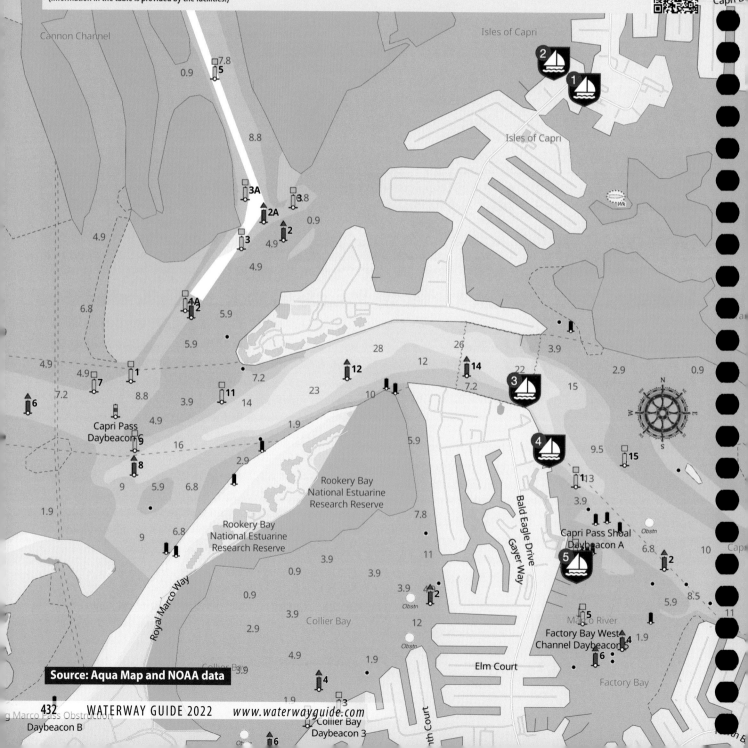

Source: Aqua Map and NOAA data

Marco Island, FL

MARCO ISLAND AREA		Largest Vessel	VHF	Total Slips	Approach/ Dockside Depth	Floating Docks	Gas/ Diesel	Repairs/ Haulout	Min/Max Amps	Pump-Out Station
1. Esplanade Marina **WiFi** **onSpot**	(239) 394-6333	66	16	77	6.0 / 6.0	F			30 / 50	P
2. Rose Marina **WiFi**	(239) 394-2502	160	9	109	7.0 / 8.0	F	GD	RH	30 / 100	P
3. Marco Island Marina **WiFi** **onSpot**	(239) 776-2986	110	16	121	7.0 / 6.5	F			30 / 100	P
4. Riverside Marina at Marco Island Yacht Club **WiFi**	(239) 399-0199	125	16	27	7.0 / 6.0	F			30 / 200+	P

WiFi Wireless Internet Access **onSpot** Dockside WiFi Facility
Visit www.waterwayguide.com for current rates, fuel prices, website addresses and other up-to-the-minute information.
(Information in the table is provided by the facilities.)

Scan here for more details:

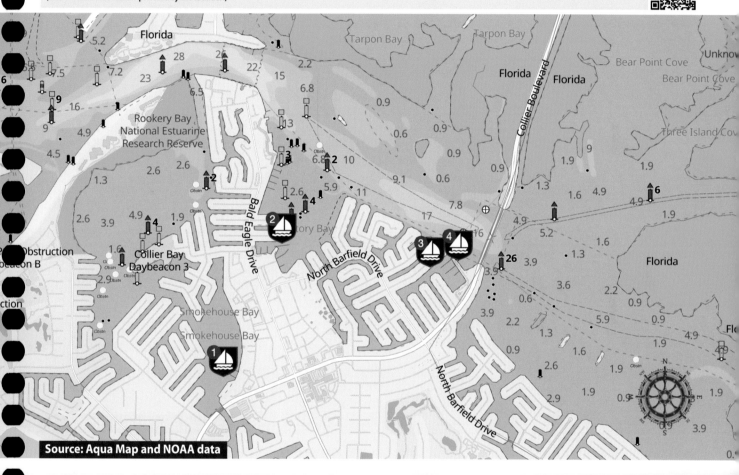

Source: Aqua Map and NOAA data

Famous Dome Houses in Marco Island

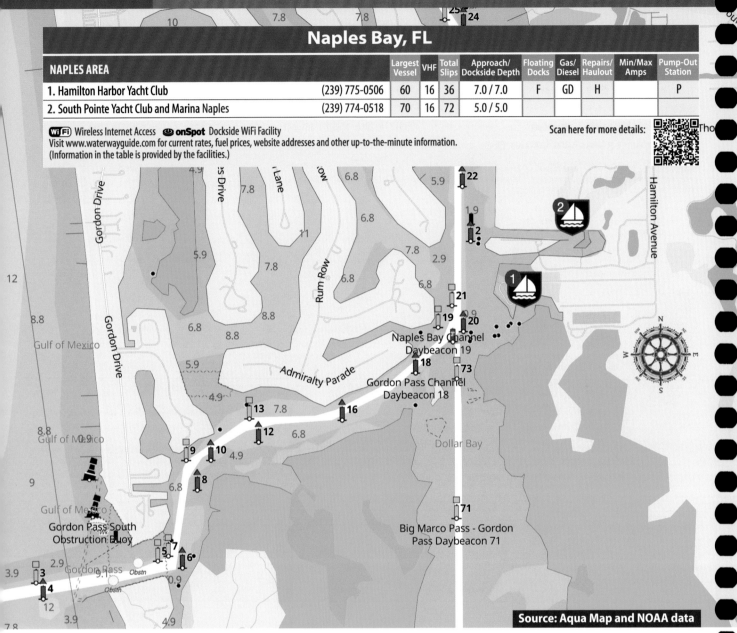

Naples Bay, FL

NAPLES AREA		Largest Vessel	VHF	Total Slips	Approach/ Dockside Depth	Floating Docks	Gas/ Diesel	Repairs/ Haulout	Min/Max Amps	Pump-Out Station
1. Hamilton Harbor Yacht Club	(239) 775-0506	60	16	36	7.0 / 7.0	F	GD	H		P
2. South Pointe Yacht Club and Marina Naples	(239) 774-0518	70	16	72	5.0 / 5.0					

WiFi Wireless Internet Access **onSpot** Dockside WiFi Facility
Visit www.waterwayguide.com for current rates, fuel prices, website addresses and other up-to-the-minute information.
(Information in the table is provided by the facilities.)

Scan here for more details:

Source: Aqua Map and NOAA data

have live entertainment 7 days a week and happy hour from 4:00 to 6:00 p.m. Snook Inn can accommodate vessels up to 60 feet. (They also offer free transportation from other marinas.)

Marina at Factory Bay is on the Big Marco River past Collier Bay (if heading to the bridge). Past flashing red "14" and the Snook Inn pick up the side channel at green daybeacon "1." Marina at Factory Bay is between green daybeacons "3" and "5." Hail the dockmaster for assistance tying up and to arrange a long-term or transient stay on their floating docks. There is limited transient dockage; call ahead.

The busy Rose Marina is in the southwestern corner of Factory Bay and may be hailed on VHF Channel 16 for reservations and directions. They have slips to accommodate all varieties and lengths of vessels including wider catamarans. They have a well-stocked store and are busy with rental boats coming and going.

If you are looking for quiet surroundings, Marco Island Marina on the south side at the Marco Island Bridge is a very nice stop. The well-marked entrance is approximately 3 miles from Capri Pass past the stanchion of power lines and has 7-foot MLW approach depths. They have the usual amenities. From the facility a walk of less than 1 mile leads to groceries, a Post Office and a West Marine (1089 N. Collier Blvd., 239-642-7060).

Anchorage: Once you work your way into Collier Bay proceed to daybeacon "7" and then enter the protected anchorage with good holding in Smokehouse Bay. There is 10 feet MLW and very good holding. Just follow channel markers closely and stay nearer the docking side of the channel for more depth. This anchorage is located in a residential neighborhood. Grocery shopping is easily accessed by passing under the west span of the Marco Island Bridge and landing at the convenient dinghy dock located beside the Winn-Dixie Supermarket.

Factory Bay also has good holding with 10 to 12 feet MLW. A sandbar splits the bay but there is plenty of water around the edge. Anchor in the southeast side by red daybeacons "2" and "4" for good protection. You can also anchor in the Big Marco River to the northwest of flashing green "15" in 10 to 12 feet MLW. This is fairly exposed; expect wakes.

◼ TO NAPLES

From Marco Island to Naples is another opportunity to choose between an Inland Passage and an Outside Passage. Again, the Inland Passage is only viable for extreme shoal-draft vessels with an air-draft of less than 55 feet. Most cruising size vessels take the Outside Passage.

To Naples–Outside Passage

Naples is known for high-end shopping, sophisticated dining and an abundance of golf courses. The Naples Pier is a popular fishing and dolphin-spotting destination and the miles of fine white "sugar" sand and calm waters make the beaches here especially desirable.

NAVIGATION: Use NOAA Chart 11430. The 7-nm passage outside is

fairly straightforward. Exiting Capri Pass be sure to clear flashing green "3" before turning northward to avoid the shoals extending off Sea Oat Island. Parallel Keewaydin Island to the well marked but slightly tricky entrance to Gordon Pass. It is best to line up for the channel well offshore. Use flashing reds "4" and "6" as a range on entry.

A rock jetty on the south side of Gordon Pass extends 100 yards into the Gulf of Mexico. Favor the south side of the channel along the jetty. With onshore winds and outgoing tide it can be challenging for slow or underpowered vessels. The encroaching shoals and jetties make this narrow entrance a bad place for an engine failure. Pass close to flashing red "6" on entry then turn north once clear of green daybeacon "7" to avoid the shoal off the northern spit (visible at low tide).

To reach Naples turn north up the Gordon River at green daybeacon "21." Shoals fringe the dredged channel so stay within the well-marked channel.

To Naples–Inland Passage

Naples is known for high-end shopping, sophisticated dining and an abundance of golf courses. The Naples Pier is a popular fishing and dolphin-spotting destination and the miles of fine white "sugar" sand and calm waters make the beaches here especially desirable.

For shoal-draft vessels the inside route from Capri Pass to Gordon Pass is delightful. The route of protected by a series on barrier islands and traverses some nature reserves. There is limited development along this route and during breaks in the

sometimes-heavy boat traffic you will feel you've stumbled into a wilderness area. But this passage is not known for boater courtesy and you may experience some wakes from boats passing close by at full throttle.

There are spots as shallow is 3.5 feet MLW but with the 2- to 3-foot tidal range deeper vessels can pass through the 9-nm route on a rising tide. Our Cruising Editor, who draws 4.8 feet, passed through at three-quarter tide in the spring of 2020 without making contact. You may also experience a "sleigh ride" on a rising tide for the passage north. A side trip or overnight stay in Rookery Bay will enhance the visit. Birdwatchers should keep the binoculars handy.

NAVIGATION: Use NOAA Chart 11430. The route northward starts by taking the north branch at the green-over-red daybeacon in Capri Pass initially towards the Iles of Capri Pass. Beware of the shifting sandbar to port near green daybeacon "1." Reduced speed is advised until the turn north. At green daybeacon "3" turn north as the channel deepens near Johnson Island. You will find deeper water closer to Cannon Island as you proceed through Calhoun Channel.

⚠ NOAA Chart 11430 bears the warning, "This area is subject to continual change," referring to the area from Capri Pass to just past Little Marco Island (green daybeacon "33"). Watch your depth sounder and proceed at reduced speed.

Naples Bay, FL

NAPLES AREA		Largest Vessel	VHF	Total Slips	Approach/ Dockside Depth	Floating Docks	Gas/ Diesel	Repairs/ Haulout	Min/Max Amps	Pump-Out Station
1. Naples Yacht Club WiFi	(239) 262-7301	130	16	88	8.0 / 6.0	F	GD		30 / 200+	P
2. Naples City Dock	(239) 213-3070	200	16	79	9.0 / 9.0	F	GD		30 / 100	P
3. Coastal Marine Fuel Dock	(239) 263-4525		16		/		GD			P
4. Naples Boat Club Marina WiFi	(239) 263-2774	110	16	47	8.0 / 8.0	F	GD	RH	30 / 100	P
5. MarineMax Naples Yacht Center	(239) 262-1000	65	16		6.0 / 6.0			RH	50	
6. Naples Sailing & Yacht Club WiFi	(239) 774-0424	65	16	75	6.0 / 6.0	F	GD		30 / 100	
7. Marina at Naples Bay Resort WiFi	(239) 530-5134	90	68	97	5.5 / 5.5	F	G		30 / 50	P
8. Gulf Shores Marina	(239) 774-0222	35	16	110	4.0 / 4.0	F	G	RH	50	

WiFi Wireless Internet Access   onSpot Dockside WiFi Facility
Visit www.waterwayguide.com for current rates, fuel prices, website addresses and other up-to-the-minute information.
(Information in the table is provided by the facilities.)

Scan here for more details:

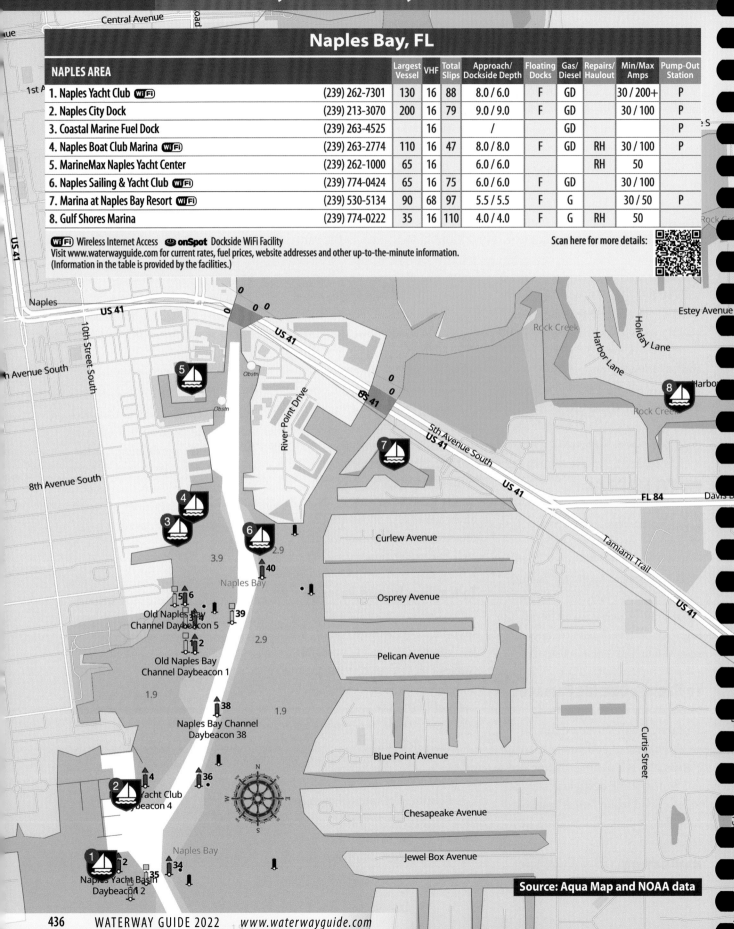

Source: Aqua Map and NOAA data

Naples Bay, FL

NAPLES AREA		Largest Vessel	VHF	Total Slips	Approach/ Dockside Depth	Floating Docks	Gas/ Diesel	Repairs/ Haulout	Min/Max Amps	Pump-Out Station
1. Walker's Hideaway Marina of Naples **WiFi**	(239) 213-1441			25	/	F	GD	RH		

WiFi Wireless Internet Access **onSpot** Dockside WiFi Facility
Visit www.waterwayguide.com for current rates, fuel prices, website addresses and other up-to-the-minute information.
(Information in the table is provided by the facilities.)

Scan here for more details:

The channel shallows abruptly between green day beacons "17" and "19" where you may find 4-foot MLW depths. Look back occasionally to check channel alignment through this dredged segment. Expect some shoaling inside the marked channel through to green daybeacon "33." In the spring of 2020 a very shallow spot was observed near red daybeacon "20" (approximately 3.5 feet MLW). Pay strict attention to the channel markers. Between green daybeacons "33" and "47" the route follows a deeper, natural channel.

About halfway along (red daybeacon "46") you pass Rookery Bay, a major wildlife sanctuary and will likely encounter local fishing boats. Many choose to anchor in Rookery Channel to enjoy the natural beauty. This channel initially has good depth and provides some refuge from the wakes of passing powerboats.

At green daybeacon "47" the route again enters a narrow, dredged channel. Expect the shallowest parts of the passage in Dollar Bay between red daybeacons "64 and 68," where you may encounter spots with depths as low as 3 feet MLW. For most cruising vessels passage is only possible if you past this stretch near high tide.

The Gordon River leading to Naples used to be a "no-wake" zone from Gordon Pass to the Route 41 Bridge (10-foot fixed vertical clearance). The "no-wake" zone now extends from flashing red "34" (south of the Naples Yacht Club) to the bridge and is frequently ignored by "weekend warriors."

Dockage/Moorings: Dock space is usually available at Naples' numerous marinas but local marina operators recommend calling ahead for slip or mooring reservations particularly during the peak periods (holidays and weekends).

Hamilton Harbor Yacht Club and South Pointe Yacht Club and Marina are south of Naples and convenient to Gordon Pass. Hamilton Harbor Yacht Club offers first-class services and amenities including concierge service, waterfront dining, an on-site Ship's Store, maintenance and repair services and discounted marine fuel. Call ahead to check on slip availability.

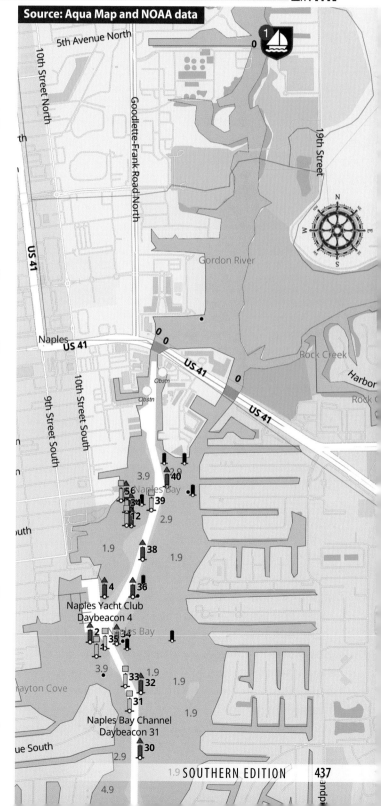

Source: Aqua Map and NOAA data

Cocohatchee River, FL

WIGGINS PASS		Largest Vessel	VHF	Total Slips	Approach/ Dockside Depth	Floating Docks	Gas/ Diesel	Repairs/ Haulout	Min/Max Amps	Pump-Out Station
1. Pelican Isle Yacht Club	(239) 566-1606	55	16	190	5.0 / 4.5	F	GD		30 / 50	P
2. Cocohatchee River Park Marina	(239) 514-3752	30	16	39	6.0 / 6.0		GD		30 / 50	P

WiFi Wireless Internet Access **onSpot** Dockside WiFi Facility
Visit www.waterwayguide.com for current rates, fuel prices, website addresses and other up-to-the-minute information.
(Information in the table is provided by the facilities.)

Scan here for more details:

Source: Aqua Map and NOAA data

Boat slips to 72 feet are available for sale or lease at South Pointe Yacht Club and Marina and allows you access to the pool and common area. There is 5-foot MLW dockside and approach depths.

Farther north after flashing red "32" is Naples Yacht Club with slips (to 130 feet). The club practices reciprocity with other clubs. Naples City Dock has slips as well as 12 moorings in two well-protected coves. It is mandatory that you receive a (free) pump-out service before picking up the mooring. There is easy access to pump-out service at the fuel dock. You cannot stay more than four days at the dock or on a mooring in accordance with a city ordinance. The floating dinghy dock is on the same side of the pier as the mooring field.

In a convenient location on Naples Bay at red daybeacon "40" is the full-service Naples Boat Club Marina with wet slips, dry rack boat storage plus a restaurant, yacht sales and service. MarineMax Naples Yacht Center offers large and small repairs but no transient slips.

Naples Sailing & Yacht Club at the south end of the island in the Gordon River offers reciprocity to members of other recognized yacht clubs. Marina at Naples Bay Resort on the east side of the river has resort amenities. There are four restaurants on the marina grounds and they offer kayak, stand-up paddleboard and bicycle rentals.

North of the **U.S. 41 Bridge** Gordon River is Gulf Shores Marina to the east off Rock Creek, a family-owned and -operated yacht brokerage. To the north on the Gordon River is Walker's Hideaway Marina of Naples with boat rentals and storage. Even farther north on a canal of the Gordon River is Hinckley Yacht Services–Naples. They provide mobile services and indoor boat storage. None of these maintain reserved transient slips.

Anchorage: You can drop the hook on the south side of Umbrella Island across from red daybeacon "12" where you will find 8 to 14 feet MLW. You can avoid some wakes by tucking in between Little Marco Island and Keewaydin Island south of green daybeacon "33." The anchorage in Rookery Channel east of green daybeacon "47" is a popular spot. The deepest water (6 to 8 feet MLW) is about 0.5 mile in. From here you can explore the nature reserve by dinghy.

After entering Gordon Pass turn north between red daybeacons "10" and "12." A charted bar with 4-foot MLW depths crosses the entrance. Enter the first canal to the east and anchor in a well-protected cove in 9-foot MLW depths among beautiful homes. There is no place to land a dinghy. A second option is to proceed into Gordon Pass to green daybeacon "21" turn northwest and then southwest into the first cove. You will be well protected from all sides in 7-foot MLW depths. There is no shore access here but you may find beach access just east of red daybeacon "22."

■ TO FORT MYERS BEACH

Gordon Pass to Big Carlos Pass

There is no protected inside route between Naples and Estero Bay. Be sure you have adequate daylight and favorable weather before embarking on the 19 nm passage from Gordon

Pass to Big Carlos Pass (23.5-nm passage from Gordon Pass to the deeper Matanzas Pass entrance).

NAVIGATION: Use NOAA Charts 11427 and 11430. There are a few obstructions and hazards along this coastline so stay about 2 nm off the beach. In particular expect some shoals extending from the inlets along the coast. In good weather the Gulf of Mexico is calm and easy to transit but in winter months, when the winds are often out of the northwest or north it can get rough. If the winds are northwest at more than 12 knots, you may want to wait it out in Naples. Pick your weather wisely and there should be no problem.

Controlling depths in the marked channel from New Pass to Big Carlos Pass are reported to be 4 feet MLW with a 2.5-foot tidal range. Note there is a fixed bridge with a vertical clearance of 30 feet on this route. For vessels drawing 4 feet or less daybeacons lead from Wiggins Pass for a distance of just under 0.5 mile into the Cocohatchee River where dockage is available.

Dockage: Once through Wiggins Pass controlling channel depths to the marinas are 4 to 5 feet MLW. Pelican Isle Yacht Club just inside Wiggins Pass can accommodate vessels to 55 feet with depths to 4.5 feet MLW. They have pump-out service at each slip and the marina offers a free shuttle to Gulf beaches and complimentary use of kayaks and stand-up paddleboards. Directly across from Pelican Isle is Cocohatchee River Park Marina, which has slips for boats 30 feet or smaller.

Anchorage: About 5.7 miles north of Gordon Pass narrow Doctors

Pass can serve as a harbor of refuge. The area is well marked; favor the center. Once inside, Moorings Bay has 3 to 6 feet MLW with good holding and all-around protection. There are no services for transients.

Big Carlos Pass to Fort Myers Beach–Outside Passage

NAVIGATION: Use NOAA Chart 11427. From Big Carlos Pass set a course for the flashing white Morse (A) 16-foot-high marker "SC." From that point you should be able to pick out 16-foot flashing red buoy "2" approximately 1 mile to the north-northwest and quick flashing red "4" beyond. Keep red markers to starboard entering San Carlos Bay. Beware of the dangerous shoals that extend 3 nm south from Sanibel Island. This shoal structure has been growing in recent years and depths may be shallower than charted in this area.

Due north from quick flashing red "4" lies the well-marked entrance channel leading off from San Carlos Bay into Matanzas Pass, which begins with flashing green "1." Keep red markers to starboard southbound through the pass. Starting at red daybeacon "6" the channel makes a large U-turn to the south behind the northwestern hook of Estero Island. The channel runs close to Estero Island. There are spoils areas and shoals to the east.

Currents can be swift in the Matanzas Pass channel depending on the tide. Expect heavy marine traffic between Estero Island and San Carlos Island. **SR 865 Matanzas Pass Bridge** (65-foot fixed vertical clearance) crosses the channel about 2 nm from the entrance.

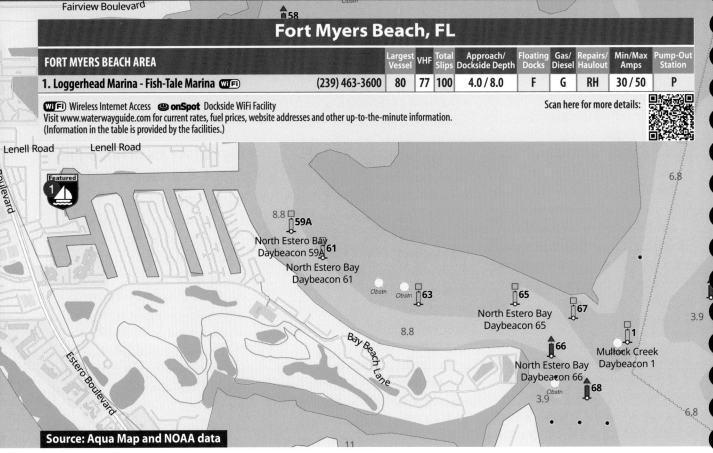

Fort Myers Beach, FL

FORT MYERS BEACH AREA		Largest Vessel	VHF	Total Slips	Approach/ Dockside Depth	Floating Docks	Gas/ Diesel	Repairs/ Haulout	Min/Max Amps	Pump-Out Station
1. Loggerhead Marina - Fish-Tale Marina (WiFi)	(239) 463-3600	80	77	100	4.0 / 8.0	F	G	RH	30 / 50	P

(WiFi) Wireless Internet Access (onSpot) Dockside WiFi Facility
Visit www.waterwayguide.com for current rates, fuel prices, website addresses and other up-to-the-minute information.
(Information in the table is provided by the facilities.)

Scan here for more details:

Source: Aqua Map and NOAA data

Big Carlos Pass to Fort Myers Beach–Inland Passage

NAVIGATION: Use NOAA Chart 11427. If you are hugging the coastline about 1 nm offshore from Naples, you should be aware that shoals project well offshore from Big Carlos Pass. If you are trying to reach Estero Bay and Fort Myers Beach, you can enter at Big Carlos Pass but the channel location moves and you may want to wait for a lead-in boat to follow. Although charts indicate controlling depths of 4 to 6 feet MLW some claim the channel carries about 8 feet MLW. While the bottom here is constantly shifting reports suggest the channel follows the contour lines of Lovers Key on approach from the south. It is best to call ahead to nearby Estero Bay Boat Tours (VHF Channel 79) for an update on directions and controlling depths

Big Carlos Pass (SR 865) Bridge (23-foot closed vertical clearance) opens on signal except from 7:00 p.m. to 8:00 a.m. daily, when it need not open. Once past Carlos Point and under the bridge daybeacons guide your passage either north or south through the natural and historic beauty of Estero Bay. To reach Fort Myers Beach turn north between green daybeacon "67" and red

daybeacon "68." This channel is well marked but note that you must keep red markers to port heading northward.

The route north follows the northeast shore of Estero Island to the Matanzas Pass, which leads on to Fort Myers Beach. There are numerous hazards outside the marked channel so take care to maintain alignment.

Dockage: Loggerhead Marina–Fish Tale Marina is a small marina and restaurant on Estero Island in a channel behind Coon Key. They report 4-foot MLW approach depths. Call ahead for slip availability. Approximately halfway along Estero Island you will encounter the full-service Snook Bight Yacht Club & Marina. The marina offers ample boater services and amenities including repair, maintenance and restoration; waterfront dining; and a well-stocked Ship's Store.

The first marina you will encounter before Matanzas Pass is the family-friendly Pink Shell Beach Resort and Marina, which is set on 12 lush acres. The marina can accommodate vessels up to 120 feet on floating docks. Guests at the marina are welcome to the resort's numerous amenities including the pool and beach club, a fitness center and water sport rentals. (Be sure to ask about their grocery service.) They are also a stop on the

Fort Myers Beach, FL

FORT MYERS BEACH AREA		Largest Vessel	VHF	Total Slips	Approach/ Dockside Depth	Floating Docks	Gas/ Diesel	Repairs/ Haulout	Min/Max Amps	Pump-Out Station
1. Snook Bight Yacht Club & Marina 📶	(239) 765-4371	70	16	74	6.5 / 6.5	F	GD	RH	30 / 50	P

📶 Wireless Internet Access 📶 **onSpot** Dockside WiFi Facility
Visit www.waterwayguide.com for current rates, fuel prices, website addresses and other up-to-the-minute information.
(Information in the table is provided by the facilities.)

Scan here for more details:

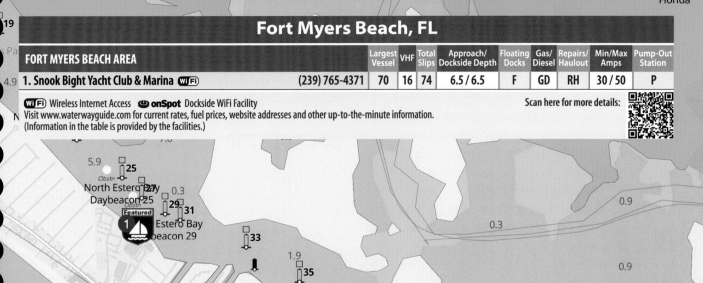

Source: Aqua Map and NOAA data

shuttle route for easy access to the island. As always call in advance for reservations.

The complex of white buildings of Moss Marina is highly visible to the south adjacent to daybeacon "17." Transient berths are available on their floating docks but make advance reservations particularly during the winter months. They also have multiple fueling stations. It is a short walk to fine dining and the beach.

Soon after you pass under the bridge on the south shore is Matanzas Inn Bayside Resort and Marina with 16 slips for boats up to 60 feet. They also manage the 70 mooring balls of the City of Fort Myers Yacht Basin. The marina provides restrooms/ showers and a dinghy dock for those who rent a mooring and a pump-out boat is available (by appointment). Diversified Yacht Services on the

Fort Myers Beach

north shore before the SR 865 Matanzas Pass Bridge sells parts and offers services plus has a tackle shop. Just south of the bridge on the north shore is Gulf Star Marina, which caters to sportfishing boats and offers dry storage, may have space for you. Call ahead for slip availability.

Continuing along the north shore south of the bridge, Olsen Marine Service Inc. and Gulf Marine Ways & Supply offer large and small repairs (but no transient slips). A little farther along the channel is Ballard Oil Co., a fuel dock with gas and diesel fuel at great prices. At the end of the harbor (beyond the shrimp fleet) is Salty Sam's Marina, which specializes in dry storage, boat rentals and boat detailing services. They have some transient space or tie up for a bite at one of the two on-site restaurants.

Anchorage: Boats anchor east of the bridge in the unmarked south channel (not in the northern Matanzas Pass channel). You can also drop the hook in 5 to 7 feet MLW east of red daybeacon "4" in Matanzas Pass on the north side of the unnamed island.

■ NEXT STOP

Fort Myers Beach is a is a genuine nautical crossroad. It is a pivotal location for vessels making passages farther north up the west coast of Florida or entering the Okeechobee Waterway and cruising all the way to its east coast terminus at the ICW in Stuart. (The Okeechobee Waterway is covered in detail in Chapter 6.)

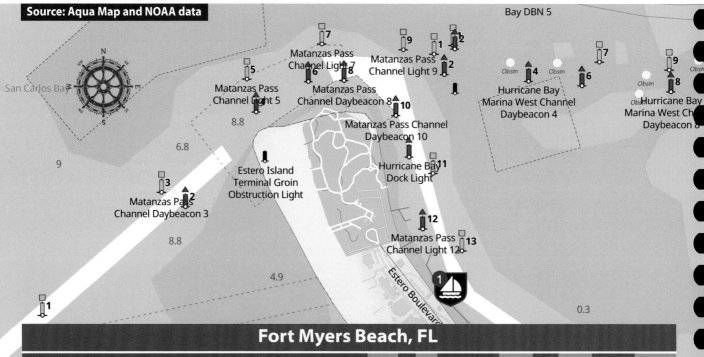

Source: Aqua Map and NOAA data

Fort Myers Beach, FL

FORT MYERS BEACH AREA		Largest Vessel	VHF	Total Slips	Approach/ Dockside Depth	Floating Docks	Gas/ Diesel	Repairs/ Haulout	Min/Max Amps	Pump-Out Station
1. Pink Shell Beach Resort and Marina (WiFi)	(239) 463-8620	120	16	41	15.0 / 8.5	F		R	30 / 100	P
2. Moss Marina (WiFi) 17	(239) 765-6677	140	16		12.0 /	F	GD	R	30 / 100	P
3. Matanzas Inn Bayside Resort and Marina (WiFi)	(239) 463-9258	60	16	16	12.0 / 8.0				30 / 50	P
4. Diversified Yacht Services	(239) 765-8700		16	20	/	F	GD	RH	30 / 50	P
5. Gulf Star Marina	(239) 872-2106	55	16	20	17.0 / 8.0		G	RH	30 / 50	P
6. Olsen Marine Service Inc.	(239) 463-6750	55	16		6.0 / 6.0			RH	50	
7. Gulf Marine Ways & Supply	(239) 463-6166	130		2	10.0 / 10.0			RH	50	
8. Ballard Oil Company (WiFi)	(239) 463-7677				/					
9. Salty Sam's Marina (WiFi)	(239) 463-7333	225	16	130	14.0 / 12.0	F	GD	RH	30 / 100	P

(WiFi) Wireless Internet Access (onSpot) Dockside WiFi Facility
Visit www.waterwayguide.com for current rates, fuel prices, website addresses and other up-to-the-minute information.
(Information in the table is provided by the facilities.)

Scan here for more details:

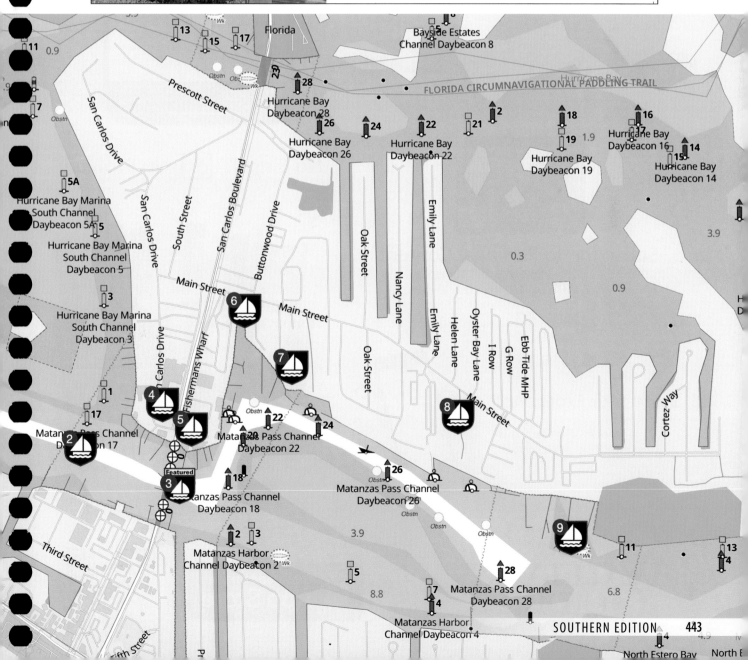

Florida

11 0.9

7

Obstn

Prescott Street

230

Florida

13 15 17

Bayside Estates
Channel Daybeacon 8

28
Hurricane Bay
Daybeacon 28

26
Hurricane Bay
Daybeacon 26

24

22
Hurricane Bay
Daybeacon 22

21 2

18
Hurricane Bay
Daybeacon 19 19 1.9

16
17 Hurricane Bay
Daybeacon 16 14 15
Hurricane Bay
Daybeacon 14

San Carlos Drive

5A
Hurricane Bay Marina
South Channel
Daybeacon 5A 5

Hurricane Bay Marina
South Channel
Daybeacon 5

3
Hurricane Bay Marina
South Channel
Daybeacon 3

San Carlos Drive

South Street

San Carlos Boulevard

Buttonwood Drive

Oak Street

Emily Lane

Nancy Lane

Helen Lane

Emily Lane

Oyster Bay Lane

I Row

G Row

Ebb Tide MHP

3.9

0.3

0.9

Main Street

Main Street

Oak Street

6

San Carlos Drive

Fishermans Wharf

4
5

1
17
Matanzas Pass Channel
Daybeacon 17

2

3
Featured

7

22
Matanzas Pass Channel
Daybeacon 22

24

18
Matanzas Pass Channel
Daybeacon 18

26
Matanzas Pass Channel
Daybeacon 26

Obstn

8

Main Street

Cortez Way

9

11 13

Third Street

2 3
Matanzas Harbor
Channel Daybeacon 2

5

3.9

Obstn

28
Matanzas Pass Channel
Daybeacon 28

8.8

6.8

7
4
Matanzas Harbor
Channel Daybeacon 4

North Estero Bay

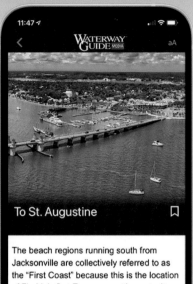

ICW **Mile 0-Mile 87**

■ TO CHARLOTTE HARBOR

Traveling north from Fort Myers Beach a skipper can choose between two passages: inside along the GIWW or outside up the Gulf of Mexico. Unless you must hurry to meet a deadline and are in a powerboat that can hit high double numbers we suggest you take the protected and infinitely more interesting GIWW route inside.

Coverage of Fort Myers, the Caloosahatchee River and the Okeechobee Waterway from Stuart is in the chapter "Side Trip on the Okeechobee Waterway."

Sanibel Island to Charlotte Harbor– Outside (Gulf) Route

NAVIGATION: Use NOAA Charts 11425, 11426 and 11427. Mariners running the Gulf of Mexico to Charlotte Harbor or points north need only to choose the best weather and go. The only complications along this route are the shoals and bars that extend out from many areas of the shoreline and form an integral part of virtually every pass and inlet on Florida's West Coast. Be sure you are standing sufficiently offshore to clear them, which may make the trip somewhat longer than cutting up Pine Island Sound. Staying 3 to 4 nm off the coastline should get the job done.

To reach the Gulf for the trip north head south down the marked channel that goes underneath Sanibel Causeway Boulevard 'B' Span Bridge. Well-charted shoals extend most of the way from Point Ybel south to the San Carlos Bay Morse (A) marker "SC," where it becomes safe to turn west as long as the weather and water won't sweep you into the shallow

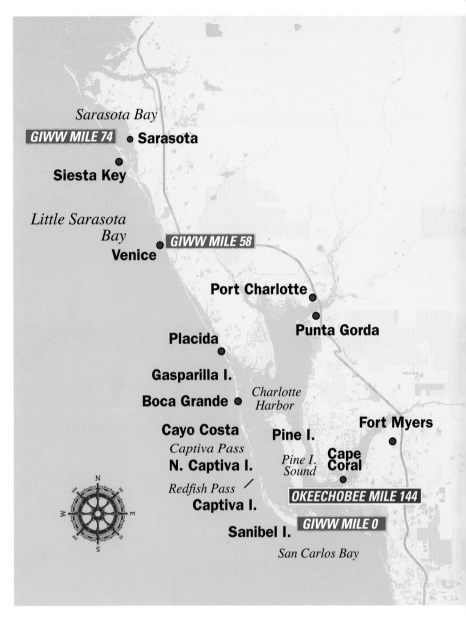

areas. Curve north with the sweep of Sanibel Island and lay a course that will take you to the Boca Grande flashing red bell buoy "2" (roughly 4.5 nm outside the entrance to Charlotte Harbor; GPS coordinates: N 026° 39.846'/W 082° 19.565').

If not planning to stop at Charlotte Harbor, entering a target waypoint just offshore of your target destination will provide the distance and after a close double-check along the path a "stay outside" line for quick visual reference. Venice provides a clean, well-marked inlet if visiting Sarasota, although we have received reports of shoaling at the end of the north jetty before flashing green "1." Deep-draft vessels should use caution while transiting the area. Using the two passes closest to Sarasota (New Pass and Big Sarasota Pass) definitely requires local knowledge.

San Carlos Bay, FL

PUNTA RASSA		Largest Vessel	VHF	Total Slips	Approach/ Dockside Depth	Floating Docks	Gas/ Diesel	Repairs/ Haulout	Min/Max Amps	Pump-Out Station
1. Sanibel Harbour Yacht Club- PRIVATE	(239) 333-4200	48	16	4	/ 6.0		GD			
2. Royal Shell Port Sanibel Marina WiFi	(239) 437-1660	65	16	95	4.0 / 5.0		GD	H	30 / 50	P
SANIBEL ISLAND										
3. Sanibel Marina WiFi	(239) 472-2723	70	16	65	6.0 / 6.0		GD	R	50	P

WiFi Wireless Internet Access　onSpot Dockside WiFi Facility
Visit www.waterwayguide.com for current rates, fuel prices, website addresses and other up-to-the-minute information.
(Information in the table is provided by the facilities.)

Scan here for more details:

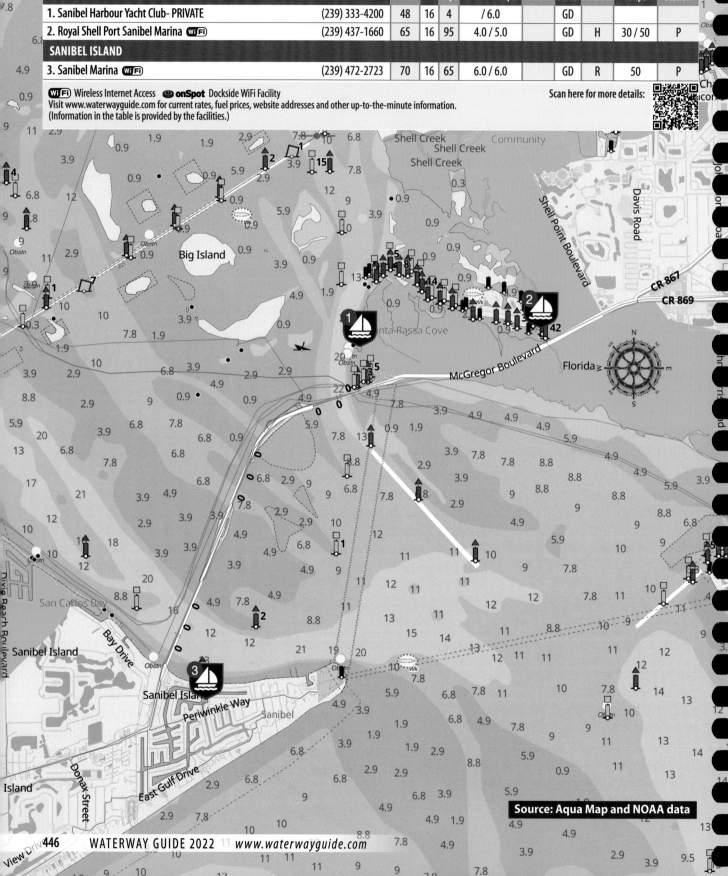

Source: Aqua Map and NOAA data

NO WAKE ZONE

No Wake Zones, Idle Speed Zones and various Speed Limit restrictions are in effect throughout the waterways included in this chapter. Exercise diligence in knowing the regulations by observing signs and other markers. Enforcement is always present. As always, be courteous to other vessels and avoid manatees and other marine life.

Sanibel Island–GIWW Mile 0

A string of barrier islands including Sanibel, Captiva, North Captiva and Cayo Costa separate Pine Island Sound from the Gulf of Mexico. Together the islands form a shallow crescent lying at an angle to the currents. That accident of shape and location causes what are said to be the world's most prolific shell deposits and the resultant "Sanibel stoop" of the island's visitors. More than 300 varieties of shells have been found on these beaches. The best shelling is at low tide after a storm when winds and waves have washed a new supply up on the beaches. Sanibel Island can have as many as four tides a day.

> A Sanibel Island law prohibits collectors from taking live shells, living starfish and sand dollars.

The best way to see Sanibel Island is on the miles of bicycle paths. Rental bikes are readily available from numerous sources on the island. You will want to visit the historic Sanibel Lighthouse at Point Ybel (1884) southeast from the marina and its beach and a fishing pier. The tree-lined main thoroughfare, Periwinkle Way, takes you to the Sanibel Historical Village and Museum (950 Dunlop Rd., 239-472-4648), which showcases the island's history. Tours (for a fee) are held at 10:30 a.m. and 1:30 p.m. based on docent availability.

The only public landing on the island other than dropping the hook and landing by dinghy is at Sanibel Marina. If you want to explore the island by land you will need to obtain permission to tie up your dinghy at the marina.

NAVIGATION: Use NOAA Chart 11426 or 11427. To reach the GIWW from Fort Myers Beach head west from Matanzas Pass. If your vessel requires more than 26 feet of vertical clearance, you will have to go through **Sanibel Causeway Boulevard 'A' Span Bridge** (70-foot fixed vertical clearance) on the Punta Rassa (northeast) side

of the bay. If you can navigate the 26-foot fixed vertical clearance you can use the **Sanibel Causeway Boulevard 'C' Span Bridge**. (**Sanibel Causeway Boulevard 'B' Span Bridge** has 9-foot fixed vertical clearance.)

To reach the high span ('A') from flashing green "1" at Matanzas Pass steer a course of 282° magnetic to flashing red "6" indicating the start of the channel to the Caloosahatchee River and the Okeechobee Waterway. Follow the channel from flashing red "6" through the bridge and then to flashing red "14" leaving it to the east. Shortly past that red lighted aid watch for green daybeacon "15" to the southwest and flashing green "101" to the northeast, which mark the end of the Okeechobee Waterway and the beginning of the GIWW (Mile 0). Turn southwest at green can "1" and pick up the well-marked channel as described above.

If you plan on transiting span 'C' (26-foot fixed vertical clearance) from Matanzas Pass, set a course of 265° magnetic from flashing green "1" when leaving the Matanzas Pass channel to flashing red "2" on the Sanibel Island side of the entrance to San Carlos Bay a distance of about 2.75 nm. Once under the 'C' span and about 2.5 miles up the well-marked channel you will pick out the 16-foot high, quick flashing green "11" for the GIWW channel.

A little less than 1 mile to the southwest you will see red daybeacon "2" marking the entrance to the channel to Sanibel Marina. Be careful making your approach. The sandy bottom is always shifting. It is best to enter at half-tide or better and call ahead for the latest local information. Enter the channel heading south and stay to the west side to avoid the obvious shoal at the first canal to the east. Continue south for Sanibel Marina's fuel dock.

Dockage: Just north of the eastern end of the fixed bridge (span 'A') west of Punta Rassa you may find a berth at Royal Shell Port Sanibel Marina. They report 4-foot MLW approach depths; call ahead for assistance with directions. They offer charters and boat rentals so expect traffic. Nearby Sanibel Harbour Yacht Club is private.

A snug harbor is available at the full-service Sanibel Marina, the only marina on the island. The marina monitors VHF Channel 16 and has transient slips for vessels up to 70 feet in an unhurried, palm-fringed setting. They have all the usual amenities plus laundry and some of the best water in the area, thanks to a reverse-osmosis water treatment system. There is a Ship's Store on site with a large inventory of boat necessities and clothing.

Pine Island Sound, FL

CAPTIVA ISLAND		Largest Vessel	VHF	Total Slips	Approach/ Dockside Depth	Floating Docks	Gas/ Diesel	Repairs/ Haulout	Min/Max Amps	Pump-Out Station
1. 'Tween Waters Island Resort & Spa MM 11.0	(239) 472-5161	100	16	41	6.0 / 6.0		GD		30 / 50	P
2. Jensen's Twin Palm Cottages and Marina (WiFi) MM 12.0	(239) 472-5800	25	16	20	5.0 / 5.0		G			

WiFi Wireless Internet Access **onSpot** Dockside WiFi Facility
Visit www.waterwayguide.com for current rates, fuel prices, website addresses and other up-to-the-minute information.
(Information in the table is provided by the facilities.)

Scan here for more details:

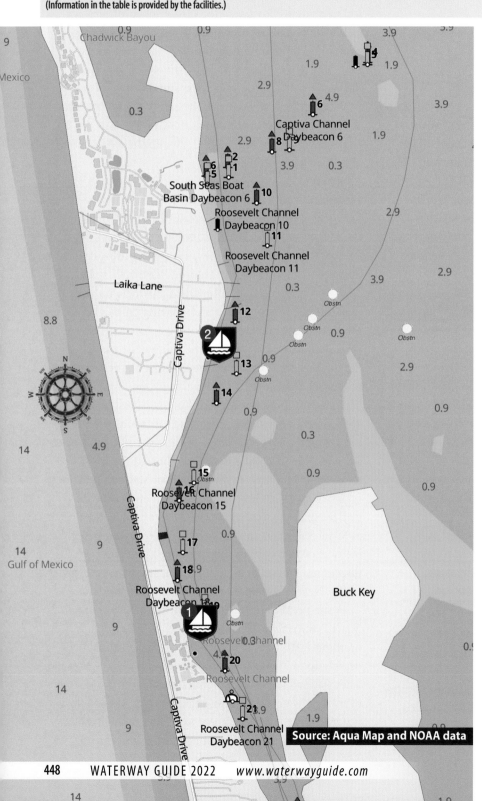

Source: Aqua Map and NOAA data

The on-site Gramma Dot's may have space for you while you eat lunch. Call ahead to the dockmaster on VHF Channel 16 or 239-472-8138.

Anchorage: The Sanibel Island anchorage just off Sanibel Marina has 9 to 14 feet MLW. This offers easy access to the shore but no amenities. There is a pocket of deeper water to the north in Matanzas Pass that has easy access, good depth and good holding. It is exposed to wind from the south but is perfectly acceptable for short stops. There is a nice day anchorage for a swim and lunch at the south end of Sanibel Island. It is exposed so stay overnight only in settled weather.

Vessels often anchor in the deeper water slot between Kitchel Key and Fisherman Key in 7 to 11 feet MLW. Watch the shoal to starboard when entering. Boats also anchor north on the outside of Punta Rassa Cove with at least 8-foot MLW depths. Both of these anchorages are fairly exposed but will suffice during settled weather.

Side Trip: J.N. "Ding" Darling National Wildlife Refuge– GIWW Mile 5.3

The 6,354-acre J.N. "Ding" Darling National Wildlife Refuge takes up much of 12-mile-long Sanibel Island mainly along the northern (Pine Island Sound) side. The refuge also serves as headquarters for several small wildlife refuges on nearby

Pine Island Sound, FL

CAPTIVA ISLAND		Largest Vessel	VHF	Total Slips	Approach/ Dockside Depth	Floating Docks	Gas/ Diesel	Repairs/ Haulout	Min/Max Amps	Pump-Out Station
1. South Seas Island Resort & Marina (WiFi) MM 13.6	(888) 777-3625	120	16		6.0 / 6.0		GD		30 / 100	P

(WiFi) Wireless Internet Access (onSpot) Dockside WiFi Facility
Visit www.waterwayguide.com for current rates, fuel prices, website addresses and other up-to-the-minute information.
(Information in the table is provided by the facilities.)

Scan here for more details:

islands. During the nesting season mariners are asked not to land on these rookery islands.

The refuge offers nature walks and an interpretive center. Even the most casual visitor will inevitably see alligators, anhinga ("snakebirds"), roseate spoonbills, snowy egrets, wood storks and great blue herons. Pink flamingos are seen quite often as well. The park is open daily from 10:00 a.m. to 4:00 p.m. For more information visit J.N. "Ding" Darling National Wildlife Refuge or call 239-472-1100.

Anchorage: J.N. "Ding" Darling National Wildlife Refuge offers an excellent anchorage possibility during settled weather in the cove due south of flashing red "16" (situated south of York Island). It is exposed to east through north winds with room for several boats. This is easily accessed off the channel. Watch your charts while entering for one shallow shoal. Holding is excellent in sand and mud close to Sanibel Island's mangrove shoreline in at least 6 feet MLW with good holding. It's a very scenic anchorage and a great spot to explore.

Pine Island Sound to North Captiva Island–GIWW Mile 4 to Mile 18.5

Liberally dotted with small islands and protected from the open Gulf of Mexico by a string of barrier islands Pine Island Sound runs about 15 miles to the mouth of Charlotte Harbor at Boca Grande Pass. Many of the small islands in the sound are part of the Pine Island National Wildlife Refuge and are closed to public access to protect the wildlife. Along this stretch you will see many ospreys tending their large nests.

NAVIGATION: Use NOAA Charts 11426 and 11427. Sailors in auxiliary-powered sailboats know the "Miserable Mile" well. Here the tide sweeps in and out directly across the arrow-

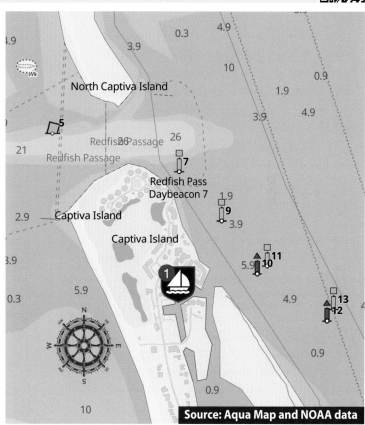

Source: Aqua Map and NOAA data

straight channel and strong crosscurrents are likely. Allow for the set and line up markers fore and aft. The channel is well marked and easy to follow. Be especially careful crossing south of Matlacha (pronounced "Mat-la-shay") Pass. The channel cuts off to the northwest just past flashing green "5" (when headed west). Do not stray too far to the west into 2 to 3 foot MLW. The currents are very strong and the channel is prone to silting around that same green daybeacon "5" and green daybeacon "9." One nautical mile farther west the problem worsens near where the channel bends to the northwest around the south end of Pine Island. Northerly winds tend to encourage the buildup of silt in the area.

The channel runs a jagged course often at an angle to the swift current through pools of relatively deep water interspersed with great shallow bays. Exercise caution. Stay to mid-channel, take navigational aids in order and do not try any shortcuts. In

Pine Island Sound between flashing green "23" and red daybeacon "24" at about Mile 8 power lines cross the channel with a charted vertical clearance of 95 feet at the main channel.

Just to the north of Sanibel is Captiva Island, about 6 miles long and separated from Sanibel Island by Blind Pass, which is crossed by a 7-foot fixed vertical clearance bridge. Heading north up Pine Island Sound at red daybeacon "38" a course of about 215° magnetic brings you back through shoal water to the little village of Captiva where cruisers will find marinas and amenities.

Shifting, shoaling Redfish Pass divides Captiva Island from North Captiva Island. This pass should only be used with current local knowledge. If you choose to exit or enter the Gulf of Mexico here call South Seas Island Resort & Marina for advice. Remember that currents are strong in this area and shoaling persists. Boca Grande Pass, a good exit to the Gulf of Mexico, is the preferred pass and is only 6 miles to the north.

North Captiva Island is accessible only by boat. A marked channel runs north from Captiva Pass across the GIWW toward Charlotte Harbor but do not use it as a shortcut unless yours is a very shallow-draft boat. This channel shoals in its upper reaches to about 5 feet MLW. In the rest of the channel depths run 7 to 13 feet MLW with occasional spots for anchoring. Although used by fishers with local knowledge Captiva Pass–between North Captiva Island and Cayo Costa–is unmarked and subject to change.

Dockage: Honor the red markers (controlling depth is 6.5 feet MLW) for 'Tween Waters Island Resort & Spa tucked in behind Buck Key. To reach the 41-slip marina turn west at red daybeacon "38" of the GIWW and proceed on a course of 215° magnetic (for about 1.0 mile) to locate Roosevelt Channel's flashing red "2." Follow that to green daybeacon "19." (Better yet, call ahead for directions and follow them.) Transients have free access to the resort including beach access, a pool complex, spa and lively pub-style bar (with entertainment most nights). They also have kayak and stand-up paddleboard rentals. Farther up the channel is Jensen's Twin Palm Cottages and Marina with a laid-back, relaxed atmosphere. Call ahead for slip availability.

A channel marked with daybeacons leads from the GIWW between red daybeacon "38" and flashing green "39" to South Seas Island Resort & Marina. The channel leading into the marina is well marked and they can accommodate vessels to 120 feet. This is a first-rate facility with resort amenities. All vessels must announce entry upon arrival at the entrance marker on VHF Channel 16.

Anchorage: At the southern tip of Pine Island sits the central point for fishing on the lower sound, St. James City. Fishing camps and small boat marinas abound here along with shallow water and numerous private markers that can be confusing to the stranger. You can anchor south of St. James City by the mangroves in 8 to 9 feet MLW and dinghy to shore. There are also several restaurants directly on the main (Monroe) canal you can dinghy to for a visit.

Chino Island to the north in Pine Island Sound offers protection from easterly and northerly winds with good holding. Leave the GIWW at flashing green "23" and you will find 7- to 8-foot MLW depths almost to the shore. You may receive a few wakes from vessels traveling the GIWW and locals who use this area for fishing and a shortcut to nearby canals. You can anchor anywhere off the channel in Pine Island Sound where deeper water is indicated on the charts.

Two anchorage areas are located behind Buck Key at Captiva Island. You can also drop the hook at green daybeacon "21" or at green daybeacon "17" in 4 to 5 feet MLW.

The anchorage at the northern tip of North Captiva Island is a beautiful location in fair weather but is fully exposed from northeast through south-southeast. North Captiva has no cars, just sand roads for foot, bike and golf cart traffic. Off the southeast tip of Cayo Costa Key an anchorage is within a dinghy-pull of the beaches at both North Captiva Island and Cayo Costa. Both anchorages have 7 to 10 feet MLW.

Side Trip: Cabbage Key–GIWW Mile 22

Just west of the GIWW channel Cabbage Key lies in the lee of Cayo Costa. This delightful and unspoiled island is accessible only by boat and offers ample opportunity for observing nature in all its forms. For bird and nature enthusiasts the bird watching and nature walk should not be missed. It is best to begin at the top of Cabbage Key's walk-up water tower for an overview of the island. Easily followed trails traverse Cabbage Key's connected shell mounds, revealing representative varieties of subtropical trees, shrubs, plants and bird life.

Nesting ospreys are abundant as are telltale signs of the Florida gopher tortoise.

A great exploration by dinghy gives you access to the front beach of Cabbage Key by way of The Tunnel. If you are anchored northeast of flashing red "60" proceed south around Cabbage Key to Murdock Bayou. Go almost to the end of Murdock Bayou and you will see a small, open area in the mangroves on the west side. There is enough room to tie a couple of dinghies to the mangroves. Walk through the tunnel of mangroves to the path that leads to the beach. (Watch for alligators.) It is a great place to picnic and enjoy the white sandy beach. In north winds depths through The Tunnel and Murdock Bayou may be too shallow even for dinghies.

Dockage: Reached by the privately marked entry channel just west of green daybeacon "61" is the classic old Florida island retreat, Cabbage Key Inn, which sits upon a 38-foot-high Calusa shell mound. One hundred acres of tropical vegetation surround the historic restaurant, inn and rental cottages. The marina sits at the base with 25 slips.

Opposite Cayo Costa north of the GIWW at about flashing red "60" is the private island of Useppa. Accessible only by water, Useppa Island Club has been established as a private club. They do not accept transients; you must be a member or a guest of a member.

Anchorage: A large, popular anchorage is available off the GIWW between flashing red "60" and red daybeacon "62" near the west side of Useppa Island. This anchorage can sometimes be uncomfortable from wakes of passing boats, especially on weekends but the scenery is beautiful. It is also somewhat exposed to wind so caution should be used when anchoring. The advantages of this anchorage far outnumber the disadvantages.

Cayo Costa–GIWW Mile 18.5 to Mile 25

Spanish fishermen from Havana gave 6-mile-long Cayo Costa its name (translated as "Coastal Key"). Located at the north end of Pine Island Sound on the south side of Boca Grande Pass, this almost-uninhabited island (home to a swine of feral pigs) is accessible only by boat.

Both Punta Blanca Island and Cayo Costa are part of Cayo Costa State Park. At the northern end of Punta

Cabbage Key Cottage

Pine Island Sound, FL

PINE ISLAND		Largest Vessel	VHF	Total Slips	Approach/ Dockside Depth	Floating Docks	Gas/ Diesel	Repairs/ Haulout	Min/Max Amps	Pump-Out Station
1. Cabbage Key Inn (WiFi) MM 21.5	(239) 283-2278	85	16	25	8.0 / 6.0				30 / 50	

Scan here for more details:

(WiFi) Wireless Internet Access **onSpot** Dockside WiFi Facility
Visit www.waterwayguide.com for current rates, fuel prices, website addresses and other up-to-the-minute information.
(Information in the table is provided by the facilities.)

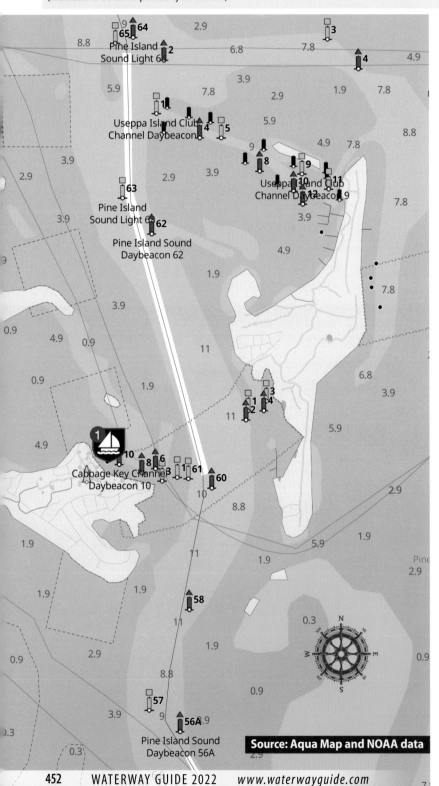

Blanca Island (between the two islands) is Pelican Pass and Pelican Bay. Although the Pelican Pass entrance may at first appear a bit dicey, it is well worth the effort. With caution and a little help from the tide boats drawing up to 5 feet can normally get through Pelican Pass into Pelican Bay.

NAVIGATION: Use NOAA Chart 11427. To reach Pelican Bay from red daybeacon "74" travel southwest toward the tip of the beach on Cayo Costa. Stay to within about 75 feet of the sand beach and just past the little sign in the water turn slightly east and follow the beach up into Pelican Bay. You will find 5 to 6 feet MLW in the pass. When inside Pelican Bay pay attention to your depth sounder as there are several very shallow areas.

If feeling particularly adventuresome, take your dinghy and look for the unmarked small but deep creek on Cayo Costa that opens into a small lake of about 200 yards in diameter. The depth in the creek is more than adequate for dinghies. There is a small dock on the lake that was once used for loading supplies on the island. You can land your dinghy there and explore. It is very pretty and worth the effort!

Dockage: Cayo Costa State Park headquarters is here with daytime dockage for small boats (25 feet and under) and some free overnight dockage (no hookups). The park extends to the Gulf side of the island where there are not only beautiful beaches but also cabins and camping. Transportation across the island is by foot, tram or rental bike. The beaches on the Gulf side are very popular for shelling.

Anchorage: At Mile 22.5 at the southern tip of Punta Blanca Island is a

Pine Island Sound, FL

PINE ISLAND		Largest Vessel	VHF	Total Slips	Approach/ Dockside Depth	Floating Docks	Gas/ Diesel	Repairs/ Haulout	Min/Max Amps	Pump-Out Station
1. Cayo Costa State Park	(941) 964-0375				6.0 / 6.0	F				

WiFi Wireless Internet Access **onSpot** Dockside WiFi Facility
Visit www.waterwayguide.com for current rates, fuel prices, website addresses and other up-to-the-minute information.
(Information in the table is provided by the facilities.)

Scan here for more details:

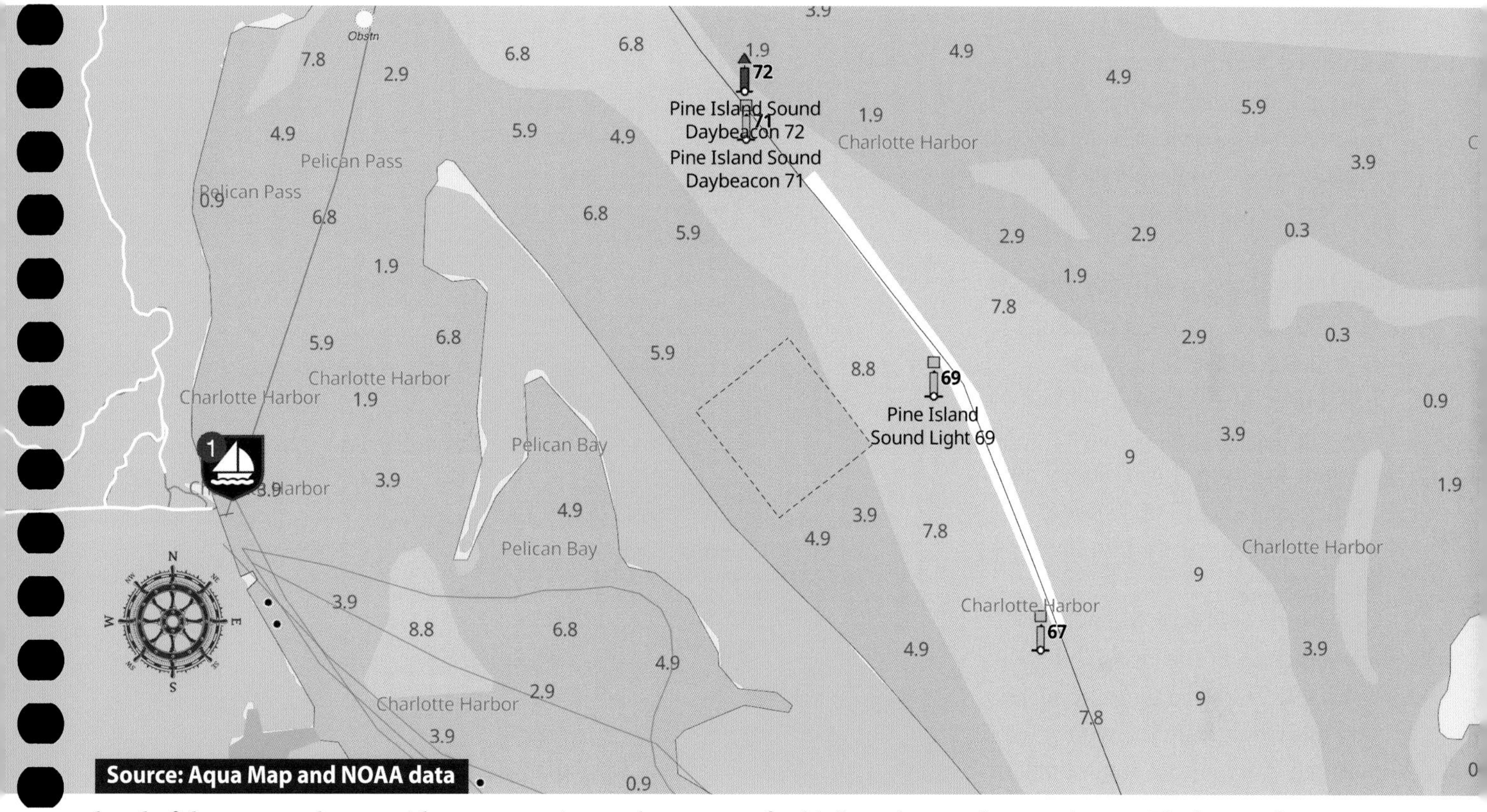

Source: Aqua Map and NOAA data

bowl of deep water that provides an attractive anchorage. The adventurous skipper can take up to a 6-foot draft vessel completely around the point where there is an exceptionally cozy anchorage. The downside of the equation is that this anchorage has poor ventilation and is best in winter months.

You can anchor in Pelican Bay in 7 to 8 feet MLW with plenty of swinging room and really good holding. This is a very popular anchorage so it can get crowded on weekends. The seasonal manatee population is robust and there are many places to explore in the dinghy.

Pine Island (North)–GIWW Mile 25

The largest island off Florida's Gulf Coast Pine Island offers a small-town atmosphere amid mangroves, three aquatic preserves and acres of palm, tropical plants and fruit groves. The waters of Pine Island Sound provide not only some of the finest fishing in Florida but are a haven for birdwatchers and nature lovers. The heart of Pine Island is a collection of homegrown shops, galleries, fish markets and residences.

NAVIGATION: Use NOAA Chart 11427. Matlacha Pass carries a marked but shallow, crooked channel north between Pine Island and the mainland to Charlotte Harbor. Controlling depth is about 3 feet MLW and a 32-foot-high power cable and the **Matlacha Pass (SR 78) Bridge** cross the pass. The bridge has 9-foot closed vertical clearance but opens on signal. This passage is not recommended but can be safely explored from the northern entrance.

Dockage: At the northwestern end of Pine Island is Wilson Cut, which leads to Safe Harbor Pineland. They have slips but you may access some skinny water on your way in. Wait for a high tide if you require more than 30 inches. Be sure to go follow all the marks on the way in or out...Don't cut corners. On the north end of Matlacha

Pine Island Sound, FL

PINE ISLAND		Largest Vessel	VHF	Total Slips	Approach/ Dockside Depth	Floating Docks	Gas/ Diesel	Repairs/ Haulout	Min/Max Amps	Pump-Out Station
1. Safe Harbor Pineland	(239) 283-3593	38	16	30	4.5 / 7.0		G	RH		

WiFi Wireless Internet Access **onSpot** Dockside WiFi Facility

Visit www.waterwayguide.com for current rates, fuel prices, website addresses and other up-to-the-minute information. (Information in the table is provided by the facilities.)

Scan here for more details:

Pass just before the bridge is Olde Fish House Marina. Originally a fish packing house, this marina, seafood market and full-service restaurant is family-owned and -operated. Call ahead for slip availability.

Charlotte Harbor–GIWW Mile 25

About 60 miles southeast of Tampa Bay, Charlotte Harbor is a wide, elbow-shaped bay carrying 9-foot MLW depths to Punta Gorda at the mouth of the Peace River. Stretching 20 miles long and 10 miles wide, Charlotte Harbor offers a lot for the cruising boater.

Charlotte Harbor is formed by the confluence of the Peace and Myakka Rivers. Tidal range averages 2 feet but winds from the west reportedly can increase water levels as much as 5 feet. The open sweep and relatively uniform depths of water in Charlotte Harbor provide a welcome change from the narrow, shoal-bordered GIWW. The high sandbars that protect the shoreline limit opportunities for gunkholing but both the Peace and Myakka Rivers compensate for that weakness by offering opportunities for scenic dinghy trips.

On the southern shore of the Peace River is the charming boating community of Punta Gorda. It comprises 60 miles of canals that meander through well-kept neighborhoods and lead to Charlotte Harbor. The city has a historic

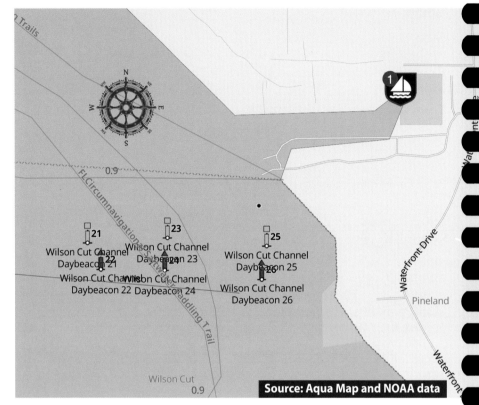

Source: Aqua Map and NOAA data

district with over 150 significant historical residential and commercial structures along its brick-lined streets. Along the Punta Gorda coastline of Charlotte Harbor is Harborwalk, a scenic pedestrian- and bicycle-friendly riverside walkway lined with palm trees, brick pavers and park amenities.

Charlotte Harbor is a good place for daysailing and has variable winds. Yacht clubs in the area are involved year-round in sailboat racing and offer privileges to members of reciprocating clubs. When entering any marina in Charlotte Harbor be sure to stay inside the well-marked channels. The water can be very shallow outside of them.

NAVIGATION: Use NOAA Chart 11427. The Peace River enters Charlotte Harbor from the northeast. It is very shallow (7 to 8 feet MLW) and marked for only about 6 miles but its channel is navigable to the town of Hull located 15 miles upriver. With just 3-foot MLW depths this stretch calls for local knowledge and the snags and heavy growths of hyacinths in the upper river require extra caution. Two 45-foot fixed vertical clearance bridges (**Tamiami Trail Bridges** and **I-75 Bridges**) cross the Peace River at the entrance. If you can get under the lower bridge,

Pine Island Sound, FL

MATLACHA		Largest Vessel	VHF	Total Slips	Approach/ Dockside Depth	Floating Docks	Gas/ Diesel	Repairs/ Haulout	Min/Max Amps	Pump-Out Station
1. Olde Fish House Marina	(239) 282-9577				12.0 / 5.0					

WiFi Wireless Internet Access **onSpot** Dockside WiFi Facility
Visit www.waterwayguide.com for current rates, fuel prices, website addresses and other up-to-the-minute information.
(Information in the table is provided by the facilities.)

Scan here for more details:

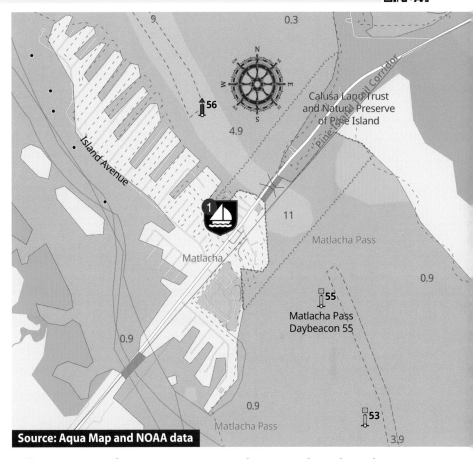

Source: Aqua Map and NOAA data

the 60-foot overhead power lines won't be an issue.

Wandering through dense woodland the Myakka River runs from the northwest from Myakka Lake to Charlotte Harbor. Boats drawing 3 feet or less with less than 25-foot clearance and armed with local knowledge can travel about 17 miles up the Myakka River. Three nautical miles up the river the **SR 776 Bridge** sets the 25-foot fixed vertical clearance limit. Past Myakka State Park in the upper reaches of the Myakka River there is a wilderness reminiscent of the Everglades. This is home to large alligators, feral hogs, eagles, deer, rattlesnakes and even the very rare Florida panther.

Dockage/Moorings: Opposite Boca Grande Channel and midway up the eastern shore of Charlotte Harbor the large (525-slip) Safe Harbor Burnt Store is a very popular stop. Flashing red "6" leads off the approach from Charlotte Harbor and is then followed by flashing red "2" and a series of daybeacons into the protected harbor. The inlet channel has been dredged and ongoing maintenance is evident. This is more to this facility than its dockage and restaurant (Cass Cay). This is home to a tight-knit community of boaters who return year after year. Taxis are available for the relatively lengthy ride to Punta Gorda for provisioning.

Fishermen's Village Marina is located on upper Charlotte Harbor with no bridges or other restrictions to the Gulf of Mexico and is within

walking distance of Historic Punta Gorda. This is a very popular spot for transients to spend the winter and spring months. The well-kept marina also has courtesy docks for day-trippers and a long dinghy dock.

Laishley Park Municipal Marina has floating concrete slips and a mooring field just past the (Tamiami Trail Bridges). Be sure to call in advance for availability. A pump-out boat comes twice a week to the mooring field. They also have a day use-only dock. Laishley Park is the site of many festivals

and activities throughout the year. Punta Gorda Marina to the north is strictly a repair/storage facility (no transient slips). On the north side of the Peace River at the mouth is Charlotte Harbor Yacht Club, which recognizes reciprocity from other clubs. Call ahead for availability.

Marine repair and storage facilities (no transient slips) can be found on a series of canals (6 miles long) off the Santa Cruz Waterway on the Myakka River located on the northwestern shore of Charlotte Harbor including Safe

Charlotte Harbor, FL

PUNTA GORDA AREA		Largest Vessel	VHF	Total Slips	Approach/ Dockside Depth	Floating Docks	Gas/ Diesel	Repairs/ Haulout	Min/Max Amps	Pump-Out Station
1. Safe Harbor Burnt Store WiFi	(941) 637-0083	100	16	525	8.0 / 8.0	F	GD	RH	30 / 100	P

WiFi Wireless Internet Access · **onSpot** Dockside WiFi Facility
Visit www.waterwayguide.com for current rates, fuel prices, website addresses and other up-to-the-minute information.
(Information in the table is provided by the facilities.)

Scan here for more details:

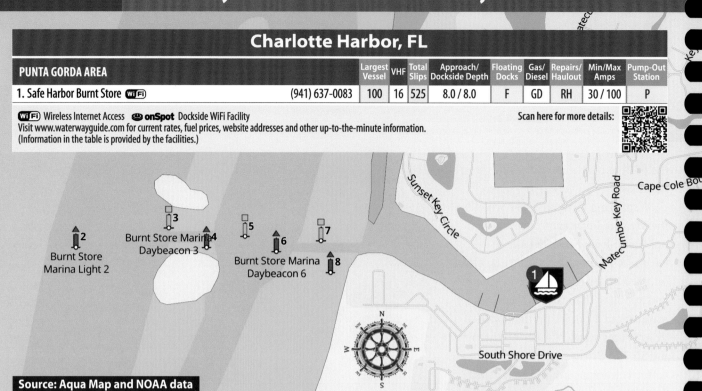

Source: Aqua Map and NOAA data

Charlotte Harbor, FL

PUNTA GORDA AREA		Largest Vessel	VHF	Total Slips	Approach/ Dockside Depth	Floating Docks	Gas/ Diesel	Repairs/ Haulout	Min/Max Amps	Pump-Out Station
1. Fishermen's Village Marina WiFi	(941) 575-3000	125	16	111	7.0 / 5.0		GD		30 / 100	P

WiFi Wireless Internet Access · **onSpot** Dockside WiFi Facility
Visit www.waterwayguide.com for current rates, fuel prices, website addresses and other up-to-the-minute information.
(Information in the table is provided by the facilities.)

Scan here for more details:

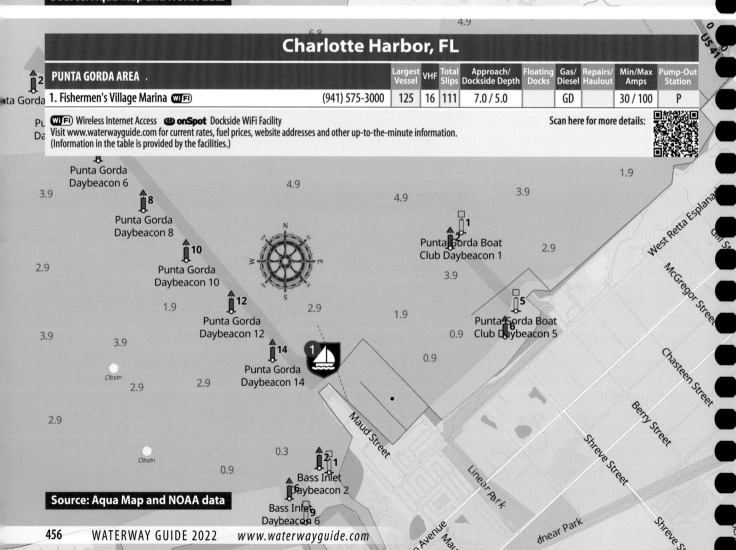

Source: Aqua Map and NOAA data

Charlotte Harbor, FL

PUNTA GORDA AREA		Largest Vessel	VHF	Total Slips	Approach/ Dockside Depth	Floating Docks	Gas/ Diesel	Repairs/ Haulout	Min/Max Amps	Pump-Out Station
1. Laishley Park Municipal Marina **WiFi**	(941) 575-0142	80	16	94	7.0 / 7.0	F			30 / 50	P
2. Punta Gorda Marina Charlotte Harbor	(941) 639-2750	60			5.0 / 5.0			RH		

WiFi Wireless Internet Access **onSpot** Dockside WiFi Facility
Visit www.waterwayguide.com for current rates, fuel prices, website addresses and other up-to-the-minute information.
(Information in the table is provided by the facilities.)

Scan here for more details:

Source: Aqua Map and NOAA data

Punta Gorda Wildlife Reserve

Charlotte Harbor, FL

PUNTA GORDA AREA		Largest Vessel	VHF	Total Slips	Approach/ Dockside Depth	Floating Docks	Gas/ Diesel	Repairs/ Haulout	Min/Max Amps	Pump-Out Station
1. Charlotte Harbor Yacht Club WiFi	(941) 629-5131	60	16	18	4.0 / 6.0		GD		30 / 50	P

WiFi Wireless Internet Access **onSpot** Dockside WiFi Facility
Visit www.waterwayguide.com for current rates, fuel prices, website addresses and other up-to-the-minute information.
(Information in the table is provided by the facilities.)

Scan here for more details:

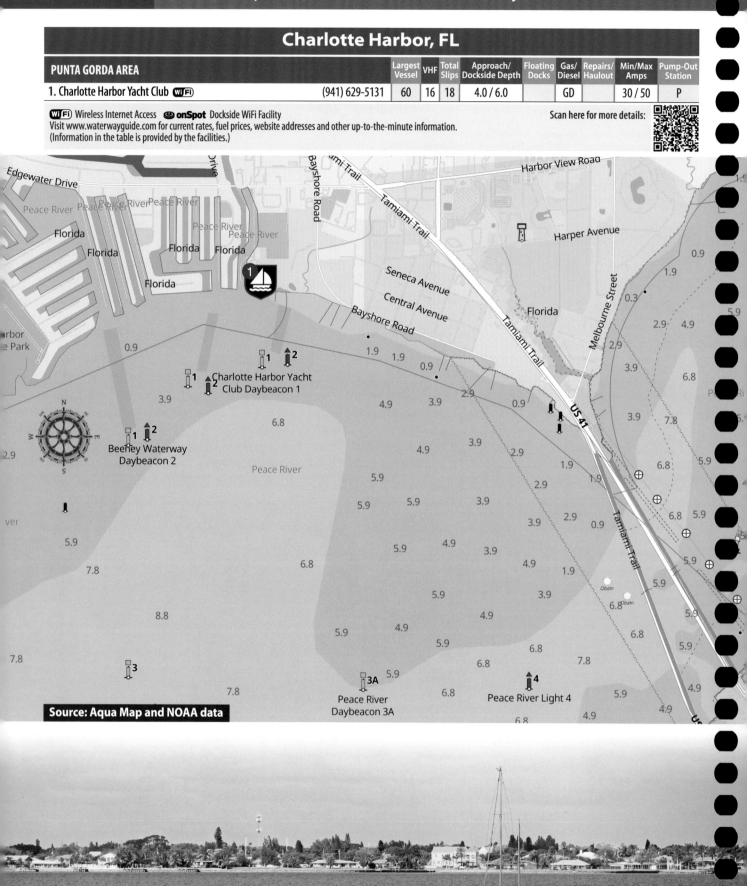

Source: Aqua Map and NOAA data

Charlotte Harbor, FL

MYAKKA RIVER		Largest Vessel	VHF	Total Slips	Approach/ Dockside Depth	Floating Docks	Gas/ Diesel	Repairs/ Haulout	Min/Max Amps	Pump-Out Station
1. Safe Cove Boat Storage	(941) 697-9900	65	63	15	6.0 / 7.0		GD	RH	30	P
2. Charlotte Harbor Boat Storage WiFi	(941) 828-0216	55			/			RH		

WiFi Wireless Internet Access **onSpot** Dockside WiFi Facility
Visit www.waterwayguide.com for current rates, fuel prices, website addresses and other up-to-the-minute information.
(Information in the table is provided by the facilities.)

Scan here for more details:

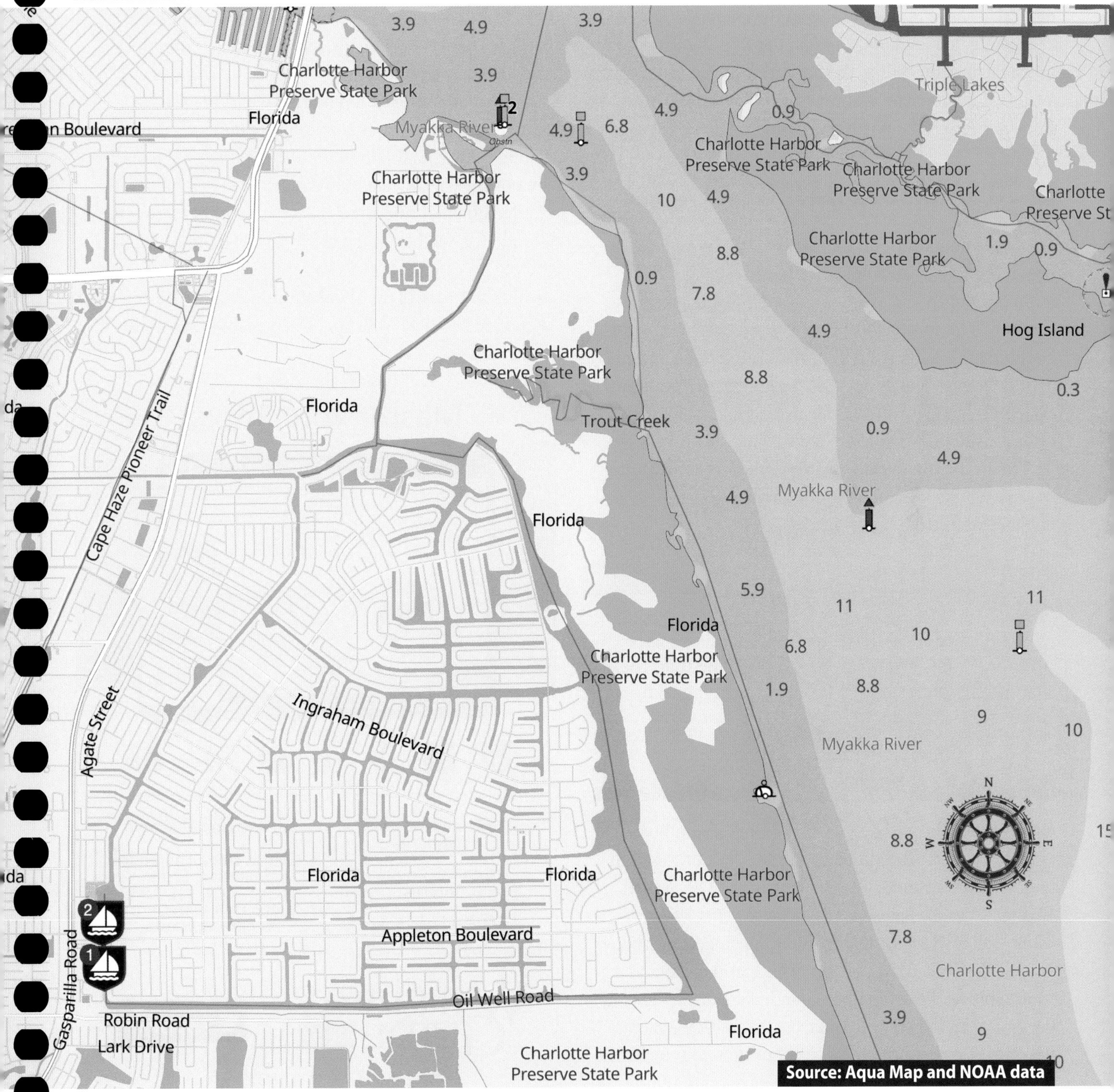

Cove Boat Storage and Charlotte Harbor Boat Storage. Nearby is Fuel Buddy To Your Boat with convenient fuel service (no slips). Schedule your fuel delivery and they will come to you.

Anchorage: You need to be adventuresome to anchor on the Peace River. If you travel beyond the 12-foot fixed vertical clearance bridge, you will find plenty of anchorages in at least 4 feet MLW and miles of unspoiled natural scenery. Be sure to stay in the channel.

A protected anchorage lies on the Myakka River near green daybeacon "9" (at the beginning of the Santa Cruz Waterway). Here you will find 5 to 7 feet MLW with protection from the north and west.

■ TO SARASOTA BAY

Those running north on the GIWW will find the bays beginning to narrow somewhat. Shores are closer and more developed and you should watch the markers carefully. The channel from Boca Grande and Charlotte Harbor winds sufficiently to maintain interest. Channel depths average 7 to 11 feet MLW although depths are extremely shallow outside the marked channel where the birds are often able to walk in the shallows.

The inside route from Charlotte Harbor to Sarasota Bay is well marked and not too heavily congested with manatee or boating safety areas.

NO WAKE ZONE

The 25-mph speed zone in the GIWW channel ("Slow-Speed/Minimum-Wake" within a specified distance from the shore) is more the rule than the exception. Pay close attention to posted signs in these slow-speed restriction areas.

Option: Outside (Gulf) Route via Boca Grande Pass

NAVIGATION: Use NOAA Chart 11425. From Boca Grande Pass, shoal-draft boats (5-foot draft or less) can use the shortcut route (known locally as "The Swash Channel") to Big Sarasota Pass. The channel leads to deep water well inshore of the big ship route. To follow The Swash Channel around the tip of Gasparilla Island you should proceed west in Boca Grande Pass until you reach the end of an old concrete pier, bearing 340° magnetic. Pass the pier about 50 to 100 feet out in 8- to 9-foot MLW depths avoiding the long shoal that runs off to the south-

southeast. Once clear of the shoal you will find 10- to 11-foot MLW depths.

Note that if you are returning to Charlotte Harbor from the Gulf of Mexico in a brisk northwesterly with an outgoing tide, Boca Grande Pass can appear reasonably docile until you are almost next to the piers when you can be in breaking waves before you know it. (The waves break away from you and are hard to recognize.) It is wise to avoid The Swash Channel in such conditions because there is no "wiggle room" there. Current local knowledge is advisable.

The safer approach to entering Charlotte Harbor particularly if the water is rough is to enter via the ship channel. The shoals along the ship channel particularly on the northwest side need to be monitored carefully as the charted channel runs very close to them. If entering Boca Grande Channel from the north, take care to come all of the way to green buoy "3" and red nun buoy "4" before turning in to avoid the shoal entirely. You will be at about the Three Nautical Mile line. Deeper water lies to the

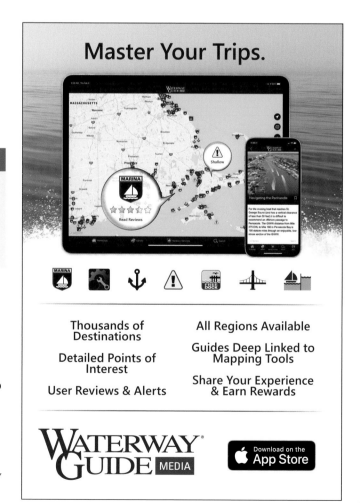

Gasparilla Sound, FL

BOCA GRANDE AREA		Largest Vessel	VHF	Total Slips	Approach/ Dockside Depth	Floating Docks	Gas/ Diesel	Repairs/ Haulout	Min/Max Amps	Pump-Out Station
1. Boca Grande Marina (WiFi) MM 28.5	(941) 964-2100	150	16	20	6.5 / 6.5		GD		30 / 100	P
2. The Gasparilla Inn & Club MM 29.5	(941) 964-4620	50		24	6.0 / 4.5	F	GD	RH	50	

(WiFi) Wireless Internet Access **onSpot** Dockside WiFi Facility
Visit www.waterwayguide.com for current rates, fuel prices, website addresses and other up-to-the-minute information.
(Information in the table is provided by the facilities.)

Scan here for more details:

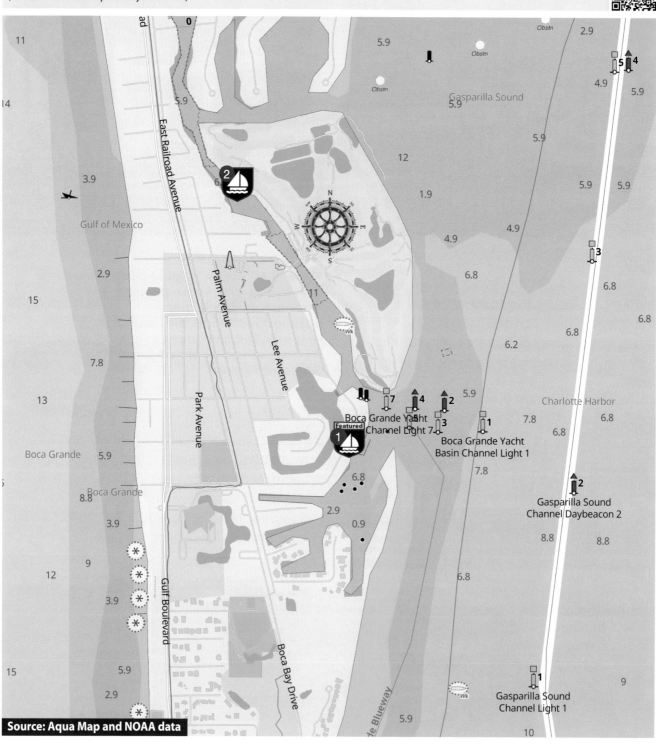

Gasparilla Sound, FL

BOCA GRANDE AREA		Largest Vessel	VHF	Total Slips	Approach/ Dockside Depth	Floating Docks	Gas/ Diesel	Repairs/ Haulout	Min/Max Amps	Pump-Out Station
1. Uncle Henry's Marina **WiFi** MM 32.8	(941) 964-0154	90	16	58	6.0 / 9.0		GD		30 / 200+	P

WiFi Wireless Internet Access **onSpot** Dockside WiFi Facility
Visit www.waterwayguide.com for current rates, fuel prices, website addresses and other up-to-the-minute information.
(Information in the table is provided by the facilities.)

Scan here for more details:

south side of the channel if you need to get out of the way of commercial vessels.

Big Sarasota Pass has reasonably good depths for most cruising boats but is subject to shoaling. Follow the charted marks. Be sure to call ahead for local information. Towing services are really good about giving information as is the Sarasota Yacht Club website (www.sarasotayachtclub.org).

Boca Grande Area–GIWW Mile 27 to Mile 36

Boca Grande on the south end of Gasparilla Island makes a good stop. In a bygone era Boca Grande was a winter resort and fishing retreat for northern socialites and tycoons. For the most part the gracious old homes they once occupied have been faithfully maintained, preserving the elegance of the past. Those in the entertainment business seem to favor the Gasparilla Inn for its privacy and good manners as well as the absolutely charming atmosphere. (You must book a room to dock there.) This is a wonderful stop and shouldn't be missed if time permits (941-964-4620).

NAVIGATION: Use NOAA Chart 11425. The Boca Grande Channel, one of the primary inlets from the Gulf, runs between Cayo Costa and Gasparilla Island forming the entrance to Charlotte Harbor. The channel is easy to navigate, deep, well marked and lighted and is one of the primary, important passes on the stretch between Naples and Tampa.

To cross Boca Grande Channel from the GIWW inside flashing red "76" (off the northeast point of Cayo Costa) and flashing green "1" (off the eastern shore of Gasparilla Island) are the important markers. If heading north, follow a bearing of about 350° magnetic after leaving flashing red "76" to the east. The channel carries 10 to 12 feet MLW and is well marked.

Located about a quarter of the way up Gasparilla Island when you are headed north is

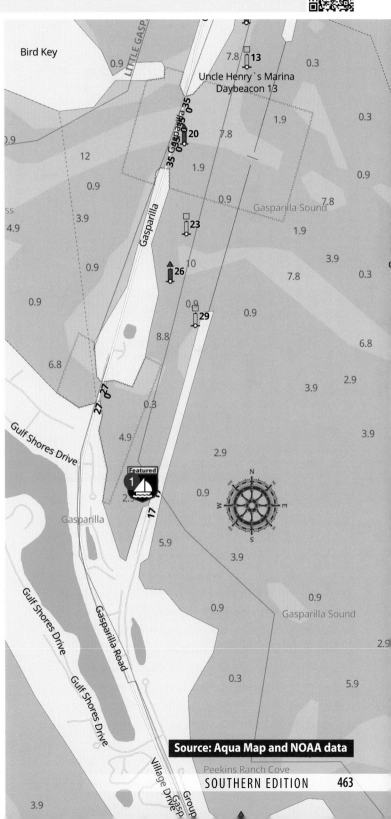

Source: Aqua Map and NOAA data

Gasparilla Sound, FL

BOCA GRANDE AREA		Largest Vessel	VHF	Total Slips	Approach/ Dockside Depth	Floating Docks	Gas/ Diesel	Repairs/ Haulout	Min/Max Amps	Pump-Out Station
1. Gasparilla Marina **WiFi**	(941) 697-2280	100	16	225	7.0 / 6.0	F	GD	RH	30 / 100	P

WiFi Wireless Internet Access **onSpot** Dockside WiFi Facility
Visit www.waterwayguide.com for current rates, fuel prices, website addresses and other up-to-the-minute information.
(Information in the table is provided by the facilities.)

Scan here for more details:

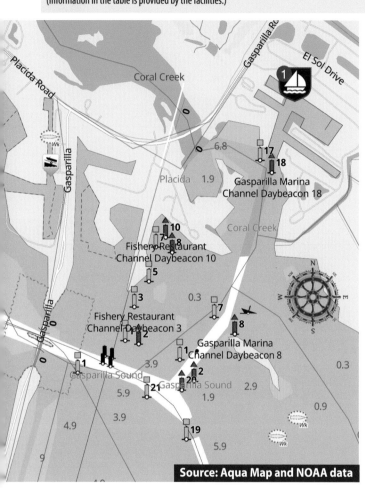

Source: Aqua Map and NOAA data

what is designated on some charts (e.g., Navionics) as "yacht basin." This is not a business but the location of Boca Grande Marina. Use 16-foot flashing green "1" to line up red daybeacon "2" and green daybeacon "3" to enter the channel into the harbor. The channel carries 7 to 9 feet MLW. On entering the Boca Grande Bayou to starboard, flashing green "7" should be given a wide berth because of the encroaching sandbar. Controlling depths are 6 feet MLW in Boca Grande Bayou.

Continuing north on the GIWW and Gasparilla Sound near the town of Placida the waterway channel doglegs farther west toward a pair of bridges at green daybeacon "19." Pass through the permanently opened railway bridge just past green daybeacon "21" then leave green daybeacon "1" to the south as you approach the **Boca Grande Swing Bridge** at GIWW Mile 34.3.

Boca Grande Swing Bridge opens on signal except 7:00 a.m. to 6:00 p.m., Monday through Friday, when the draw need only open on the hour and half-hour. On Saturdays, Sundays and federal holidays the draw opens every 15 minutes. Vessels must request an opening. Be sure to check the Coast Guard *Local Notice to Mariners* (www.navcen.uscg.gov) for schedule changes or use VHF Channel 09 to get in touch with the bridgetender.

⚠

When approaching from the Gulf, Gasparilla Pass is not recommended. This is an access used by local fishers with a lot of local knowledge and very shallow-draft boats. The area around the pass is riddled with charted 2- to 3-foot MLW spots and the entire north side of the pass has a 1-foot MLW bar on its border. Use Boca Grande Pass instead.

Dockage: Boca Grande Marina has secure berths and a full range of amenities for visiting boaters inside the yacht basin. Guests will enjoy friendly dockside assistance, a well-stocked Ship's Store and waterfront casual dining (inside or out). This facility is located just 0.5 mile from downtown and offers golf cart rentals.

Arriving at the northern tip of Gasparilla Island along the GIWW from the south transients can find dockage at Uncle Henry's Marina. Turn southwest between the open railroad bridge and the Boca Grande Swing Bridge. (Note that private green daybeacon "1" may be missing.) The quiet, peaceful Uncle Henry's Marin) can accommodate vessels up to 80 feet. There is a covered patio and grill and Kappy's Market is adjacent for groceries and golf cart rentals The entrance has 6 to 7 feet MLW and a 1.5- to 2-foot tidal

Lemon Bay, FL

LEMON BAY AREA		Largest Vessel	VHF	Total Slips	Approach/ Dockside Depth	Floating Docks	Gas/ Diesel	Repairs/ Haulout	Min/Max Amps	Pump-Out Station
1. Loggerhead Marina - Palm Harbour Marina (WiFi) MM 38.5	(941) 697-4356	65	16	90	7.0 / 6.0		GD	RH	30 / 50	P
2. Cape Haze Marina MM 39.0	(941) 698-1110	70	16	105	6.0 / 9.0	F	GD	RH	30 / 50	P

WiFi Wireless Internet Access   **onSpot** Dockside WiFi Facility
Visit www.waterwayguide.com for current rates, fuel prices, website addresses and other up-to-the-minute information.
(Information in the table is provided by the facilities.)

Scan here for more details:

range. With a wind out of the north depths will be less. Pay attention to the tide tables; deep-draft vessels should call Uncle Henry's (941-964-0154) for a current report. There has been some silting along both sides of this access passage so honor all markers and stay as close to center channel as possible.

At flashing red "20" on the GIWW a channel leads off to the mainland side past the mouth of Coral Creek to Gasparilla Marina with slips to 40 feet in an enclosed basin. The marina has an on-site restaurant.

Anchorage: Anchorage is limited around Gasparilla Island and any available space is often filled with local boats on permanent moorings. You can go north from flashing green "7" in Boca Grande Key and drop the hook in the small basin before the fixed 13-foot fixed vertical clearance bridge. Be prepared to drop your anchor, back down on it and then tie off on the mangroves with a stern line to stop your swing in the tight quarters.

At Mile 36 Cape Haze offers a quiet, protected anchorage northeast of red daybeacon "30" in 7- to 9-foot MLW depths surrounded by private homes. Set your anchor carefully as the bottom is soft mud. There is a small canal that leads to the north and the tidal current may swing you more than the wind. There is only enough room for two or three boats to anchor comfortably. In short watch your depths, set your anchor well and if there are three boats already there, you may want to choose to find another spot.

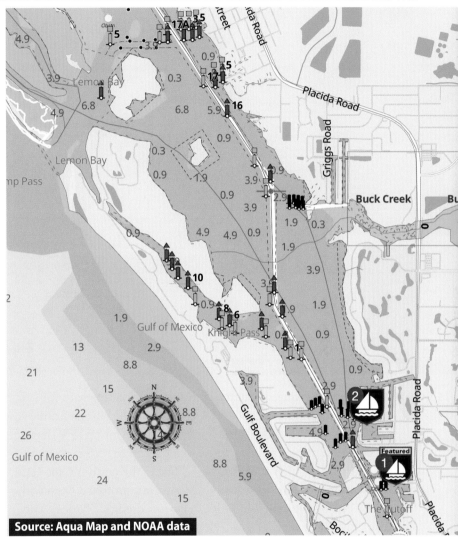

Source: Aqua Map and NOAA data

Boca Grande to Lemon Bay–GIWW Mile 36 to Mile 50

NAVIGATION: Use NOAA Chart 11425. Beyond Little Gasparilla Island and Placida Harbor the GIWW threads through a series of small islands to a narrow 2.25-mile straight stretch called The Cutoff, leading into Lemon Bay. Once in Lemon Bay the GIWW swings to the northeast shore and opens up for a 7.5-mile narrow straightaway through shallow water to the end of the bay. Green daybeacon "17A" keeps you on the straight and narrow where other daybeacons indicate the channel leading to Stump Pass, which opens to the Gulf. Private navigational aids are relocated as

Lemon Bay, FL

LEMON BAY AREA		Largest Vessel	VHF	Total Slips	Approach/ Dockside Depth	Floating Docks	Gas/ Diesel	Repairs/ Haulout	Min/Max Amps	Pump-Out Station
1. Stump Pass Marina MM 40.8	(941) 697-4300	50	66	300	4.5 / 4.0		GD	RH	30 / 50	

WiFi Wireless Internet Access **onSpot** Dockside WiFi Facility
Visit www.waterwayguide.com for current rates, fuel prices, website addresses and other up-to-the-minute information.
(Information in the table is provided by the facilities.)

Scan here for more details:

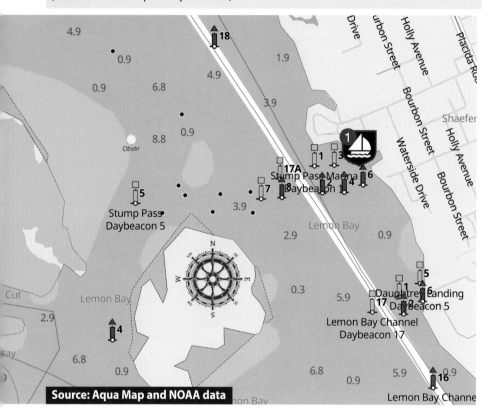

Source: Aqua Map and NOAA data

channel conditions change in Stump Pass, which requires local knowledge.

At GIWW Mile 43.5 is the **Tom Adams Bridge** (26-foot closed vertical clearance), which opens on signal. The **Manasota Bridge** (26-foot closed vertical clearance) at Mile 49.9 also opens on signal.

Dockage: Marinas in Lemon Bay tend to be small, unpretentious and friendly but are geared to handle cruising boats. Two marinas are located near Mile 38 before the GIWW enters Lemon Bay at The Cutoff. The sheltered Loggerhead Marina–Palm Harbour Marina located on the mainland side near green daybeacon "7" is a boutique,

resort-style marina with full amenities. The marina features dry stack storage for up to 40 feet and wet slips up to 65 feet.

Just to the north is Cape Haze Marina in a protected basin with a narrow, dredged channel. The marina has transient dockage and can accommodate vessels to 70 feet. Their Cabana pool and spa is a great place for relaxing and enjoying the sun.

At green daybeacon "17A" just off the GIWW at Mile 40.8 is the large, full-service Stump Pass Marina. This family-friendly facility includes a waterfront restaurant, bait shop and the repair and servicing of all brands of marine engines. Note that dockside

depths are reported as 4 feet MLW.

Royal Palm Marina is tucked away to the north at Mile 45.8 with transient dockage, dry storage and boat sales. The on-site Snook's Bayside Bar & Grill (941-475-3712) is open daily for lunch and dinner and has panoramic views and a waterfront tiki bar.

Anchorage: Anchorages in the area include one at the north end of Thorton Key and one on the south side of Peterson Island (Mile 40.9) at Manasota Key. Both offer good holding and protection.

At Mile 43.3 on the west side of the GIWW is a large, quiet anchorage with 7- to 10-foot MLW depths at Englewood Beach. The anchorage is reached by heading southwest between lighted red daybeacon "22" and the Tom Adams Bridge. Buildings around the anchorage help to protect visiting yachts from buffeting winds. If you continue south hugging the mangroves, you will be sheltered from all directions. Watch depths closely. A convenience store and souvenir shop, dive shops, restaurants and the beach are across the street. To the north of Tom Adams Bridge is an anchorage at Lemon Bay with 6 feet MLW and excellent holding at Mile 44.5 east of red daybeacon "26."

Lemon Bay to Venice–GIWW Mile 50 to Mile 65

About 15 miles south of Sarasota, Venice is one of Florida's younger

Lemon Bay, FL

LEMON BAY AREA		Largest Vessel	VHF	Total Slips	Approach/ Dockside Depth	Floating Docks	Gas/ Diesel	Repairs/ Haulout	Min/Max Amps	Pump-Out Station
1. Royal Palm Marina **WiFi**	(941) 475-6882	80	16	160	6.0 / 9.0		GD	RH	30 / 50	P

WiFi Wireless Internet Access   **onSpot** Dockside WiFi Facility

Visit www.waterwayguide.com for current rates, fuel prices, website addresses and other up-to-the-minute information.
(Information in the table is provided by the facilities.)

Scan here for more details:

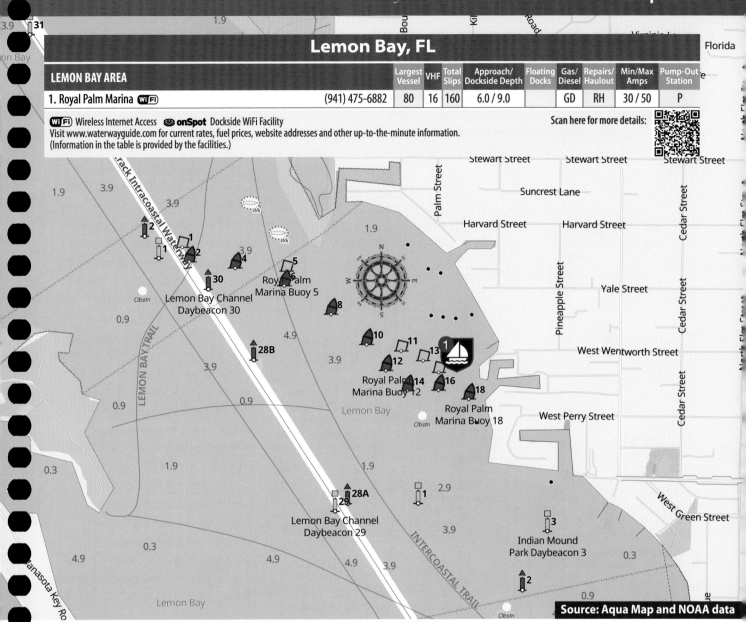

Source: Aqua Map and NOAA data

Lemon Bay Area

Venice Inlet, FL

VENICE AREA		Largest Vessel	VHF	Total Slips	Approach/ Dockside Depth	Floating Docks	Gas/ Diesel	Repairs/ Haulout	Min/Max Amps	Pump-Out Station
1. MarineMax of Venice MM 55.1	(941) 485-3388	68	16	60	12.0 / 9.0		GD	RH	30 / 50	P

WiFi Wireless Internet Access **onSpot** Dockside WiFi Facility
Visit www.waterwayguide.com for current rates, fuel prices, website addresses and other up-to-the-minute information. (Information in the table is provided by the facilities.)

Scan here for more details:

Source: Aqua Map and NOAA data

towns. You will find boutiques, a theater and a variety of dining options around a central green, which was planned in the 1920s with a Mediterranean theme. As you can imagine there are several good Italian restaurants here. You shouldn't leave Venice feeling hungry.

It is a short walk to one of the widest and loveliest beaches on Florida's west coast from the marinas. Fossilized sharks' teeth–either gray or black and with a triangular shape– are abundant here.

NAVIGATION: Use NOAA Chart 11425. Past Lemon Bay at Mile 53 the GIWW becomes a long, high-banked land cut, which runs through a corner of the Venice Municipal Airport. Watch for water-soaked debris in the cut. There is little tidal flushing action to move it out and it can be a nuisance.

At GIWW Mile 54.9 the **Tamiami Trail (Circus) Bridges** (25-foot vertical clearance) open on signal. This is followed by the **Venice Avenue Bridge** at Mile 56.6 (30-foot vertical clearance), which opens on signal except from 7:00 a.m. to 4:30 p.m., Monday through Friday, when it opens at 10, 30 and 50 minutes past the hour. (Note that the bridge need not open between 4:35 p.m. and 5:35 p.m.)

Entering Venice waters the first bridge is the **KMI (Hatchett Creek) Bridge** at GIWW Mile 56.9, which has 30-foot closed vertical clearance and restricted openings year-round. It opens on signal except from 7:00 a.m. to 4:20 p.m., Monday through Friday (except federal holiday), when the draw need only open on the hour and at 20 and 40 minutes past the hour (except between 4:25 p.m. and 5:25 p.m. when the bridge need not open). On weekends and holidays it opens from 7:30 a.m. to 6:00 p.m. on the hour and at 15, 30 and 45 minutes past the hour. Call ahead on VHF Channel 09.

After leaving the land cut the GIWW runs through Roberts Bay. Lightly powered vessels should be cautious of the strong currents flowing in and out of Venice Inlet, which cross the route and create some navigational challenges. Shoaling is a recurrent condition even though the Army Corps of Engineers advises that 9-foot MLW depths are maintained in Venice Inlet. The inlet is jettied and easily navigable except when strong westerly winds oppose an ebbing tide.

North of Venice the GIWW continues its sheltered path behind Casey Key through the **Albee Road Bridge** (14-foot closed vertical clearance) at Mile 59.3. Boaters who require an opening should radio ahead on VHF Channel 09 before entering the channel. The **Blackburn Point Bridge** (9-foot closed vertical clearance) at Mile 63 is a swing bridge

Venice Inlet, FL

CASEY KEY		Largest Vessel	VHF	Total Slips	Approach/ Dockside Depth	Floating Docks	Gas/ Diesel	Repairs/ Haulout	Min/Max Amps	Pump-Out Station
1. Gulf Harbor Marina MM 59.0	(941) 488-7734	45	16		10.0 / 6.0		GD	RH	30	
2. Escape at Casey Key Resort & Marina MM 59.0	(941) 218-3199	50		14	10.0 / 4.0				30 / 50	

WiFi Wireless Internet Access **onSpot** Dockside WiFi Facility
Visit www.waterwayguide.com for current rates, fuel prices, website addresses and other up-to-the-minute information.
(Information in the table is provided by the facilities.)

Scan here for more details:

and opens on signal. Note that the bridgetender has to walk out to the middle to turn (open) the bridge. Passage through both bridges is on an angle in tight quarters (51-foot horizontal clearance) with little maneuvering room on either side so use caution.

Blackburn Bay outside the GIWW at Mile 60 is very shallow and has only limited tie-ups. Proceed with caution and definitely do not attempt transiting this area at night. The course crosses Little Sarasota Bay, the approach to Sarasota.

Overall the GIWW is well marked and maintained and if you keep to the middle of the channel, you should encounter no problems.

Dockage: Marine supplies are available at GIWW Mile 55.1 at MarineMax of Venice with a well-stocked Ship's Store and repairs. They may have space for you; call ahead. Fisherman's Wharf Marina at GIWW Mile 57 has been serving the boating community since 1949. They offer all amenities and floating docks for monthly and yearly rentals and might be able to make room for you for a night or two but do call ahead. They have a pet-friendly restaurant on site and Fisherman's Wharf Tiki Hut is on the water near the docks for your fishing and boating needs. It is just a short walk over the bridge to historic downtown Venice.

At Mile 58 between quick-flashing green "13" and red daybeacon "14" a privately marked channel leads west toward the private Venice Yacht Club (with reciprocal privileges for members of the Florida Yacht Council only). Located just opposite the Venice Yacht Club docks is a small city dock (Higel Marine Park) that five or six boats could tie to for the day but you must vacate the dock between midnight and 6:00 a.m.

Conveniently situated just inside the Venice Inlet, Crow's Nest Marina & Restaurant can accommodate boats up to 140 feet and offers the usual cruiser amenities plus a laundry and a very popular on-site restaurant. It is an easy walk to the beach and rental

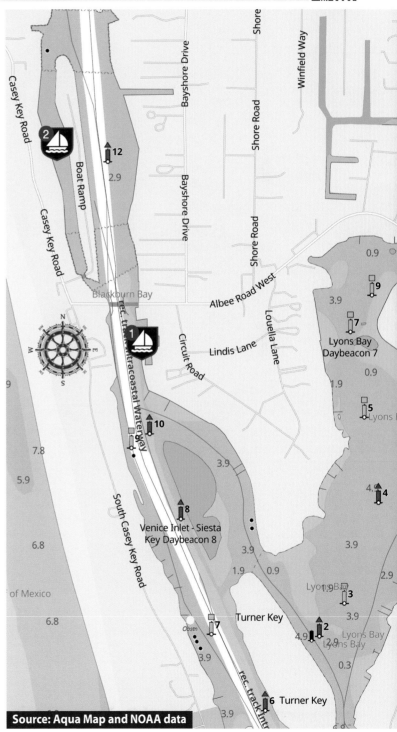

Source: Aqua Map and NOAA data

Venice Inlet - Siesta

Venice Inlet, FL

VENICE AREA		Largest Vessel	VHF	Total Slips	Approach/ Dockside Depth	Floating Docks	Gas/ Diesel	Repairs/ Haulout	Min/Max Amps	Pump-Out Station
1. Fisherman's Wharf Marina of Venice WiFi MM 57.0	(941) 486-0500	100	16	57	8.0 / 7.0	F	GD		30 / 100	P
2. Venice Yacht Club MM 57.5	(941) 483-3625	100	16	67	10.0 / 10.0		GD		30 / 100	P
3. Crow's Nest Marina & Restaurant WiFi MM 58.0	(941) 484-7661	140	16	34	12.0 / 12.0		GD		30 / 100	P

WiFi Wireless Internet Access   onSpot Dockside WiFi Facility
Visit www.waterwayguide.com for current rates, fuel prices, website addresses and other up-to-the-minute information.
(Information in the table is provided by the facilities.)

Scan here for more details:

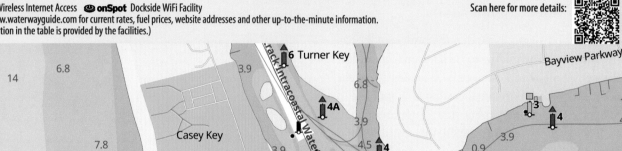

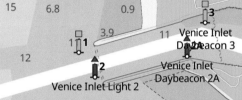

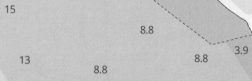

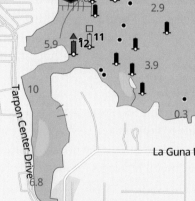

Source: Aqua Map and NOAA data

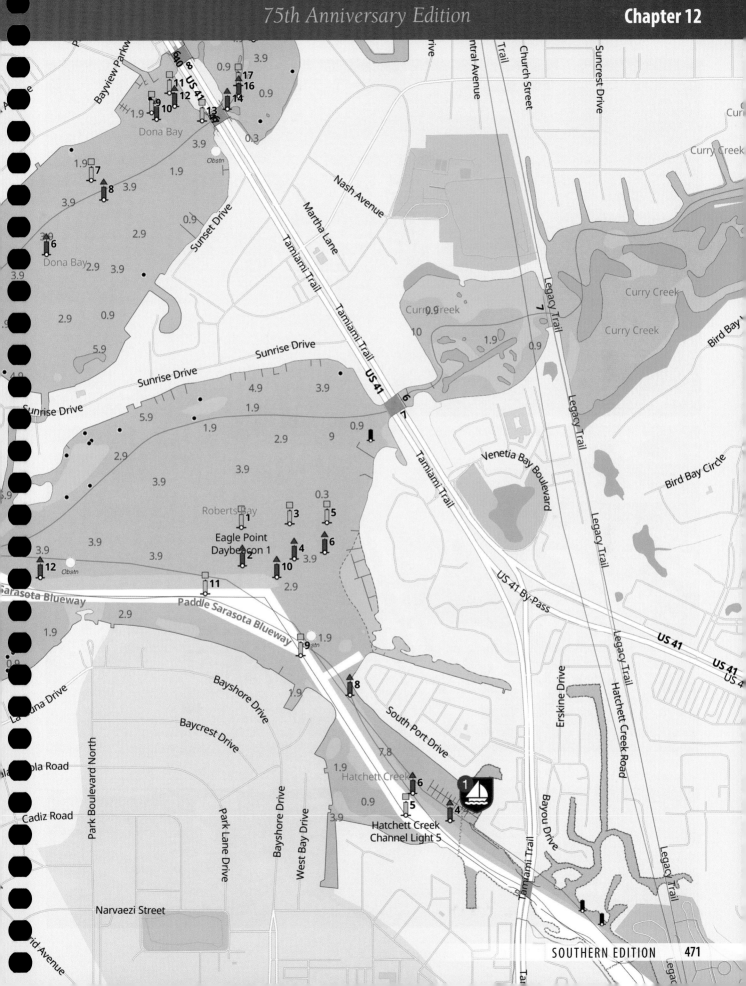

Casey Key

Gulf of Mexico

Crow's Nest Marina & Restaurant

GIWW

Venice

© Mapbox, © OpenStreetMap

WATERFRONT VIEWS

FRESH SEAFOOD

LOCATED HERE

• Easy Access to the Gulf
• Located Inside the Venice Inlet on Deep Water
• Paddleboard & Kayak Rentals
• Marine Charts, Live & Frozen Bait, Beer, Wine
• FIRST CLASS Dockhands to Help YOU!

THE CROW'S NEST

MARINA RESTAURANT TAVERN

1968 Tarpon Center Dr. Venice FL, 34285 | Marker 7 | Marina: 941-484-7661 | CrowsNest-Venice.com

Little Sarasota Bay, FL

SIESTA KEY		Largest Vessel	VHF	Total Slips	Approach/ Dockside Depth	Floating Docks	Gas/ Diesel	Repairs/ Haulout	Min/Max Amps	Pump-Out Station
1. Bayfront Yacht Works & Marina MM 66.0	(941) 349-9449	50		25	5.0 / 5.0		G	RH		
2. Hidden Concierge	(941) 927-4800	40		25	6.0 / 6.0	F	G	RH	30	

WiFi Wireless Internet Access **onSpot** Dockside WiFi Facility
Visit www.waterwayguide.com for current rates, fuel prices, website addresses and other up-to-the-minute information.
(Information in the table is provided by the facilities.)

Scan here for more details:

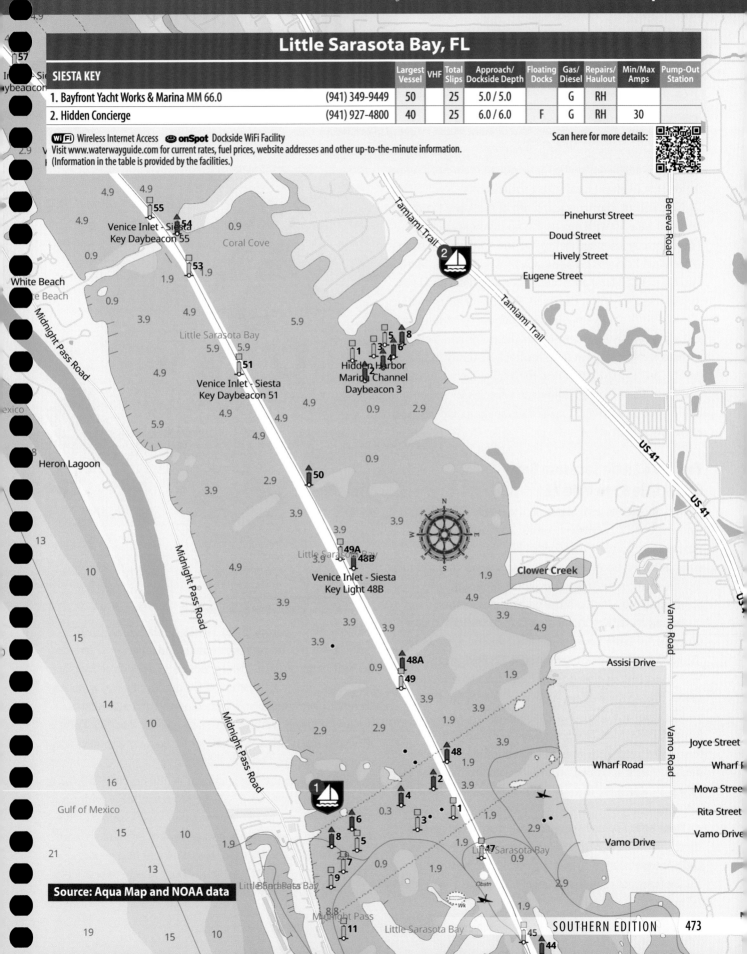

Source: Aqua Map and NOAA data

Little Sarasota Bay, FL

SIESTA KEY		Largest Vessel	VHF	Total Slips	Approach/ Dockside Depth	Floating Docks	Gas/ Diesel	Repairs/ Haulout	Min/Max Amps	Pump-Out Station
1. Safe Harbor Siesta Key	(941) 349-1970				/		GD	R		

WiFi Wireless Internet Access **onSpot** Dockside WiFi Facility
Visit www.waterwayguide.com for current rates, fuel prices, website addresses and other up-to-the-minute information.
(Information in the table is provided by the facilities.)

Scan here for more details:

bikes are available for the 1.5-mile ride to town (well worth the ride). Call ahead for docking instructions.

Gulf Harbor Marina is just south of the Albee Road Bridge at Mile 59 with repairs but no transient dockage. This is strictly a storage facility. On the north side of the Albee Road Bridge is Escape at Casey Key Resort & Marina. Two slips (to 50 feet) are available for non-hotel guests as well as those staying at the resort. Resort amenities include a heated pool, a fully-appointed clubhouse (with kitchen) and access to kayaks, stand-up paddleboards and bicycles.

Anchorage: You can drop the hook in Venice at green daybeacon "15" (Mile 58) near the Venice Yacht Club and free dock. There is good holding in 6 feet MLW with a sand bottom but it somewhat exposed to the north and east and to GIWW wakes.

Venice to Little Sarasota Bay– GIWW Mile 65 to Mile 72

Writers and artists congregate on the slender, heavily wooded Siesta Key between Venice and Sarasota. Large private estates and deluxe condos line the waterway, each with their own dock. Siesta Beach is a favorite and facilities include picnic areas, restrooms, concession stands, a playground, trails and tennis and volleyball courts.

Behind Siesta Key the narrow, dredged GIWW runs up the center of Little Sarasota Bay until the bay narrows to the north. At the **Stickney Point (SR 72) Bridge** at GIWW Mile 68.6 (18-foot closed vertical clearance) the route moves over to the western shore then swings out into the middle again at Roberts Bay. At the northern end of Siesta Key at GIWW Mile 71.6 is the **Siesta Drive Bridge** (25-foot closed vertical clearance). Both bridges follow the same schedule and open on signal except from 6:00 a.m. to 7:00 p.m., when the draw need only open on the hour and half hour (daily).

Dockage: There are several small marinas along this stretch of the GIWW that cater to small center consoles and pontoon boats. Marinas with facilities and slips to handle transient cruisers are largely located in Venice and in

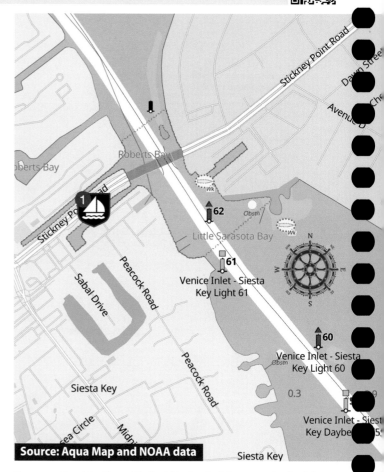

Source: Aqua Map and NOAA data

Sarasota Bay. Bayfront Yacht Works & Marina at Mile 66 is a Suntex Marina offering boat rentals and an array of services, as well as dry storage. Call for details. Across Little Sarasota Bay is the protected channel of Hidden Concierge, which is primarily a storage and launching site that also offers repairs and some services. Just south of the Stickney Point Bridge is Safe Harbor Siesta Key with boat rentals, sales and storage. Call ahead for slip availability.

Anchorage: You can anchor at White Beach at Mile 67.4 west of green daybeacon "55" in 5 to 6 feet MLW with good holding. This is somewhat exposed to wakes from passing boats. There is another anchorage west of green daybeacon "79" at Mile 71 (Siesta Key). Here you will find good holding in 5 to 6 feet MLW. In the busy season expect jet skis, wake boarders and boats towing all manner of floats.

America's Waterway Guide Since 1947

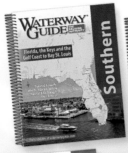
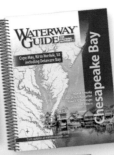
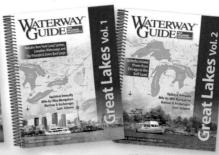
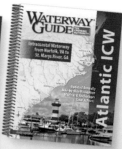

Southern — Florida, the Keys and the Gulf Coast to Bay St. Louis

Cape May, NJ to Norfolk, VA Including Delaware Bay

Chesapeake Bay

Great Lakes Vol. 1 — Includes New York Canal System, Canadian Waterways and The Triangle & Down East Loops

Great Lakes Vol. 2 — Includes Islands Rivers from Chicago to the Gulf Coast

Atlantic ICW — Intracoastal Waterway from Norfolk, VA to St. Marys River, GA

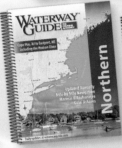

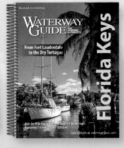

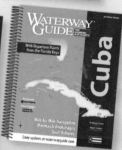

Northern — Cape May, NJ to Eastport, ME including the Hudson River

Bahamas — Including Turks and Caicos

Florida Keys — From Fort Lauderdale to the Dry Tortugas

Western Gulf Coast — Lake Pontchartrain & New Orleans to South Padre Island, TX

Cuba — With Departure Points from the Florida Keys

Skipper Bob Publications

- Cruising Comfortably on a Budget
- Bahamas Bound
- Anchorages Along the Intracoastal Waterway
- Cruising the New York Canal System

SKIPPER BOB Publications

- Cruising the Gulf Coast
- Cruising America's Great Loop
- Cruising the Rideau & Richelieu Canals

SKIPPER BOB Publications

- Marinas Along the Intracoastal Waterway
- Cruising the Trent-Severn Waterway, Georgian Bay and North Channel
- Cruising from Chicago to Mobile

SKIPPER BOB Publications

The iOS App from Waterway Guide

To St. Augustine

The beach regions running south from Jacksonville are collectively referred to as the "First Coast" because this is the location of Florida's first European settlements. It vigorously competes with the Gold Coast, the Sun Coast and the Treasure Coast for developer and tourist dollars. The area begins a parade of shoreside communities

< Previous   Next >

Waterway Explorer Magazine

The Explorer web app
waterwayguide.com

WATERWAY® GUIDE MEDIA

No Signal? **No Problem!**
DOWNLOAD CONTENT

GOIN' ASHORE

SARASOTA, FL

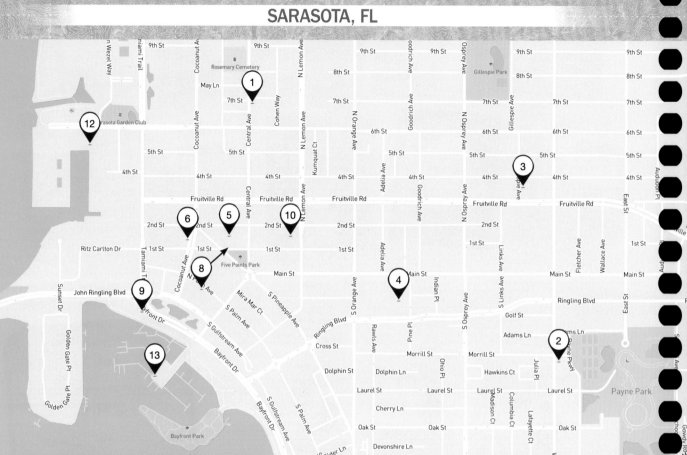

In 1929, John Ringling chose Sarasota as winter headquarters for his "Greatest Show on Earth" circus, and even though the circus has moved on, the Ringling legacy is very much alive here. The Ringling Museum of Art (5401 Bay Shore Rd., 941-359-5700) is a Renaissance-style palace that the circus king built to house his art collection. In addition to the 31 galleries of art, the Ringling includes a 66-acre bayfront garden, the Ringling's 56-room mansion and a circus museum. Next to his museum, Ringling reconstructed an 18th-century Italian theater with stones brought piece by piece from Asolo, Italy. Throughout the year, visitors can see plays and operas in the playhouse built for Queen Catherine.

SERVICES

1. **Animal Medical Clinic at Rosemary**
   650 Central Ave. #2 (941-955-0136)

2. **Veterinary Center of Sarasota**
   311 S. Washington Blvd. (941-952-1900)

3. **Sarasota County Visitor Information Center**
   1945 Fruitville Rd. (941-706-1253)

4. **Sarasota Post Office**
   1661 Ringling Blvd. (941-331-4221)

5. **Selby Library**
   1331 1st St. (941-861-1100)

ATTRACTIONS

6. Florida Studio Theater
Live theater and a full food and drink menu in five venues in one location at 1241 N. Palm Ave. (941-366-9000).

7. Marie Selby Botanical Gardens
Bayfront oasis with tropical plants, a conservatory and a garden museum at 900 S. Palm Ave. (941-366-5731).

8. Sarasota Opera House
Familiar and unusual opera productions performed in an ornate circa-1926 theater (61 N. Pineapple Ave., 941-328-1300).

9. Unconditional Surrender
One in a series of sculptures replicating an iconic photo taken of a sailor and nurse kissing in Times Square at the end of World War II. Located on the way to City Island on Bayfront Dr.

SHOPPING

10. Whole Foods Market
Eco-minded grocery chain with natural and organic items and other products (1451 1st St., 941-316-4700).

11. Publix Super Market
Full-service grocery store for provisioning (groceries, deli and bakery items) at 2031 Bay St. (941-366-4089).

MARINAS

12. Hyatt Regency Sarasota
1000 Blvd. of the Arts (941-812-4063)

13. Marina Jack
2 Marina Plaza (941-955-9488)

The Ringling Museum

Sarasota Bay, FL

SARASOTA AREA		Largest Vessel	VHF	Total Slips	Approach/ Dockside Depth	Floating Docks	Gas/ Diesel	Repairs/ Haulout	Min/Max Amps	Pump-Out Station
1. Marina Jack **WiFi** MM 73.5	(941) 955-9488	228	16	298	8.0 / 8.0	F	GD		30 / 100	P
2. Bird Key Yacht Club **WiFi**	(941) 953-4455	50	16	42	12.0 / 8.0		GD		30 / 50	P
3. Sarasota Yacht Club **WiFi**	(941) 365-4191	120	16	113	16.0 / 10.0		GD		30 / 50	P
4. Sarasota Sailing Squadron	(941) 388-2355				10.0 / 9.0				30	
5. MarineMax Sarasota	(941) 388-4411				10.0 / 6.0		GD	H		

WiFi Wireless Internet Access **onSpot** Dockside WiFi Facility
Visit www.waterwayguide.com for current rates, fuel prices, website addresses and other up-to-the-minute information.
(Information in the table is provided by the facilities.)

Scan here for more details:

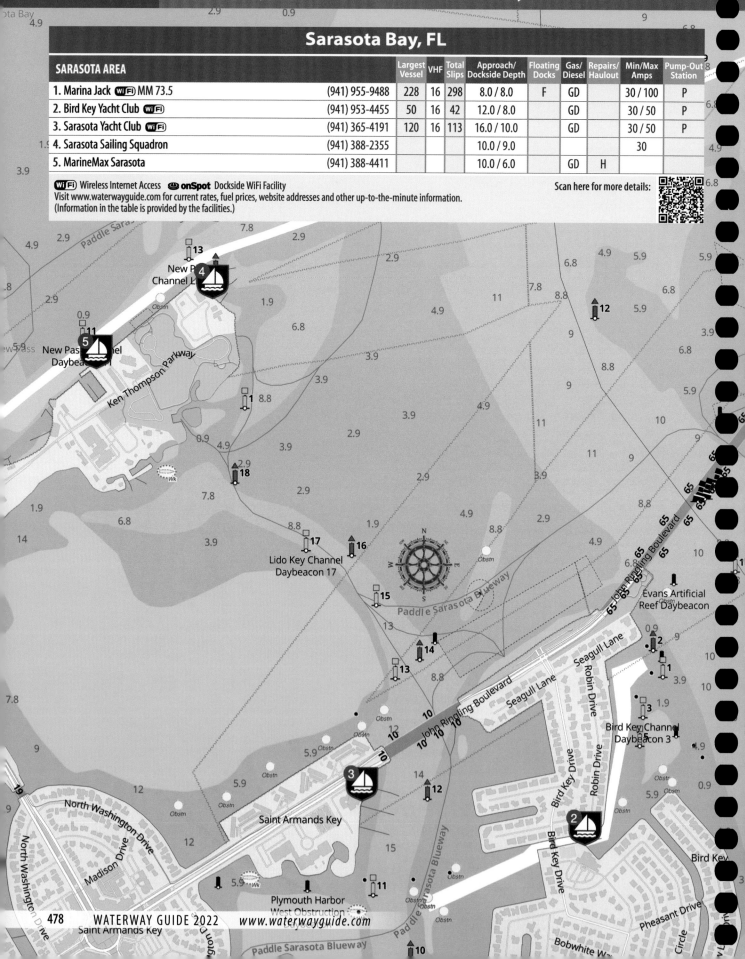

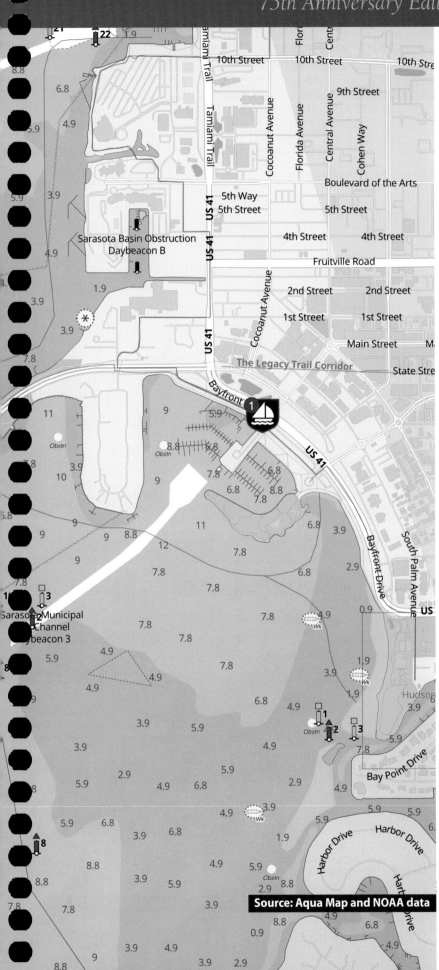

Source: Aqua Map and NOAA data

Sarasota Bay–GIWW
Mile 72 to Mile 87.4

At Siesta Key off to port heading north after clearing Little Sarasota Bay the Sarasota area officially begins around Mile 71 and then continues for about 15 miles. The passage starts with a well-marked stretch through the shoals of Roberts Bay and ends with the exit through Longboat Key Pass to the north of Sarasota Bay.

This section of the GIWW traverses a sophisticated, fast-growing region and is a popular layover spot for cruising boats. As such, facilities are plentiful, ranging from fishing camps to marina resorts, and all manner of boating needs and repairs can be handled here. As the mainland's focal point for a cluster of offshore island resorts (linked to it by causeways) Sarasota acts as the hub of an important agricultural and cattle-ranching district but is most proud of its cultural image.

The low purple building on the east side of Sarasota Bay just north of the causeway is the Van Wezel Theatre of Performing Arts (pronounced "Vann WAY-zull"). At about Mile 77 also on the east side you can see the coral-colored mansion of John Ringling (of circus fame). For details on these and other attractions, see "Goin' Ashore: Sarasota, FL" in this chapter.

NAVIGATION: Use NOAA Chart 11425. After traversing Roberts Bay the GIWW widens amidst a variety of marine facilities and then passes under the **Ringling Causeway (SR 789) Bridge** at Mile 73.6 with a fixed vertical clearance of 65 feet. Ringling Causeway crosses three Sarasota Bay keys (Bird, Coon and St. Armands) to link Lido Key to the mainland. The bridge span between Bird Key and Coon Key is fixed with only a 10-foot vertical clearance. From flashing green "13" north of the causeway Sarasota Bay opens up both in width and–in certain areas–depth.

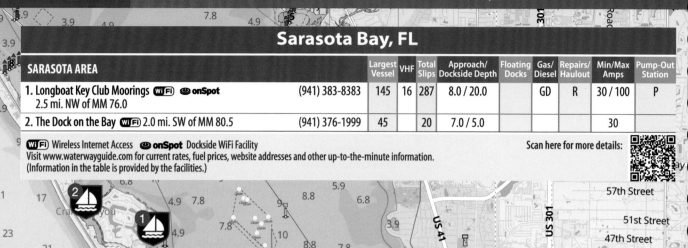

Sarasota Bay, FL

SARASOTA AREA		Largest Vessel	VHF	Total Slips	Approach/ Dockside Depth	Floating Docks	Gas/ Diesel	Repairs/ Haulout	Min/Max Amps	Pump-Out Station
1. Longboat Key Club Moorings **WiFi** ⊜ **onSpot** 2.5 mi. NW of MM 76.0	(941) 383-8383	145	16	287	8.0 / 20.0		GD	R	30 / 100	P
2. The Dock on the Bay **WiFi** 2.0 mi. SW of MM 80.5	(941) 376-1999	45		20	7.0 / 5.0				30	

WiFi Wireless Internet Access   ⊜ **onSpot** Dockside WiFi Facility
Visit www.waterwayguide.com for current rates, fuel prices, website addresses and other up-to-the-minute information.
(Information in the table is provided by the facilities.)

Scan here for more details:

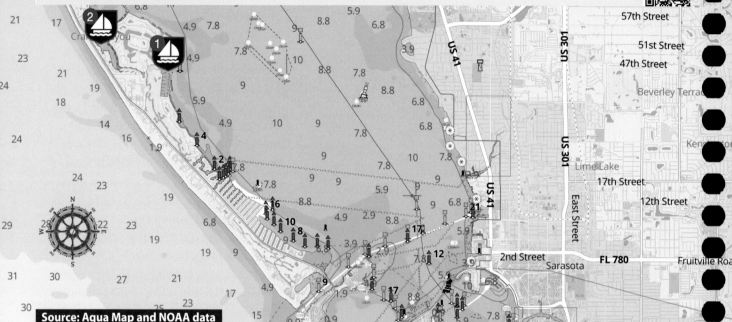

Source: Aqua Map and NOAA data

Sarasota Bay, FL

SARASOTA AREA		Largest Vessel	VHF	Total Slips	Approach/ Dockside Depth	Floating Docks	Gas/ Diesel	Repairs/ Haulout	Min/Max Amps	Pump-Out Station
1. Ramada by Wyndham Sarasota **WiFi** 1.5 mi. NE of MM 78.5	(941) 203-6439	70	16	78	4.0 / 6.0	F	GD	R	30 / 50	P
2. Sara Bay Marina **WiFi** 1.5 mi NE of MM 78.5	(941) 359-0390	50		60	4.0 / 4.0	F		RH	30 / 50	P

WiFi Wireless Internet Access   ⊜ **onSpot** Dockside WiFi Facility
Visit www.waterwayguide.com for current rates, fuel prices, website addresses and other up-to-the-minute information.
(Information in the table is provided by the facilities.)

Scan here for more details:

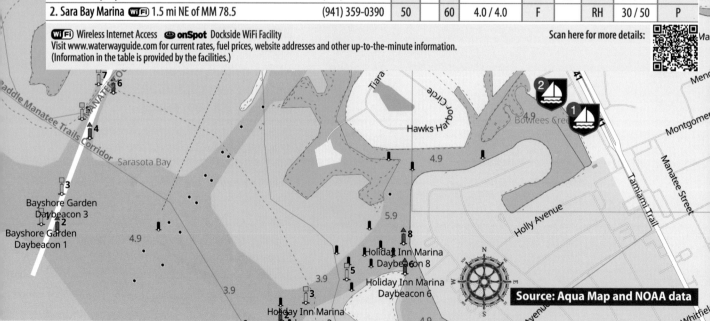

Source: Aqua Map and NOAA data

Sarasota Bay, FL

LONGBOAT PASS		Largest Vessel	VHF	Total Slips	Approach/ Dockside Depth	Floating Docks	Gas/ Diesel	Repairs/ Haulout	Min/Max Amps	Pump-Out Station
1. Cannons Marina MM 83.5	(941) 383-1311				5.0 / 5.0		G	R		

WiFi Wireless Internet Access   **onSpot** Dockside WiFi Facility

Visit www.waterwayguide.com for current rates, fuel prices, website addresses and other up-to-the-minute information. (Information in the table is provided by the facilities.)

Scan here for more details:

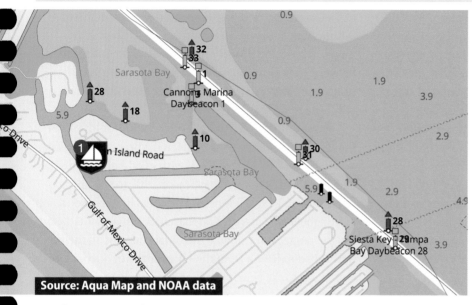

Source: Aqua Map and NOAA data

After New Pass (not recommended due to shoaling) Longboat Key shields Sarasota Bay from the Gulf of Mexico and opens wide with central controlling depths of 7 to 12 feet MLW. Watch out for strong crosscurrents to and from Longboat Pass. The 17-foot closed vertical clearance **Longboat Pass (SR 789) Bridge** crosses the pass (opens on request). A call to a towboat captain for local knowledge is wise.

In this area the GIWW runs a straight line down the middle of Sarasota Bay with markers along this stretch spaced about 2 miles apart. At flashing green "17" (near the midpoint of Longboat Key at Mile 80) the route turns sharply west and Sarasota Bay narrows. Along this stretch the GIWW follows a dredged path through shoal water (1- and 2-foot MLW depths outside the channel). You must observe all aids to navigation very carefully!

Dockage/Moorings: Many of Sarasota's marine facilities are on the mainland near the Ringling Causeway, in Whittaker Bayou and clustered around New Pass.

Tucked in behind Island Park, Marina Jack (a Suntex Marina) is at the doorstep to downtown Sarasota. Full amenities include laundry facilities, concierge service, a shuttle and a well-stocked Ship's Store. There are several on-site options for waterfront dining. The Sarasota Mooring Field has 85 moorings for vessels to 80 feet. It is run by Marina Jack and includes all the marina amenities and access to a dinghy dock.

South of the Ringling Causeway before Lido Key are Bird Key Yacht Club and Sarasota Yacht Club, both of which may have transient space for reciprocating yacht club members only. Be sure to call ahead.

Sarasota Sailing Squadron on Lido Key welcomes visiting sailors. Facilities include shower facilities, temporary mast-up storage and docking, boat ramps and hoist, and beachfront access. MarineMax Sarasota provides boat repair and service as well as yacht brokerage.

To get farther from the crowd take a mooring at the 287-slip Longboat Key Club Moorings. To reach its channel steer 255° true from flashing green "15." On this course point toward the one farthest south of the three high-rise condominiums where you will encounter the privately maintained entrance channel to the facility. Dockage provides access to the resort facilities including tennis and a spa as well as the on-site Portofino Ristorante & Bar.

The 20-slip The Dock on the Bay is also on Longboat Key in the Buttonwood Harbor area and may have transient space for vessels to 40 feet with basic amenities and a pool. Call ahead.

At red daybeacon "16" in Sarasota Bay, steer a course of 038° magnetic for 1.5 nm to access the entrance markers to the Ramada by Wyndham Sarasota, which has a long seawall for tie-ups and an on-site restaurant. This facility shares an entrance with Sara Bay Marina, which is primarily a boat sales facility. Be aware that there is only 4 feet MLW on the approach near low tide. Head towards the house with a white roof and chimney take a hard left and hug the right shoreline.

Cannons Marina at Mile 83.5 (Longboat Pass) is a sales/service facility and offers no transient dockage.

Anchorage: Many transient and local boats anchor in Sarasota Bay. You can anchor southwest of Marina Jack on the outside of Island Park but you must be at least 150 feet outside and away from any of the moorings. You will be exposed to weather coming out of the north and west.

Privately owned Bickel's Bayou is offered for transient cruiser use and is located on the north (mainland) side of the Ringling Causeway (SR 789) Bridge. Be sure to anchor only in the area exposed to the west and not in the rest of the basin. The access channel has a controlling depth of about 6 feet MLW. Approach from the GIWW directly eastward towards the basin where you will find 9 feet MLW. Leave enough space in the central channel for other boats to access the rest of the basin. Shallow-draft vessels should leave the deeper areas for those with deeper keels. There is no shore access here. Please do not trespass on private land.

Dinghy access is available at the Ringling Bridge Causeway Park or the public boat ramp at 10th Street to the north of the anchorage. Anchor light regulations are enforced after dark.

Another anchorage is between Otter Key and Lido Key where you will find at least 6 feet MLW with good holding in sand and mud with all-around protection.

Off New Pass Cove is a lovely anchorage in well-protected New Pass Cove at green daybeacon "9." Coming from the GIWW you must be able to pass under the **New Pass (SR 789) Bridge** (23-foot closed vertical clearance) or wait for an opening. From 7:00 a.m. to 6:00 p.m. the bridge need only open on the hour, 20 minutes past the hour and 40 minutes past the hour. From 6:00 p.m. to 7:00 a.m., the bridge will open on signal if at least a 3-hour notice is given to the drawtender. There is no more than 4 feet MLW at the entrance to the cove. Enter between the "No Wake" sign and the shore nearest the bridge. Once you enter there is 9 feet MLW and some crab pots to dodge.

Closer to the north end of Longboat Key at Mile 78.4 there is an anchorage west of green daybeacon "15" where you will find 7 to 11 feet MLW with good holding in sand and mud. Just before red daybeacon "40" to the north a good anchorage in 13-foot MLW depths lies behind the tip of Longboat Key just off Longbeach. A restaurant is within dinghy range. You can take the dinghy almost all the way down Bishop Bayou from the Long Boat Key anchorage and tie up to the cement wall on the left side to access a shopping plaza with groceries, a liquor store, a Post Office and a restaurant.

■ NEXT STOP

Continuing north, cruisers will next encouter Anna Maria Island and the popular Tampa-St. Petersburg area. Beyond that, Clearwater and its famous resort beaches beckon.

Lido Key

Mile 88-Mile 150

◼ TAMPA BAY AREA

One of the great natural harbors of the world Tampa Bay extends about 25 miles north to south and about 10 miles east to west. It has two major cities (Tampa and St. Petersburg) and several large rivers that meander in from the east and north. Fringing the west side of the coast and extending northward is a pencil-thin chain of barrier islands with resort communities famous for their Gulf shore beaches.

Tampa Bay comprises three vast bodies of water–Tampa Bay proper, Old Tampa Bay to the northwest and Hillsborough Bay to the northeast–all providing excellent cruising. Lower Tampa Bay opens to the Gulf of Mexico but enjoys the protection of barrier islands. Old Tampa Bay reaches northwest from Tampa Bay to the shoal water around Safety Harbor and Mobbly Bay. Hillsborough Bay branches off to the northeast between Interbay Peninsula and the mainland to serve the city of Tampa, Ybor City and Davis Islands with their extensive shipping and industrial areas.

From the open mouth of Tampa Bay, St. Petersburg lies due north with metropolitan Tampa to the northeast. Each dominates one of the two big peninsulas that pierce the bay. Pinellas to the west extends about 45 miles from the southern edge of St. Petersburg almost to Tarpon Springs. MacDill Air Force Base occupies the southern tip of Interbay, the second peninsula (about 3 miles wide and 10 miles long).

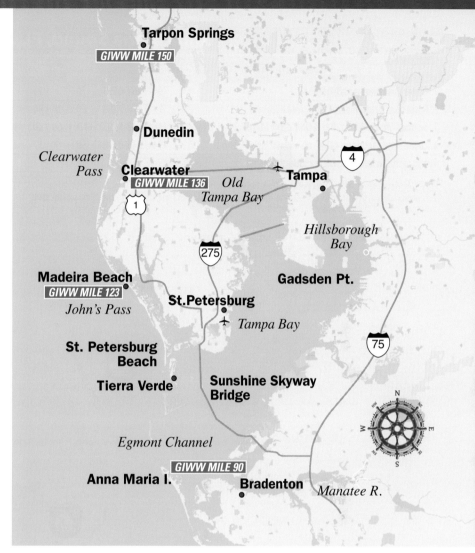

For the cruising skipper Tampa Bay is a welcome change from the confines of the GIWW. Here there are some 300 square miles of cruising waters, Gulf fishing, interesting ports, pleasant anchorages, good yacht facilities and superb sailing.

NO WAKE ZONE

No Wake Zones, Idle Speed Zones and various Speed Limit restrictions are in effect throughout the waterways included in this chapter. Exercise diligence in knowing the regulations by observing signs and other markers. Enforcement is always present.

As always, be courteous to other vessels and avoid manatees and other marine life.

Anna Maria Island– GIWW Mile 89.2

Lovely Anna Maria Island is noted for its white sandy beaches, good tarpon fishing and premium restaurants. The island lies between Sarasota Bay on the south, Anna Maria Sound (separating the island from the mainland at the towns of Cortez and Bradenton) and Tampa Bay on the north. Cruisers can reach Tampa Bay and points north either directly from the Gulf of Mexico or via the inside GIWW route from Sarasota Bay.

Anna Maria Sound, FL

BRADENTON BEACH AREA		Largest Vessel	VHF	Total Slips	Approach/ Dockside Depth	Floating Docks	Gas/ Diesel	Repairs/ Haulout	Min/Max Amps	Pump-Out Station
1. Cortez Cove Marina **WiFi** MM 87.2	(941) 761-4554	70		35	7.0 / 7.0			RH	30 / 50	
2. Bradenton Beach Marina **WiFi** MM 87.2	(941) 778-2288	60	16	40	6.0 / 4.0		GD	RH	30 / 50	P
3. Seafood Shack Marina, Bar & Grill **WiFi** MM 87.2	(386) 643-5555	120	68	68	14.0 / 12.0		GD		30 / 50	
4. Cove Sound Moorings **WiFi** **onSpot** MM 87.2	(941) 216-0398	50	9	57	/				30	
5. Loggerhead Marina - Cortez Village Marina	(941) 795-3625	38			/	F	G	RH		

WiFi Wireless Internet Access　**onSpot** Dockside WiFi Facility
Visit www.waterwayguide.com for current rates, fuel prices, website addresses and other up-to-the-minute information.
(Information in the table is provided by the facilities.)

Scan here for more details:

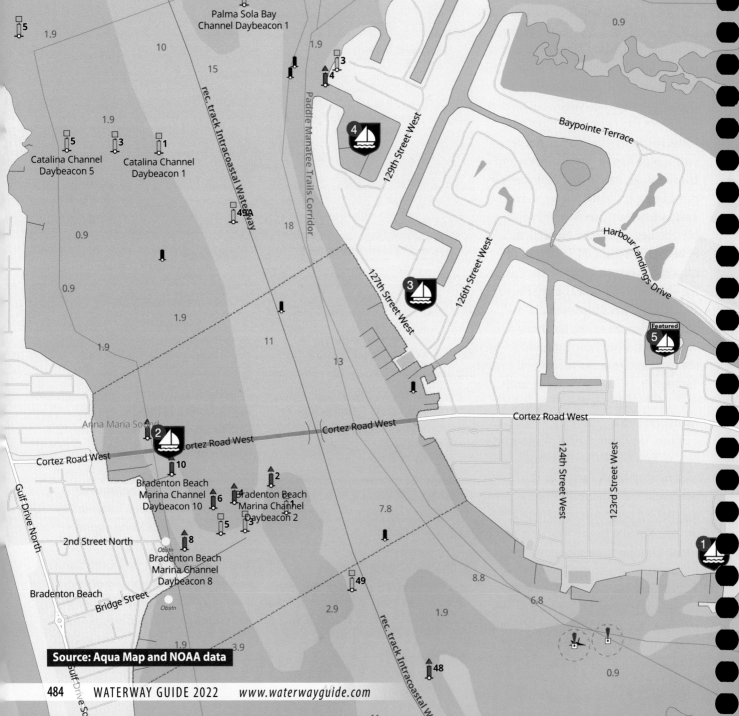

Anna Maria Sound, FL

ANNA MARIA ISLAND		Largest Vessel	VHF	Total Slips	Approach/ Dockside Depth	Floating Docks	Gas/ Diesel	Repairs/ Haulout	Min/Max Amps	Pump-Out Station
1. Galati Yacht Basin 1.0 mi W of MM 91.8	(941) 778-0755	105	16	60	7.0 / 7.0		GD	RH	50	P

WiFi Wireless Internet Access **onSpot** Dockside WiFi Facility
Visit www.waterwayguide.com for current rates, fuel prices, website addresses and other up-to-the-minute information.
(Information in the table is provided by the facilities.)

Scan here for more details:

NAVIGATION: Use NOAA Charts 11415 and 11425. Traveling north from Sarasota Bay there is no "quick" route north by going out into the Gulf of Mexico at Longboat Pass. Just stay on the inside. Even with a couple of bascule bridges that will have to open on the GIWW you will save time and fuel. The inside route will bring you into Tampa Bay at red daybeacon "68."

Two bascule bridges cross the GIWW on this stretch before reaching Tampa Bay: the **Cortez (SR 684) Bridge** (Mile 87.4, 22-foot closed vertical clearance) and the **Anna Maria (SR 64/Manatee Avenue West) Bridge** (Mile 89.2, 24-foot closed vertical clearance). Both open on signal except from 6:00 a.m. to 7:00 p.m. daily, when the draw need only open on the quarter hour and three quarter hour. The GIWW channel cuts through shoals in much of Anna Maria Sound and at red daybeacon "52" starts swinging toward Perico Island just south of the Anna Maria Bridge.

A back range at Mile 90 helps you stay in the center of the channel until you reach the sand bar charted as "The Bulkhead," which is marked by flashing red "64" at Mile 92. After leaving red daybeacon "68" the water is deep and you can head into Tampa Bay, go up the Manatee River to the east or turn due west for the continuation of the GIWW across the bay. You can also head into the channel through Key Royale Bar to Bimini Bay on the northeast end of Anna Maria Island.

Dockage: South of the Cortez Bridge on the mainland side of the GIWW at Mile 87 is Cortez Cove Marina, which has a lift and offer repairs. This is primarily a boatyard with few amenities. To the west of the GIWW on the south side of the Cortez Bridge is Bradenton Beach Marina, which has 15 reserved transient slips. They also permit DIY work in their boat yard.

Immediately after the Cortez Bridge a dredged channel on the eastern shore leads to Loggerhead Marina–Cortez Village Marina. They offer dry storage slips with valet boat service, wet slips with lifts, an on-site service department and a boat brokerage.

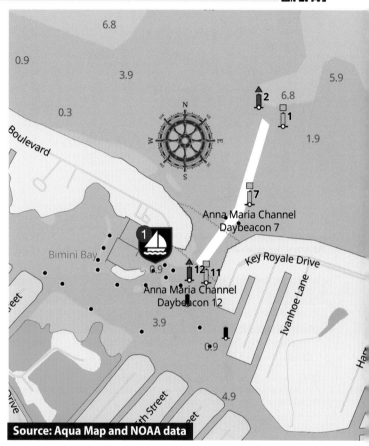

Source: Aqua Map and NOAA data

Shortly after flashing red "48" and the Cortez Bridge on the eastern shore is Seafood Shack Marina, Bar & Grill, a popular waterfront restaurant and marina with transient slips. The helpful dockmaster answers on VHF Channel 16. They also offer over 400 feet of dedicated dockage for restaurant guests (two hour complimentary mooring while you dine). To the north is Cove Sound Moorings with slips to 50 feet.

Waterline Marina Resort & Beach Club, Autograph Collection on Anna Maria Island is a modern resort with "old Florida authenticity." Boaters (with vessels up to 45 feet) can enjoy resort amenities including laundry facilities and a resort-style pool. Eliza Ann's Coastal Kitchen (941-238-6264) is on site serving breakfast, lunch and dinner plus brunch on Saturday and Sunday and a daily happy hour.

Anna Maria Sound, FL

ANNA MARIA ISLAND		Largest Vessel	VHF	Total Slips	Approach/ Dockside Depth	Floating Docks	Gas/ Diesel	Repairs/ Haulout	Min/Max Amps	Pump-Out Station
1. Safe Harbor Pier 77 **WiFi**	(941) 761-4200	50		55	/	F	GD		30 / 50	P

WiFi Wireless Internet Access **onSpot** Dockside WiFi Facility
Visit www.waterwayguide.com for current rates, fuel prices, website addresses and other up-to-the-minute information.
(Information in the table is provided by the facilities.)

Scan here for more details:

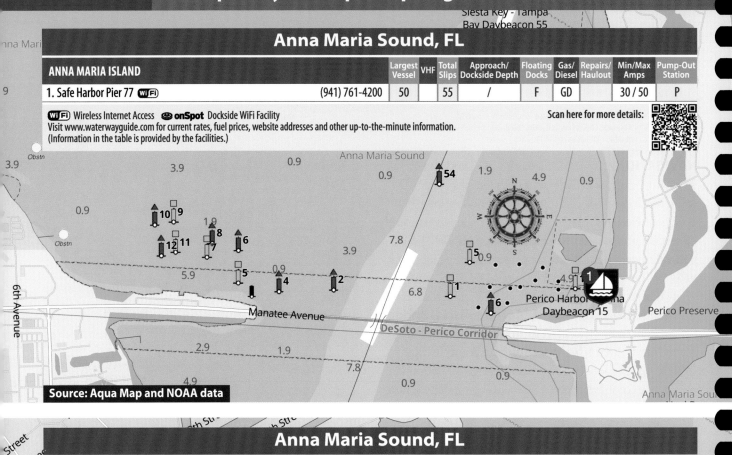

Source: Aqua Map and NOAA data

Anna Maria Sound, FL

ANNA MARIA ISLAND		Largest Vessel	VHF	Total Slips	Approach/ Dockside Depth	Floating Docks	Gas/ Diesel	Repairs/ Haulout	Min/Max Amps	Pump-Out Station
1. Waterline Marina Resort & Beach Club, Autograph Collection **WiFi**	(888) 849-2642	30	16	50	5.0 / 4.0				30 / 50	

WiFi Wireless Internet Access **onSpot** Dockside WiFi Facility
Visit www.waterwayguide.com for current rates, fuel prices, website addresses and other up-to-the-minute information.
(Information in the table is provided by the facilities.)

Scan here for more details:

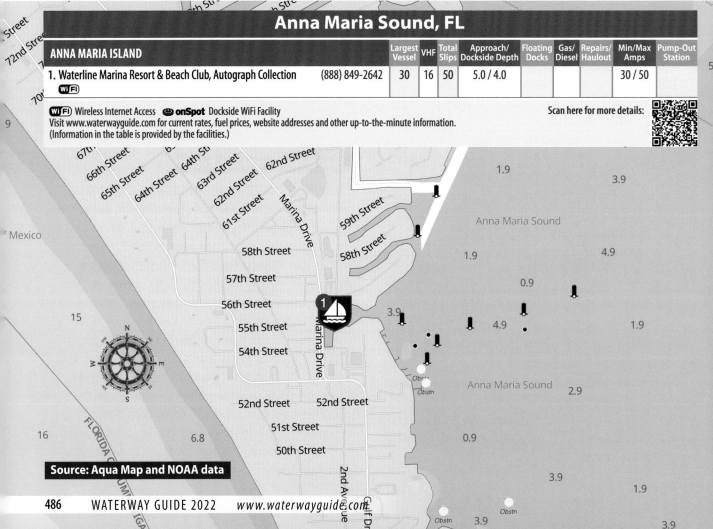

Source: Aqua Map and NOAA data

To the northwest on Anna Maria Island, Galati Yacht Basin is a yacht brokerage in Bimini Bay featuring a Ship's Store with an excellent parts department. If you are coming into Bimini Bay for the first time, it is easy to get confused by the marina markers. To enter the basin go out of Anna Maria Sound northbound past quick flashing green "67" then hang a sharp left heading west for a little more than a 0.5 mile to flashing green "1." To port will be the markers to Bimini Bay, which are privately maintained.

Safe Harbor Pier 77 at Perico Island boasts a dry-stack building rated to withstand 175 mph winds. Call ahead for slip availability.

Anchorage: It is possible to anchor on the west side of the Cortez (SR 684) Bridge in 4 to 8 feet MLW. Be sure not to swing into the channel.

Option: Crossing Tampa Bay via GIWW

On clear days the high-level **Bob Graham Sunshine Skyway Bridge**, the span of which forms a 15-mile-long highway across lower Tampa Bay, is clearly visible from The Bulkhead. The span is 425 feet high at the top of the two cable towers and it has a charted fixed vertical clearance of 180 feet at the center. Small manmade islands (called dolphins) flank the 12 columns that support the Sunshine Skyway Bridge nearest the shipping channel. Their function is to deflect ships that might wander out of the channel. Half of the old southbound span, damaged when struck in 1980, remains on both sides as fishing piers.

After crossing The Bulkhead at read daybeacon "68" you will face about 4.5 miles of open water across

Tampa Bay to the continuation of the GIWW on the north side of the bay. Flashing red "70" near Mile 95 is a useful checkpoint on this open-water run. When crossing the main shipping channel remember that commercial shipping traffic has the right-of-way and stay alert. With its long fetch this stretch can kick up an uncomfortable chop.

The Sunshine Skyway Channel is on the opposite side of the main (Mullet Key) channel and is marked by flashing green "1." Exercise caution when crossing the busy channel.

Shoaling to 5 feet MLW has been observed in the Sunshine Skyway Channel. The shoaling extends 40 to 50 feet into the channel to the southwest of red daybeacon "14." Deep-draft vessels should exercise caution while transiting the area.

Side Trip: Egmont Key– GIWW Mile 95

Square in the middle of the entrance to Tampa Bay lies Egmont Key, 3 miles off the tip of Anna Maria Island. The island is a bird sanctuary and you will also see a lot of gopher tortoises, which are on the endangered species list. Unfettered wandering is discouraged. Egmont Key is a popular daytime anchorage that gets crowded on the weekends in the summer. You can anchor close to shore on the southeast end of the island and dinghy in. As an overnight anchorage the waters on the east side off Egmont may be uncomfortable when an evening breeze kicks in and creates a lee shore. The bottom is hard sand with good holding.

The Manatee River & Bradenton, Tampa Bay

Manatee River's main city, Bradenton, is a popular layover port for those who want to explore the river and other waters. The protected marina basin has good depths and includes slips for liveaboards and weekenders alike.

NAVIGATION: Use NOAA Charts 11415 and 11425. From the exit at The Bulkhead in Anna Maria Sound, a sharp turn to the east around red daybeacon "68" leads to the mouth of the lovely Manatee River, one of Tampa Bay's finest cruising and gunkholing areas.

The almost-tropical Manatee River has a well-marked, deep channel (8-foot MLW depths), interesting side streams to explore by dinghy and friendly towns to visit. The entrance channel threads through shoals but a series of ranges are strategically placed to keep the mariner from finding those shoals. When traveling in from the north be aware of the shoal that is north of quick-flashing red "4" stay close to the buoy but inside the channel. Follow the markers closely until you are past DeSoto Point marked by flashing red "12" where there is ample water. Continuing up the river be aware of flashing red "14" and green daybeacon "15" as there are shoals growing in and around the markers. Give them a wide berth.

At Bradenton three bridges cross the Manatee River within 1 mile of each other. The first is the **8th Avenue West Bridge** (known locally as the Green Bridge), which has 41-foot fixed vertical clearance; the second (**CSX Railroad Bridge**) is untended and usually open (5-

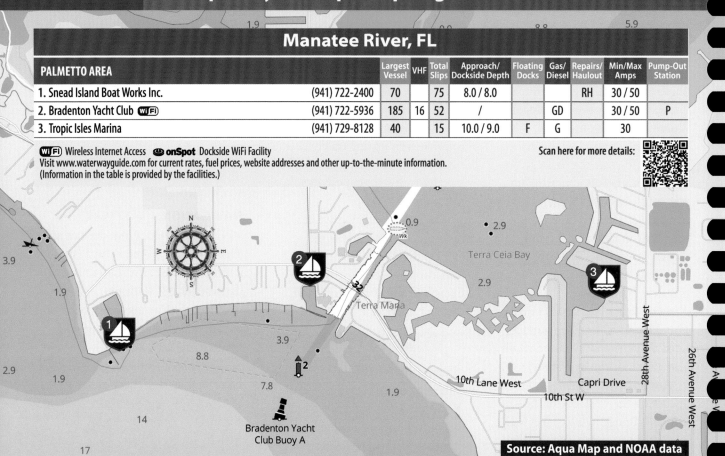

Manatee River, FL

PALMETTO AREA		Largest Vessel	VHF	Total Slips	Approach/ Dockside Depth	Floating Docks	Gas/ Diesel	Repairs/ Haulout	Min/Max Amps	Pump-Out Station
1. Snead Island Boat Works Inc.	(941) 722-2400	70		75	8.0 / 8.0			RH	30 / 50	
2. Bradenton Yacht Club (WiFi)	(941) 722-5936	185	16	52	/		GD		30 / 50	P
3. Tropic Isles Marina	(941) 729-8128	40		15	10.0 / 9.0	F	G		30	

(WiFi) Wireless Internet Access   **onSpot** Dockside WiFi Facility
Visit www.waterwayguide.com for current rates, fuel prices, website addresses and other up-to-the-minute information.
(Information in the table is provided by the facilities.)

Scan here for more details:

Source: Aqua Map and NOAA data

DeSoto National Park

Manatee River, FL

PALMETTO AREA		Largest Vessel	VHF	Total Slips	Approach/ Dockside Depth	Floating Docks	Gas/ Diesel	Repairs/ Haulout	Min/Max Amps	Pump-Out Station
1. Safe Harbor Regatta Pointe **WiFi**	(941) 729-6021	120	16	350	10.0 / 10.0		GD		30 / 50	P
2. Twin Dolphin Marina **WiFi**	(941) 747-8300	105	16	225	12.0 / 9.0	F	GD		30 / 100	P

WiFi Wireless Internet Access **onSpot** Dockside WiFi Facility
Visit www.waterwayguide.com for current rates, fuel prices, website addresses and other up-to-the-minute information.
(Information in the table is provided by the facilities.)

Scan here for more details:

foot closed vertical clearance); and the third (**Hernando Desoto Bridge**) has 40-foot fixed vertical clearance.

The upper Manatee River east of these three bridges offers some cruising options and holds depths of 10 feet MLW or better to the **I-75 Bridges** at Ellenton (40-foot fixed vertical clearance). After that depths shallow considerably and venturing farther is not recommended.

The Braden River opens to the south 2 nm beyond the last of the bridges. This is a lush and scenic stream with plenty of wildlife but it is unmarked and full of shoals. Slim water and a fixed bridge with 10-foot vertical clearance limit exploration by bigger boats but fine gunkholing by dinghy.

Dockage: Snead Island Boat Works Inc. located on the north bank of the river opposite red flashing "14" is locally known for their excellent repair service. They can handle all types of maintenance and repair services. Membership in a reciprocal yacht club is required at the friendly Bradenton Yacht Club east of McKay Point (northeast of red daybeacon "14"). They offer elegant as well as casual dining in its spacious formal dining room.

Between Snead Island and Palmetto a land cut beside the Bradenton Yacht Club leads into Terra Ceia Bay. This channel has depths of about 5 feet MLW and a fixed bridge with a 13-foot vertical clearance restricting access for some to the small boat repair facilities beyond the bridge including Tropic Isles Marina.

Directly on the Manatee River west of the Hwy. 41 Bridge is the well-equipped and well-appointed Safe Harbor Regatta Pointe, which accommodates transient guests with upscale amenities and three waterfront restaurants. Bicycles are available for loan at the marina store to get to the grocery store located a few blocks away.

Directly across the river and close to downtown Bradenton is Twin Dolphin Marina with transient dockage at floating docks. The marina is located at green daybeacon "21" and red daybeacon "22." The marina has a single-opening entrance configuration through its breakwaters. Be sure to sound your horn going in or

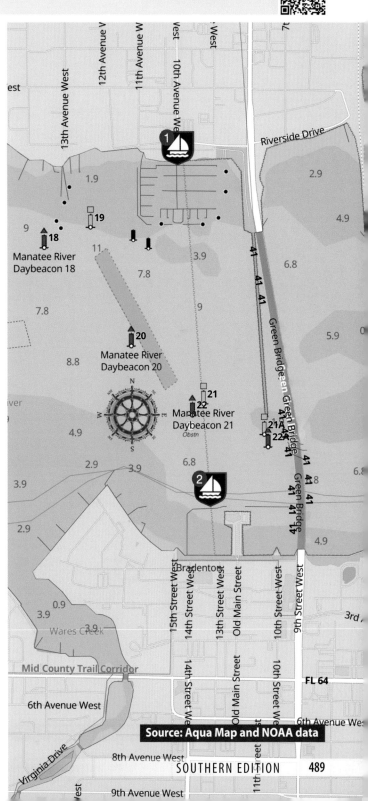

Manatee River, FL

PALMETTO AREA		Largest Vessel	VHF	Total Slips	Approach/ Dockside Depth	Floating Docks	Gas/ Diesel	Repairs/ Haulout	Min/Max Amps	Pump-Out Station
1. Tarpon Pointe Marina	(941) 745-1199	38			13.0 / 5.0	F	G	R		
2. Riviera Dunes Marina **WiFi** **onSpot**	(941) 981-5330	110	16	219	9.0 / 18.0	F	GD		30 / 100	P

WiFi Wireless Internet Access **onSpot** Dockside WiFi Facility
Visit www.waterwayguide.com for current rates, fuel prices, website addresses and other up-to-the-minute information.
(Information in the table is provided by the facilities.)

Scan here for more details:

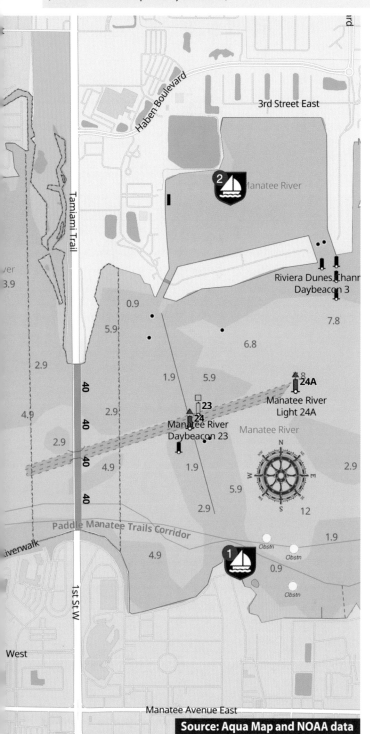

Source: Aqua Map and NOAA data

coming out. Tarpon Pointe Marina offers services and repairs (no transient slips) farther east after the three bridges (40 foot vertical clearance) on the south side of the Manatee River.

On the opposite (north) shore is the full-service and well-maintained Riviera Dunes Marina, which can accommodate vessels to 120 feet with resort amenities including two heated pools, on-site laundry facilities, pump-out service at each slip or at the fuel dock and individual bathrooms with showers. Riviera Dunes Dockside offers casual upscale cuisine and live entertainment Wednesday through Sunday. There are two supermarkets, banks, a pharmacy and an auto parts store within walking distance.

Anchorage: Follow the channel past flashing red "12" then turn west into the cove behind Desoto Point (Holy Hole), being mindful of the charted shoal in the center of the cove. (This is called "holy hole" due to the three crosses on shore.) There is plenty of room for several boats to anchor despite the shoal. This anchorage is protected except from the east and carries 9 to 10 feet MLW. You can land your dinghy to visit the DeSoto National Memorial Park.

A second anchorage is across the river at McKay Point east of Snead Island Boat Works Inc.. Depths range from 6 to 9 feet MLW but protection is good only from north winds. Farther upriver boats anchor just west of the bridge on either the Bradenton side (near red daybeacon "22") or the Palmetto side (east of red daybeacon "18"). Both have good holding in mud in a least 7 feet MLW. Expect a strong current.

Little Manatee River & Apollo Beach, Tampa Bay

NAVIGATION: Use NOAA Chart 11416. About 15 miles north of Manatee River on Tampa Bay is Little Manatee River. From the Manatee River channel follow the main ship channel to flashing red "6D" and head for lighted "LM" at the mouth of the river. Head north for

Hillsboro Bay, Tampa Bay, FL

LITTLE MANATEE RIVER		Largest Vessel	VHF	Total Slips	Approach/ Dockside Depth	Floating Docks	Gas/ Diesel	Repairs/ Haulout	Min/Max Amps	Pump-Out Station
1. Village Marina at Little Harbor	(813) 645-2288	65	16	100	6.0 / 10.0			R	30 / 50	
2. Antiqua Cove at Little Harbor WiFi	(813) 645-2288	75	16	105	8.0 / 10.0	F	GD	R	30 / 50	
3. Shell Point Marina WiFi	(813) 645-1313	60		43	6.0 / 9.0		G	RH	30	P

WiFi Wireless Internet Access　**onSpot** Dockside WiFi Facility
Visit www.waterwayguide.com for current rates, fuel prices, website addresses and other up-to-the-minute information.
(Information in the table is provided by the facilities.)

Scan here for more details:

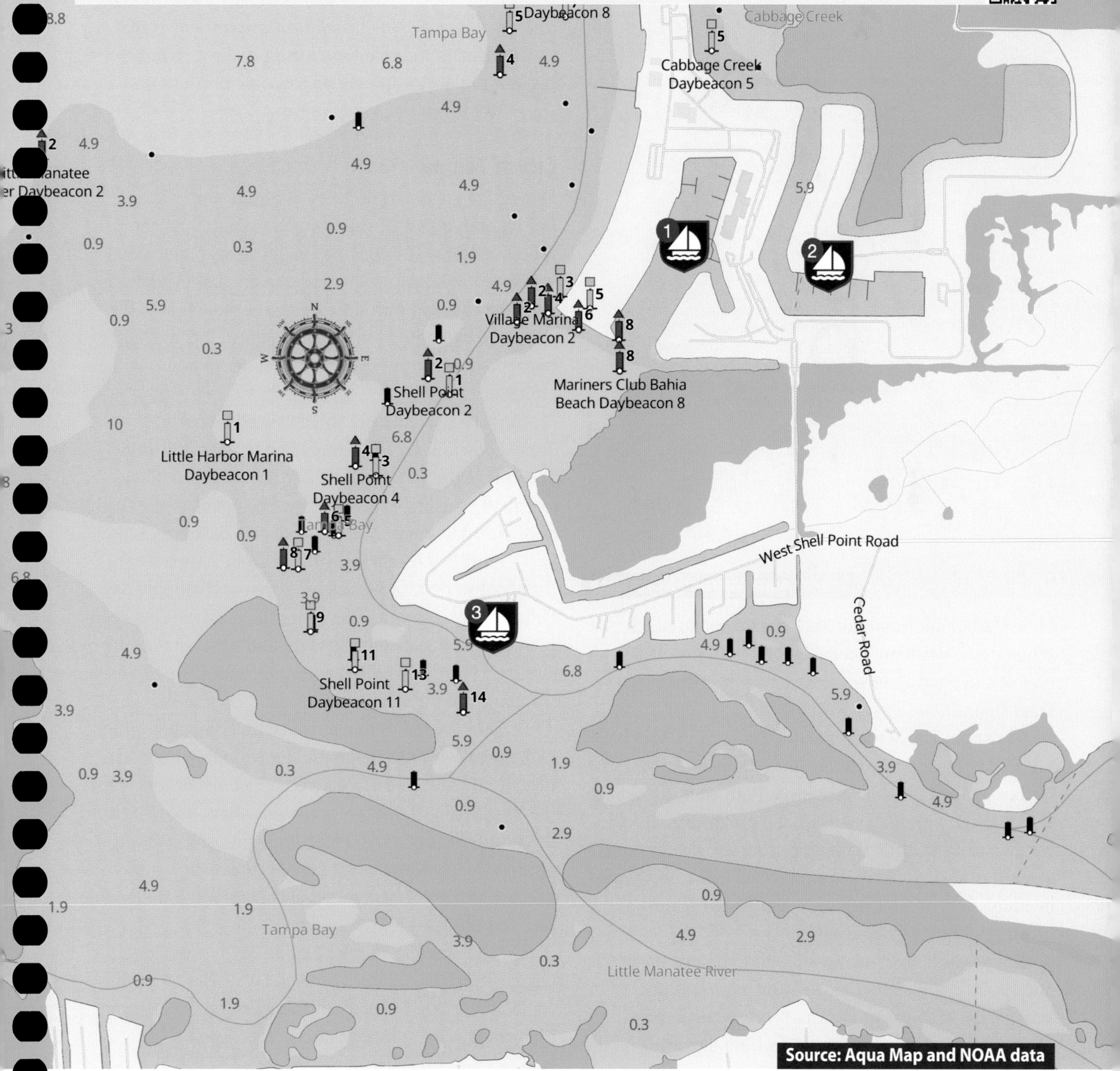

Source: Aqua Map and NOAA data

Hillsboro Bay, Tampa Bay, FL

APOLLO BEACH		Largest Vessel	VHF	Total Slips	Approach/ Dockside Depth	Floating Docks	Gas/ Diesel	Repairs/ Haulout	Min/Max Amps	Pump-Out Station
1. Lands End Marina (WiFi)	(813) 645-5594	100		105	10.0 / 10.0		GD	RH	30 / 50	P
2. Apollo Beach Marina	(813) 645-0720	40		12	8.0 / 5.0			H	30	

(WiFi) Wireless Internet Access   **onSpot** Dockside WiFi Facility
Visit www.waterwayguide.com for current rates, fuel prices, website addresses and other up-to-the-minute information.
(Information in the table is provided by the facilities.)

Scan here for more details:

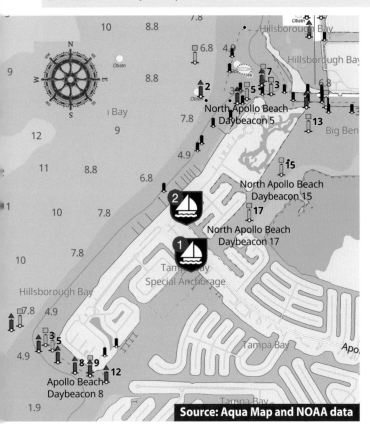

Source: Aqua Map and NOAA data

Little Harbor and south for Shell Point. Apollo Beach is just to the north on Tampa Bay and is approached on a southeasterly course from the Cut "C" Channel range light.

Dockage: The Marinas at Little Harbor manages both Village Marina at Little Harbor and Antiqua Cove at Little Harbor on the Little Manatee River. Both offer dry storage and dockage with full amenities and multiple restaurants. Antiqua Cove at Little Harbor has concrete floating slips and offers repairs. This is in a protected basin surrounded by multi-story condos making it a great hurricane hole. A beach is within walking distance.

To the south near the mouth of the Manatee River, Shell Point Marina provides wet slips as well as dry storage, bottom jobs and marina services (including DIY). Apollo Beach Marina is approached from the north via the

Big Bend Channel. This facility is usually full with long-term rentals so be sure to call first for transient availability.

There is no room for anchoring in these tight harbors. It's best to take a slip here or continue north to Boca Ciega Bay if you must anchor out.

City of Tampa

One of the great natural harbors of the world Tampa Bay extends about 25 miles north to south and about 10 miles east to west. It has two major cities (Tampa and St. Petersburg) and several large rivers that meander in from the east and north. Fringing the west side of the coast and extending northward is a pencil-thin chain of barrier islands with resort communities famous for their Gulf shore beaches.

Tampa Bay comprises three vast bodies of water–Tampa Bay proper, Old Tampa Bay to the northwest and Hillsborough Bay to the northeast–all providing excellent cruising. Lower Tampa Bay opens to the Gulf of Mexico but enjoys the protection of barrier islands. Old Tampa Bay reaches northwest from Tampa Bay to the shoal water around Safety Harbor and Mobbly Bay. Hillsborough Bay branches off to the northeast between Interbay Peninsula and the mainland to serve the City of Tampa, Ybor City and Davis Islands with their extensive shipping and industrial areas.

St. Petersburg lies due north from the open mouth of Tampa Bay with metropolitan Tampa to the northeast. Each dominates one of the two big peninsulas that pierce the bay. Pinellas to the west extends about 45 miles from the southern edge of St. Petersburg almost to Tarpon Springs. MacDill Air Force Base occupies the southern tip of Interbay, the second peninsula (about 3 miles wide and 10 miles long).

For the cruising skipper Tampa Bay is a welcome change from the confines of the GIWW. Here there are some 300 square miles of cruising waters, Gulf fishing, interesting ports, pleasant anchorages, good yacht facilities and superb sailing.

Hillsboro Bay, Tampa Bay, FL

TAMPA AREA		Largest Vessel	VHF	Total Slips	Approach/ Dockside Depth	Floating Docks	Gas/ Diesel	Repairs/ Haulout	Min/Max Amps	Pump-Out Station
1. Davis Island Yacht Club-PRIVATE	(813) 251-1158	55		114	10.0 / 8.0	F		H	30	

WiFi Wireless Internet Access **onSpot** Dockside WiFi Facility
Visit www.waterwayguide.com for current rates, fuel prices, website addresses and other up-to-the-minute information.
(Information in the table is provided by the facilities.)

Scan here for more details:

NAVIGATION: Use NOAA Chart 11415 and 11416. To get to Tampa from The Bulkhead at the exit of Anna Maria Sound set a course of 022° magnetic for flashing red buoy "70" well out in Tampa Bay at GIWW Mile 95. Continue on the same heading until you pick up quick-flashing red buoy "26" at Mullet Key Channel, the big ship route up Tampa Bay. Go under the center spans of the Bob Graham Sunshine Skyway Bridge (known locally as the Meisner Bridge). You may then follow the Big Ship Channel the 20 to 25 miles all the way northeast to the City of Tampa.

Most of the marine facilities are on the Seddon Channel between Harbor and Davis Islands. At the end of Davis Islands is a park that offers a small beach area, off-leash area for dogs, picnic area, canoe launch and boat ramps.

Dockage: Nearly all of the dockage at Harbour Island, which is in downtown Tampa, is private. Other private facilities in the area include Tampa Yacht & Country Club (at Ballast Point) and Davis Island Yacht Club (at Davis Islands). The municipal Marjorie Park Yacht Basin located on the channel between Harbor and Davis Islands is a full-service facility with slips and easy access to mass transit.

There are 27 slips at Tampa Convention Center Transient Docks. Tie up at one of two floating docks for a few hours or stay overnight.

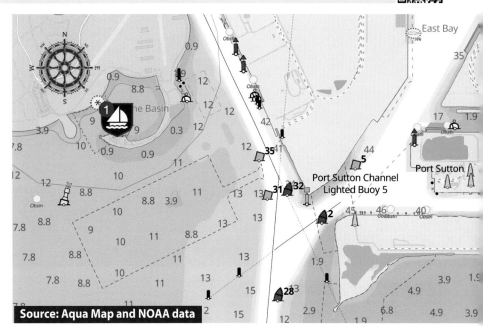

Source: Aqua Map and NOAA data

(Note that North Dock has no power and water but South Dock does.) There are black-out dates due to construction and special events so call ahead for a reservation. This facility is very convenient to the sights, sounds and activities of downtown Tampa and Ybor City.

Marriott Tampa Water Street Hotel & Marina is located on Garrison Channel between the **S. Franklin Street Bridge** and the **S. Meridian Avenue Bridge**, both with charted 10-foot fixed vertical clearance. (According to the marina the vertical clearance is actually closer to 18 feet MLW.) They may have transient slips on their floating docks for those who can navigate the bridge but call well in advance to check availability. This facility offers resort amenities including laundry facilities, a gym and a pool.

Plan to take a slip. There is no room to anchor in the Seddon or Garrison Channels.

Old Tampa Bay

On the opposite side of Interbay Peninsula from the City of Tampa is Old Tampa Bay, which is crossed by three bridges. Marine facilities are located at Port Tampa before the southernmost (twin) **Gandy Bridges** with 43-foot vertical clearance.

Dockage: The full-service Port 32 Tampa has wet slips and dry stack storage plus outboard repairs and service. Westshore Yacht Club is part of a condominium complex that has transient slips on floating docks for vessels up to 150 feet on floating slips. Guests have access to the waterfront Bay Club with a spa, fitness center, pools and dining.

Tampa Bay Area

Hillsboro Bay, Tampa Bay, FL

TAMPA AREA		Largest Vessel	VHF	Total Slips	Approach/ Dockside Depth	Floating Docks	Gas/ Diesel	Repairs/ Haulout	Min/Max Amps	Pump-Out Station
1. Marjorie Park Yacht Basin **WiFi**	(813) 259-1604	90	16	51	21.0 / 9.0	F	GD		30 / 50	P
2. Tampa Convention Center Transient Marina	(813) 444-7728	160		19	19.0 / 19.0	F			30 / 50	
3. Marriott Tampa Water Street Hotel & Marina **WiFi**	(813) 314-1006	60	16	32	19.0 / 19.0	F			30 / 50	

WiFi Wireless Internet Access　**onSpot** Dockside WiFi Facility
Visit www.waterwayguide.com for current rates, fuel prices, website addresses and other up-to-the-minute information.
(Information in the table is provided by the facilities.)

Scan here for more details:

City of St. Petersburg

Facilities of one kind or another line all sides of the peninsula in St. Petersburg (often referred to as St. Pete). Boaters heading up Tampa Bay reach the marinas at the south end first but there are also facilities downtown on the east side of the peninsula and in Boca Ciega Bay on the west side. See more at "Goin' Ashore: St. Petersburg, FL" in this chapter.

NAVIGATION: Use NOAA Charts 11411, 11415 and 11416. Two routes, both clearly marked on NOAA Chart 11416, lead from Anna Maria Sound to St. Petersburg. Starting from The Bulkhead set a course of 022° magnetic for flashing red "70" well out in Tampa Bay at Mile 95. Continue on the same heading until you pick up flashing red buoy "26" at Mullet Key Channel, the big ship route up Tampa Bay.

The western approach to St. Petersburg follows Mullet Key Channel eastward through the high-rise **Bob Graham Sunshine Skyway Bridge**. Leave the channel at flashing green buoy "3B" with a bearing of about 5° magnetic. After leaving a 27-foot-high quick-flashing red to the east you should pick up the twin, 16-foot-high flashing green "1" and flashing green "2." At quick-flashing green "3" continue north on the marked channel to access the facilities on the east side of the peninsula.

You can head into Bayboro Harbor at flashing green "S." Coast Guard ships and cruise ships come here so the water is deep. Keep north for the marinas at the three yacht basins (North, Central and South).

To continue to Boca Ciega Bay, turn west to flashing green "1" and take the channel under the 65-foot fixed vertical clearance span of the Sunshine Skyway Bridge until it converges with the northbound channel to St. Petersburg at red daybeacon "14."

Source: Aqua Map and NOAA data

Old Tampa Bay, FL

PORT TAMPA AREA		Largest Vessel	VHF	Total Slips	Approach/ Dockside Depth	Floating Docks	Gas/ Diesel	Repairs/ Haulout	Min/Max Amps	Pump-Out Station
1. Port 32 Tampa **WiFi**	(813) 831-1200	80	16	25	25.0 / 12.0	F	GD	RH	30 / 50	P
2. Oasis Marinas at Westshore Yacht Club **WiFi** **onSpot**	(813) 831-7002	150	16	149	25.0 / 8.0	F			30 / 100	P

WiFi Wireless Internet Access   **onSpot** Dockside WiFi Facility
Visit www.waterwayguide.com for current rates, fuel prices, website addresses and other up-to-the-minute information.
(Information in the table is provided by the facilities.)

Scan here for more details:

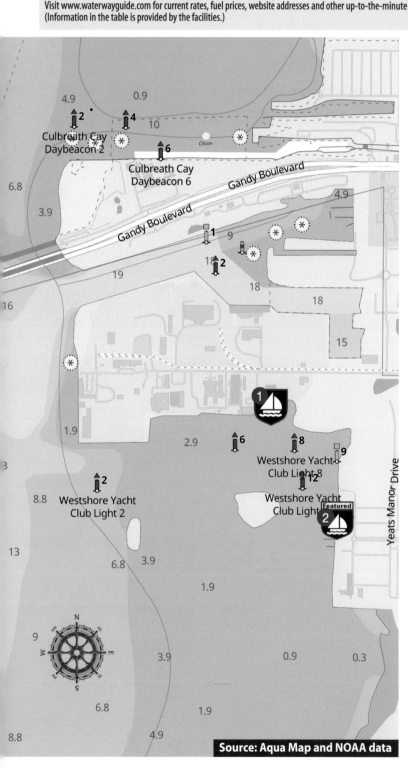

Source: Aqua Map and NOAA data

Be advised that if you are trying to avoid easterly winds out in Tampa Bay you will have them right on your nose from green daybeacon "13A." It is several miles to the northbound channel.

> In case you haven't guessed, this is a great place for a good set of binoculars for sorting out the different channel markers.

Dockage/Moorings: Renaissance Vinoy Resort Marina near the big pink historic Vinoy Hotel in the North Basin is a Marriott property with 74 concrete boat slips for vessels of up to 130 feet and offering resort amenities. Nearby St. Petersburg Yacht Club is private. Anchoring is not allowed in the North Basin (also known as Vinoy Basin).

The large (650-slip) St. Petersburg Municipal Marina in the Central Basin offers transient slips to 100 feet and all the usual amenities including laundry facilities. The trolley system has stops close by but most everything is within walking distance.

The St. Petersburg Municipal Marina manages 13 moorings in the Central Basin in 14 to 16 feet MLW. Call ahead of your arrival to make sure a mooring will be available. There is a handy dinghy dock nearby and great access to the city.

Safe Harbor Harborage Marina at Bayboro is around the bend from downtown but close to a trolley stop so you can get around if needed. The mega-yacht marina offers deep-water transient slips protected by an 800-foot breakwater. They also boast a resort-style pool and Tiki hut.

To the south at the end of the entrance channel are Sailor's Wharf Yacht Yard, Embree Marine and Salt Creek Marina. These are all repair and maintenance facilities (no transient slips). Call in advance.

Tampa Bay, FL

ST. PETERSBURG AREA		Largest Vessel	VHF	Total Slips	Approach/ Dockside Depth	Floating Docks	Gas/ Diesel	Repairs/ Haulout	Min/Max Amps	Pump-Out Station
1. Renaissance Vinoy Resort Marina **WiFi**	(727) 824-8022	130	16	74	12.0 / 12.0				30 / 100	P
2. St. Petersburg Municipal Marina	(727) 893-7329	125	16	650	12.0 / 12.0		GD		30 / 100	P
3. St. Petersburg Yacht Club-PRIVATE **WiFi**	(727) 822-3227	120	16	60	10.0 / 14.0		GD		30 / 100	

WiFi Wireless Internet Access **onSpot** Dockside WiFi Facility
Visit www.waterwayguide.com for current rates, fuel prices, website addresses and other up-to-the-minute information.
(Information in the table is provided by the facilities.)

Scan here for more details:

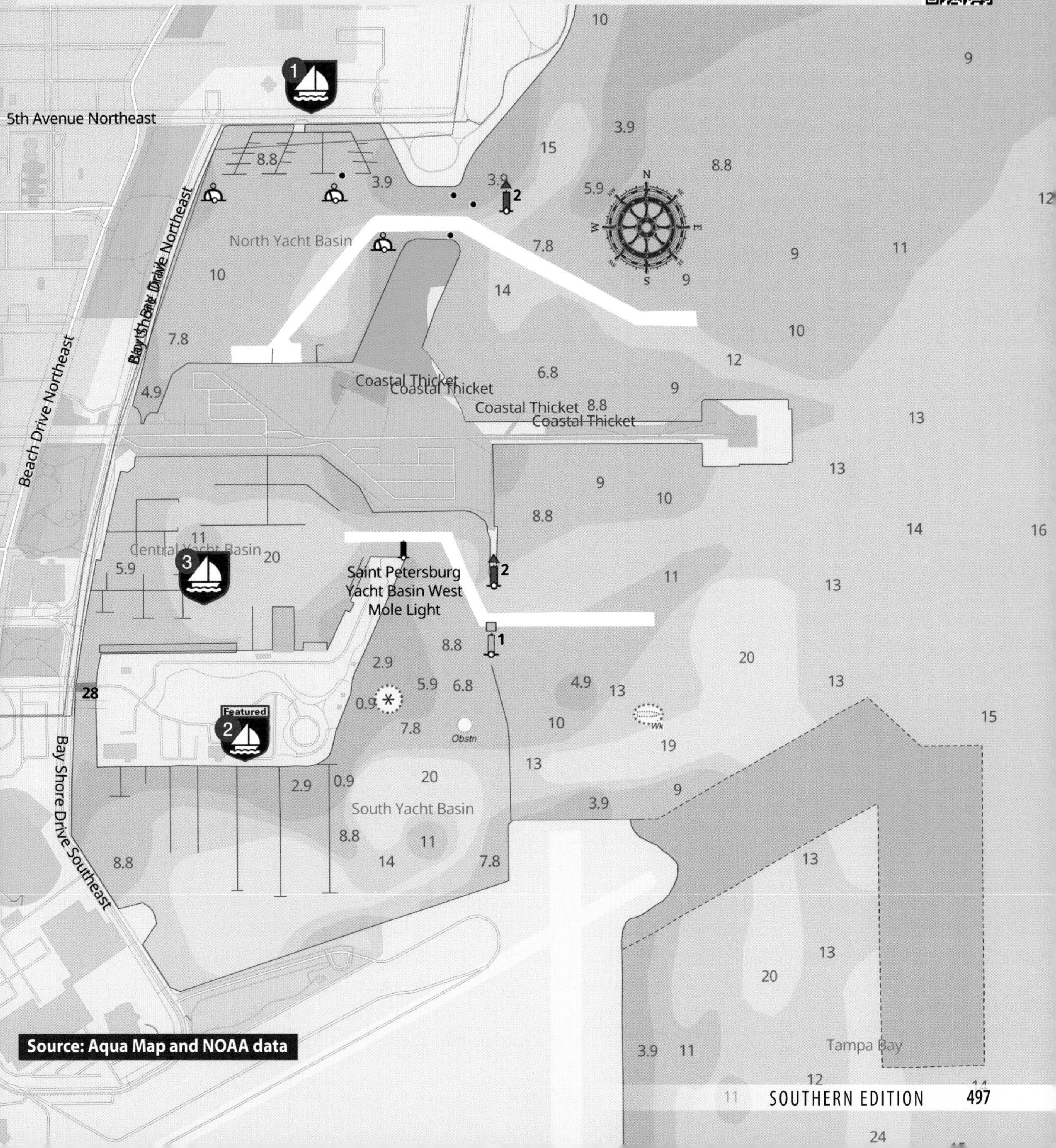

Source: Aqua Map and NOAA data

GOIN' ASHORE

ST. PETERSBURG, FL

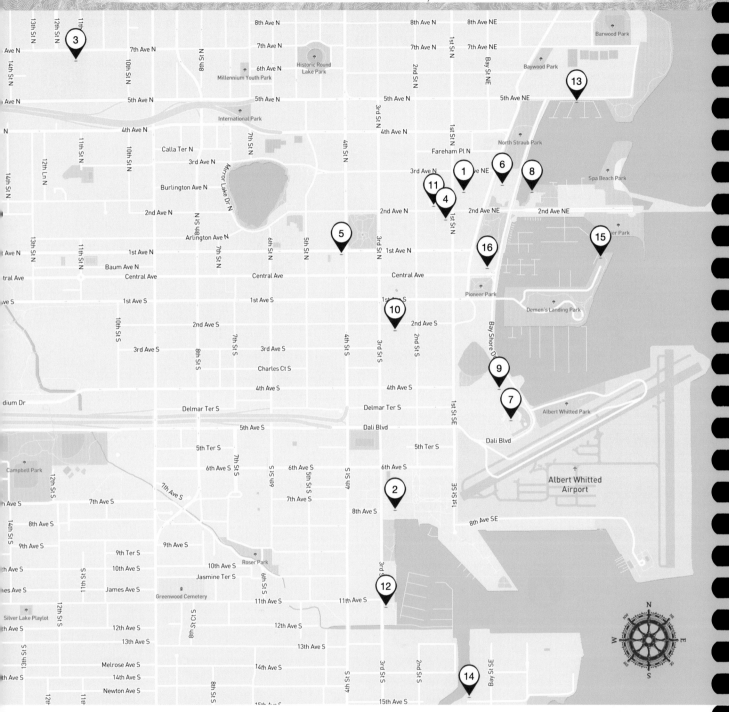

As with most larger cities, St. Petersburg boasts an exciting arts and food scene, professional sporting events, a variety of museums and a serious nightlife. Not only does St. Pete have the largest public waterfront park system of any U.S. city, it's also an easy city to negotiate by foot or public transportation. The downtown "Looper" trolley (727-821-5166) stops at many of the tourist spots and downtown locations every 15 minutes for a nominal charge. The public bus service (PSTA, 727-540-1800) can get you around the rest of the city in all-electric buses.

SERVICES

1. Downtown St. Pete Vet Clinic
111 2nd Ave. NE, Unit 113 (727-755-7387)

2. Nelson Poynter Memorial Library
140 7th Ave. S. (727-873-4405)

3. St. Anthony's Hospital
1200 7th Ave. N. (727-825-1100)

4. St. Pete Store & Visitors Center
100 2nd Ave. N. #150 (727-388-0686)

5. St. Petersburg Post Office
3135 1st Ave. N. (727-322-6632)

ATTRACTIONS

6. Museum of Fine Arts
Daily guided tours of expansive fine art and
photography collection at 255 Beach Dr. NE
(727-896-2667).

7. The Dali
Houses the largest collection of works of Salvador
Dali outside of Europe, including paintings,
sculpture, holograms and art glass. Don't miss the
hedge maze and melting clock benches
(1 Dali Blvd., 727-823-3767).

8. St. Petersburg Museum of History
Artifacts, photos and an exhibit on the beginning of
commercial air travel at 335 2nd Ave. NE
(727-894-1052).

9. The Mahaffey Theater
Hosts the Florida Orchestra, ballet, performing
artists and traveling Broadway plays at
400 1st St. S. (727-892-5767)

SHOPPING

10. Publix Super Market
Full-service grocery store for provisioning
(groceries, deli and bakery items) at
250 3rd St. (727-822-1125).

11. Sundial St. Pete
Outdoor mall with upscale shopping and dining
in the downtown center featuring three-story tall
sundial (153 2nd Ave. N., 727-800-3201).

MARINAS

12. Harborage Marina
1110 3rd St. S. (727-821-6347)

13. Renaissance Vinoy Resort Marina
501 5th Ave. NE (727-824-8022)

14. Salt Creek Marina
107 15th Ave. SE (727-895-4481)

15. St. Petersburg Municipal Marina
500 1st Ave. SE (727-893-7329)

16. St. Petersburg Yacht Club
11 Central Ave. (727-822-3873)

Salvador Dali Museum

Tampa Bay, FL

ST. PETERSBURG AREA		Largest Vessel	VHF	Total Slips	Approach/ Dockside Depth	Floating Docks	Gas/ Diesel	Repairs/ Haulout	Min/Max Amps	Pump-Out Station
1. Safe Harbor Harborage WiFi	(727) 821-6347	300	16	340	24.0 / 12.0	F	GD		30 / 200+	P
2. Sailor's Wharf Yacht Yard	(727) 823-1155	80		23	10.0 / 9.0	F		RH	30 / 50	
3. Embree Marine	(727) 896-0671	70			7.0 / 7.0			RH	30 / 50	
4. Salt Creek Marina WiFi	(727) 895-4481	72		12	10.0 / 9.0			RH	30 / 50	

WiFi Wireless Internet Access **onSpot** Dockside WiFi Facility
Visit www.waterwayguide.com for current rates, fuel prices, website addresses and other up-to-the-minute information.
(Information in the table is provided by the facilities.)

Scan here for more details:

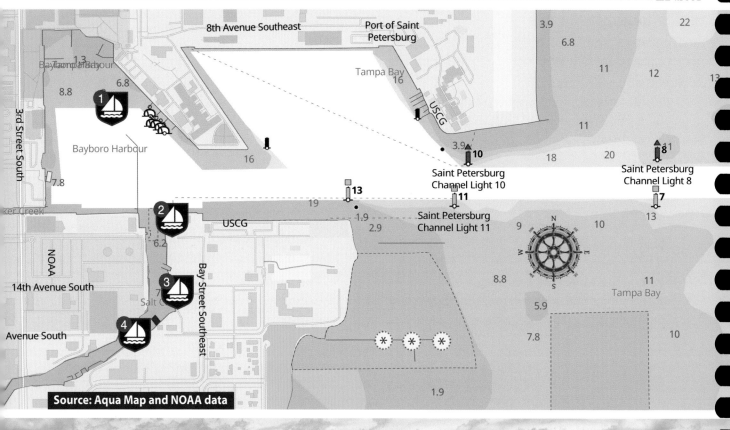

Source: Aqua Map and NOAA data

St. Petersburg Area

Boca Ciega Bay, FL

MAXIMO POINT		Largest Vessel	VHF	Total Slips	Approach/ Dockside Depth	Floating Docks	Gas/ Diesel	Repairs/ Haulout	Min/Max Amps	Pump-Out Station
1. Magnuson Hotel Marina Cove - Closed Until Sometime in 2022 (WiFi) MM 110.3	(727) 867-1151	55		32	5.0 / 8.0				30 / 50	
2. Loggerhead Marina - St. Petersburg Marina (WiFi) onSpot	(727) 867-2600	60		143	5.0 / 5.0	F	GD	RH	30 / 50	P

(WiFi) Wireless Internet Access   onSpot Dockside WiFi Facility
Visit www.waterwayguide.com for current rates, fuel prices, website addresses and other up-to-the-minute information.
(Information in the table is provided by the facilities.)

Scan here for more details:

Southern Boca Ciega Bay

NAVIGATION: Use NOAA Chart 11411. There are two routes to reach boating facilities on the west side of the Pinellas Peninsula. Those who can clear **Pinellas Bayway Structure 'A' Bridge** (with 18-foot fixed vertical clearance) can use the shortcut past Cats Point off the straight-line extension of the Sunshine Skyway Channel. Otherwise follow the GIWW channel through **Pinellas Bayway Structure 'E' Bridge** (25-foot vertical clearance) and then **Pinellas Bayway Structure 'C' Bridge** (65-foot fixed vertical clearance).

> The Pinellas Bayway Structure 'E' Bridge has been replaced with a new (in 2021) 65-foot vertical clearance fixed bridge. Be aware that there could be some activity in the area related to this construction.

Just north of the Pinellas Bayway Bridges is a shoal spot that sometimes catches the unwary. It is well marked but it is recommended that you stay alert. Flashing red "26" and red "26A" lead past the shoal.

Dockage: On the back side of Maximo Point at the south end of Pinellas Peninsula is Magnuson Hotel Marina Cove, which is part of an 18-acre resort. Turn north at green daybeacon "13" to reach

the marina. The marina accepts transients up to 55 feet. Just to the north Loggerhead Marina– St. Petersburg Marina is located in Frenchman Creek. They can accommodate vessels up to 60 feet and provide hurricane-rated dry storage in their well-protected harbor. They also have a pool and this location provides easy access to restaurants, shopping and activities.

South of the Structure 'C' Bridge and just to the west of Structure 'E' Bridge, Tierra Verde Marina has 10 reserved transient slips to 60 feet and offers dry storage. To the south off Pass-A-Grille Channel is Port 32 Tierra Verde with dry stack storage, wet slips and a full range of services. On the opposite side of the channel is The Pass-A-Grille Marina with limited amenities but a great location near beaches and shopping.

■ TO TARPON SPRINGS

The GIWW runs from Tampa Bay to Anclote Key via Boca Ciega Bay at the mouth of the Anclote River leading to Tarpon Springs. Tarpon Springs on the Anclote River marks the end of the Florida GIWW at Mile 150.

> The GIWW picks back up in the The Big Bend section of this guide, where mileages are measured east and west of Harvey Lock, LA, notated as EHL or WHL.

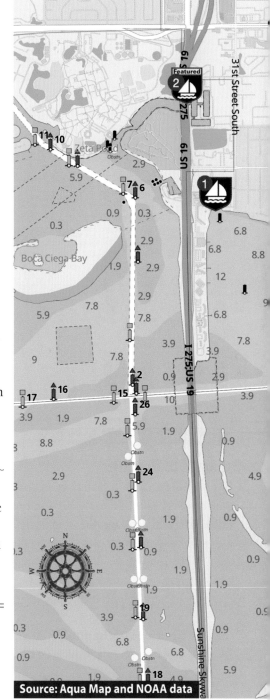

Source: Aqua Map and NOAA data

Boca Ciega Bay, FL

PASS-A-GRILLE AREA		Largest Vessel	VHF	Total Slips	Approach/ Dockside Depth	Floating Docks	Gas/ Diesel	Repairs/ Haulout	Min/Max Amps	Pump-Out Station
1. Tierra Verde Marina MM 113.0	(727) 866-0255	42	75	34	20.0 / 15.0	F	GD	RH	30 / 50	
2. Port 32 Tierra Verde **WiFi** **onSpot** MM 113.0	(727) 867-0400	120	72	115	12.0 / 12.0	F	GD	RH	15 / 50	P
3. The Pass-A-Grille Marina **WiFi** MM 113.8	(727) 360-0100	50	16	20	20.0 / 15.0	F	GD	RH	30 / 100	

WiFi Wireless Internet Access **onSpot** Dockside WiFi Facility
Visit www.waterwayguide.com for current rates, fuel prices, website addresses and other up-to-the-minute information.
(Information in the table is provided by the facilities.)

Scan here for more details:

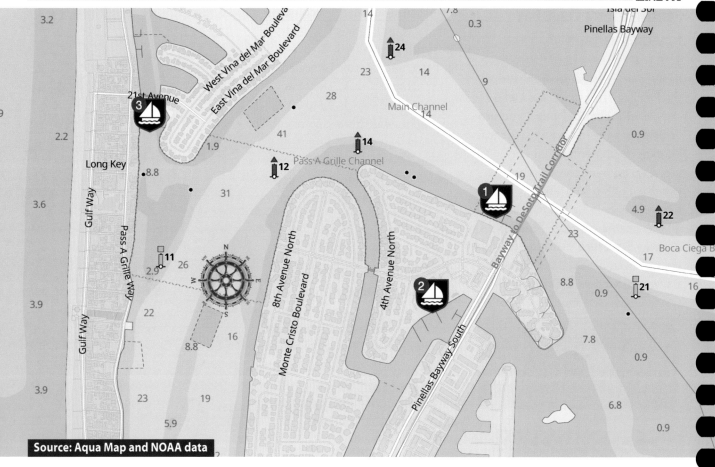

Source: Aqua Map and NOAA data

Passes to the Gulf

From Tampa Bay to Clearwater any one of several inlets affords easy access from the GIWW to and from the Gulf of Mexico (in good weather and daylight).

- **Passage Key Inlet:** Follow the charts closely and stay in deep water. Not marked so be aware that there could be hazards. Should only be attempted with local knowledge. A better route is Southwest Channel.
- **Southwest Channel:** Well marked and deep inlet into Tampa Bay. Carries a lot of commercial traffic so stay alert and pay attention. Remember, tonnage rules!

- **North Channel (just north of Tampa Bay):** Well marked and leads from the Gulf to Pass-a-Grille Channel.
- **Pass-A-Grille Channel:** Watch for shoaling and keep clear of the north side.
- **Johns Pass:** Connects with the GIWW between Mitchell and Sunshine beaches and is crossed by **Johns Pass Drawbridge** (with closed vertical clearance of 27 feet at the center of the channel). The bridge opens on request.

Boca Ciega Bay, FL

GULFPORT & PASADENA		Largest Vessel	VHF	Total Slips	Approach/ Dockside Depth	Floating Docks	Gas/ Diesel	Repairs/ Haulout	Min/Max Amps	Pump-Out Station
1. Gulfport Municipal Marina **WiFi** 1.5 mi. NE of MM 115.0	(727) 893-1071	45	16	250	7.0 / 6.0	F	GD	R	30 / 50	P

WiFi Wireless Internet Access **onSpot** Dockside WiFi Facility
Visit www.waterwayguide.com for current rates, fuel prices, website addresses and other up-to-the-minute information.
(Information in the table is provided by the facilities.)

Scan here for more details:

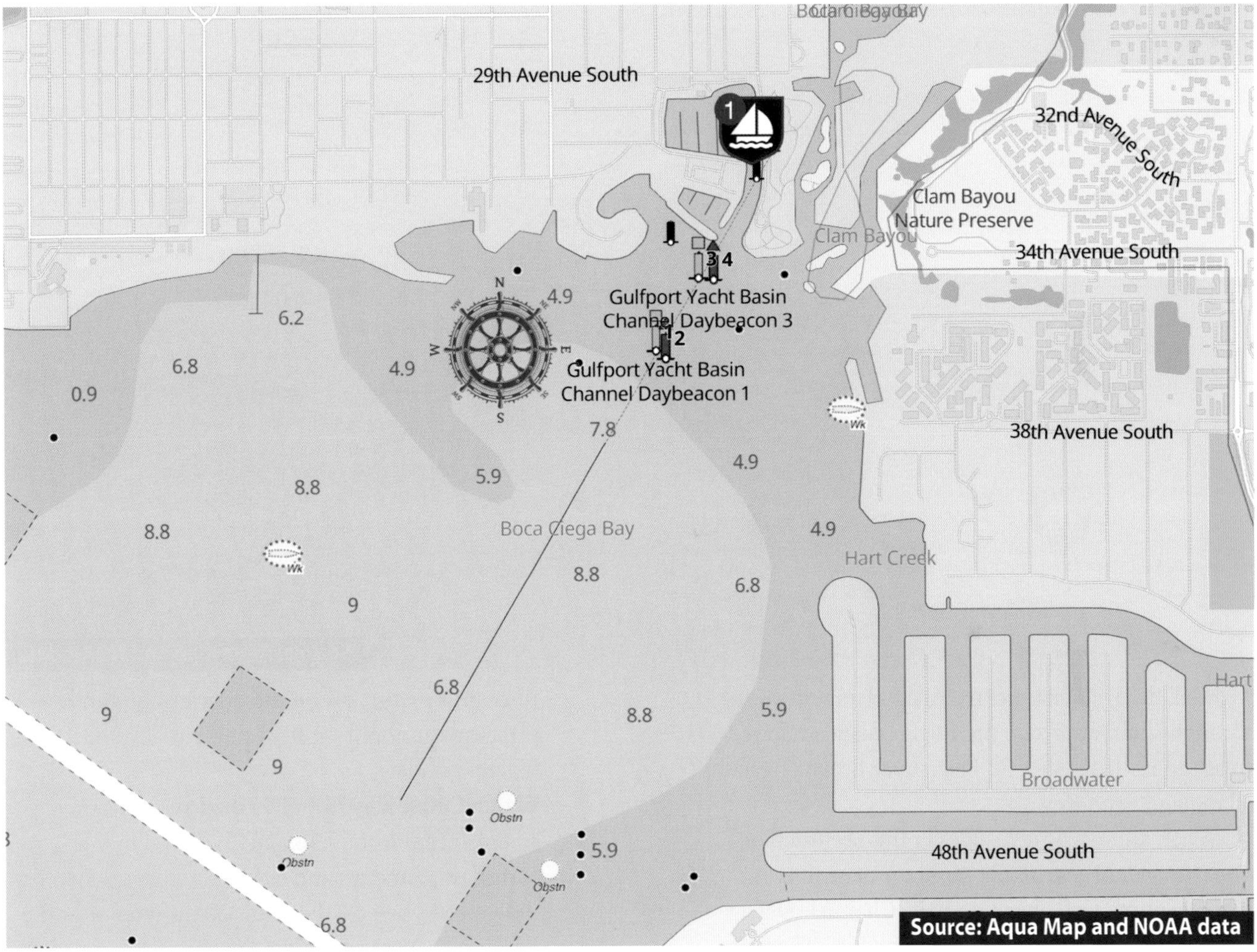

Source: Aqua Map and NOAA data

All vessels operating with more than a 3-foot draft are advised to use extreme caution when transiting inbound and outbound of Johns Pass due to an encroaching shoal to the north in the vicinity of green can "3" in the entry channel from the Gulf. Shoaling has also been observed in the channel between flashing red "8" and "10." The shoaling is from center of the channel towards the red side. This inlet tends to shoal rapidly. Calling for local knowledge from one of the tow services would be wise.

• **Clearwater Pass:** Located about 13 nm north of Johns Pass. Leads right into the heart of Clearwater proper. The 74-foot fixed vertical clearance **Clearwater Pass (SR183) Bridge** spans the pass. This is the preferred channel unless you have solid local knowledge for the others.

Boca Ciega Bay to The Narrows–GIWW Mile 114 to Mile 126

The GIWW runs from Tampa Bay to Anclote Key and the Tarpon Springs area through well-marked Boca Ciega Bay. From Boca Ciega Bay the GIWW is a well-

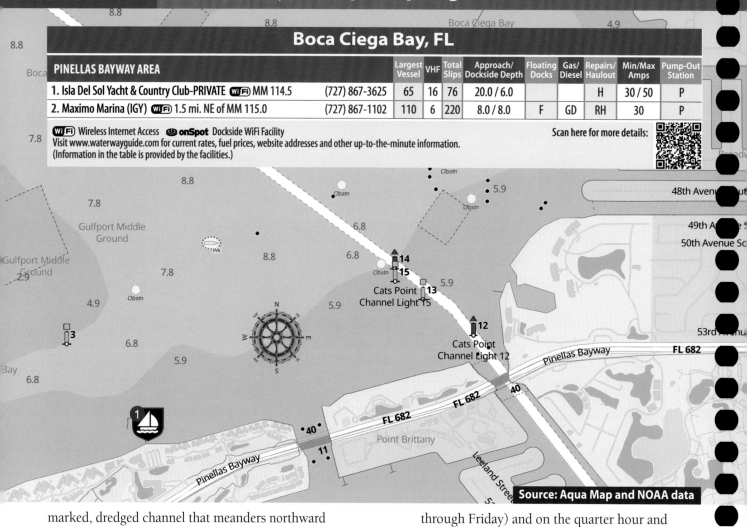

Boca Ciega Bay, FL

PINELLAS BAYWAY AREA		Largest Vessel	VHF	Total Slips	Approach/ Dockside Depth	Floating Docks	Gas/ Diesel	Repairs/ Haulout	Min/Max Amps	Pump-Out Station
1. Isla Del Sol Yacht & Country Club–PRIVATE **WiFi** MM 114.5	(727) 867-3625	65	16	76	20.0 / 6.0			H	30 / 50	P
2. Maximo Marina (IGY) **WiFi** 1.5 mi. NE of MM 115.0	(727) 867-1102	110	6	220	8.0 / 8.0	F	GD	RH	30	P

WiFi Wireless Internet Access   **onSpot** Dockside WiFi Facility
Visit www.waterwayguide.com for current rates, fuel prices, website addresses and other up-to-the-minute information. (Information in the table is provided by the facilities.)

Scan here for more details:

Source: Aqua Map and NOAA data

marked, dredged channel that meanders northward through shallows inside the barrier islands referred to as the Holiday Isles–St. Petersburg Beach, Treasure Island and Sand Key.

When approaching bridges in this section bide your time and leave ample room for maneuvering while waiting. Call ahead on VHF Channel 09 if you are in doubt of the opening schedule. There are three bascule bridges on the GIWW with varying restrictions and schedules:

- **Corey Causeway (SR 693) Bridge** (23-foot vertical clearance) opens on signal except from 8:00 a.m. to 7:00 p.m., Monday through Friday, and 10:00 a.m. to 7:00 p.m., Saturdays, Sundays and federal holidays, when the draw need only open on the hour, 20 minutes after the hour and 40 minutes after the hour.
- **Treasure Island Causeway Bridge** opens on signal except from 7:00 a.m. to 7:00 p.m., when the draw need open on the hour, 20 minutes after the hour and 40 minutes after the hour (Monday through Friday) and on the quarter hour and three-quarter hour on Saturday, Sunday and federal holidays.
- **Welch Causeway (SR 699) Bridge** opens on signal except from 9:30 a.m. to 6:00 p.m. on Saturdays, Sundays and federal holidays, when the draw need open on the hour, 20 minutes after the hour and 40 minutes after the hour.

Dockage: North of the Pinellas Bayway is Isla Del Sol Yacht & Country Club, which is private but social and dining facilities are open to transient members of any reciprocal yacht club. Maximo Marina (IGY) is to the east and just north of Cats Point and the Structure 'A' Bridge. This facility has covered and open slips (including four megayacht slips). Within two blocks from Maximo Marina is a grocery store, several banks and a few restaurants.

To reach Gulfport and its boating facilities turn to the northeast at GIWW Mile 114.5 just before flashing red "26." Slow down and take care as you round red daybeacon "2" and head carefully for green daybeacon "3." The red flashing light marks a shoal. Gulfport

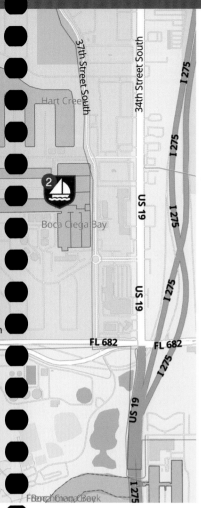

Municipal Marina has a full complement of transient facilities in its well-protected basin. It is a short walk to the center of downtown Gulfport and the trailhead for the Pinellas Trail is only 1 mile away.

The friendly Pasadena Yacht & Country Club to the north is private but recognizes reciprocity from other clubs. MarineMax St. Petersburg is in a protected basin and offers repairs. Call ahead for slip availability. The well-maintained Pasadena Marina offers 125 full-service slips both covered and open accommodating boats up to 55 feet. Call ahead for transient availability.

There are full-service municipal marinas and facilities on both shores from Johns Pass at Mile 121 north to Sand Key including Blind Pass Marina, John's Pass Marina, Madeira Bay Docks, Inc., Snug Harbor Inn and Madeira Beach Municipal Marina. Slips and repairs are available here. There are also motels and on-the-water restaurants with dockage while you dine.

To the northeast of Turtlecrawl Point between two fixed bridges (32-foot vertical clearance on first bridge) is the friendly Bay Pines Marina with slips and some services and repairs.

> We have been told that you are only allowed to stay aboard your boat for three days in this area. If you plan to stay longer call ahead before your arrival.

Anchorage: One popular spot in Boca Ciega Bay near the Gulfport Municipal Marina has 5 to 7 feet MLW and the other to the northwest has 6 to 10 feet MLW. These offer protection from all but southern blows. Expect lots of weekend boat traffic and snuggle up to the east shore.

To anchor closer to St. Pete Beach, proceed west between green daybeacon "31" and red daybeacon "30"

from flashing red "32" then anchor where the chart shows 7- to 8-foot MLW depths. Proceed between the last two "No-Wake" markers to find the best depths. Expect wakes from boats coming inshore via Pass-A-Grille Channel.

Just north of the Treasure Island Bridge at green daybeacon "17" turn west and stay north of the charted spoil area for the well-protected Treasure Island anchorage. Depths around the spoil are roughly 4 to 6 feet MLW and the bottom is sand. Highly visible west of the GIWW on St. Pete Beach is the renovated Don CeSar Hotel, a longtime landmark for mariners.

Finally you can anchor north of the Welch Causeway (SR 699) Bridge (Mile 122.1) in 7 feet MLW with good holding. Dinghy back to the first channel by the bridge (past the American Legion building) to the day dock to access restaurants and shopping.

The Narrows–GIWW Mile 126 to Mile 130

NAVIGATION: Use NOAA Chart 11411. Nine nautical miles south of Clearwater the GIWW enters the well-named Narrows, a deep but narrow channel connecting Boca Ciega Bay to Clearwater Harbor, which is comparatively broad and open. At the northern end of the GIWW approaching Clearwater the waterway tends to narrow and bridges and shoaling become more frequent. Boats with significant draft should be very cautious.

Park Boulevard (SR 248) Bridge at Mile 126.0 has a 20-foot closed vertical clearance and opens on request. The **Indian Rocks Beach (CR 694) Bridge** at Mile 129.3 has a 25-foot closed vertical clearance and opens on request.

Dockage: Indian Springs Marina at GIWW Mile 129 is a yacht brokerage and dry boat storage facility. Call ahead for slip availability. Harbourside Marina, part of a Holiday Inn & Suites, is near the Indian Rocks Beach (CR 694) Bridge with transient slips and access to hotel amenities. Largo Intercoastal Marina at Mile 129.6 is a dry dock facility with a few slips and some repairs.

Clearwater Harbor–GIWW Mile 130 to Mile 136

Although divided by the GIWW channel, Clearwater and Clearwater Beach constitute one very boat-minded community. Boaters find it an increasingly important port of call both as a base of operations from which to enjoy the nearby resort attractions and also as a layover stop. The yacht services and elegant marinas here are mostly

Boca Ciega Bay, FL

GULFPORT & PASADENA		Largest Vessel	VHF	Total Slips	Approach/ Dockside Depth	Floating Docks	Gas/ Diesel	Repairs/ Haulout	Min/Max Amps	Pump-Out Station
1. Pasadena Yacht & Country Club-PRIVATE WiFi onSpot MM 116.5	(727) 543-4086	110	16	89	8.5 / 10.5				50 / 100	
2. MarineMax St. Petersburg	(727) 343-6520	75	16	130	8.0 / 6.0	F		RH	30 / 100	P
3. Pasadena Marina WiFi MM 116.0	(727) 343-4500	56		125	6.0 / 6.0				30 / 50	P

WiFi Wireless Internet Access onSpot Dockside WiFi Facility
Visit www.waterwayguide.com for current rates, fuel prices, website addresses and other up-to-the-minute information.
(Information in the table is provided by the facilities.)

Scan here for more details:

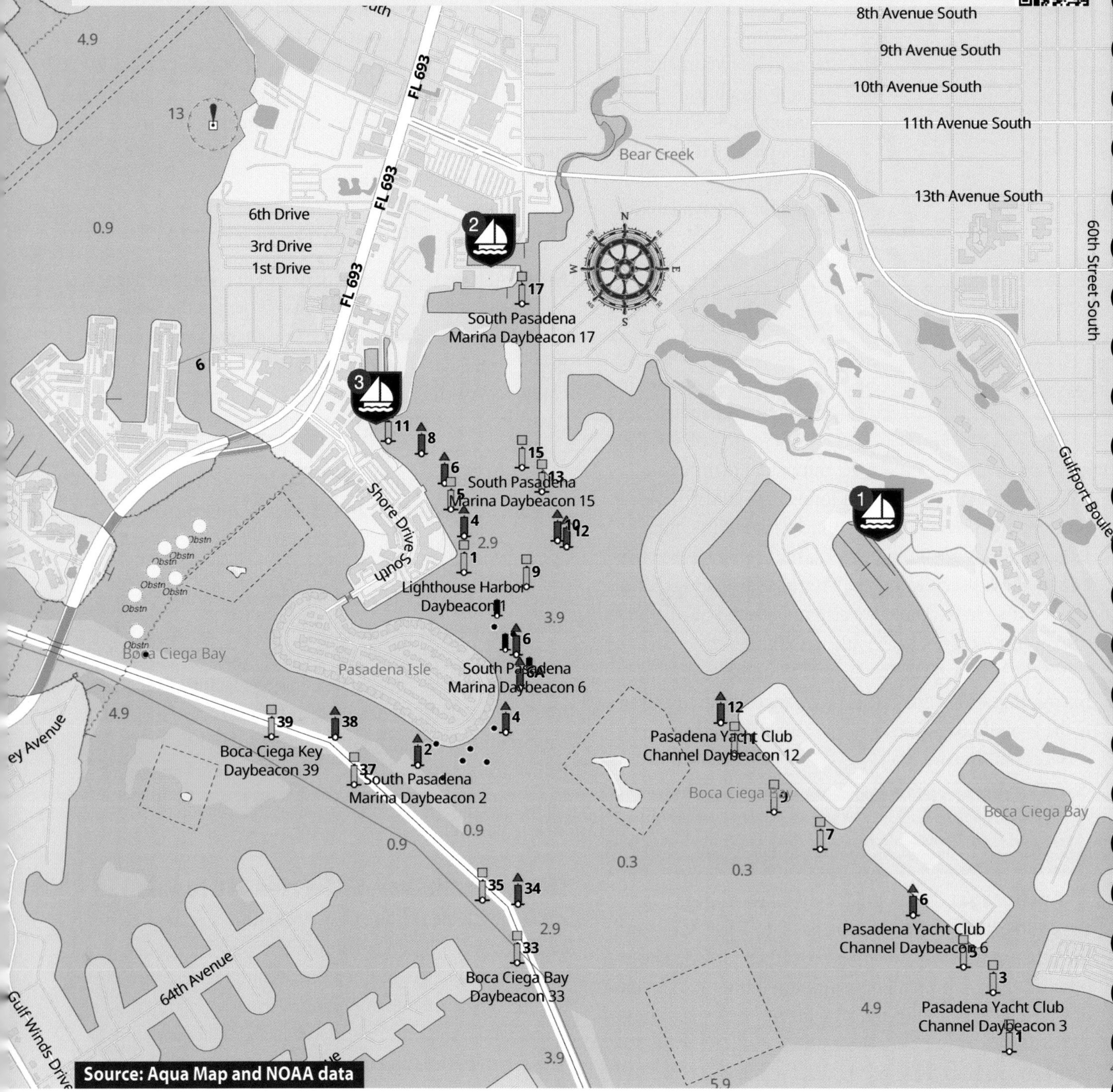

Source: Aqua Map and NOAA data

Boca Ciega Bay, FL

JOHNS PASS AREA		Largest Vessel	VHF	Total Slips	Approach/ Dockside Depth	Floating Docks	Gas/ Diesel	Repairs/ Haulout	Min/Max Amps	Pump-Out Station
1. Blind Pass Marina MM 118.5	(727) 360-4281	55	16	110	/	F		H	30 / 50	P

WiFi Wireless Internet Access **onSpot** Dockside WiFi Facility

Visit www.waterwayguide.com for current rates, fuel prices, website addresses and other up-to-the-minute information.
(Information in the table is provided by the facilities.)

Scan here for more details:

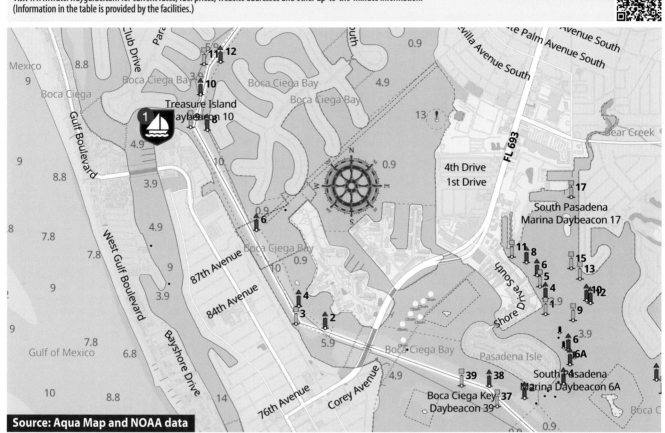

Source: Aqua Map and NOAA data

Boca Ciega Bay

Gulfport

Boca Ciega Bay, FL

JOHNS PASS AREA		Largest Vessel	VHF	Total Slips	Approach/ Dockside Depth	Floating Docks	Gas/ Diesel	Repairs/ Haulout	Min/Max Amps	Pump-Out Station
1. John's Pass Marina WiFi 1 mi. S of MM 121.4	(727) 367-3835	75	16	34	10.0 / 5.0	F	GD		30 / 50	
2. Madeira Bay Docks, Inc. WiFi	(727) 639-2862	80		44	8.0 / 10.0	F		RH	30 / 50	P
3. Snug Harbor Inn 1.0 mi. S of MM 121.4	(727) 395-9256	50		6	6.0 / 5.0			RH		

WiFi Wireless Internet Access   onSpot Dockside WiFi Facility
Visit www.waterwayguide.com for current rates, fuel prices, website addresses and other up-to-the-minute information.
(Information in the table is provided by the facilities.)

Scan here for more details:

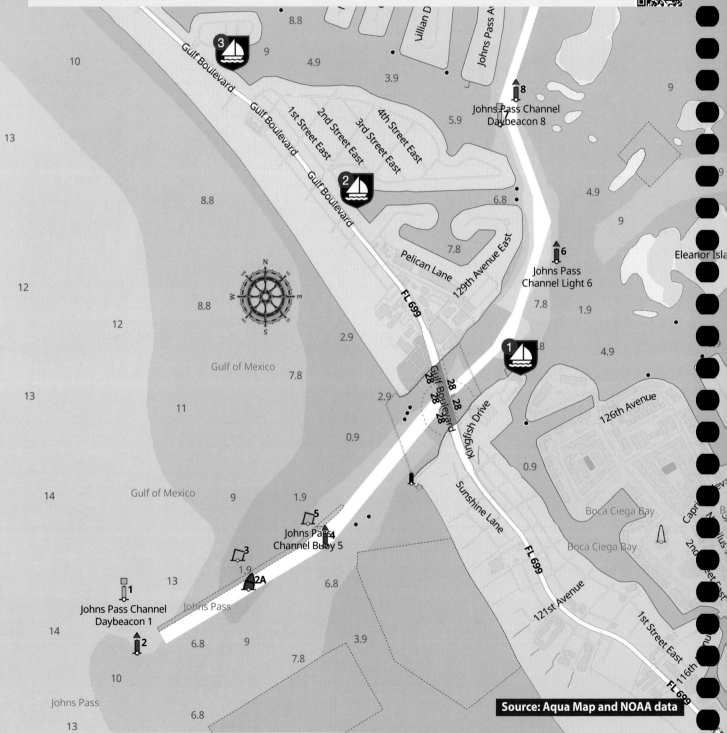

 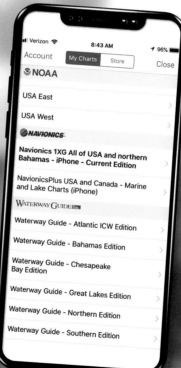 

Boca Ciega Bay, FL

JOHNS PASS AREA		Largest Vessel	VHF	Total Slips	Approach/ Dockside Depth	Floating Docks	Gas/ Diesel	Repairs/ Haulout	Min/Max Amps	Pump-Out Station
1. Madeira Beach Municipal Marina MM 122.2	(727) 399-2631	100	16	80	6.0 / 11.0	F	GD	R	30 / 50	P
2. Bay Pines Marina ⓦⓘⒻⓘ 1.5 mi. NE of MM 120.5	(727) 392-4922	50	16	60	5.0 / 7.0	F	G	RH	30 / 50	P

ⓦⓘⒻⓘ Wireless Internet Access   🔵onSpot Dockside WiFi Facility
Visit www.waterwayguide.com for current rates, fuel prices, website addresses and other up-to-the-minute information.
(Information in the table is provided by the facilities.)

Scan here for more details:

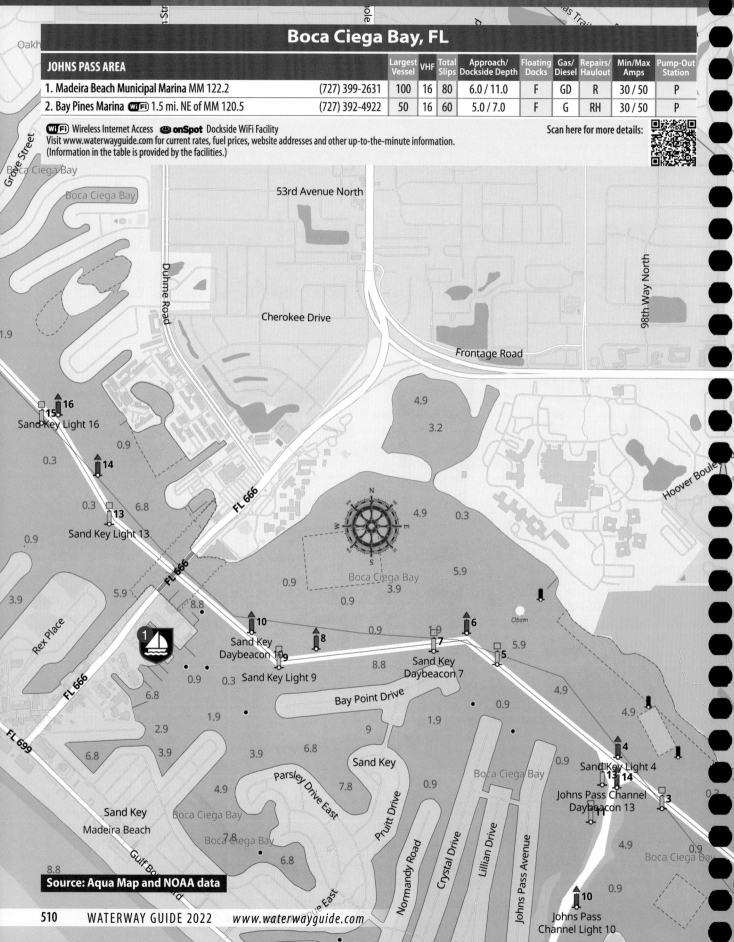

Source: Aqua Map and NOAA data

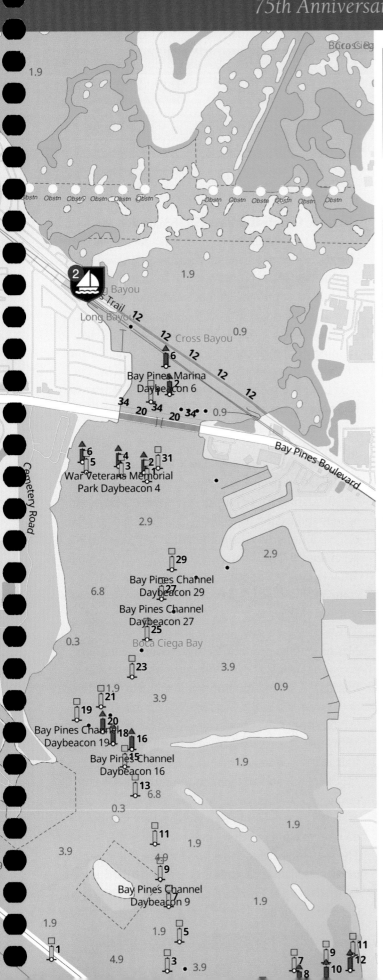

1.9

Clearwater Harbor, FL

INDIAN SHORES		Largest Vessel	VHF	Total Slips	Approach/ Dockside Depth	Floating Docks	Gas/ Diesel	Repairs/ Haulout	Min/Max Amps	Pump-Out Station
1. Indian Springs Marina MM 129.0	(727) 595-2956	40		48	4.5 / 4.5	F	G	RH	30	
2. Harbourside Marina (WiFi) MM 129.4	(727) 517-3652	70	16	50	8.0 / 6.0				30 / 50	
3. Largo Intercoastal Marina MM 129.6	(727) 595-3592	35		381	4.0 / 4.0	F	G	RH	50	P

(WiFi) Wireless Internet Access (onSpot) Dockside WiFi Facility
Visit www.waterwayguide.com for current rates, fuel prices, website addresses and other up-to-the-minute information.
(Information in the table is provided by the facilities.)

Scan here for more details:

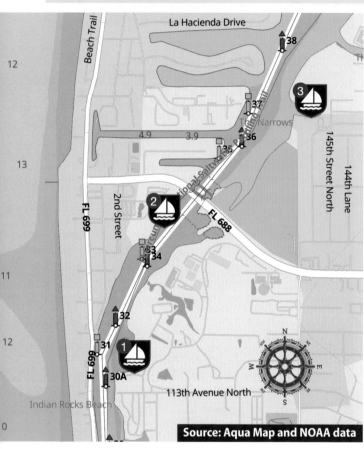

Source: Aqua Map and NOAA data

deep water and capable of handling the largest boats that travel the GIWW. Marinas and repair installations are busy but transient berths are generally available.

NAVIGATION: Use NOAA Chart 11411. At the northern end of the GIWW approaching Clearwater the waterway tends to narrow and bridges and shoaling become more frequent. Boats with significant draft should be very cautious. The best access to Clearwater from the Gulf of Mexico is through Clearwater Pass just south of Clearwater. This is one of the west coast's better daytime passes and it is easy to use in good weather. North of the causeway the channel has shoaled; proceed with caution.

When approaching from Clearwater Pass 16-foot-high, flashing red "8" is followed by the 74-foot fixed vertical

clearance **Clearwater Pass (SR183) Bridge**. At flashing red "14" turn north and into the channel marked by red daybeacon "2" and green daybeacon "3." A well-marked channel will take you to green daybeacon "9" where you will turn west into the channel leading to the Clearwater Municipal Marinas.

You can also turn east into the well-marked channel running parallel to the causeway to green daybeacon "1" where that channel merges with the GIWW. The next bridge to the north on the GIWW is **Clearwater Memorial Causeway (SR 60) Bridge** (74-foot fixed vertical clearance).

Dockage: Approaching from the GIWW channel, Clearwater Municipal Marinas (Clearwater Harbor Marina) is on the mainland side at green daybeacon "1." A sizable charter boat fleet is berthed here as well as tour and fishing boats of all sizes. The marina takes reservations and the helpful marina staff can usually accommodate transients on the floating docks. The Jolly Trolley (727-445-1200) stops in front of the marina complex and provides a convenient ride to the grocery store or the beach.

On the beach side, facilities include Chart House Marina and the private Clearwater Yacht Club (only accepting members of reciprocating yacht clubs in Florida). A second location of the municipal marina is at the west end of the Clearwater Memorial Causeway (SR 60) Bridge. A second city-owned facility, Clearwater Municipal Marinas (Clearwater Beach Marina), has ample transient space and all the usual amenities.

The beach and all the requisite surf shops, resort restaurants and souvenir stores are nearby. The celebration of sunset (much like in Key West) is held nightly at Pier 60 from two hours before until two hours after sunset. The festivities include street performers, crafts, outdoor movies and fabulous sunsets (weather permitting).

Anchorage: There are more anchoring choices in Clearwater Harbor than in Boca Ciega Bay beginning at

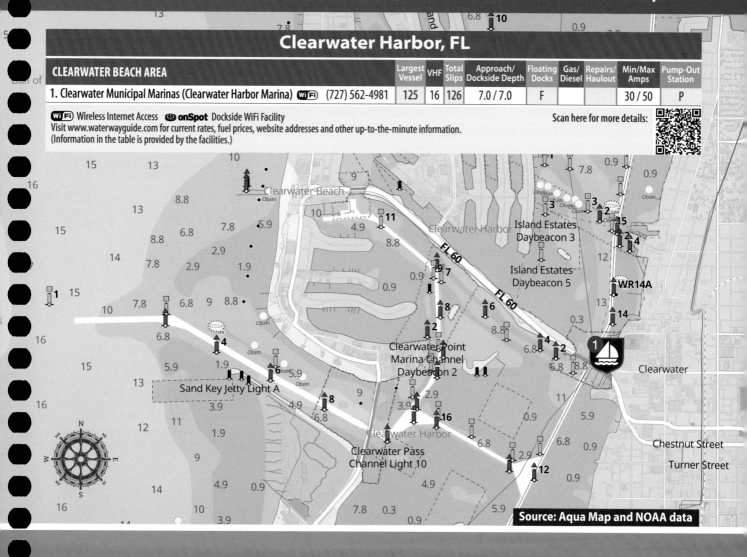

Clearwater Harbor, FL

CLEARWATER BEACH AREA	Largest Vessel	VHF	Total Slips	Approach/ Dockside Depth	Floating Docks	Gas/ Diesel	Repairs/ Haulout	Min/Max Amps	Pump-Out Station
1. Clearwater Municipal Marinas (Clearwater Harbor Marina) **WiFi** (727) 562-4981	125	16	126	7.0 / 7.0	F			30 / 50	P

WiFi Wireless Internet Access **onSpot** Dockside WiFi Facility
Visit www.waterwayguide.com for current rates, fuel prices, website addresses and other up-to-the-minute information.
(Information in the table is provided by the facilities.)

Scan here for more details:

Source: Aqua Map and NOAA data

(Chart labels) Clearwater Beach · Clearwater Harbor · Island Estates Daybeacon 3 · Island Estates Daybeacon 5 · WR14A · Clearwater Point Marina Channel Daybeacon 2 · Sand Key Jetty Light A · Clearwater Pass Channel Light 10 · Clearwater Harbor · Clearwater · Chestnut Street · Turner Street · FL 60

Clearwater Pass

Clearwater Harbor, FL

CLEARWATER BEACH AREA		Largest Vessel	VHF	Total Slips	Approach/ Dockside Depth	Floating Docks	Gas/ Diesel	Repairs/ Haulout	Min/Max Amps	Pump-Out Station
1. Chart House Marina WiFi	(727) 449-8007			26	7.0 / 7.0				30 / 50	
2. Clearwater Yacht Club WiFi MM 136.0	(727) 447-6000	70	16	42	7.0 / 7.0				30 / 50	
3. Clearwater Municipal Marinas (Clearwater Beach Marina) WiFi	(727) 562-4955 x2	125	16	207	7.0 / 12.0	F	GD		30 / 100	P

WiFi Wireless Internet Access **onSpot** Dockside WiFi Facility
Visit www.waterwayguide.com for current rates, fuel prices, website addresses and other up-to-the-minute information.
(Information in the table is provided by the facilities.)

Scan here for more details:

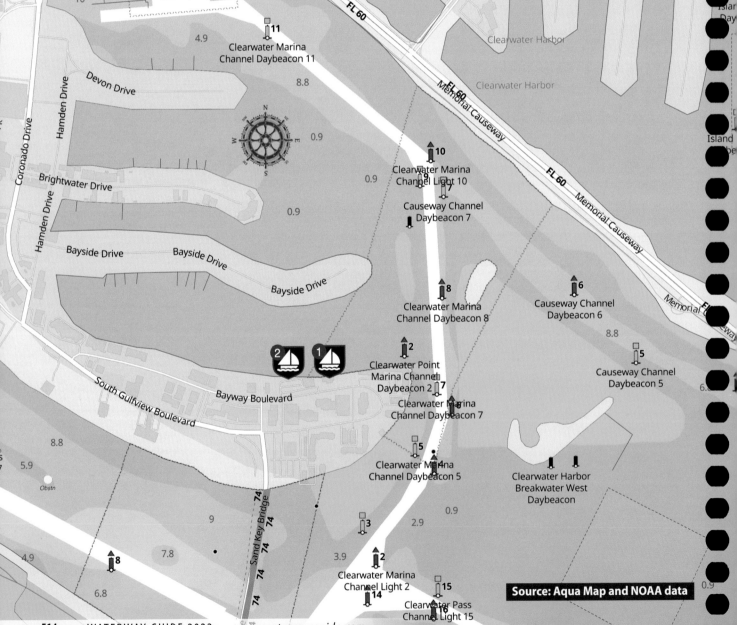

Source: Aqua Map and NOAA data

Clearwater Harbor, FL

DUNEDIN AREA		Largest Vessel	VHF	Total Slips	Approach/ Dockside Depth	Floating Docks	Gas/ Diesel	Repairs/ Haulout	Min/Max Amps	Pump-Out Station
1. Dunedin Municipal Marina MM 139.0	(727) 298-3030	70	16	194	5.0 / 4.5				30 / 50	P

WiFi Wireless Internet Access **onSpot** Dockside WiFi Facility
Visit www.waterwayguide.com for current rates, fuel prices, website addresses and other up-to-the-minute information.
(Information in the table is provided by the facilities.)

Scan here for more details:

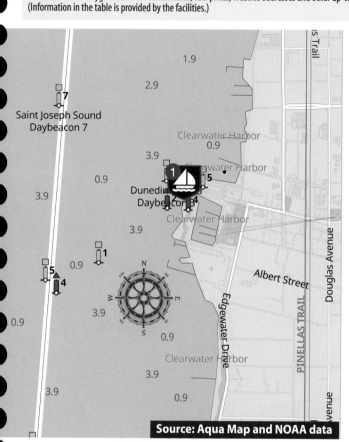

Saint Joseph Sound
Daybeacon 7

Clearwater Harbor

Dunedin
Daybeacon

Clearwater Harbor

Clearwater Harbor

Albert Street

Douglas Avenue

Edgewater Drive

PINELLAS TRAIL

Clearwater Harbor

Source: Aqua Map and NOAA data

GIWW Mile 131.9. On the northern side of the **Belleair Beach Causeway Bridge** (75-foot fixed vertical clearance) you will find 7 to 8 feet MLW with good holding in sand. There is about a 3-foot tide here. Use bow and stern anchors to ride the wakes from the nearby launch ramp and the GIWW.

Clearwater Yacht Club has an anchorage with 6 to 9 feet MLW. You can also anchor on either side of the west side of the **SR 60 (Clearwater Harbor) Bridge** (14-foot fixed vertical clearance) in 6 to 10 feet MLW.

Dunedin Area–GIWW Mile 136 to Mile 150

St. Joseph Sound is home to Dunedin and several beaches including Honeymoon Island and Caladesi Island State Park (accessible only by boat). Dunedin is one of the few open waterfront communities from Sarasota to Cedar Key where buildings do not completely obscure the view of

the waterway and the Gulf of Mexico beyond from the highway. There is also a lack of large commercial signage to obscure the view and no franchise restaurants or chain retail stores.

> Pinellas Trail, a 39-mile-long bicycle and pedestrian trail that traverses Pinellas County, bisects downtown Dunedin. A large portion of the trail lies on the former roadbed of the Orange Belt Railway, the first railroad in Pinellas County, which arrived in 1888.

NAVIGATION: Use NOAA Chart 11411. The **Dunedin Causeway Drawbridge** (opens on signal) crosses the GIWW at Mile 141.9. The bridge has an observed closed vertical clearance of 18 feet even though it is charted as 24-foot vertical clearance.

> ⚠ The Coast Guard has made several changes to the aids to navigation in this area that may not be reflected on older NOAA charts. Proceed with caution.

Dockage: Dunedin Municipal Marina has a busy boat ramp, day docks and transient slips and is within walking distance to Dunedin's restaurants and shopping. Loggerhead Marina–Marker 1 Marina offers slips and dry racks and caters to sportfishing vessels. Located immediately south of the Dunedin Causeway Drawbridge, this facility is close to downtown Dunedin with good restaurants and groceries as well as the Pinellas Trail.

To the north of the bridge is Palm Harbor, which is shown on the NOAA chart as "Smith Bayou." This is not cruise boat territory (slips to 42 feet maximum). To access the facilities here turn east at green daybeacon "17" and follow the privately marked channel toward the large dry stack buildings. Home Port Marina has slips (to 42 feet) and a marine service center and is the site of the popular waterfront Ozona Blue Grilling Co. (727-789-4540).

George's Marina is on the northeast side of the harbor with slips to 40 feet. Ozona Fish Camp to the north can accommodate vessels to just 37 feet.

Clearwater Harbor, FL

DUNEDIN AREA			Largest Vessel	VHF	Total Slips	Approach/ Dockside Depth	Floating Docks	Gas/ Diesel	Repairs/ Haulout	Min/Max Amps	Pump-Out Station
1. Loggerhead Marina - Marker 1 **WiFi** 0.5 mi. E of MM 141.5	(727) 733-9324		65	16	150	6.0 / 6.0		GD		30 / 50	P

WiFi Wireless Internet Access **onSpot** Dockside WiFi Facility

Visit www.waterwayguide.com for current rates, fuel prices, website addresses and other up-to-the-minute information. (Information in the table is provided by the facilities.)

Scan here for more details:

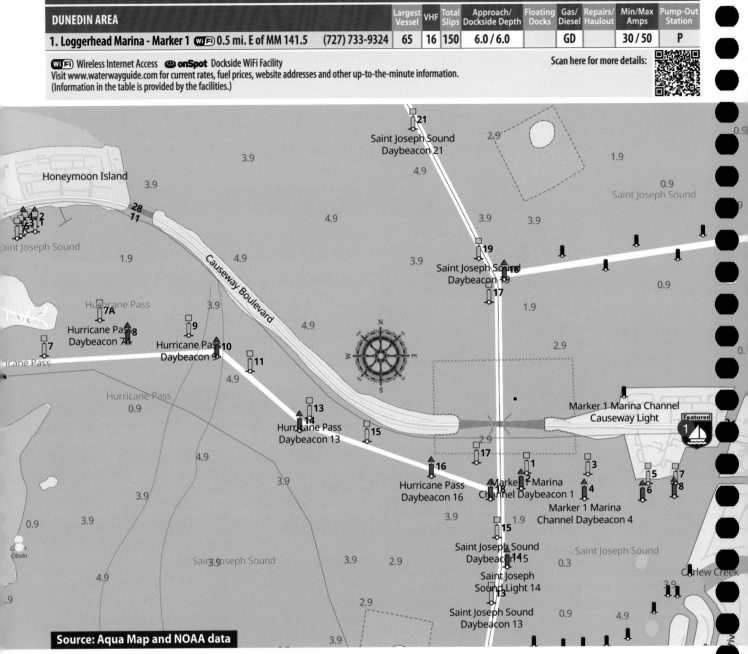

Source: Aqua Map and NOAA data

Side Trip: Caladesi Island State Park

Caladesi Island State Park has trails and a quiet beach that is rated among the best in the world. There are 108 slips in the isolated Caladesi Island State Park Marina. To get to Caladesi Island turn west just south of the Dunedin Causeway Drawbridge (green daybeacon "17") and then follow the Honeymoon Island Channel to a separate buoyed channel into Seven Mouth Creek. Only three slips here are wider than 11 feet; however, there are three "T" docks for larger boats. Average depths on the approach

and dockside are reported at 4 feet MLW so you may need to travel at high tide, go slowly and obtain up-to-date local knowledge. This is a great place to tuck away for a day or two or just visit for a night. Call ahead for reservations.

Anclote Key–GIWW Mile 150

About 3 miles north of Clearwater the barrier islands fall away and the GIWW enters unprotected St. Joseph Sound and the approach to Anclote Key. After this final stretch on the GIWW boaters continuing north beyond Anclote Key

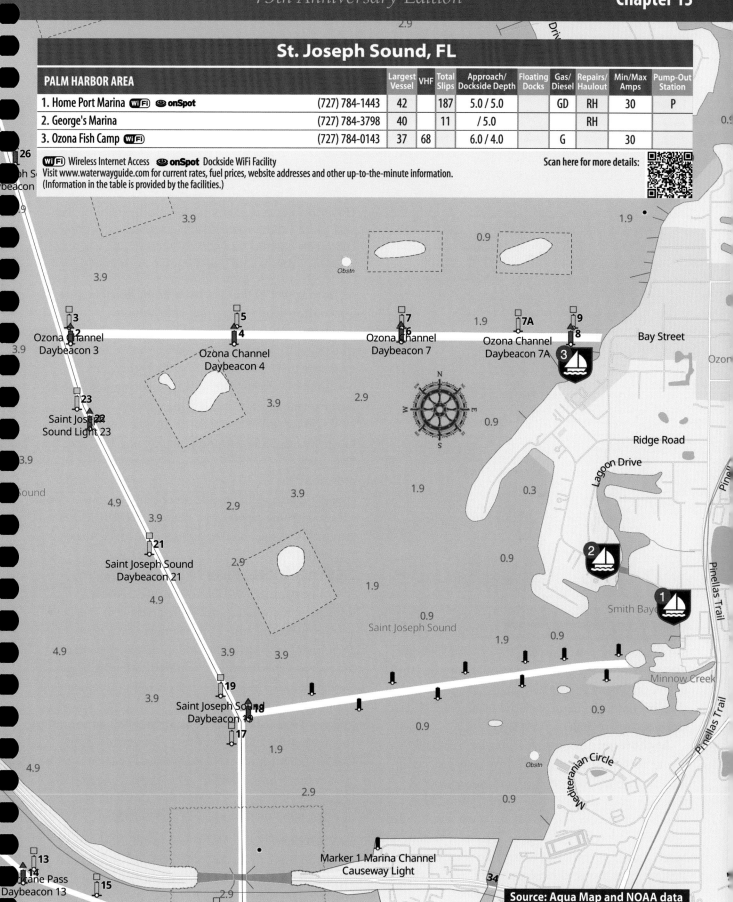

St. Joseph Sound, FL

PALM HARBOR AREA		Largest Vessel	VHF	Total Slips	Approach/ Dockside Depth	Floating Docks	Gas/ Diesel	Repairs/ Haulout	Min/Max Amps	Pump-Out Station
1. Home Port Marina **WiFi** ● onSpot	(727) 784-1443	42		187	5.0 / 5.0		GD	RH	30	P
2. George's Marina	(727) 784-3798	40		11	/ 5.0			RH		
3. Ozona Fish Camp **WiFi**	(727) 784-0143	37	68		6.0 / 4.0		G		30	

WiFi Wireless Internet Access   ● onSpot Dockside WiFi Facility
Visit www.waterwayguide.com for current rates, fuel prices, website addresses and other up-to-the-minute information.
(Information in the table is provided by the facilities.)

Scan here for more details:

Source: Aqua Map and NOAA data

Clearwater Harbor, FL

DUNEDIN AREA		Largest Vessel	VHF	Total Slips	Approach/ Dockside Depth	Floating Docks	Gas/ Diesel	Repairs/ Haulout	Min/Max Amps	Pump-Out Station
1. Caladesi Island State Park Marina	(727) 469-5918			108	4.0 / 4.0	F			30	

WiFi Wireless Internet Access **onSpot** Dockside WiFi Facility

Visit www.waterwayguide.com for current rates, fuel prices, website addresses and other up-to-the-minute information. (Information in the table is provided by the facilities.)

Scan here for more details:

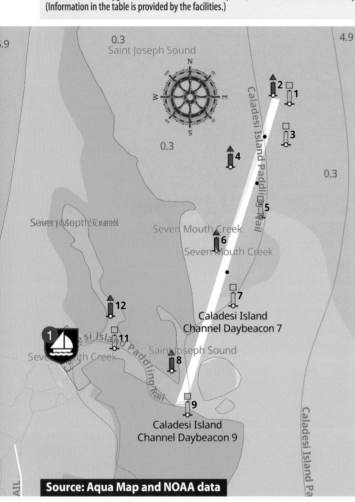

Source: Aqua Map and NOAA data

and the Anclote River have two choices: You may cross the open Gulf of Mexico for about 140 nm to Carrabelle or you can follow a series of several markers relatively close in-shore around the Big Bend section of Florida for about 160 or 165 miles to Carrabelle.

Anchorage: A popular anchorage in St. Joseph Sound is Three Rooker Bar, a narrow C-shaped island located between Honeymoon Island and Anclote Key about 2.5 miles offshore from Tarpon Springs. Three Rooker's white sand beaches line the north and seaward sides of the island and offer some of the best shelling and beachcombing anywhere. The bay side of the island's shallow water teems with fish and birds. This is a well-protected anchorage from all but east winds.

Enter the anchorage around the north end of the bar, being careful to avoid shoaling encroaching on the navigable channel near red daybeacon "36" where depths as low as 2 to 5 feet MLW have been reported.

Drop anchor in the crescent near the beach in 4- to 8-foot MLW depths over a soft mud bottom. Use the depth sounder and line-of-sight navigation to avoid the white sand bars that run out from the beach. On holiday weekends this normally placid anchorage becomes a maelstrom of activity with jet skis, small outboards and a floating hamburger stand all vying for space.

It is also possible to anchor at Anclote Key (Mile 151) in 8 to 10 feet MLW with excellent holding and protection from the west. Anclote Key Preserve State Park has no provisions but the 403-acre park is home to at least 43 species of birds including the American oystercatcher, bald eagle and piping plover. A picturesque 1887 lighthouse stands as a sentinel on the southern end of the island.

Side Trip: Anclote River to Tarpon Springs

In reality, there are two Tarpon Springs. Both are intimately interrelated and well worth a visit. The sponge docks, the unbroken string of Greek restaurants and charming shops along Dodecanese Boulevard and the marinas are one aspect, while the other (historic downtown Tarpon Springs) is a charming complement to the docks. From November to early spring you will find manatees make their home in the shallow Spring Bayou close to downtown. Craig Park offers a great vantage point for observing these gentle giants. It only takes a short dinghy ride to get to the Bayou but it becomes a non-motorized area so you will need to row in and around the bayou to view the manatees.

NAVIGATION: Use NOAA Chart 11411. A range helps you through the big offshore shoal around the entrance to the Anclote River. (If you cannot see the onshore light, locate quick-flashing green "1.") Channel

Anclote River, FL

TARPON SPRINGS AREA		Largest Vessel	VHF	Total Slips	Approach/ Dockside Depth	Floating Docks	Gas/ Diesel	Repairs/ Haulout	Min/Max Amps	Pump-Out Station
1. Anclote Village Marina (WiFi) MM 150.0	(727) 937-9737	55		20	5.0 / 7.0	F	GD	R	30 / 50	

(WiFi) Wireless Internet Access (onSpot) **onSpot** Dockside WiFi Facility
Visit www.waterwayguide.com for current rates, fuel prices, website addresses and other up-to-the-minute information.
(Information in the table is provided by the facilities.)

Scan here for more details:

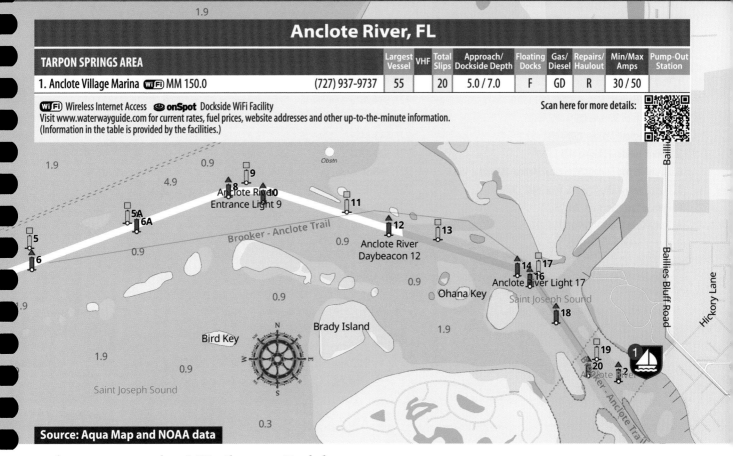

Source: Aqua Map and NOAA data

markers are no more than 0.75 miles apart. For help in orienting you will see a tall, power plant chimney on the north side of the Anclote River entrance visible from 22 nm at sea (on a clear day). The chimney, illuminated by flashing lights at night, is plotted on NOAA Chart 11411 ("STACK") and mentioned in the U.S. Coast Pilot.

Respect the shoal south of Anclote Key. When entering the GIWW south of Anclote Key or entering the Anclote River give flashing green "7" near Mile 150 a wide berth. Older charts may not show the extension of the shoal southward. When traveling in this area it is important to keep your charts current and your depthsounder on. Refer to the latest NOAA charts for the most up-to-date information.

Take it easy going upriver the 3 miles to Tarpon Springs and observe the posted Idle-Speed/No-Wake Zone. There are many boats at slips in the river and your wake can cause serious damage. Commercial fishing and sponging boats also use the channel. The Cut C range's eastern mark is partially obscured by trees. Favor the southern side of the channel to avoid the shoal.

Severe shoaling has been observed in the vicinity of Anclote River turning basin daybeacons "51" and "53" at Tarpon Springs. Mariners are advised to use extreme caution while transiting the area.

Dockage: Just as you enter the river on the northeast side is the 20-slip Anclote Village Marina. With some transient slips and "high and dry" storage for smaller boats this is a convenient stopping place if you do not have time to go upriver. Opposite green daybeacon "39" on the northeast side, Port Tarpon Marina has a convenient fuel dock just off the river channel and transient slips. The on-site restaurant, Davidsons Dockside (727-487-0100), serves breakfast, lunch and dinner daily. Next door, Anclote Harbors Marina welcomes cruising boats up to 45 feet.

In a basin to the east the full-service Anclote Isles Marina can accommodate vessels to 85 feet and has all the usual amenities. The 18-slip Belle Harbour Marina has a few slips and storage options. Pitman Yacht Services is located on a peninsula next to Belle Harbour, a full-service

Anclote River, FL

TARPON SPRINGS AREA		Largest Vessel	VHF	Total Slips	Approach/ Dockside Depth	Floating Docks	Gas/ Diesel	Repairs/ Haulout	Min/Max Amps	Pump-Out Station
1. Port Tarpon Marina **WiFi** MM 150.0	(727) 937-2200	75	16	58	9.0 / 9.0	F	GD	RH	50 / 100	
2. Anclote Harbors Marina **WiFi** MM 150.0	(727) 934-7616	45	16	30	9.0 / 6.0		G	RH	30 / 50	
3. Anclote Isles Marina **WiFi** MM 150.0	(727) 939-0100	85	16	70	8.0 / 7.0				30 / 100	P
4. Belle Harbour Marina **WiFi** MM 150.0	(727) 943-8489	50	16	18	6.0 / 5.0	F	G	RH	30 / 50	P
5. Tarpon Landing Marina MM 150.0	(727) 937-1100	65		50	5.0 / 6.0		GD	R	30 / 50	P
6. City of Tarpon Springs Municipal Marina **WiFi** MM 150.0	(727) 946-5658	50	16	21	11.0 / 10.0				30 / 50	
7. River Energy- The New F & Y Inc. MM 150.0	(727) 937-4351	200	1		12.0 / 12.0		D		50	
8. Pitman Yacht Services MM 150.0	(727) 942-1495	45			10.0 / 6.0		GD	RH	50	
9. Turtle Cove Marina **WiFi** MM 150.0	(727) 934-2202	50	16	56	5.0 / 6.0	F	GD	H	30 / 50	P
10. Tarpon Springs Yacht Club	(727) 934-2136	60		18	/					

WiFi Wireless Internet Access **onSpot** Dockside WiFi Facility
Visit www.waterwayguide.com for current rates, fuel prices, website addresses and other up-to-the-minute information.
(Information in the table is provided by the facilities.)

Scan here for more details:

Source: Aqua Map and NOAA data

boat yard and yacht maintenance facility offering all types of restorations and repairs.

Staying at any of the marinas on the north side of the river means you will need to arrange for transportation if you wish to get to the sponge docks and restaurants, most of which are on the south side of the river. The exception is Tarpon Landing Marina from which sponge docks and Greek restaurants are a short walk across the fixed **SR 19 Alternate Hwy. Bridge** to the south side of the river. The marina caters to anglers and weekend boaters. (Call ahead.) Capt'n Jack's Waterfront Bar and Grille (727-944-3346) is at the head of the slips with casual dining in a tropical atmosphere.

At the end of the navigable portion of the river the City of Tarpon Springs Municipal Marina is on the south side of the river. Its location at the east end of the sponge docks is ideal for exploring Tarpon Springs. Reservations are a must.

River Energy–The New F & Y Inc. is an oil company with a 200-foot marine dock for refueling (diesel only). They can accept vessels to 200 feet at their docks. Call ahead.

To reach the full-service Turtle Cove Marina, turn and follow the channel, favoring the north side. The marina channel (to port) is marked with private floating reds and greens. Stay in the channel. After about 100 yards it opens up into the marina area. Turtle Cove Marina is a full-service facility with floating docks and pump-out service at every slip.

Tarpon Springs Yacht Club, located before the Beckett Bridge (25-foot vertical clearance), is private but welcomes members of reciprocating yacht clubs.

Anchorage: An anchorage with 6-foot MLW depths is located by the river's entrance east of green daybeacon "17" at Anclote River just beyond the power plant stack. There is a nearby park with a boat ramp and restrooms.

Up the river in Tarpon Springs some boats anchor in front of the City of Tarpon Springs Municipal Marina but shoaling and traffic may be a problem and it is not recommended.

■ NEXT STOP

Mile 150 at Tarpon Springs on the Anclote River marks the end of the Florida GIWW. The GIWW picks back up in Carrabelle, FL, where mileages are measured from the east (EHL) and west (EHL) of Harvey Lock, LA. Beyond Anclote Key lies the intriguing Big Bend (or Nature Coast).

Sponge Diver Memorial in Tarpon Springs

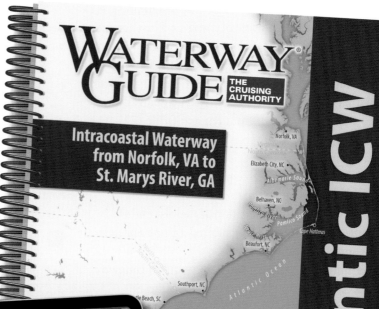

Section 4

Upper Gulf Coast

Chapter 14: The Big Bend: Anclote Key to Carrabelle **Chapter 16:** Mobile Bay, AL to Bay St. Louis, MS
Chapter 15: The Florida Panhandle

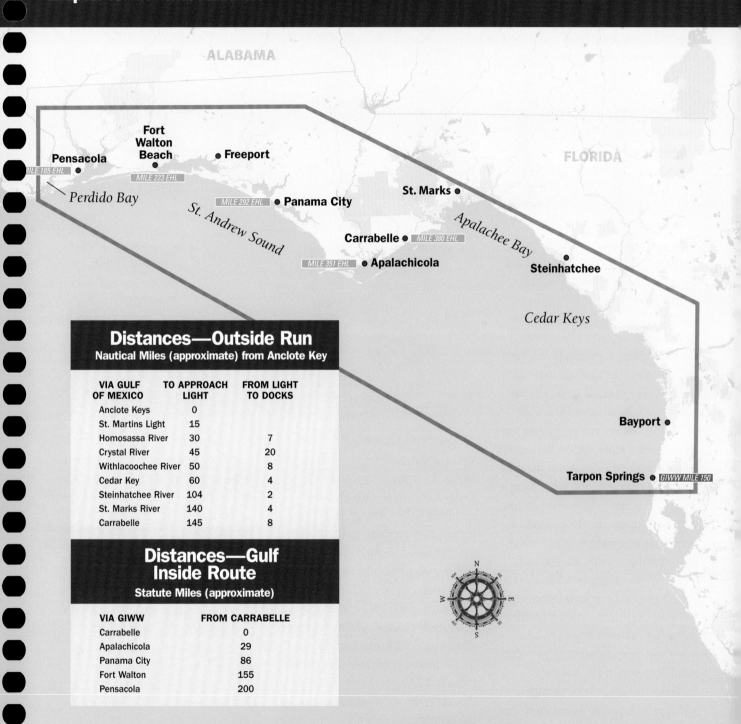

ALABAMA

FLORIDA

Fort
Walton
Beach
Freeport

Pensacola
MILE 185 EHL
MILE 223 EHL

St. Marks

Perdido Bay

St. Andrew Sound
MILE 292 EHL Panama City

Carrabelle *MILE 380 EHL*

Apalachee Bay

MILE 351 EHL Apalachicola

Steinhatchee

Cedar Keys

Distances—Outside Run
Nautical Miles (approximate) from Anclote Key

VIA GULF OF MEXICO	TO APPROACH LIGHT	FROM LIGHT TO DOCKS
Anclote Keys	0	
St. Martins Light	15	
Homosassa River	30	7
Crystal River	45	20
Withlacoochee River	50	8
Cedar Key	60	4
Steinhatchee River	104	2
St. Marks River	140	4
Carrabelle	145	8

Bayport

Tarpon Springs *GIWW MILE 150*

Distances—Gulf Inside Route
Statute Miles (approximate)

VIA GIWW	FROM CARRABELLE
Carrabelle	0
Apalachicola	29
Panama City	86
Fort Walton	155
Pensacola	200

ICW Mile 150-Mile 350 EHL

■ NAVIGATION NOTES

The 350-nm stretch from the Anclote Keys to Carrabelle across the Big Bend (also called "The Nature Coast") has no protected inside route. To transit the Big Bend area mariners must make the trip across open waters in the Gulf of Mexico. For the second half, from Carrabelle on to Florida's Panhandle, you can travel the GIWW (inside) or continue outside in the Gulf. The more interesting GIWW route connects big bays and sounds that are protected by narrow, wooded barrier islands.

Along the west coast shore from Anclote Key almost to Carrabelle the Gulf of Mexico is relatively shallow and the coastline low and indistinct. It is possible to safely make the Big Bend Passage and never lose sight of land. If you are running along the shore, keep a close eye on the depth sounder and tide charts and the little buoys for crab pots and lobster traps.

This is a fine sailing area but boats with deep drafts should be wary of the shoals and reefs, many of which are oyster bars, some littered with rocks. When sailing in difficult waters for which you have little knowledge and past experience, it may be safer to be farther out than nearer to land.

Brown pelicans are tricky neighbors here. They have a tendency to deface buoy numbers and a pelican perched on a green can buoy may, from a distance, change the outline to that of a red nun buoy. Get in the habit of checking floating marks carefully.

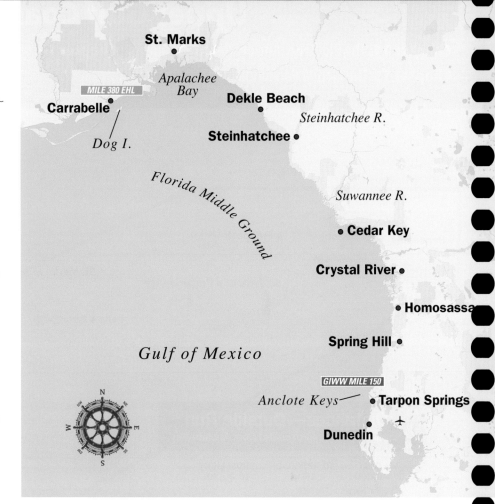

The Coast Guard station on the Withlacoochee River at Yankeetown (about 17 miles southeast of Cedar Key) covers this area and monitors VHF Channel 16. This station also operates and maintains three vessels for emergency search and rescue. In addition to VHF, the station can be reached by telephone at 352-447-6900.

A small change in latitude creates a perceptible difference in the weather of this region compared to southern Florida. The upper Gulf Coast of Florida is the only coastal section of the state that experiences a noticeable winter. Depending on the marine facility and location, boating season in the Upper Gulf Coast may run from Memorial Day to Labor Day. It gets chilly in the winter but it is still possible to enjoy these uncrowded, clear waters, award-winning beaches and boating-oriented communities.

NO WAKE ZONE

No Wake Zones, Idle Speed Zones and various Speed Limit restrictions are in effect throughout the waterways included in this chapter. Exercise diligence in knowing the regulations by observing signs and other markers. Enforcement is always present. As always, be courteous to other vessels and avoid manatees and other marine life.

Choice of Routes

A trip through the Big Bend starts with making choices regarding your route:

1. Travel an outside route in deeper water from Anclote Key or Clearwater Beach. Plan your arrival for daylight. Weather will be a serious consideration. You need a boat capable of the offshore passage and a captain and crew with the ability and confidence to make the voyage.

2. Travel an inside route closer to shore and find safe harbor before dark. Chart a careful course and do not travel after sunset. These are shallow waters! Know where you are going to go, how you are going to get there and the condition of the water all along the route before you leave the dock.

NAVIGATION: Use NOAA Chart 1114A. Let's start by drawing course lines. Most of your cruising will be in Gulf waters so all distances are measured in nautical miles (nm). All routes will start from Anclote Key's 16-foot high, flashing red buoy "2" at N 28° 15.089'/W 82° 52.896'. Its location is 2.6 nm at 290° from the north end of Anclote Key or 2.6 nm at 277° from 15-foot high, flashing red "4."

Along both direct offshore routes you will be as much as 45 nm from land. Channel entrances to find shelter from weather are probably too far away and too dangerous to navigate in inclement weather. Waiting for an agreeable weather window will make a big difference in the comfort and safety of your trip along this course. The average cruising boat may want to wait for winds that are less than 10 knots with sea conditions less than 4 feet. Westerly winds are the least desirable. If winds are blowing greater than 15 knots, wait 24 hours after they fall below 10 knots before you depart.

Outside Route from Anclote Key to Carrabelle:

From Anclote Key's 16-foot high, flashing red "2" draw a rhumb line all the way to East Pass's Carrabelle Channel flashing red buoy "2" at N 29° 44.541'/W 84° 39.199'. The distance is 130 nm at a course of 313° magnetic.

Outside Route from Clearwater to Carrabelle:

From the west end of Clearwater Pass's 20-foot flashing green "1" at N 27° 58.270'/W 82° 50.840' draw a rhumb line to Carrabelle Channel flashing red buoy "2." This course will take you 142.5 nm on a course of 323° magnetic.

Inside Route:

1. Anclote Key's 16-foot high, flashing red "2" to St Martins Outer Shoal 16-foot high, lighted buoy flashing red "10" at N 28° 25.864'/W 82° 55.076'. The distance is 11 nm on a course of 354° magnetic.

2. St. Martins Outer Shoal 16-foot high, flashing red "10" to Crystal River flashing red buoy "2" at N 28°.47.542'/W 82°.58.571' (13 nm west of Homosasssa). The distance is 21.4 nm on a course of 350° magnetic.

3. Crystal River flashing red "2" to Seahorse Reef's 31-foot high, flashing white at N 28° 58.518'/W 83° 09.182'. Do not get too close to this light as it marks a shoal. The distance is 14.4 nm on a course of 319° magnetic.

4. Seahorse Reef's 31-foot high, flashing white to Ochlockonee Shoal's flashing red buoy "24" at N 29° 51.485'/W 84° 10.318'. The distance is 75 nm at a course of 314° magnetic.

5. Ochlockonee Shoal's flashing red buoy "24" to Carrabelle Channel flashing red buoy "2" at N 29° 44.541'/W 84° 39.199'. The distance is 26 nm on a course of 254° magnetic.

Note: A rhumb line follows the shortest distance between two points on the globe, which isn't always the same thing as the shortest distance across a stretched-flat Mercator chart. The more area a chart covers, the less likely it is that a straight line produces the shortest route.

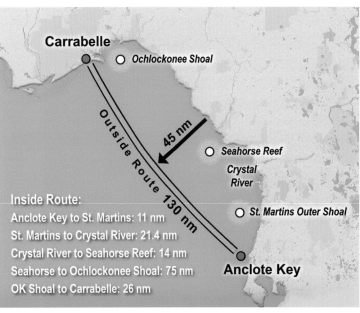

Planning Your Stops

For vessels traveling along an inside route by day consider the following as possible ports for shelter before the sun goes down. Do not attempt to enter these channels after the sun goes down. All distances are total daily nautical miles from point of departure to an anchorage or marina at the end of each day.

Daily distance of approximately 50 nm:

1. Anclote Key to Hernando Beach*–25 nm
2. Hernando Beach to Crystal River–50 nm
3. Crystal River to Yankeetown–30 nm
4. Yankeetown to Suwannee River–50 nm
5. Suwannee to Steinhatchee–40 nm
6. Steinhatchee to St. Marks–60 nm
7. St. Marks to East Pass–40 nm

(*Note: It is possible to go directly from Hernando Beach to Yankeetown, a distance of 50 nm. The channel is shallow and it can take more time to find deep water and work your way in to the Withlacoochee River.)

Daily distance of approximately 60 nm:

1. Anclote Key to Crystal River–55 nm
2. Crystal River to Suwannee River–55 nm
3. Suwannee River to Steinhatchee–40 nm
4. Steinhatchee to St. Marks–60 nm
5. St. Marks to East Pass–45 nm

(Alternate Route)
Daily distance of approximately 60 nm:

1. Anclote Key to Yankeetown–55 nm
2. Yankeetown to Suwannee–50 nm
3. Suwannee River to Steinhatchee–40 nm
4. Steinhatchee to East Pass–70 nm

Daily distance of approximately 80 nm:

1. Anclote to Suwannee River–75 nm
2. Suwannee River to Steinhatchee–40 nm
3. Steinhatchee to East Pass–70 nm

(Note that it is possible to go directly from Suwannee to East Pass, a distance of 90 nm.)

Electronic charting has made rhumb lines easy to create but it is more complicated for those going long distances using small scale paper charts. To plot a rhumb line by hand cut all the meridians at the same angle.

Chart your course as you navigate. It is unlikely that your compass course will be exactly as those above. Keep a constant eye on your depth. Watch your time. These are difficult waters to navigate at night.

⚠️ It is advisable to call ahead and ask for local knowledge if possible. Navigational information about shoals, location of river channels, aids to navigation and water depths are ever changing. Electronic charts are updated regularly but not after every storm. Remember that the only true, up-to-date indicator of depth comes from your depth sounder.

You can plot a course closer to shore by using entrance buoys to the various river channels. The caveat here is to make sure when plotting the course that your bearing does not carry you over shoals your vessel cannot negotiate. If weather is fair and winds are no more than 10 to 15 knots from the east, northeast or southeast, seas should be less than 4 feet.

Option: Offshore Crossing to St. George Island

You can travel outside in the Gulf of Mexico by following the coastline all the way to Pensacola. If you don't plan to cruise the Big Bend area, running the 130- to 140-nm rhumb line directly from Tarpon Springs or Clearwater to the St. George Island East Pass entrance buoy for Carrabelle can save a lot of time but only an able boat enjoying good weather should attempt this passage. Many cruisers prefer to follow a route closer to the coastline. The Big Bend markers that provided an inshore route closer to the coastline have been discontinued but there are channel entrance markers that can be used to run a course closer to shore.

Before setting out make sure your boat is seaworthy and your engine is sound. Know your compass error. Have the latest charts on board. There have been numerous changes to the navigation aids in recent years. Plot your courses carefully and stick to them along this route. The land is low lying and it can be a long stretch between the navigation aids as you traverse this coastline. Always track your position by both dead reckoning and GPS.

There are some remote sections of this coast and even though you are not far offshore, you may be far from help. A registered Emergency Position Indicating Radio Beacon (EPIRB) is an excellent addition to your safety equipment.

Unless you are very experienced run only in daylight. It is particularly important to have daylight while you are within 20 nm or so off the Florida coast as the crab pots can be very thick.

■ TO CEDAR KEY

Anclote Key to St. Martins Outer Shoal (Homosassa)

St. Martins Reef runs along the coast north from Anclote Key for some 40 nm. The shoals of this reef extend over 10 nm offshore. St. Martins Outer Shoal 16-foot high, flashing red "10" marks the outer limit of the shallow water. Many of the rocks and shoals are identified by private markers. Cruisers without local knowledge should approach the coast with care and deep-draft vessels should stand out in deeper waters. Smaller boats with drafts of 3 to 4 feet can usually follow the coast and find smooth water by keeping about 7 nm offshore.

Hernando Beach is a potential stop between Anclote and Crystal River. This is a small community with restaurants within walking distance and Hernando Beach Marina has a small Ship's Store.

The Homosassa River is another possible stopover, although it is a comparatively narrow and shallow waterway with winding channels and unforgiving oyster bars and rock beds. It has some great fishing for both salt and freshwater species, thanks to the headwater springs. This phenomenon is possible because the mineral content in the spring water resembles minerals found in salt water. The village of Homosassa is an attractive fishing center that grows more popular each year. More than 20 fishing guides operate year-round. Fishers should remember that the river qualifies as freshwater so a fishing license is required.

NAVIGATION: Use NOAA Chart 11409. To reach Hernando Beach travel the distance from Anclote Key's 16-foot high, flashing red "2" to St Martins Outer Shoal 16-foot high, flashing red "10" for 11 nm at 350° magnetic. From St. Martins Outer Shoal 16-foot high, flashing red "10" set a course of 60° magnetic for 8.5 nm to the private Oc flashing 14-foot marker. Then proceed 3.5 nm at 58° magnetic to a point where you can turn toward the Hernando Beach Channel. The channel entrance is 1 nm at 142° magnetic. Controlling channel depth is reported as 4 feet MLW; however, mariners with local knowledge say it is common for boats with drafts of 5 feet to use the channel.

For Homosassa from St. Martins Outer Shoal 16-foot high, flashing red "10" set a course of 18° magnetic for 16.5 nm to Homosassa Bay entrance 16-foot high, flashing red buoy "2" at N 28° 41.435'/W 82° 48.641'. Keep a close eye on your depth. Avoid the shoals to the southeast between that and red daybeacon "2A." Steer a careful, direct course between the first three reds as there are shallows to both sides.

The route winds its way to the fishing village of Homosassa about 4 miles upriver. The channel into the Homosassa River is narrow and shallow with depths reported from 3.5 to 7 feet MLW. Be aware that you may encounter many fast moving small fishing boats.

Local mariners report depths of 3 feet MLW at what they call "Hells Gate," a very narrow passage close to the entrance of the marked channel to Homosassa. Proceed with great care. Currents can be strong.

Dockage: Hernando Beach Marina has transient slips; however, be aware that their widest slip is 14 feet. Blue Pelican Marina is primarily a dry stack facility and may not have transient space; call ahead for slip availability and to verify that shoaling is not a problem in this well-marked channel. MacRae's of Homosassa has slips as well as a hotel, bait house (for anglers) and a riverfront tiki bar. They report 3-foot MLW dockside depths so call ahead if that is a concern.

St. Martins Outer Shoal to Crystal River

Crystal River and Crystal Bay are located 45 nm north of Anclote River and 23 nm southeast of Cedar Key. A marked channel leads from the Gulf through Crystal Bay and the Crystal River 6 nm to Kings Bay and the town of Crystal River. Crystal River is Florida's second largest system of natural springs with a daily flow of about 3 million cubic yards of water at a constant temperature of 72 degrees. When the water temperature drops in the Gulf of Mexico manatees move to the warmer waters of the Crystal River. Crystal River is one of the few places where you can swim with manatees.

NAVIGATION: Use NOAA Chart 11409. From St Martins Outer Shoal 16-foot high, flashing red "10" continue on a course of 353° magnetic for 21.4 nm to Crystal River flashing red buoy "2" at N 28° 47.542'/W 82° 58.571'.

Watch for rocks inside the channel at Crystal River close to red daybeacon "8." Local knowledge advises favoring green daybeacon "7."

As local channels and rivers go, Crystal River is navigable and King's Bay is worth the trip. Depths are posted from 5 to 8 feet MLW from flashing red buoy "2" through the channel and the river. Local mariners say the depth is actually

closer to 6 to 9 feet MLW. Depths can drop dramatically during periods of north winds.

Dockage:

Use caution approaching Twin Rivers Marina on the Salt River and check your height; the charted overhead power cables have a 47-foot vertical clearance.

At the junction of the Salt and Crystal Rivers you will find Twin Rivers Marina. This is the only complete, full-service boatyard in Crystal River. Water depth to the marina and dockside is 5 feet MLW. Pete's Pier Inc. is located in the City of Crystal River at Kings Bay. They have some transient slips reserved for vessels to 80 feet. There are golf carts on hand for going into town for provisions. A grocery store, fish market, liquor store and a laundry are all about 1 mile from the waterfront. You can get a bite to eat at Crackers Bar and Grill (352-795-3999), which has a fun tiki hut with live entertainment on the weekends.

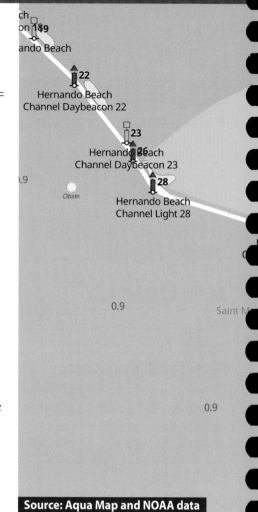

Source: Aqua Map and NOAA data

Little Pine Island Bay, FL

HERNANDO BEACH		Largest Vessel	VHF	Total Slips	Approach/ Dockside Depth	Floating Docks	Gas/ Diesel	Repairs/ Haulout	Min/Max Amps	Pump-Out Station
1. Hernando Beach Marina	Hernando Beach	(352) 596-2952	45		31	4.0 / 4.0	F	GD	RH	30	
2. Blue Pelican Marina		(352) 610-9999	30		4	4.0 / 4.0	F	G	RH		

 Wireless Internet Access 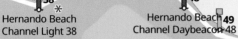 **onSpot** Dockside WiFi Facility
Visit www.waterwayguide.com for current rates, fuel prices, website addresses and other up-to-the-minute information.
(Information in the table is provided by the facilities.)

Scan here for more details:

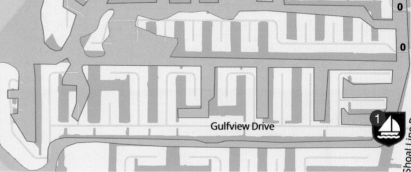

Hernando Beach Area

Crystal River, Homosassa River, FL

HOMOSASSA		Largest Vessel	VHF	Total Slips	Approach/ Dockside Depth	Floating Docks	Gas/ Diesel	Repairs/ Haulout	Min/Max Amps	Pump-Out Station
1. MacRae's of Homosassa **WiFi**	(352) 628-2602	35	16	10	6.0 / 3.0	F	G	R	30	

WiFi Wireless Internet Access   **onSpot** Dockside WiFi Facility
Visit www.waterwayguide.com for current rates, fuel prices, website addresses and other up-to-the-minute information.
(Information in the table is provided by the facilities.)

Scan here for more details:

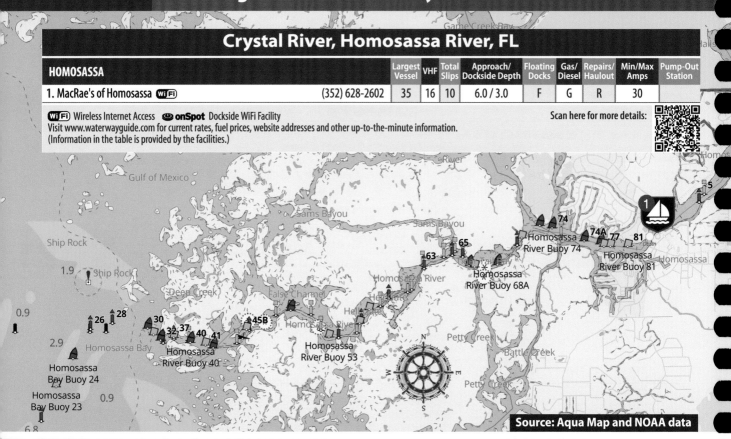

Source: Aqua Map and NOAA data

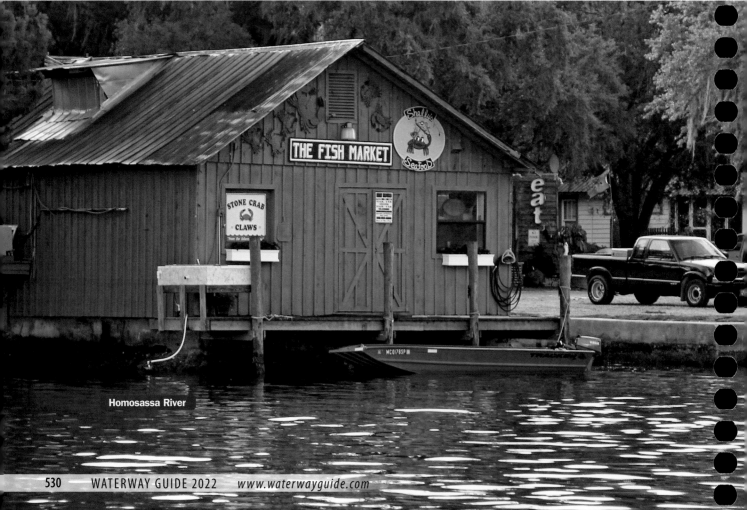

Homosassa River

Crystal River, Homosassa River, FL

CRYSTAL RIVER		Largest Vessel	VHF	Total Slips	Approach/ Dockside Depth	Floating Docks	Gas/ Diesel	Repairs/ Haulout	Min/Max Amps	Pump-Out Station
1. Twin Rivers Marina WiFi	(352) 795-3552	60	68	53	5.0 / 8.0	F	GD	RH	30 / 50	
2. Pete's Pier Inc.	(352) 795-3302	80	68	92	8.0 / 8.0		GD	H	30 / 50	P

WiFi Wireless Internet Access onSpot Dockside WiFi Facility
Visit www.waterwayguide.com for current rates, fuel prices, website addresses and other up-to-the-minute information.
(Information in the table is provided by the facilities.)

Scan here for more details:

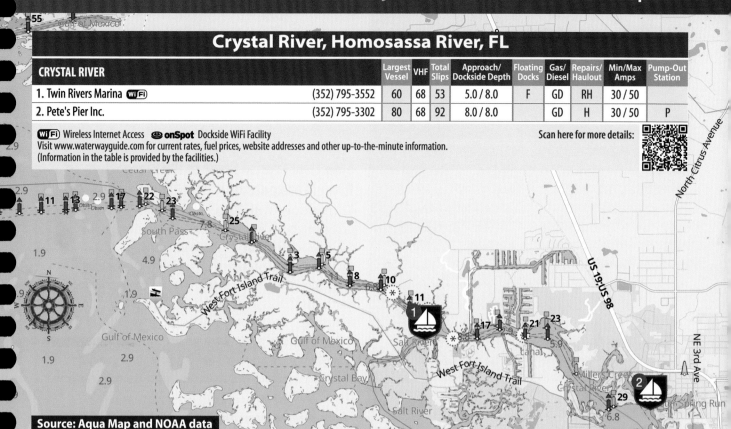

Source: Aqua Map and NOAA data

Master Your Trips.

Thousands of Destinations

Detailed Points of Interest

User Reviews & Alerts

All Regions Available

Guides Deep Linked to Mapping Tools

Share Your Experience & Earn Rewards

WATERWAY GUIDE MEDIA

Download on the App Store
Free Download

Swim with the Manatees

Crystal River is Florida's second largest system of natural springs with a daily flow of about 3 million cubic yards of water at a constant temperature of 72°. When the water temperature drops in the Gulf of Mexico manatees move to the warmer waters of the Crystal River. This area may host Florida's largest population of manatees.

Do not leave this area without checking out the spectacular caverns nearby. You can look down from King's Bay and see springs 60 feet under the surface. This is the only place where you can legally swim with manatees in the wild in the U.S. (during designated times). Be respectful of the manatees and remember that <u>you</u> are in <u>their</u> waters.

We recommend going with a local guide who can take you to the manatee "hot spots" and who will also educate you about them, giving you a more full experience and a greater understanding of these gentle creatures.

Another option is to board a free bus tour to Three Sisters Spring during the Florida Manatee Festival, held the third weekend in January in downtown Crystal River. Tours run continuously during the Festival. Manatee boat tours are also available for a nominal charge to take you out into Kings Bay and other favorite hangouts of the manatees.

Anchorage: You can anchor anywhere in the wide part of Kings Bay with good holding and protection with plenty of room to swing. There is a full 3-foot tidal range with 3 feet MLW. From here you can kayak or dinghy to the springs or to Pete's Pier Inc. where there is a dock for small boats at the restaurant.

Side Trip: Crystal River to Withlacoochee River (Yankeetown)

There are two Withlacoochee Rivers in Florida. The other one flows from Georgia and empties into the Suwannee River. Big Bend's Withlacoochee River empties into the Gulf of Mexico 17 nm southeast of Cedar Keys. Yankeetown is the primary boating community on the river. It is a very small fishing and winter resort 3 nm above the mouth. The river is navigable for 8 miles upstream where it intersects with a bridge with a fixed vertical clearance of 10 feet. This is an easily navigable channel and river. The river itself is worth the trip to Yankeetown.

> You need to work your way through the well-marked confusion of the Cross Florida Geenway into the channel for the Withlacoochee River. Officially named the Marjorie Harris Carr Cross Florida Greenway, this planned conduit was intended to stretch 110 miles from the Gulf of Mexico (GIWW) to St. John's River (and the ICW) in Palatka. Only two sections were completed before the project was abandoned in 1992.

NAVIGATION: Use NOAA Charts 11408 and 11409. Back on your inside course through the Big Bend leave Crystal River flashing red buoy "2" at N 28° 47.542'/W 82° 58.571' on a course of 3° magnetic. Travel with a watchful eye on the depth sounder for 8 miles to the flashing red "4" at N 28° 55.512'/W 82° 58.004'. The Cross Florida Barge Canal runs in an easterly direction. Follow the canal to flashing green "17" where a channel will branch off to the right and a channel will go slightly left or straight. Take the channel straight ahead using flashing red "20" to set yourself in the new channel.

At flashing green "23" take a course of 36° magnetic and make for the 16-foot high, quick-flashing green "1" to take the Withlacoochee River Entrance channel. Green daybeacon "25" will be south as will red daybeacon "26." The channel winds with rocks on both sides. From green daybeacon "3" it is about 8 miles to Yankeetown. Depths for the channel, canal and river are reported

Withlachoochee River, FL

YANKEETOWN		Largest Vessel	VHF	Total Slips	Approach/ Dockside Depth	Floating Docks	Gas/ Diesel	Repairs/ Haulout	Min/Max Amps	Pump-Out Station
1. Yankeetown Marina	(352) 302-4725	50	16	50	6.0 / 6.0				50	
2. B's Marina & Campground (WiFi)	(352) 447-5888	60		12	12.0 / 12.0		GD		30	
3. Riverside Marina & Cottages (WiFi)	(352) 447-2980	60		15	25.0 / 6.0				30	

(WiFi) Wireless Internet Access   (onSpot) Dockside WiFi Facility
Visit www.waterwayguide.com for current rates, fuel prices, website addresses and other up-to-the-minute information.
(Information in the table is provided by the facilities.)

Scan here for more details:

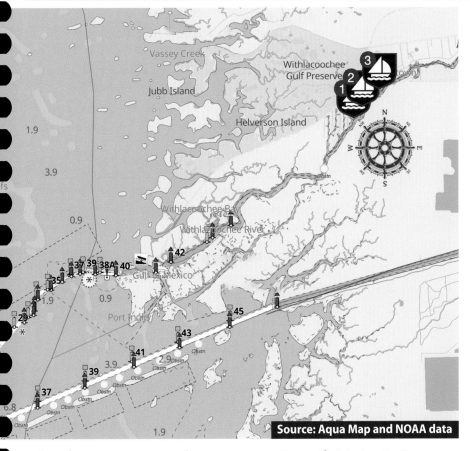

Source: Aqua Map and NOAA data

Crystal River to Seahorse Reef (Cedar Key)

The Cedar Keys are a group of low sandy islets covered with mangrove trees and pelicans...lots of pelicans. The outermost islet is Seahorse Key, where the white tower of an abandoned lighthouse stands on its south side. The lighthouse is visible from offshore.

Cedar Key is a small town on Way Key, located roughly one-third of the way between Anclote Key and Carrabelle. The island was named for the stand of cedar trees that once grew here and are now gone (logged out) and now the town subsists on fishing, both commercial and sport. Cedar Key is the top U.S. producer of farm-raised clams. You can find out more at the museum at the Cedar Key Museum State Park, which offers a nature trail, a 1920s home and artifacts depicting Cedar Key's history as a busy port.

NAVIGATION: Use NOAA Chart 11408. Resume your course for this route at Crystal River flashing red buoy "2" at N 28° 47.542'/W 82° 58.571'. Leave flashing red "2" on a course of 341° magnetic and travel for 17 nm to Cedar Key's 16-foot high, flashing green "1" at N 29° 04.000'/W 083° 04.500'. Depths in the channel are at least 7 feet MLW but you must follow the well-marked channel carefully. Study an up-to-date chart in

to be 5 feet MLW or more. The Withlacoochee definitely fits the bill for those wanting to take the path less traveled.

Dockage: This is a great place to visit off the beaten path but do not expect high-end docks or resort amenities. This is a remote location. Yankeetown Marina has 6-foot MLW approach and dockside depths. It is followed by B's Marina & Campground, which has cabins, pontoon boats, kayaks and bikes for

rent. Riverside Marina & Cottages is a camping and RV resort with covered and open transient slips. They also rent pontoon boats and kayaks for further exploration. Call ahead as there is limited transient dockage here.

Anchorage: Sailboats have been seen anchoring near the **Hwy. 19 Bridge** (40-foot fixed vertical clearance) on the Cross Florida Greenway.

Cedar Key, FL

CEDAR KEY		Largest Vessel	VHF	Total Slips	Approach/ Dockside Depth	Floating Docks	Gas/ Diesel	Repairs/ Haulout	Min/Max Amps	Pump-Out Station
1. Cedar Key Marina II	(352) 543-6148		11		6.0 / 6.0			RH		

WiFi Wireless Internet Access   **onSpot** Dockside WiFi Facility
Visit www.waterwayguide.com for current rates, fuel prices, website addresses and other up-to-the-minute information.
(Information in the table is provided by the facilities.)

Scan here for more details:

Source: Aqua Map and NOAA data

detail before you enter and you should have no difficulty.

Seahorse Reef extends for 11 nm from Seahorse Key and is a dangerous shoal with little depth. The outer end of the reef is marked by a 31-foot high, flashing white daybeacon "7M" (N 28° 58.310'/W 83° 09.130'). The shoal between red daybeacons "10" and "12" is building out into the channel. When transiting this area give red daybeacon "12" a wide berth favoring the western (Seahorse Key) side of the channel.

⚠️ Be careful! Several unwary visitors seeking a shortcut have been grounded by the S-curve in the winding channel.

Also pay close attention at the junction of Ship and Northwest Channels just past Grassy Key. Sorting out the maze of shoals and lights demands serious concentration. Go slowly, attempt no shortcuts and be aware of the currents.

When leaving Cedar Key northbound take Northwest Channel, which leaves the main channel at quick-flashing red "30" about 1 nm from the town dock off Grassy Key. Do not attempt Northwest Channel on a low tide if your draft exceeds 4 feet or during darkness or rough water conditions. Shoaling is particularly acute between green daybeacon "17A" and flashing red "18" and also between flashing green "19" and red daybeacon "20." Prominent marks on Cedar Key are a radio tower and 140-foot municipal water tank.

Dockage: Cedar Key Marina II provides small boat dockage and dry storage as well as engine repair. They also sell boats and motors and offer some repairs. What they do not offer is transient slips.

Anchorage: It is possible to anchor in depths around 8 feet MLW on the north side of Atsena Otie Key. Feel your way in cautiously. The island is part of the Cedar Keys National Wildlife Refuge. The cut between the two halves of the island provides a great place to paddle a kayak.

Another alternative is to anchor just southwest of the fishing pier at Cedar Key (out of the channel) in 8 to 14 feet MLW, and then dinghy in under the bridge to the small-boat docking area in the basin. Because of the strong tidal current in the anchorage, you may want to use a two-anchor Bahamian moor.

All of these anchorage are exposed to wind and tide with little protection. You should only anchor here in fair weather. This is not cruising boat territory.

■ TO CARRABELLE

It is just over 83 miles from Cedar Keys to the St. Marks River. Two good stopovers are the Suwanee and Steinhatchee Rivers. The Suwanee River originates in Georgia's Okefenokee Swamp and meanders about 280 miles before reaching the Gulf of Mexico. This is Old Florida territory and you won't find much here except the beauty of the river and the 70-plus springs that feed millions of gallons of water into it every day.

> The tannin-stained water of the Suwanee River was the inspiration for Stephen Foster's Suwannee River from "Old Folks at Home," which is Florida's official state song.

Suwannee River to St. Marks

NAVIGATION: Use NOAA Chart 11407. On approach from the Gulf of Mexico there are three passes or channels into the Suwannee, which can be confusing.

East Pass: Approaching from the south you will pass Derrick Key Gap at the south end of Suwannee Reef and Suwannee Sound. Depths in East Pass are about 2 feet MLW. You may see small fishing boats using the Pass but you shouldn't be tempted to enter.

West Pass: Sometimes referred to as Alligator Pass by locals, this is the first marked channel. You may see small boats coming and going from West Pass. At high tide it should carry depths of 4 feet or more but it is not recommended for a cruising boat.

Main Pass: Often referred to as Wadley Pass, this is the northernmost of the three channels and the preferred one. Depths are posted at a controlling depth of 3 feet MLW; however, we have received reports of at least 5 feet MLW. Keep in mind that if a north wind is blowing and a winter front is coming through, depths can drop considerably.

Leaping Sturgeons!

The Suwannee River appears to support the largest viable population of Gulf sturgeon according to the Florida Fish and Wildlife Conservation Commission (FWC). Biologists estimate the annual population at 10,000 to 14,000 fish, averaging approximately 40 pounds each.

The sturgeon can be hazardous to boaters as they tend to leap unexpectedly straight up and out of the water, turning sideways and landing with a loud noise. Much like deer hit by cars, jumping sturgeon are sometimes struck by boats. A large sturgeon can weigh more than 100 pounds so impact with a fast-moving boat can cause serious injury to both boat passengers and the sturgeon alike. Numerous people have been injured in accidental collisions with the jumping sturgeon on the Suwannee River.

Sturgeon can leap more than 7 feet out of the water and jumping occurs most frequently in mid-summer (May through August) when sturgeon are fasting. Researchers have determined that the sturgeon jump to communicate with other fish and to gulp air to fill their swim bladders. This allows the sturgeon to maintain neutral buoyancy.

FWC officials have initiated a public awareness campaign to alert boaters to the risks of jumping sturgeon and recommended that boaters slow down to reduce the risk of impact and to have more reaction time if a jumping sturgeon is encountered. And boaters are always encouraged to wear their life jackets at all times while on the water. To report sturgeon collisions call 888-404-FWCC (3922).

Suwannee River, FL

SUWANNEE		Largest Vessel	VHF	Total Slips	Approach/ Dockside Depth	Floating Docks	Gas/ Diesel	Repairs/ Haulout	Min/Max Amps	Pump-Out Station
1. Gateway Marina WiFi	(352) 542-7349	70	16	200	10.0 / 6.0	F	GD	H	30	P
2. The Suwannee Marina	(352) 542-9159	38		20	7.0 / 7.0	F	G	R		

WiFi Wireless Internet Access   onSpot Dockside WiFi Facility
Visit www.waterwayguide.com for current rates, fuel prices, website addresses and other up-to-the-minute information.
(Information in the table is provided by the facilities.)

Scan here for more details:

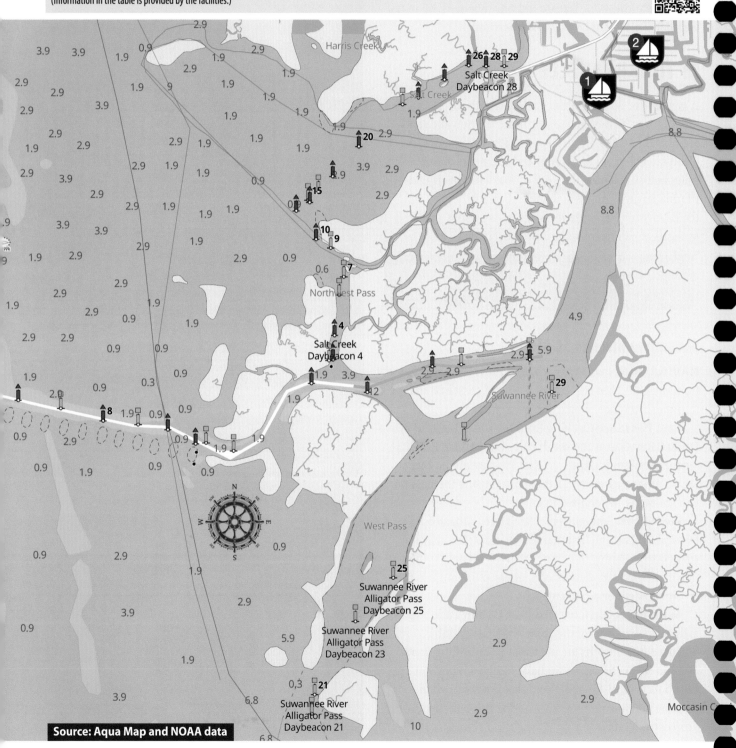

Cyprees trees on the Suwannee River

To access Main Pass starting at daybeacon green "1" at the entrance of the Crystal River Channel, travel 2 nm on a course of 269° magnetic. Then follow a course of 281° magnetic for 20 nm to the 31-foot tower, flashing "7M" at Sea Horse Reef. Be mindful to avoid the markers as you pass the Cross Florida Greenway.

From Sea Horse Reef travel on a course of 352° magnetic for 20 nm. Then navigate to 68° magnetic for 0.5 nm to the entrance channel for the Main/Wadley Pass to the Suwannee River. The total distance from the Crystal River Channel entrance to the Main/Wadley Pass channel entrance is 42 nm. Follow the channel markers into the Suwanee River. Depths in the river average 15 feet MLW.

Shoaling in the Suwanee River channel has been observed between red daybeacon "10" and "12." Entrance during high tide is recommended.

The average cruising boat should be able to enter the river (at high tide) and travel the 34 miles or so upriver to Fanning Springs, where you will encounter the 34-foot fixed vertical clearance Hwy. 19 Bridge.

Should you choose to explore the river be wary of the unmarked shoal, Jack's Reef, about 13 miles above the river entrance and 3.7 miles north of Fowlers Bluff. The reef occupies about two thirds of the east bank with depths as shallow as 1 foot MLW. Stay close to the west bank where you will find depths of more than 10 feet MLW. The location of Jack's Reef is identified on some charts.

A 25-mile trip upriver will take you to Manatee Springs and the State Park dock. It is possible to anchor in the river and enjoy all the park has to offer.

Dockage: Gateway Marina is a houseboat community with 10 reserved for transients. Call ahead for approach depths and space availability. The Suwannee Marina has a popular on-site restaurant. Call ahead. You can tie up at Salt Creek Restaurant (352-542-7072) at the town of Suwannee (north of Barbree Island on Salt Creek) if you plan to dine there. Choose from the large deck with water views, cozy indoor bar or cool outdoor tiki bar.

Anchorage: Anchorage opportunities are boundless along the Suwannee River. North and west of Hog Island carries at least 5 feet MLW and excellent holding in mud. Salt Creek has 5 feet MLW with good holding in mud. Both provide all-around protection.

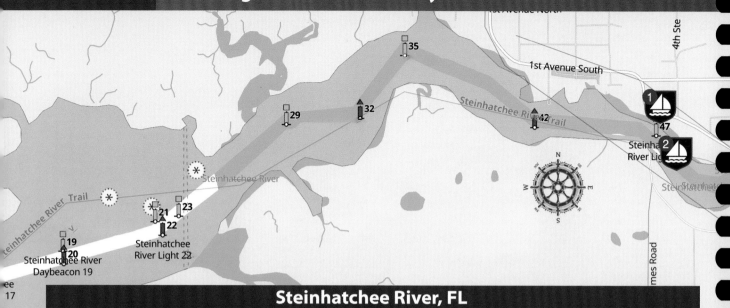

Steinhatchee River, FL

STEINHATCHEE		Largest Vessel	VHF	Total Slips	Approach/ Dockside Depth	Floating Docks	Gas/ Diesel	Repairs/ Haulout	Min/Max Amps	Pump-Out Station
1. Sea Hag Marina **WiFi**	(352) 498-3008	45	9	20	5.0 / 8.0	F	GD	RH	30 / 50	
2. Good Times Motel & Marina **WiFi**	(352) 498-8088	45	9	50	9.0 / 9.0	F	GD		30	
3. Steinhatchee River Inn and Marina (Formerly River Haven Marina & Motel) **WiFi**	(352) 498-0709	70	10	51	3.5 / 10.0	F	G	RH	30 / 50	P

WiFi Wireless Internet Access **onSpot** Dockside WiFi Facility
Visit www.waterwayguide.com for current rates, fuel prices, website addresses and other up-to-the-minute information.
(Information in the table is provided by the facilities.)

Scan here for more details:

Steinhatchee River

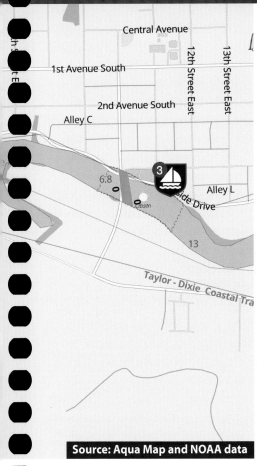

Source: Aqua Map and NOAA data

Steinhatchee River

NAVIGATION: Use NOAA Chart 11407. From the inside route through the Big Bend leave the Cross Florida Barge Canal red buoy "2" on a course of 335° magnetic. Stay on this course for 40 nm until you are standing out from Bull Cove.

At Bull Cove keep a distance from shore of about 6 nm. Keep a close eye on the depth sounder to make sure you avoid shoals that extend as far as 4 nm from the coast. From Bull Cove change course to 17° magnetic and run 7.5 nm to Steinhatchee River light green "1" at N 29° 39.357'/W 83° 27.347'. Flashing green "1" marks the entrance to the channel for Steinhatchee River. Controlling depth is 5 feet MLW. The channel is narrow in places but depths of 6 feet MLW or more are common.

This one of the more accessible ports of call along Florida's Big Bend. The interesting fishing village of Steinhatchee (pronounced "STEEN-hatchee") supports several seafood plants.

Dockage: Sea Hag Marina in Steinhatchee is able to accommodate a few shallow-draft boats in transient slips. They report 5-foot MLW approach depths; call ahead. They have a large Ship's Store, Gift & Dive Shop. Good Times Motel & Marina across the river has limited transient space (three slips). There is a motel, bar and grill and a fishing-centered store on site.

River Haven Marina & Motel is above the **10th Street Bridge** (25-foot fixed vertical clearance). They report 3.5-foot MLW approach depths. Call ahead for slip availability, directions and updated knowledge about water depths. They also have a motel and rent small boats and kayaks for exploring the upper reaches of the river.

Anchorage: An anchorage is located on the outside of the bend several hundred feet beyond red daybeacon "36" in 6- to 7-foot MLW depths. The holding is soupy but protection from all directions is excellent. Anchorage is also available just above Sea Hag Marina after daybeacon red "48" (may be missing) before the 10th St. Bridge (25-foot fixed vertical clearance).

St. Marks

Four rivers flow into the eastern Apalachee Bay: St. Marks, Aucilla, Econfina and Fenholloway. Residential and commercial development is minimal along this part of the coast. This is truly a part of "old Florida." From Cedar Key it is 83 miles to the St. Marks River. The town of St. Marks is 5.5 miles above the river entrance. The Visitor Center is at 15 Old Palmetto Path (850-925-0400) just 1.7 miles from Shields Marina.

Wakulla Springs is less than 10 miles away. This immense freshwater spring reaches a maximum depth of 185 feet and more than 600,000 gallons flow from the spring every minute, literally creating the Wakulla River.

NAVIGATION: Use NOAA Charts 11406, 11407, 11408 and 11405. A good reference for a route to St. Marks is to begin at the Cross Florida Greenway approach flashing red "2" located 4 nm southwest of the Seahorse Reef's 31-foot high, flashing white. From Barge Canal flashing red "2" set a course of 322° magnetic for 76 nm to Ochlockonee Shoal's flashing red "24." From there it is 9.5 nm on a course of 3° magnetic to the red and white "SM" buoy at the entrance of the St. Marks Channel.

St. Marks is easily accessible from Steinhatchee. From 30-foot flashing green "1" marking the entrance to the Steinhatchee River Channel, set a course of 273° magnetic for 9 nm to the yellow special purpose buoy at Steinhatchee Reef at N 29° 39.893'/W 83° 37.823'. Depths at the reef are charted at 15 feet at MLW. From Steinhatchee Reef your course is 306° magnetic for 36 nm to the red and white Morse (A) buoy "SM" marking the entrance to the St. Marks River.

Well before arriving at Morse (A) buoy "SM" you will see the 82-foot-high St. Marks Lighthouse (no longer lighted) on shore but do not shortcut this leg. The well-marked entry channel twists and turns through a maze of shoals. Daylight passage should present no problems but avoid

St. Marks Lighthouse

going in at night. The single orange range marker is used in conjunction with the St. Marks Lighthouse. Lining both up will keep you in mid-channel from flashing green "1" to the first dogleg at green can buoy "3A." (Note that green can "3" may be missing.)

St. Marks has a straightforward channel and river. Both are wide, well-marked and carry enough depth (at least 6 feet MLW) to accommodate most cruising boats that have made it this far.

Dockage: Up the St. Marks River is Shields Marina selling new and used boats and motors. Their Ship's Store is over 6,000 square feet and sells fishing tackle and gear, as well as electronics, nautical charts and more. They have limited (two) reserved transient slips on floating docks. Two restaurants, a Post Office and a small grocery store are within easy walking distance of the marina.

St. Marks Yacht Club is on the Wakulla River, which branches off the St. Marks River south of the town. They accept non-members if space is available. There are no amenities nearby but the small Wakulla River Park is next door with some trails and a pavilion. A call ahead to the marinas is essential here based on the minimal number of reserved transient slips.

Anchorage: About 1 mile above the marinas around the first bend, the St. Marks River offers an anchorage completely different from the usual Gulf Coast beaches. Tropical plants line both riverbanks, wildlife abounds and you can anchor in complete solitude. Be sure to install your screens and apply plenty of insect repellent. You should have minimum 6-foot MLW depths.

St. George Sound, FL

ST. MARKS		Largest Vessel	VHF	Total Slips	Approach/ Dockside Depth	Floating Docks	Gas/ Diesel	Repairs/ Haulout	Min/Max Amps	Pump-Out Station
1. St. Marks Yacht Club	(850) 925-6606	50		25	7.0 / 7.0	F			50	
2. Shields Marina	(850) 925-6158	65	16	100	12.0 / 10.0		GD	RH	50	P

WiFi Wireless Internet Access **onSpot** Dockside WiFi Facility
Visit www.waterwayguide.com for current rates, fuel prices, website addresses and other up-to-the-minute information.
(Information in the table is provided by the facilities.)

Scan here for more details:

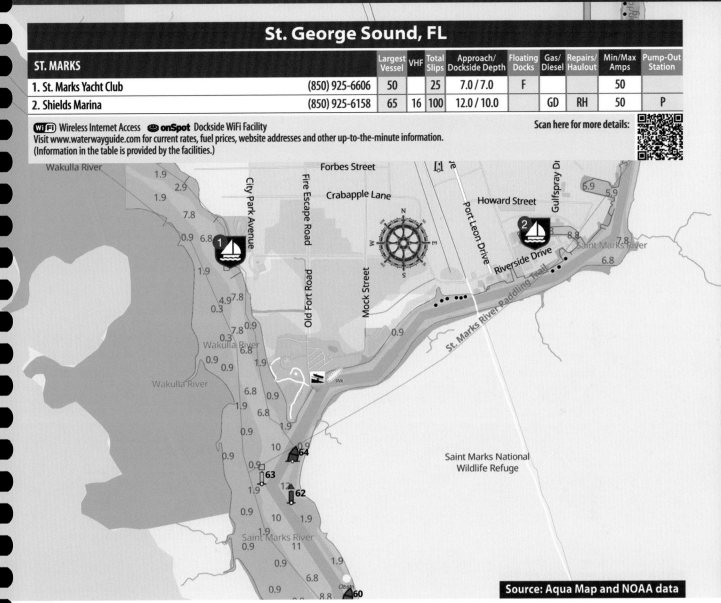

Source: Aqua Map and NOAA data

Alligator Harbor

NAVIGATION: Use NOAA Chart 11405. To reach Alligator Harbor take your departure from flashing red bell buoy "26" south of South Shoal. From there take a course of 312° magnetic to flashing green "1" at the northeast end of Dog Island Reef. At this point you can alter course to 350° magnetic. After just more than 3 nm you will pick up red flashing "2" marking the entrance to Alligator Harbor. Follow the daybeacons all the way to the Alligator Point Marina.

Dockage: Watch your depth. Shoals at the entrance to Alligator Point Marina are charted at 3 to 5 feet MLW. The marina is primarily for small fishing boats but transient slips to 45 feet are available. They have a Ship's Store with fishing tackle and boating accessories. The draw here is

the white sandy beach. End of the World Oasis–a seasonal on-site tiki hut–will cook your catch on site or you can choose from their (mostly grilled) menu (850-349-2058).

Anchorage: A protected anchorage can be found inside Bay Mouth Bar near red daybeacon "22" in at least 7 feet MLW or off Wilson Beach (on the north side of the harbor) in 8 to 10 feet MLW.

Ochlocknee Shoal to Carrabelle

East Pass into St. George Sound marks the end of the trek across Florida's Big Bend. Once again cruising boats with a vertical clearance of less than 50 feet can choose to travel the GIWW or go offshore in the Gulf of Mexico.

To the west is the port city of Apalachicola and to the east is the port city of Carrabelle. Carrabelle is the closest

St. George Sound, FL

ALLIGATOR HARBOR		Largest Vessel	VHF	Total Slips	Approach/ Dockside Depth	Floating Docks	Gas/ Diesel	Repairs/ Haulout	Min/Max Amps	Pump-Out Station
1. Alligator Point Marina	(850) 349-2511	45	16	45	4.0 / 5.0	F	GD		30 / 50	

WiFi Wireless Internet Access **onSpot** Dockside WiFi Facility
Visit www.waterwayguide.com for current rates, fuel prices, website addresses and other up-to-the-minute information.
(Information in the table is provided by the facilities.)

Scan here for more details:

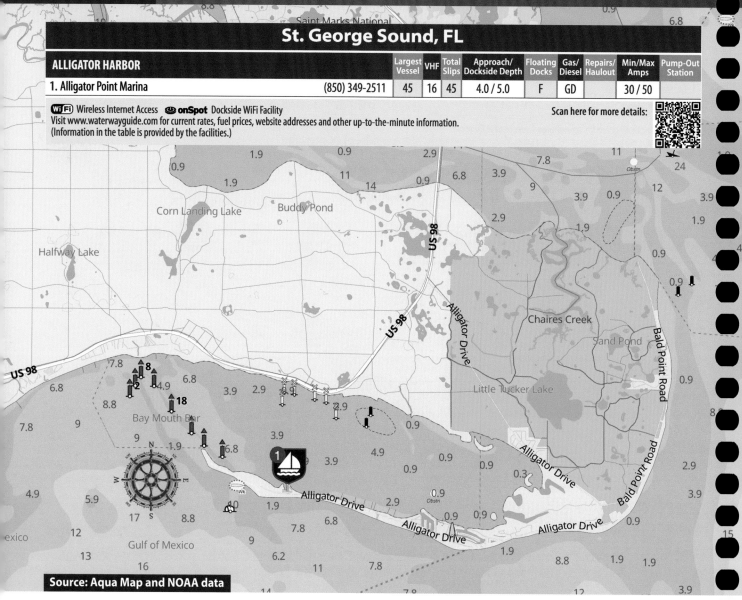

Source: Aqua Map and NOAA data

to East Pass. It is an excellent stop for boats looking for a place to rest after crossing The Big Bend. Carabelle is a friendly fishing village that feels like a step back in time. See more at "Goin' Ashore: Carrabelle, FL" in this chapter.

NAVIGATION: Use NOAA Charts 11401, 11404 and 11405. The inside route runs from Ochlockonee Shoal's flashing red "24" to the East Pass entrance to St. George Sound and on to Carrabelle. For the cruising boaters coming from St. Marks, your transit begins at the red and white "SM" entrance buoy for the St. Marks River. From the "SM" buoy travel on a course of 183° magnetic for 9.5 nm to Ochlockonee Shoal's flashing red "24" at N 29° 51.500'/W 84° 10.300'.

From there travel a course of 250° magnetic for 9.3 nm to flashing red "26" at N 29° 47.500'/W 84° 20.000'. From

flashing red "26" change course to 265° magnetic for 17 nm to flashing red "2" at N 29° 44.500'/W 84° 39.200' marking the entrance to East Pass and St. George Sound.

East Pass, one of the better Florida west coast passes, leads 5 nm through St. George Sound to the Carrabelle River. Follow the marked channel through East Pass and note the northeastern jog at flashing red "12." Stay in the marked marina channel to Carrabelle. Be aware that the tide here is up to 3 feet and tie up accordingly.

Dockage: Three marinas offer transient dockage 1 mile north of the GIWW on the Carrabelle River. MS Dockside Marina & Boatyard offers boat yard services on Timber Island. Across the river, the full-service C-Quarters Marina has slips for transient boats to 53 feet. Their Ship's Store is open daily from dawn to dusk. Many locals

St. George Sound, FL

CARRABELLE		Largest Vessel	VHF	Total Slips	Approach/ Dockside Depth	Floating Docks	Gas/ Diesel	Repairs/ Haulout	Min/Max Amps	Pump-Out Station
1. MS Dockside Marina & Boatyard	(850) 697-3337	65	16	22	16.0 / 9.0	F		RH	30 / 50	
2. C-Quarters Marina **WiFi** GIWW 380.0 mi. EHL	(850) 697-8400	80	16	67	12.0 / 9.0		GD	R	30 / 50	P
3. The Moorings of Carrabelle **WiFi** GIWW 380.0 mi. EHL	(850) 697-2800	150	16	150	15.0 / 9.0		GD		30 / 50	P
4. Carrabelle Boat Club-PRIVATE	(850) 697-5500			18	/			H		

WiFi Wireless Internet Access　**onSpot** Dockside WiFi Facility
Visit www.waterwayguide.com for current rates, fuel prices, website addresses and other up-to-the-minute information.
(Information in the table is provided by the facilities.)

Scan here for more details:

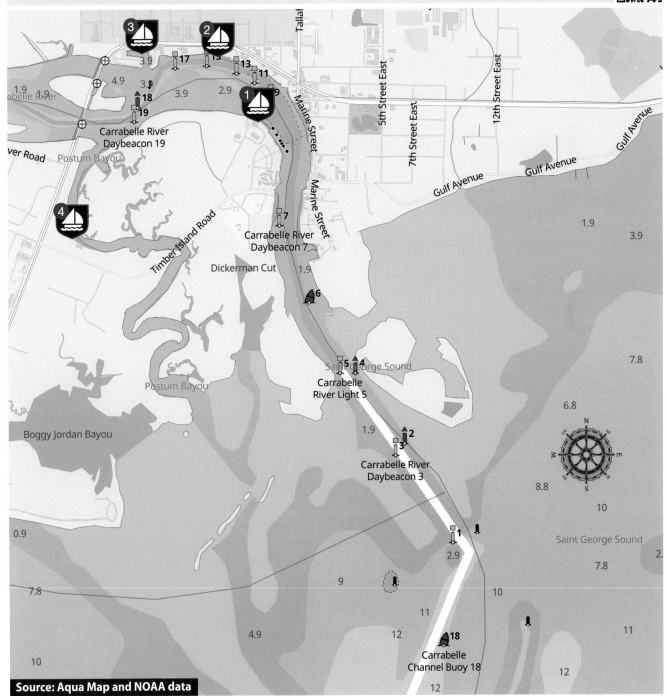

Source: Aqua Map and NOAA data

GOIN' ASHORE

CARRABELLE, FL

Carrabelle is a small, quiet town known for relaxing, boating, fishing, hunting, friendly people and white sand beaches. The eastern panhandle area of Florida is largely undeveloped and unspoiled. Land and water adventure tours are available for hiking, kayaking, off-road trails, fishing and sightseeing.

SERVICES

1. Carrabelle Post Office
93 Tallahassee St. (850-697-3339)

2. Carrabelle Visitor Center
105 St. James Ave. (850-697-2585)

3. Franklin County Public Library
311 St. James Ave. (850-697-2366)

4. Weems Medical Center East
110 5th St. E. (850-697-2345)

ATTRACTIONS

5. Carrabelle Bottle House
A unique lighthouse and cottage made entirely of bottles is at 604 SE Ave. F (850-697-9620). Best seen at dusk when it is lit from inside.

6. Carrabelle History Museum
Thousands of local artifacts are housed in the Old Carrabelle City Hall (circa 1933) at 106 SE Ave. B (850-697-2141).

7. World's Smallest Police Station

This police station at 102 Ave. A N. is located in an actual phone booth and has an interesting and amusing history. A replica of the booth is on display across the street from the Visitor Center at 105 St. James Ave.

SHOPPING

8. Gulfside IGA Plus

Convenient grocery store for provisioning located at 812 NW Ave. A (386-752-0067).

9. Ace Hardware

Well-stocked hardware store with household tools, supplies and more at 712 Ave. A N. (850-697-3332).

MARINAS

10. C-Quarters Marina

501 St. James Ave. (850-697-8400)

11. MS Dockside Marina

292 Graham Dr. (850-697-3337)

12. The Moorings of Carrabelle

1000 Ave. A N. (850-697-2800)

congregate here in the mornings and evenings on the well-known front porch for coffee or a cold beverage. The Moorings of Carrabelle has transient slips in an enclosed basin plus an on-site hotel, complimentary bicycles and continental breakfasts. There is no public transportation but groceries, hardware and several restaurants are easily accessible.

Anchorage: You can anchor in the main river at Carrabelle in 5-foot MLW depths south of green marker "17." Be sure not to block the channel.

Side Trip: Dog Island Anchorage

Due south of the Carrabelle River is Dog Island with numerous anchoring possibilities. Just inside the hook of the west end of Dog Island you can anchor at Shipping Cove, an excellent spot in deep water (charted at 17 to 20 feet MLW). A small embayment at the northeast end of Dog Island can provide limited shelter. Tysons Harbor, also at the northeast end of Dog Island, offers protection from all but northwest winds. The 6-foot-plus channel leading to the small ferry dock is narrow but well marked. Stay in the center and watch for the abruptly shoaling edges.

There are no amenities ashore. The island's hospitable owners allow cruising mariners to explore the beaches but please stay off private docks and property. A portion of the island is a bird breeding and nesting area, posted with "Keep Out" signs. Please honor them. (The posted section does not include the beach.)

■ NEXT STOP

We will leave the Big Bend area and enter the Florida Panhandle. Here you will need to decide if you are going to travel outside in the Gulf of Mexico by following the coastline all the way to Pensacola or take the 200-statute mile inside (GIWW) route. Fixed bridge heights of 50 feet will prevent most sailboats from using at least part of the inside route.

Mile 375-Mile 170 EHL

■ NAVIGATION NOTES

For the cruising boat that reaches St. George Sound (and has a vertical clearance of less than 50 feet) it is difficult to recommend an offshore passage to Pensacola. The GIWW distance from Mile 375 EHL to Mile 180 in Pensacola Bay is 195 statute miles through an enjoyable, low-stress section of the GIWW.

The more interesting GIWW route connects big bays and sounds that are protected by narrow, wooded barrier islands. From Carrabelle to Pensacola there are 200 statute miles of inside cruising with occasional passes to the Gulf of Mexico. Fixed bridge heights of 50 feet will prevent most sailboats from using some of the inside route.

The offshore passage from East Pass must go around the shoals that extend from Cape St. George and Cape San Blas. The offshore distance from Mile 375 EHL to the entrance at Pensacola Bay is 158 nm.

Along the panhandle of Florida a rather unique change occurs to tides. West of St. George Sound/Apalachicola Bay, there are only two tides per 24 hours (one high and one low, called diurnal tides), while east of this demarcation the tides are the normal four per 24 hours (two highs and two lows). Very few places on the planet can claim this distinction.

NO WAKE ZONE

No Wake Zones, Idle Speed Zones and various Speed Limit restrictions are in effect throughout the waterways included in this chapter. Exercise diligence in knowing the regulations by observing signs and other markers. Enforcement is always present. As always, be courteous to other vessels and avoid manatees and other marine life.

Offshore Route: East Pass to Pensacola

From the flashing red "2" at the end of East Pass set a course of about 230° magnetic for 25 nm to avoid the shoals at Cape St. George and Cape San Blas. Then set a course of about 295° magnetic for 130 nm (for a total distance of 155 nm) to Pensacola.

Depths range from 10 to 12 feet MLW but shoaling is possible so be sure to keep an eye on your depth sounder. There are three bridges with a fixed vertical clearance of 50 feet: **Dupont (U.S. 98) Bridge** in East Bay (Mile 295.4 EHL), **Brooks Memorial Bridge** at Fort Walton Beach (Mile 223 EHL) and **Navarre Beach Causeway (CR 399) Bridge** (Mile 206.6 EHL).

There are two inlets that will allow you to break the trip into two days to enjoy this part of the Emerald Coast. The well-marked inlet at St. Andrews Bay is 80 nm from East Pass.

The channel at Destin is 120 nm from East Pass and is passable but not as well marked. It has a controlling depth

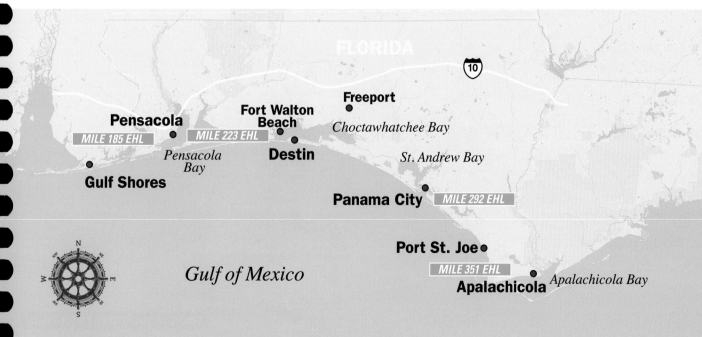

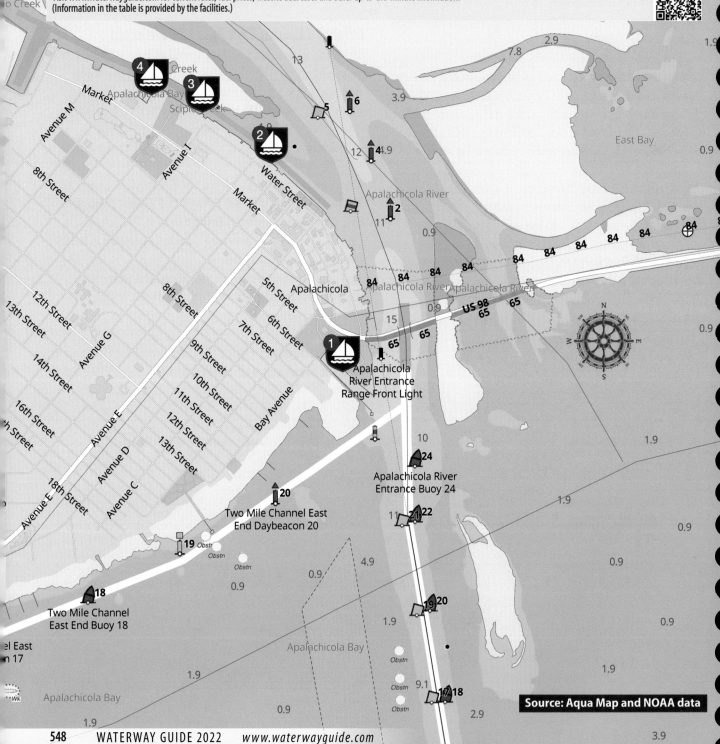

Apalachicola River, FL

APALACHICOLA		Largest Vessel	VHF	Total Slips	Approach/ Dockside Depth	Floating Docks	Gas/ Diesel	Repairs/ Haulout	Min/Max Amps	Pump-Out Station
1. Battery Park Marina GIWW 351.0 mi. EHL	(850) 653-9319	50			6.0 / 5.0				50	P
2. Apalachicola Marina, Inc. WiFi GIWW 351.0 mi. EHL	(850) 653-9521	100	16	3	15.0 / 12.0				30 / 50	
3. Water Street Hotel and Marina WiFi GIWW 351.0 mi. EHL	(850) 653-3700	55	16	19	12.0 / 8.0	F			50	
4. Scipio Creek Marina WiFi GIWW 351.0 mi. EHL	(850) 653-8030	100	16	14	12.0 / 10.0		GD	RH	30 / 50	

WiFi Wireless Internet Access   onSpot Dockside WiFi Facility
Visit www.waterwayguide.com for current rates, fuel prices, website addresses and other up-to-the-minute information.
(Information in the table is provided by the facilities.)

Scan here for more details:

Apalachicola

of 6 feet MLW and a width of 50 feet. From this channel you can reach marine facilities before the fixed **William T. Marler (U.S. 98/SR 30) Bridge** with 49-foot vertical clearance, which crosses the pass.

An alternate (and recommended) offshore route is to enter St. George Sound at East Pass and proceed 52 (statute) miles along the GIWW to Port St. Joe. To reach Port St. Joe turn to the southwest at Mile 328 EHL at the Gulf County Canal. (There are signs at this intersection.) The offshore run from Port St. Joe to the entrance at Pensacola Bay is 100 nm on a course of 283° magnetic.

This area of the Gulf is used extensively by the U.S. Air Force. Along the entire route you will be passing by and over areas marked as missile testing, unexploded ordnance and fish havens. Check the latest *Local Notice to Mariners* for updates.

■ TO PANAMA CITY

From Carrabelle to Florida's Panhandle you can travel the GIWW (inside) or continue outside in the Gulf. Note that the inside route is in shallow waters! Know where you are going to go, how you are going to get there and the condition of the water all along the route before you leave the dock.

Apalachicola–GIWW Mile 351 EHL

A worthwhile layover along this stretch of the GIWW is Apalachicola with a village-like atmosphere, excellent local oysters and unique shopping opportunities within walking distance of the marinas. It is a pleasant trip through St. George Sound and Apalachicola Bay to the unique and beautiful City of Apalachicola. See details on attractions and amenities at "Goin' Ashore: Apalachicola, FL" in this chapter.

GOIN' ASHORE

APALACHICOLA, FL

Apalachicola is a small southern town with a strong maritime culture. A walking tour will take you past cotton warehouses from the 1800s, a sponge exchange, a maritime museum and meticulously restored Victorian homes nestled amid moss-draped live oaks. As an interesting side note, several of the larger houses in Apalachicola were originally built in Port St. Joe (40 miles to the west) but were moved after a yellow fever outbreak in the 1800s.

SERVICES

1. Apalachicola Bay Chamber of Commerce & Visitor Center
17 Ave. E (850-653-9419)

2. Apalachicola Margaret Key Library
80 12th St. (850-653-8436)

3. Apalachicola Post Office
20 Ave. D, Ste. 101.
(850-653-9554)

4. George E. Weems Hospital
137 12th St. (850-653-1525)

ATTRACTIONS

5. Apalachicola Center for History, Culture & Art
Artist exhibits, events, films, lectures, classes and workshops, cultural events and programs are housed in this restored 1830s cotton warehouse at 86 Water St. (850-653-1458).

6. Apalachicola Maritime Museum
Active boating excursions, adventure programs, boat building and restoration, and educational programs at 103 Water St. (850-653-2500).

7. The Gibson Inn
"Front porch sitting" has been going on since 1907 in this "cracker" style structure characterized by a metal roof and a wraparound porch. Lodging, a bar and fine dining at 51 Ave. C (850-653-2191).

8. Raney House Museum
Local historical artifacts are housed in the 1800s home of cotton-trader David G. Raney at 128 Market St. (850-653-1700).

SHOPPING

9. Down Town Books and Purl
Find a wide selection of books and exquisite yarns plus games and diversions at 67 Commerce St.(850-653-1290).

10. Piggly Wiggly
Full-service grocery chain 1 mile from the waterfront at 130 Ave. E (850-653-8768).

11. The Tin Shed

This literal "shed" contains a comprehensive collection of antique and used nautical equipment and items plus shells, wood carvings and apparel at 170 Water St. (850-653-3635).

MARINAS

12. Apalachicola Marina, Inc

119 Water St. (850-653-9521)

13. Battery Park Marina

1 Bay Ave. (850-653-9319)

14. Scipio Creek Marina

301 Market St. (850-653-8030)

15. Water Street Hotel & Marina

329 Water St. (850-653-3700)

NAVIGATION: Use NOAA Chart 11404. If you go into Carrabelle, you will have to come back out the same way. After exiting the Carrabelle River and retracing your course into St. George Sound pick up flashing red "2" (Mile 374 EHL) just inside East Pass. Flashing red "6" becomes visible about 2.5 miles to the southwest. From here the GIWW is clearly marked as it jogs south by southwest at flashing red "20" for about 2 miles to flashing red "28" (Mile 365 EHL) where it resumes its southwest direction.

From that point it is a straight shot southwest for about 9.3 miles under the fixed **Bryant Patton (SR 300) Bridge** at Mile 361.4 EHL (65-foot vertical clearance) over Apalachicola Bay at Bulkhead Shoal (red nun buoy "48"). Watch your depths carefully in the area of Bulkhead Shoal where the oyster beds come right to the edge of the channel. The channel is especially narrow on the east side of the bridge so keep an eye on the markers ahead and behind to keep from crabbing into the shallows. The bridge is the boundary of demarcation between St. George Sound and Apalachicola Bay.

After traversing much of Apalachicola Bay at flashing red "76" make a 90-degree turn north and follow the GIWW about 3.5 miles to red nun buoy "24" marking the entrance to the Apalachicola River and the town of Apalachicola.

Dockage: After passing red nun buoy "24" and just south of the fixed **John Gorrie Memorial (U.S. 98/319) Bridge** at Mile 351.4 EHL (65-foot vertical clearance) the Apalachicola municipal marina (Battery Park Marina) is in a basin to port. Transient slips are available to 50 feet with the usual amenities. There are several busy boat ramps here and the docks are open to wakes left by passing boaters so be sure to use ample spring lines and fenders. The well-regarded Apalachicola Marina, Inc. may be small in size (three total slips on a 150-foot face dock) but it's big on service and sells some marine supplies. A supermarket, drug store and restaurants are within easy walking distance.

Most of the other transient facilities are located farther north along with various fuel docks and a waterfront hotel (Water Street Hotel and Marina) with newly renovated dock space. Their 19 transient slips on floating docks can accommodate power or sailboats up to 55 feet in length. J. V. Gander Distributors, Inc. sells gas and diesel fuel but has no transient space.

Take care while fueling and docking as the Apalachicola River can have a strong current depending on tidal flow.

If you want to get away from GIWW traffic, the well-regarded Scipio Creek Marina is a popular stopover for cruisers. (The "c" is silent in Scipio.) There is less tidal current here than at the facilities located directly on the Apalachicola River. The full-service marina is located to the northwest of the river at green-red can "A" with slips, an on-site store and a restaurant. Motels, restaurants and provisions are within a three-block walk.

Anchorage: It is possible to anchor in Apalachicola just north of the John Gorrie Bridge. Here you will find 9 to 12 feet MLW with good holding. You will be exposed to wakes so be sure to anchor well out of the channel. There are also anchorages at Shell Point on St. George Island (GIWW Mile 365 EHL) in 7 to 10 feet MLW.

Apalachicola to White City–GIWW Mile 351 to Mile 329 EHL

The GIWW leaves Apalachicola Bay and the Gulf of Mexico at Mile 350 EHL and winds along on the scenic Apalachicola River, undulating generally northwest to the **Apalachicola Northern Railroad Bridge** at Mile 347.0 EHL (11-foot closed vertical clearance, usually open). Keep a sharp eye out for tree limbs and other floating debris. Again, a night passage is not recommended.

NAVIGATION: Use NOAA Charts 11393, 11401 and 11402. From the mouth of the Apalachicola River the GIWW is well marked. Past red daybeacon "30" the Apalachicola River turns north and the GIWW continues along the Jackson River to Lake Wimico at Mile 340 EHL.

You will soon take a hairpin turn to the south past flashing green "9" just west of Mile 345 EHL and about 1 mile later take a sharp curve to the west and proceed to Lake Wimico at Mile 340 EHL and green daybeacon "3" and red daybeacon "4." The course for the straight shot across the lake is about 310° magnetic. Follow the daybeacons carefully as the spoil areas are close to the narrow channel.

At flashing green "15" enter Searcy Creek at the end of Lake Wimico (Mile 335 EHL). Follow the well-marked channel from here about 6 miles to the **Elgin Bayless (SR 71) Bridge** (65-foot fixed vertical clearance) at Mile 329.3 EHL. The waterway is relatively wide and deep and offers an enjoyable view as you traverse swamp country (described on the some charts as "impenetrable," "cypress" and "low swampy area").

A little over 1.5 miles from the bridge you must choose to continue on the GIWW to Panama City or turn southwest on the Gulf County Canal to Port St. Joe, St. Joseph Bay and the Gulf.

Dockage: The free White City Dock is in the adjacent park. It is posted as no overnight dockage. Tie up to either the seawall or floating dock. There are restrooms on site and a convenience store with minimal supplies 1 mile north on the highway. The bulkhead is subject to wakes from GIWW traffic.

Anchorage: Just after the Jackson River splits off from the Apalachicola there is an excellent protected anchorage in 8 feet MLW at the junction of Saul Creek and the Saul Creek Cutoff (northeast at Mile 345 EHL between green daybeacon "7" and red "8"). There is some shoaling on the left bank when turning in so stay more right of center when leaving the GIWW. Depths exceed 30 feet MLW in much of this lovely creek. For optimum holding use your depth sounder to find an appropriate depth to set the hook. Alligators and birds are abundant.

After exiting Lake Wimico into Searcy Creek, the oxbow around the island at Mile 334 EHL normally carries 10 feet MLW or better and provides an excellent secluded anchorage.

Side Trip: North on the Apalachicola River

Boaters seeking a side trip can follow the Apalachicola River upstream through a few miles of heavily wooded swampland to the St. Marks, East and Brothers Rivers after exiting the GIWW at red daybeacon "30" (GIWW Mile 346 EHL). There is ample depth here for smaller vessels. (Controlling depths of 9 to 10 feet MLW are available to St. Marks Island.) The really adventurous can navigate the river up to the Jim Woodruff Dam at Chattahoochee but obtain local knowledge before embarking.

Option 1: White City to Panama City–GIWW Mile 329 to Mile 290 EHL

NAVIGATION: Use NOAA Charts 11390, 11391 and 11393. From White City the GIWW continues to run clean, wide and deep with no need for navigational aids. At about Mile 318 EHL it becomes the South Prong of Wetappo Creek and continues beneath

Overstreet (SR 386) Bridge at Mile 315.4 EHL (65-foot fixed vertical clearance) to about Mile 314 EHL where it joins the North Prong and becomes Wetappo Creek.

At this point aids to navigation appear again, starting with green daybeacon "1" at about Mile 313 EHL and continuing down the Wetappo Creek and into Big Cove. At that same green daybeacon "1" eastbound vessels need to stay alert as the channel bends southeast here and the small bay to the south can be confused with the GIWW.

On this part of your journey you will be passing a bay that leads to Sandy Creek just past GIWW Mile 310 EHL and past Raffield Island to the south (at 3 feet mean sea level). During strong southerlies the narrow channel leading west to the sharp turn at GIWW Mile 310 EHL (flashing red "28") can pose serious difficulties to barge traffic. If meeting a tow along this stretch be sure to coordinate on VHF Channel 13 to clarify your intentions. As a matter of practical concern we recommend you have your VHF radio cycling between VHF Channels 16 and 13 on this section of the GIWW.

Study the chart carefully for the run up East Bay to Panama City. Flashing green "29" (Mile 294.2 EHL) off Parker Bayou should be left to starboard here as the GIWW buoy system gives way to the Panama City buoy system (red-right-returning from the Gulf). This can be confusing as red buoys are now on your port side as you travel west switching back to red on the right with flashing red "6" off Buena Vista Point west of Panama City.

There is a 4-foot-deep MLW shoal charted just northeast of the channel at red daybeacon "38" off Piney Point (Mile 300.75).

The GIWW channel continues southwest from Raffield Island and turns west at red daybeacon "44" to Murray Point. Near GIWW Mile 306 EHL favor the southwestern side of the channel to avoid oyster reefs on the northeast side (generally marked with "Danger" signs). Just past Long Point on East Bay is the **Dupont (U.S. 98) Bridge** at Mile 295.4 (50-foot fixed vertical clearance). From here to Panama City the GIWW runs through relatively deep water (25 to 35 and even 40 feet).

Anchorage: Between White City and Panama City on the GIWW a pleasant, protected overnight anchorage is located on Wetappo Creek at GIWW Mile 314.5. Just around the first bend of the creek, you can safely anchor over a soft mud bottom in about 10 feet MLW. Due to the strong current a Bahamian moor is appropriate here, preferably on the side of the river by the marshlands.

In East Bay, Walker Bayou (GIWW Mile 307.5 EHL), Murray Bayou (GIWW Mile 305.7 EHL) and California Bayou (GIWW Mile 302 EHL) are options for anchoring. Northeast of the GIWW across from Cedar Point in East Bay is Laird Bayou (GIWW Mile 299.5 EHL). This anchorage provides ample protection from north winds in 6 to 8 feet MLW with plenty of room to swing. One cove over is Callaway Bayou with good holding in 8 feet MLW and all-around protection.

Option 2: White City to Panama City–Gulf Canal & Gulf Route

NAVIGATION: Use NOAA Charts 11389, 11393 and 11401. About 1.5 miles from White City at about GIWW Mile 328 EHL the Gulf Canal cuts off 90 degrees south and extends 5 miles southwest from the waterway to Port St. Joe on St. Joseph Bay. The controlling depth is 12 feet MLW and there is a 75-foot fixed **U.S. 98/SR 30 Bridge** near the exit to St. Joseph Bay.

The channel from Port St. Joe to the Gulf is clearly marked in St. Joseph Bay. Turn northwest at the intersection with the ship channel and then north to get around St. Joseph Point at the tip of St. Joseph Peninsula and out of St. Joseph Bay. You will be doing this incrementally with the last straight run to the southwest until you get into the Gulf of Mexico and 30-plus feet of water.

To get to the entrance buoy (RW "SA") off Panama City, steer northwest. The distance is 21 miles. The "SA" stands for either St. Andrew or St. Andrews depending on whether you are looking at a chart or listening to the locals. It is best to be flexible.

Dockage: The marina at Port St. Joe Marina is partially open after extensive hurricane renovation. Amenities currently include transient slips and dry boat storage (under construction). Captain's Cove Marina is primarily a dry storage facility but they may have space for you. Call ahead. Family-owned Mexico Beach Marina to the north of Port St. Joe has slips and a well-equipped Ship's Store.

Anchorage: Just north of the Gulf Canal where it intersects with St. Joseph Bay is an anchorage in 8 to 9 feet MLW at Highland View in front of the tank (shown on the NOAA chart).

St. Joseph Bay, FL

ST. JOSEPH BAY AREA		Largest Vessel	VHF	Total Slips	Approach/ Dockside Depth	Floating Docks	Gas/ Diesel	Repairs/ Haulout	Min/Max Amps	Pump-Out Station
1. Port St. Joe Marina - TEMP. CLOSED (WiFi) GIWW 327.5 mi. EHL	(850) 227-9393	120	16	114	15.0 / 7.0		GD		30 / 50	P
2. Captain's Cove Marina	(850) 227-3357				12.0 / 12.0		GD	R	30 / 50	

(WiFi) Wireless Internet Access (onSpot) Dockside WiFi Facility
Visit www.waterwayguide.com for current rates, fuel prices, website addresses and other up-to-the-minute information.
(Information in the table is provided by the facilities.)

Scan here for more details:

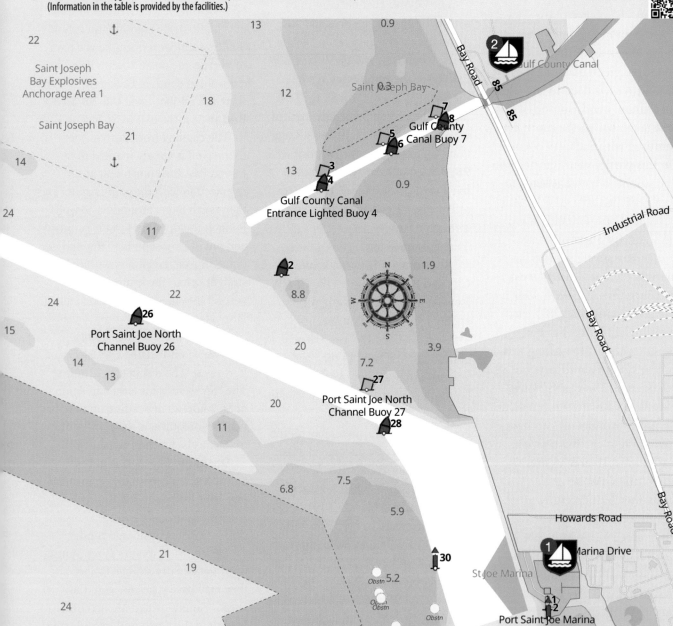

Source: Aqua Map and NOAA data

St. Joseph Bay, FL

ST. JOSEPH BAY AREA		Largest Vessel	VHF	Total Slips	Approach/ Dockside Depth	Floating Docks	Gas/ Diesel	Repairs/ Haulout	Min/Max Amps	Pump-Out Station
1. Mexico Beach Marina **WiFi**	(850) 867-9125		16	34	/ 6.0			RH	30	

WiFi Wireless Internet Access **onSpot** Dockside WiFi Facility
Visit www.waterwayguide.com for current rates, fuel prices, website addresses and other up-to-the-minute information.
(Information in the table is provided by the facilities.)

Scan here for more details:

You can drop the hook in Eagle Harbor on the inland side of St. Joseph Peninsula. This is a beautiful, remote deep-water anchorage. Dinghy into the St. Joseph Peninsula State Park to access the hiking trails and beach.

Panama City–GIWW Mile 290 EHL

It's no surprise that a city with the slogan "Where life sets sail" is a popular boater destination. Panama City welcomes cruisers year-round. Check in with the friendly staff at Destination Panama City Visitors Center at 1000 Beck Ave. (850-215-1700) when you arrive. They can point you to the unique art galleries and specialty shops, a thriving music scene and dining opportunities that range from casual dockside cafés to upscale eateries, with local Gulf oysters as the fare of choice.

Panama City boasts a large year-round charter fishing fleet, party boats, fishing piers, diving and surf fishing. Gulf fishing has greatly improved in the area thanks to conservation efforts and inshore light-tackle catch-and-release fishing on the bay has become very popular. Boaters can also enjoy the area's sparkling white sugar sand beaches, rated as some of the finest in the country.

NAVIGATION: Use NOAA Chart 11389 and 11390. Shell Island, the barrier island forming the southern side of the main pass from the Gulf of Mexico into St. Andrew Bay, provides shelter for Panama City, which is a major harbor for transient yachts. The cut itself is considered one of the best deep-water channels on the Gulf Coast.

St. Andrew Bay, one of Florida's finest bays and home to Panama City, is deep and almost landlocked. The well-marked exit to the Gulf of Mexico is a land cut through St. Andrews Park that has a rock jetty. The Navy operates a lab on the west end of the bay and south of the Hathaway (US 98) Bridge at Mile 284.6 EHL (65-foot fixed vertical clearance). You will frequently see helicopters, hovercraft and some esoteric "special ops" equipment here.

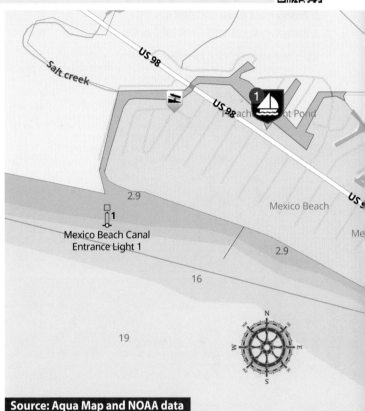

Source: Aqua Map and NOAA data

St. Andrew Bay, FL

		Largest Vessel	VHF	Total Slips	Approach/Dockside Depth	Floating Docks	Gas/Diesel	Repairs/Haulout	Min/Max Amps	Pump-Out Station
BUENA VISTA POINT										
1. St. Andrews Marina - FUEL ONLY-NO DOCKAGE GIWW 287.0 mi. EHL	(850) 872-7240		16		15.0 / 8.0		GD			P
GRAND LAGOON										
2. Lighthouse Marina WiFi GIWW 280.0 mi. EHL	(850) 625-2728	70	16	50	8.0 / 8.0		GD	R	30 / 50	
3. Treasure Island Marina GIWW 280.0 mi. EHL	(850) 234-6533	70	16	85	8.0 / 6.0		GD	RH	30 / 50	P
4. Pirates Cove Marina WiFi GIWW 280.0 mi. EHL	(850) 234-3939	60	16	400	6.0 / 8.0		GD	RH	30 / 50	

WiFi Wireless Internet Access onSpot Dockside WiFi Facility
Visit www.waterwayguide.com for current rates, fuel prices, website addresses and other up-to-the-minute information.
(Information in the table is provided by the facilities.)

Scan here for more details:

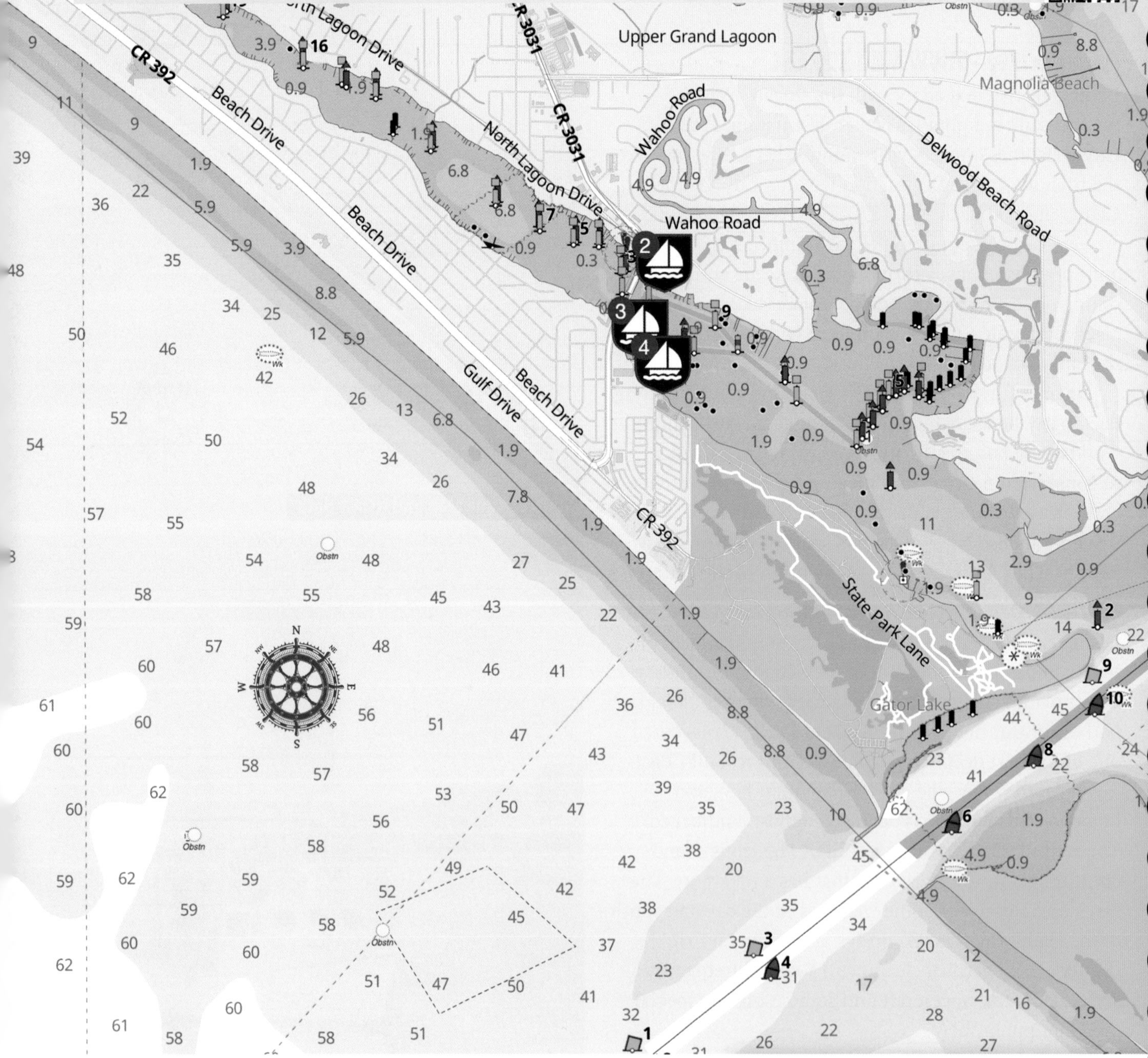

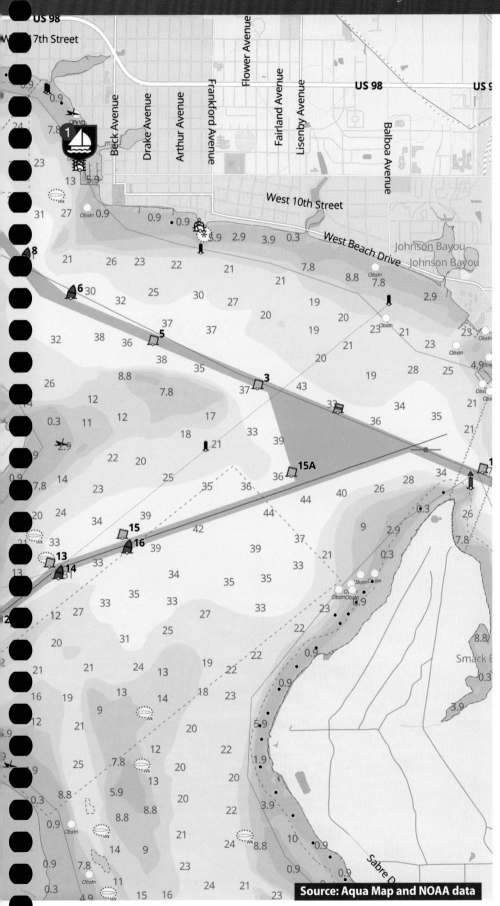

Source: Aqua Map and NOAA data

Dockage: Panama City is probably the best-equipped harbor north of Tampa and St. Petersburg and berths are usually available except on holiday weekends. It is a good idea, particularly during the season, to call ahead and reserve a berth. There are facilities throughout the area beginning from the east at Watson Bayou (north of flashing green "25") and extending west to flashing red "14" off Dyers Point.

Panama City Marina and St. Andrews Marina (fuel only) at Buena Vista Point (0.5 mile north of flashing red "6") were still closed at press time due to storm damage. Call ahead to check the operational status of the facilities in this area.

Anchorage: Along this stretch of the GIWW from the Dupont Bridge to Panama City virtually any cove well away from the channel offers good anchorage. Pitts Bayou and Parker Bayou on the north side of Long Point are viable anchorages. Pearl Bayou to the south is a nice anchorage that could be considered a hurricane hole.

Watson Bayou also offers 360-degree protection and good holding in 8 to 10 feet MLW. Farther west of Watson Bayou on the southern side of the GIWW (near flashing red "20"), Redfish Point and Smack Bayou offer protection from southerly winds with good holding in 8 to 9 feet MLW with a sandy mud bottom. You can get in pretty close to shore at Redfish Point for great protection. Expect to hear jets flying over in the mornings. Bunkers Cove is across the water with at least 9-feet MLW depths if you need northerly protection. West of Watson Bayou you will find some anchoring room in Massalina Bayou. The drawbridge at the entrance (7-foot closed vertical clearance) opens on demand 24 hours a day.

Shell Island has some excellent anchorages off the beach over a hard sand-and-shell bottom. If boat wakes from the channel bother you, head farther east on the island. Be wary of the charted sandbars between Davis Point and Shell Island. If your depth sounder shows less than 7-foot MLW depths you are either too close to the island or too far north over the Camel Humps.

Side Trip: Grand Lagoon

Grand Lagoon, immediately inside and west of St. Andrews Inlet, offers an interesting side trip. Lighthouse Marina, Treasure Island Marina and Pirates Cove Marina are here. Call ahead for slip availability and amenities. The anchorage at Grand Lagoon has 10 to 13 feet MLW with good holding in sand. It is open and exposed, however, to the southeast and wakes. Note that jets flying overhead (often early in the morning) is pretty typical of the entire area.

■ TO PENSACOLA BAY

From Panama City westbound cruisers will find about 12 miles of relatively trouble-free transit through West Bay then about 16.5 miles of transit through a land cut known to some as the "Grand Canyon" before ending up in wide Choctawhatchee Bay.

NAVIGATION: Use NOAA Charts 11385 and 11390. When westbound from Panama City and approaching the **Hathaway (U.S. 98) Bridge** at Mile 284.6 EHL (65-foot fixed vertical clearance) stay well off the 17-foot high, flashing red "14" off Dyers Point (Audubon Island) as shoaling off the small island reaches into the marked channel.

West Bay channel buoys from green can "23" through run nun "38" before the Hathaway Bridge were reportedly off station at press time. Exercise caution and seek local knowledge, if possible.

The GIWW opens up after the Hathaway Bridge. Heading north give flashing green "5" at Shell Point a wide berth. From there the GIWW curves northwest through West Bay, cuts under the **West Bay Creek (SR 79) Bridge** at Mile 271.8 EHL (65-foot fixed vertical clearance) and then enters the relatively narrow channel of West Bay Creek, the start of the land cut known as the "Grand Canyon." For purposes of careful navigation, however, you may assume that you are in narrow circumstances at flashing green "15" at GIWW Mile 275 EHL.

While in the Grand Canyon watch aids to navigation and your course carefully as shoal water with depths of 2 to 4 feet MLW runs very close to either side of the channel. The narrow channel persists past green daybeacon "39" (just past West Bay Creek (SR 79) Bridge) where the aids to navigation cease. The channel here runs relatively wide and deep for about 16.5 miles to GIWW Mile 254.5 EHL at the entrance to Choctawhatchee Bay.

Occasionally when high winds are expected on Choctawhatchee Bay you will find westbound barges waiting inside the Grand Canyon at about GIWW Mile 254 EHL for better conditions. Cautious mariners might follow suit. Tying up to a commercial barge here is entirely possible, if you make a proper approach to the towboat's skipper.

In the event of strong crosswinds make it a point to check with any tows (VHF Channel 13) in the channel east of the **Clyde B. Wells & Choctawhatchee Bay (U.S. 331/SR 83) Bridges** at Mile 250.4 EHL (65-foot fixed vertical clearance) as the narrow channel may require coordinated meeting or passing. Barges, especially empty ones, are exceptionally difficult to handle for towboat operators in heavy wind and current.

While the cut is frequently dredged to 10.5-foot MLW depths, shoaling is chronic so hold to the center except when passing and realize that if you hug the shore too closely while passing you will likely run aground in soft mud. Also use particular caution when transiting after strong winds or heavy rain when large pine trees can break away from the nearly vertical banks and float downstream.

Anchorage: Burnt Mill Creek at Mile 277.7 EHL on the northern shore of West Bay has 7 to 9 feet MLW. If you need it you can find anchorage in 7 feet MLW over good holding ground in the lee of the causeway on either side of the Choctawhatchee Bay Bridge at Mile 250.3.

Choctawhatchee Bay, FL

CHOCTAWHATCHEE BAY AREA		Largest Vessel	VHF	Total Slips	Approach/ Dockside Depth	Floating Docks	Gas/ Diesel	Repairs/ Haulout	Min/Max Amps	Pump-Out Station
1. Fisherman's Boatyard	(850) 835-4848				/			RH		
2. Freeport Marina and Yacht Club **WiFi** GIWW 249.0 mi. EHL	(850) 835-2035	55	9	50	15.0 / 10.0	F	G		30	P

WiFi Wireless Internet Access **onSpot** Dockside WiFi Facility
Visit www.waterwayguide.com for current rates, fuel prices, website addresses and other up-to-the-minute information.
(Information in the table is provided by the facilities.)

Scan here for more details:

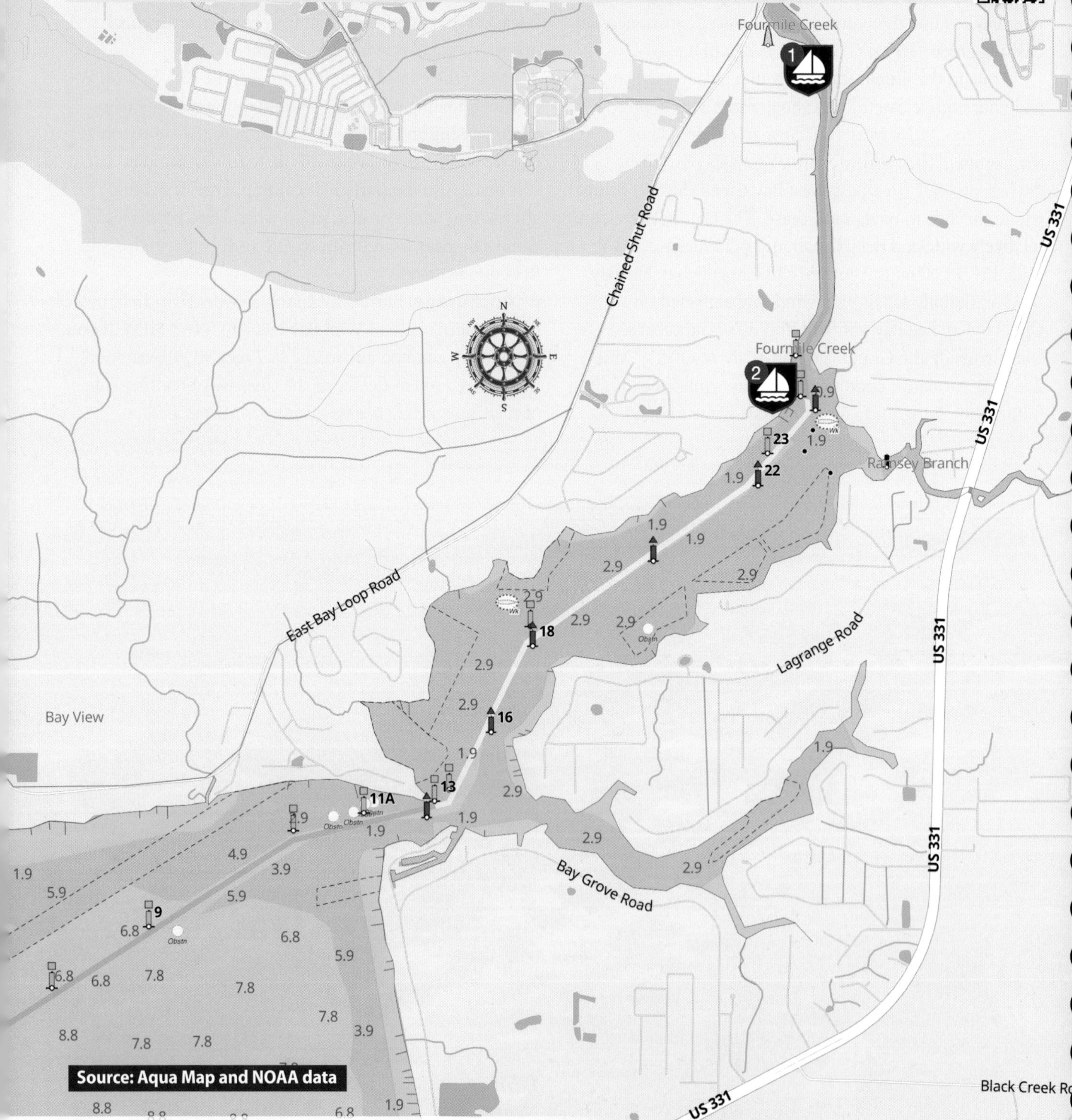

Source: Aqua Map and NOAA data

Choctawhatchee Bay, FL

CHOCTAWHATCHEE BAY AREA		Largest Vessel	VHF	Total Slips	Approach/ Dockside Depth	Floating Docks	Gas/ Diesel	Repairs/ Haulout	Min/Max Amps	Pump-Out Station
1. Sandestin's Baytowne Marina **WiFi** GIWW 240.0 mi. EHL	(850) 267-7773	130	16	120	8.0 / 7.0		GD	R	30 / 100	P

WiFi Wireless Internet Access **onSpot** Dockside WiFi Facility
Visit www.waterwayguide.com for current rates, fuel prices, website addresses and other up-to-the-minute information.
(Information in the table is provided by the facilities.)

Scan here for more details:

Choctawhatchee Bay–GIWW Mile 253.5 to Mile 225 EHL

NAVIGATION: Use NOAA Chart 11385. As you travel into Choctawhatchee Bay from the east the water deepens from about 9 to 38 feet MLW but is generally shallow along its southern shore. Be cautious passing Tucker Bayou (Mile 254 EHL) at the entrance (or, as in this case, exit) of the Grand Canyon as it sometimes shoals to 3-foot MLW depths or less at its mouth.

The route is closely pegged with markers for the first 5 to 6 mile but as the bay broadens and deepens, buoys thin out. Markers are used mainly to indicate shallows to the south and these should be given a wide berth due to the possibility of shoaling. There is room to roam in this large, open bay (about 30 miles long and 3 to 5 miles wide) but be aware that it can get rough in hard easterly or westerly blows due to

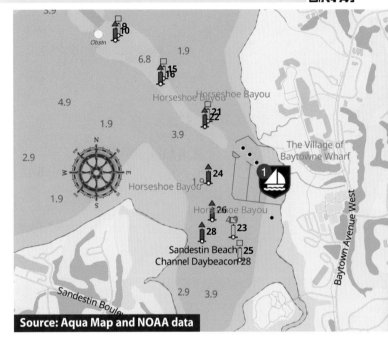

Source: Aqua Map and NOAA data

Choctawhatchee Bay, FL

CHOCTAWHATCHEE BAY AREA		Largest Vessel	VHF	Total Slips	Approach/ Dockside Depth	Floating Docks	Gas/ Diesel	Repairs/ Haulout	Min/Max Amps	Pump-Out Station
1. Legendary Marine GIWW 234.0 mi. EHL	(850) 990-2010	50	16	350	8.0 /	F	GD	RH	30 / 50	P

WiFi Wireless Internet Access **onSpot** Dockside WiFi Facility
Visit www.waterwayguide.com for current rates, fuel prices, website addresses and other up-to-the-minute information.
(Information in the table is provided by the facilities.)

Scan here for more details:

the east-west fetch. The approach to the 64-foot fixed vertical clearance **Mid-Bay (SR 293) Bridge** (Mile 234.2 EHL) is well marked from both east and west.

Dockage: In La Grange Bayou off the north side of the Choctawhatchee Bay are two marinas with limited services: Fisherman's Boatyard (repairs only) and Freeport Marina and Yacht Club with a few slips, a Ship's Store and boat and RV storage.

Near the center of the long Choctawhatchee Bay south of Mile 239 EHL in Horseshoe Bayou is the full-service Sandestin's Baytowne Marina, part of a large resort community that stretches from the bay to the beach. The gated community offers marina guests all resort amenities. The Village of Baytowne Wharf has

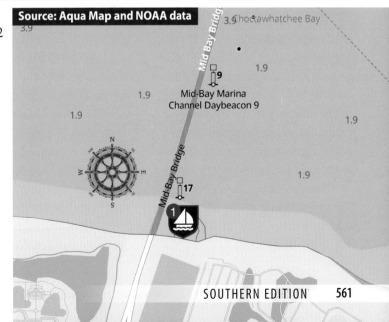

Source: Aqua Map and NOAA data

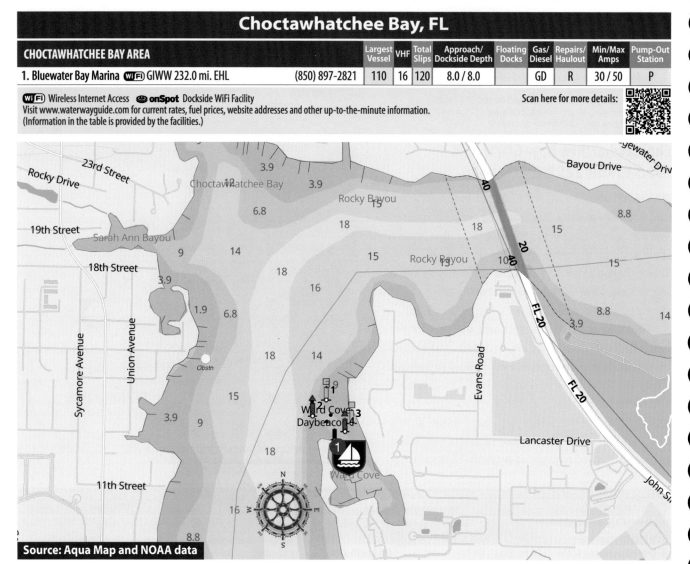

Choctawhatchee Bay, FL

CHOCTAWHATCHEE BAY AREA				Largest Vessel	VHF	Total Slips	Approach/ Dockside Depth	Floating Docks	Gas/ Diesel	Repairs/ Haulout	Min/Max Amps	Pump-Out Station
1. Bluewater Bay Marina (WiFi) GIWW 232.0 mi. EHL			(850) 897-2821	110	16	120	8.0 / 8.0		GD	R	30 / 50	P

(WiFi) Wireless Internet Access (onSpot) Dockside WiFi Facility
Visit www.waterwayguide.com for current rates, fuel prices, website addresses and other up-to-the-minute information.
(Information in the table is provided by the facilities.)

Scan here for more details:

Source: Aqua Map and NOAA data

many charming shops and boutiques, restaurants, nightclubs, art galleries and other facilities.

To approach Sandestin's Baytowne Marina, head south once you are clear of Four Mile Point and line up for flashing green "1" and flashing red "2" at the beginning of the entrance to the facility. Be careful to avoid the shoal depths when approaching shore to the east. Located at the southeastern foot of the Mid-Bay Bridge is Legendary Marine, which is primarily a boat brokerage. Call ahead for slip availability.

After passing under the Mid-Bay Bridge (Mile 234.2 EHL) and flashing red "58" head northwest a little more than 3 miles along the northern shore to flashing green "1" and turn north for Rocky Bayou. Ward Cove is to the east as you approach Rocky Bayou on the north side of Choctawhatchee Bay. Green daybeacon "1" and flashing red "2" mark the entrance to Ward Cove and Bluewater Bay Marina. This is a full resort complex with slips, repairs and an outstanding Ship's Store. They also offer "high and dry" boat storage. Nearby Emerald

Coast Marine Group is a full-service boatyard.

Anchorage: Rocky Bayou on the north shore provides a scenic anchorage. To enter Rocky Bayou follow the directions above for Bluewater Bay Marina but pass Ward Cove. The anchorage offers 12 to 14 feet MLW with protection from the south and only a small amount of fetch from the north before the charted 20-foot fixed vertical clearance bridge. A tighter but even more protected (except from the south) option is in the northwest fork in 7 to 10 feet MLW. You can

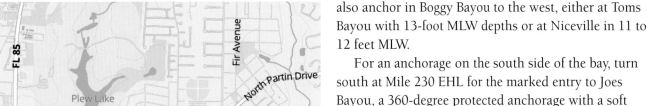

Choctawhatchee Bay, FL

CHOCTAWHATCHEE BAY AREA		Largest Vessel	VHF	Total Slips	Approach/ Dockside Depth	Floating Docks	Gas/ Diesel	Repairs/ Haulout	Min/Max Amps	Pump-Out Station
1. Emerald Coast Marine Group (WiFi) GIWW 231.0 mi. EHL	(850) 389-8318	65	16	60	15.0 / 8.0		GD	RH	50	P

(WiFi) Wireless Internet Access   onSpot Dockside WiFi Facility
Visit www.waterwayguide.com for current rates, fuel prices, website addresses and other up-to-the-minute information.
(Information in the table is provided by the facilities.)

Scan here for more details:

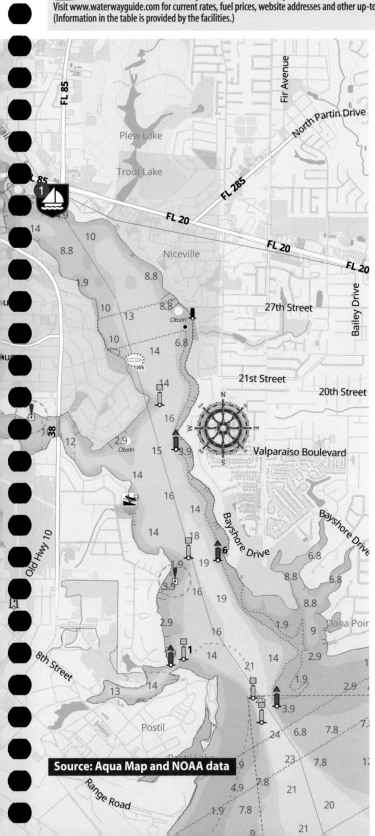

Source: Aqua Map and NOAA data

also anchor in Boggy Bayou to the west, either at Toms Bayou with 13-foot MLW depths or at Niceville in 11 to 12 feet MLW.

For an anchorage on the south side of the bay, turn south at Mile 230 EHL for the marked entry to Joes Bayou, a 360-degree protected anchorage with a soft mud bottom and depths of 10 feet MLW or more.

Destin–GIWW Mile 227 EHL

Destin lies just north and east of the Choctawhatchee Bay Entrance from the Gulf on the barrier peninsula sheltering the bay on the south. Destin is renowned for its sparkling beaches, crystal-clear waters and seaside resort activities, which are accessible year-round, thanks to an average air temperature of 67.3° maximum with a minimum average of 52.2° from October through March. Full-service marinas, waterfront hotels and restaurants abound.

This is sportfishing country and Destin sponsors numerous tournaments each year. The entire month of October is devoted to the more than 50-year-old Destin Fishing Rodeo (www. destinfishingrodeo.org). Big game fish ply the Loop Current that circulates clockwise in the Gulf of Mexico and that current comes relatively close to shore near Destin. The rodeo draws thousands of expectant anglers who search the offshore waters, inshore bays and bayous for prize-winning fish worth thousands of dollars.

NAVIGATION: Use NOAA Chart 11385. The main docking area in Destin is immediately south and east of the fixed bridge over the Choctawhatchee Bay entrance from the Gulf (south of the GIWW). The charted vertical bridge clearance at the William T. Marler (US 98/SR 30) Bridge (locally known as the Destin Bridge) is 49 feet but there have been reports that 48 feet is closer to reality so sailors should use caution if their vessel's mast height is more than that.

If entering East Pass from the Gulf, care should be taken when crossing the bar if there is a swell running. Also note that buoys are not charted in the Choctawhatchee Bay entrance channel as constant shoaling necessitates frequent relocation. This is a pass

Choctawhatchee Bay, FL

DESTIN		Largest Vessel	VHF	Total Slips	Approach/ Dockside Depth	Floating Docks	Gas/ Diesel	Repairs/ Haulout	Min/Max Amps	Pump-Out Station
1. Destin Marina	(850) 837-2470	30		10	6.0 / 6.0		G			
2. HarborWalk Marina GIWW 230.0 mi. EHL	(850) 650-2400	85	16	52	10.0 / 6.0	F	GD		30 / 50	P
3. Destin Fisherman's Co-op GIWW 230.0 mi. EHL	(850) 654-4999	100		40	8.0 / 8.0		D	RH	30	

WiFi Wireless Internet Access **onSpot** Dockside WiFi Facility
Visit www.waterwayguide.com for current rates, fuel prices, website addresses and other up-to-the-minute information.
(Information in the table is provided by the facilities.)

Scan here for more details:

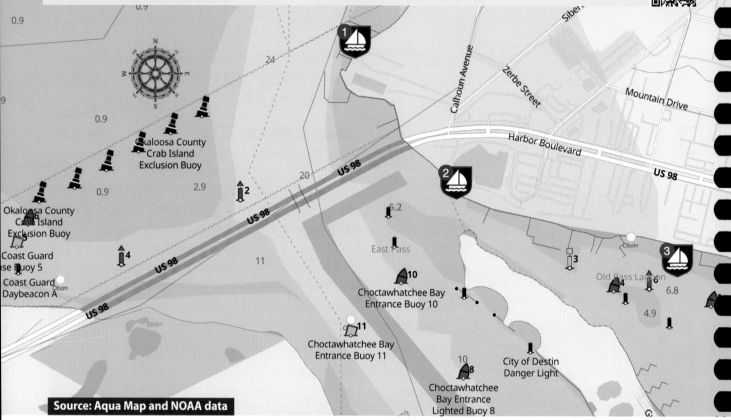

Source: Aqua Map and NOAA data

Okaloosa County Crab Island Exclusion Buoy

Okaloosa County Crab Island Exclusion Buoy

Coast Guard ... se Buoy 5

Coast Guard ... Daybeacon A

East Pass

Choctawhatchee Bay Entrance Buoy 10

Choctawhatchee Bay Entrance Buoy 11

Choctawhatchee Bay Entrance Lighted Buoy 8

City of Destin Danger Light

East Pass

Destin

Crab Island

that needs to be negotiated with local knowledge, in flat water, with good visibility and during reasonable tides.

To enter the main Destin Harbor (commonly called Old Pass Lagoon) turn sharply to east after passing under the bridges (or before if coming from the Gulf). The channel into the large harbor is narrow but well-marked with daybeacons. It runs between the mainland to the north and the protective sandbar to the south.

Marine facilities line the northern shore of the harbor. The pristine beaches and dunes of Santa Rosa Island are located across the peninsula on the Gulf side. Because of the substantial development along the beach, you will have to search for a public beach access.

Dockage: Along the north shore of the harbor Destin Marina (located north of the bridge) has newly rebuilt docks but few amenities. It is, however, within walking distance of downtown. Transient dockage

is available at HarborWalk Marina located southeast of the bridge and on the north side of Destin Harbor. This facility gets high marks from cruisers for the friendly and helpful staff. Provisions are within walking distance of the marina.

The entrance is a little tricky to Destin Harbor. Turn directly after passing under bridge and follow the (unlit) channel, staying closer to the north side of harbor. Destin Fisherman's Co-op is located on the north side of the harbor and can accommodate vessels to 100 feet. This is primarily a sportfishing charter site so call ahead for slip availability. Many locally popular eating establishments also offer dockage with everything from snacks to gourmet meals.

Anchorage: Destin Harbor provides excellent anchorage with no surge. You can anchor on the southwest side of the harbor or just off Harbor Docks Restaurant (850-837-2506) to the east. There are restaurants all around with dinghy

docks. A municipal water taxi service is available during the summer months. Note that the harbor is a No-Discharge Zone.

Side Trip: Crab Island

Although more of a submerged sandbar than an island, Crab Island attracts hundreds of boaters who wade in 1- to 4-foot-deep clear waters in search of sea life. Located on the north side of the Destin Bridge it is open to the inflow and outflow of the crystal clear water from the Gulf yet protected from the surf and waves. Crab Island is only accessible by boat (or kayak or stand-up paddleboard).

There are several floating businesses where you can find food, drinks, live music and even a playground for kids. Although Crab Island is accessible year round, the floating vendors are typically only open from March through October. By the way, you cannot buy alcoholic beverages here but you can bring your own (and many do).

Choctawhatchee Bay, FL

FORT WALTON BEACH		Largest Vessel	VHF	Total Slips	Approach/ Dockside Depth	Floating Docks	Gas/ Diesel	Repairs/ Haulout	Min/Max Amps	Pump-Out Station
1. Two George's Marina (WiFi) GIWW 225.0 mi. EHL	(850) 651-0510	125	16	134	32.0 / 8.0		GD	RH	30 / 50	P

(WiFi) Wireless Internet Access　(onSpot) Dockside WiFi Facility
Visit www.waterwayguide.com for current rates, fuel prices, website addresses and other up-to-the-minute information.
(Information in the table is provided by the facilities.)

Scan here for more details:

Source: Aqua Map and NOAA data

Fort Walton Beach–GIWW Mile 224 EHL

Fort Walton Beach combines the many charms of a major seaside resort and is well worth a cruising layover. Besides the swimming and snorkeling in crystal-clear water, the area is an angler's delight.

Need a break from the water? This captivating town is a shopper's bonanza with antiques stores, novelty shops, boutiques, upscale dress shops and bookstores. Golf and tennis facilities abound and there is an eclectic variety of restaurants and nightclubs. This is also home to Eglin Air Force Base, a military facility that's larger than the entire state of Rhode Island.

NAVIGATION: Use NOAA Chart 11385. The channel at Fort Walton Beach is well marked on the approach from the east. Flashing green "1" and red nun "2" are almost 2 miles west of the entrance to North Channel. The GIWW narrows considerably on the west side

Choctawhatchee Bay, FL

FORT WALTON BEACH		Largest Vessel	VHF	Total Slips	Approach/ Dockside Depth	Floating Docks	Gas/ Diesel	Repairs/ Haulout	Min/Max Amps	Pump-Out Station
1. Adventure Marina (WiFi) GIWW 223.0 mi. EHL	(850) 581-2628	130	16		8.0 / 8.0		G	RH	30 / 50	
2. Emerald Coast Boatyard	(850) 244-2722				9.0 / 7.0			RH		
3. Fort Walton Beach Yacht Basin GIWW 222.0 mi. EHL	(850) 244-5725	50	16	94	9.0 / 7.0		G		30 / 50	P

(WiFi) Wireless Internet Access　(onSpot) Dockside WiFi Facility
Visit www.waterwayguide.com for current rates, fuel prices, website addresses and other up-to-the-minute information.
(Information in the table is provided by the facilities.)

Scan here for more details:

Choctawhatchee Bay, FL

NAVARRE		Largest Vessel	VHF	Total Slips	Approach/ Dockside Depth	Floating Docks	Gas/ Diesel	Repairs/ Haulout	Min/Max Amps	Pump-Out Station
1. East River Smokehouse Navarre	(850) 939-2802			48	5.0 / 4.0					

WiFi Wireless Internet Access   **onSpot** Dockside WiFi Facility
Visit www.waterwayguide.com for current rates, fuel prices, website addresses and other up-to-the-minute information.
(Information in the table is provided by the facilities.)

Scan here for more details:

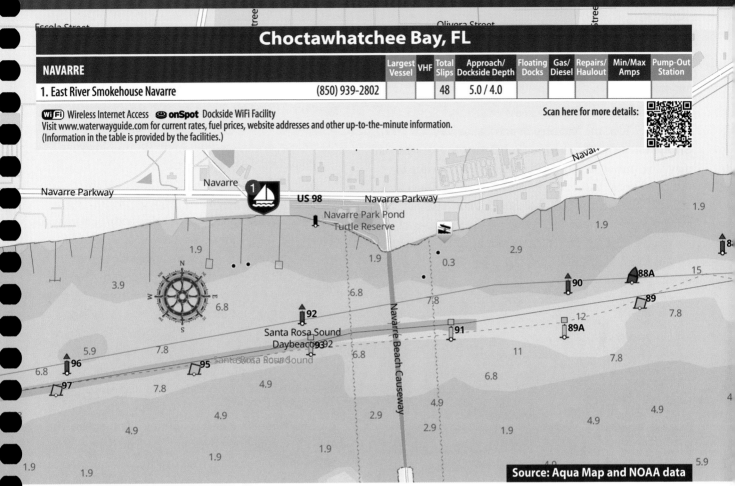

Source: Aqua Map and NOAA data

of **Brooks Memorial Bridge** (50 foot fixed vertical clearance) at Mile 223.1 EHL and you will come across a series of floating marks that will get that point across to you quite well.

Dockage: Although off the "main drag," transient space may be found on the eastern shore of the entrance to Garnier Bayou, approximately 2 miles northwest of GIWW Mile 225 EHL. A well-marked channel entrance with a tall, cylindrical water tower serves as a beacon to Two George's Marina at Shalimar Yacht Basin, a full-service repair facility with slips on five landscaped acres. While Cinco and Garnier Bayous offer a number of marine facilities, the 19-foot fixed vertical clearance **Elgin Parkway Bridge** limits access to both. Adventure Marina on the west side of Brooks Memorial Bridge is a boat brokerage with a complete service department. Call ahead for slip availability.

One-half mile west of Brooks Memorial Bridge, Fort Walton Beach offers a free pump-out station at a city park on the north side. You are welcome to stay overnight but there are no amenities. Depth at the dock's T-head is 6 feet MLW but it is considerably shallower near the shore.

This is a busy waterway and there is not much room for anchoring except near the free dock so why not tie up?

Emerald Coast Boatyard on the north side of the GIWW at Mile 222 EHL offers repairs but no transient slips. Fort Walton Beach Yacht Basin has some transient space reserved (for vessels to 50 feet). Call ahead for slip availability in this area.

The Narrows & Santa Rosa Sound– GIWW Mile 223 to Mile 189 EHL

From the southwestern terminus of Choctawhatchee Bay, west of Fort Walton Beach, the GIWW enters a section known as The Narrows. This waterway, which is actually the eastern end of Santa Rosa Sound, is appropriately named.

Although well marked, the channel twists back and forth through shallows for about 6 miles before it widens somewhat as it approaches Santa Rosa Sound proper. As the GIWW winds through Santa Rosa Sound to Pensacola Bay, you will see an abundance of attractive homes along the mainland side with beach communities dotting the barrier side.

Pensacola Bay, west of Deer and Fair Points, has always been considered one of Florida's largest and safest harbors. It has served as a heavy weather refuge for commercial and naval ships as well as smaller craft.

NAVIGATION: Use NOAA Charts 11378 and 11385. At Mile 206.7 EHL the **Navarre Beach Causeway (CR 399) Bridge** has a charted fixed vertical clearance of 50 feet but may have only a 48-foot fixed vertical clearance due to tide conditions. East of the bridge between flashing green "87" and flashing red "88" is a shoal into the channel so favor the green (south) side.

While transiting The Narrows monitor VHF Channels 16 and 13 for barge traffic to avoid a "squeeze" when meeting with an oncoming barge.

- "Passing one whistle" means that you and the tow agree to alter course to starboard and pass port-to-port.
- "Passing two whistles" means that you are altering course to port and will pass starboard-to-starboard.

If you ask the skipper of the tow what is best for him, you will likely get extreme cooperation. Remember that barges are not maneuverable like your pleasure craft so give the barge traffic the benefit of the doubt.

⚠️

Near Mile 200 EHL note that red daybeacon "124" marks a shoal encroaching into the channel. Some charts do not show this marker. At this point you should switch to NOAA Chart 11378.

At Mile 205 EHL the GIWW emerges from shoal territory into Santa Rosa Sound. Although the GIWW does move through some shoal areas in Santa Rosa Sound (5- and 6-foot MLW depths), for the most part it carries respectable depths of 13 to 17 feet MLW all the way to the **Bob Sikes (Pensacola Beach/SR 399) Bridge** at Mile 189.1 EHL.

Dockage: On the west side of the Navarre Beach Causeway (CR 399) Bridge at Mile 206.7 EHL (north shore) is East River Smokehouse Navarre with 48 slips and 4-foot MLW dockside depths. They also have excellent ribs and live music on weekends. Call ahead for slip availability.

Anchorage: Anchorages abound in The Narrows. Mary Esther at GIWW Mile 219.7 EHL has at least 4 feet MLW and good holding. On Santa Rosa Island there are four main anchorages:

- Mile 217.4 EHL just west of green daybeacon "51"
- Mile 215 EHL by green daybeacon "69"
- Mile 213.9 EHL on the south shore at Manatee Point (red daybeacon "74A")
- Mile 208.6 EHL on the north shore at Lower Pritchard Long Point by green daybeacon "85"

All of these these anchorages have a sandy bottom with good holding. What they do not have is shore access.

You can also drop the hook on either side of the Navarre Beach Causeway (CR 399) Bridge (Mile 206.7 EHL) at green daybeacon "89" on the south shore just east of the bridge or at "93" on the west side of the bridge.

Juana's Pagodas & Sailors' Grill (850-939-1092) next to the boat ramp on the west side of the bridge has a great little beach (with chair and umbrella rentals) and serves breakfast, lunch and dinner daily. They also rent all types of watercraft from Waverunners to Hobie Cats.

Santa Rosa Sound, which is not much wider than The Narrows, has numerous coves and good anchorages along its shores. Be sure to check your depths and remember the effect of the wind on tides as the anchorages may be somewhat more shallow than charted.

■ TO PERDIDO BAY

The Pensacola Bay area not only has beautiful beaches there are also historic forts and the National Museum of Naval Aviation (850-452-3604, www.navalaviation.com). The area blends the influences of the outstanding beach, extensive military history, active art scene and hikeable woodlands create a destination where there's something for everyone.

Pensacola Bay is relatively narrow (3 miles) and stretches in an east-west direction for about 22 miles. On its west side Escambia Bay and East Bay extend some 10 miles north. Pensacola Bay carries depths of 20 to 50 feet but the bays to the north run 9 to 12 feet (at MLW) with more extensive shoals as you go north. Many marine facilities are located in Sabine Bay, located just west of the Bob Sikes (Pensacola Beach/SR 399) Bridge (65-foot fixed vertical clearance) at GIWW Mile 189.1 EHL.

Pensacola Beach & Little Sabine Bay

NAVIGATION: Use NOAA Charts 11378. Keep within all channel markers if you are entering Pensacola Bay from the Gulf of Mexico on the Caucus Channel. This good all-weather passage is subject to shoaling, which is almost always well marked.

A principal mark for the entrance is the 171-foot conical brick Pensacola Light. Currents can be significant in this channel, especially at the 90-degree turn into the Bay. The Pensacola Coast Guard Station is 1 mile east of Pensacola Light.

For westbound skippers, as you enter Pensacola Bay note that after passing flashing green "145" (at about GIWW Mile 184.2 EHL) the buoys shift to that of the Pensacola Ship Channel (red-right-returning for vessels in-bound from the Gulf). Thus, if traveling the GIWW from this point across Pensacola Bay to the Pensacola Landcut and then re-entering the GIWW at about GIWW Mile 179.5 EHL, you should leave red markers to port and green to starboard. (These markers carry the appropriate small yellow triangles and squares indicating their dual role as GIWW route markers.)

Dockage: Immediately east of the Pensacola Beach Bridge at GIWW Mile 189.1 EHL on the north side of Santa Rosa Sound is the 40-slip Santa Rosa Yacht & Boat Club offering transient dockage. Just past the bridge, if you turn south and run parallel to it, you will see channel markers for Little Sabine Bay. Pensacola Beach Marina is the first marina on the port side after entering Little Sabine Bay. It provides a few transient slips, fishing charters, dolphin cruises and boat rentals. Expect the docks to be busy in the summer months.

Just to the south in Little Sabine Bay is Sabine Marina, which may also have transient space and is home to the Frisky Dolphin Sunset Oyster Bar & Grill (850-934-3141).

Six miles northeast of the GIWW on the west side of the Commercial Port of Pensacola is Sayville Harbor with marine facilities just three blocks from downtown Pensacola. The slips at Palafox Pier Yacht Harbor are on floating piers with deep water. Other amenities include a small Ship's Store. The 24-slip Baylen Slips Marina may also have transient space on their floating docks. There is no room for anchoring here.

Anchorage: Quiet Water Beach Pier is a free dock (no services) at Pensacola Beach to the east of the Pensacola Beach Bridge. If the dock is full, you can anchor nearby at Quiet Water Beach in 7 to 11 feet MLW. It is also possible to anchor in Little Sabine Bay (west of the bridge) in 5 to 11 feet MLW. This is a tight area.

English Navy Cove on the north shore of Santa Rosa Sound carries 11 to 15 feet MLW. Expect wakes from large fishing vessels.

Bayou Chico

One mile southwest of the Port of Pensacola is a channel running northwest to Bayou Chico (GIWW Mile 185 EHL), which has full-service boatyards with facilities to handle most repairs and a number of full-service marinas. The 65-foot fixed vertical clearance **Bayou Chico (SR 292) Bridge** crosses Bayou Chico.

Dockage: South of the bridge in Bayou Chico is the private Pensacola Yacht Club. They recognize reciprocal privileges from yacht clubs throughout Florida, all along the Gulf Coast and in many southeast cities with GYA lake-based yacht clubs.

Pensacola Bay Area

Pensacola Bay, FL

PENSACOLA BEACH AREA		Largest Vessel	VHF	Total Slips	Approach/ Dockside Depth	Floating Docks	Gas/ Diesel	Repairs/ Haulout	Min/Max Amps	Pump-Out Station
1. Santa Rosa Yacht & Boat Club (WiFi) GIWW 189.0 mi. EHL	(850) 934-1005	70	16	40	8.0 / 8.0		GD		30 / 100	P
2. Pensacola Beach Marina - Temporarily closed due to hurricane damage (WiFi) GIWW 189.0 mi. EHL	(850) 932-0304	100	16	30	/		GD		30 / 50	P
3. Sabine Marina (WiFi) GIWW 189.0 mi. EHL	(850) 932-1904	57	16	64	9.0 / 8.0				30 / 50	P

(WiFi) Wireless Internet Access   onSpot Dockside WiFi Facility
Visit www.waterwayguide.com for current rates, fuel prices, website addresses and other up-to-the-minute information.
(Information in the table is provided by the facilities.)

Scan here for more details:

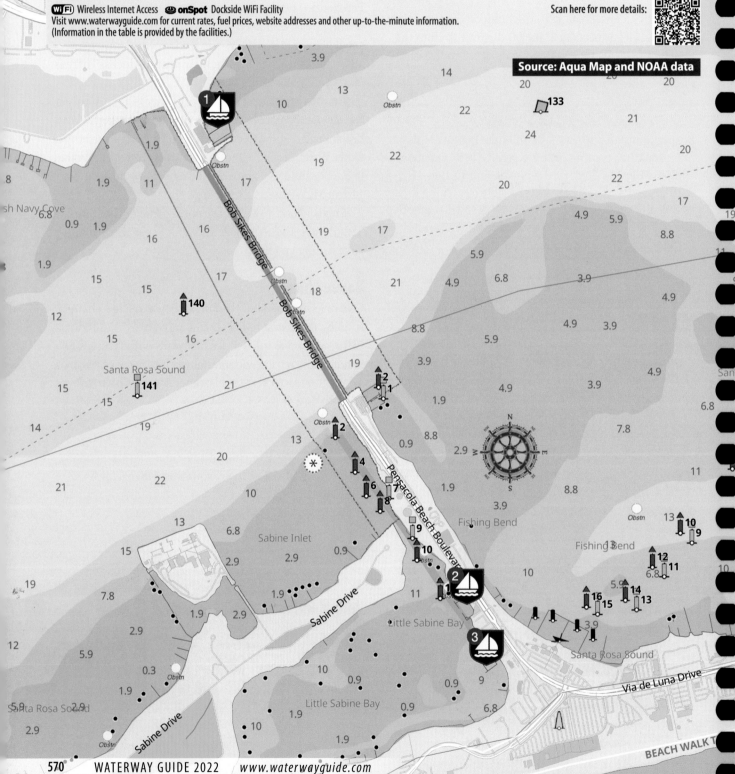

Source: Aqua Map and NOAA data

Pensacola Bay, FL

SAYVILLE HARBOR		Largest Vessel	VHF	Total Slips	Approach/ Dockside Depth	Floating Docks	Gas/ Diesel	Repairs/ Haulout	Min/Max Amps	Pump-Out Station
1. Seville Harbour Marina 186 EHL	(850) 432-9620	50	16	43	7.0 / 7.0				30	
2. Palafox Pier Yacht Harbor (WiFi) GIWW 186.0 mi. EHL	(850) 432-9620	175	16	88	20.0 / 13.0	F	GD		30 / 50	P
3. Baylen Slips Marina - Temp closed due to damage from Hurricane Sally (WiFi)	(850) 432-9620	55	16	24	20.0 / 13.0	F	GD		30 / 50	P

(WiFi) Wireless Internet Access onSpot Dockside WiFi Facility
Visit www.waterwayguide.com for current rates, fuel prices, website addresses and other up-to-the-minute information.
(Information in the table is provided by the facilities.)

Scan here for more details:

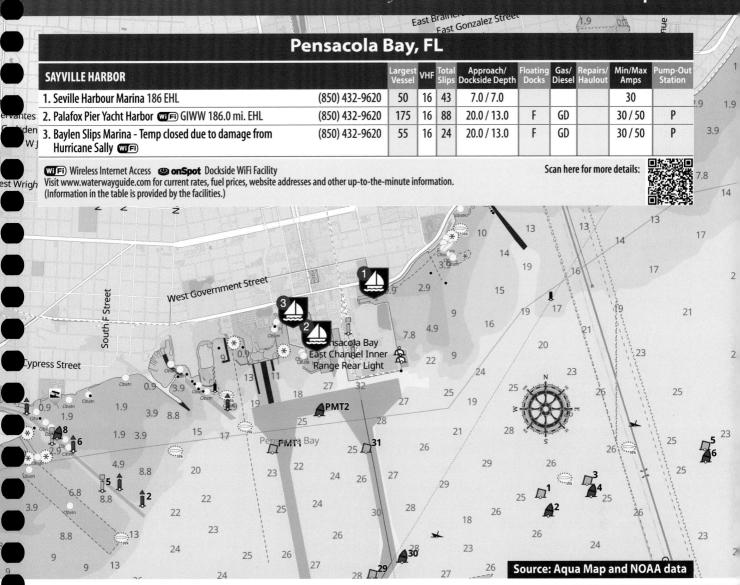

Source: Aqua Map and NOAA data

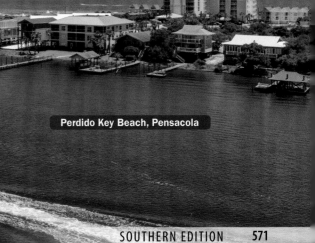

Perdido Key Beach, Pensacola

MarineMax Pensacola is a yacht brokerage with one transient slip. To the south-southwest before the bridge are the 52-slip Yacht Harbor Marina and 64-slip Palm Harbor Marina. Both have deep-water slips on floating docks.

Beyond the high-rise Bayou Chico (SR 292) Bridge, full-service repairs and transient dockage is available at Pelican's Perch Marina & Boatyard. This family-owned facility has floating docks and maintains a comprehensive listing of qualified local marine contractors. Call ahead for slip availability.

Past Pelican's Perch is Bell Marine Service offering service and repairs. The well-protected Island Cove Marina has a barbecue area and a community kitchen. Call ahead for slip availability. A little farther up Bayou Chico is the Pensacola Shipyard Marina & Boatyard, a full-service marina and boatyard facility.

Anchorage: In Bayou Chico you can anchor north of the marinas in 9 to 11 feet MLW with good holding in mud and all-around protection. The public boat ramp before the Bayou Chico Bridge allows access to the main road. Shopping is a two-mile walk west or you can take the bus.

Bayou Grande at Jones Point to the southwest has 9-foot MLW depths and offers good protection from wind and wakes. Anchor in the basin before the Murray Road Bridge (14-foot fixed vertical clearance).

Big Lagoon–GIWW Mile 179 to Mile 172 EHL

Continue west from Pensacola Bay into the GIWW. The intersection is about 1 mile from the exit into the Gulf of Mexico. It is a run of about 8 to 10 miles from Fort McRee at Pensacola's Gulf entrance to the Alabama line at about Mile 170 EHL. Ahead on the GIWW are some fabulous anchorages, great waterfront restaurants and fine repair facilities.

NAVIGATION: Use NOAA Chart 11378. As mentioned before traffic here can get confusing because the markers change to red-right-returning for vessels inbound from the Gulf to Pensacola to the GIWW (red on the north or land side and green on the south or Gulf side).

After flashing green "15" in the middle of the Caucus Channel between Forts Pickens and Barrancus, head west-southwest to green can "1" and flashing red "2" to transit the short and narrow but well-marked passage known locally as the Pensacola Land Cut (about Mile 178 to Mile 179 EHL) leading to Big Lagoon.

Be careful not to confuse green can buoy "1" with green can buoy "13" just to its south, which is a marker for the Caucus Channel. You can also line up the range markers to get to the land cut, which leads into Big Lagoon. As you enter keep an eye out for shoaling caused by strong tidal currents through the Caucus Channel. The shallows are easily seen on sunny days but if it is overcast, they will be harder to make out so stay to the center except to pass. Wait if you see a barge entering the pass. There is not much room in there.

Anchorage: There is a great anchorage at Fort McRee in 10 to 13 feet MLW in Big Lagoon at GIWW Mile 178.4 EHL. This is adjacent to Fort McRee so expect to see planes flying overhead. Dinghy to the beaches on the Bay or Gulf side. This anchorage is somewhat exposed to the west.

Redfish Point is a good anchorage south of the GIWW that is well

Pensacola Bay, FL

PENSACOLA AREA		Largest Vessel	VHF	Total Slips	Approach/ Dockside Depth	Floating Docks	Gas/ Diesel	Repairs/ Haulout	Min/Max Amps	Pump-Out Station
1. Pensacola Yacht Club-PRIVATE GIWW 185.0 mi. EHL	(850) 433-8804	100	16	58	8.0 / 8.0		GD		30 / 50	P
2. MarineMax Pensacola (WiFi) GIWW 185.0 mi. EHL	(850) 477-1112	60	16	60	6.0 / 4.0	F	GD	RH	30 / 50	P
3. Yacht Harbor Marina (WiFi) GIWW 185.0 mi. EHL	(850) 455-4552	65	16	52	9.0 / 6.5	F	D		30 / 50	P
4. Palm Harbor Marina - Pensacola (WiFi) GIWW 185.0 mi. EHL	(850) 455-4552	70		64	9.0 / 6.5	F			30 / 50	P
5. Pelican's Perch Marina & Boatyard (WiFi) GIWW 185.0 mi. EHL	(850) 453-3471	50			15.0 / 6.0	F		RH	30 / 50	P
6. Bell Marine Service GIWW 185.0 mi. EHL	(850) 455-7639	48		20	5.0 / 6.0			R	30	
7. Island Cove Marina (WiFi) GIWW 185.0 mi. EHL	(850) 455-4552	75		94	7.0 / 6.0				30 / 50	P
8. Pensacola Shipyard Marina & Boatyard (WiFi) GIWW 185.0 mi. EHL	(850) 439-1451	200		52	18.0 / 7.0	F	D	RH	30 / 100	P

(WiFi) Wireless Internet Access   (onSpot) Dockside WiFi Facility
Visit www.waterwayguide.com for current rates, fuel prices, website addresses and other up-to-the-minute information.
(Information in the table is provided by the facilities.)

Scan here for more details:

Source: Aqua Map and NOAA data

protected in most weather. Turn south before flashing red "10," which marks a very shallow shoal. You can anchor as close to shore as your draft permits in hard sand. You can also turn north at red "10" to access Trout Point (mainland side) with 11 feet MLW and good holding.

If you continue to flashing green "15" and double back toward the beach on Perdido Key, you will find 12-foot MLW depths with good holding. For a bit of shore side recreation swim or dinghy to the beach. The Gulf beach is a short walk across the dunes, which are part of the Gulf Coast Island National Seashore Park. This is a favorite weekend getaway for locals but there is a bothersome chop during a northerly.

You can anchor before the bridge at Siguenza Cove (Mile 172 EHL) in 5 to 7 feet MLW. This is somewhat exposed to the east and wakes.

Perdido Bay–GIWW Mile 172 to Mile 170 EHL

From Big Lagoon it is a short trip to Perdido Bay, sliced down the middle by the state line separating Florida from Alabama. Perdido Bay offers a variety of enticements for the cruising yachtsman.

NAVIGATION: Use NOAA Chart 11378. Leaving either the anchorage or the marinas, as you approach the left turn at the west end of Big Lagoon be careful not to shortcut the channel as flashing red "12" is well up in the cove and hard to see.

The area southeast of green can buoy "11" is shallow (which will be evident by the pelicans walking on the bar) so favor the center of the channel to avoid joining the many who have run aground here. Follow the markers because this entire area is surrounded by shoal water.

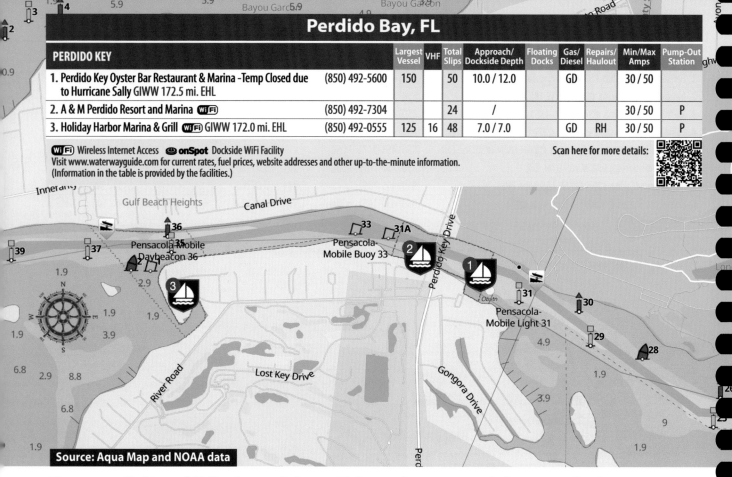

Perdido Bay, FL

PERDIDO KEY		Largest Vessel	VHF	Total Slips	Approach/ Dockside Depth	Floating Docks	Gas/ Diesel	Repairs/ Haulout	Min/Max Amps	Pump-Out Station
1. Perdido Key Oyster Bar Restaurant & Marina -Temp Closed due to Hurricane Sally GIWW 172.5 mi. EHL	(850) 492-5600	150		50	10.0 / 12.0		GD		30 / 50	
2. A & M Perdido Resort and Marina (WiFi)	(850) 492-7304			24	/				30 / 50	P
3. Holiday Harbor Marina & Grill (WiFi) GIWW 172.0 mi. EHL	(850) 492-0555	125	16	48	7.0 / 7.0		GD	RH	30 / 50	P

(WiFi) Wireless Internet Access (onSpot) **onSpot** Dockside WiFi Facility
Visit www.waterwayguide.com for current rates, fuel prices, website addresses and other up-to-the-minute information.
(Information in the table is provided by the facilities.)

Scan here for more details:

Source: Aqua Map and NOAA data

After a turn at flashing red "16" and green daybeacon "15" you will see the Gulf Beach Highway (SR 292) Bridge at Mile 171.8 EHL with a 73-foot fixed vertical clearance.

After flashing green "35" at Mile 170 EHL, enter the open but shoaled area between Perdido Key (FL) and Ono Island (AL). The GIWW is well marked as it extends along the northern side of Ono Island and Innerarity Peninsula. From flashing green "57" the GIWW swings north into Perdido Bay. The last of Florida, Innerarity Point, will be to the north and the first part of Alabama, Ono Island, is to the south. (Contrary to popular belief, not all of Alabama is west of Florida.)

Dockage: Immediately before the bridge on your left is the Perdido Key Oyster Bar Restaurant & Marina, LLC (at green daybeacon "31"). They offer slips and a face dock for larger vessels (to 150 feet). The restaurant serves lunch and dinner, has an outdoor bar and frequently host live music. Just after the bridge is the 24-slip A & M Perdido Resort and Marina, an RV resort with condos and a marina. Call ahead for slip availability.

If you are in need of repairs or a break, just 0.5 mile west of the bridge and immediately past flashing green "35" you can turn south and follow the private markers a short distance to Holiday Harbor Marina & Grill. The marina offers transient dockage and a popular waterfront restaurant. Use lots of fenders to cushion wakes from the GIWW. They are either the last marina in Florida heading west or the first marina in Florida heading east, depending on your perspective.

Anchorage: Tarkiln Bay (Mile 166.3 EHL) on the east shore of Perdido Bay offers 7- to 9-foot MLW depths and protection from all but southwest winds. On the western side of Perdido Bay there are anchorages at Soldier Creek and Palmetto Creek, which offer protection from the north and good holding in mud.

■ NEXT STOP

From here you will be entering the waters of Alabama's Gulf Coast and the vast delta of Mobile Bay, where those traveling the Great Loop will exit the inland river system.

Mile 170 EHL–Mile 40 EHL

■ MOBILE BAY AREA

West of the Pensacola Inlet you will enter the GIWW, pass Sherman Cove to the north and enter Big Lagoon. As you approach Mobile Bay, you are entering a vast delta basin fed by many rivers. These rivers feed into the bay and spread across the area to comprise the second largest drainage basin in the U.S. with the largest being the Mississippi River Delta. The GIWW to the west promises adventures with a rich history, scenic beauty and endless opportunities to entice the cruising boater.

Along this stretch of the GIWW you will cross into Alabama waters. The waterway route from the Alabama border at Mile 170 EHL through Mile 160 EHL is a wonderland of excellent protected anchorages including Perdido Bay, Terry Cove, Cotton Bayou, Soldier Creek, Roberts Bayou, Ingram Bayou and Wolf Bay. Check your charts and pick any one of these for a pleasant, protected overnight stop.

There are also plenty of marinas in the area, along with repair facilities, restaurants and other amenities. Until you get to Mobile Bay the only water-accessible town is

Orange Beach, AL, named for the orange groves that once were plentiful there.

NO WAKE ZONE

No Wake Zones, Idle Speed Zones and various Speed Limit restrictions are in effect throughout the waterways included in this chapter. Exercise diligence in knowing the regulations by observing signs and other markers. Enforcement is always present. As always, be courteous to other vessels and avoid manatees and other marine life.

Orange Beach Area

Spanish explorer Carlos Sequenza was looking for a permanent base when he stumbled upon Perdido Bay, which means "lost" in Spanish. Presumably Perdido Bay was named "lost" because of its narrow entrance. Pirates reportedly once favored the bay and the many coves and bayous in the area because they made good hiding places. Citizens using picks and shovels opened the Perdido Pass Inlet from the Gulf in Orange Beach proper in 1906.

NAVIGATION: Use NOAA Chart 11378. At Mile 170 EHL, heading west on the GIWW, the tip of private Ono Island appears to the south as you cruise the straight

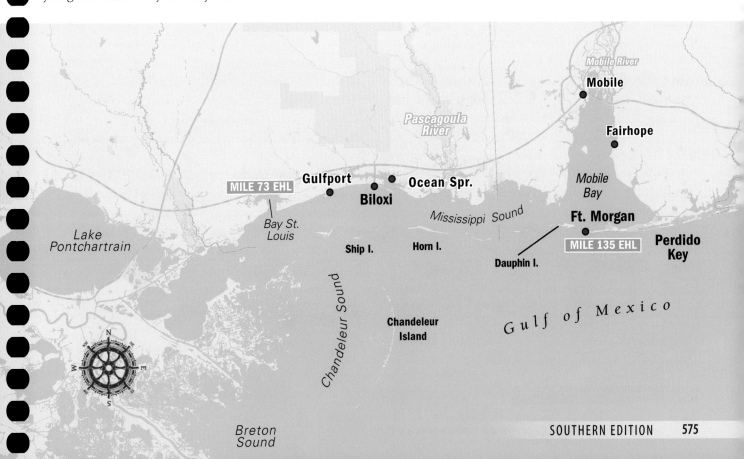

Perdido Bay, FL to Bon Secour Bay, AL

ORANGE BEACH AREA		Largest Vessel	VHF	Total Slips	Approach/ Dockside Depth	Floating Docks	Gas/ Diesel	Repairs/ Haulout	Min/Max Amps	Pump-Out Station
1. Reel Surprise Marina GIWW 167.0 mi. EHL	(251) 981-5423	68	16	46	5.0 / 5.0		GD			
2. Zeke's Landing Marina GIWW 163.0 mi. EHL	(251) 981-4044	100	69	50	7.0 / 7.0		GD	H	50	P
3. Saunders Marine Center - Orange Beach WiFi	(251) 981-3700	75		1	6.0 / 6.0			RH	30 / 50	P
4. Orange Beach Marina WiFi GIWW 163.0 mi. EHL	(251) 981-4207	130	16	161	9.0 / 8.0		GD	RH	30 / 100	P
5. Safe Harbor Sportsman WiFi GIWW 163.0 mi. EHL	(251) 981-6247	140	19	100	12.0 / 8.0		GD	RH	30 / 100	P

WiFi Wireless Internet Access **onSpot** Dockside WiFi Facility
Visit www.waterwayguide.com for current rates, fuel prices, website addresses and other up-to-the-minute information.
(Information in the table is provided by the facilities.)

Scan here for more details:

Source: Aqua Map and NOAA data

westward line of the GIWW to the entrance to Perdido Bay. At flashing green "57" turn north to explore Perdido Bay or southwest to explore Bayou St. John.

From flashing green "57" on the GIWW there is a marked channel extending from the GIWW through Bayou St. John to Perdido Pass to the Gulf of Mexico. The pass has a 9-foot MLW controlling depth and **Perdido Pass (SR 182) Bridge** has a 54-foot fixed vertical clearance. This pass is a popular well-marked gateway to and from the Gulf of Mexico.

A number of restaurants and marinas are located in the bays and bayous on the way to Perdido Pass. To visit Perdido Pass turn southwest off the GIWW at flashing green "57" then head for green daybeacon "17," which is the last buoy of the Perdido Pass Inlet channel. Pass between green daybeacon "17" (which will be to the west) and quick flashing red "18" (to the east) and then continue that orientation toward Perdido Pass as you

come around to the west. Note that at the beginning of this channel there are several private markers to a small cut into Ono Island to the south, which you should not follow.

If you want to explore marinas and facilities in Cotton Bayou, Terry Cove or Johnson Cove, make a soft turn further west at green can buoy "1" making sure not to cut the shallows between that and red nun buoy "8" for the Perdido Pass Channel. Parallel the Perdido Pass (SR182) Bridge by running west on its north side.

At the western end of the Perdido Pass (SR182) Bridge there are two channels–one that goes farther west into Cotton Bayou and the other going north from red nun buoy "8" and green can buoy "9." This will take you into both Terry Cove and Johnson Cove.

If you choose to enter Cotton Bayou, be careful of shoal water. Downtown Orange Beach amenities can be reached from the bayou. There is a moderate current here

Perdido Bay, FL to Bon Secour Bay, AL

ORANGE BEACH AREA			Largest Vessel	VHF	Total Slips	Approach/ Dockside Depth	Floating Docks	Gas/ Diesel	Repairs/ Haulout	Min/Max Amps	Pump-Out Station
1. Bear Point Harbor	WiFi	GIWW 165.0 mi. EHL	(251) 981-2327	47	16	83	12.0 / 6.0		GD		30 / 50	P
2. Barber Marina	WiFi	GIWW 163.0 mi. EHL	(251) 987-2628	125	16	155	12.0 / 12.0	F	GD	RH	30 / 200+	P
3. Pirates Cove Marina & Restaurant		GIWW 165.0 mi. EHL	(251) 987-1224	65		16	10.0 / 10.0				30	P

WiFi Wireless Internet Access onSpot Dockside WiFi Facility
Visit www.waterwayguide.com for current rates, fuel prices, website addresses and other up-to-the-minute information.
(Information in the table is provided by the facilities.)

Scan here for more details:

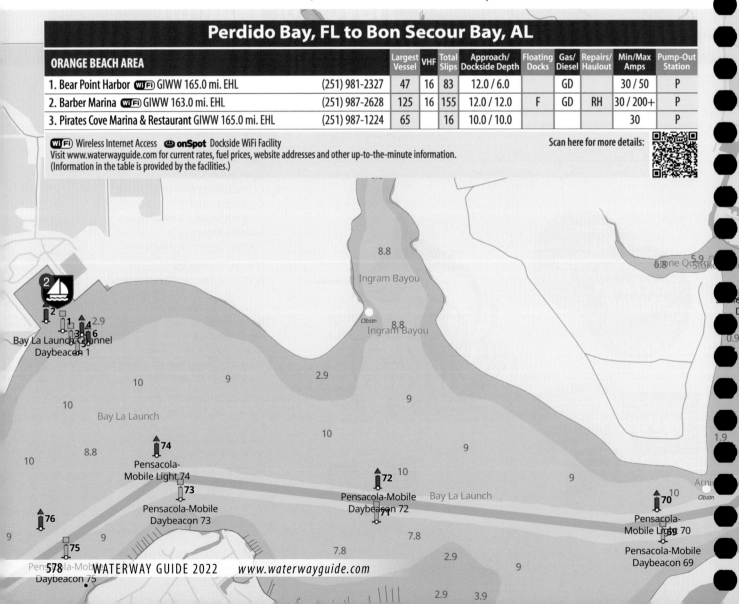

as you pass the inlet so be careful. Boaters with deep-draft vessels should use caution in Cotton Bayou; keep an eye on your depth sounder. Six-foot MLW depths have been observed here even though the chart shows differently.

Dockage: Reel Surprise Marina and Zeke's Landing Marina can accommodate a few transient vessels on the south side of Cotton Bayou. Both cater to charter fishing boats and Zeke's Landing Marina boasts the largest charter fleet on the Gulf Coast.

If you are heading up to Terry Cove from either Cotton Bayou or Perdido Pass, you will pass a boat ramp on the west headland and just past this boat ramp, flashing red "12." For Orange Beach Marina look due west (about 150 to 200 yards) for green daybeacon "1" and red daybeacon "2." This privately marked channel curves southward and then westward along private docks and residences. Follow it keeping red to starboard and at the very end you will see the marina's private channel, running due south.

The full-service Orange Beach Marina has plenty of transient dockage in a secluded and fully protected harbor. They offer all the usual amenities plus charters. A full-service boatyard, Saunders Marine Center–Orange Beach, is on site.

Safe Harbor Sportsman Marina on the north shore of Johnson Cove or eastern end of Terry Cove is easy to reach. At flashing red "12" in Johnson Cove carefully proceed north by northeast but give flashing red "12" a wide berth to avoid shoals lying east of the marker. The marina offers dry storage and some transient slips.

Anchorage: There is an anchorage at Bayou St. John at Mile 167 EHL with 7 to 8 feet at MLW and excellent holding in sand. (Somewhat exposed to the west.)

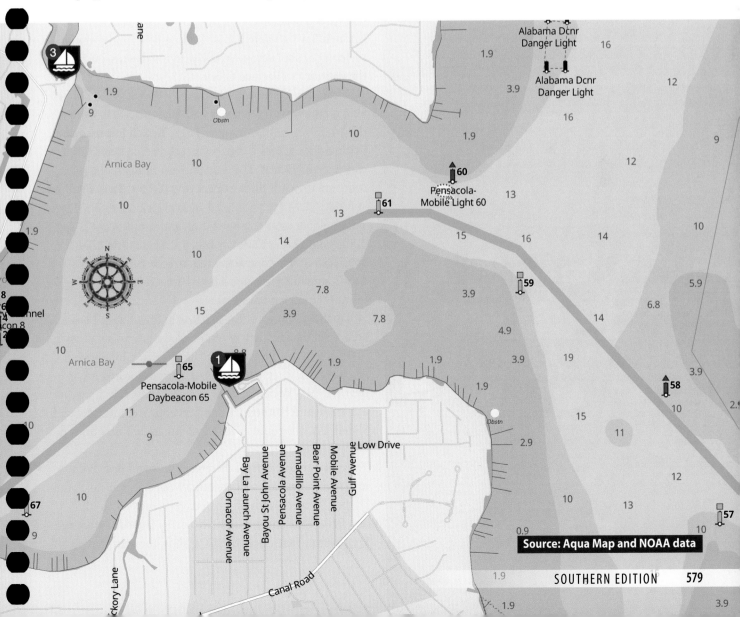

Source: Aqua Map and NOAA data

Exploring Perdido Bay

Spanish explorer Carlos Sequenza was looking for a permanent base when he stumbled upon Perdido Bay, which translates as "lost." Pirates reportedly once favored the narrow entrance of the bay and the many coves and bayous in the area that made good hiding places. Citizens using picks and shovels opened up Perdido Pass Inlet from the Gulf in Orange Beach proper in 1906.

We recommend you start your exploration of this area at the Orange Beach Welcome Center at 23685 Perdido Beach Blvd. (251-974-1510). The staff will undoubtedly tell you about the 222-acre Wharf Resort, which contains a full-service marina on the GIWW, condominiums, several restaurants, a variety of specialty and retail shops, a 10,000-seat amphitheater, a movie theater and a record-height (112-foot) Ferris wheel.

There are concerts, festivals and sporting events every weekend. Coastal Alabama Business Chamber coordinates the annual National Shrimp Festival on the second weekend in October, drawing more than 200,000 people to Pleasure Island at the Gulf Shores Beach Boardwalk for four days of live music, savory foods and numerous booths featuring arts and crafts of all kinds.

Perdido Bay to Bon Secour Bay–GIWW Mile 151 EHL

There are many "must-see" spots off the GIWW, particularly for gunkholers. Many cruisers have a problem when they visit this bountiful area in that they do not want to leave. Some who plan to stay for a week or so stay several weeks or even permanently.

NAVIGATION: Use NOAA Chart 11378. Reversing course toward the GIWW, as you leave Bayou St. John you can safely cut across from green daybeacon "17" (which will be to the west) to GIWW flashing red "58" (leave to the east as you are back on the GIWW westbound) at Mile 166 EHL.

The channel around Mill Point is well marked but is narrow and shallow on the edges. A sharp watch is required. Once in Arnica Bay the channel opens up–particularly to the north–before it closes down again off Hatchett Point at flashing red "68." From flashing red "68" to red daybeacon "90" the GIWW is relatively open through Bay La Launch, past Sapling Point and through the straight shot across Wolf Bay to red daybeacon "90" at the entrance to Portage Creek.

From here (Mile 160 EHL) the GIWW is bordered by land all the way to Oyster Bay at Mile 152.5 EHL. Along this route you will pass under **Foley Beach Expressway Bridge** at Mile 158.7 EHL, which has a fixed vertical clearance of 73 feet. The next and last bridges along this route are the **Gulf Shores Parkway (SR 59) Twin Bridges** at Mile 154.9 EHL with fixed vertical clearances of 73 feet.

A tugboat crew change station and supply store is east of the Gulf Shores Parkway Bridges. There is an Idle-Speed/No-Wake Zone along this stretch. Shrimp boats and barges sometimes tie up to both banks east of the bridge to wait out inclement weather.

Dockage: Most of the marinas in the Orange Beach area welcome transients (and there are several small ones not listed here). These and the facilities at Gulf Shores, AL, are the last recreational boat marinas located on or near the GIWW east of New Orleans. Full-service marinas at Mobile and Fairhope, AL; Biloxi and Gulfport, MS; and Slidell, LA, all require side trips of up to 20 miles from the GIWW proper.

After curving around the green buoys off Bear Point into Arnica Bay you will encounter the 83-slip Bear Point Harbor, located south of green daybeacon "65" at Mile 165 EHL. This has traditionally been a favorite stopover for cruising boats. In addition to slips, they also have a well-stocked Ship's Store and a restaurant on site.

At Mile 165 EHL Pirates Cove Marina & Restaurant has 16 reserved transient slips. You will see the entrance to the marina docks and boatyard off to the west as you approach the narrow cut into Roberts Bayou. Barber Marina is located north off the GIWW at Mile 163 EHL (at red daybeacon "74") in Bay La Launch. This marina can accommodate boats on floating docks, offers boat sales, dry storage, services and a boatyard with four marine lifts. There are no amenities here outside of the marine complex.

Activity increases on the GIWW as you approach Gulf Shores. The 210-slip The Wharf Marina is located on the shore at the high-rise Foley Beach Expressway Bridge at Mile 158.8 EHL. This marina offers resort amenities including shopping, golf, dining and entertainment in addition to slips on floating docks.

The full-service Saunders Yachtworks–Gulf Shores is located at GIWW Mile 155.5 EHL. They can handle most any service, repair or refit. Call ahead for slip availability.

Homeport Marina is located at Mile 155.0 EHL, just east of the Gulf Shores Parkway Bridges with room for transients on floating docks. They offer all the usual amenities plus the on-site LuLu's (www.lulubuffett.com/restaurant), the original of three locations operated by Lucy Buffett (Jimmy's sister). There is a 120-foot-long dock in front of the restaurant where you can tie up if you are stopping to eat. The daily "count-down to sunset" is not to be missed.

Fort Morgan Marina is southwest of Bon Secour Bay with dock store, dry storage, transient slips and private charters. Tacky Jacks 2 (www.tackyjacks.com/locations-fm) is located here.

Anchorage: You can anchor just to the west of Bear Point Harbor and dinghy in. This is open and exposed to the north and west as well as wakes. Almost due north on the opposite side of Arnica Bay (GIWW Mile 165 EHL) is Roberts Bayou, commonly known both to cruisers and locals as "Pirates Cove." There is a narrow entrance with private markers leading to the bayou. While the narrow entrance may seem intimidating, there is plenty of depth. There is a spot at the mouth of the bayou and the end

Gulf Shores Area, AL

GULF SHORES	Largest Vessel	VHF	Total Slips	Approach/ Dockside Depth	Floating Docks	Gas/ Diesel	Repairs/ Haulout	Min/Max Amps	Pump-Out Station
1. The Wharf Marina **WiFi** GIWW 158.8 mi. EHL (251) 224-1900	150	16	210	10.0 / 10.0	F	GD	R	30 / 200+	P

WiFi Wireless Internet Access **onSpot** Dockside WiFi Facility
Visit www.waterwayguide.com for current rates, fuel prices, website addresses and other up-to-the-minute information.
(Information in the table is provided by the facilities.)

Scan here for more details:

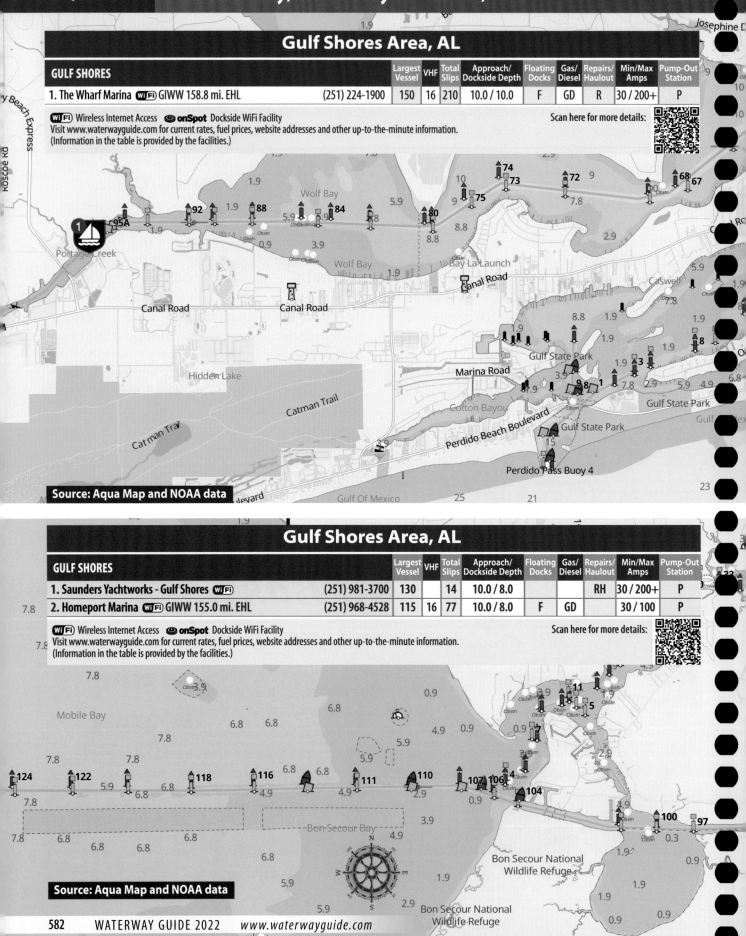

Source: Aqua Map and NOAA data

Gulf Shores Area, AL

GULF SHORES	Largest Vessel	VHF	Total Slips	Approach/ Dockside Depth	Floating Docks	Gas/ Diesel	Repairs/ Haulout	Min/Max Amps	Pump-Out Station
1. Saunders Yachtworks - Gulf Shores **WiFi** (251) 981-3700	130		14	10.0 / 8.0			RH	30 / 200+	P
2. Homeport Marina **WiFi** GIWW 155.0 mi. EHL (251) 968-4528	115	16	77	10.0 / 8.0	F	GD		30 / 100	P

WiFi Wireless Internet Access **onSpot** Dockside WiFi Facility
Visit www.waterwayguide.com for current rates, fuel prices, website addresses and other up-to-the-minute information.
(Information in the table is provided by the facilities.)

Scan here for more details:

Source: Aqua Map and NOAA data

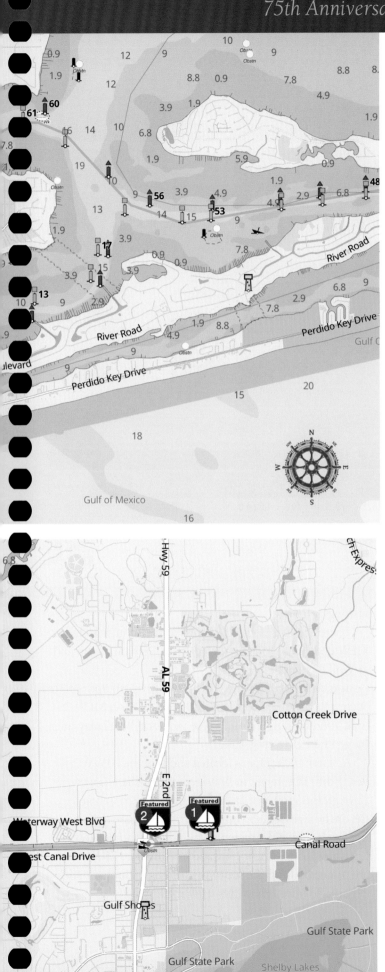

Gulf Shores Area, AL

BON SECOUR BAY		Largest Vessel	VHF	Total Slips	Approach/ Dockside Depth	Floating Docks	Gas/ Diesel	Repairs/ Haulout	Min/Max Amps	Pump-Out Station
1. Fort Morgan Marina GIWW 135.0 mi. EHL	(251) 540-2628	70	16	70	4.0 / 4.0		GD	H		P

WiFi Wireless Internet Access   **onSpot** Dockside WiFi Facility
Visit www.waterwayguide.com for current rates, fuel prices, website addresses and other up-to-the-minute information.
(Information in the table is provided by the facilities.)

Scan here for more details:

Source: Aqua Map and NOAA data

of the entrance channel that narrows to one boat width so plan ahead. Roberts Bayou is a popular anchorage for cruisers and locals. As in any anchorage that is already or might become crowded, it is a good idea to buoy your anchor with a trip line, not only so someone will not drop their hook over your rode, but to prevent snarling and tangling in tight quarters.

Larger boats can find 8-foot MLW depths just past the sharp bend to the left at the head of Ingram Bayou in Bay La Launch (GIWW Mile 162.5 EHL). Turn right at red daybeacon "72" and then proceed straight into Ingram Bayou, right down the center of the channel. There is shoaling on either side of this excellent, all-weather anchorage but 9-foot MLW depths hold most of the way in. Once inside you will be surrounded by total greenery and quiet (except on a busy weekend) and there is usually a breeze to keep the bugs away. Keep an eye out for visiting dolphins.

There are also plenty of places to anchor in 5- to 8-foot MLW depths at Wolf Bay including in Graham Bayou and at Wolf Bay Lodge.

You can anchor up the Bon Secour River off Bon Secour Bay by red daybeacon "38" in 4 to 7 feet MLW with good holding in mud. Note that local boats may buzz by you here throwing wakes.

A better anchorage is located south of the GIWW near Edith Hammock in Bon Secour Bay. There is a cut through the spoil area at flashing green "123" to reach the anchorage. Watch your chart and take care to avoid the fish haven and submerged pilings as you head toward the water tower. Anchor in sand in 7 to 9 feet MLW. You are protected from the southwest through southeast and exposed to northerly winds. Holding is good.

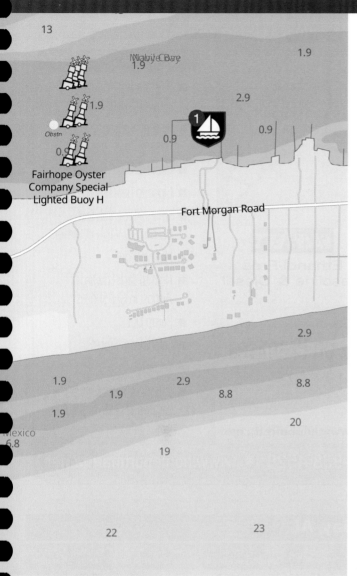

NAVIGATION: Use NOAA Charts 11376 and 11378. Bon Secour Bay lies at the southeasterly reaches of Mobile Bay. Continuing west on the GIWW enter Bon Secour Bay from the Bon Secour River at the 17-foot flashing green "103" and red nun buoy "104."

You can cruise north into Mobile Bay by leaving the GIWW and navigating through the open waters of the Bay, or continue east and turn north when you enter the Main Ship Channel. The GIWW tracks west across lower Mobile Bay and crosses the Main Ship Channel at flashing red "26" on the channel (Mile 133.75 EHL).

The ship channel provides a well-defined, well-marked route to follow north. You can leave the channel almost anywhere. It is bordered by spoils but local boaters say the depth over the spoils is about 10 feet MLW. You may choose to leave the GIWW for a shorter route but be aware that this requires navigating the more open shallow waters of the Bay. Eastbound cruisers will almost surely choose the Main Ship Channel, which is a shorter route to the north and east.

The alternative route is to leave the GIWW at green "129" (Mile 145 EHL) on a course of 337° magnetic. Continue for 10 miles to the 30-foot flashing red "2" at Mullet Point. Continue on a course of 337° magnetic for another 7.25 miles to the 37-foot flashing red "4" at Great Point Clear. Leave the charted shoals to the east.

> The northern entrance into Mobile Bay marks the end of the inland river system portion of the Great Loop. The Loop trail turns east and follows the Florida Panhandle but do not overlook the intrigue of continuing westward.

■ MOBILE BAY

Mobile Bay sits on the northern Gulf Coast, 40 miles west of Pensacola and 90 miles northeast of South Pass at the Mississippi River. It is the approach to the City of Mobile and to the Alabama and Tombigbee Rivers. The Bay has depths of 7 to 12 feet MLW outside the dredged channels.

> Mobile Bay is shallow and with its long fetch running south to north, it can build substantial waves. It will be rough in 15-knot winds and dangerous in winds at greater speeds.

The best way to cover cruising in Mobile Bay is through a literary "tale of two shores." The eastern shore is anchored by the quintessential southern City of Fairhope and the western shore by the bustling Port of Mobile.

Mobile Bay–Gulf Approach

The Gulf approach to the Bay is 3 miles wide and is bordered by Mobile Point on the east and Pelican Point on the west. Stay in the dredged channel to avoid shoals that extend 4 miles south (into the Gulf) on both sides. The Port of Mobile is 25 miles to the north. Expect heavy traffic.

High-rise condominiums are prominent along the shoreline and can be seen on approach. West of the entrance is a chain of low, wooded islands for 50 nm. The black conical tower that is Sand Island Light is the most prominent landmark near the entrance at 131 feet. On the east side of the entrance the pentagon-shaped walls of Fort Morgan at Mobile Point are clearly visible. To the

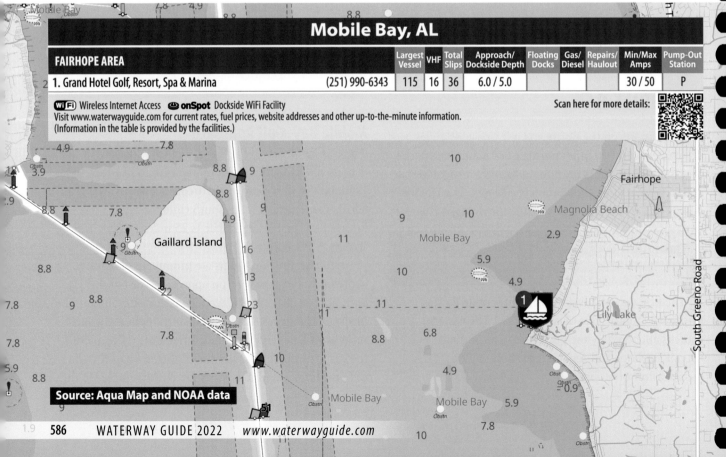

Mobile Bay, AL

FAIRHOPE AREA		Largest Vessel	VHF	Total Slips	Approach/ Dockside Depth	Floating Docks	Gas/ Diesel	Repairs/ Haulout	Min/Max Amps	Pump-Out Station
1. Grand Hotel Golf, Resort, Spa & Marina	(251) 990-6343	115	16	36	6.0 / 5.0				30 / 50	P

WiFi Wireless Internet Access **onSpot** Dockside WiFi Facility
Visit www.waterwayguide.com for current rates, fuel prices, website addresses and other up-to-the-minute information.
(Information in the table is provided by the facilities.)

Scan here for more details:

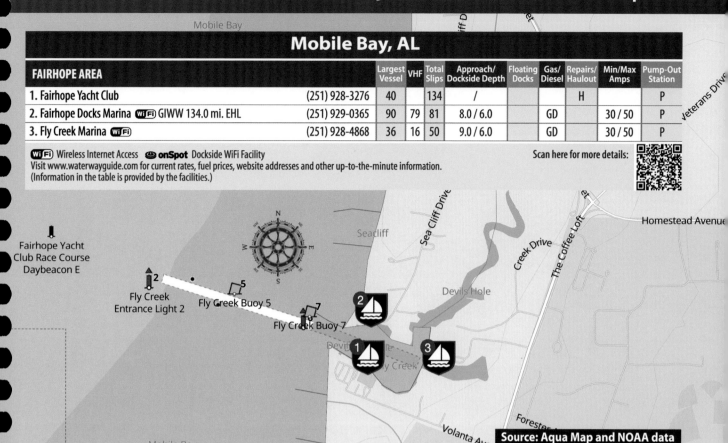

Mobile Bay, AL

FAIRHOPE AREA		Largest Vessel	VHF	Total Slips	Approach/ Dockside Depth	Floating Docks	Gas/ Diesel	Repairs/ Haulout	Min/Max Amps	Pump-Out Station
1. Fairhope Yacht Club	(251) 928-3276	40		134	/			H		P
2. Fairhope Docks Marina (WiFi) GIWW 134.0 mi. EHL	(251) 929-0365	90	79	81	8.0 / 6.0		GD		30 / 50	P
3. Fly Creek Marina (WiFi)	(251) 928-4868	36	16	50	9.0 / 6.0		GD		30 / 50	P

(WiFi) Wireless Internet Access (onSpot) Dockside WiFi Facility
Visit www.waterwayguide.com for current rates, fuel prices, website addresses and other up-to-the-minute information.
(Information in the table is provided by the facilities.)

Scan here for more details:

Source: Aqua Map and NOAA data

west of the entrance a spherical, elevated tank 2 miles west of Fort Gains on the east end of Dauphin Island at Pelican Point is clearly visible.

Mobile Bay–Eastern Shore

The allure of the east is its attractive, character-filled communities including beautiful Fairhope. Read more at "Goin' Ashore: Fairhope, AL" in this chapter. If you are continuing north, turn to starboard on a course of 142° magnetic. The Town of Fairhope is 4 miles farther on this course then 1 mile to the east.

To reach the marinas at Fly Creek continue a course of 142° magnetic for 1 mile then turn east for 1 mile. If you want to continue a northerly trek in the Bay, it is best to go west to the ship channel.

Dockage: For the Grand Hotel Golf, Resort, Spa & Marina use the charted Point Clear approach and follow the daybeacons that line the entrance channel. The depth in the channel and in the harbor is at least 7 feet MLW. This upscale location has dockage for vessels to 115 feet with resort amenities.

Stay to the south side of channel as you enter Fly Creek to avoid the 3-foot shoal. Fairport Yacht Club is the first facility to starboard (south). They welcome visiting

boats from reciprocal clubs to their facility. The municipal Fairhope Docks Marina is on the north side of the channel with covered and open slips and the usual amenities. Approach depths are 8 feet MLW. The family-owned and -operated Fly Creek Marina is located further up the creek. This marina–like many others on the eastern shore– is heavily populated by sailboats. It is a tidy, clean marina in a lovely wooded area and the only dry storage facility on the eastern shore.

Port of Mobile

The City of Mobile has a busy commercial waterfront. There is heavy barge traffic from the Tennessee-Tombigbee Waterway, on the northern end of Mobile Bay near the mouth of the Mobile River. There is also a cruise ship terminal, which adds to waterfront traffic.

Mobile is a cultural center with numerous festivals, museums and historical sites. One attraction worth mentioning is GulfQuest National Maritime Museum of the Gulf of Mexico (www.gulfquest.org), which is dedicated to the rich traditions, history and culture of the Gulf. The museum has 90 interactive exhibits, simulators and theaters covering an array of maritime topics including early settlements and trade routes,

GOIN' ASHORE
FAIRHOPE, AL

There is much to intrigue and delight visiting cruisers to Mobile Bay's eastern shore. The people who began the initial experimental community were a freethinking, intellectual group. Fairhope continues to attract artists, philosophers, musicians, and writers. The town boasts independent bookstores and hardware stores in the thriving downtown district. Unique art galleries, shops and restaurants abound. An Art Walk featuring art exhibits and musical entertainment is held the first Friday of every month in downtown Fairhope. Between 20 and 30 venues are open between 6:00 p.m. and 8:00 p.m. for the Art Walk.

SERVICES

1. Colony Animal Clinic
359 Morphy Ave. (251-928-7728)

2. Fairhope Post Office
509 Fairhope Ave. (251-990-3623)

3. Fairhope Public Library
501 Fairhope Ave. (251-928-7483)

4. Fairhope Welcome Center
20 N. Section St. (251-928-5095)

5. Thomas Hospital
750 Morphy Ave. (251-928-2375)

ATTRACTIONS

6. Fairhope Museum of History
Highlights the unique history of Fairhope in a
Spanish Mission Revival structure originally built in
1928 (24 N. Section St., 251-929-1471).

7. Marietta Johnson Museum
Tells the story of Marietta Johnson who founded
Fairhope's first school, the School for Organic
Education, in 1907. The visionary educator and
author boasted "no tests, no grades, no shoes" at
10 S. School St. (251-990-8601).

SHOPPING

8. Ace Home Center
Full-service hardware store for parts and tools at 560
Fairhope Ave. (251-990-6665).

9. Greer's Fairhope Market
Market with quality meat and produce with deli
counter (75 S. Section St., 251-928-8029).

10. Rae's Kitchen Fairhope
Freshly made sandwiches and wraps to go for lunch
(11:00 a.m. to 2:00 p.m.) plus casseroles, meals and
salads to go until 5:30 p.m. (weekdays) and 2:00 p.m.
Saturday (closed on Sundays) at 460 N. Section St.
(251-210-6135).

MARINAS

11. Fairhope Docks Marina
848 Sea Cliff Dr. (251-929-0365)

12. Fairhope Yacht Club
101 Volanta Ave. (252-928-3276)

13. Fly Creek Marina
831 N. Section St. (251-928-4868)

Mobile Bay, AL

DOG RIVER AREA		Largest Vessel	VHF	Total Slips	Approach/ Dockside Depth	Floating Docks	Gas/ Diesel	Repairs/ Haulout	Min/Max Amps	Pump-Out Station
1. Fowl River Marina	(251) 973-2670	50	16	60	5.0 / 5.0	F	GD		50	P

WiFi Wireless Internet Access **onSpot** Dockside WiFi Facility
Visit www.waterwayguide.com for current rates, fuel prices, website addresses and other up-to-the-minute information. (Information in the table is provided by the facilities.)

Scan here for more details:

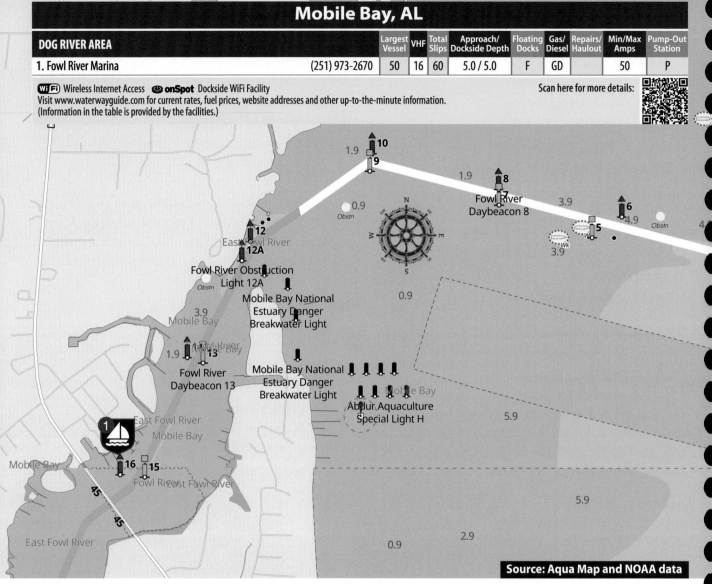

Source: Aqua Map and NOAA data

marine archeology and shipwrecks, marine life, weather and hurricanes, marine and coastal environments, maritime commerce and shipbuilding, ship navigation and communication, offshore oil/gas platforms and much more. The museum is located at 155 S. Water St. (251-436-8901).

Anchorage: There are several anchorages north of Mobile on the Mobile River. These are covered in more detail in the Great Lakes Vol. 2 edition of Waterway Guide.

> Note: It would be best if you and your pet don't swim here. There seem to be more and more alligators every year, and there's no need to feed the wildlife!

Mobile Bay–Western Shore

On the western shore of Mobile Bay boaters will find work-a-day marinas with good basic services but few amenities. Some, however, are within convenient reach to downtown Mobile, either by rental car or marina courtesy car.

NAVIGATION: Use NOAA Chart 11376. All cruising boats visiting the western shore will want to move north in the large ship channel. Boats heading west across Bon Secour Bay can leave the GIWW at the 17-foot flashing green "147." Set a course of 298° magnetic for 6.5 miles to a cut through the spoil into the ship channel. Follow the same course through the cut for 1.5 miles and enter the ship channel at the 17-foot flashing red "34."

Mobile Bay, AL

DOG RIVER AREA		Largest Vessel	VHF	Total Slips	Approach/ Dockside Depth	Floating Docks	Gas/ Diesel	Repairs/ Haulout	Min/Max Amps	Pump-Out Station
1. Beachcomber Marina	(251) 443-8000	65		96	9.0 / 16.0			RH	30	
2. Grand Mariner Marina & Restaurant **WiFi** GIWW 134.0 mi. EHL	(251) 443-7160	200		100	15.0 / 12.0		GD	RH	30 / 50	
3. Turner Marine Supply Inc. **WiFi**	(251) 476-1444	100	16	150	8.0 / 7.0			RH	30 / 50	
4. Dog River Marina and Boat Works Inc. **WiFi** GIWW 134.0 mi. EHL	(251) 471-5449	200	16	100	8.0 / 10.0		GD	RH	30 / 100	P
5. Dockside Marina Dog River	(251) 479-2772				/				30 / 50	P

WiFi Wireless Internet Access **onSpot** Dockside WiFi Facility
Visit www.waterwayguide.com for current rates, fuel prices, website addresses and other up-to-the-minute information.
(Information in the table is provided by the facilities.)

Scan here for more details:

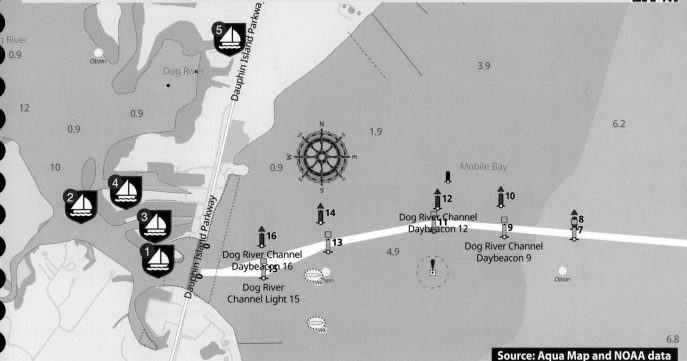

Source: Aqua Map and NOAA data

Boats coming from the west through Pass Aux Heron can leave the GIWW at red nun "10" and green can "9" after passing under the Dauphin Island Causeway Bridge. Set a course of 61° magnetic for 5 miles to the cut entering the ship channel. Follow the same course for 1.5 miles and enter the ship channel at the 17-foot flashing green "33."

Moving north in the ship channel for 8 miles you will come to a cut in the spoil just before 17-foot flashing green "49." To access the facilities on the western shore at Fowl River, exit the ship channel before green "49" on a course of 275° magnetic for 4.3 miles to the channel entry at green daybeacon "1" and flashing red "2."

Further north (2.7 miles) in the ship channel you will pass the Hollinger Island and Theodore Ship Channel, opposite the 17-foot flashing red "54." The channel leads to an industrial complex with no facilities for cruising boats.

Continuing north past the 17-foot flashing green "63" and red "64" for 5 miles where you will intersect the channel to Dog River to the west. Enter the channel between green daybeacon "1" and red daybeacon "2." Stay in the channel on a heading of about 305° magnetic for 2.5 miles to green daybeacon "5." Channel depths are charted at 6.5 feet at MLW. Turn west at green "5" and follow the channel for 2 miles to the Dog River Bridge (73-foot fixed vertical clearance). Several marinas are located just under the bridge.

Dockage: Working clockwise around Mobile Bay from the southwest corner, the channel into Fowl River is well marked. Fowl River Marina is located 0.5 miles upriver on the north side at red daybeacon "16," before

Mobile Bay, AL

DOG RIVER AREA		Largest Vessel	VHF	Total Slips	Approach/ Dockside Depth	Floating Docks	Gas/ Diesel	Repairs/ Haulout	Min/Max Amps	Pump-Out Station
1. River Yacht Basin Marina **WiFi**	(251) 776-4435	70		75	6.0 / 6.0				30 / 50	

WiFi Wireless Internet Access **onSpot** Dockside WiFi Facility
Visit www.waterwayguide.com for current rates, fuel prices, website addresses and other up-to-the-minute information.
(Information in the table is provided by the facilities.)

Scan here for more details:

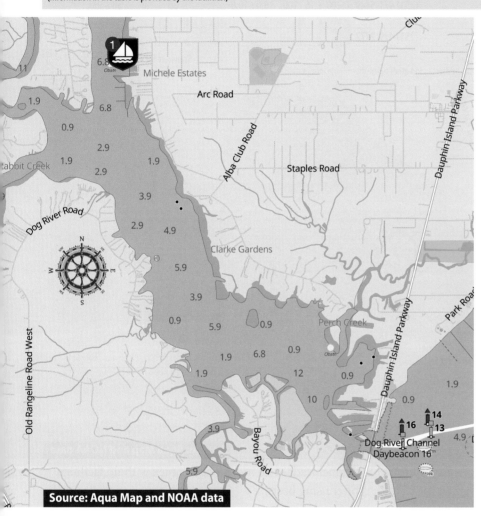

Source: Aqua Map and NOAA data

the 45-foot fixed vertical clearance East Fowl River (SR 193) Bridge. The Pelican Reef (www.thepelicanreef.com) seafood restaurant is on site (251-973-2670).

There is a cluster of marinas on Dog River to the north on the western shore of Mobile Bay, roughly two-thirds of the way up the ship channel from the pass entering Mobile Bay. Marinas are on each side of the river within 100 yards of the Dog River Bridge.

Beachcomber Marina is the first marina on the south side of the bridge. They have transient slips, a dry dock and a restaurant. Grand Mariner Marina & Mariner Restaurant is the second facility south of the bridge when heading upriver. This full-service marina has ample dockage and a well-respected restaurant.

The full-service Turner Marine Supply Inc. is about 150 yards past the bridge on the north shore with yacht sales, slips and repairs. The full-service Dog River Marina and Boat Works Inc. is on the same side a little farther north around the curve. This is a working boatyard offering a comprehensive range of services. The complex hosts all manner of services and a West Marine.

To the north is Dockside Marina Dog River in a quiet, protected harbor. This marina is usually fully booked and has a waiting list so call ahead. The inviting stretch of beach and easy access for larger boats in a family-friendly environment are the main draws. Three miles upriver from the bridge is River Yacht Basin Marina, which may have space for you. This is a quiet marina with mostly covered docks.

Anchorage: There is room to anchor up the East Fowl River in 6 to 8 feet MLW if you can fit under the 45-foot fixed East Fowl River Bridge. Dog River offers a good anchorage near River Yacht Basin Marina. Anchor in 6 to 7 feet MLW according to wind direction.

■ TO BAY ST. LOUIS

West of Mobile Bay the GIWW opens up to the Mississippi Sound, a bay-like expanse of water between the mainland and a string of barrier islands known as the Gulf Islands National Seashore. This open stretch of waterway extends from east to west for 85 miles.

Mississippi Sound, MS

DAUPHIN ISLAND		Largest Vessel	VHF	Total Slips	Approach/ Dockside Depth	Floating Docks	Gas/ Diesel	Repairs/ Haulout	Min/Max Amps	Pump-Out Station
1. Dauphin Island Marina **WiFi** GIWW 127.8 mi. EHL	(251) 861-2201	60	16	90	6.0 / 6.0		GD	H	30 / 50	P

WiFi Wireless Internet Access **onSpot** Dockside WiFi Facility
Visit www.waterwayguide.com for current rates, fuel prices, website addresses and other up-to-the-minute information.
(Information in the table is provided by the facilities.)

Scan here for more details:

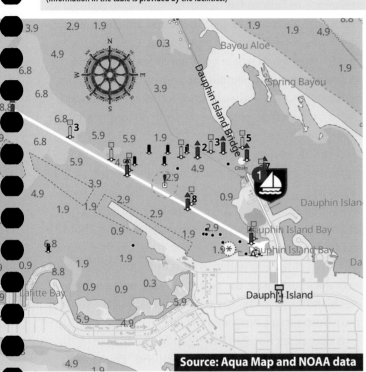

Source: Aqua Map and NOAA data

The width of the sound is 10 to 12 miles. This long stretch and significant width when combined with a 15-knot wind will result in considerable chop. When the winds blow over 15 knots consider staying in a safe harbor or looking for shelter if you find yourself underway in these conditions. Wait for fair weather and this can be a very enjoyable and rewarding cruising area worth exploring in detail. Sunrise over the beaches of Horn Island has been heralded as truly spectacular.

Shoreside facilities are limited. The number and quality of destinations is growing, however, due to both the popularity of the area as well as the ongoing rebuilding effort from past hurricanes. Pleasure boaters should keep in mind that traveling west from this point will increase the frequency of encounters with commercial vessels, most often towboats. Give these vessels a wide berth, particularly in shallower waters and narrow channels. As suggested earlier it is advisable to monitor both VHF Channels 13 and 16. Additionally Automatic Identification System (AIS) is used extensively on the GIWW.

Gulf inlets (referred to in these waters as "passes") are not all trustworthy. Only the three inlets at Pascagoula, Biloxi and Gulfport provide reliable access to the Gulf of Mexico. Throughout Mississippi Sound there are constant dredging operations. Stay alert.

Dauphin Island–GIWW Mile 130 EHL

On the west side of the entrance to Mobile Bay, Dauphin Island with its long sandy spit to the west is the first of the barrier islands running from Mobile Bay to New Orleans. Of the many recreational and boating centers in the Mobile area Dauphin Island is the closest to the GIWW. The island is a pleasant and interesting stopover with a sizable marina, anchorages along the entire length of the island and excellent beaches.

On Dauphin Island, less is more. The little island is well known and much loved for being less congested than other Gulf Coast resorts. It's also noted for its breathtaking sunsets, pristine beaches, walking and biking trails, bird sanctuaries, charter fishing boats, ferry across Mobile Bay, outdoor recreation and historic sites. Truth is, Dauphin Island is awash in history.

Dauphin Island is home to Fort Gaines (251-861-3607), once a Confederate stronghold used to defend the east entrance to Mobile Bay. The fort is located at the east end of the island and is now a historic site and museum. Nearby is Dauphin Island Sea Lab, Alabama's marine education and research center (251-861-2141). The lab operates the Estuarium, an extensive public aquarium, displaying features of coastal Alabama's ecosystems: the Delta, Mobile Bay and the Gulf of Mexico.

NAVIGATION: Use NOAA Chart 11378. It is possible to enter Dauphin Island Bay via two channels. Middle Ground is the first channel for boats heading west across Mobile Bay. Middle Ground is on the east side of the island by Fort Gains at Pelican Point. (This entrance is referred to locally as "Billy Goat Hole.") Move west through the channel in the spoil areas at flashing green "25" and flashing red "26." Local knowledge suggests that depth over the spoils is about 10 feet MLW. Turn south to the well-marked channel through Billy Goat Hole. You will pass a Coast Guard Station and ferry dock just inside the entry. Depths are charted at 4.5 feet MLW. (Check the latest chart.)

> ⚠️ Significant post-hurricane shoaling has been reported in the vicinity of the entrance to Pelican Bay and the Pelican Bay Fish Haven. Charted depths are reportedly no longer accurate. Mariners transiting the area are advised to use extreme caution.

The second channel is Aux Heron's Channel, 1.6 miles west of the **Dauphin Island Causeway Bridge** (fixed 83-foot vertical clearance) at Mile 127.8 EHL. Entrance via this second channel is limited by the Dauphin Island Bridge with 25-foot fixed vertical clearance.

At red "22" in the Aux Heron's Channel leave the GIWW on a southeast course and pick up flashing green "1" marking the entrance to a channel to Bayou Aloe. Proceed on a southeast course past the 17-foot flashing red "2" and green "3." The next marker should be flashing green "1" leading into a privately marked channel to Chugae Point and the clearly visible Dauphin Island Causeway Bridge. Depths are charted at 4.5 feet at MLW.

Dockage: The only marina here is Dauphin Island Marina, a full-service facility welcoming transients. It would be prudent to call ahead for reservations and the latest information on markers and water depths. Many charters and tours leave from here. Motels, restaurants and groceries are a short walk from the marina.

Anchorage: Dauphin Island has many fine anchorages protected from southerly winds but not from the north. Hurricane Rita broke through the middle of Dauphin Island, leaving a breach in the island. Keep this in mind when deciding where to anchor.

On the south side of the island you can find a quiet anchorage in Pelican Bay. Leave the main ship channel at green "15" and navigate past the shoals at Pelican Island, which has become more of a peninsula, then into the smaller bay/lagoon where you should find good holding. As previously noted, significant post-hurricane shoaling has been reported at the entrance to Pelican Bay and in the bay. Charted depths are reportedly no longer accurate. Proceed with caution.

If you need someplace close to the channel entrance on the east side of the island, you can also anchor in Billy Goat Hole. Move west through the channel in the spoil areas at flashing green "25" and flashing red "26." Local knowledge suggests that depth over the spoils is about 10 feet MLW. Turn south to the well-marked channel through Billy Goat Hole. You will pass a Coast Guard Station and ferry dock just inside the entry. Put your bow on the beach and carry an anchor to shore to make sure you stay away from service boats and the ferry.

A deeper anchorage (6 to 9 feet MLW) is at Confederate Pass, also on the eastern end. This is well protected and marked and is within dinghy distance of a restaurant; however, it is usually occupied by commercial boats. Other options are Bayou Aloe with good holding in sand (very shallow) and near green daybeacon "27" to the west in 7 to 9 feet MLW.

Dauphin Island

Mississippi Sound, MS

PASCAGOULA		Largest Vessel	VHF	Total Slips	Approach/ Dockside Depth	Floating Docks	Gas/ Diesel	Repairs/ Haulout	Min/Max Amps	Pump-Out Station
1. Pascagoula Inner Harbor Marina	(228) 938-6694	40		60	7.0 / 3.0				30 / 50	P

WiFi Wireless Internet Access **onSpot** Dockside WiFi Facility

Visit www.waterwayguide.com for current rates, fuel prices, website addresses and other up-to-the-minute information. (Information in the table is provided by the facilities.)

Scan here for more details:

Source: Aqua Map and NOAA data

Pass Aux Heron to Pascagoula Bay–GIWW Mile 125 EHL to 104 EHL

Pascagoula is primarily a commercial shipping port. The harbor is located about 9 miles north of Horn Island Pass and is one of the important deep water ports on the Gulf Coast. The city, which is located at the mouth of the Pascagoula River, is home to many large industries, which contribute to commercial ship traffic.

NAVIGATION: Use NOAA Charts 11367, 11372, 11373, 11374 and 11375. From Mobile Bay the GIWW passes through Pass Aux Herons Channel at Dauphin Island Causeway Bridge and then enters Mississippi Sound. When leaving the channel at Mile 124 EHL most markers are lighted and elevated, although some are up to 4 miles apart. Pay close attention to compass headings and position fixes on the long run between markers.

The next 70 or more miles are a long and only partially protected passageway. Natural depths of 12 to 18 feet MLW are found throughout the sound and a channel from Mobile Bay to New Orleans is regularly dredged. Stay in the channel to GIWW Mile 118.5 EHL at 17-foot flashing red "40" and green "41." The next channel marker is

17-foot flashing green "5" at GIWW Mile 114 EHL at a distance of 4.5 miles on a course of about 255° magnetic. Chart your course to stay in or close to the GIWW channel through the rest of the sound.

It is 10.5 miles from the large ship channel at Horn Island Pass to Pascagoula. North in the Pascagoula Channel you will encounter a Y at flashing red "36." To port is the route to Pascagoula; to starboard is Bayou Casotte.

Dockage: Pascagoula Inner Harbor Marina is at Lake Yazoo and has limited space. They report 3-foot MLW dockside depths so call ahead. Also off of the Pascagoula River to the north and west is the Mary Walker Marina, catering mostly to sportfishermen (reporting 5-foot MLW dockside depths) but welcoming to transients of all kinds.

Anchorage: It is possible to anchor in Lake Yazoo in 5 feet MLW with all-around protection. Another option is north of the CSX Transportation Railroad Bridge (8-foot vertical clearance, usually open) and the US 90 Bridge (80-foot fixed vertical clearance), where you will find 8 to 15 feet of depth. This is easy to reach with a wide, sparsely occupied river.

Mississippi Sound, MS

GAUTIER		Largest Vessel	VHF	Total Slips	Approach/ Dockside Depth	Floating Docks	Gas/ Diesel	Repairs/ Haulout	Min/Max Amps	Pump-Out Station
1. Mary Walker Marina **WiFi** GIWW 96.0 mi. EHL	(228) 497-3141	50		150	6.0 / 5.0		GD		30 / 50	P

WiFi Wireless Internet Access **onSpot** Dockside WiFi Facility
Visit www.waterwayguide.com for current rates, fuel prices, website addresses and other up-to-the-minute information.
(Information in the table is provided by the facilities.)

Scan here for more details:

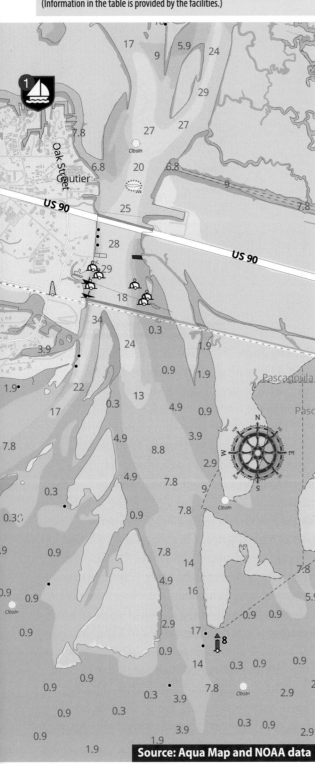

Source: Aqua Map and NOAA data

Pascagoula Bay to Biloxi Bay– GIWW Mile 104 EHL to Mile 87.5 EHL

Biloxi is a city on a peninsula jutting east into Mississippi Sound. The port is accessible from the Gulf through Dog Keys Pass and Little Dog Keys Pass and from the GIWW, which passes through Mississippi Sound about 6 miles south of the city. It is an important sportfishing and resort area with a large commercial seafood industry. Keesler Air Force Base and a large veteran's hospital are at the west end of the city. The waterfront on the sound is protected by Deer Island and the harbor in Back Bay of Biloxi is landlocked.

NAVIGATION: Use NOAA Charts 11372, 11373 and 11374. Cross the Pascagoula Channel at flashing green "29" and flashing red "30." Continue west in the Mississippi Sound and the next GIWW mark will be flashing green "1" in 4.4 miles. From here, continue for 2 miles to 17-foot flashing red "2" and 17-foot flashing green "3." Turn to star-board (north) on a course of about 320° magnetic for 2.5 miles to 17-foot flashing green "5A." The GIWW makes this turn to the north to avoid the shoals at Middle Ground and will shoal slightly (8 to 12 feet MLW) until you reach flashing green "5." Continue west for 9 miles to Biloxi Bay Channel.

At Mile 87.5 EHL follow the Biloxi Ship Channel into Biloxi Bay and turn to port at green daybeacon "35" and flashing red "26." Do not drift outside the channel as the water depth is as low as 2 to 4 feet MLW on the edges with an oyster shell bottom. Deer Island is south of the channel. Heading west-southwest the channel opens up to the Biloxi waterfront and many marine facilities at flashing red "26."

Eastbound cruisers can return to the GIWW along the Biloxi Ship Channel, as described above. Westbound cruisers can save some time by continuing along the Biloxi Channel extending east to west along the city and then changing direction to the south toward the GIWW.

From the Biloxi waterfront travel west to flashing red "12" and then turn south to green daybeacon "5" and flashing red "6." This section of the channel is 150 feet wide and 6 feet deep with a soft mud bottom. The Biloxi Ship Channel continues north into Back Bay of Biloxi. Three bridges cross the channel. The first is the Biloxi Bay (US 90) Bridge with a fixed 95-foot vertical clearance;

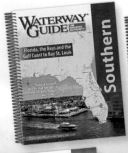
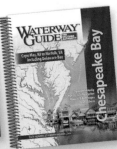
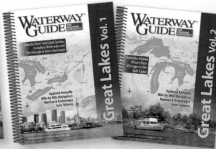
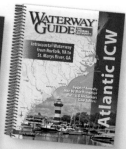
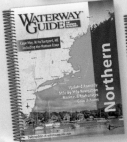

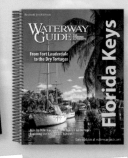
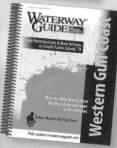

Mississippi Sound, MS

BILOXI		Largest Vessel	VHF	Total Slips	Approach/ Dockside Depth	Floating Docks	Gas/ Diesel	Repairs/ Haulout	Min/Max Amps	Pump-Out Station
1. Point Cadet Marina GIWW 88.0 mi. EHL	(228) 436-9312	100	16	246	12.0 / 10.0	F	GD		30 / 50	P
2. Biloxi Schooner Pier Complex **WiFi** GIWW 88.0 mi. EHL	(228) 435-6320			27	10.0 /	F			30 / 50	P
3. Biloxi Small Craft Harbor	(228) 374-6600	50	16	124	/		GD		30 / 50	P

WiFi Wireless Internet Access   **onSpot** Dockside WiFi Facility
Visit www.waterwayguide.com for current rates, fuel prices, website addresses and other up-to-the-minute information.
(Information in the table is provided by the facilities.)

Scan here for more details:

Source: Aqua Map and NOAA data

Shrimp Boats in Biloxi

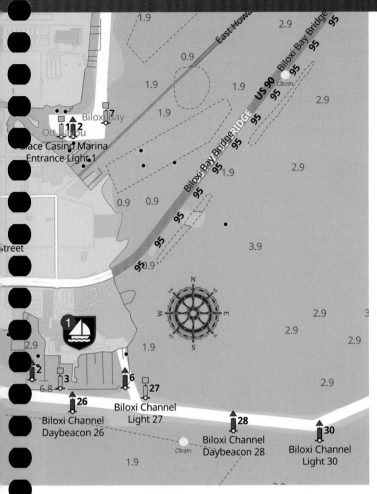

Biloxi Bay to Gulfport–GIWW Mile 87.5 to Mile 69 EHL

Gulfport is one of Mississippi's most successful commercial ports and a major center for tourism. For the cruising boater Gulfport features casinos, restaurants, museums and the ferry to Ship Island, all near the marinas.

NAVIGATION: NOAA Chart 11372. Cross the Biloxi Bay Channel in Mississippi Sound south of green daybeacon "1" and flashing red "2." Set a course to the west for 15 miles to Gulfport Sound Channel. The first marker you will see is the flashing red Ship Island Light ("S") in 5.5 miles.

Continue west 5.5 miles to flashing red "4" then 4 miles to the well-marked Gulfport Sound Channel. Pass between flashing green "43" and flashing red "44" and then travel along Gulfport Shipping Channel to flashing red "62." From here follow the channel markers. There is only one tidal cycle per day here with a very small tidal range of just over 1 foot.

Dockage: The friendly Gulfport Municipal Marina is a deep-water marina that can accommodate vessels up to 140 feet. This modern facility offers easy access (no bridges to negotiate) and all the usual amenities plus security, wide fairways and full-length finger piers. They offer a 24-hour fuel dock and a beautiful white sand beach right on the Gulf. Casinos and downtown restaurants are within walking distance.

Long Beach Harbor is about 3 miles to the west of Gulfport. The friendly marina may have transient space for you and reports 8-foot MLW dockside and approach depths.

Anchorage: Drop the hook north of Long Beach Harbor in 8 to 9 feet MLW with excellent holding in soft mud. Keep in mind that this is exposed to the south.

Gulfport to Bay St. Louis–GIWW Mile 69 to Mile 54 EHL

At the western entrance to St. Louis Bay the town of Bay St. Louis is the last of the Mississippi coastal resorts. Visiting shallow-draft vessels will find many suitable anchorages and fine fishing here.

NAVIGATION: Use NOAA Chart 11372. From GIWW Mile 54 EHL at the junction of Marianne Channel and the Grand Island Channel travel 5 miles north to flashing red

the second is an abandoned bridge (now used as a fishing pier) with channel sections removed, and the third is a CSX Transportation Railroad Bridge with a 14-foot closed vertical clearance (opens on signal).

Dockage: The municipal Point Cadet Marina at the eastern tip of Biloxi offers transient berths. The Biloxi Schooner Pier Complex, 0.5 mile west of Point Cadet, includes some transient slips at the Maritime & Seafood Industry Museum facility. This complex is walking distance to several casinos. It is also the home base of the two historic Biloxi Schooners, replicas of turn-of-the-century oyster ships that make daily sails around Mississippi Sound.

Anchorage: You can drop the hook anywhere in Back Bay. For northeast protection, anchor in deep water (at least 14 feet) at Big Lake west of the Popps Ferry Road Bridge. The 25-foot closed vertical clearance bridge will open on signal except from 7:30 a.m. to 9:00 a.m. and from 4:30 p.m. to 6:00 p.m., Monday through Friday (except federal holidays), when the draw need not open for the passage of vessels.

Mississippi Sound, MS

GULFPORT			Largest Vessel	VHF	Total Slips	Approach/ Dockside Depth	Floating Docks	Gas/ Diesel	Repairs/ Haulout	Min/Max Amps	Pump-Out Station
1. Gulfport Municipal Marina-MS WiFi		(228) 867-8721	140	16	327	12.0 / 11.0		GD		30 / 100	P

WiFi Wireless Internet Access　onSpot Dockside WiFi Facility

Visit www.waterwayguide.com for current rates, fuel prices, website addresses and other up-to-the-minute information.
(Information in the table is provided by the facilities.)

Scan here for more details:

Source: Aqua Map and NOAA data

MISSISSIPPI GULF COAST'S FINEST MARINA

GulfportMarina.com　　Marina@Gulfport-MS.gov

VHF 16　　**(228) 236-8070**
(228) 236-8071　　**24 HRS.**

30°21'48.0"N　89°05'17.5"W

✔ Quick access from the Gulf, no bridges
✔ Protected basin with deep-water slips
✔ 319 slips, all with full-length finger piers
✔ Dockage available for vessels up to 140 feet
✔ 24-hour fuel dock & store
✔ Air-conditioned showers & laundry
✔ 30/50/100A power, free WiFi, pumpout
✔ Short walk to restaurants & casinos

$1 per foot transient rate

Loopers & Liveaboards Welcome!

Mississippi Sound, MS

PASS CHRISTIAN		Largest Vessel	VHF	Total Slips	Approach/ Dockside Depth	Floating Docks	Gas/ Diesel	Repairs/ Haulout	Min/Max Amps	Pump-Out Station
1. Pass Christian East Harbor Expansion	(228) 452-5128	70	16	164	10.0 / 10.0		GD		30 / 50	P
2. Pass Christian Harbor GIWW 60.0 mi. EHL	(228) 452-5128	100		164	10.0 / 10.0		GD		30 / 50	P
3. Pass Christian Yacht Works	(228) 245-9987				/			RH		

WiFi Wireless Internet Access **onSpot** Dockside WiFi Facility
Visit www.waterwayguide.com for current rates, fuel prices, website addresses and other up-to-the-minute information.
(Information in the table is provided by the facilities.)

Scan here for more details:

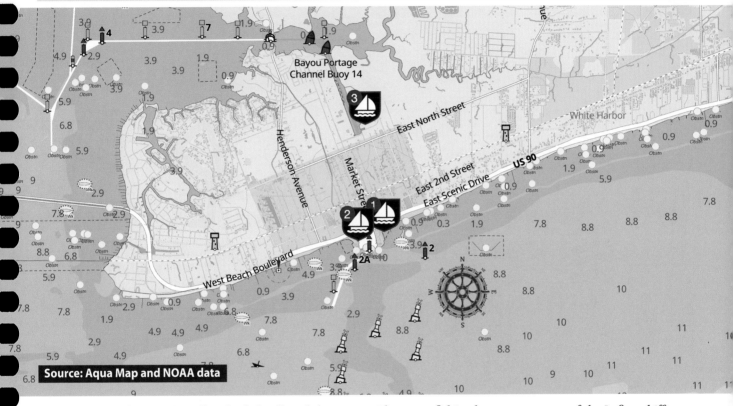

Source: Aqua Map and NOAA data

"2" (west side of Square Handkerchief Shoal) and then 2.5 miles to the Bay St. Louis Railroad Bridge (13-foot closed vertical clearance), which opens on signal. This is followed by the Bay St. Louis (US 90) Bridge (85-foot vertical clearance).

Bayou Caddy, located along the shoreline just a few miles west of Bay St. Louis, is mostly a commercial fishing port. Carefully follow the 50-foot-wide channel (5.5-foot MLW depths) into the bayou, which itself has 6-foot MLW depths. The atmosphere is very friendly toward visiting pleasure boaters. Many interesting hours can be spent watching the commercial and private fishermen as they come and go.

Heron Bay just northwest of Lighthouse Point and north of flashing green "3" may look like a good anchorage or fishing hole but note its shallow depths.

The many fishing boats you see are of the Lafitte skiff type, which draw less than 2 feet.

Dockage: There are two marked channels leading to the pleasant and well-protected Pass Christian Harbor, located about 4 miles east of Bay St. Louis. The eastern channel reportedly has better depths. Both Pass Christian Harbor and the Pass Christian East Harbor Expansion have slips. Water and pump-out service are available at each slip but the restrooms are public at these municipal marinas.

Less than 5 nm to the west Bay St. Louis Municipal Harbor is conveniently located between the bridges and offers transient slips for vessels up to 110 feet with full amenities. The new Pier 5, which will house 43 new slips for larger boats, will be at the east end of the harbor. (Construction in progress at press time.) Shopping and restaurants are nearby as is beach access.

Mississippi Sound, MS

BAY ST. LOUIS		Largest Vessel	VHF	Total Slips	Approach/ Dockside Depth	Floating Docks	Gas/ Diesel	Repairs/ Haulout	Min/Max Amps	Pump-Out Station
1. Bay St. Louis Municipal Harbor WiFi	(228) 467-4226	110	16	214	8.0 / 8.0		GD	R	30 / 100	P
2. Bay Marina & R.V. Park WiFi 55 EHL	(228) 466-4970	50	16	75	5.0 / 5.0		G	R	30 / 50	P

WiFi Wireless Internet Access **onSpot** Dockside WiFi Facility
Visit www.waterwayguide.com for current rates, fuel prices, website addresses and other up-to-the-minute information.
(Information in the table is provided by the facilities.)

Scan here for more details:

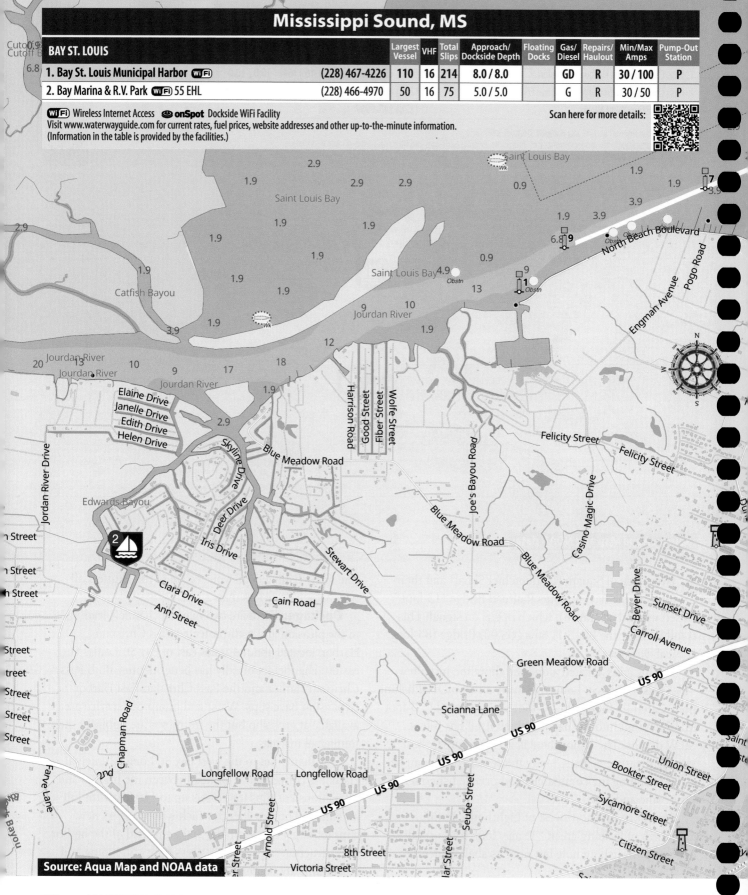

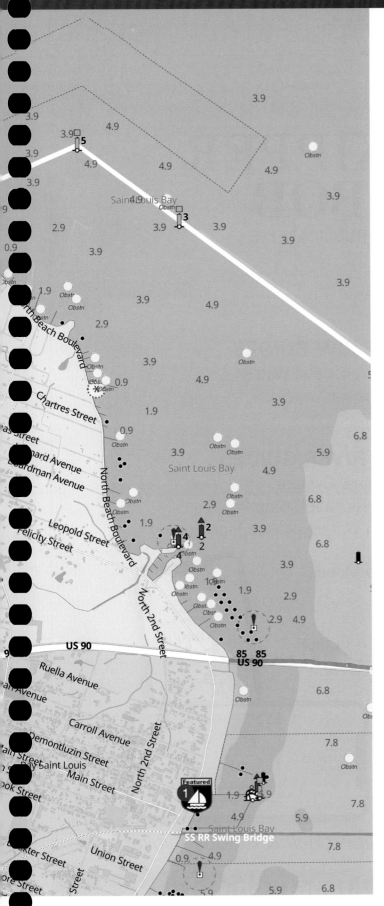

■ NEXT STOP

You have reached the end of our *Waterway Guide Southern* edition coverage but not necessarily the end of your voyage. From here you can continue westward to New Orleans, the Louisiana low country and the windswept Texas coast all the way to Mexico. This area is detailed in our *Western Gulf Coast* edition.

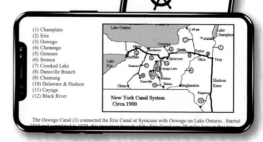

Goin' Ashore Index

Inlets Index